D0843425

*Temple Beth David*

6100 Hefley Street
Westminster, CA 92683
(714) 892-6623

# THE TORAH
## FOR
# FAMILY READING

The Torah for Family Reading reflects the conviction that the Bible would be read with increased ease and enjoyment if only the difficulties found in most English translations were removed.

The language of *The Torah for Family Reading* eliminates obscurities and archaic expressions so that every reader can understand the text. In addition, each book of the Bible is divided into logical parts that are identified by descriptive titles to guide the reader. Each book, as well as each group of books, has a brief introduction in which the historical background of the section is given and specific problems are discussed. The result is a beautiful, modern rendering of the most sacred literature of the Jewish people.

In this edition of the Hebrew Scriptures, every chapter is accounted for, yet all duplications, specifications, detailed descriptions of rituals, and genealogies have been relegated to summarized notes at the end of the volume. The principal laws are given separately in a summary, alphabetically arranged, and all obvious redundancies are omitted.

*The Torah for Family Reading* is intended not to displace traditional versions but rather to encourage, through easier comprehension, a revival of family reading of this centuries-old work that so profoundly affects our lives and shapes our moral behavior.

# THE TORAH
## FOR
## FAMILY READING

The Five Books of Moses

תּוֹרָה

The Prophets

נְבִיאִים

The Writings

כְּתוּבִים

𝒜

## JASON ARONSON INC.
*Northvale, New Jersey*
*London*

ISBN 0-87668-915-2
Library of Congress Catalog Number 86-70620

Manufactured in the United States of America. Jason Aronson Inc. offers books and cassettes. For
information and catalog write to Jason Aronson Inc., 230 Livingston Street, Northvale, New Jersey 07647.

# INTRODUCTION

The reader must realize at the outset that the Torah[1] is not a *book* but, rather, a *collection of many books;* and that it is a *collection of many diverse books.* It contains books of law, books of history, personal narratives, short stories, prophecies, riddles, philosophical dissertations, descriptions of rituals, parables, psalms, dramatic debates, letters, and gnomic poetry. The "books" vary in length from the Psalter, which contains 150 psalms in nearly 2,500 verses and 44,000 words, and the almost as long Book of Ezekiel, to the Book of Obadiah, which is only one chapter or less than 700 words in length.

These varied books were written by authors unequal in literary talent and differing in their depth of perception. Some books bear the name of one author (Isaiah, for instance), though the text makes it evident that parts were written by another, or several others, who lived many years later.

Furthermore, the books of the Torah cover a period of many centuries, and were written and rewritten over a period of many centuries. And the *time of* the writing was not always the *time covered in* the writing. There are fragments in the earlier books of the Bible, such as the Song of Deborah, which some scholars ascribe to about 1250 B.C.E.; other sections, like some of the Psalms, are placed fully eleven centuries later. Between the time that the first and the last parts of the Bible were written and assembled, great changes took place in the manners, customs, laws, ethical concepts, and very language of the people who wrote these books, for no nation or institution or language in the history of humankind has ever remained unchanged for a thousand years. And those changes were reflected in the writings. But the reader unaware of this fact is under-

---

[1]The Hebrew word *Torah* is of the same root as the word *hora'ah*, meaning instruction or teaching. The term has at least four definitions: (1) the Five Books of Moses; (2) the Hebrew Scriptures (known by many as the Old Testament); (3) the entire body of Jewish sacred writings; and (4) the metaphysical blueprint of existence. In this volume, we use the term in the second sense.

standably puzzled by seeming contradictions in some of the laws or ethical teachings.

The books of the Torah, written by many authors in diverse literary forms, treating a wide variety of topics, and produced over a period of ten to twelve centuries...would create difficulties enough (as would any anthology covering such a period) even if the individual contributions were presented chronologically. But the books of the Torah do not always appear in the chronology of the time in which they were written; nor do they follow throughout the chronology of the time covered by the books.

At the very beginning, in the first two chapters of Genesis, the reader is confronted with two accounts of the creation of man. In the first chapter the account tells how God created man in His own image, "male and female he created them. And God blessed them and God said to them, 'Be fruitful, and multiply, and replenish the earth.'" In the next chapter, the account relates how God created Adam out of the dust of the ground, and later caused a deep sleep to fall upon him, and then created woman out of one of Adam's ribs. Further on in Genesis (12:11–20) the reader comes upon the account of Abraham, who in Egypt states that his wife is his sister. Eight chapters further the same story is given in almost identical language, with the difference that the king of Egypt is replaced by King Abimelech of Gerar. After another six chapters this story reappears, but with the change that Isaac and Rebekah replace Abraham and Sarah in King Abimelech's court. Chronicles I and II recall events already given in Samuel and Kings, though from a different point of view. Jeremiah (chapter 52) repeats with slight variations events recorded in II Kings (chapters 24–25). The examples of duplication can be extended, and each, in turn, tends to puzzle the reader.

More confusing than the duplications are the seeming contradictions. How Jacob's name was changed to Israel is told twice within three chapters, but the explanations differ (Genesis 32:22–28 versus 35:10). In the Ten Commandments, graven images of any kind are forbidden; but later on, Moses is commanded to set up a serpent of brass so that those bitten by poisonous snakes may be healed by looking at the image (Exodus 20:4 versus Numbers 21:8). In the story of Sodom and Gomorrah, Lot tries to placate the wicked men of his city by offering his "two daughters who have not known man." Yet six verses later Lot goes out to speak "to his sons-in-law, who married his daughters" (Genesis 19:8 versus 19:14). Joseph is sold by his brothers to the Ishmaelites, but eight verses later he is brought down to Egypt by Midianites—a people of an entirely different nationality (Genesis 37:28 versus 37:36). And almost all the factual data in Chronicles differ substantially from the same facts as presented in Samuel and Kings.

If the reader is puzzled by the duplications and perplexed by the seeming contradictions, he or she is often distracted by the genealogies, redundancies, and detailed specifications and identifications.

Early in Genesis the reader encounters the first of the genealogies, entitled "the book of the generations of Adam" (Genesis 5). From there on the narrative is frequently interrupted by genealogy following genealogy, twenty-eight in all, which vary in length from the brief succession from Ruth to David, as given in Ruth 4:18–22, to the lengthy genealogy of the sons of Azel, as given in the first nine chapters of I Chronicles.

Some redundancies derive from the identification of places and names. As a mark of respect and honor, a man highly regarded would often be identified by his father's name, his grandfather's name, the tribe to which he belonged, and, finally, the place of his birth. And this information is often repeated each time the name appears. Other forms of redundancy arise from the style of writing in an early period, such as the form: "And he carried away all his cattle, and all his goods which he had gotten, the cattle of his getting, which he had gotten in Padan-Aram" (Genesis 31:18).

An added distraction to the reader is the detailed specification with which the Torah abounds, such as is given on the building of Noah's ark (Genesis 6:14–16); the building and furnishing of the tabernacle (Exodus 21–31); and the measurements of the future Temple in Jerusalem, as given in the vision of Ezekiel (40–48). Then, too, there are lists of census-takers, laws concerning the prohibition of idol-worship, laws on what people priests were permitted to marry, descriptions of sacrifices in the Temple, enumeration of the men of war of King David and of King Solomon, and so on—all of which, while of interest to the people of those times, and to theologians and scholars, hold little interest for the contemporary reader.

Added to the difficulties already enumerated, the consecutive reading of the Bible is impeded by occasional transpositions of verses and chapters. Before the days of printing, books were copied by hand. Because books are highly perishable, copies were transcribed generation after generation. And it frequently happened that a copyist at some time skipped one or several verses because the next passage began with an identical word or phrase. When the scribe realized his error, he continued to the end of the passage, then inserted the part he had omitted, since erasures were forbidden. Such transpositions may account for the confusion, for instance, in II Samuel 4–9. Sometimes, it is surmised by certain scholars, the transposition involved a whole chapter. The Joseph story, for example, is suddenly interrupted by an unrelated incident about Judah, Joseph's older brother, and his daughter-in-law Tamar (Genesis 38), which clearly belongs elsewhere. And Isaiah's call to prophecy (Isaiah 6) quite clearly belongs at the beginning of that book and not after Chapters 1–5, where it now appears.

Another handicap for the reader is the lack of any signposts in the Torah that would indicate where one story, law, record, ritual, or poem ends and another begins. In some parts this causes only slight confusion, but in others it creates utter bewilderment. In Genesis, for example, although it appears as a continuous narrative in fifty chapters and nearly 40,000 words, the perceptive reader quickly discerns that the book is a collection of some twenty-five stories in a historical progression. But in Isaiah, a book of equal length, we have the work of three or more poet-prophets who lived in different times, who were even further apart in their stature as poets, and who treated a wide diversity of topics—and all these are given in sixty-six chapters without a break. Even the most perceptive reader would have difficulty knowing when he or she had finished one poem, on one topic, and started on another.

To all these impediments were added a number of others that arose out of the translations of the Torah.

In Biblical times the Hebrew language was written without vowels or punctuation. Even those who knew the language intimately came upon instances where a word or phrase was subject to different readings, in which case the meaning of an entire passage would change, since the reader supplied the missing vowels. To meet this problem, a group of scholars called the Masoretes evolved a system of vowels for the Hebrew language, consisting of dots and dashes placed under or above the consonants. The Masoretes agreed among themselves as to how disputed passages or words should be read, and fixed them with their system of vowels. This system of Hebrew vowels was evolved about the seventh century A.D., and the text to which they were first affixed is known as the Massorah.

But the Torah was translated into Greek long before the Massorah was available, and the King James or Authorized Version of the Bible, with which we are familiar, was translated not from the Hebrew, but from the Greek translation. And there are discrepancies between the Greek and the Massorah.

Because there are no capital letters in Hebrew, in order to mark the beginning of a sentence the Hebrew letter *v* was often attached to the first word in the sentence. This *v* was translated as meaning *and*—with the result that the word "and" appears over thirty-five thousand times in the Hebrew Scriptures, a great number of them in places where no connective is necessary.

Throughout the Torah we also find a play on words that is inevitably lost in translation. Statements appear about Adam, Eve, Cain, Abel, Abraham, Sarah, Jacob, Naomi, and so on that can be understood only if the meaning of these names in Hebrew is understood. For instance, in Ruth 1:20 we read: "Call me not Naomi, call me Mara; for God dealt bitterly with me." This has meaning only when the reader knows that in Hebrew Naomi means "the sweet" or "the pleasant," and Mara means "the bitter."

Elsewhere passages play on the sound of the words in the original Hebrew, and the meaning is not clear in translation. In Amos 8:1–2, for instance, the prophet sees a basket of summer fruit in a vision; then follows this passage: "And he [God] said, 'Amos, what do you see?' And I said, 'A basket of summer fruit.' Then the Lord said to me, 'The end is come upon my people Israel.'" What we have here is a play on the word *kaitz* (summer) and *keytz* (end), which is lost in translation.

Then, too, there are idiomatic expressions in Hebrew, as there are in every language, that are untranslatable. How would we translate into Chinese or Prakrit such American idioms as "make the fur fly" or "take pot luck"? We would only create bewilderment by a literal translation. And this was also true of the Torah when certain idiomatic expressions were translated literally.

Still another difficulty arose that was caused neither by the original text nor by the translation but, rather, by the natural obsolescence of all languages. The Bible in the Authorized Version (still the most beautiful English translation) has archaisms which have accumulated as changes have occurred in the English language. Since the time when the Bible was first translated, the English language has changed perceptibly. As a result we find in the Authorized Version the word "abject" used for "outcast," "base" for "lowly," "carriage" for "baggage," "enlarge" for "to free," "forward" for "to corrode," "garner" for "barn," and so on down the alphabetical list to "with" for "twig" and "wot" for "know." Some words are no longer used, and are puzzling; other words have changed their meaning so completely that they carry a meaning which is the opposite from the meaning they conveyed in their day—like "let," which was used for "detain."

Yet, despite all the difficulties occasioned by the various authorships and editorships of the books, the duplications and contradictions, the redundancies and transpositions; the problems created by translation from Hebrew into Greek and from Greek into seventeenth-century English—a long, long passage from the innermost soul of a distant and ancient people into a region so different from the place of its origin—the glowing warmth and guiding light of the Torah have not diminished. And this enduring greatness is easily recognized by old and young, once the obstacles are removed.

The present version of the Torah was undertaken in the conviction that, with most of the impediments removed, it would be read with ease and enjoyment by many who have turned away from it because of its obstacles, and that they would find in it the spiritual sustenance it has given generation after generation.

In *The Torah for Family Reading* every chapter is accounted for. Yet it is considerably shorter than any of the standard versions, because all duplications, specifications, and detailed descriptions of rituals and genealogies have been relegated to summarized notes at the end of the book; the principal laws are given separately in a summary, alphabetically arranged; and all obvious redundancies are omitted altogether.

In language *The Torah for Family Reading* approximates the Authorized King James Version more closely than any other version in English. That is to say, the Hebrew Scriptures were compared word for word and sentence for sentence with the Authorized Version, and preference was given to the time-honored and familiar text, unless the difference involved accuracy of meaning or clarity of thought. All obscurities and archaisms were eliminated, so that every member of the family who can read, can read the text without difficulty.

Each book of the Torah is divided into logical parts and identified by descriptive titles to guide the reader.

Transposition within the text has been made where imperative for the sake of logical continuity.

Each group of books, and each book, is preceded by a brief introduction in which the historical background of the section is given and the specific problems of that book are discussed.

*The Torah for Family Reading* is intended not to displace or replace the traditional versions but, rather, to encourage, through easier reading, a revival of family reading of this centuries-old work that so profoundly affects our lives and shapes our moral behavior.

# CONTENTS

xi

# CONTENTS

# CONTENTS

PART THREE: THE BOOKS OF THE PROPHETS
*An Anthology of Four Centuries of Hebrew Prophecy (293)*

ISAIAH (I): *The Eloquent (299)*

ISAIAH (II): *The Comforter (316)*

ISAIAH (III): *Poet of Great Faith (327)*

xvi

# CONTENTS

## PART ONE

# The Five Books of Moses
## תורה

*From Creation to the Conquest of Canaan*

❑ How long ago the books of the Hebrew Bible were assembled in the form we have them now, and when they were canonized in their present order, remains in dispute. Some modern scholars claim that many of the books of the Prophets and of the Historical Chronicles were in existence before any of the Five Books were recorded. Yet these Five Books assumed a prominence in the Hebrew Scriptures unequaled by any of the others, and became the core of Judaism and Hebrew ethics.

For nearly twenty-five hundred years the Hebrew Bible has been traditionally divided into three parts: The Five Books of Moses; The Prophets; and The Other Sacred Writings, called in Greek Hagiographa. And the first part, though only about a fifth of the Hebrew Bible in length, was accorded from the start an incomparable eminence.

In Hebrew, the Five Books became known as Torah, a word meaning "law" or "instruction" — in which divine law or divine instruction is implied. Though the word Torah is now often used for the whole Bible as well as the vast literature which grew up around it, specifically the word refers to the Five Books. The Greek word for this part of the Bible is Pentateuch, which means "the five books," but is used as a term for a single work with five parts; for in Hebrew, the Five Books, by whatever name they were known, were always regarded as five parts of a single work.

On the Holy Scroll used in Hebrew worship, the Five Books alone are inscribed. This work, written by hand on parchment in a strictly prescribed manner, is divided into weekly portions according to the number of weeks in a year or leap year; and every Sabbath morning the portion prescribed for that week is read during the service. (Though in Hebrew there are no names for the days of the week other than for the Sabbath day, each week in the year has a name — a name derived from the first part of the portion of the Five Books read on that particular Sabbath.) In ancient times the reading of the Five Books lasted three years; but the Jews of Babylonia instituted the division of the Five Books so that they are completed within each year's liturgical readings.

5

And each new cycle of the reading is celebrated in a gay holiday known as "The Rejoicing of the Law" (Simhath Torah).

In Orthodox Judaism, every word in the Five Books is regarded as immutable, and the redundancies and repetitions as intentional and necessary for effective emphasis. But to the reader who comes to the Bible for its ethics and literature, the Five Books present in concentrated form all the difficulties treated earlier in the Introduction. Here the distinctive styles of the Jahwistic, Eloistic, Priestly, Deuteronomic and other documents collated in the Bible are so evident that a number of distinguished scholars have been able to chart each part to its origin. And the almost insurmountable difficulties which the original Hebrew text at times presents to the translator might be indicated in one example:

The first sentence in the Bible, as everyone knows, reads, "In the beginning God created the heaven and the earth." But in the original Hebrew text, as Rashi, the great commentator on the Bible, points out, the word "heaven" (*hashumayim*) could also be read as two words (*hash a-mayim*), in which case the meaning would be changed to: "In the beginning God created fire, and water, and earth" — a significant difference. This was, of course, recognized by the early scholars of the Bible; and in that great and voluminous commentary on the Five Books, the Midrash Rabah, we find the explanation that the heavens were made of fire and water, and therefore the beginning of Creation is given correctly whichever way we read it.

From the first sentence in Genesis to the last in Deuteronomy, we are confronted with a variety of difficulties. Some of these are the problems presented by the many duplications which vary enough to seem, or to be, in contradiction with each other. And throughout — even in the English translation — are evident the diverse materials selected from earlier texts, each retaining the language peculiarities of the time in which it was written, and each retaining its distinctive approach and style.

Considering the entanglement of ambiguities, duplications, differences in thought and language patterns, and scribal errors, it is astounding that the Five Books as we have them today still have such vital unity and such persuasive clarity as a code, and as great literature.

The reader who wishes to get the full significance of the Five Books might do well to disregard the ambiguities, which have resulted in a mountain of commentaries, and read them as a unified work with a single theme and a single objective, built around the central figure: Moses. They should be read for what, as literature, they really are: a great narrative of an emancipator and lawgiver, of a prophet of prophets, who, though he lived so many centuries ago, still profoundly influences our lives.

Read as a unified work, the Five Books assume extraordinary literary structure.

Genesis becomes the necessary prelude, with the Age of the Patriarchs introducing the times and circumstances of Moses' youth.

Exodus gives briefly the childhood of one born into slavery and accidentally reared in a palace, who learns early of his origins and of the evils of slavery. In his youth he kills a man and flees to the desert for safety. But he cannot escape his conscience — not because of the man he killed, but because of the evils of slavery for which he killed the man. Then the narrative gives the struggle of Moses with himself, with his people, and finally with Pharaoh; culminating in the bitter triumph of seeing his people emancipated from slavery only to dream of the fleshpots of Egypt, and to descend to the worship of a golden calf.

Leviticus may at first seem an interpolation of later times (which in the order of the growth of the Bible it probably was), but when read as part of the narrative of Moses it takes its place in showing the character of the lawgiver who abhorred slavery but who could not conceive of freedom and a free people without order and without obedience to law. The many ordinances on priestly offerings, the ceremonies concerning ordination of priests, and the definitions of what may or may not be eaten — all these are not unrelated to the lofty Code of Holiness, and the proclamation about the Jubilee, symbol of freedom, ringing out the injunction: "Proclaim liberty throughout the land unto all the inhabitants thereof!" This stirring injunction has echoed throughout the centuries in the hearts of men, and is inscribed upon the American Liberty Bell.

Numbers follows Leviticus as logically as a change in weather follows a storm. The short stormy period — of revolt against slavery; of the exodus of a people from the land in which they had dwelt for many generations; of two tests, one at the Red Sea and the other at the foot of Mount Sinai, where the Law is defined — this short stormy period is over. Now begins the slow and painful period when a nation born in slavery must be molded into a nation of courageous freemen, worthy of the Lord their God. Numbers covers thirty-eight long and tedious years, years full of trouble and personal tragedy in the life of Moses. During this time his sister Miriam and his brother Aaron die; a dreadful revolt must be harshly subdued and the people quieted; the laws of daily living must be effectively repeated and inscribed on the minds of the people; and in between there are wars to be fought and negotiations to be carried on with people whose lands must be crossed. Finally the leader and his people arrive at the border on the Jordan, and there Moses realizes that he will not be permitted to enter the Promised Land. And Moses sets about to prepare a successor who will lead the people in their conquest of Canaan, and to prepare the people to accept the authority of that successor.

Deuteronomy, the climax and completion of the narrative, covers a very short period. It consists of three great discourses by Moses, his song, and his blessing of the tribes — apparently the traditional act for a departing leader. Deuteronomy is written with a greater eloquence and a more profound love for mankind than is evident in the preceding books. The style and content give the calm and mature expression of a great and aging man who reviews the days of his life without regret, but with sadness, and with the implied fear that his labors may come to nought if the people forget what he has taught them. Most of Deuteronomy, like all orations, should be read aloud to elicit the richness of phrasing and the sonority of the underscored promises and threats.

The Five Books of Moses, read as a great and ancient epic about a prophet and the people he created with the Law and with his dream of freedom and justice and love, will make clear to the reader why the Psalmist broke out into such joyous praise (Psalm 119) in his tribute to the Book of the Law:

"O Lord, my soul breaks with longing for your judgments at all times! Turn away my eyes from vanity, and quicken me on your way; and take not the word of truth ever out of my mouth. For how sweet are your words to my palate — sweeter than honey in my mouth!" (

# GENESIS
## The Story of Early Mankind

❡ Genesis gives the story of mankind from Creation to the death of Joseph, a period according to the Bible of some twenty-two centuries, and is primarily concerned with the Hebraic record of the ten generations from Adam to Noah; from Noah's son Shem to his descendant Abraham, ten generations removed; and from Abraham to the sons of Jacob. Genesis contains more stories that have had a universal appeal, undiminished through the centuries, than all the rest of the books of the Hebrew Bible. These stories have been retold thousands of times, in a thousand tongues, in prose and in poetry, in nursery rhymes and complex scholarly explorations, in brief quatrains and lengthy novels; and they constantly reappear as themes of contemporary literature and films. This book gives the early days of mankind in an exciting sequence of dramatic stories, often presented symbolically or allegorically, which endure in our memories beyond any other historical document. Within the confines of this rather small book are related the origins of many human institutions: how people began to wear clothes, why man must labor for his food, the conflict between the farmer and the shepherd, the rise of the various languages and nations, the distinction between human rights and property rights, and a host of others. And they are presented in story form, with an exceptional simplicity and a startling economy of words.

Here we encounter the familiar stories of Adam and Eve's expulsion from the Garden of Eden; Cain's murder of his brother Abel; the confusion of tongues at the tower of Babel; Noah's ark and the great flood; Abraham's covenant with God; the destruction of Sodom and Gomorrah; the conflict between the brothers Jacob and Esau; the tragedy of Dinah and Shechem; climaxed by the magnificent story of Joseph, dreamer of dreams, wise and incorruptible, who rose from slavery to the highest appointment in the land of Egypt.

In Hebrew this book is called simply, "In the Beginning" (B'reshith), after the opening phrase: "In the beginning God created the heaven and the earth." We know the book by its Greek title, Genesis, which carries the same meaning. Though the story of Creation appears at the beginning of the Bible, scholars find mounting evidence that it may have come late in order of composition. But whatever the time of its composition, Genesis logically belongs at the beginning, as the foundation stone for the structure of the Bible. ⟨[

## The Story of Creation

1-2   In the beginning God created the heaven and the earth. The earth was without form, and void; and darkness was upon the face of the deep; and the winds of God moved upon the face of the waters. Then God said, "Let there be light." And there was light. God saw that the light was good, and he divided the light from the darkness. God called the light Day, and the darkness he called Night.

And the evening and the morning were the first day.

Then God said, "Let there be a firmament in the midst of the waters and let it divide them." And God made the firmament, and divided the waters which were below from the waters which were above. And God called the firmament Heaven.

And the evening and the morning were the second day.

Then God said, "Let the waters under the heaven be gathered together in one place, and let the dry land appear." And it was so. God called the dry land Earth, and the waters that were gathered together he called Seas. Then God said, "Let the earth bring forth grass, the herbs yielding seed, and the fruit trees yielding fruit, each after its kind." And it was so. The earth brought forth grass, the herbs yielding seed, and the fruit trees yielding fruit, each after its kind. And God saw that it was good.

And the evening and the morning were the third day.

Then God said, "Let there be lights in the heaven to divide the day from the night; and let them be as signs for the days, and the seasons, and the years; and let them give light upon the earth." And it was so. God made two great lights, the greater light to rule the day, and the lesser light to rule the night; and he made the stars also.

And the evening and the morning were the fourth day.

Then God said, "Let the waters bring forth abundantly moving creatures that have life, and birds that may fly above the earth in the open firmament of heaven." Thus God created great whales and every creature which lives in the water, after their kind, and every winged bird after its kind. And God blessed them, saying, "Be fruitful and multiply."

And the evening and the morning were the fifth day.

Then God said, "Let the earth bring forth living creatures, each after its kind — cattle, and creeping things, and wild beasts of the earth." And it was so. And God saw that it was good.

Then God said, "Let us make man in our image, after our likeness; and let him have dominion over the fish of the sea, and over the birds of the air, and over all the living things upon the earth."

And the Lord God formed man out of the dust of the ground, and breathed into his nostrils the breath of life; and man became a living being. Then God planted a garden eastward in Eden. And out of the ground God made to grow every tree that is pleasant to the sight, and its fruit good to eat, and in the midst of the garden he made to grow the tree of life, and the tree of knowledge of good and evil. God took the man, and put him in the garden of Eden to care for it; and God said to him, "Of every tree in the garden you may freely eat, except of the tree of knowledge of good and evil. You must not eat of the fruit of that tree, for on the day you eat of it, you shall surely die."

Then God said, "It is not good that the man should be alone; I will make a helpmate for him." So God caused a deep sleep to fall upon the man, whom he called Adam; and while he slept, God took one of his ribs, and closed up the place with flesh. Out of the rib which God took from Adam, he made a woman and brought her to the man.

And Adam said, "This is now bone of my bones, and flesh of my flesh; she shall be called woman, because she was taken out of man." Therefore shall a man leave his father and his mother and cling to his wife, and they shall be one flesh. And they were both naked, the man and his wife, but they were not ashamed.

God blessed them, saying, "Be fruitful and multiply; replenish the earth, and rule over it. And have dominion over every living thing that moves upon the earth." And God said, "Behold, I have given you every herb bearing seed, and every tree whose fruit yields seed. These shall be your food. And to every beast of the earth, to every bird of the air, and to everything that moves upon the earth in which there is life, I have given the green herb for food."

God saw everything that he had made, and behold, it was very good. And the evening and the morning were the sixth day.

Thus on the sixth day the heaven and the earth, and all their host, were completed. And on the seventh day God rested. And God blessed the seventh day and sanctified it, because on that day God rested from all his work.[1]

## The Great Temptation

3        Now the serpent was craftier than any other beast of the field, and he said to the woman: "Did God command you not to eat the fruit of every tree in the garden?"

The woman answered, "We may eat of the fruit of all the trees of the garden; but of the tree in the center of the garden, God said: 'You shall not eat of it, neither shall you touch it, lest you die.'"

The serpent said to her, "Surely you would not die, for God knows that on the day you eat of it your eyes will be opened, and you shall be as gods, knowing good and evil."

When the woman saw that the tree was pleasant to the eye, and a tree to be desired to make one wise, she took of its fruit and ate, and she also gave some to her husband, and he ate. Then the eyes of both of them were opened, and they knew that they were naked. So they sewed fig leaves together and made themselves aprons.

Then they heard the voice of the Lord God, walking in the garden in the cool of the day, and Adam and his wife hid themselves from the presence of God among the trees of the garden.

God called to Adam, "Where are you?"

And Adam answered, "I heard your voice in the garden, and I was afraid because I was naked, so I hid myself."

God said, "Who told you that you were naked? Have you eaten of the tree of which I commanded you not to eat?"

And Adam answered, "The woman whom you gave to be with me, she gave me some fruit from the tree, and I ate it."

Then God said to the woman, "What have you done?"

[1] See GENESIS, Chapters 1 and 2, in Notes and Excisions.

And the woman answered, "The serpent beguiled me, and I did eat."

God said to the serpent, "Because you have done this, you shall be accursed! Upon your belly shall you crawl, and dust shall you eat all the days of your life! And I will put enmity between you and the woman and between her seed and your seed. They shall bruise your head, and you shall bruise their heel."

To the woman, God said, "I will greatly multiply your sorrows. In pain shall you bring forth your children; your will shall be subject to your husband's, and he shall rule over you."

And to Adam, God said, "Because you have listened to the voice of your wife, and have eaten of the tree of which I commanded you not to eat, the ground shall be cursed. Thorns and thistles shall it bear for you, and in the sweat of your brow shall you bring forth your food out of the ground till the day you return to it. For dust you are, and to dust shall you return."

Adam named his wife Eve (Life), because she was the mother of all the living. And for Adam and his wife God made garments of skins, and clothed them.

Then God reflected, "Behold, the man has become as one of us, knowing good and evil. If he should put forth his hand and eat also of the tree of life, he will live forever."

Therefore, the Lord God sent him out of the garden of Eden, to till the ground from which he had been taken. He drove out the man, and at the east of the garden of Eden he placed angels, with flaming swords which turned in every direction to bar the way to the tree of life.

## The First Murder

4-5    Adam knew Eve his wife, and she conceived, and bore Cain. And she conceived again, and bore his brother Abel. Abel grew up and became a keeper of sheep, while Cain was a tiller of the ground. And in the course of time Cain the farmer brought of the fruit of the ground an offering to the Lord; and Abel the shepherd brought an offering of the firstlings of his flock. God accepted Abel's offering, but for Cain's offering he showed no regard. Then Cain was angered and his countenance fell.

God said to him, "Why are you angry and why has your countenance fallen? If you do what is right, will you not be accepted? And if you do what is wrong, the sin will be at your door. For your younger brother is subject to you, and you rule over him."

Cain quarreled with his brother Abel; and when they were in the field, Cain rose up against Abel and slew him.

God called out to Cain, "Where is Abel your brother?"

And he answered, "I know not. Am I my brother's keeper?"

God said to him, "What have you done? The voice of your brother's blood cries out to me from the ground. And now you shall be cursed upon the earth which has opened its mouth to receive your brother's blood. Henceforth, when you till the soil, it shall not yield to you its strength. A fugitive and a wanderer shall you be upon the earth."

And Cain cried out to the Lord, "My punishment is greater than I can bear. This day you have driven me out, and your face will be hidden from me. I shall be a fugitive, and whoever comes upon me will slay me."

Then the Lord said to him, "Whoever slays Cain shall have vengeance taken on him sevenfold." And God put a mark upon Cain, lest any coming upon him should kill him.

Then Cain went out from the presence of the Lord. And he dwelt in the land at the east of Eden.[2]

Adam knew his wife again, and she bore him a son, and they named him Seth. "For," said Eve, "God has given me another son to take the place of Abel, whom Cain slew."

The days of Adam after he became the father of Seth were eight hundred years, and he had other sons and daughters. All the days that Adam lived were nine hundred and thirty years. And then he died.[3]

## Noah's Ark

6-10   And it came to pass, when men began to multiply on the face of the earth, and daughters were born to them, that the sons of God saw the daughters of men were fair, and took them as wives. In those days there were giants on the earth; for when the daughters of men bore children to the sons of God, the same became mighty men, who were of old the men of renown.

[2] See GENESIS, Chapter 4, in Notes and Excisions.
[3] See GENESIS, Chapter 5, in Notes and Excisions.

God saw that man's wickedness was great, and that every thought in man's heart was only for evil. And God regretted that he had made man, and his heart was grieved.

God reflected, "My spirit shall not always strive with man, for he is only flesh. I will destroy man whom I have created. I shall efface him, and the beasts and the creeping things and the birds of the air, for I regret that I have made them."

But Noah had found favor in the eyes of the Lord. For Noah was a just man and perfect in his generation. And God said to Noah, "The time has come for the end of all flesh, because they have filled the earth with corruption and violence. Therefore make yourself an ark of gopher wood, and make rooms in the ark, and cover it inside and out with pitch. The length of the ark shall be three hundred cubits; and with lower, second, and third stories shall you make it. For behold, I will bring a flood upon the earth, and every living thing that is upon it shall perish. But with you I will establish my covenant; and you shall enter the ark, you and your sons and your wife, and your sons' wives with you. And of every living thing, two of every sort, male and female, shall you bring into the ark to keep them alive with you. And take with you of all food that is eaten, as food for you and for them."

Thus Noah did; according to all that God commanded him, so did he. Then Noah went into the ark with his sons and his wife and his sons' wives. And of everything that lives upon the earth there went in two and two into the ark, the male and the female, as God had commanded Noah.

After seven days the waters of the flood came upon the earth. And on the same day the fountains of the great deep burst, and the windows of heaven opened. And the rain fell upon the earth forty days and forty nights. The waters increased greatly and bore up the ark, and the ark floated on the face of the waters. And the waters rose upon the earth until all the high hills were covered. The waters prevailed, and covered all the mountains under the whole heaven. And all in whose nostrils was the breath of life perished. Only Noah remained alive, and those that were with him in the ark.

The waters covered the earth a hundred and fifty days. And at the end of that time God remembered Noah and all that were with him in the ark. And God made a wind to pass over the earth, and stopped up the fountains of the deep, and closed the windows of heaven, and the waters abated. On the seventeenth day of the seventh month, the ark came to rest upon the mountains of Ararat. The waters decreased steadily; and on the first day of the tenth month, the tops of the mountains were seen.

At the end of forty days after the ark came to rest, Noah opened a window and sent forth a dove. But the dove could find no rest for the sole of her foot, because the waters still covered the face of the whole earth, and she returned to the ark. Noah put out his hand and took her in. Seven days later Noah again sent out the dove, and again she returned to him in the evening. But lo, in her mouth was an olive leaf freshly plucked, so Noah knew that the waters were abating. Noah waited another seven days, and again sent out the dove, which returned to him no more. Then Noah removed the covering of the ark, and looked, and behold, the face of the earth was dry.

Then God said to Noah, "Come out of the ark, you and your wife and your sons, and your sons' wives with you. Bring out with you every living thing, that they may breed abundantly, and be fruitful, and multiply upon the earth."

Noah came out of the ark, and all those that were with him; and he built an altar to the Lord, and placed burnt offerings upon the altar. The Lord smelled the sweet offering and reflected, "I will not again curse the ground for man's sake; neither will I again smite every living thing, as I have done. As long as the earth endures, seedtime and harvest, cold and heat, summer and winter, day and night shall not cease."

God blessed Noah and his sons, saying, "Be fruitful and multiply and replenish the earth. The fear of you shall be upon every beast on land, and every bird of the air, and upon all the fish in the sea. Every moving thing that lives shall be food for you. Only flesh with the lifeblood in it you must not eat. For I will require an accounting of your own lifeblood, and of every man will I require an accounting of the life of his brother man. Whoever sheds man's blood, by man shall his blood be shed, for in the image of God made he man."

God said to Noah and his sons, "Behold I establish my covenant with you, and with your descendants after you, that there shall never again be a flood to destroy the earth. And this is the sign of my covenant for all generations: When I bring clouds over the earth, I shall set my rainbow on the cloud; and I will look upon it and remember the covenant between me and every living creature that is upon the earth."

Noah lived three hundred and fifty years after the flood; and when he reached the age of nine hundred and fifty years, he died.

The sons of Noah who went with him out of the ark were Shem, and Ham, and Japheth, and of them was the whole earth populated.[4]


## The Confusion of Tongues

11     Now the whole earth was of one language, and of one speech.
        And in time, as men journeyed from the East, they found a plain in the land of Shinar; and they dwelt there.

They said to one another, "Come, let us make bricks, and burn them thoroughly." And they used bricks for stone, and bitumen for mortar. Then they said, "Come, let us build ourselves a city, and a tower whose top may reach to heaven; and let us make a name for ourselves."

The Lord came down to see the city and the tower which the children of men were building. And God reflected, "Behold, they are one people and they have one language, and this is what they begin to do. Later nothing will restrain them in whatever they resolve upon. Come, let us go down and confound their language, that they may not understand one another's speech."

So the Lord scattered them abroad upon the face of all the earth, and they left off building the city.

Therefore it was called Babel; for it was there that the Lord confounded the languages of the nations, and from there he scattered the people abroad over the whole earth.[5]


## Abraham's Trials

11-12   Now these are the generations of Terah (a descendant of Noah's
        son Shem). Terah became the father of Abraham, Nahor, and Haran; and Haran was the father of Lot. Haran died in the city of his nativity, in Ur of the Chaldees. And Terah took Abraham, his son, and Lot, his grandson, and Sarah, wife of Abraham, and they went from Ur of the Chaldees toward Canaan; they came to Haran and dwelt there. And Terah died in Haran.

And the Lord said to Abraham, "Depart from your country, and from your kindred, and from your father's house, and go to a land that I will

[4] See GENESIS, Chapters 9-10, in Notes and Excisions.
[5] See GENESIS, Chapter 11, in Notes and Excisions.

show you. And I will make of you a great nation, and bless you, and make your name great. I will bless him who blesses you, and curse him who curses you, and in you shall all the families of the earth be blessed."

So Abraham left, as the Lord had commanded him. Abraham was seventy and five years old when he departed from Haran. And he took Sarah his wife, and Lot his nephew, with all their substance and the servants they had acquired in Haran; and they went into the land of Canaan, as far as Shechem in the plain of Moreh.

There the Lord appeared to Abraham and said, "To your descendants will I give this land." And there Abraham built an altar to the Lord, who had appeared to him. Then Abraham went on to a mountain east of Bethel, and pitched his tent with Bethel on the west, and Ai on the east; and there he built another altar to the Lord.

And Abraham journeyed on, still going toward the south.

Now there was a grave famine in the land, so Abraham went down to dwell in Egypt. And as he was about to enter Egypt, he said to Sarah his wife, "I know that you are beautiful to look upon. When the Egyptians see you they will say, 'This is his wife,' and they will kill me that they may take you from me. Say to them that you are my sister, that it may go well with me for your sake."

And it came to pass that when Abraham came into Egypt, the princes of Pharaoh saw that Sarah was very beautiful, and she was taken to Pharaoh's house. Pharaoh treated Abraham well for her sake, and gave him sheep, and oxen, and asses, and camels, and menservants and maidservants. But the Lord plagued Pharaoh and his household with great plagues because of Abraham's wife.

Then Pharaoh summoned Abraham and said, "What have you done to me? Why did you not tell me that she was your wife? Why did you say, 'She is my sister'?"

Abraham answered, "Because I thought, 'Surely the fear of God is not in this place, and they will slay me so that they may take my wife from me.' And, indeed, she is my sister, for she is the daughter of my father but not the daughter of my mother; and she became my wife."

Pharaoh said, "Behold your wife! Take her, and go your way!"

Then Pharaoh ordered his men concerning Abraham, and they saw him on his way, with his wife, and Lot, and all that they had. And they went out of Egypt and journeyed as far as Bethel, to the place where his tent had been before, to the place of the altar he had built; and there Abraham called on the name of the Lord.

## Abraham and Lot Separate

*13-15*   Abraham was now very rich in cattle, in silver, and in gold. And
Lot, who went with Abraham, also had flocks, and herds, and
tents. The land was not sufficient to support them both, for their substance was so great; and strife arose between the herdsmen of Abraham's
cattle and the herdsmen of Lot's cattle. Then Abraham said to Lot, "Let
there be no strife between us, or between your herdsmen and mine, for
we are kinsmen. Is not the whole land spread out before you? Separate
yourself from me, I pray you, and if you will go to the left, I will go to
the right; or if you depart to the right, then I will go to the left."

Lot lifted his eyes and beheld in the east the plain of Jordan, well
watered like the garden of the Lord. So Lot chose the plain of Jordan,
and he journeyed east. Thus they separated the one from the other.
Abraham dwelt in the land of Canaan, and Lot settled in the plain of
Jordan and pitched his tents as far as Sodom. Now the men of Sodom
were wicked, and sinners before the Lord.

After Lot departed, the Lord said to Abraham, "Now lift up your eyes
and look from the place where you are to the north, and the south, and
the east, and the west; for all the land which you see before you I shall
give to you and to your descendants forever. And I will make your offspring as numerous as the dust of the earth, so that if a man can number the dust of the earth, then shall your descendants also be numbered.
Arise, walk through the land in the length of it and in the breadth of it,
for I will give it to you."

So Abraham moved his tent to the oaks of Mamre, at Hebron, and
there he built an altar to the Lord.[6]

## The Birth of Ishmael

*16*   Now Sarah, Abraham's wife, bore him no children. And after they
had dwelt in Canaan ten years, Sarah said to her husband, "Behold, the Lord has restrained me from bearing. I pray you, go in to my
maid, that I may obtain children through her." And she took Hagar, her
Egyptian maid, and gave her to Abraham to be his wife.

When Hagar knew that she was with child, she began to despise her

[6] See GENESIS, Chapters 14-15, in Notes and Excisions.

mistress. And Sarah said to Abraham, "I have given my maid to you, and now that she has conceived I am despised in her eyes. May the Lord judge between you and me!" But Abraham answered, "Your maid is in your hands; do with her as it pleases you."

Sarah dealt harshly with Hagar, and she fled. An angel of the Lord found her beside a spring of water in the wilderness, on the way to Shur. He said to her, "Where do you come from? And where do you go?" She answered, "I am fleeing from the face of my mistress Sarah."

And the angel said to her, "Return to your mistress and submit yourself to her. For behold, you shall bear a son, and you shall name him Ishmael, because the Lord has heard your affliction. His hand will be against every man, and every man's hand will be against him."

Hagar returned and bore Abraham a son, and they named him Ishmael. And Abraham was fourscore and six years old when Ishmael was born to him.

## The Covenant of Circumcision

17    When Abraham was ninety and nine years old, the Lord appeared to him and said, "I am the Almighty God. Walk before me with integrity. And I will make a covenant between me and you."

Abraham fell on his face, and God talked with him, saying, "Behold, my covenant is with you, and you shall be the father of many nations. I will give to you, and to your descendants after you, the land in which you are a stranger, all the land of Canaan, for an everlasting possession. And this is my covenant, which you shall keep, you and your descendants, from generation to generation: Every male child among you shall be circumcised — every male child among you that is eight days old shall be circumcised — he that is born in your house, and he that is bought with money from a stranger. And the uncircumcised child shall be cut off from his people, for he has broken my covenant."

Then God said to Abraham, "As for Sarah your wife, I will bless her and give her a son, and she shall be a mother of nations."

Abraham fell upon his face and laughed, and said in his heart, "Shall a child be born to him who is a hundred years old? And shall Sarah, who is ninety years old, bear a child?"

And God said, "Sarah your wife shall bear you a son, and you shall call him Isaac. And I will establish my covenant with him and with his descendants forever."

Then God left off talking with him, and went up from Abraham.

Abraham took Ishmael his son, and all the males that were born in his house or bought with his money, and circumcised them on the selfsame day, as God had commanded him. Abraham himself was ninety-nine years old when he was circumcised, and Ishmael his son was thirteen years old.[7]

## The Visit of the Angels

18    The Lord appeared to Abraham in the plains of Mamre, as he sat at the tent door during the heat of the day. When he lifted his eyes and looked, lo, three men were coming toward him. Abraham ran to meet them and bowed to the ground, and said, "My lords, if I have found favor in your eyes, pray do not pass by your servant. Let a little water be brought, and wash your feet, and rest yourselves under the tree; and I will bring a morsel of bread to refresh you. After that you shall go your way."

They answered, "Do as you have said."

Abraham hastened into the tent to Sarah, and said, "Make ready quickly three measures of fine meal, knead it, and make cakes upon the hearth." Then he went to the herd and chose a calf tender and good, which he gave to a servant to prepare. Abraham took butter and milk and the meat which had been made ready and set it before his guests; then he stood nearby under the tree to serve them as they ate.

The angels said to him, "Where is Sarah your wife?" And he answered, "She is in the tent." One of them said, "I will return to you when the season comes again, and, lo, Sarah your wife shall have a son."

Now Sarah heard this, for she was at the tent door which was behind him, and she laughed to herself.

The Lord said to Abraham, "Why did Sarah laugh? Is there anything too difficult for the Lord? At the time appointed I will return, and Sarah shall have a son."

And Sarah denied, saying, "I laughed not." For she was afraid.

But he said, "No. You did laugh."

Then the men rose and were ready to leave, and they looked toward

[7] See GENESIS, Chapter 17, in Notes and Excisions.

21

Sodom. And Abraham went along with them to accompany them part of the way. The Lord reflected, "Shall I hide from Abraham what I am about to do, seeing that Abraham shall become a great and mighty nation, and all the nations of the earth shall be blessed in him?"

And the Lord said to Abraham, "Because the outcry against Sodom and Gomorrah is great, and their sin is very grave, I will go down to see whether they have done evil according to the outcry against them."

The two angels turned and went toward Sodom, while Abraham still stood before the Lord. Abraham drew near and said, "Will you destroy the just with the wicked? Perhaps there are fifty just men within the city. Will you not spare the place for the sake of fifty? For it would be far from you to slay the righteous with the wicked."

And the Lord said, "If I find in Sodom fifty righteous men, then I will spare the place for their sakes."

Abraham answered, "Behold now, I, who am but dust and ashes, have taken upon myself to speak to the Lord! Perhaps there shall lack five of the fifty righteous. Will you destroy all the city for want of five?"

And the Lord said, "If I find there forty and five righteous men, I will not destroy the city."

Abraham spoke again. "Perhaps only forty will be found there?"

And God said, "I will not destroy it for the forty's sake."

Abraham answered, "Oh let not the Lord be angry, and I will speak. Perhaps thirty will be found there."

And the Lord said, "I will not do it for the sake of the thirty."

Then Abraham said, "Behold, I have taken it upon myself to speak to the Lord! Perhaps only twenty will be found there."

And God said, "I will not destroy the city for the sake of the twenty."

Abraham said, "Oh let not the Lord be angry and I will speak but this once. Perhaps only ten will be found there."

And the Lord said, "Then I will not destroy the city for the sake of the ten."

And the Lord went his way, and Abraham returned to his place.

## The Destruction of Sodom

19-20　In the evening the two angels came to Sodom. Lot was sitting at the gate of the city, and when he saw them, he rose to meet them, and bowed with his face to the ground and said, "My lords, I pray you turn in to your servant's house, and wash your feet and stay for the night; and in the morning you may rise early and go on your way."

They answered, "No, we will spend the night in the street."

But Lot urged them. So they went to his house, and he prepared a feast for them, and they ate. But before they lay down for the night, the men of Sodom, both young and old, surrounded the house and called out to Lot, "Where are the men who came to you tonight? Bring them out to us!"

Lot came out and shut the door after him, and said, "I pray you, my brothers, do not be so wicked. Behold, I have two daughters who have known no man. Let me bring them out to you. Only do no harm to these men, for they have come under the shelter of my roof."

They shouted, "Stand back!" And they said, "This fellow, who came as a sojourner, sets himself up as a judge. Now we will deal worse with you than with them!" And they pressed heavily against Lot to break down the door. But the men within pulled Lot into the house and shut the door. Then they struck those outside with blindness, both young and old, so that they wearied themselves groping to find the door.

And the two said to Lot, "Take out of this place all your kindred, and whatever you have in this city. For the Lord has sent us to destroy it."

So Lot went out, and he said to the men who were to marry his daughters, "Arise! Flee this place! For the Lord will destroy the city!" But they thought that Lot was mocking them.

At dawn the angels hurried Lot, saying, "Take your wife and your daughters and flee, lest you be consumed with the city." But Lot lingered. Then the men seized his hand, and the hand of his wife, and the hands of his two daughters, and brought them outside the city. And they said, "Flee, nor look behind you, nor tarry in the plain. Flee to the mountains, lest you be destroyed."

Then God rained upon Sodom and Gomorrah brimstone and fire out of heaven. And he overthrew those cities, and destroyed all the inhabitants and all that grew upon the ground.

But Lot's wife looked back to see what was behind her, and she became a pillar of salt.

In the morning Abraham got up early and went out to the place where he had stood before the Lord. He looked toward Sodom and Gomorrah and toward all the land of the plain, and lo, the smoke rose up from the land like the smoke of a furnace.

# Lot's Daughters

Lot went up and dwelt in the cave of a mountain, and his two daughters dwelt with him. And the firstborn said to the younger: "Our father is old, and there is not another man on earth to come in to us after the manner of all the earth. Come, let us make our father drink wine, and we will lie with him, that we may preserve the seed of our father."

That night they made their father drink wine; and the firstborn went in and lay with her father; and he perceived not when she lay down nor when she arose. On the morrow, the firstborn said to the younger, "Let us make our father drink wine this night also; and you go in and lie with him, that we may preserve the seed of our father."

They made their father drink wine that night also; and the younger arose and lay with him; and he perceived not when she lay down nor when she arose.

Thus were both the daughters of Lot with child by their father. The firstborn bore a son, and called him Moab. The same is the father of the Moabites to this day. The younger also bore a son, and she called him Ben-ammi. The same is the father of the children of Ammon to this day.[8]

# Hagar's Exile

21 Sarah conceived and bore Abraham a son in his old age, at the time of which God had spoken to him. Abraham called his son Isaac; and he circumcised him when he was eight days old, as God had commanded. And Abraham was a hundred years old when Isaac was born.

The child grew and was weaned, and on the day of the weaning Abraham gave a great feast. But Sarah saw the son of Hagar the Egyptian mocking. Therefore she said to Abraham, "Cast out this bondswoman and her son, for the son of this servant shall not share in the inheritance with my son."

This was unjust in Abraham's sight because of his son Ishmael. But God said to him, "Be not grieved because of the boy and because of his mother, for through Isaac shall your descendants carry your name. And

[8] See GENESIS, Chapter 20, in Notes and Excisions.

because the child of the bondswoman is your son, of him also will I make a nation."

Abraham rose early in the morning, and took bread, and a skin filled with water, and gave it to Hagar, putting it on her shoulder. Then he gave her the child and sent her away. She departed, and wandered in the wilderness of Beersheba. When the water was gone, Hagar cast the child under one of the bushes. And she went and sat down a good way off, the distance of a bowshot. "For," she said, "I cannot bear to look upon the death of my child." And she lifted up her voice and wept.

An angel of God called to Hagar out of heaven: "Fear not, Hagar, for God has heard the voice of your child. Arise, lift him up and hold him, for I will make of him a great nation." And God opened her eyes and she saw a well of water. She went and filled the skin with water, and gave some to the boy to drink. And God was with them.

The boy grew up, and became an archer. He dwelt in the wilderness of Paran, and his mother took a wife for him from the land of Egypt.[9]

## Abraham's Test

22 And it came to pass after these things that God tested Abraham in this way: He said to him, "Abraham, take your son, your only son Isaac, whom you love, and go to the land of Moriah, and offer him there as a burnt offering on one of the mountains which I will show you."

Abraham rose early in the morning, saddled his ass, took two of his young men with him, and Isaac his son; and after he had cut the wood for the burnt offering, he started out for the place of which God had told him. On the third day of their journey, Abraham lifted his eyes and saw the place afar off. He said to his young men, "Abide here with the ass, and I and the boy will go yonder to worship." He took the wood for the sacrifice and laid it upon Isaac his son, and he carried in his hand the fire and the sacrificial knife. Then they both went off together.

On the way Isaac said, "My father, behold the fire and the wood, but where is the lamb for a burnt offering?" And Abraham answered, "My son, God will provide a lamb for the burnt offering."

So they went on together until they reached the place of which God had told him. Abraham built an altar there, and placed the wood on it in order, and he bound Isaac and laid him on the altar, upon the wood.

[9] See GENESIS, Chapter 21, in Notes and Excisions.

Then Abraham took up the sacrificial knife and stretched out his hand to slay his son.

But an angel of the Lord called out to him from heaven, "Abraham! Abraham!"

Abraham answered, "Here am I!"

And the angel said, "Lay not your hand upon the boy! For now I know that you fear God, seeing that you have not withheld your son, even your only son."

Abraham lifted his eyes and looked, and behold, behind him a ram was caught in a thicket by his horns.

Abraham went and took the ram, and sacrificed him as a burnt offering in the place of his son.

The angel called to Abraham a second time, saying, "'Because you have done this, and have not withheld from me your son, even your only son,' says the Lord, 'I will bless you and multiply your offspring like the stars of the heaven and like the sand on the seashore, and they shall possess the gate of their enemies, and in them shall all the nations of the earth be blessed.'"

So Abraham returned to the young men, and they went together to Beersheba, where Abraham dwelt.

## Sarah's Death

23    Sarah lived a hundred and twenty-seven years; and she died in Hebron, in the land of Canaan. And Abraham mourned for Sarah, and he wept for her.

Then Abraham rose up from before his dead, and went to the sons of Heth, and said to them, "I am a stranger and a sojourner among you. Give me possession of a burying-place with you, that I may bury my dead." And they answered him, "My lord, you are a mighty prince among us. In the choicest of our sepulchers bury your dead. None of us will withhold from you his sepulcher." Abraham bowed down to the people of the land, and he said to them, "Entreat Ephron, the son of Zohar, that he may give me the cave of Machpelah, which is at the end of his field. For as much as it is worth, let him give it to me in your presence as a burying-place."

Now Ephron was sitting in their midst, and he answered Abraham in the hearing of the sons of Heth, and of all those who went in at the gate of the city, "My lord, hear me: the field is yours and the cave that is in it.

In the presence of my people I give it to you; bury your dead." Abraham bowed down before the people. And he said to Ephron in their hearing, "I pray you, hear me: I will give you the price of the field; accept it from me, and I will bury my dead there." Ephron answered, "My lord, a piece of land worth four hundred shekels in silver, what is that between you and me? Bury your dead."

Abraham weighed out for Ephron the silver which he had named; and the field of Machpelah, and the cave in it, and all the trees in the field, were made over to Abraham in the presence of the people, and before all those who went in at the gate of the city.

After this, Abraham buried Sarah his wife in the cave of the field of Machpelah before Mamre, which is Hebron, in the land of Canaan.


## Isaac Takes a Bride

24     When Abraham was old and stricken with age, he said to the steward of his household, "Put your hand under my thigh, and swear by the God of heaven and earth that you will not take a wife for my son from the daughters of the Canaanites, but you will go to my native country and my kindred to bring a wife for my son Isaac."

The steward asked, "If the woman is not willing to follow me to this land, shall I take your son back to the land from which you came?" And Abraham answered, "If the woman is not willing to follow you, you shall be free from this oath; but see to it that you do not take my son there." Then the steward put his hand under his master's thigh, and swore to obey him.

Abraham's steward took ten of his master's camels laden with gifts, and departed, and he went to Mesopotamia, to the city of Nahor. He arrived at the outskirts of the city toward evening, at the time when the women came out to draw water, and he made the camels kneel down near a well.

And the steward prayed, "O God of my master Abraham, show kindness to him. Behold, I stand here by the well and the daughters of the men of the city come out to draw water. Let it come to pass that the maiden to whom I shall say, 'Let down your pitcher, that I may drink,' shall reply, 'Drink, and I will give water to your camels also'; and let that maiden be the one you have chosen for your servant Isaac. Thus shall I know that you have shown kindness to my master."

Before he had done praying, behold, a maiden came out with a pitcher on her shoulder, and she was very fair to look upon. She went down to the well and filled her pitcher; and the steward ran up to her and said, "Pray, let me drink a little water from your pitcher." She answered, "Drink, my lord." And she hastened to lower the pitcher upon her hand. When he had finished drinking, she said, "I will draw water for your camels also, until they have done drinking." And she hastened to empty her pitcher into the trough, and ran again to the well to draw water, and drew for all the camels.

And the man, wondering at her, held his peace.

When the camels had done drinking, the steward took a gold ring of half a shekel weight, and two gold bracelets, and gave them to her, saying, "Tell me, whose daughter are you? And is there room in your father's house for us to lodge in?" She answered, "I am Rebekah, daughter of Bethuel, the son of Nahor, brother to Abraham. And we have both straw and fodder enough, and there is room for you to lodge in." The man bowed his head and thanked the Lord, while the maiden ran home to tell of these happenings.

Now Rebekah had a brother named Laban. When Laban saw the ring and the bracelets upon his sister's hands, he ran to find the man at the well and said to him, "Come, blessed of the Lord, why do you stand outside? For I have prepared the house, and space for the camels."

The steward came into the house; the camels were ungirded and given straw and fodder; water was brought for the steward and his men to wash their feet; and food was set before them. But the steward said, "I will not eat until I have told you of my errand." Laban answered, "Speak on."

And when the steward had finished telling them of his vow to his master Abraham, Laban and Bethuel said, "This thing proceeds from the Lord; we dare not say to you anything bad or good. Behold, Rebekah is before you. Let her be Isaac's wife, as the Lord has spoken."

Abraham's steward bowed his head when he heard their words, and he worshiped the Lord. Then he brought out ornaments of silver, and ornaments of gold, and festive garments, and gave them to Rebekah; and he also gave precious things to her brother and her mother. Then they ate and drank, and tarried all night.

In the morning the steward said, "Now let us leave, and return to my master." But Rebekah's brother and her mother answered, "Let the maiden abide with us a few days longer; after that she shall go with you."

The steward said, "Detain me not, seeing that the Lord has prospered my errand; let me return to my master." And they answered, "We will call Rebekah and ask her." They called her and asked, "Will you go with this man?" And she said, "I will go."

They blessed Rebekah; and sent her off with her maidservants and her nurse; and they rode upon the camels and followed Abraham's steward.

Now Isaac dwelt in the south country, and at eventide he went out to meditate in the fields. He lifted his eyes, and behold, his father's camels were coming. When Rebekah saw Isaac, she alighted from the camel. For she had asked the steward, "Who is this man who walks in the field to meet us?" And he answered, "It is my master Isaac." Therefore she took a veil and covered her face.

Then the steward told Isaac all that he had done. And Isaac brought Rebekah into his mother Sarah's tent, and she became his wife, and he loved her. And Isaac was comforted after his mother's death.[10]

## Jacob and Esau

25-28 Isaac was forty years old when he took as his wife Rebekah, the daughter of Bethuel. And he prayed to the Lord for his wife, because she was barren. The Lord answered his prayer and Rebekah conceived. And behold, twins struggled within her. She inquired of the Lord why it was so, and the Lord said to her, "Two nations are in your womb, and two manner of people shall be born to you: one shall be stronger than the other, and the elder shall serve the younger."

When the time of her delivery came, Rebekah gave birth to twins. And the first came out red, covered all over with hair like a garment, and they named him Esau; and after that came his brother, holding on to Esau's heel, and they named him Jacob.

The boys grew up. Esau became a skillful hunter, a man of the open field, while Jacob was a plain man, a breeder of cattle. Isaac loved Esau, because he ate of his venison; but Rebekah loved Jacob.

Once Jacob was cooking a pottage of red lentils when Esau came in from the hunt, faint with hunger. Esau said to his brother, "Feed me of that red pottage, I pray you, for I am famished." Jacob replied, "First

[10] See GENESIS, Chapter 25, in Notes and Excisions.

sell me your birthright." And Esau said, "I am dying of hunger, so what shall this birthright profit me?" Jacob said, "Swear to me." And Esau swore to him. Then Jacob gave his brother bread and the pottage of lentils; and Esau ate his fill, and rose up and went his way. Thus did Esau show contempt for his birthright.

And Esau took as his wife Judith, daughter of Beeri the Hittite, and Basemath, daughter of Elon the Hittite, who were a grief to Isaac and Rebekah.

Now when Isaac was old and his eyes were so dim that he could not see, he sent for his older son Esau and said to him, "My son, behold, I am old, and I know not the day of my death. Therefore, I pray you, take your quiver and your bow, and go out and bring me some venison. Make me savory food such as I love, that I may eat and bless you before I die."

Rebekah overheard what Isaac said to his son Esau. And when Esau went off to the field to hunt, she said to her son Jacob, "I heard your father speak to your brother, saying, 'Bring me venison, that I may eat and bless you before my death.' Now, my son, obey my voice. Go to the flock and bring me two good kids of the goats, and I will make savory food for your father such as he loves. And you shall take it to him, that he may eat, and that he may bless you before he dies."

Jacob said to Rebekah his mother, "Esau my brother is a hairy man, and I am smooth. If my father touches me, I shall seem a deceiver, and bring down upon myself a curse instead of a blessing."

His mother answered, "Upon me be your curse, my son. Only obey me." So he went and brought the kids, and his mother prepared savory food such as his father loved. Then Rebekah took fine garments belonging to her eldest son Esau, and put them upon Jacob, her younger son; and she put skins of the kids upon his hands and the smooth part of his neck. Then she placed into his hands the food she had prepared.

Jacob went to his father and said, "My father!" And Isaac said, "Here am I. Who are you, my son?" And Jacob said to his father, "I am Esau your firstborn. I have done as you bade me. Sit up and eat of my venison, that your soul may bless me." Isaac asked, "How is it that you found it so quickly, my son?" And Jacob answered, "Because the Lord your God brought it to me." Then Isaac said, "Come near, I pray you, that I may touch you, my son, that I may know whether you are my very son Esau or not."

Jacob went near Isaac his father, and the blind man touched him and said, "The voice is the voice of Jacob, but the hands are the hands of Esau. Are you my very son Esau?" Jacob answered, "I am." Isaac ate of the food and drank of the wine his son had brought him. Then he said, "Come near now and kiss me, my son." Jacob came near and kissed him. And Isaac smelled his garments and blessed him, saying, "Ah, the smell of my son is like the smell of a field which the Lord has blessed! Therefore, may God give you of the dew of heaven and of the fat of the earth. May the nations bow down to you, and may you be lord over your brothers. Cursed be everyone who curses you, and blessed be everyone who blesses you."

After Isaac had blessed Jacob, and Jacob had scarcely left the presence of his father, Esau came in from the hunt. He also had prepared savory food and brought it to his father. He said, "Let my father sit up, and eat of his son's venison, and bless me." Isaac asked, "Who are you?" And he answered, "I am your son, your firstborn, Esau."

Isaac trembled exceedingly and said, "Who then was he that brought me venison before you came? I ate of it, and I blessed him."

When Esau heard the words of his father, he cried out with a great and bitter cry, "Bless me, me also, O my father!"

And Isaac said, "Your brother came with guile and has taken away the blessing of the firstborn."

Esau said to his father, "Have you but one blessing, my father?" And he lifted up his voice and wept.

Isaac his father answered, "By your sword shall you live, and serve your brother. But it shall come to pass that you shall break his yoke from off your neck."

After that Esau hated Jacob because of the blessing with which his father had blessed him; and he said in his heart, "The days of mourning for my father are at hand; then I will slay my brother Jacob." Rebekah knew what was in Esau's heart and she sent for Jacob, and said to him, "Your brother Esau comforts himself with plans to kill you. Therefore, my son, flee to Laban my brother in Haran. Tarry with him until your brother's anger turns away from you and he forgets what you have done to him. Then will I send for you."

And Rebekah went to Isaac and said, "If Jacob takes a wife from the daughters of Heth, such as are the women of this land, what good will my life be to me?"

Isaac summoned Jacob, and charged him, "You shall not take a wife from the daughters of Canaan. Arise, go to the house of Bethuel, your mother's father, and take a wife from the daughters of Laban, your mother's brother. And may the Lord bless you."

Thus Isaac sent Jacob away to Haran, where dwelt Laban, son of Bethuel, the brother of Rebekah.[11]

## Jacob's Ladder

28     Jacob left Beersheba and went toward Haran. On the way he stopped at a certain place, because the sun had set, and he tarried there all night. He took a stone to use as a pillow and lay down to sleep. And he dreamed that a ladder was set up on the earth, the top of which reached to heaven; and behold, the angels of God were ascending and descending on it. And the Lord stood above it, and said, "I am the Lord, the God of Abraham and the God of Isaac your father. The land upon which you lie, to you will I give it, and to your descendants as an inheritance. And your descendants shall be as numerous as the dust of the earth, and spread to the west, and to the east, and to the north, and to the south; and in you, and in them, shall all the families of the earth be blessed. Behold, I am with you, and will keep you in all the places to which you go, and will bring you again into this land."

Jacob awoke from his sleep, and said, "Surely the Lord is in this place, and I knew it not." And he was afraid, and said, "How awesome is this place! This is none other than the house of God, and this the gateway to heaven!" He rose early and took the stone he had used for a pillow, and set it up as a pillar, and poured oil upon the top of it. And he named that place Bethel (The House of God). And Jacob vowed, "If God will be with me in the way that I go, so that I may come again to my father's house in peace, then shall the Lord be my God, and this stone, which I have set up as a pillar, shall be God's house, and of all that you give me I will surely give the tenth to you."

## Jacob in Laban's House

29     Jacob journeyed on, and he came into the land of the people of the east. In a field he beheld three flocks of sheep lying beside a well, and a great stone lay upon the well's mouth. Jacob said to the

[11] See GENESIS, Chapter 26, in Notes and Excisions.

shepherds, "My brothers, where do you come from?" They answered, "We are from Haran." And Jacob asked, "Do you know Laban, the son of Nahor?" They said, "We know him." Then Jacob asked, "Is all well with him?" And they answered, "It is well — and behold, here comes Rachel his daughter with the sheep!"

Jacob said to them, "The sun is still high, nor is it time for the cattle to be gathered together. Why do you not water the sheep, and go and feed them?" They answered, "We cannot until all the flocks are gathered together, and until they roll the stone from the well's mouth. Then we water the sheep."

And while he yet spoke with them, Rachel came near with her father's sheep. When Jacob saw Rachel, he went up and rolled the stone from the well's mouth, and watered her flock. Then he told Rachel that he was Rebekah's son. And Jacob kissed Rachel, and lifted up his voice and wept.

Rachel ran off to tell her father. And when Laban heard the tidings of his sister's son, he hastened to meet Jacob, and embraced him and brought him home. Jacob told Laban all that had happened to him. And Laban said, "Surely you are my bone and my flesh." And Jacob dwelt with him for the space of a month.

Then Laban said to Jacob, "Because you are my sister's son, should you therefore serve me for nothing? Tell me, what shall your wages be?"

Now Laban had two daughters; the name of the elder was Leah, and the name of the younger was Rachel. Leah was weak-eyed, but Rachel was beautiful. Jacob loved Rachel, and he said to Laban, "I will serve you seven years for Rachel, your younger daughter." Laban answered, "It is better that I give her to you than to another. Abide with me."

Jacob served seven years for Rachel; and they seemed to him but a few days, for the love he had for her.

Then Jacob said to Laban, "Give me my wife, since I have fulfilled my years of service to you."

Laban gathered together all the men of the place and gave a wedding feast. And during the dark of the evening he took Leah to Jacob's chamber. In the morning Jacob saw that it was Leah, and he said to Laban, "What have you done? Did I not serve you for Rachel? Why then have you deceived me?" Laban answered, "It is not the custom in our country to give the younger in marriage before the firstborn. Fulfill Leah's wedding week, and after that I shall give you Rachel also, and you shall serve me another seven years."

Jacob served Laban another seven years. And he loved Rachel more than Leah.

## Jacob Departs Secretly

29-31   And when the Lord saw that Leah was not loved, he gave her children; but Rachel was barren. Leah bore a son, and she called him Reuben. She bore another son, and named him Simeon. And she bore a third son, whom she named Levi. Then she conceived again and bore a son, and she called him Judah.

Rachel envied her sister, and said to Jacob, "Give me children, or I shall die!" But Jacob's anger kindled against her, and he said, "Am I in God's stead, who has withheld children from you?"

Rachel gave her handmaid Bilhah to Jacob as his wife, and said, "I may have children through her." And Bilhah conceived and bore Jacob a son. Rachel said, "God has heard me, and has given me a son." Therefore she named him Dan. Bilhah bore Jacob a second son. And Rachel said, "I have wrestled with my sister, and I have prevailed," and she named him Naphtali.

When Leah saw that she had stopped bearing children, she gave her handmaid Zilpah to Jacob as his wife. And Zilpah bore Jacob a son. Leah said, "Fortune has come!" and she named him Gad. Zilpah bore Jacob a second son. And Leah said, "Happy am I!" and she named him Asher.

Leah conceived, and bore Jacob a fifth son. And she called him Issachar. And when Leah bore a sixth son to Jacob, she said, "God has endowed me with a good dowry," and she called him Zebulun. Afterward she bore a daughter, whom she named Dinah.

Then God remembered Rachel, and she conceived, and bore a son. And she said, "God has taken away my reproach." She named him Joseph, saying, "The Lord shall add to me another son."

When Rachel had borne Joseph, Jacob said to Laban, "Send me away, that I may return to my own country. Give me my wives and my children, for whom I have served you, and let me go." Laban answered, "If I have found favor in your eyes, stay a while longer, for I know the Lord has blessed me for your sake." But Jacob said to him, "You know I have served you well; for it was little you had before I came, and the Lord has blessed you since my coming, and your flocks have increased greatly. When shall I provide for my own household?" Laban asked, "What shall I give you?"

Jacob answered, "You need not give me anything. If you will do this thing for me, I will again feed and tend your flock: I will pass through all your flocks and remove the speckled and spotted cattle, and all the brown among the sheep, and all the spotted and speckled among the goats, and after this my wages shall be the spotted and speckled of the herd."

That day Laban removed all the goats that were ring-streaked and spotted, or that were speckled and spotted, and every one that had any white in it, and all the brown among the sheep, and he gave them to his sons. Then he set three days' journey between them and the flocks fed by Jacob.

But Jacob took boughs of green poplar and of the hazel and chestnut trees, and peeled white streaks in them. Then he set up the boughs at the watering troughs where the flocks came to drink. And the flocks bred among the boughs and brought forth young that were ring-streaked, speckled and spotted. Jacob's possessions increased exceedingly, and he acquired much cattle, and servants, and camels, and asses.

Then Jacob heard that Laban's sons were saying, "Jacob has taken away all that was our father's, and from that which belonged to our father he has gained his wealth." And Jacob saw that Laban had changed toward him.

Jacob sent for Rachel and Leah to come to the field where he cared for his flocks, and said to them, "Your father's face is not toward me as before. And you know that I have served him with all my power. Your father has deceived me and changed my wages ten times, but God did not suffer him to harm me. In a dream the angel of God spoke to me, saying, 'Arise, and return to the land of your kindred.'"

Rachel and Leah answered, "Whatever God has commanded you, do."

Then Jacob rose, and set his children and his wives upon camels, and went off with all his cattle and all the substance he had gained, to go to Isaac his father in the land of Canaan. He stole away secretly, and passed over the river, and set his face toward Mount Gilead.

Three days later Laban was told that Jacob had fled. He took his kinsmen with him and pursued Jacob for seven days, and they overtook him at the mountain.

Laban said to Jacob, "What have you done, that you fled secretly and carried off my daughters like captives taken by the sword? Why did you not tell me, that I might send you away with merriment and song? But you did not permit me even to kiss my daughters and my grandchildren! You were foolish in so doing, and it is in the power of my hand to harm you. But the God of your father spoke to me last night in a dream and warned me not to speak to you either good or bad. And now, though you would be gone because you long for your father's house, yet why have you stolen my gods?"

Jacob knew not that Rachel had stolen her father's household gods, and he answered, "I fled secretly for fear you would take your daughters from me by force. But as to the gods, with whomever you find them, let him not live."

Laban searched Jacob's tent, and Leah's tent, and the tents of the maid-servants; but he found not the images. Then he entered Rachel's tent. Now Rachel had taken the images and put them in a camel's saddle, and sat down on it. As Laban sought all over her tent Rachel said to her father, "Let it not displease my lord that I cannot rise up before you, for the illness of women is upon me." So Laban searched on, but found not the images.

Jacob grew angry and chided Laban, "What is my sin that you have so hotly pursued me? You have searched through all my household goods, yet what have you found belonging to you? Twenty years have I been in your house; I served you fourteen years for your daughters and six years for the cattle; and you have changed my wages ten times. If the God of my father had not been with me, you would surely have sent me away now empty-handed."

Laban answered, "These women are my daughters and these children are my grandchildren, and these cattle are my cattle, and all that you have is mine. But what can I do to these, my daughters, or to the children they have borne? Come, let us make a covenant, you and I."

Jacob took a stone and set it up as a pillar. And his kinsmen gathered stones and made a heap, and they ate there. And Laban said, "Let this pillar be a witness between us that I will not pass over this heap to you, and you will not pass over this heap to me, for harm."

Then Jacob offered a sacrifice upon the mountain and called his kinsmen to eat with him. And they ate, and tarried there all night. Early in the morning Laban rose, and kissed his grandchildren and his daughters, and blessed them.

Laban departed and returned to his place. And Jacob went on his way.

## The Meeting with Esau

32-33 Jacob sent messengers ahead of him to Esau his brother in the
land of Seir. He said to them, "Speak to my lord Esau, and say,
'Thus says your servant Jacob: "I have dwelt with Laban until now; and
I have oxen and asses, flocks and servants; and I have sent to tell my
lord, that I may find grace in your sight."'"

The messengers returned and said, "We brought your message to your
brother Esau, and he comes to meet you, and four hundred men come
with him."

Then Jacob was frightened and greatly distressed. He divided the people that were with him into two camps, and also the flocks and herds
and camels; so that if Esau came upon one camp and struck it, the other
might escape. And Jacob prayed: "O God of my father Abraham and my
father Isaac, I am not worthy of the least of the mercies you have shown
your servant, for I passed over this Jordan with only my staff, and now I
have become two companies. Deliver me from the hand of my brother
Esau, for I fear that he comes to destroy me, and the mothers with their
children."

Then Jacob took as a present for Esau two hundred she-goats and
twenty he-goats, two hundred ewes and twenty rams, thirty milch camels
with their colts, forty cows and ten bulls, twenty she-asses and ten
foals.

And he delivered each drove separately to a servant, and said, "Pass on
ahead of me, and leave a space between drove and drove. When Esau
my brother meets the first drove and asks, 'Whose are these animals? And
where are you going?' you shall answer, 'They are your servant Jacob's,
which he has sent as a present to my lord Esau. And behold, your servant
Jacob is behind us.'" Thus he instructed the second servant, and the
third, and all that followed the droves. For Jacob sought to appease
Esau with the present that went before him.

So the present went ahead, while Jacob stayed that night in the camp.
During the night he arose, and took his wives and his children, and
sent them across the ford of the Jabbok. Then he sent across the brook all
that belonged to him.

Jacob was left alone.

And there appeared a man who wrestled with him in silence all through
the night until the break of day. When the stranger saw that he could

not overpower Jacob, he touched the hollow of his thigh; and Jacob's thigh was out of joint as he wrestled on. Then the man said, "Let me go, for day is breaking." But Jacob said, "I will not let you go unless you bless me." And the man said to him, "Your name shall no longer be Jacob, but Israel (Prince of God). For you have power with God and with men." Then Jacob asked him, "What is your name?" And he said, "Why do you ask for my name?" And he blessed Jacob.

Jacob named the place Peniel (The Face of God), for he had seen God there face to face, yet lived. When the sun rose Jacob left, and he limped because the sinew of his thigh had shrunk.

Therefore the children of Israel do not eat of the sinew of the thigh to this day.

When Jacob lifted his eyes and saw Esau coming with four hundred men, he divided the children with their mothers, and placed the hand-maids and their children foremost, Leah and her children after them, and Rachel and Joseph last. Then he went on ahead of them, and bowed to the ground seven times until he came near his brother.

Esau ran to meet him and embraced him, and fell on his neck and kissed him, and they wept.

Then Esau looked up and saw the women and the children, and he asked, "Who are these with you?" Jacob answered, "The children whom God has graciously given your servant." Then the maidservants came near, they and their children, and they bowed; Leah also, with her children, came near, and they bowed; and after them came Joseph and Rachel, and they bowed. Esau asked, "What is the meaning of all the droves which I met?" And Jacob answered, "They are to find grace in the sight of my lord." But Esau said, "I have enough, my brother; keep what you have for yourself." Jacob said, "No, I pray you receive my present. For now that I have seen your face it is as though I had seen the face of God. Take the blessing that I brought to you, because God has dealt graciously with me and because I have enough." Thus Jacob urged him, and Esau took it.

Esau said, "Let us go on with our journey, and I will go with you." But Jacob replied, "My lord knows that the children are tender, and the flocks and herds are with young; and if they are overdriven one day, the whole flock will die. Let my lord go on ahead, and I will follow slowly at the pace the children and the flocks can endure."

So Esau returned to Seir. And Jacob journeyed to Succoth, where he built a house, and made booths for his cattle; therefore the place is called

Succoth. And from there Jacob went to Shalem, a city of Shechem, which is in the land of Canaan.

## Dinah and Shechem

34    Now Dinah, the daughter Leah had borne to Jacob, went out to visit the daughters of Shalem. And when Shechem, son of Prince Hamor the Hivite, saw her, he took her and lay with her. And his soul yearned for Dinah, the daughter of Jacob, for he loved her, and he spoke gently to her. And he said to his father, "Get me this maiden for my wife."

Jacob heard that Shechem had seduced Dinah, but his sons were away with the flocks and he held his peace until they returned. When they came in from the fields and heard of it, the men were grieved, and they were very angry, for such a thing ought not to be done in Israel.

Hamor came to speak with them, and said, "The soul of my son Shechem longs for Dinah your sister. Pray let her become his wife. Make marriages with us. Give your daughters to us, and take our daughters for yourselves, if you are to dwell with us. Our land is before you; dwell and trade in it, and gather possessions in our midst."

And Shechem said, "Let me find grace in your eyes, and whatever you ask I will give you. But let me have Dinah as my wife."

The sons of Jacob answered deceitfully because he had forced their sister, and they said to Shechem and Hamor, "We cannot give our sister to one who is not circumcised, for that would be a reproach to us. But we will give our consent if every male in this city will be circumcised. Then we will give our daughters to you, and take your daughters to ourselves, and we will become one people. But if you will not be circumcised, then we will take our sister and we will leave."

Their words pleased Hamor and Shechem. They went out to the gate of their city and counseled with their men, saying, "Jacob and his sons are peaceable; therefore let them dwell in the land, for it is large enough for us and for them. Let us take their daughters in marriage and let us give them our daughters. But they will consent to dwell with us, and to become one people, only if every male among us will be circumcised as they are."

All who went out of the gate of the city agreed with Hamor and Shechem his son, and every male was circumcised.

On the third day, when the males were ill, Simeon and Levi, Dinah's brothers, each took a sword and boldly came upon the city, and slew all the males. And they slew Hamor and Shechem, and took Dinah out of Shechem's house. Then they carried off the sheep and oxen and cattle, and all that was in the city and in the field. And the little ones and the wives they took captive. All this the sons of Jacob did because of the wrong done to their sister.

Jacob said to them, "You have made me odious to the inhabitants of the land. Now if they should gather against me, my numbers being few, I shall be destroyed, I and my household."

But they answered, "Should we have allowed him to deal with our sister as with a harlot?"

## Rachel's Death

.35-36  God said to Jacob, "Arise, go up to Bethel and dwell there, and build an altar to God, who appeared to you when you fled from the face of Esau your brother."

So Jacob said to his household, and all who were with him, "Put away the strange gods that are among you, purify yourselves, change your garments, and let us go up to Bethel; and I will build there an altar to God, who answered me in the day of my distress."

They gave Jacob all the strange gods which they had, and all the earrings which were in their ears, and Jacob hid them under an oak that grew near Shechem. Then they set out on their journey. And the terror of God fell upon the cities round about them, so that Jacob and his sons were not pursued.

Thus Jacob came to Bethel in Canaan, he and all the people who were with him. And he built there an altar. And there Deborah, Rebekah's nurse, died, and she was buried under an oak at Bethel.

Jacob and his household journeyed on from Bethel; and they were only a little distance from Ephrath when Rachel, who was about to give birth to a child, began to have pains. In the midst of her hard labor, the midwife said to her, "Fear not; you shall have another son." And as Rachel's soul was departing, for she died, she named her son Ben-oni (Son of My Sorrow). But his father called him Benjamin (Son of My Right Arm). Thus Rachel died; and she was buried on the road to Ephrath, which is Bethlehem. And Jacob set up a stone pillar upon her grave which is there to this day.

Jacob and his household journeyed on, and came at last to Hebron, where Isaac dwelt.

The days of Isaac were one hundred and fourscore years; and he died and was gathered to his people, being old and full of days. And his sons Esau and Jacob buried him.[12]

# The Story of Joseph

## Joseph's Dreams

37-38   Jacob dwelt in the land of Canaan. And Joseph his son, who was seventeen years old, tended the flock with his brothers, the sons of Bilhah and Zilpah; and he brought an evil report of them to his father. Now Jacob loved Joseph more than any of his other children, and he made him a coat of many colors. Joseph's brothers saw that their father loved him most, and they hated him and could not speak to him peaceably.

Then Joseph dreamed a dream and told it to his brothers, and they hated him still more. For he had said, "Hear this dream which I have dreamed; behold, we were binding sheaves in the field, and lo, my sheaf arose and stood upright, and your sheaves stood round about and bowed to mine."

His brothers said to him, "Shall you indeed reign over us?" And they hated him even more for his dream and for his words.

Then Joseph dreamed another dream and told it to them: "Behold, I dreamed that the sun and the moon and eleven stars paid homage to me." But when he told this to his father and his brothers, Jacob rebuked him: "What is the meaning of this dream that you have dreamed? Shall I and your mother and your brothers bow down to you?"

His brothers envied him, but his father pondered the meaning of his words.

One day Joseph's brothers went to pasture their father's flock in Shechem. And Jacob said to Joseph, "Go, see whether all is well with your brothers, and with the flock, and bring me word of them." So Joseph left the vale of Hebron and went to Shechem. A man found him wandering about in the field, and asked, "What do you seek?" Joseph answered, "I seek my brothers. Tell me, I pray you, where they feed their flock." And the man said, "They have gone from here, for I heard them say, 'Let us go to Dothan.'"

[12] See GENESIS, Chapter 36, in Notes and Excisions.

Joseph went to seek his brothers in Dothan, and found them there. When they saw him afar off, before he came near them, they said one to another, "Behold, the dreamer comes here. Let us slay him and cast him into a pit, and we will say a wild beast devoured him. Then we shall see what will become of his dreams."

But Reuben said, that he might save Joseph from them and return him to his father, "Let us shed no blood, but cast him into this pit in the wilderness."

And when Joseph came up to his brothers, they stripped him of his coat of many colors and cast him into the pit; and the pit was empty, there was no water in it.

Then they sat down to eat. When they raised their eyes, behold, a caravan of Ishmaelites came toward them from Gilead, with camels bearing spices and balm and myrrh down to Egypt.

Judah said to his brothers, "What have we to gain if we slay our brother and conceal his blood? Come, let us sell him to the Ishmaelites, and let not our hand be upon him; for he is our brother and our flesh." And his brothers were content. They drew Joseph out of the pit and sold him to the Ishmaelites for twenty pieces of silver, and the merchants took Joseph with them down to Egypt.

When Reuben returned to the pit and found Joseph was not in it, he rent his clothes, and he returned to his brothers and said, "The boy is gone! And I, how can I ever go home?"

The brothers took Joseph's coat and dipped it in the blood of a kid of the goats. Then they brought the coat to their father and said, "This have we found. Is it your son's coat?"

Jacob cried out, "It is my son's coat! A wild beast has devoured him!" He rent his garments and put on sackcloth, and mourned his son for many days. All his sons and daughters tried to comfort him; but he refused to be comforted, and he said, "I shall go down into the grave mourning my son." [13]

## Joseph in Potiphar's House

39 Joseph was brought down to Egypt; and Potiphar, an officer of Pharaoh, captain of the Egyptian guard, bought him from the Ishmaelites. Joseph lived in the house of his master the Egyptian, and his master saw that the Lord was with him and that all he did prospered.

[13] See GENESIS, Chapter 38, in Notes and Excisions.

Joseph found favor in Potiphar's eyes and was made overseer of the house, and his master entrusted everything to him.

Now Joseph was exceedingly handsome, and after some time had passed, his master's wife cast her eyes upon him, and she said, "Lie with me."

But he refused, and said to his master's wife, "Behold, my master has committed everything he has to my care. There is no one in this house above me. Nor has he withheld anything from me, except you, because you are his wife. How then can I do this great wickedness, and sin against God?"

She spoke to Joseph day after day, but he would not listen to her, to lie with her or to be with her. And it came to pass about this time that Joseph went into the house to his work, and none of the men of the household were within. So she caught him by his garment, saying, "Lie with me." But he left his garment in her hand and fled.

And when she saw that he had left his garment in her hand, she called out to those in the house, "See, Potiphar has brought among us a Hebrew to mock us. He came in to lie with me, and when I cried out with a loud voice, he left his garment with me and fled."

She laid the garment beside her until Potiphar came home. Then she said to him, "The Hebrew servant whom you brought us came in to mock me, and when I cried out, he left his garment with me and fled."

Potiphar's wrath was kindled. And he took Joseph and put him in the prison where the king's prisoners were held, and there Joseph remained.

But the Lord was with Joseph and showed him mercy, and gave him favor in the sight of the keeper of the prison. The keeper committed to Joseph's care all the prisoners, and put him in charge of whatever was done there.

And everything Joseph did, the Lord made to prosper.

## Dreams of the Cupbearer and the Baker

40    At the time these events came to pass, Pharaoh's cupbearer and baker offended their master, and they were put in the prison where Joseph was confined. The captain of the guard placed them in Joseph's charge, and he served them.

After a time in the prison, both the cupbearer and the baker dreamed a dream on the same night. And when Joseph came in to them in the morning and looked at them, behold, they were sad. He asked, "Why are you so sad today?" And they answered, "We have each dreamed a dream, and there is no one to interpret them." Joseph said, "Do not interpretations belong to God? Tell me your dreams, I pray you."

The chief cupbearer said to Joseph: "In my dream I saw a vine with three branches. And it seemed as though it budded, and blossoms shot up, and the clusters ripened into grapes. Pharaoh's cup was in my hand, and I took the grapes and pressed them into Pharaoh's cup and placed it in his hand."

Joseph said to him, "This is the meaning of your dream: The three branches are three days; within three days Pharaoh will lift up your head and restore you to your place, and you shall put Pharaoh's cup into his hand as you did before. Remember me when it goes well with you, I pray you, and mention me to Pharaoh, and deliver me out of this prison; for indeed, I have done nothing for which they should put me in this dungeon."

When the chief baker heard that the interpretation was good, he said to Joseph: "In my dream I had three white baskets which I carried on my head. The uppermost basket was full of all manner of baked foods for Pharaoh, but the birds ate them out of the basket on my head."

Joseph said, "This is the meaning of your dream: The three baskets are three days; within three days Pharaoh will lift your head from off you and hang it upon a tree, and the birds will eat your flesh."

Three days later, which was Pharaoh's birthday, the king gave a feast for all his servants, and to it the cupbearer and baker were summoned. The king restored the cupbearer to his post, but he hanged the baker, as Joseph had foretold.

Yet the cupbearer did not remember Joseph, but forgot him.


## Joseph Made Governor of Egypt

41      Two full years later, Pharaoh dreamed a dream; and behold, he stood upon the banks of a river, and out of the river came seven well-favored and well-fattened cows, and they fed in a meadow. Then seven other cows came up out of the river, ill-favored and lean-fleshed, and they devoured the seven fat cows. Yet after they had finished eating, they were still lean, as at the beginning. And Pharaoh awoke. When he fell asleep again, he dreamed a second time; and behold, seven ears of grain came up upon one stalk, all full and good. Then another seven

ears, withered and blasted by the east wind, sprang up after them; and the seven thin ears devoured the seven full ears.

In the morning Pharaoh's spirit was troubled. He sent for all the magicians of Egypt, and for all the wise men, and told them his dreams. But none could interpret them.

Then the cupbearer said to Pharaoh, "I remember now that when the king was angry with his servant and imprisoned me with the chief baker we dreamed a dream on the same night, the baker and I. And there was with us a young Hebrew, servant to the captain of the guard, who interpreted our dreams to us. And as he interpreted them, so it was."

Pharaoh sent for Joseph, and they hastily brought him out of the prison. Joseph shaved and changed his garments, and came before Pharaoh. And the king said to Joseph, "I have dreamed a dream, and there is no one who can interpret it. I have heard it said of you that when you hear a dream, you can interpret it." And Joseph said, "Only God can give Pharaoh an answer."

And then Pharaoh told Joseph his dreams. Joseph said, "The two dreams of Pharaoh are one: God has shown the king what he is about to do. The seven fat cows and the seven full ears of grain are seven good years; the seven lean cows and the seven withered ears are seven years of famine. Behold, there come seven years of great plenty throughout Egypt; and there shall arise after them seven years of famine; and all the plenty shall be forgotten when famine consumes the land. The dream was doubled because God will shortly bring this to pass. Therefore let Pharaoh find a man discreet and wise, and appoint him over the land of Egypt. And let Pharaoh select officers to gather a fifth part of all food during the good years to come, to store up against the seven years of famine."

And Pharaoh said to Joseph, "Since God has shown you all this, there is none more discreet and wise than you. You shall have charge of my household, and according to your word shall my people be ruled. Only in regard to the throne will I be greater than you."

Pharaoh took off his ring and put it on Joseph's finger. He arrayed him in fine linen and put a gold chain about his neck. And he said, "I, Pharaoh, decree that no man shall lift his hand or foot in all the land of Egypt without you!" And Pharaoh changed Joseph's name to Zaphenath-paneah (Revealer of Secrets), and gave to him in marriage Asenath, the daughter of Poti-pherah, priest of On.

Joseph was thirty years old when he came before Pharaoh. And he went out from the presence of the king and journeyed throughout the land of Egypt. In the seven years of plenty Joseph stored up the food in the cities, the food of the fields which were round about every city. And the grain so gathered was like the sands of the sea, beyond measure or number.

Before the years of famine came, two sons were born to Joseph. The first-born he called Manasseh (Forgetfulness). "For," said he, "God has made me forget my hardships, and my father's house." And the second he called Ephraim (The Fruitful). "For," said he, "God has made me fruitful in the land of my affliction."

The seven years of plenty came to an end, and the seven years of want began, as Joseph had predicted. There was famine in all lands; but in the land of Egypt there was bread. And when the land of Egypt was famished, and the people cried out to Pharaoh for bread, he said, "Go to Joseph, and what he says to you, do."

Joseph opened all the storehouses and sold grain to the Egyptians. And people from many countries came into Egypt to buy grain, for hunger gripped many lands.

## Joseph and His Brothers

42-45  When Jacob learned that there was grain in Egypt, he said to his sons, "Why do you look at one another? Go down there and buy grain for us, that we may live and not die." And ten of Joseph's brothers went down to buy grain in Egypt.

Now Joseph was governor over the land; he it was who sold the grain to the peoples of other countries. So Joseph's brothers came, and bowed down before him with their faces to the ground. Joseph saw his brothers and he recognized them; but he treated them as if he were a stranger, and spoke harshly to them, saying, "Where do you come from?" And they answered, "From the land of Canaan, to buy food." Joseph remembered the dreams which he had dreamed in his youth, and he said to them, "You are spies! You have come to spy out the nakedness of the land!" They answered, "No, my lord! Your servants have come to buy food. We are twelve brothers, all sons of one man in the land of Canaan. The youngest is with his father, and one is no more." Joseph said, "In this way you shall prove that you are not spies. Send one of you to fetch your youngest brother, and the rest of you shall be kept in prison until the truth of your words is proven; or else, by the life of Pharaoh, surely you are spies!"

And he put them all together in prison for three days.

On the third day, Joseph said to them, "If you are upright men, let only one of you remain in prison while the rest of you carry grain to your starving households. But bring your youngest brother to me, so that your words may be verified, and you shall not die."

They said one to another, "We are guilty concerning our brother. We saw the anguish of his soul when he besought us, yet we would not listen to him. Therefore has this misfortune come upon us." And Reuben said, "Did I not say to you, 'Do not sin against the child'? But you would not listen. And now, behold, his blood is required of us."

They knew not that Joseph understood them, for he spoke to them only through an interpreter. And he went away from them and wept. When he returned he took Simeon, and bound him before their eyes. And Joseph gave orders privately to fill their sacks with grain, and replace every man's money in his sack, and to give them provisions for the journey.

The brothers loaded their asses with the grain and departed. And when they came home to Jacob their father in the land of Canaan, they told him all that had befallen them. Then they emptied their sacks, and behold, each man's bundle of money was in his sack. When they and their father saw the bundles of money, they were afraid.

Jacob said to his sons, "You have bereaved me. Joseph is no more, and Simeon is no more, and now you would take Benjamin away." Reuben said to his father, "Slay my two sons if I do not bring him back to you." But Jacob said, "Benjamin shall not go down with you. His brother is dead, and if any harm should befall Benjamin on the way, then you would bring down my gray hairs with sorrow to the grave."

Now the famine was grave in the land. And when they had eaten all the grain which they had brought from Egypt, their father said to them, "Go down again, and buy us a little food."

Judah answered him, "The man solemnly warned us, saying, 'You shall not see my face unless your brother is with you.' If you will send Benjamin with us we will go, but we cannot go down without him."

Jacob asked, "Why did you tell him that you have another brother?" And they answered, "He asked us, 'Is your father alive? Have you another brother?' And we told him. Could we know that he would say, 'Bring your brother down'?"

And Judah said to his father, "Send the boy with us and we will arise and go, that we may live and not die, we and you and our little ones. I will be surety for him, and of my hand shall you require him. If I fail to bring him back to you, let me bear the blame forever."

Their father answered, "If it must be, then do it now. And carry down to the man a present of the best of our fruit, and a little balm, a little fragrant honey, spices, and nuts and almonds. Take double the money: money for grain and the money you found in your sacks — perhaps it was an oversight. Take also your brother, and go again to the man. And may God Almighty grant you mercy before him that he may release your other brother and return Benjamin to me."

They took the present, and they took double the money, and Benjamin their brother; and they went down to Egypt and stood before Joseph. And when Joseph saw Benjamin with them, he said to the steward of his household, "Take these men to my home, for they shall dine with me today." And the steward did as Joseph bade him.

The brothers were afraid when they were brought to Joseph's house, and they said, "Because of the money that was returned in our sacks, he may seek occasion against us and take us as slaves."

They crowded around Joseph's steward at the door of the house and said, "O sir, we did indeed come down the first time to buy food; but when we opened our sacks, behold, each man's money was in the mouth of his sack in full weight. We brought that money back. And we do not know who put the money in our sacks." He answered, "Peace be with you; fear not! Your God must have given you treasure in your sacks. For I received your money."

And he went and brought Simeon to them, and took them into Joseph's house and gave them water to wash their feet; and he gave their asses fodder.

When Joseph came home, the brothers brought out their present and they bowed down before him. He asked them, "Is your father well, the old man of whom you spoke?" And they replied, "Your servant our father is in good health." Then they bowed again in homage to him.

Joseph lifted his eyes and saw his brother Benjamin, his mother's son, and asked, "Is this your younger brother, of whom you spoke to me?"

And to Benjamin he said, "May God be gracious to you, my son!"

Then Joseph hastily sought a place to be alone, for his heart yearned at the sight of his brother. He entered his chamber and wept there. Then he washed his face and came out, and controlled himself and said, "Set out the food."

The food was set out separately for him, and separately for his brothers, and separately for the Egyptians who ate with him. For the Egyptians regarded it an abomination to eat with the Hebrews. The brothers were seated before him, the firstborn according to his birthright, and the youngest according to his youth; and the brothers marveled at this. They were served portions from the food before him, and Benjamin's portions were five times greater than any of the others. And they all drank until they were merry.

Then Joseph privately ordered his steward, "Fill the men's sacks with food, as much as they can carry, and put each man's money in the mouth of his sack. And place my silver cup, together with his grain money, in the sack of the youngest." And the steward did so.

As soon as the morning was light, the brothers were sent on their way.

When they had scarcely left the city, Joseph said to his steward, "Up, follow the men! And when you overtake them, say to them, 'Why have you rewarded good with evil? Why have you stolen the cup from which my lord drinks, and by which he divines? You have done a wicked thing!' "

So the steward overtook them and accused them. And they said to him, "God forbid that your servants should do such a thing! Behold, the money which we found in our sacks we brought back to you from the land of Canaan; why then should we steal silver or gold from your lord's house? The one upon whom the stolen cup is found, let him die; and we also will be my lord's slaves."

The steward said, "Only he with whom it is found shall be a bondsman, and the rest of you shall be blameless."

Then each one speedily took down his sack and opened it. The steward searched, beginning with the eldest and ending with the youngest, and the cup was found in Benjamin's sack.

The brothers rent their garments, and they loaded the asses again and returned to the city. They went to Joseph's house and fell before him on the ground. Joseph said, "What deed is this that you have done?" And Judah answered, "What can we say to you, my lord? How shall we clear ourselves? God has found out the iniquity that is in us. Behold, we are my lord's slaves." And Joseph said, "God forbid that I should do so! Only he in whose hand the cup was found shall be my slave. As for the rest, go home in peace to your father."

Then Judah came near him and said, "O my lord, let not your anger burn against your servant, for you are even as Pharaoh! My lord asked his servants, 'Have you a father, or a brother?' And we said to my lord, 'We have a father, an old man, and a child of his old age, a little one, whose brother is dead; and he alone is left of his mother, and his father loves him.' And you said, 'Bring him down to me that I may set my eyes upon him.' And we said to my lord, 'The boy cannot leave his father, for if he should leave him, his father would die.' But you said, 'Unless your youngest brother comes with you, you shall see my face no more.' We told these words to your servant my father. And he said, 'You know that if you take this son from me, and harm befalls him, you will bring down my gray hairs with sorrow to the grave.' Therefore when I return to your servant my father, and he sees that the boy is not with me, he will die. I pray you, therefore, to let your servant remain as a slave to my lord instead of the boy, and let him go back with his brothers."

Then Joseph could not restrain himself any longer, and he cried out to the people who stood about him, "Let everyone withdraw from me!" And when they were alone with him, Joseph said to his brothers, "I am Joseph! Does my father still live?"

But his brothers could not answer him, for they were dismayed by his presence.

Joseph said to them, "Come near me." And they came near. He said, "I am Joseph your brother, whom you sold into Egypt. Be not grieved nor angry with yourselves because you sold me, for God sent me here to preserve life. The famine has been in the land for two years, and there are to be five more years in which there will be no plowing and no reaping. God sent me here before you to save your lives; so it was not you who sent me here, but God. He has made me a father to Pharaoh and a ruler throughout Egypt. Make haste now and go to my father, and say to him, 'Thus says your son Joseph: "Come down to me and dwell in the land of Goshen; and you shall be near me, you and your children and your children's children, and your flocks and your herds and all that you have. Here I will nourish you, for there are to be still five more years of famine." ' "

And Joseph fell upon his brother Benjamin's neck and wept, and Benjamin wept with him. Then he kissed all his brothers, and after that his brothers talked with him.

When it became known in Pharaoh's house that Joseph's brothers had come, it pleased Pharaoh and the men of his court. And Pharaoh said to

Joseph, "Say to your brothers, 'Load your beasts and go to the land of Canaan, and take your father and your households and come to me, and I will give you of the fat of the land of Egypt.'"

So Joseph's brothers went up out of Egypt and came into the land of Canaan to Jacob their father, and said to him, "Joseph is alive, and he is governor over all the land of Egypt." Jacob's heart fainted, for he believed them not. Then they told him every word that Joseph had said to them, and the spirit of Jacob their father revived. He said, "Joseph my son is alive! I will go and see him before I die!" [14]

## Jacob in Egypt

*46-49*　Joseph made ready his chariot, and went up to Goshen to meet his father; and he fell upon his neck and wept a good while. And Jacob said to Joseph, "Now I can die in peace, since I have seen your face and know you are alive."

Joseph came to Pharaoh and said, "My father and my brothers, their flocks, and their herds, and all they have, have come from the land of Canaan and are now in the land of Goshen." And he took five of his brothers and presented them to Pharaoh. Pharaoh asked his brothers, "What is your occupation?" And they answered, "Your servants are shepherds." Pharaoh said to Joseph, "Let your father and your brothers dwell in the best of the land of Egypt; in the land of Goshen let them dwell; and if you know of able men among them, put them in charge of my herds."

Then Joseph brought in Jacob his father and presented him to the king, and Jacob blessed Pharaoh.

Jacob was one hundred and thirty years old when he came to Egypt, and he lived there seventeen years. And when the time drew near that Jacob must die, he sent for his son Joseph and said to him, "If I have found favor in your sight, put your hand under my thigh and promise that you will not bury me in Egypt. For I wish to lie with my fathers, and to be buried in their burying-place." Joseph answered, "I will do as you ask." And Jacob said, "Swear to me." So Joseph swore to him.

Then Jacob called for his sons and said, "Gather around me, that I may bless you before I die:

"REUBEN, you are my firstborn, my might and the beginning of my

[14] See GENESIS, Chapter 46, in Notes and Excisions.

strength; to you belongs the excellency of dignity and of power. But you are as unstable as water; and because you are wanting, you shall not excel.

"SIMEON and LEVI are brothers — instruments of cruelty are their tools. In their anger they slew a man, and in their wrath they tore apart an ox. Cursed be their anger, for it is fierce; and their wrath, for it is cruel. I will divide them in Jacob and scatter them in Israel.

"JUDAH, you are he whom your brothers shall praise. Your hand shall be on the neck of your enemies, and to you shall your brothers bow down. Judah is a young lion; who shall dare to rouse him? The scepter shall not depart from him. He shall bind his foal to the vine, and wash his garments in the blood of the grape; his eyes shall sparkle from wine, and his teeth gleam white from milk.

"ZEBULUN shall dwell at the shore of the sea and be a haven for ships, and his border shall be at Zidon.

"ISSACHER, like a strong ass crouching between two burdens, saw that a rest was good and that the land was pleasant, so he bowed his shoulder to the load and became a faithful servant.

"DAN shall judge his people as one of the tribes of Israel. He shall be like a serpent along the wayside, like a viper that strikes at the horse's heels so that the rider falls backward.

"GAD shall be overcome by a troop, but he shall overcome at the last.

"ASHER shall yield royal delicacies, and his bread shall be nourishing.

"NAPHTALI is a doe set free, and he speaks pleasant words.

"JOSEPH is the fruitful bough of a tree beside the river whose branches arch over the wall. His arms have been made strong by the hands of the Almighty God of Jacob. The blessings of your father upon the head of Joseph, prince among his brothers.

"BENJAMIN is a ravenous wolf: in the morning he shall devour his prey, and in the evening he shall divide his spoil."

All these are the twelve tribes of Israel, and this is how their father Jacob spoke to them and blessed them; each according to his blessing did he bless them. And then Jacob died and was gathered to his fathers.

Joseph fell upon his father's face, and wept over him and kissed him. And Joseph ordered the physicians to embalm his father. They embalmed him; and after the forty days were fulfilled, the days required for those who are embalmed, the Egyptians mourned Jacob for threescore days and ten. And when the days of mourning were over, Jacob's sons carried him to the land of Canaan and buried him in the cave of Machpelah, which Abraham bought as a burial-place in the fields near Mamre.[15]

## "So Died Joseph . . ."

50    When Joseph's brothers saw that their father was dead, they said to each other, "If Joseph hates us, now that our father is dead he will repay us for all the evil we have done to him." Therefore they said to him, "Before he died, your father commanded us to say to you: 'Joseph, forgive the trespass of your brothers and their sin, I pray you, for they did evil to you.'"

Joseph wept when he heard these words. His brothers fell down before him and said, "Behold, we are your servants." And Joseph answered, "Fear not! For am I in the place of God to judge you? You thought evil against me; but God meant it for good, to bring about this day when so many are saved from starvation. Therefore, fear not! I will nourish you and your little ones." And he comforted them and spoke kindly to them.

Joseph dwelt in Egypt, he and his father's house, and Joseph lived until he was one hundred and ten years old. He saw Ephraim's children of the third generation, and the grandchildren of Manasseh.

Then Joseph said to his brothers, "I die. And God will surely visit you and bring you out of this land to the land which he promised to Abraham, to Isaac and to Jacob. Promise me that then you will carry up my bones from here." And he took an oath from them on this.

So Joseph died, and they embalmed him; and he was put into a coffin in Egypt.

[15] See GENESIS, Chapter 48, in Notes and Excisions.

# EXODUS
## *The Story of a Great Emancipation*

⟨ Exodus is sharply divided into two almost equal parts: The first twenty chapters give the stirring saga of a daring emancipator, who freed his people from bondage in Egypt and led them through desert and wilderness to establish a covenant between them and the Lord their God. The remaining twenty chapters contain a collection of diverse laws and ordinances, many of which are no longer practiced, and a detailed description of the tabernacle and its priesthood. The name of the book is derived from the great narrative of the man Moses, his childhood, his adventures, and the seemingly insurmountable difficulties he overcame in winning the confidence of his people in Egypt, and bringing about their release from Pharaoh.

In Hebrew this book is known as "Names" (Sh'mos), for the book opens with: "Now these are the names of the sons of Israel, who came into Egypt with Jacob." Exodus is the Greek name of the book and means "The Departure."

While Genesis covers a period of many centuries and gives the stories of a number of people, Exodus covers a relatively short space of time and concentrates on the adventures of the spirit of one man, born in slavery, who was destined to influence the history of mankind.

The laws and ordinances in Exodus, as well as in the succeeding three Books of Moses, permeate the remainder of the Moses story—from the time the children of Israel receive the Ten Commandments at Sinai to the day on which Joshua ben Nun leads them into the Promised Land. These laws, covenants, ordinances and observances became the core of the Hebrew religion, and some of them became the foundation of Western law and ethics. The Ten Commandments received by Moses on Mount Sinai now occupy a central and supreme place in the ethical sys-

54

tems of three great living religions: Judaism, Christianity, and Mohammedanism. ⟨[

## The Wicked Pharaoh

1      Joseph died, and all his brothers, and all that generation. But the children of Israel were fruitful and multiplied and became exceedingly mighty, and they filled the land. Then there arose a new king over Egypt who knew not Joseph. And the king said to his people, "Behold, the children of Israel are more and mightier than we. And if there should be war, they might join our enemies against us and escape from the land."

So they appointed taskmasters to oppress them, and to have them build for Pharaoh the treasure cities Pithom and Raamses. The Egyptians forced the children of Israel to serve them in heavy bondage, and made their lives bitter with hard labor in all manner of service in the field. Yet the more they were afflicted, the more they multiplied and grew.

Pharaoh sent for the Hebrew midwives and said to them, "When you act as midwife to a Hebrew woman, if the infant is a son you shall kill him, and if it is a daughter, then she may live."

But the midwives feared God and they saved the children. So the king of Egypt summoned them again and said, "Why have you done this, and let the male infants live?" And the midwives replied, "Because the Hebrew women are unlike the Egyptian women; for they are lively, and their infants are born before the midwives reach them."

Then Pharaoh issued a command to the children of Israel, saying "Every son that is born to you, you shall cast into the river, and every daughter you shall permit to live."

## The Birth of Moses

2      Now there went a man of the house of Levi, and married a woman of the house of Levi; and the woman gave birth to a son. And when the mother saw that he was a goodly child, she hid him for three months. When she could hide him no longer, she took a basket woven of bulrushes and coated it with pitch; and she placed the child in it, and

set it down among the reeds at the bank of the river. And the child's sister stood a little way off to see what would happen to him.

Soon afterwards Pharaoh's daughter came down to bathe in the river. And when she noticed the basket among the bulrushes, she sent a maid to fetch it. She opened it and saw the child; and behold, the child wept. She was moved by pity and said, "This must be one of the Hebrew infants." And the child's sister came forward and asked, "Shall I go and call a nurse of the Hebrew women, that she may nurse the child for you?" Pharaoh's daughter answered, "Go." And the girl went, and called the child's mother.

Pharaoh's daughter said to the woman, "Take this child and nurse it for me, and I will pay you your wages." The mother took the child and nursed it. And the child grew; and she brought him to Pharaoh's daughter, and he became her son.

Pharaoh's daughter named him Moses (He Who Was Drawn Out). "For," she said, "I drew him out of the water."

## Moses in Midian

2    In the course of time, when Moses had grown up, he went out among his brothers, the children of Israel, and he saw their suffering. One day he witnessed an Egyptian lashing a Hebrew. Moses looked this way and that way, and when he saw there was no one about, he slew the Egyptian and hid him in the sand.

The next day when he went out, Moses came upon two of the Hebrews quarreling. And Moses said to the one in the wrong, "Why do you strike your companion?" He answered, "Who made you a prince and a judge over us? Do you intend to kill me, as you killed the Egyptian?"

Then Moses was afraid, and he said to himself, "Surely this thing is known." And when Pharaoh heard of the matter, he sought to slay Moses. But Moses learned of Pharaoh's intent and fled to the land of Midian; and when he reached that land, he sat down beside a well.

Now the priest of Midian had seven daughters; and they came to the well and drew water, and filled the troughs for their father's flock. Then some shepherds came up and drove them away, but Moses went to their aid and helped them water their flock. When they returned home, their father, Jethro, asked, "How is it that you are home so soon today?" They answered, "An Egyptian protected us from the shepherds, and drew water for our flock." Jethro asked his daughters, "Where is this man? Why have you left him? Go, call him, that he may eat with us."

Moses came, and he was content to dwell in Jethro's house; and the priest gave his daughter Zipporah to Moses in marriage. She bore a son to Moses, and he named the child Gershom (A Stranger There). "For," he said, "I have been a stranger in a strange land."

In the process of time the king of Egypt died. But the children of Israel still suffered in their bondage; and they cried out, and their cry came up to God. And God remembered his covenant with Abraham, Isaac and Jacob. And God looked upon the children of Israel.

## The Burning Bush

**3-4**    Now Moses tended his father-in-law's flock. And one day he led the flock to the edge of the desert, and came to the foot of Mount Horeb, the mountain of God. And an angel of the Lord appeared to him in a flame of fire out of the midst of a bush. Moses looked, and behold, the bush burned in the fire but was not consumed. He said to himself, "I will turn aside to watch this wondrous sight."

As Moses neared, God called to him from the midst of the burning bush, "Moses, Moses!" He answered, "Here am I." And God said, "Draw not nigh; put off your shoes; for the place on which you stand is holy ground. I am the God of your fathers, the God of Abraham, the God of Isaac, and the God of Jacob!"

Moses hid his face, for he feared to look upon God. And the Lord said, "I have seen the suffering of my people, who are slaves in Egypt; I have heard their cry and I know their sorrows. I have come down to deliver them from the Egyptians, and to bring them out of that land to a good land and large, flowing with milk and honey. Come now, and I will send you to Pharaoh, that you may bring my people out of Egypt."

Moses said, "Who am I, that I should go to Pharaoh, and that I should bring the children of Israel out of Egypt?" And God said, "I will be with you; and this shall be the proof that I have sent you: When you have brought the people out of Egypt, you shall serve God upon this mountain."

Moses said, "When I go to the people and say to them, 'The God of your fathers has sent me to you,' and they ask 'What is his name?' — what shall I tell them?" And God said to him, "Say to them, 'I AM has sent me to you!' For I AM WHO I AM. This is my name forever. Go, and gather the elders of Israel and say to them, 'The God of your fathers has appeared to me, saying, "I shall take you out of your affliction in Egypt, to the land of the Canaanites, and the Hittites, and the Amorites, and the Perizzites, and the Hivites, and the Jebusites, to a land flowing with milk and honey." ' And they will listen to you. Then shall you take the elders to the king of Egypt, and say to him, 'We beseech you to let us go for three days' journey into the wilderness, that we may sacrifice to the Lord our God.' The king will not let you go, and I will stretch out my hand and smite Egypt with all my wonders. After that he will let you go."

Moses answered, "What if they will not believe me, and say, 'The Lord has not appeared to you'?"

The Lord said, "What is that in your hand?" "A staff," said Moses. And God said, "Cast it upon the ground." Moses cast it upon the ground, and it turned into a serpent; and Moses fled. But the Lord commanded, "Put out your hand and take it by the tail." Moses caught the serpent by the tail, and it turned into a staff in his hand.

Then the Lord said, "Now put your hand into your bosom." Moses did so; and when he took his hand out, behold, it was leprous and white as snow. God said, "Put your hand into your bosom again." Moses put his hand in again, and when he drew it out it was once again like the rest of his body.

And God said, "If they will not believe you at the first sign, they will believe you at the second. And if they will not believe you after these two signs, then take water from the river and spill it upon dry ground, and the water will turn into blood before their eyes."

Moses said, "O my Lord, I pray you, do not send me. For I am slow of speech and slow of tongue. I am not a man of words, neither heretofore, nor since you have spoken to your servant." And the Lord said to him, "Who has made man's mouth? Who makes a man dumb or deaf, or seeing, or blind? Is it not I, the Lord? Now, therefore, go; and I will teach you what to say."

But Moses answered, "O Lord, I pray you, send another more fit than I."

God's anger kindled against Moses, and he said, "Is not Aaron the Levite your brother? I know that he can speak well. And behold, he comes to meet you. He shall be your spokesman to the people. And you shall take this staff with which to perform the signs."

Moses returned to Jethro, his father-in-law, and said, "Pray let me go, that I may return to my kinsmen who are in Egypt to see whether they still live." And Jethro replied, "Go in peace."

## The Ten Plagues

*4-12*    Moses took his wife and his sons and set out for the land of Egypt. And he carried the staff of God in his hand. Then the Lord appeared to Aaron, saying, "Go into the wilderness to meet your brother Moses." Aaron went, and he met Moses at the mount of God, and kissed him. And Moses told Aaron all the words of the Lord, who had sent him.

Moses and Aaron went on to Egypt together, and they spoke there to the elders of the children of Israel, and told them all that the Lord had commanded. And they showed the signs in the sight of the people. The people believed; and when they heard that the Lord had seen their suffering, they bowed their heads and worshiped.

Afterward Moses and Aaron went to Pharaoh, and said to him, "Thus says the Lord God of Israel, 'Let my people go, that they may hold a feast to me in the wilderness.'" Pharaoh asked, "Who is this Lord, that I should obey his voice and let Israel go? I know not the Lord, nor will I let Israel go. And why do you keep the people from their tasks?"

On the same day Pharaoh commanded the taskmasters of the people, "You shall no longer give the people straw to make the brick as before; let them go and gather straw for themselves. But the number of bricks which each must make shall not be diminished. For they are idle; that is why they cry, 'Let us go and sacrifice to our God!' Let more work be laid upon them, so they will have no time to listen to lying words." And the taskmasters obeyed.

So the people were scattered abroad through the land to gather stubble, and Pharaoh's taskmasters beat them and demanded, "Why have you not fulfilled your task and made the same number of bricks, both yesterday and today, as you have made before?"

The officers over the children of Israel saw the plight of their people, and they went to Moses and Aaron and said, "The Lord look upon you and judge you. For you have put a sword into the hands of Pharaoh and his servants with which to slay us."

Moses said to the Lord, "Lord, why have you sent me? For since I came to Pharaoh to speak in your name, he has done evil to your people; nor have you delivered them at all."

59

Then the Lord said to him, "Now you shall see what I will do to Pharaoh, for he shall let them go, and he shall drive them out of his land. I am the Lord. And I appeared to Abraham, to Isaac, and to Jacob by the name of God Almighty, and my name JEHOVAH (HE WAS, HE IS, HE SHALL BE — THE ETERNAL ONE) was not known to them. I established my covenant with them to give them the land of Canaan, the land of their pilgrimage, in which they were strangers. Now I have heard the moaning of the children of Israel, whom the Egyptians keep in bondage, and I have remembered my covenant. Therefore, go to the children of Israel, and say to them, 'The Lord will bring you out from under the burdens of the Egyptians and will redeem you with an outstretched arm. And he will take you as his people; and he will be your God.'"

Moses went and spoke thus to the children of Israel, but they turned away from him in the anguish of their spirit. And Moses said to the Lord, "Behold, the children of Israel will not listen to me. How then shall Pharaoh listen to me?"

The Lord God said to Moses, "See, I have made you as a god to Pharaoh, and Aaron your brother as your prophet. You shall tell him all that I command you, and Aaron your brother shall speak to Pharaoh. But I will harden Pharaoh's heart and multiply my signs and wonders in the land of Egypt, that the Egyptians shall know I am the Lord when I stretch forth my hand and bring out the children of Israel from among them."

Moses was fourscore years old, and Aaron fourscore and three, when they spoke to Pharaoh.[1]


*The Plague of Blood.* Moses and Aaron went into the presence of Pharaoh, and they did as the Lord had commanded. Aaron threw down his staff in front of Pharaoh and his courtiers, and it became a serpent. Then Pharaoh sent for his wise men and sorcerers, and they did in like manner with their enchantments. Each man threw down his staff, and the staffs became serpents. But Aaron's staff swallowed up theirs. When Pharaoh saw this, his heart hardened, so that he would not listen to Moses and Aaron.

The Lord said to Moses, "Seek out Pharaoh in the morning; lo, he goes down to the river; and you shall stand at the river's bank and say to him, 'The Lord God of the Hebrews has sent me to you, saying: "Let my people go, that they may serve me in the wilderness." Behold, if you do not

[1] See EXODUS, Chapter 6, in Notes and Excisions.

hear me now, I will strike the waters of the river with this staff in my hand, and the water shall turn into blood.'"

And Moses and Aaron did so. Aaron lifted his staff and struck the waters of the river within sight of Pharaoh and his courtiers, and the waters turned into blood. The fish died, and the river became foul, and the Egyptians could not drink of it.

The Egyptians dug around the river for clear water to drink; and the magicians of Egypt with their enchantments turned the water into blood. And when Pharaoh saw this, he turned and he went into his house. And the plague of blood lasted seven days.

*The Plague of Frogs.* Again the Lord spoke to Moses and said, "Go to Pharaoh and say to him, 'Thus says the Lord, "Let my people go, that they may serve me." And if you refuse to let them go, I will smite your land with frogs. The frogs shall come up from the river and enter your house, and your bedchamber and your bed, and come into your ovens and into your kneading troughs, and they shall swarm over you and your people.'"

Moses and Aaron did as the Lord commanded. And Aaron stretched out his staff over the streams, the ponds, and the rivers of Egypt; and the frogs came up, and they covered the land.

The magicians did so also with their enchantments, and brought frogs upon the land of Egypt. But Pharaoh sent for Moses and Aaron and said to them, "Entreat the Lord to take away the frogs, and I will let your people go."

Moses cried out to the Lord to rid the land of the frogs which he had brought upon Pharaoh, and the frogs died in the houses and the villages and the fields. Then the frogs were gathered up in great heaps, and the land stank.

When Pharaoh saw that there was respite from the frogs, he hardened his heart, as the Lord had said.

*The Plague of Lice.* The Lord said to Moses, "Say to Aaron, 'Stretch out your staff and strike the dust of the ground, that it may become lice.'" Aaron did so, and the dust became lice and covered man and beast throughout the land.

The magicians tried to bring forth lice out of the dust with their enchantments, but they could not. Then they said to Pharaoh, "This is the finger of God!" But Pharaoh's heart was hardened, and he would not listen to them.

*The Plague of Insects.* And the Lord said to Moses, "Appear before Pharaoh early in the morning when he goes down to the river, and say to him, 'Thus says the Lord: "Let my people go, that they may serve me. Else I will send swarms of insects upon you and your people; and your houses shall be full of them. On that day I will set apart the land of Goshen, in which my people dwell, so that no insects shall be there. Thus shall you know I am the Lord"'"

And the Lord did so; and great swarms of different kinds of insects came into Pharaoh's house and the houses of his courtiers; and the whole land of Egypt was devastated by them.

Pharaoh summoned Moses and Aaron, and said, "Go, sacrifice to your God within the land." Moses answered, "Let us go three days' journey into the wilderness, and sacrifice to the Lord our God as he will command us."

Pharaoh said, "I will let you go, that you may sacrifice to the Lord your God in the wilderness, only you shall not go very far away. And pray for me."

Moses left Pharaoh's presence, and prayed to the Lord to remove the swarms of insects; and the Lord did so: there remained not one. But this time also Pharaoh's heart hardened, and he would not let the people go.

*The Plague of Murrain.* Then the Lord said to Moses, "Go to Pharaoh and tell him, 'Thus says the Lord God of the Hebrews: "Let my people go that they may serve me." For if you refuse, and still hold them, the hand of the Lord will fall upon your cattle in the field, upon the horses, upon the asses, upon the camels, upon the oxen and the sheep. They shall all be stricken with a severe murrain. Tomorrow the Lord shall do this thing.'"

And the Lord did so on the morrow. All the cattle of Egypt were stricken and died. Only of the cattle of the children of Israel there died not one. But the heart of Pharaoh was stubborn, and he did not let the people go.

*The Plague of Boils.* The Lord said to Moses and to Aaron, "Take handfuls of ashes from the furnace, and let Moses throw them heavenward within sight of Pharaoh. The ashes shall become a fine dust that will cover the whole land of Egypt, and it will bring boils upon man and upon beast." They did as God commanded them; and boils broke out upon man and beast. And the magicians could not stand before Moses because of the boils, for the boils were upon the magicians as well as upon all the other Egyptians.

But the Lord hardened the heart of Pharaoh, and he would not listen to Moses and Aaron.

*The Plague of Hail.* The Lord said to Moses, "Appear before Pharaoh early in the morning, and say to him, 'Thus says the Lord God of the Hebrews: "Let my people go, that they may serve me. Else on the morrow, I will stretch out my hand and cause a hailstorm such as has never been known in Egypt since the day it was founded."'"

On the morrow Moses stretched out his staff toward heaven and the Lord sent thunder and hail, and fire ran along the ground. So that there was hail, and fire mingled with the hail. And the hail struck every herb in the field, and broke every tree. And the flax and the barley were struck down, for the barley was in the ear and the flax was in bloom. Only in the land of Goshen, where dwelt the children of Israel, there was no hail.

Pharaoh sent for Moses and Aaron, and said to them, "I have sinned! The Lord is righteous, and I and my people are wicked. Pray to the Lord, that there may be an end to these mighty thunderings and hail; and I will let your people go, and you shall stay no longer."

Moses went out of the city and stretched his hands out to the Lord; and the thunder and hail ceased, and the rain no longer poured upon the earth. But when Pharaoh saw that the thunder and hail had ceased, his heart hardened, and he would not let the children of Israel go.

*The Plague of the Locusts.* Then Moses and Aaron came before Pharaoh and said, "Thus says the Lord God of the Hebrews, 'How long, how long will you refuse to humble yourself before me? Let my people go, that they may serve me. For if you refuse, behold, tomorrow I will bring the locust upon your land, and whatever escaped the hail the locust shall eat.'"

Pharaoh's courtiers cried out, "How long shall this man be a snare to us? Let him and his people go, that they may serve their God. For by their plagues they have almost destroyed our land."

Pharaoh said to Moses and Aaron, "Who are those among you that will go to serve your God?" And Moses said, "We will go with our young and with our old, with our sons and with our daughters; with our flocks and with our herds will we go." Pharaoh answered, "Your men may go to serve your God. But if you take your little ones with you, evil will lie in wait for you." And Moses and Aaron were driven out of Pharaoh's presence.

Moses stretched out his staff over the land of Egypt, and the Lord sent an east wind all day and all night; and when morning came the sky was dark with locusts. They ate every herb of the field and all the fruit of the trees which the hail had left; and not a green thing remained throughout the whole land.

Pharaoh sent in haste for Moses and Aaron, and said, "I have sinned against the Lord your God and against you! Forgive my sin only this once, and entreat the Lord your God to take away the locusts."

Moses went out of Pharaoh's presence and entreated the Lord. And a mighty west wind came which swept the locusts into the Red Sea, and there remained not one locust in all the land of Egypt.

But the Lord hardened Pharaoh's heart, so that he would not let the children of Israel go.

*The Plague of Darkness.* And the Lord said to Moses, "Stretch out your hand toward heaven, that darkness may descend over the land of Egypt." Moses stretched out his hand, and upon the land fell darkness, a darkness so thick that it could be felt; and for three days the darkness endured, and the people could not see one another, nor dared to leave their places. Yet the children of Israel had light in their dwellings.

Pharaoh sent for Moses, and said, "You may go to serve your Lord and you may take the children with you, but your flocks and your herds must remain behind." Moses answered, "Our cattle must go with us, for we shall need them as sacrifices, and we know not with what we must serve our God until we come there."

Pharaoh said to him in anger, "Go away from me, and take heed never to see my face again, for on the day you see my face you shall die!" Moses answered, "As you have spoken: I will see your face again no more."

*The Death of the Firstborn.* The Lord said to Moses, "I will bring one more plague upon Pharaoh and upon Egypt. Afterwards he will let my people go. And when he lets you go, he shall drive you out altogether. Speak now in the ears of the people, and let every man borrow of his neighbor, and every woman of her neighbor, jewelry of silver and jewelry of gold."

Moses spoke to the people and said, "Thus says the Lord, 'At midnight I will go out into the midst of Egypt, and all the firstborn in the land shall die — from the firstborn of Pharaoh, who sits upon his throne, to the firstborn of the servant at the mill, even to the firstborn of the cattle. But against the children of Israel not even a dog shall bark, that you may know the Lord does put a difference between the Egyptians and Israel.' "

And it came to pass that at midnight the Lord struck down all the firstborn of the land. And Pharaoh rose up in the night, he and all his courtiers and the people, and there was a great cry throughout Egypt — for there was not a house where there was not one dead. Pharaoh sent for Moses and Aaron during the night, and said to them, "Rise up and leave! Go serve the Lord, as you have said. Take your children, and your flocks and your herds, and be gone; and ask a blessing for me also."

## The Passover Memorial

12-13    The Lord had said to Moses and Aaron in the land of Egypt, "This month shall be the first month of the year for you. And on the tenth day of this month let every man in the congregation of Israel take a lamb and keep it until the fourteenth day of the month. Then the whole assembly of the congregation of Israel shall kill their lambs in the evening. And they shall take of the blood and put it on the two doorposts and the lintel of the houses in which they eat them. And they shall eat the meat that night, roasted by fire; and with unleavened bread and bitter herbs they shall eat it. And they shall eat it with their loins girded, their shoes on their feet, their staffs in their hands; and they shall eat it in haste. For on that night I will pass through the land of Egypt and smite all the firstborn of the land; but when I see the blood on the doorposts, I will *pass over*, and the plague shall not be upon Israel when I smite the land of Egypt. And this day shall forever be to you as a memorial day, and you shall keep it as a feast to the Lord from generation to generation. Seven days there shall be no leaven in your houses; and he who eats leavened bread from the first to the seventh day, that soul shall be cut off from Israel.

"You shall observe the feast of unleavened bread, for on this selfsame day I brought you out of the land of Egypt. And when you observe this ordinance in time to come, and in the land which the Lord will give you as he has promised, and your children ask, 'What is the meaning of this feast?' you shall say to them, 'It is a memorial of the Lord's passover, for he *passed over* the houses of the children of Israel in Egypt, and spared our houses when he smote the Egyptians.'"

The children of Israel did as the Lord had commanded Moses and Aaron. And it came to pass that at midnight, on the fourteenth day of the first month, the children of Israel left Egypt. They journeyed from Rameses to Succoth, about six hundred thousand men on foot, besides children. And a mixed multitude went with them, and flocks, and herds of cattle. They baked unleavened cakes of the dough which they had brought out of Egypt for it was not leavened because they were thrust out of Egypt and could not tarry to prepare for themselves any food.

And Moses took the bones of Joseph with him, for Joseph had taken an oath from the children of Israel, saying, "God will surely visit you, and you shall carry my bones away from here with you."

Moses said to the people, "Remember this day in which you came out of Egypt, out of the house of bondage. For with a strong arm the Lord brought you out of this place. Let this day be remembered forever as a token upon your arm and as frontlets between your eyes, for by the hand of the Lord were we freed from our bondage in Egypt!"

Now the children of Israel had dwelt in Egypt four hundred and thirty years. On the selfsame day that the four hundred and thirty years came to an end, on the fourteenth night of the first month, all the hosts of the Lord departed from Egypt. And this is the night of the Lord to be observed by the children of Israel in all generations.

## The Song of Moses

13-15   When Pharaoh let the people go, God led them not by the way of the land of the Philistines, which was near, but by the way of the wilderness of the Red Sea. "For," said God, "when the people see war, they may regret their departure and wish to return to Egypt."

And the Lord went before them by day in a pillar of cloud to guide them, and by night in a pillar of fire to give them light. Thus they could journey by day and by night; and the pillar of cloud by day and the pillar of fire by night was always at the head of the people.

The king of Egypt was told that the children of Israel had fled, and he and his courtiers said, "Why have we released Israel from serving us?" And the king chose six hundred chariots from all the chariots of Egypt, and there was a captain over each one of them; and they pursued the children of Israel, and overtook them where they were encamped by the sea, beside Pi-ha-hiroth.

When the children of Israel lifted up their eyes and saw the Egyptians pursuing them, they were frightened and cried out to Moses, "Were there no graves left in Egypt that you brought us away to die in the wilderness?" Moses answered them, "Fear not; stand still and see how the Lord will save you. For these Egyptians whom you see today, you shall see again no more forever."

Moses stretched out his hand over the sea; and the Lord swept back the sea with a strong east wind all that night, and turned the sea into dry land; and the waters of the sea were divided. Then the children of Israel went into the midst of the sea upon the dry ground, and the waters rose like walls on the right and on the left of them.

The Egyptians pursued them to the middle of the sea; all Pharaoh's horses, his chariots, and his horsemen. But Moses again stretched out his hand over the sea, as the Lord commanded him, and the waters returned. They covered the chariots and the horsemen and all the host of Pharaoh that had followed them into the sea, and there remained alive not so much as one of them.

Thus the Lord saved Israel that day from the Egyptians; and the people feared the Lord, and believed the Lord and his servant Moses.

Then Moses and the children of Israel sang this song to the Lord:

"I will sing to the Lord, for he has triumphed gloriously! The Lord is my strength and my song; he has become my salvation. The horse and his rider has he hurled into the sea; Pharaoh's chariots and his captains has he cast into the Red Sea. They went down into the depths like a stone; the deep waters cover them.

"Your right hand, O Lord, glorious in power, your right hand, O Lord, shatters the enemy. In the greatness of your majesty you have overthrown those who rose up against you; you loose your wrath, and they are consumed like stubble. At the blast of your nostrils the waters gathered together, the floods stood upright, the depths congealed in the heart of the sea.

"The enemy said in his heart: 'I will pursue, I will overtake, I will divide the spoil; my lust shall be satisfied upon them. I will draw my sword, my hand shall destroy them.' But you blew with your wind, and the sea covered them; they sank as lead in the mighty waters.

"Who is like unto you, O Lord, among the gods? Who is like you, glorious in holiness, performing wonders? In your love you led the people whom you have redeemed; you have guided them by your strength to your holy habitation.

"The nations shall hear of it, and tremble; panic shall strike the inhabitants of Philistia. The mighty men of Edom and of Moab shall be dismayed; the inhabitants of Canaan shall melt away. Fear and dread shall fall on them; because of the greatness of your arm they shall be still as a stone until your people pass over, O Lord, until your people pass over!

"Then shall you bring your people in and plant them in the mountain of your inheritance; in the sanctuary, O Lord, which your hands have established!

"The Lord shall reign forever and forever!"

And Miriam the prophetess, sister of Moses and Aaron, took a tambourine in her hand, and all the women followed her with tambourines and with dancing, while Miriam led them in song:

"Sing to the Lord, for he has triumphed gloriously; the horse and his rider has he hurled into the sea!"

## Miracles in the Desert

15-16    So Moses led Israel onward from the Red Sea, and they went into the wilderness of Shur. For three days they journeyed and found no water. And when at last they found water, they could not drink it because the water was bitter. Therefore they called the place Marah, which means Bitter. The people murmured against Moses, saying, "What shall we drink?" And he cried out to the Lord. Then the Lord showed him a tree, which Moses cast into the water, and the water became sweet.

From Marah they went on to Elim, where there were twelve springs of water and threescore and ten palm trees, and they camped there beside the waters.

On the fifteenth day of the second month after they had departed from Egypt, the children of Israel came to the wilderness of Sin, which lies between Elim and Sinai. And there all the people murmured against Moses and Aaron, and said to them, "Would that we had died a natural death in the land of Egypt, when we sat beside the fleshpots and ate bread to the full; for you have brought us into the wilderness where this whole assembly will surely perish from hunger."

Then said the Lord to Moses, "I have heard the murmuring of the people. Say to them, 'At dusk you shall eat meat; and in the morning, bread to the full. And you shall know the Lord your God.' "

At even the quails came up and covered the camp, and in the morning the ground was covered with dew. And when the dew lifted, behold, the face of the wilderness was covered with a layer as fine as hoarfrost. When the people saw it, they said one to another, *"Man-hu? Man-hu?"* ("What is it? What is it?") For they did not know what it was. And Moses said to them, "This is bread from heaven which the Lord has given us. Gather of it according to the number of persons in your tents."

The children of Israel gathered it, some more and some less. Yet those who gathered too much had none left over, and those who gathered too little suffered no lack, and everyone had his fill. The people called it *manna;* and it was white like coriander, and tasted like wafers made with honey. They gathered the manna each morning, and when the sun grew hot it melted. But if it was kept overnight, it bred worms and became foul.

On the sixth day they gathered twice as much manna. And they laid it up until morning, as Moses bade; and it did not become foul. Moses said, "Eat that today, for today is a Sabbath to the Lord; today you will not find it in the field. Six days you shall gather it, but on the seventh day, which is a Sabbath, there will be none." On the seventh day some of the people went out to gather, and they found none.

Moses said to the people, "Thus says the Lord, 'Let an omer of manna be kept for future generations, that they may see the bread from heaven with which I fed you in the wilderness, when I brought you out of the land of Egypt.' "

So Aaron took a jar and filled it with an omer of manna, to be kept for the generations to come.

And the children of Israel ate manna for forty years, until they came to an inhabited land, until they came to the borders of the land of Canaan.

## The War with Amalek

17    The children of Israel journeyed on from the wilderness of Sin and camped at a place called Rephidim. And again there was no water for the people to drink. The people quarreled with Moses and said,

"Give us water that we may not perish." Moses answered, "Why do you quarrel with me? Why do you try God's patience?" But the people thirsted for water; and they murmured against him and said, "Why have you brought us here to die of thirst?"

Moses cried out to the Lord, "What shall I do with this people? They are almost ready to stone me." And the Lord said to him, "Take your staff in your hand and go to the rock in Horeb. Behold, I will stand before you there, and you shall strike the rock, and out of it shall come water that the people may drink."

And Moses did so in the sight of the elders of Israel. And he named the place Massah-Meribah (Trial and Contention), for here the children of Israel were quarrelsome and tried the patience of the Lord, saying, "Is the Lord among us or not?"

Then came Amalek and fought with Israel at Rephidim.

Moses said to Joshua, the son of Nun, "Choose men for us to go out and fight with Amalek, while I stand on the top of the hill with the staff of God in my hand."

Joshua did as Moses commanded him; and he fought with Amalek, while Moses, Aaron, and Hur went up to the top of the hill. And it came to pass that when Moses held up his hand, Israel prevailed; but when he grew tired and lowered his hand, Amalek prevailed. As the battle went on, and Moses' hands grew very heavy, Aaron and Hur brought a stone for him to sit upon, and they held up his hands, one on the one side and the other on the other side; and so they held his hands steady until the going down of the sun.

Thus Joshua discomfited Amalek and his people with the edge of the sword.

## Jethro's Advice

18    When Jethro, the priest of Midian, heard of all that God had done for Moses and for Israel, his people, he took Zipporah, whom Moses had sent back to her father's house, and her two sons, Gershom and Eliezer, and brought them to Moses in the wilderness where he was encamped at the mount of God.

Moses went out to meet his father-in-law, and bowed before him, and after they had inquired after each other's welfare, they entered the tent. There Moses told Jethro of all that had happened to the children of Israel along the way, and how the Lord had saved them. Jethro rejoiced and said, "Blessed be the Lord for his goodness in delivering you from the Egyptians. Now I know that the Lord is greater than all other gods." And he took a burnt offering and sacrifices for God; and Aaron came, and all the elders of Israel, to break bread with Jethro before God.

On the morrow Moses sat to judge the people, and they stood about him waiting from morning until evening. When Jethro saw this, he asked, "Why do you sit alone and the people stand about you from morning until evening?"

Moses answered, "Because the people come to me to inquire of God. And when they have differences between them, they come to me and I judge between one and another and I make known to them the statutes of God and his laws." Jethro said to him, "You will surely wear away, both you and the people, for this task is too heavy for you; you are not able to perform it alone. Listen to my voice, and I will give you counsel. Select from among the people able men such as fear God, men of truth who hate greed; and appoint them as rulers of thousands, of hundreds, and of fifties and of tens. Teach them the ordinances and laws, and show them the way they must walk. And let them judge the people at all times. Every important matter they shall bring to you, but every small matter they shall judge themselves; so shall it be easier for you and they will bear the burden with you. If you do this, you will be able to endure; and the people also will go their way in peace."

Moses listened to the voice of his father-in-law. He chose able men, and made them heads over the people, rulers of thousands, of hundreds, of fifties and of tens. And they judged the people at all times. The hard cases they brought to Moses, but every small matter they judged themselves.

Then Moses let his father-in-law depart, and Jethro went his way to his own land.

## The Ten Commandments

19-20   In the third month after the children of Israel had gone out of Egypt, they came into the wilderness of Sinai. And they encamped there at the foot of the mountain, while Moses went up to God.

And the Lord called to him out of the mountain, "Thus shall you speak to the house of Jacob and say to the children of Israel: 'You have seen what I did to the Egyptians, and how I bore you on the wings of eagles and brought you to myself. Now, therefore, if you will indeed listen to my voice and keep my covenant, you shall be my own treasure from among all peoples; for all the earth is mine, and you shall be to me a kingdom of priests and a holy nation.'"

And Moses came down and called together the elders of Israel, and set before them all these words which the Lord had commanded him. And the people answered together, "All that the Lord has spoken we will do."

Moses returned with the words of the people to the Lord. And the Lord said to him, "Lo, I shall appear to you in a thick cloud, that the people may hear when I speak with you, and believe you forever. Go to the people, and sanctify them today and tomorrow, and let them wash their garments and be ready by the third day. For on the third day the Lord will come down in the sight of all the people upon Mount Sinai."

Moses went down from the mountain to the people, and sanctified them; and they washed their garments. And on the morning of the third day there were thunder and lightning, and a thick cloud upon the mount, and the voice of a clarion exceedingly loud, so that all the people who were in the camp trembled. Moses brought the people out of the camp to meet with God, and they stood at the foot of the mount. Now Mount Sinai was hidden in smoke, because the Lord descended upon it in fire; and the smoke of it ascended like the smoke of a furnace, and the whole mountain quaked. And as the voice of the clarion sounded long, and grew louder and louder, Moses spoke, and God answered him by a voice. The Lord came down upon Mount Sinai and called Moses to the top of the mount, and Moses went up.

And God spoke these words:

I AM THE LORD YOUR GOD, who brought you out of the land of Egypt, out of the house of bondage. You shall have no gods before me.

YOU SHALL NOT MAKE ANY IMAGE or any likeness of anything that is in heaven above, or on the earth below, or that is in the water under the earth. You shall not bow down to them, nor serve them; for I the Lord your God am a jealous God, visiting the iniquity of the fathers upon the children to the third and fourth generation of those who hate me, but showing mercy to the thousandth generation of those who love me and keep my commandments.

YOU SHALL NOT TAKE THE NAME OF THE LORD YOUR GOD IN VAIN, for the Lord will not hold him guiltless who takes his name in vain.

REMEMBER THE SABBATH DAY, to keep it holy. Six days shall you labor and do all your work; but the seventh day is a Sabbath to the Lord your God: on it you shall not do any work, you, nor your son, nor your daughter, nor your manservant, nor your maidservant, nor your cattle, nor the stranger who is within your gates. For in six days the Lord made heaven and earth, the sea, and all that is in them, and on the seventh day he rested. Therefore the Lord blessed the Sabbath day and made it holy.

HONOR YOUR FATHER AND YOUR MOTHER, that your days may be long upon the land which the Lord your God gives you.

YOU SHALL NOT COMMIT MURDER.

YOU SHALL NOT COMMIT ADULTERY.

YOU SHALL NOT STEAL.

YOU SHALL NOT BEAR FALSE WITNESS against your neighbor.

YOU SHALL NOT COVET your neighbor's house; you shall not covet your neighbor's wife, nor his manservant, nor his maidservant, nor his ox, nor his ass, nor anything that is your neighbor's.

All the people perceived the thundering and the lightning, and the voice of the clarion, and the mountain smoking; and the people trembled and moved away and stood afar off. They said to Moses, "You speak to us and we will listen, but let not God speak to us lest we die."

And Moses said to them, "Fear not, for God has come to test you, that the fear of him may be with you and you sin not."

The people stood afar off, but Moses drew near to the thick darkness where God was.

## Walls of the Covenant

21-23   The Lord said to Moses, "Now these are the judgments which you shall set before the children of Israel:

*On Murder:* "Whoever strikes a man so that he dies shall be put to death. But if he did not lie in wait for the man, then I will appoint a place to which he may flee. If a man comes upon his neighbor to slay him with guile, you shall take him even from my altar, that he may die."

*On Injury:* "If men struggle, and hurt a woman with child so that she loses her child, and no other harm follows, the guilty shall be fined according to the husband's demand and as the judges determine. But if harm to the woman follows, then the guilty man shall give life for life, eye for eye, tooth for tooth, hand for hand, foot for foot, burning for burning, wound for wound, stripe for stripe."

*On Battery*: "And if a man strikes his slave, male or female, and an eye is destroyed, the slave shall go free for the sake of the eye; and if a man knocks out his slave's tooth, he shall let the slave go free for his tooth's sake."

*On Manumission*: "If you buy a Hebrew slave, he shall serve you six years; and in the seventh he shall go out free. If he came in by himself, he shall go out by himself; if he came in married, then his wife shall go out with him. But if the master has given him a wife, and she has borne him sons and daughters, the wife and the children shall belong to her master, and he shall go out by himself."

*On Filial Respect*: "He who strikes his father or his mother shall be put to death."

*On Seduction*: "If a man entices a girl who is not betrothed, and lies with her, he shall endow her to be his wife. If her father refuses to let the girl marry him, he shall pay money equal to the dowry for virgins."

*On Treatment of Strangers*: "You shall not wrong a stranger, nor oppress him; for you know the heart of a stranger, seeing that you were strangers in the land of Egypt."

*On Treatment of the Widow and the Orphan*: "You shall not afflict the widow or the fatherless child. If you do afflict them, your wives shall become widows, and your children fatherless."

*On Usury and Pledges*: "If you lend money to any of my people who is poor, you shall not take interest from him. And if you take your neighbor's garment as a pledge, you shall return it to him before the sun goes down, for that is the covering for his body; in what else shall he sleep?"

*On False Rumors and False Witness*: "Keep far from a false matter. You shall not give rise to a false report. You shall not join hands with the wicked, to be an unrighteous witness."

*On Conscience*: "You shall not follow the multitude to do evil."

*On Partiality*: "You shall not withhold justice due to your poor; nor shall you favor a poor man in his cause because of his poverty."

*On Bribery*: "You shall take no gift, for a gift blinds the wise and perverts the words of the just."

*On Stray Cattle*: "If you come upon your enemy's ox or ass going astray, you shall bring it back to him. If you see the ass of one who hates you lying under its burden, you shall help him with it."

*On Pitfalls*: "When a man opens a pit or digs one, and fails to cover it, and an ox or an ass falls into it, the owner of the pit shall make it good and pay for the beast; and the dead beast shall be his."

*On Fines for Theft*: "If a man steals an ox or a sheep, and kills it or sells it, he shall restore five oxen for an ox, and four sheep for a sheep."

*On Grazing Fines*: "If a man causes a field or vineyard to be grazed over, or lets his beast feed in another man's field, he shall give of the best of his own field and his own vineyard, and shall make restitution."

*On Fire Law*: "If a fire breaks out and catches in thorns, so that the shocks of grain or the standing grain or the fields are consumed, he who caused the fire shall surely make restitution."

*On Hired Animals*: "If a man hires a work-animal from his neighbor, and it is hurt or dies, the owner not being with it, the hirer shall make it good. But if the owner was with it, he shall not make it good, because it was a hired animal and came for its hire."

*On First Fruits and the Firstborn*: "You shall not delay to offer the first of your ripe fruits. The firstborn of your sons you shall give to me. And thus shall you do with your oxen and your sheep: Seven days shall it be with its dam, and on the eighth day you shall give it as an offering to me."

*On the Jubilee*: "Six years shall you sow your land and gather its yield, but in the seventh year you shall let it rest, that the poor among you may eat; and what they leave the beasts of the field shall eat. In like manner you shall deal with your vineyards and your olive orchards."

*On the Day of Rest*: "Six days shall you do your work, and on the seventh day you shall rest, that your ox and your ass may rest, and the son of your servant and the stranger may be refreshed."

*On Feasts*: "Three times in the year you shall keep a feast to me. You shall keep the feast of unleavened bread; and the feast of the first fruits of your labor in the field; and you shall keep the feast of the ingathering at the end of the year, when you have gathered in from the field the fruit of your labor."

"Behold, I shall send an angel before you to guard you on the way, and to bring you to the place which I have prepared. Obey his voice, for my name is with him. And when my angel brings you to the Amorites, the Hittites, the Perizzites, the Hivites, the Jebusites, and the Canaanites, and I cut them off, you shall not bow down to their gods nor serve them, but you shall overthrow them and break their images.

"You shall serve only the Lord your God, and I will bless your bread and your water, and free you from sickness, and you will live the full number of your days.

"The fear of me will go on before you and destroy your enemies. I shall drive them out until you have inherited the borders I have set for you from the Red Sea to the sea of the Philistines, and from the desert to the river Euphrates. For I will deliver the inhabitants of the land into your hand." [2]

# The Tables of the Law

**24-31** Moses came and told the people all the words of the Lord, and all the ordinances, and the people answered with one voice, "All that the Lord has commanded us we will do."

And Moses wrote all the words of the Lord. He rose early the next morning, and built an altar at the foot of the mountain, and twelve pillars, according to the twelve tribes of Israel. And he sent young men of the children of Israel, who sacrificed peace offerings of oxen to the Lord. Moses took half of the blood of the offerings and put it in basins, and half of the blood he sprinkled on the altar.

Then he took the book of the covenant and read it in the hearing of the people, and they responded, "All that the Lord has said, we will do, and we will obey." Moses took the blood from the basins and sprinkled it on the people, and said, "Behold, the blood of the covenant which the Lord has made with you in accordance with these words."

Then Moses went up, and with him Aaron, and Nadab and Abihu, the sons of Aaron, and seventy elders of Israel. And they saw the God of Israel; and under his feet there was as it were a pavement of sapphire stone, like the heaven in clearness. And the Lord said to Moses, "Come up to me on the mountain, and I will give you tablets of stone with the laws and commandments I have written, that you may teach them."

So Moses rose up with his servant Joshua, and went up the mount of God. And he said to the elders, "Tarry here for us until we come again; and behold, Aaron and Hur are with you; whoever has a matter to be judged, let him go to them."

Then Moses went up on the mountain, and a cloud covered the mountain. The glory of the Lord settled on Mount Sinai, and the cloud covered it six days; and on the seventh day he called to Moses out of the midst of

[2] See EXODUS, Chapters 21-23, in Notes and Excisions.

the cloud. Now the appearance of the glory of the Lord was like a devouring fire on the top of the mountain in the sight of the people of Israel. And Moses entered the cloud. And he remained on the mountain forty days and forty nights.

And the Lord said to Moses, "Ask the children of Israel to bring me an offering, and from every man whose heart makes him willing you shall receive the offering for me. And this is the offering you shall take from them: gold and silver and brass; blue and purple and scarlet, and fine linen; rams' skins dyed red; acacia wood; oil for the lamps; spices for the anointing oil and the fragrant incense; onyx stones, and stones to be set in the ephod and the breastplate. And let them make me a sanctuary, that I may dwell in their midst. And exactly as I instruct you, both as to the pattern of the tabernacle and of all its instruments, even so shall you make it."

And the Lord gave to Moses, when he had finished speaking with him upon Mount Sinai, the two tablets of testimony, tablets of stone, written with the finger of God.[3]

## The Golden Calf

32-34    When the people saw that Moses delayed coming down from the mount, they gathered around Aaron and said, "Up, make us a god who shall go on ahead of us. As for this Moses, the man who brought us up out of Egypt, we know not what has become of him."

Aaron answered, "Take off the golden earrings which are in the ears of your wives, of your sons and of your daughters, and bring them to me." The people brought the golden earrings to Aaron, and he melted them and fashioned them with a tool into a golden calf. And the people said, "This is your god, O Israel, who brought you out of the land of Egypt!"

When Aaron saw this, he built an altar before it, and proclaimed, "Tomorrow shall be a feast day to the Lord." On the morrow the people rose early, and made sacrifices of burnt offerings and peace offerings; and they sat down to eat and to drink, and they rose up to make merry.

And the Lord said to Moses, "Go down; for your people, whom you brought out of the land of Egypt, have quickly turned aside from the way which I commanded them to follow. They have made for themselves a golden calf and worship it, and sacrifice to it, and say, 'This is your god, O

[3] See EXODUS, Chapters 25-31, in Notes and Excisions.

Israel, who brought you up out of the land of Egypt!' Behold, they are indeed a stubborn people. Now leave me, that my wrath may consume them, but of you I will make a great nation."

And Moses besought the Lord his God, "Lord, why does your wrath burn against your people, whom you have brought out of Egypt with a mighty hand! Why should the Egyptians say, 'He brought them out to slay them in the mountains, and to consume them from the face of the earth'? Turn from your fierce wrath, and repent of this evil against your people. Remember Abraham, Isaac, and Jacob, your servants, to whom you did swear, 'I will multiply your descendants like the stars of heaven, and this land that I have spoken of will I give your descendants to inherit forever.'"

The Lord repented of the evil which he had thought to do to his people. And Moses turned, and went down from the mount with the two tablets in his hand. The tablets were written on both sides, and the writing was the writing of God.

As Moses came near the camp he saw the calf, and the people dancing; and his anger blazed, and he threw down the tablets, and broke them at the foot of the mount. Then he took the calf which they had made and ground it to powder, and strewed the powder upon the water and made the children of Israel drink of it.

Moses said to Aaron, "What did the people do to you, that you have brought so great a sin upon them?" And to the people Moses said, "You have sinned a great sin. Now I will go up to the Lord; perhaps I can make atonement for you."

Moses returned to the Lord and said, "The people have sinned a great sin, for they have made for themselves a god of gold. Yet now, will you not forgive their sin? And if not, I pray you, blot me out of your book which you have written." The Lord said to him, "Whoever has sinned against me, him will I blot out of my book. And now go; lead the people to the place of which I have spoken to you, to the land which I promised to Abraham, to Isaac and to Jacob, saying, 'To your descendants will I give it.' Behold, I will send an angel before you, but I will not go up in your midst. And say to the children of Israel, 'You are a stubborn people! If I should go into your midst for one moment, I would consume you.'"

When the children of Israel were told of these words they mourned, and they stripped themselves of their ornaments.

Moses took the tabernacle and pitched it outside the camp, afar off, and called it the tabernacle of the congregation. And everyone who sought the Lord went into the tabernacle. Whenever Moses went out of the camp to the tabernacle, all the people rose up, and each man stood at his tent door and looked after Moses until he had entered the tabernacle. And as Moses entered, the people saw the pillar of cloud descend and stand at the tabernacle door; and the people worshiped, each man at the door of his tent. Thus the Lord spoke to Moses face to face, as a man speaks to his friend.

And Moses said to the Lord, "If I have found grace in your sight, I pray you, show me now your ways, that I may know you; and consider this nation your people." And the Lord said to him, "My presence shall go with you and I will give you peace. Hew two tablets of stone like the first, and I will write upon them the words that were on the first tablets, which you broke. Be ready in the morning, and present yourself to me at the top of the mount."

Moses hewed two tablets of stone like the first; and he rose early in the morning and went up Mount Sinai with the two tablets in his hands. And the Lord descended in a cloud and proclaimed: "The Lord, the Lord God, the God of mercy and forgiveness, slow to anger, abounding in goodness and truth, extends his mercy to thousands and forgives transgressions, iniquity and sin; but he will not clear the impenitent, visiting the iniquity of the fathers upon the children to the third and fourth generation."

Moses made haste, and bowed his head toward the earth and worshiped.

And the Lord said to him, "Write the words of my covenant with you and with Israel." And Moses was there with the Lord forty days and forty nights; he neither ate bread nor drank water. And he wrote upon the tablets the words of the covenant, the ten commandments.

When Moses came down from Mount Sinai with the two tablets in his hands, Aaron and the children of Israel saw that his face shone; and they were afraid to come near him. Then Moses covered his face, and he spoke to the children of Israel, and gave them in commandment all that the Lord had spoken with him on Mount Sinai.

# Preparation of the Tabernacle

**35-40** Moses assembled the children of Israel and said to them, "The Lord has commanded you, saying, 'Whoever is of a willing heart, let him bring the Lord's offering; and let every wise-hearted man among you come and make the tabernacle: its tent and its covering, its clasps and bars, its pillars and sockets, the ark and its staves, the ark cover and the veil of the screen, the table and all its vessels, the candelabra and the lamps, the incense altar and the screen for the door at the entrance of the tabernacle, the altar with its grating of brass and all its vessels, the hangings of the court, and the garments for ministering in the holy place."

The people departed from the presence of Moses. And everyone whom his spirit made willing brought the Lord an offering for the work of the tabernacle, and for the service within it, and for the holy garments. And all the women who were wise-hearted brought what they had spun, of blue, of purple, of scarlet, and of fine linen. And the rulers brought onyx stones and the stones to be set, for the ephod and the breastplate; and the spices and the oil for the light and for the anointing oil, and for the sweet incense.

Then Moses called Bezalel and Oholiab, and every able man in whose heart the Lord had put wisdom, and they wrought all the work of the sanctuary. And on the first day of the first month, in the second year, the tabernacle was reared up. Moses laid its sockets and put in its bars and reared up its pillars. And he spread the tent over the tabernacle, and put the covering of the tent over it. Then he took the tablets of testimony and put them in the ark. And he brought the ark into the tabernacle, and set up the veil of the screen and screened the ark of the testimony, as the Lord had commanded.

He put the table in the tent of the congregation, northward, and set a row of bread in order on it before the Lord. And he put the lampstand opposite the table, southward, and lighted the lamps before the Lord. Then he put the golden altar before the veil, and burnt on it incense of sweet spices. And he caused all things to be done as the Lord had commanded. So Moses finished the work.

Then a cloud covered the tent of the congregation, and the glory of the Lord filled the tabernacle. And Moses was not able to enter the tabernacle because the cloud abode upon it.

And whenever the cloud rose up from the tabernacle, the children of Israel went onward in their journey. But if the cloud did not rise, then they journeyed not until the day that it rose.

For the cloud of the Lord rested upon the tabernacle by day, and fire by night, in the sight of all the house of Israel, throughout all their journeying.[4]

[4] See EXODUS, Chapters 35-40, in Notes and Excisions.

# LEVITICUS
## The Code of the Priests

⟨ In Hebrew this book is known by two names: "He Called" (Va-yikra), based on the opening sentence: "And God called to Moses and spoke to him"; and sometimes "The Law of the Priests" (Toras Kohanim), from which the Greek name Leviticus derives, meaning essentially the same thing: "The Law of the Priests" or "The Code of the Priests."

The Code is clearly of a very late date and was formalized centuries after the laws which are given in the preceding or subsequent books of the Pentateuch. Much of it repeats what has been said before, or concerns itself with rites and ceremonies that have not been observed since the destruction of the temple in Jerusalem nearly twenty centuries ago.

However, adherents of Judaism still follow, more or less strictly, the laws concerning what may or may not be eaten, and whom one may or may not marry among next of kin; and they observe the holidays prescribed in the Bible.

And embedded, as it were, in the vast amount of varied legislation and minute instructions on such matters as the manner of offering a sacrificial ram, or the type of garment to be worn by the priest when he enters the sanctuary, are two startling chapters known as "The Code of Holiness," which give briefly a résumé of the important laws and ethical principles which are to serve as guides for the people of the Book. The teachings of truth and justice, humility and kindness, respect for elders, and consideration for the stranger are summarized here in stirring precepts. And, like a rare gem in a royal diadem, appears one commandment which sums up the whole of the Holy Law and turns the rest into commentary and elaboration:

*You shall not hate your brother in your heart, nor shall you rebuke*

*him so as to cause sin upon him. You shall seek no vengeance, nor bear a*
*grudge, but you shall love your neighbor as yourself."* [1] ⟨[

# The Dietary Laws

*11-17*    The Lord said to Moses and to Aaron, "Say to the children of
Israel, 'These are the living things which you may eat among all
the beasts that are upon the earth: those that are cloven-hoofed and
chew the cud you may eat. Nevertheless, you shall not eat of those that
chew the cud but are not cloven-hoofed, such as the camel, the cony and
the hare; nor shall you eat of those that are cloven-hoofed but do not
chew the cud, such as the swine. They are unclean to you.

"'And these among the creatures of the waters you may eat: all those
that have fins and scales, whether in the seas or in the rivers. But all the
living creatures in the waters that have not fins and scales shall be unclean to you.

"'And these among the birds shall not be eaten: the eagle, the ossifrage,
the osprey, the vulture, the kite, the falcon, the raven after its kind, the
ostrich, the owl, the hawk, the gull, the cormorant, the great owl, the
swan, the pelican, the stork, the heron, the lapwing, and the bat, each
after its kind. These shall be abhorrent to you; and all winged creatures
that creep or go upon all fours shall also be abhorred by you. Yet among
the winged things that go upon all fours, which have legs joined above
their feet with which to leap upon the earth, these you may eat: the
locust, the cricket and the grasshopper, each after its kind. All other
winged, swarming things which have four feet shall be abhorrent to you.
And every creeping thing that creeps upon the earth shall not be eaten.

"'This is the law of the beast and of the bird and of every living creature that moves in the waters and that swarms upon the earth: to distinguish between the clean and the unclean; between that which may be
eaten and that which may not be eaten.

"'And if any man of the house of Israel, or any strangers who sojourn
among you, eats any manner of blood, I will cut him off from among his
people. For the soul of all made of flesh is in the blood. Therefore any
man who hunts and catches a beast or bird that may be eaten, shall first

---

[1] See LEVITICUS, Chapters 1-10, in Notes and Excisions.

draw out its blood and cover it with dust; for you shall eat no manner of blood!' " [2]

## Unlawful Marriages

18 And the Lord said to Moses, "Say to the children of Israel, 'You shall not follow the customs of the land of Egypt where you dwelt, nor shall you follow the customs of the land of Canaan to which I shall bring you. You shall keep my statutes and my ordinances and live by them: I am the Lord!

" 'None of you shall approach in marriage any who are near of kin. You may not marry your father, or your mother, or your sister, or your brother, or your half sister, or your half brother, or your son's children or your daughter's children, or your uncle or your aunt, or your son-in-law or your daughter-in-law; nor shall you marry your brother's widow, if she has borne him children; nor shall you take a woman in marriage as a rival to her sister, during her sister's lifetime.

" 'You shall not give any of your children to pass through the fire to Molech, and so profane the name of your God. I am the Lord.

" 'You shall not lie with a man as with a woman; it is an abomination. You shall not lie with any beast; it is perversion.

" 'For by all these have the nations I am casting out defiled themselves before you. Therefore did I punish their iniquity, and the land vomited out its inhabitants. Do none of these abominations, lest the land vomit you out also.' "

## The Code of Holiness

19-22 And the Lord said to Moses, "Say to the congregation of Israel, 'You shall be holy, for I the Lord your God am holy!

" 'Every one among you shall revere his father and his mother. You shall rise up before the hoary head, and honor the face of the old man.

" 'You shall not steal, nor deal falsely, nor lie one to another. And you shall not swear by my name falsely: I am the Lord.

" 'You shall not oppress your neighbor, nor defraud him. The wages of him who is hired shall not abide with you all night until the morrow.

[2] See LEVITICUS, Chapters 12-17, in Notes and Excisions.

" 'You shall do no injustice in weight or in measure. Just weights and balances shall you have.

" 'And when you reap the harvest of your land, you shall not wholly reap the corners of your field, nor gather the gleanings after your harvest. And you shall not glean your vineyard, nor gather its fallen fruit; you shall leave them for the poor and the stranger.

" 'You shall not curse the deaf, nor put a stumbling block before the blind.

" 'You shall do no injustice in judgment; you shall not be partial toward the person of the poor, nor favor the person of the mighty, but in righteousness shall you judge your neighbor.

" 'You shall not be a talebearer; neither shall you stand idly by the blood of your neighbor.

" 'You shall not hate your brother in your heart, nor shall you rebuke him so as to cause sin upon him.

" 'You shall seek no vengeance, nor bear a grudge, but you shall love your neighbor as yourself: I am the Lord.

" 'You shall keep my Sabbaths, and reverence my sanctuary.

" 'And when a stranger dwells in your land, you shall not wrong him. The stranger among you shall be to you as the home-born among you, and you shall love him as yourself.' " [3]

## The Holidays

**23-24**  The Lord said to Moses, "Speak to the children of Israel and say to them, 'These are my appointed feasts:

*The Sabbath.* " 'Six days shall work be done, but the seventh day is a Sabbath of solemn rest, a holy convocation; you shall do no manner of work on that day: it is the Sabbath of the Lord in all your dwellings.' "

*The Passover.* " 'The fourteenth day of the first month, at dusk, is the Lord's Passover. And on the fifteenth day of the same month is the feast of unleavened bread; seven days you shall eat unleavened bread. The first day of this feast you shall have a holy convocation; you shall do no manual work; and on the seventh day you shall do no manual work.' "

*Shabuoth* or *Feast of Weeks:* " 'When you come into the land which I give you, and reap the harvest of it, then you shall bring a sheaf of the first fruits of your harvest to the priest; and he shall bring the sheaf be-

[3] See LEVITICUS, Chapters 21-22, in Notes and Excisions.

fore the Lord to be accepted for you. And you shall count from the
day you have brought the first fruit seven weeks, seven Sabbaths shall
be complete, and on the morrow after the seventh Sabbath it shall be
fifty days (the Pentecost), and you shall present a new meal offering to
the Lord. And you shall make a proclamation on the selfsame day; it
shall be a holy convocation to you and a day on which you shall do no
labor.'"

*Rosh Hashanah (The New Year):* "'The first day of the seventh month
shall be a solemn rest to you, a memorial proclaimed with the blowing of
the trumpets. You shall do no work of any kind on that day, but you
shall bring a burnt offering to the Lord.'"

*Day of Atonement:* "'The tenth day of this seventh month shall be
your day of atonement, a day of holy convocation, when you shall search
your souls. You shall do no manner of work on that day, for it is a day
when you make atonement before the Lord your God.'"

*Succoth* or *Feast of Tabernacles:* "'On the fifteenth day of this seventh
month is the Feast of Tabernacles, which shall last seven days. The first
day shall be a holy convocation, a solemn rest; and the eighth day shall be
a day of solemn rest. On the first day you shall take the boughs of goodly
trees, branches of palm trees and willows of the brook; and you shall
dwell in booths seven days; all who are Israelites born shall dwell in
booths, that your generations may know that I made the children of Israel
dwell in booths when I brought them out of the land of Egypt.'" [4]

## The Jubilee Year

25-27    And the Lord said to Moses, "Say to the children of Israel, 'When
you come into the land which I give you, then shall the land keep
a Sabbath to the Lord. Six years you shall sow your field, and six years
you shall prune your vineyard and gather in the harvest. But in the
seventh year you shall neither sow your field nor prune your vineyard.
That which grows of itself you shall not reap, and the grapes of your un-
dressed vine you shall not gather; it shall be food for your slaves, and your
maid, and your hired servant, and the stranger who sojourns with you, and
for your cattle and the beast in the land. And if you ask, "What shall we
eat the seventh year, since we may not sow nor reap?" know that my blessing upon you in the sixth year shall yield a harvest for three years. You

[4] See LEVITICUS, Chapter 24, in Notes and Excisions.

shall sow on the eighth year, and still eat of the old harvest until the new harvest comes in.

"'And you shall count seven sabbaths of years, seven times seven years, a space of forty and nine years; and you shall hallow the fiftieth year, and proclaim liberty throughout the land to all its inhabitants. It shall be a jubilee for you; and in that year you shall return to every man his possession, and you shall return every man to his family.

"'The land shall not be sold forever, for the land belongs to the Lord, and you are strangers and sojourners with God! In all the land you possess you shall grant a redemption of the land. If your brother becomes poor and sells some of his possessions, any of his kin may come to redeem it. And if the man has no one to redeem it, that which he sold shall remain in the hand of him who bought it until the year of jubilee; and in the jubilee it shall return to him who sold it.

"'If your brother becomes poor, then you shall relieve him. You shall not lend him money at interest, nor give him food for profit. And if your brother becomes poor and is sold to you, you shall not compel him to serve you as a slave; but as a hired servant shall he be to you. And in the year of the jubilee he, and his children with him, shall return to his own family and to the possession of his fathers. For I am the Lord your God who brought you out of the land of Egypt to give you the land of Canaan, and to be your God!'" [5]

[5] See LEVITICUS, Chapters 26-27, in Notes and Excisions.

# NUMBERS
## *Wanderings in the Wilderness*

❡ Because this book begins with the numbering of the children of Israel after their exodus from Egypt, the early translators of the Bible named it Numeri, or Numbers. But its original Hebrew title, "In the Wilderness" (Bamidbar) is more appropriate to the contents. For this book, which opens with a census in preparation for war, goes on as the recital of a thirty-eight-year-long migration of a people through desert and wilderness, and among hostile nations — a journey full of tribulation in the lives of the people and in the life of their aging leader Moses. During this trek through the wilderness they encounter so many disheartening obstacles, they are afflicted with such plagues and diseases, that often they even regret having left their house of bondage. By the time the people finally reach the borders of Canaan, Miriam and Aaron have died, and Moses is aware that his own end, too, is near, and that though his eyes can look across and see the promised land beyond the Jordan, he will not walk upon it.

The book contains memorable literary episodes in the story of Miriam's and Aaron's resentment of Moses, their brother; in the report of the men sent to spy out the land beyond the Jordan; and the narrative, touched with humor, of Balaam and Balak.

The Book of Numbers is also remarkable for what it does not tell, for here we have a record evidently written many centuries after the events it describes. In almost all such national records, the remote and trying days, when seen through the lens of elapsed time, turn into a golden era, with all the cowardice, rebellion and doubts in the hearts of men erased and forgotten; and the heroes emerge as of giant stature, spotless, their every victory blotting out defeats or compensating for them tenfold. Not so in this book. Underscored throughout are the sins and weaknesses of

88

the people: their jealousies and doubts; their greater concern with the needs of the day than with the dream of the future; the envy that arises even in the heart of Miriam and of Aaron; the rebellion of Korah and his followers, who argue that every member of the congregation is holy, and therefore Moses and the priests should not be regarded as above the congregation. Even Moses is shown as growing impatient at times, and angry at times — though steadfast in faith and courage, and never deviating from his mission.

Numbers becomes the second part of the trilogy on Moses — a trilogy of which Exodus is the first book and Deuteronomy the last. These three books, together, give us the great biography of a man whose memory will remain green as long as mankind seeks freedom, and justice, and the way of the Lord. ❴[

## Preparation for War

*1-9*    In the second year after they had come out of the land of Egypt, on the first day of the second month, the Lord spoke to Moses in the wilderness of Sinai, in the tabernacle of the congregation, saying, "Number all the males of Israel by their families, from twenty years old and upward. You shall number them by their hosts, and with you there shall be a man from each tribe, each one the head of his father's house. And you and Aaron shall number all those able to go forth to war."

Moses and Aaron assembled the people and numbered them, and those numbered were six hundred and three thousand and five hundred and fifty. But the Levites were not numbered among those chosen to go to war. For the Lord said to Moses, "Only the tribe of Levi you shall not number, for you shall appoint them over the tabernacle and over all that belongs to it; and they shall carry the tabernacle, and they shall minister in it, and encamp round about it. When the tabernacle is to set forward, the Levites shall take it down; and when the tabernacle is to be pitched, the Levites shall set it up; and the stranger who comes near shall be put to death."

Then Moses and Aaron numbered each man by his own standard, with the ensign of his father's house; and the tribes assembled under their standards in camps pitched round about the tabernacle.

On the east side, toward the rising of the sun, the standard of the camp of Judah was raised, and next to Judah were the camps of the men of

Issachar and Zebulun. And all those numbered in the camp of Judah came to one hundred and eighty-six thousand and four hundred. These were to be the first to set out.

On the south side was raised the standard of the camp of Reuben, and with Reuben were the men of Simeon and Gad. And all those numbered in the camp of Reuben were one hundred and fifty-one thousand and four hundred and fifty. These were to be the second to set out.

Then came the tabernacle of the congregation with the camp of the Levites, encamped in the midst of the camps, every man in his place by his standard. And they were to be the next to set out.

On the west side was raised the standard of the camp of Ephraim, and with Ephraim were the men of Manasseh and Benjamin. And those numbered in the camp of Ephraim were one hundred and eight thousand and one hundred. They were to go forward in the third rank.

The standard of the camp of Dan was raised on the north side, and with Dan were the men of Asher and Naphtali. And those numbered in the camp of Dan were one hundred and fifty-seven thousand and six hundred. They were to set out last.

Thus the children of Israel did according to all that the Lord commanded Moses. Thus they pitched their camps by their standards, and thus they set out, each according to the house of his father.

And the Lord said to Moses, "Say to Aaron and to his sons, 'Thus shall you bless the children of Israel; you shall say to them: "The Lord bless you and keep you; the Lord make his face to shine upon you, and be gracious to you; the Lord lift up his countenance upon you, and give you peace."' So shall they put my name upon the children of Israel, and I will bless them." [1]

## The Silver Trumpets

10     The Lord spoke to Moses, saying, "Make for yourselves two trumpets of beaten silver, that you may use them in calling the congregation together or for the camps to set out. When both trumpets are blown the people shall assemble at the door of the tabernacle. And if but one trumpet is blown, then only the leaders, who are rulers of thousands, shall come to you.

"When you blow an alarm, the camps on the east shall go forward.

[1] See NUMBERS, Chapters 1-9, in Notes and Excisions.

When you blow an alarm the second time the camps on the south side shall set out. But when the congregation is to be gathered together, you shall blow, but not sound an alarm.

"And the sons of Aaron, the priests, shall blow the trumpets. And if you go to war in your land against the adversary who oppresses you, then you shall sound an alarm with the trumpets; and you shall be remembered before the Lord your God, and saved from your enemies.

"Also on the day of your gladness, and on your appointed feasts, and at the new moon, you shall blow the trumpets over your burnt offerings and the peace offerings, that they may serve you for remembrance before your God."

## The Cry for Meat

9-11    On the day that the tabernacle was completed, a cloud came down and covered it; and in the evening the cloud had the appearance of fire until the morning. So it was always; the cloud covered it by day, and the appearance of fire by night. When the cloud lifted from the tabernacle, the children of Israel set out on their journey; and when the cloud came down on the tabernacle, they stopped and pitched their camp. And so it was, that whether it was day or night when the cloud rose, they journeyed. And when the cloud tarried upon the tabernacle, whether it was two days, or a month, or a year, the children of Israel abode in their tents, and journeyed not. Thus they rested at the command of the Lord, and they journeyed at the command of the Lord.

And when they reached a place called Taberah, the mixed multitude among them and the children of Israel wept, and said, "We remember the fish we ate in Egypt; and the cucumbers, and the melons, and the leeks, and the onions, and the garlic. But now there is nothing at all before our eyes excepting this manna!"

Moses heard the people weep, each man at the door of his tent. And he said to the Lord, "Why have you laid this burden upon your servant? Did I beget them, that you should say to me, 'Carry them in your bosom as a father carries a nursing child, and take them to the land promised to their fathers'? They weep before me, and say, 'Give us meat, that we may eat!' I am not able to carry this people alone; the burden is too heavy for me. And if you deal thus with me, I pray you kill me outright, if I have found favor in your sight, for I can no longer endure my wretchedness."

The Lord said to him, "Gather seventy of the elders of Israel and bring them to the tabernacle, that they may stand there with you. And I will take of the spirit which is upon you and put some on them, so that they may bear the burden of the people with you. Then say to the people, 'You have wept, and you have said, "Would that we were given meat to eat, for it was well with us in Egypt." Therefore the Lord will give you meat and you shall eat. And you shall not eat one day, or two days, or five, or ten, or twenty days, but you shall eat meat a whole month, until it comes out at your nostrils and becomes loathsome to you, because you have rejected the Lord who is among you, and have wept before him, saying, "Why came we out of Egypt?" ' "

And Moses said, "The people number six hundred thousand on foot, and you have said, 'I will give them meat, that they may eat a whole month'! If all the flocks and herds were slaughtered for them, would that suffice them? Or if all the fish in the sea were gathered in nets for them, would that suffice them?"

And the Lord said to Moses, "Has the Lord's hand grown short? You shall see now whether or not my word shall come to pass."

Moses told the people the words of God; and he gathered seventy of the elders of Israel and set them round about the tabernacle. And the Lord came down in a cloud, and took some of the spirit that was upon Moses and put it upon the elders. And when the spirit came to rest upon them, they prophesied. But after that they did not prophesy again.

But two of those on whom the spirit rested (the name of the one was Eldad, and the name of the other was Medad) continued to prophesy in the camp. And a young man ran to Moses and told him, "Eldad and Medad are prophesying in the camp!" Joshua, son of Nun, the minister of Moses from his youth up, said, "My lord Moses, forbid them!" But Moses answered, "Are you jealous for my sake? Would that all the Lord's people were prophets, and that the spirit of the Lord were put upon them all!"

Moses returned to the camp, he and the elders of Israel. And there went forth a great wind from the Lord, which brought quails from the sea, and let them fall near the camp, about a day's journey on this side and a day's journey on the other side; and they lay round about the camp, two cubits high upon the earth. The people gathered the quails all that day, and all the night, and all the next day, and they spread the meat round about the camp. But while the meat was still between their teeth, the wrath of the Lord kindled against them, and the Lord struck the people with a very great plague. Those who lusted for meat died, and were buried there. And the place was named Kibroth-hattaavah (The Grave of Lust).[2]

## The Rebuke of Miriam and Aaron

12    Miriam and Aaron spoke against Moses because of the Cushite woman he had married; for he had married a Cushite woman. They said, "Has the Lord indeed spoken only by Moses? Has he not spoken also by us?" And the Lord heard it. Now, the man Moses was very humble, more humble than any other man upon the face of the earth. And the Lord spoke suddenly to Moses, and to Aaron, and to Miriam, saying, "Come out, you three, to the tabernacle of the congregation." They three came out. Then the Lord came down in the pillar of cloud and stood at the door of the tabernacle, and called Aaron and Miriam; and they both came forward. And he said, "Hear now. If there is a prophet among you, I, the Lord, make myself known to him in a vision and speak with him in a dream. But not so with my servant Moses! With him I speak mouth to mouth, plainly, and not in dark speeches; and he beholds the face of the Lord. Why then were you not afraid to speak against my servant Moses?"

The cloud lifted from off the tabernacle; and behold, Miriam was leprous and white as snow. Aaron said to Moses, "Alas, my lord, lay not upon us the sin which we have sinned. We have done foolishly. And let not our sister be as one dead!"

Moses cried to the Lord, "Heal her now, O God, I beseech you!" And the Lord said, "If her father had but spat in her face, would she not have been ashamed seven days? Therefore let her be shut out from the camp seven days, and after that let her be received in again."

Miriam was shut out of the camp for seven days, and the people did not journey until Miriam was brought in again.

## The Report of the Spies

13-15    And the Lord said to Moses, "Select twelve men, one from each tribe, and send them to spy out the land of Canaan, which I give to the children of Israel."

[2] See NUMBERS, Chapter 10, in Notes and Excisions.

Moses selected twelve men, and among them, from the tribe of Judah, he chose Caleb, son of Jephunneh; and from the tribe of Ephraim he chose Joshua, son of Nun. And he said, "Go up to the mountains of the south and see whether the people who dwell there are strong or weak, whether they are few or many, what the land is in which they dwell, whether it is good or bad, whether they dwell in tents or in strongholds, and whether or not there is wood in the land. Be of good courage, and bring us some of the fruit of the land." For this was the time of the first ripe grapes.

So the men set out; and they went into the south, and came to Hebron, an ancient city which was built seven years before the ancient city Zoan in Egypt. Then they came to the valley of Eshcol, where they cut down a branch with a single cluster of grapes so large that two men carried it between them upon a pole. There they gathered also pomegranates and figs. And after forty days the men returned.

They came before Moses and Aaron and the whole congregation encamped in the wilderness of Paran, and showed them the fruit. They said, "The land to which you sent us is indeed a land which flows with milk and honey, and here is some of its fruit. But the people who dwell there are fierce, and their cities are fortified and very great. Moreover, we saw there a giant race, sons of the giant Anak; and we seemed like grasshoppers beside them. The Amalekites dwell in the southland; the Hittites and the Jebusites and the Amorites dwell in the mountains; and the Canaanites dwell near the sea."

Caleb quieted the people and said, "Let us go up at once to possess this land, for we are well able to overcome it!"

But the others who had gone with him said, "We are not able to go up against them, for they are stronger than we."

The people wept, and they murmured against Moses and Aaron. And they said one to another, "Let us choose a captain who will lead us back to Egypt."

Moses and Aaron fell on their faces before the assembly. And Joshua and Caleb rent their garments and said to the people, "The land which we passed through is an exceedingly good land. If the Lord delights in us, he will bring us into this land and give it to us. Only do not rebel against the Lord, nor fear the people of this land. For their defense is removed from them since the Lord is with us. Fear them not."

But the congregation wanted to stone them.

Then the glory of the Lord appeared at the tabernacle before all the children of Israel. And the Lord said to Moses, "How long will this people provoke me? How long will it be before they trust in me? I will smite them with pestilence and disinherit them. And I will make of you a greater nation and mightier than they."

Moses said to the Lord, "If you kill the people whom you delivered in your might from the Egyptians, the nations who have heard of your fame will say, 'Because the Lord was not able to bring the people into the land which he promised them, he has slain them in the wilderness.' Pardon their iniquity, I beseech you, according to the greatness of your mercy, as you have forgiven them even until now!"

And the Lord said, "I have pardoned them, according to your word. But those men who have seen my glory and my signs and have not listened to my voice shall not see the land which I promised to their fathers. Say to them, 'Your children shall wander in the wilderness for forty years, according to the number of days in which you searched out the land. But my servant Caleb, because he followed me fully, and Joshua, the son of Nun, I will bring into the land and their descendants shall possess it.' Tomorrow turn back to the wilderness, and set out by way of the Red Sea."

Moses told these words to the children of Israel, and the people mourned greatly.

In the morning they rose early and went up to the top of the mountain, saying, "Lo, we are here, and we will go to the place which the Lord has promised, for we have sinned." But Moses said to them, "Why do you again transgress the Lord's command? It shall not prosper. Go not, for the Lord is not with you, and you shall fall by the sword."

But they presumed to go up, although the ark of the covenant of the Lord, and Moses, departed not out of the camp. And the Amalekites and the Canaanites who dwelt in that hill country came down and smote them, and pursued them to Hormah.[3]

## Korah's Revolt

16-19    Now Korah, the son of Izhar, a Levite, and Dathan and Abiram and On, sons of the tribe of Reuben, with two hundred and fifty of the assembly, men of renown in the congregation, gathered together against Moses and Aaron, and said to them, "You take too much upon

[3] See NUMBERS, Chapter 15, in Notes and Excisions.

yourselves, seeing that all the congregation are holy, every one of them, and the Lord is among them. Why then do you raise yourselves above the congregation of the Lord?"

When Moses heard this he fell upon his face, and he said to Korah and his company, "In the morning the Lord will show who is his, and who is holy; and he whom the Lord chooses will come near him. This do: Take censers and put fire in them, and put incense upon them before the Lord tomorrow; and the man whom the Lord chooses, he shall be holy. Hear now, you sons of Levi, is it but a small thing to you that God has separated you from the congregation of Israel to bring you near him and to serve him in the tabernacle, that you seek the priesthood also? For what cause have you and your company assembled against the Lord? And what has Aaron done, that you murmur against him?"

Then Moses sent for Dathan and Abiram, but they refused to come. They said, "Is it a small thing that Moses brought us up out of a land flowing with milk and honey to slay us in the wilderness, that he also wishes to make himself a prince over us? We will not come."

On the morrow Korah gathered his men at the door of the tabernacle. And the glory of the Lord appeared to all the assembly. And the Lord said to Moses and to Aaron, "Separate yourselves from among this congregation, that I may consume them in a moment."

They fell on their faces and said, "O God, the God of all flesh, shall one man sin and will you be angry with the whole congregation?" And the Lord said to Moses, "Say to the congregation, 'Withdraw from the tents of these wicked men, and touch nothing of theirs, lest you be swept away in their sins.'"

So the people withdrew on every side from Korah, Dathan and Abiram, while Korah and his followers came out and stood at the door of their tents with their wives, their sons, and their little ones. Moses said, "By this you shall know that the Lord has sent me to do all these works, and that I have not done them of my own choice. If these men die the common death of all men, then the Lord has not sent me. But if the Lord causes the earth to open its mouth and swallow them up, with all that belongs to them, then you shall understand that these men have provoked the Lord."

As he finished speaking these words, the ground split asunder beneath them and swallowed up Korah and all the men who were with him, and all their households. They went down alive into the pit and the earth closed over them.

WATER FROM A ROCK

The people round about them fled at their cry, for they said, "Lest the earth swallow us also."

But on the morrow the whole congregation murmured against Moses and Aaron, saying, "You have killed the people of the Lord." And as they gathered against Moses and Aaron, they looked toward the tabernacle; and behold, the cloud covered it, and the glory of the Lord appeared. Moses and Aaron came to the front of the tabernacle. And the Lord said to Moses, "Withdraw from the midst of this congregation, that I may consume them in a moment."

And they fell on their faces. And Moses said to Aaron, "Take a censer and fill it with fire from off the altar, and put on incense, and quickly make atonement for the congregation. For the wrath of the Lord has fallen upon them; the plague has begun." Aaron did so, and made atonement for the people; and he stood between the dead and the living. And the plague was stayed.[4]

## Water from a Rock

20     The children of Israel came into the desert of Zin and abode there, and they could find no water for the congregation. They gathered together against Moses and Aaron and chided Moses, "Why have you brought the assembly of God into this evil place? It is no place for grain, or for figs, or for vines, or for pomegranates; nor is there any water to drink."

Moses and Aaron went from the presence of the assembly to the door of the tabernacle, and they fell upon their faces. And the glory of the Lord appeared to them. The Lord said to Moses, "Take the staff, and assemble the congregation, you, and Aaron your brother, and speak to the rock before their eyes; and it shall give forth water."

Moses took the staff from its place before the Lord, and when the congregation gathered in front of the rock, Moses said to them, "Hear now, you rebels! Must we fetch you water out of this rock?"

He lifted up his hand and struck the rock with his staff twice; and water gushed out abundantly, and the congregation drank, and their cattle also.[5]

[4] See NUMBERS, Chapters 17-19, in Notes and Excisions.
[5] See NUMBERS, Chapter 20, in Notes and Excisions.

# The Death of Miriam and Aaron

20    When the children of Israel came to the desert of Zin and en-
      camped in Kadesh, Miriam died; and she was buried in that place.

And Moses sent messengers from Kadesh to the king of Edom, to say
to him, "Thus says your brother Israel, 'You know all the trouble that
has befallen us; and behold, we are at Kadesh, a city in the remotest
border of your land. Let us pass, I pray you, through your country. We
will not pass through field or vineyard, nor will we drink water from the
wells. We will go along the king's highway and turn aside neither to the
right nor to the left until we have passed your border.' "

But Edom answered, "You shall not pass through, lest I come out
against you with the sword." Wherefore Israel turned away from him.

They journeyed from Kadesh, and the children of Israel, the whole congregation, came to Mount Hor. There the Lord spoke to Moses, saying,
"Take Aaron and Eleazar his son and bring them up to Mount Hor; and
strip Aaron of his garments and put them upon his son, for Aaron shall
be gathered to his people, and shall die there."

And Moses did as the Lord commanded. They went up Mount Hor
within sight of the whole congregation. Moses stripped Aaron of his garments and put them upon his son Eleazar; and Aaron died there at the
top of the mount. Then Moses and Eleazar came down. And when the
congregation saw that Aaron was dead, all the house of Israel wept for
him, and they mourned for Aaron thirty days.

# The Serpent of Brass

21    From Mount Hor the children of Israel journeyed by the way of
      the Red Sea to go around the land of Edom; and the soul of the
people was discouraged because of the difficult way. They spoke against
God, and against Moses, saying, "Why have you brought us to die in
the wilderness? There is no bread and no water, and we loathe this light
food."

Then the Lord sent among the people fiery serpents that bit them; and
many of them died. Therefore the people came to Moses and said, "We
have sinned, for we have spoken against the Lord and against you. Pray
to the Lord for us, that he may take away the serpents."

Moses prayed for the people. And the Lord said to him, "Make a fiery serpent and mount it upon a pole; and when anyone who is bitten looks upon it, he shall live." Moses made a serpent of brass and mounted it upon a pole; and when anyone was bitten by a serpent, he looked upon the brazen serpent, and he lived.[6]

# Balaam's Ass

**21-26**  The children of Israel set forward from Bamoth to the region of Moab, which is at the top of Pisgah and looks down upon Jeshimon. And they sent messengers to Sihon, king of the Amorites, saying, "Let us pass through your land. We will not turn into your fields or into your vineyards; nor will we drink of the water of the wells; and we will go only along the king's highway until we pass your border."

But Sihon would not let them pass through his land; and he, and his people, went out against Israel in the wilderness; and he fought them at Jahaz. And Israel smote him with the sword and possessed his land from Arnon to Jabbok.

When Balak, king of Moab, saw all that Israel had done to the Amorites, he was sore afraid. He said to the elders of Moab and of Midian, "Now Israel will lick up all that is round about us, as the ox licks up the grass of the field."

And he sent the elders to Balaam, the seer of Pethor, saying, "Behold, a people has come out of Egypt and they abide near me. Come therefore and curse them, for they are too mighty for me. If you curse them for me, perhaps I shall be able to defeat them and drive them out of the land; for I know that he whom you bless is blessed, and he whom you curse is cursed."

The elders of Moab and of Midian departed with gifts in their hands, and they came to Balaam and told him the words of Balak. Balaam said to them, "Lodge here this night, and on the morrow I will bring you word, as the Lord may speak to me."

But in the morning Balaam said to the elders, "Go back to your land without me, for the Lord refuses to give me leave to go with you." The messengers rose and returned to Balak, and said, "Balaam refuses to come."

Balak sent messengers again, more of them, and princes more honorable

[6] See NUMBERS, Chapter 21, in Notes and Excisions.

than the first. They came to Balaam and said, "Thus says Balak, king of Moab, 'Let nothing hinder you from coming to me; for I will promote you to great honor, and whatever you say to me I will do. Only come, I pray you, and curse this people for me!' "

Balaam answered, "Even if Balak were to give me his house full of silver and gold, I could not go against the word of the Lord to do less or more. But tarry here this night also, that I may know what the Lord will tell me to do."

And God came to Balaam that night, and said to him, "If the men have come to summon you, rise up and go with them. But only what I bid you to say shall you say, and only what I bid you to do shall you do."

Balaam rose early in the morning and saddled his ass, and went off with the princes of Moab. On the way an angel of the Lord stood in the road to bar the way. When the ass saw the angel standing in the road with a sword drawn in his hand, she turned aside and went off into a field; and Balaam struck the ass to turn her back into the road. But the angel stood in a narrow path between the vineyards which had a wall on either side. And when the ass saw the angel, she thrust herself against the wall and crushed Balaam's foot against it; and Balaam struck her again. Then the angel went on ahead and stood in a place so narrow that there was no way to turn either to the right or to the left. And when the ass saw the angel there, she lay down under Balaam. Balaam's anger kindled and he struck the ass with his staff.

Then the Lord gave speech to the ass, and she said to Balaam, "What have I done to you, that you have struck me these three times?"

Balaam answered, "Would there were a sword in my hand, for then I would kill you."

The ass said, "Am I not your ass, upon which you have always ridden? Was I ever accustomed to do so before to you?" "No," said he.

Then the Lord opened Balaam's eyes and he saw the angel standing in the road, with a sword drawn in his hand; and Balaam bowed down his head and fell upon his face. The angel said to him, "Why did you strike the ass these three times? Behold, it was I who obstructed your way because your design is perverse. The ass saw me and turned aside three times, and three times saved your life. For if she had not turned aside from me, I would surely have slain you."

Balaam answered, "I have sinned. If my journey is evil in your eyes, I will turn back."

The angel said to him, "Go with the men, but only the words that I bid you shall you speak."

So Balaam went on with the princes of Balak. And when King Balak heard that Balaam was coming, he went out to meet him at a city of Moab, on the border of Arnon. And Balak said to him, "I earnestly entreated you to come — why came you not sooner? Am I unable to repay you with honor?" Balaam answered, "Lo, now that I have come, have I the power to say anything other than the word that God puts in my mouth?"

On the morrow, Balak took Balaam to the high places of Baal, from which he could see the utmost part of the camp of Israel. Balaam said, "Build me here seven altars, and prepare me here seven bullocks and seven rams." Balak did so. And Balak and Balaam offered a bullock and a ram on each altar.

Then the Lord put words in Balaam's mouth, and the seer said, "Balak, the king of Moab, has brought me from Aram, out of the mountains of the east, saying, 'Come, curse Jacob for me and denounce Israel.' But how can I curse whom God has not cursed? How can I denounce whom the Lord has not denounced? For from the top of the rocks I see him, and from the top of the hills I behold him. Who can count the dust of Jacob, or number Israel? Let me die the death of the just, and let my end be like his!"

Balak cried out, "What have you done to me? I brought you to curse my enemies, and behold, you have blessed them!" And Balaam answered, "Must I not utter what the Lord puts in my mouth?"

Then Balak said, "Come with me to another place, from which you can see only the edge of their camp and not all of them, and curse them from there." So he took Balaam to the top of Pisgah, and built seven altars, and offered up a bullock and a ram upon each altar. Balaam said to the king, "Stand here near your burnt offering, while I go to meet the Lord yonder."

Then the Lord put words in Balaam's mouth, and the seer said, "Rise, Balak, and listen to me, O son of Zippor! Behold, I have received a command to bless. God has blessed Israel, and I cannot reverse it. He brought Israel out of Egypt and gave him the strength of a unicorn. Surely there is no enchantment against Jacob, nor any divination against Israel! And it shall be said of Jacob and of Israel, 'What hath God wrought!' Behold, a people that shall rise up like a lion!"

And Balak said to Balaam, "Neither curse them at all, nor bless them at all." But Balaam answered, "Did I not tell you that whatever the Lord puts in my mouth, that I must utter?"

Balak said, "Come, I pray you, and I will take you to another place; perhaps it will please God that you may curse Israel for me from there." And he took Balaam to the top of Peor, which looks down upon the desert. Balaam said to Balak, "Build me here seven altars, and prepare me here seven bullocks and seven rams." Balak did so, and offered a bullock and a ram upon each altar.

Then Balaam set his face toward the desert, and lifted up his eyes, and he saw Israel abiding in his tents, grouped according to the tribes; and the spirit of God came upon him. He said, "Balaam, the son of Beor, who hears the words of God, who sees the vision of the Almighty, says, 'How goodly are your tents, O Jacob; your dwellings, O Israel! They spread out like valleys, like gardens by the banks of a river, like aloes which the Lord has planted, like cedars beside the waters. Their king shall be mightier than Agag, and their kingdom exalted. Israel has the strength of a unicorn; he shall destroy his enemies; he shall pierce them through with his arrows. He lies down like a lion, who will dare stir him up? Blessed are they who bless him, and cursed are they who curse him!'"

Balak's anger kindled against Balaam, and he struck his hands together and said, "I called you to curse my enemies, and behold, you have blessed them these three times. Therefore flee to your place. I thought to promote you to great honor, but the Lord has kept these honors from you."

Balaam answered, "Did I not tell your messengers, 'Even if Balak were to give me his house full of silver and gold, I could not go against the command of the Lord to do either good or bad of my own choice'? And now, behold, I will prophesy what Israel will do to your people in the days to come.

"I, Balaam, son of Beor, who heard the words of God and saw the vision of the Almighty, say, 'A star shall rise out of Jacob, and a scepter out of Israel, and shall smite all the corners of Moab, and destroy all the children of Sheth. Edom and Seir also shall be his possession, and Israel shall do valiantly.'"

Balaam looked toward the country of Amalek, and said, "Amalek was the first of the nations, but in the end he shall perish forever." He looked toward the country of the Kenites, and said, "Strong is your dwelling place, O Kenite, for you have made your nest on a rock. Yet the Kenite shall be crushed, and Asshur shall carry you away captive. And ships shall come from the coast of Kittim and harass Asshur; and Asshur also shall perish forever."

Then Balaam rose up and returned to his place; and Balak also went his way.[7]

## The Successor to Moses

**27-31** The Lord said to Moses, "Go up into this mountain of Abarim, and look out over the land which I have given to the children of Israel. And when you have seen it, you also shall be gathered to your people, like Aaron your brother."

Moses said to the Lord, "Let the Lord, the God of the spirits of all flesh, set a man over the congregation who may come and go before them, and who may lead them out and bring them in, that the congregation of the Lord be not like sheep who have no shepherd."

And the Lord said to him, "Take Joshua, the son of Nun, a man of spirit, and lay your hand upon him. Have him stand before Eleazar the priest, and before the whole congregation; and you shall give him charge in their sight, so that the children of Israel may be obedient."

And Moses did so. He took Joshua before Eleazar the priest, and before the whole congregation; and he laid his hands upon Joshua to give him charge, as the Lord had commanded.[8]

## The Petition of Reuben and Gad

**32-36** Now the children of Reuben and the children of Gad had a very great multitude of cattle; and when they saw that the land of Jazer and of Gilead was a place for cattle, they came to Moses and to Eleazer the priest and to the elders of Israel and said, "The country which the Lord smote before the congregation of Israel is a land for cattle, and your servants have cattle. If we have found favor in your sight, let this land be given to your servants as a possession, and do not take us over the Jordan."

Moses asked, "Shall your brothers go to war while you sit here? Why do you discourage the people from going over into the land which the

[7] See NUMBERS, Chapters 25-27, in Notes and Excisions.
[8] See NUMBERS, Chapters 28-31, in Notes and Excisions.

Lord has given them? Thus did your fathers, when I sent them from Kadesh-barnea to see the land. And the Lord's anger was kindled on that day. Behold, you have risen in your fathers' stead, a brood of sinful men, to augment the fierce anger of the Lord toward Israel. For if you turn away from him now, he will again leave Israel in the wilderness, and you will destroy all this people!"

They came near Moses and said, "We will build sheepfolds here for our flocks and cities for our little ones, but we ourselves will go ready armed before the children of Israel. We will not return to our homes until every man has his inheritance."

Moses answered, "If you will do this; if you will arm yourselves, and every armed man of you will pass over the Jordan before the Lord, until he has driven out his enemies from before him and the land is subdued; then afterward you shall return, and be guiltless before the Lord and before Israel, and this land shall be your possession."

The men of Reuben and of Gad said, "We will do as you command."

And Moses gave to the men of Gad and to the men of Reuben and to half the tribe of Manasseh the kingdom of Sihon, king of the Amorites, and the kingdom of Og, king of Bashan: the land and all the cities within their boundaries.

Then the Lord said to Moses in the plains of Moab by the Jordan near Jericho, "Say to the children of Israel, 'When you pass over the Jordan into the land of Canaan, you shall drive out all the inhabitants of the land before you, and destroy all their images, and tear down all their high places. And you shall dwell in the land, for to you I have given it. You shall divide the land by lot according to your families: to the more you shall give more and to the fewer you shall give less as an inheritance; every man's share shall be in the place where the lot falls, and according to the tribes of your fathers shall you inherit.'"

And Moses commanded the children of Israel, saying, "This is the land which you shall inherit by lot, which the Lord has commanded to be given to the nine tribes and to the half tribe, for the tribes of Reuben and of Gad and half the tribe of Manasseh have received their inheritance this side of the Jordan. And the inheritance of each of the children of Israel shall not be assigned from tribe to tribe, for each one shall cling to the inheritance of his fathers. Neither shall the inheritance be assigned from one tribe to another, but each tribe shall cling to its own inheritance."

And the Lord said to Moses, "Command the children of Israel to give to the Levites cities to dwell in, and also open land round about the cities for their cattle. And of the cities which you give the Levites, six shall be cities of refuge, which you shall appoint for the man-slayer to flee to; and besides these you shall give forty and two cities. And the cities which you give them shall be from the possession of the children of Israel; from those who have many you shall take many, and from those who have few you shall take few; each tribe shall give of its cities to the Levites according to its inheritance.

"And of the cities of refuge you shall give three cities this side of the Jordan, and three cities in the land of Canaan. For the children of Israel, and for the stranger and for the settler among them, these cities shall be a refuge from the avenger, so that the man-slayer may not die until he stands before the congregation in judgment."

These are the commandments which the Lord spoke to Moses in the plains of Moab by the Jordan at Jericho.[9]

[9] See NUMBERS, Chapters 33-36, in Notes and Excisions.

# DEUTERONOMY
## The Repetition of the Law

⟨ Though the Book of Deuteronomy belongs to a very early period, and there is reason to believe that it was recorded in essence before most of the other parts of the Pentateuch, in the logical order of the narrative it belongs where it is, presenting the pinnacle in the life of Moses. The preceding book, Numbers, records his leadership for nearly forty years; this book gives only his farewell to his people. The book consists, essentially, of three great discourses, followed by a final warning in the form of a song, and ends with a blessing of the people, through their tribes, in the patriarchal tradition.

In the first discourse Moses briefly reviews highlights in the history of their wanderings and explains why he is not permitted to cross the Jordan and witness the fulfillment of his lifelong pilgrimage. The second discourse, which takes up the major part of the book, recapitulates the commandments, laws, injunctions and rituals given at Sinai and in the intervening years of wandering. But Moses does not merely repeat the law. He modifies, amplifies, and adds new laws concerning kings of Israel, prophets false and true, and a complete judicial system for cities. The amplifications and additions presented at this time have a new spirit. They are more precise in form and imbued with kindness and benevolence. Then Moses makes a final summation in the form of blessings and curses — blessings on those who keep God's laws, and curses on those who follow and serve other gods.

In the song, Moses takes as his theme: The Lord will judge his people by their faith and loyalty.

The book closes quickly and somberly with a stark account of the death of Moses, recorded, according to tradition, by his disciple and successor, Joshua ben Nun. ⟨

## The First Discourse by Moses

*1-4*    These are the words which Moses spoke to all Israel, on this side
of the Jordan, in the wilderness between Paran and Tophel, in
the land of Moab; and it was in the fortieth year, on the first day of the
eleventh month after they had come out of Egypt, and after they had
slain Sihon, king of the Amorites, and Og, king of Bashan. And Moses
spoke to the people of Israel according to all that the Lord had given
him in commandment to them, saying:

"Behold, I have set the land of the Canaanites before you; go in and
possess the land which the Lord promised to your fathers, Abraham, Isaac
and Jacob, to give to them and to their descendants after them.

"Remember now the time when we departed from Horeb and went
through all that great and terrible wilderness until we came to Kadesh-
barnea. And I said to you then, 'You have come to the hill country of the
Amorites, to the land which the Lord our God gives to us. Go up and
possess it, as the Lord of your fathers has said to you. Fear not, nor be
discouraged.' But you came near me and said, 'We will send men before
us to search out the land, and bring us word by which way we must
go up, and into which cities we shall come.' And your words pleased
me well. I took twelve men of you, one man from each tribe, and they
went up into the hill country, and came to the valley of Eshcol and
searched it out. They took some of the fruit of the land and brought it to
us, and they brought us word, saying, 'It is a good land which the Lord
does give us.'

"Yet you would not go up, but rebelled against the command of the
Lord. You murmured in your tents and said, 'The Lord seeks to deliver
us into the hand of the Amorites, to destroy us. The Amorites are
greater and taller than we; their cities are walled up to heaven; and the
sons of giants dwell among them.' Then I said to you, 'Fear not, fear not,
be not afraid of them. The Lord shall fight for you, as he did in Egypt before your eyes; and in the wilderness, where you have seen how he bore
you as a man bears his son, all the way that you went until you came to this
place!' Yet you feared, and did not believe the Lord your God, who went
before you in a cloud by day to search out a place for you to pitch your
tents, and in fire by night to show you by which way you should go.

"The Lord heard your words and was angered, and he declared, 'Surely
not one of these men of this evil generation shall see that good land

which I promised to your fathers, except Caleb, the son of Jephunneh, because he has wholly followed the Lord, and Joshua, the son of Nun, who stands before you. Moreover, your little ones, who you said would become a prey, they shall go into the land, and to them will I give it. But as for you, turn and take your journey into the wilderness by way of the Red Sea.' And you wept before the Lord, but the Lord did not give ear to you.

"So we turned and journeyed into the wilderness by way of the Red Sea, and we went about Mount Seir for many days. Then the Lord commanded us to turn northward, and to pass through the land of our kinsmen, the children of Esau, who dwell in Seir, buying our food from them with money and our water with money; and through the land of Moab, which the Lord gave to the children of Lot; and across the brook Zered.

"And the time in which we came from Kadesh-barnea until we crossed the brook Zered was thirty-and-eight years; and the generation of the men of war in our host had died out. For indeed, the hand of the Lord was against them.

"So it came to pass that then the Lord spoke to me, saying, 'When you come near the land of the children of Ammon, distress them not, for I have given their land to the children of Lot. Rise up, and pass over the valley of the Arnon. Behold, I have given into your hand Sihon the Amorite and his land; begin to possess it, and contend with him in battle. This day will I begin to put the dread of you upon the nations, who shall hear of you and shall tremble.'

"And I sent messengers to Sihon with words of peace, saying, 'Let us pass through your land. We will go along by the highway, and turn aside neither to the right nor to the left. You shall sell us food for money, that we may eat; and give us water for money, that we may drink. Only let us pass through on foot.' But Sihon would not let us pass, for the Lord hardened his spirit and made his heart obstinate. Then Sihon came out against us, to fight at Jahaz. And the Lord delivered Sihon and all his people to us, and we utterly destroyed them.

"We turned and went up toward Bashan; and Og, the king of Bashan, came out against us, he and all his people. And the Lord said to me, 'Fear him not, for I will deliver him and all his people into your hand, and you shall do to him as you did to Sihon, king of the Amorites.' So the Lord delivered into our hand Og also, and we smote him and his people until none remained.

"I commanded Joshua at that time, saying, 'Your eyes have seen all that the Lord your God has done to these two kings; so will the Lord do to all the kingdoms which you are to pass. You shall not fear them, for it is the Lord your God who fights for you.' And I besought the Lord at that time, saying, 'O Lord God, you have begun to show your servant your greatness, and your mighty hand. I pray you, let me go over and see the good land beyond the Jordan, that goodly hill country, and Lebanon!' But the Lord was displeased with me for your sake, and he said, 'Let it suffice you. Speak no more to me of this matter. Go up to the top of Pisgah, and look westward and northward and southward and eastward, and behold it with your eyes, for you shall not go over this Jordan. But charge Joshua, and encourage and strengthen him, for he shall go at the head of this people, and cause them to inherit the land which you shall see.' So we abode in the valley opposite Beth-peor.

"And now, O Israel, give heed to the statutes and to the judgments which I teach you, and do them. Behold, I have taught them to you, even as the Lord my God commanded me, that you may follow them in the land to which you go. Keep them, therefore, and do them; for that will be your wisdom and your understanding in the sight of the nations, who, when they hear all these statutes, will say: 'Surely this great nation is a wise and understanding people.' For what nation is there so close to God as to call upon him in all things? And where is the nation so great, that has statutes and ordinances so righteous as all this law which I set before you this day?

"Only take heed lest you forget the things which your eyes have seen, and lest they depart from your heart — especially the day you stood before the Lord your God at Horeb; and you came near and stood at the foot of the mountain that burned with fire to the heart of heaven. Then the Lord spoke to you out of the midst of the fire. And he declared to you his covenant, which he commanded you to perform — the ten commandments — and he wrote them upon two tablets of stone. Out of heaven he let you hear his voice, that he might instruct you. And because he loved your fathers, he chose their children after them, and brought you out of Egypt, to drive from before you nations greater and mightier than you, to bring you in, and to give you their land as an inheritance.

"Know therefore this day, and consider in your heart, that the Lord, he is God in heaven above and on the earth beneath: there is no other. Keep his commandments, that it may go well with you and with your children after you, and that you may prolong your days in the land which the Lord gives you forever." [1]

## The Second Discourse by Moses

5-26    And Moses summoned together all of Israel, and said to them:
"Hear, O Israel: the Lord our God, The Lord is One! You shall love the Lord your God with all your heart and with all your soul and with all your might. And these words which I command you this day shall be in your heart, and you shall teach them diligently to your children. Repeat them when you sit down in your house, and when you walk along the road; when you lie down in the evening, and when you rise up in the morning. Bind them as a reminder upon your arm, and they shall be as frontlets between your eyes. And you shall write them upon the doorposts and the gates of your house.

"You shall not go after other gods, the gods of the nations round about you, lest the anger of the Lord be kindled against you. Do what is right and good in the eyes of the Lord, and keep his commandments, that it may go well with you.

"And when in time to come your son asks you, 'What is the meaning of these commandments?' then you shall say to your son, 'We were slaves to Pharaoh in Egypt; and the Lord brought us out of there with a mighty hand to the land which he promised to our forefathers; and the Lord commanded us to keep these statutes, for our own good always, that he might preserve us as he has preserved us to this day.'

"For you are a holy people to the Lord your God: He did not set his love upon you, nor choose you, because you were more in number than any other people, for you were the fewest of all peoples. The Lord chose you because he loves you, and because he would keep his promise to your forefathers; therefore he redeemed you from Pharaoh.

"You shall be blessed above all people: There shall not be a male or a female barren among you or among your cattle. All sickness will the Lord take away from you, and he will put upon you none of the evil diseases you knew in Egypt.

"You shall remember the way along which the Lord led you these forty years in the wilderness, to test you, to know what was in your heart, and whether you would keep his commandments or not. He humbled you; he

[1]See DEUTERONOMY, Chapters 1-4, in Notes and Excisions.

110

let you hunger; and he fed you with manna (which you did not know before, nor did your fathers know of it before you). He did this that you might know: Man does not live by bread alone, but by the word of God does man live. The clothes upon you did not grow old, nor did your foot grow sore, these forty years. Consider then in your heart that, as a man chastens his son, so did the Lord chasten you. Therefore keep the commandments of the Lord, and walk in his ways, and revere him. For he will bring you into a good land, a land of brooks of water, of lakes, of fountains and of springs that flow in the valleys and hills; a land of wheat and barley in the field, of fig trees and pomegranates and olive in the grove, and of vineyards upon the hillside; a land in which you will eat bread in abundance, and not lack anything; a land whose stones are iron, and out of whose hills you may dig brass. And when you have eaten and are full, you shall bless the Lord your God for the good land which he has given you.

"Take heed lest, when you have eaten and are full, and have built goodly houses and dwell in them, and your herds and flocks have multiplied, you do not say in your proud heart, 'My power and the might of my hand has gotten me this wealth.' You shall remember the Lord your God: for it is he who gives you power to get wealth, that he may establish his covenant. If you at all forget the Lord, and walk after other gods to serve and worship them, I testify to you this day that you shall surely perish. Like the nations who perished before you, so shall you perish, because you would not obey the voice of the Lord your God.

"Hear, O Israel! On this day that you are to cross over the Jordan, and go in to possess the land of nations greater and mightier than yourselves, and cities fenced up to heaven, say not in your heart, 'For the sake of our righteousness has the Lord driven them out before us.' Not for the uprightness of your heart shall you possess their land; but because of their own wickedness shall the Lord drive them out before you. Understand, therefore, that this good land shall be given to you not because of your righteousness — for you are a stubborn people. Forget not how you provoked the Lord in the wilderness; and from the day you departed from Egypt until the day you came to this place you have been rebellious against the Lord.

"Even at Horeb you provoked the Lord to wrath, and he was ready to destroy you. When I went up the mount to receive the covenant which the Lord had made with you, I abode there forty days and forty nights; and I neither ate bread nor drank water. And the Lord gave me two tablets of stone written with the finger of God; and on them were all the words which the Lord had spoken out of the midst of the fire on the day of the assembly. Then the Lord said to me, 'Arise, hasten down from here; for your people have quickly turned aside from the way which I commanded them, and have made for themselves a golden image.' So I turned and came down, and the mountain burned with fire; and the two tablets of the covenant were in my hands. I looked, and behold, you had sinned against the Lord and made for yourselves a golden calf. I cast the two tablets of stone out of my hands and broke them before your eyes. And I fell down before the Lord, as at the first time, and for forty days and forty nights I neither ate bread nor drank water, because I feared that the Lord in his wrath might destroy you. But the Lord heard my prayer at that time also. And I took your sin, the calf which you had made, and burnt it with fire, and ground it into dust, and cast the dust of it into the brook that descended out of the mountain.

"And now, O Israel, what does the Lord your God require of you but to revere him, to walk in his ways, to love him and keep his commandments for your good?

"Behold, the heaven is the Lord's, and the earth also, with all that is in it. Yet the Lord set his love on your fathers, and chose their descendants after them, you above all people, as at this day. Therefore be no longer stubborn. For the Lord your God is God of gods, and Lord of lords, a great God, mighty and terrible, who is not partial and takes no reward. He executes justice for the fatherless and widow, and loves the stranger, giving him food and raiment. The Lord is your praise, and he is your God. And he has done for you these great and terrible things which your eyes have seen. Therefore, love the Lord your God and keep his commandments always.

"And if you will love the Lord your God, and serve him with all your heart and with all your soul, he will give you the rain of your land in its season, the early rain and the later rain, that you may gather in your grain and your wine and your oil. And there will be grass in the fields for your cattle, that you may eat and be full. And when you have eaten and are full, take heed that you do not forget the Lord your God, who brought you out of the house of bondage in the land of Egypt.

"Behold, I set before you this day a blessing and a curse: a blessing if you obey the Lord your God, and a curse if you turn aside out of the way which I command you this day, to follow other gods. When the Lord cuts off the nations before you, and you dwell in their land, take heed that you are not lured to follow them. For they have done for their gods every abominable thing which the Lord hates, and they have even burnt their sons and daughters in the fire to their gods.

"If there arises among you a prophet, or a dreamer of dreams, who gives you signs and performs wonders and says, 'Let us follow other gods, and let us serve them,' you shall not listen to the words of that prophet or that dreamer of dreams; but you shall put him to death because he has spoken to turn you away from the Lord. And if your brother, or your son, or your daughter, or your beloved wife, or your friend who is as dear to you as your own soul, entices you secretly, saying, 'Come, let us serve other gods,' you shall not listen to him, nor shall your eye pity him, nor shall you shield him. Your hand shall be first against him, to put him to death, and afterwards the hand of all the people. You shall stone him with stones because he has sought to draw you away from the Lord your God. And all Israel shall hear, and fear, and there shall be no more wickedness such as this among you.

"At the end of every three years you shall bring the tithe of your harvest and lay it up within your towns; and the Levite, because he has no portion or inheritance with you, and the stranger and the fatherless and the widow who are within your towns shall come and eat and be filled, that the Lord may bless you in all that you do.

"At the end of every seven years you shall grant a release. Every creditor shall release what he has lent to his neighbor. He shall not exact it of his neighbor or of his brother, because it is called the Lord's release. Of a foreigner you may exact it, but whatever of yours is with your brother, your hand shall release.

"If there is among you a poor man in the land which the Lord gives you, you shall not harden your heart nor shut your hand against him. But you shall open your hand wide and lend him sufficient for his need. For the poor will never cease out of the land; therefore, I command you, open wide your hand to help your brother, the poor and the needy.

"Three times each year shall all your males appear before the Lord your God at the place which he will choose: at the Feast of Unleavened Bread, at the Feast of Weeks, and at the Feast of Booths. And they shall not appear before the Lord empty-handed: every man shall give as he is able, according to the blessing of the Lord.

"You shall appoint judges and officers in all your towns throughout your tribes, and they shall judge the people justly.

"You shall not pervert justice; you shall not show partiality to persons;

and you shall not take a bribe, for a bribe blinds the eyes of the wise and perverts the cause of the just.

"And that which is altogether just shall you follow.

"And if any matter arises which is too difficult for you to judge, then you shall go to the priests, the Levites, and to the judge in office in those days, to consult them; and they shall declare to you the sentence of judgment. And you shall do according to all that they direct you.

"A single witness shall not rise up against a man for any wrong; only on the evidence of two witnesses or of three witnesses shall the matter be established.

"If a witness rises to testify falsely against any man, then both men of the controversy shall stand before the Lord, before the priests and the judges who are in office in those days, and the judges shall inquire diligently; and if the witness has testified falsely against his brother, then shall you do to him as he had thought to do to his brother. Thus shall you put away the evil from among you. And those who remain shall hear, and fear, and shall no more commit such evil among you.

"When you go out to battle against your enemies, and see horses and chariots, and a people stronger than you, be not afraid, for the Lord is with you. And the officers shall say to the people, 'The man who has built a new house and has not dedicated it, let him return to his house lest he die in battle and another man dedicate it. And the man who has planted a vineyard and has not eaten of its fruit, let him also return to his house lest he die in battle and another man enjoy its fruit. And the man who has betrothed a wife and has not taken her, let him return to his house lest he die in battle and another man take her.'

"And the officers shall speak further and say, 'The man who is fearful and fainthearted, let him return to his house lest the heart of his brothers melt like his heart.'

"You shall not abhor an Edomite, for he is your brother; you shall not abhor an Egyptian, because you were a stranger in his land. And their children of the third generation may enter the congregation of the Lord.

"You shall not deliver up to his master the slave who has escaped to you for safety; he shall dwell with you where it pleases him best; you shall not oppress him.

"There shall be no whore of the daughters of Israel, nor a sodomite of the sons of Israel. You shall not bring the hire of a whore or the price of a dog into the house of the Lord for any vow, for both are abominations to the Lord your God.

"No man shall take a nether millstone or an upper millstone in pledge, for that would be like taking a man's life in pledge. And when you lend your brother anything, you shall not go into his house to fetch his pledge. You shall stand outside, and the man shall bring the pledge out to you.

"You shall not oppress a hired servant, whether he is one of your brothers or one of the strangers within your towns; you shall give him his hire on the day he earns it, before the sun goes down.

"The fathers shall not be put to death for the children, nor shall the children be put to death for the fathers; every man shall be put to death for his own sin.

"And when you come into the land which the Lord gives you for an inheritance and dwell in it, you shall take some of the first of all the fruit of the earth and bring it as an offering to God. And the priest shall take it from your hand and set it down before the altar, and you shall respond before the Lord your God: 'A wandering Aramean was my father, and he went down to Egypt few in number, and he dwelt there and became a nation great and populous. And the Egyptians oppressed us and laid upon us heavy bondage. When we cried out to the Lord God of our fathers, he heard our voice and looked upon our oppression; and he brought us out of Egypt with a mighty hand, and with signs and wonders, to this land that flows with milk and honey. Now, behold, I have brought the first fruits of the land which you, O Lord, have given me.'

"And you shall set it before the Lord and worship him, and rejoice in every good thing which he has given you.

"This day you have declared that you will walk in his ways and obey his voice. And this day the Lord will take you to be his treasured people, as he has promised, and will lift you high among the nations to be a people holy to the Lord your God." [2]


## The Third Discourse by Moses

27-31    Moses gathered the elders and the priests and all the people of
        Israel, and said to them:

"I am one hundred and twenty years old this day, and can no longer go out and come in as before; also the Lord has said to me, 'You shall not go over this Jordan.' The Lord your God, he will go over before you

[2] See DEUTERONOMY, Chapters 5-27, in Notes and Excisions.

115

and destroy these nations before you; and Joshua will go over at your head, as the Lord has said.

"And on the day you pass over the Jordan to the land which the Lord gives you, you shall set up great stones and plaster them with plaster; and you shall write upon them very plainly all the words of the law.

"And if you listen to the voice of the Lord and obey his commandments, he will set you high above all the nations of the earth, and he will bless you with these blessings:

"Blessed shall you be in the city, and blessed shall you be in the field; blessed shall be the fruit of your body, and of your ground, and of your flocks and herds; blessed shall you be when you come in, and blessed shall you be when you go out.

"The Lord shall cause your enemies who come out against you one way to flee before you in seven directions. And all the people of the earth shall see that you are called by the name of the Lord, and they shall respect you.

"The Lord shall open to you the treasury of heaven, to give you rain in its season, and to bless all the work of your hands. You shall lend to many nations, but have no need to borrow.

"The Lord shall make you the head, and not the tail; you shall be above, and not beneath — if you listen to the commandments of the Lord your God, and do not turn aside to the right or to the left to follow other gods to serve them.

"But if you will not listen to the voice of the Lord your God, he will curse you with these curses:

"Cursed shall you be in the city, and cursed shall you be in the field; cursed shall be the fruit of your body, and of your ground, and of your flocks and herds; cursed shall you be when you come in, and cursed shall you be when you go out.

"The Lord shall send you confusion and vexation in all you undertake to do.

"The Lord shall smite you with madness and blindness and astonishment of heart, and you shall grope at noonday as the blind grope in darkness, and you shall be oppressed and plundered and there shall be none to save you. The heavens above you shall be brass, and the earth under your feet shall be iron.

"You shall take a wife, and another man shall lie with her; you shall build a house, and another shall dwell in it; you shall plant a vineyard, and not taste its grapes.

"Your sons and your daughters shall be given to a strange people; and your eyes shall look for them and fail with longing all day, but you shall have no power to bring them back.

"If you will not serve the Lord your God with joy and with gladness of heart, you shall serve your enemies in hunger and in thirst, in nakedness, and in want of all things; and he shall put a yoke of iron upon your neck until he has destroyed you. For the Lord shall bring against you a nation from afar, from the end of the earth, a fierce nation, swift as the eagle, speaking a tongue you do not understand, a nation that shall not regard the aged, or show favor to the young. And he shall devour your bread and your wine and your flocks until you have come to naught.

"And the Lord shall scatter you among all peoples, from one end of the earth to the other; and among these nations you shall find no ease. For the Lord shall fill your heart with fear and your mind with sorrow, and your life shall hang in doubt. In the morning you shall say, 'Would that it were evening!' And in the evening you shall say, 'Would that it were morning!' For such shall be the fear of your heart, and such the sights which your eyes shall see.

"And the Lord shall bring you to Egypt again, and there you shall offer yourselves to your enemies as slaves, but no man will buy you.

"And it shall come to pass, when all the blessings and the curses have come upon you, and you recall them among the nations where the Lord has driven you, and you return to the Lord your God, you and your children, and obey his voice with all your heart and with all your soul, then the Lord will have compassion upon you, and he will gather you from all the nations where the Lord your God has scattered you. He will bring you out of your captivity and return you to the land which your fathers possessed, and you shall possess it; and he will prosper every work of your hand; and the Lord will again rejoice over you as he rejoiced over your fathers.

"If you would but listen to the voice of the Lord your God, to keep his commandments and his statutes which are written in this book of the law; and if you would turn to the Lord your God with all your heart and all your soul.

"For this commandment which I command you this day is not written in hidden language, nor is it far off. It is not in heaven, that you should say, 'Who shall go up to heaven and bring it down for us to hear and obey?' Neither is it beyond the sea, that you should say, 'Who shall go over the sea and bring it to us that we may hear it and obey?' The word of God is very near you; it is in your mouth and in your heart, that you may do it!

"See, I have set before you this day the choice of life and death, good and evil. And I call upon heaven and earth to witness that it is now for you and your children to choose between life and death, between good and evil, between the blessing and the curse. Therefore choose life, that you and your descendants may live. Love the Lord your God and obey his voice, for he is life!"

## The Song of Moses

31-33  And the Lord said to Moses, "Behold, the day approaches when you must die. Call Joshua and present yourselves in the tabernacle."

Moses and Joshua went and presented themselves in the tabernacle of the congregation. And the Lord appeared in a pillar of cloud, and the pillar stood over the door of the tabernacle. The Lord gave Israel in Joshua's charge and said to him, "Be strong and of good courage; for you shall bring the children of Israel into the land which I promised them. And I will be with you."

And to Moses the Lord said, "Write a song and teach it to the children of Israel; put it in their mouths, that this song may be a witness for me against them."

Moses wrote this song on the same day, and he taught it to the children of Israel:

"O heavens, give ear and I will speak; O earth, hear the words of my mouth!

"My words shall fall like rain, my speech like dew, like fine rain upon the tender sprouts and like showers upon the grass; for I will proclaim the name of the Lord.

"He is the Rock, his work is perfect; a God of truth is he, just and right.

"Ask your father and he will tell you, your elders and they will declare it:

"When the Most High gave to the nations their inheritance, when he separated the sons of Adam, he set the bounds for his people, the portion of Israel, according to their number.

"In a desert land, in a wasteland, a howling wilderness, he found Israel and led him; he instructed him, and guarded him like the apple of his eye.

"As the eagle stirs up in her nest and flutters over her young, and spreads wide her great wings and bears her young upon them, so the Lord alone led Israel, and there was no strange god with him.

"He carried him to the high places of the earth, that he might feed on the increase of the field; he made him suck honey out of the stone and oil out of the flinty rock; and with butter from kine and milk from sheep, and with the fat of lambs, and with rams from the breed of Bashan he fed him; and gave him to drink the pure blood of the grape.

"But Israel grew fat; and he grew thick and became sleek; and he forsook the Lord who made him, and lightly esteemed the Rock of his salvation.

"He provoked the Lord with sacrifices to demons, and to gods whom his fathers had not dreaded.

"And the Lord said, 'I will hide my face from them, for they are a brazen generation, children in whom there is no faithfulness. I will heap evils upon them; I will spend my arrows upon them. The sword without, and terror within, shall destroy the young man and the virgin, the infant and the man of gray hairs.

" 'I would scatter them to the corners of the earth, and erase the remembrance of them from among men, were it not that their enemies should say, "Our hand, and not the Lord, has done this!"

" 'Oh that they were wise, that they understood this, that they would consider their latter end!

" 'For their vine is from the vine of Sodom, and their field is from the field of Gomorrah; their grapes are grapes of gall, their clusters are bitter; their wine is the poison of serpents and the cruel venom of asps.

" 'Vengeance is mine, and recompense,' said the Lord. 'Their foot shall slip; the day of their calamity is at hand.'

"Then the Lord shall judge his people. And he shall say, 'Where are those gods in whom you trusted, who ate the fat of your sacrifices and drank the wine of your offerings? Let them rise up and help you, and be your protection!

" 'See now that I, even I, am He, and there is no god beside me; I kill and I make alive; I wound and I heal; and none can deliver you out of my hand.

" 'My hand takes hold of judgment, and I whet my glittering sword;

and I render vengeance to my adversary, and reward those who hate me according to their hatred.'

"Sing, and rejoice, O you nations of his people! For he will avenge the blood of his servants, and he will make expiation for his land and his people."

## The Blessing of the Tribes

33  And this is the blessing with which Moses the man of God blessed Israel before his death:

"Let REUBEN live and not die, but let the men of SIMEON be few.

"Hear, O Lord, the voice of JUDAH, and bring him to his people. Contend for him, and help him against his enemies.

"Let your Thummin and your Urim be with LEVI, whom you tested at Massah, and at the waters of Meribah. Let his children teach your judgments and your law in Israel; they shall put the incense before you upon your altar, and the burnt offering. Bless his substance, O Lord, and accept the work of his hand.

"Place your hand, O Lord, upon BENJAMIN, that he may dwell in safety.

"Bless the land of JOSEPH, O Lord, with the precious things of heaven, of the sun, of the moon, of the lasting hills, and all the fullness of the earth. His glory is like the firstling bullock, and his horns are like the horns of unicorns.

"Rejoice, ZEBULUN, in your going out; and ISSACHAR, in your tents! Your children shall call the people to offer sacrifices in the mountain; for they shall suck abundance out of the seas, and hidden treasures from the deep.

"Blessed be he who enlarges GAD. For Gad is fearless as the lion. He shall come at the head of the people and execute the justice of the Lord.

"DAN is a lion's whelp, fearless as the lions of Bashan.

"O NAPHTALI, full of the blessing of the Lord, you shall possess the west and the south.

"Let ASHER be blessed with many children; let him be acceptable to his brothers; and let him dip his foot in soil rich as oil. Let his shoes be of iron and brass in war; and, even as his days shall be many, his strength shall be great.

"Happy are you, O Israel! Who is like you? You are a people saved by the Lord, who is your shield and your sword. Your enemies shall dwindle before you, and you shall tread upon their high places."

## The Death of the Prophet

34    Moses went up from the plains of Moab to the mount of Nebo, which faces Jericho. And the Lord showed him all the land of Gilead, as far as Dan, and the southland, and the plain of Jericho, city of palm trees, and as far as Zoar. And the Lord said to him, "This is the land which I promised to Abraham, to Isaac, and to Jacob, saying, 'I will give it to your descendants.' You have seen it with your eyes, but you shall not go there!"

So Moses, the servant of the Lord, died on Mount Nebo, in the land of Moab. And the Lord buried him in a valley near Beth-peor, but no man knows the place of his sepulcher to this day.

Moses was a hundred and twenty years old when he died; and his eye was not dim, nor his natural force lessened. And the children of Israel wept for Moses in the plains of Moab and they mourned for thirty days; then the days of weeping and mourning for Moses were ended.

And since that day there has not arisen a prophet in Israel like unto Moses, whom the Lord knew face to face.

## PART TWO

# The Books of the Chronicles

*The Story of Israel in Canaan*

❲ The historical books of the Bible, from Joshua to Nehemiah — more than a third of the Hebrew Scriptures — span almost a millennium, and this period of nearly a thousand years became the core and heart of the history of the Jewish people. For it was during this period that the tribes of Israel, under the leadership of Joshua, came into the land of Canaan, which they regarded as their Promised Land by divine decree; and then followed the long period of the rule by judges and kings, marked by constant harassment from enemies without, and by rifts and revolts from within. Finally the kingdom of Israel in the north was wiped out; and not long afterwards the kingdom of Judah was conquered, and its people were taken captive. Yet only half a century later, the exiled people (led by Jerubbabel and Joshua the priest, and after them by Ezra the scribe and Nehemiah the governor) returned from captivity in Babylon to learn the new concept that captivity and redemption were both to be found only in their hearts and in their souls.

Historians from Josephus to those of our own day have found in these books the most detailed and reliable source for the period in Jewish history from 1250 to 432 B.C.E.; and no historian has arisen to give us an account covering the same period comparable to the Biblical chronicles themselves. These books may lack the compact unity found in other histories of ancient times — such as the record of the conflict between two civilizations portrayed by Herodotus, and the political and military exploits during the Gallic wars as described by Julius Caesar; but even the best historical works written by the Greeks and the Romans do not have their unique intensity, or their complete objectivity in presenting the weaknesses of the heroes in the Biblical chronicles.

These records are the more remarkable since history in the conventional sense was not their purpose. The many authors of these books constantly refer to other works in which were preserved the chronicles of the kings of Judah and Israel — works which, though they have disappeared, were assumed in their day to serve as a historical account of the times. The books we have in the Bible were meant to demonstrate the

125

conflicts of a people in maintaining their adherence to divine law. That is why these Chronicles are called in the Hebrew Scriptures, "The Former Prophets."

The books in this section (from Joshua, of nearly thirteen centuries before the Christian Era, to Nehemiah, who inspired his people about eight centuries later) are to be read less as histories of judges and kings, of wars and peace pacts, of court intrigues and national catastrophes, and more as chronicles of events which reflect the trials and struggles of a people whose whole national life was evaluated in terms of their covenant with God. ⟨[

# JOSHUA
## Conquest of the Promised Land

❲ The Book of Joshua, according to some scholars, did not originally belong with the "Former Prophets" but rather with the Five Books of Moses, because it is an extension and fulfillment of the settling of the children of Israel in the Promised Land. These scholars point out that the writing and contents in Joshua more closely resemble the Five Books than any of the others in the Bible. Joshua is accorded continuation of the divine leadership of Moses; and many events in his life are similar to events in the life of his predecessor. Joshua splits the waters of the Jordan; he communes with God; and he conveys the divine commands to the people in the manner of Moses. Joshua too chides the people, and reminds them again and again not to turn away from the Lord their God; and, in his final address to the people, Joshua uses almost the identical language used by Moses in his last great discourses. Therefore, these scholars argue, the Book of Joshua should have been joined to the preceding Five Books to form the Hexateuch, which is the Greek for "The Six Books."

There are other scholars who feel that the Book of Joshua is a late interpolation by certain priests and scribes to give military proof to the prophetic words of the great emancipator and lawgiver Moses. They point to the repeated contradictions between accounts as given in Joshua and the accounts as found in the next two books, Judges and I Samuel. These scholars argue that the Book of Joshua should be placed among the apocryphal works.

However, in the structure of the Bible as we have it, the Book of Joshua belongs precisely where it is: at the beginning of the history of Israel in the Promised Land; for it forms the necessary link which connects a past, hidden beyond the curtain of ascertainable fact, with the beginning of an account which enters into discernible history — covering almost a millennium — from Joshua ben Nun to the days of Ezra and Nehemiah. ([

## *Rahab and the Spies*

**1-2**  After the death of Moses, the Lord spoke to Joshua, the son of Nun, Moses' minister, saying, "Moses my servant is dead. Now therefore arise, you and all the people with you, and cross over the Jordan into the land which I give them. Every place that the sole of your foot will tread upon, to you it shall be given, as I promised to Moses. From the wilderness and this Lebanon, as far as the great river, the river Euphrates, all the land of the Hittites, and to the Great Sea toward the going down of the sun, shall be yours. There shall be no man able to stand against you all the days of your life. As I was with Moses, so will I be with you; I will not fail you, nor forsake you. Be strong and of good courage, for to this people shall you divide as an inheritance the land which I promised to their fathers."

Then Joshua commanded the officers of the people, "Pass through the camp and say to the people, 'Prepare food, for within three days you shall pass over this Jordan to possess the land which the Lord your God gives you!'"

And Joshua sent out from Shittim two men to spy secretly, saying, "Go, view the land, especially Jericho."

The men went, and came to the house of a harlot named Rahab, and lodged there. Now the king of Jericho was told, "Behold, this night men from the children of Israel came here to search out the country." And the king of Jericho sent his men to Rahab; but Rahab had brought the two men up to the roof of the house and hidden them under stalks of flax. The king's men said to her, "Bring out the men who have entered your house, for they have come to search out the land." And she answered, "Yes, the men were here, but I knew not whence they came; and, at about the time the gate is shut, when it was dark, the men went out. Where they went I know not. Pursue them quickly, for you will overtake them." The king's men pursued them all the way to the Jordan, as far as the fords. And as soon as the pursuers had gone out, the gate to the city was shut.

Rahab came up to the men on the roof and said to them, "I know that the Lord has given you the land, because the terror of you has fallen upon all the inhabitants. For we have heard how the Lord dried up the waters of the Red Sea before you when you came out of Egypt, and what you did to the two kings of the Amorites, Sihon and Og, whom you utterly destroyed. When we heard of these things, our hearts melted, nor was there courage left in any man. Therefore, I pray you, swear to me by the Lord, since I have shown kindness to you, that you will also show kindness to my father's house, and save my father and my mother, my brothers and my sisters, and all who belong to them, and deliver us from death."

The men answered, "When the Lord gives us this land, we will deal kindly and truly with you."

Then Rahab let them down by a cord through the window, for her house was built upon the city wall, and she said to them, "Hasten to the hills lest the pursuers come upon you, and hide there three days, until they have returned. Afterward you may go on your way." The men answered, "When we come into the land, bind this line of scarlet in the window from which you have let us down; and gather into your house your father and your mother, and your brothers, and all your father's household. After that, whoever goes out of the door of your house into the street, his blood shall be upon his own head and we will be guiltless; and whoever stays with you in the house, his blood shall be on our heads if any hand is laid upon him. But if you reveal our errand, we will be released from the oath which you have made us swear."

And she said, "So be it." She sent them away, and they departed; and she bound the scarlet line in the window.

The men went off to the hills and abode there three days. And the pursuers sought them throughout all the way but found them not. Then the men descended from the hills, and came to Joshua and told him all that had befallen them. They said, "Truly the Lord has given the land into our hands, for the inhabitants are in fear of us." [1]

## Miracle at the Jordan

3-5     Joshua and all the children of Israel departed from Shittim, and came to the Jordan, and lodged there before they passed over. After three days, the officers went through the camp, and they commanded the people, "When you see the ark of the covenant carried by

[1] See JOSHUA, Chapter 1, in Notes and Excisions.

the priests, then you shall leave your place and follow it, but keep a distance of two thousand cubits between you and it. Come not near the ark, but follow it, that you may know the way by which you must go, for you have not passed this way before."

And Joshua said to the priests, "Take up the ark of the covenant and pass on ahead of the people." They took up the ark and went on ahead of the people. Then to the people Joshua said, "Behold, the ark of the covenant of the Lord of all the earth passes on before you into the Jordan. And when the soles of the feet of the priests who bear the ark of the Lord rest in the waters of the Jordan, the waters which come down from above shall be cut off, and they shall stand up in a heap."

And so it came to pass. As those who bore the ark came to the Jordan, and their feet dipped into the edge of the water (for the Jordan overflows its banks at the time of the harvest), the waters from above stopped flowing and rose up in a heap. The priests who bore the ark stood firm on dry ground in the midst of the Jordan; and there they stood while all the people passed over on dry land, and until all the people had crossed over the Jordan.

Then the Lord said to Joshua, "Choose twelve men, a man from each tribe, and command them, saying, 'Take from the midst of the Jordan, out of the place where the priests' feet stood, twelve stones, and carry them over with you, and leave them in the place where you shall lodge this night.'"

The priests who bore the ark stood in the midst of the Jordan until everything was finished that the Lord had commanded. Then the priests came up out of the Jordan, and when their feet were lifted up on the dry land, the waters of the Jordan returned to their place and overflowed the banks as before.

The people came up out of the Jordan on the tenth day of the first month, and encamped in Gilgal, on the east border of Jericho. And those twelve stones which they took out of the Jordan, Joshua set up in Gilgal.

On that day the Lord exalted Joshua in the sight of Israel; and they feared him, as they had feared Moses, all the days of his life.

## The Fall of Jericho

5-8    When all the kings of the Amorites, who were west of the Jordan, and all the kings of the Canaanites, who were by the sea, heard that the Lord had dried up the waters of the Jordan before the children of Israel until they had passed over, their hearts melted and there was no spirit in them any more.

The children of Israel encamped in Gilgal, and they kept the Passover on the fourteenth day of the month, at evening, in the plains of Jericho. And on the morrow after the Passover, on the selfsame day, they ate unleavened cakes and parched grain from the grain of the land. And the manna ceased, and the children of Israel had manna no more; but they ate of the fruit of the land of Canaan that year.

Now Jericho was sealed up because of the children of Israel; none went out and none came in. Joshua said to the people, "Pass on and march around the city, and let those who are armed go ahead of the ark of the Lord. You shall not shout, nor let your voice be heard, nor any word come out of your mouth, until the day I bid you shout; then shall you shout." To the priests he said, "Take up the ark of the covenant, and let seven priests, bearing trumpets of rams' horns, go in front of the ark of the Lord." And to the armed men he said, "Pass on ahead of the priests."

Joshua rose early in the morning, and the priests took up the ark of the Lord. The seven priests bearing trumpets went on in front of the ark, blowing the trumpets continually; and the armed men went ahead of them; and rearward came the people, following the ark. So the ark of the Lord circled the city, going about it once; and then they returned and lodged in the camp. On the second day they again marched around the city once, and then returned into the camp. So they did for six days.

On the seventh day they rose at dawn and marched around the city in the same manner; only on that day they marched around the city seven times. And at the seventh time, when the priests blew the trumpets, Joshua said to the people, "Shout! For the Lord has given you the city!" So the people shouted while the priests blew the trumpets, and when the people heard the sound of the trumpets they shouted with so great a shout that the wall of the city fell down flat. And the people went up, every man straight before him, and they took the city.

Joshua said to the two men who had spied out the country, "Go to the harlot's house and bring the woman out, and all who belong to her, as you vowed."

The young men went, and brought out Rahab, and her father and her mother, and her brothers, and all her kindred, and all their belongings, and set them outside the camp of Israel. Then they burned the city and all that was in it; only the silver and the gold, and the vessels of brass and of iron, they put into the treasury of the house of the Lord.

And Joshua charged the people with an oath, saying, "Cursed before the Lord be the man who rises up to rebuild this city of Jericho; with the loss of his firstborn shall he lay the foundation, and with the loss of his youngest-born shall he set up the gates!"

So the Lord was with Joshua, and his fame became known throughout the country.[2]

## The Guile of Gibeon

9    When the kings who were beyond the Jordan, in the hills and in the valleys and along the shore of the Great Sea, heard what Joshua had done, they gathered together with one accord to fight Joshua and Israel.

The Hivites who dwell in Gibeon heard what Joshua had done, and they went to work with guile. They put worn-out shoes upon their feet and old garments upon their backs; and loaded asses with old sacks filled with dry and moldy bread, and wineskins, worn and bound up; and they went to Joshua at Gilgal. They said to him and to the men of Israel, "We have come from a far country to seek an alliance with you."

Joshua asked them, "Who are you? And where do you come from?" And they answered, "Your servants have come from a very far country. We heard the fame of the Lord your God and all that he did in Egypt, and all that he did to the two kings of the Amorites, Sihon and Og. Our elders and the inhabitants of our country said to us, 'Take provisions with you for the journey, and go to them and say, "We are your servants; therefore make an alliance with us."' This bread we took hot on the day we departed, but now, behold, it is dry and moldy; and these wineskins, which were new when we filled them, are now torn; and our garments and shoes are worn out because of the very long journey."

The men of Israel partook of their food, and did not ask counsel from

[2] See JOSHUA, Chapters 7-8, in Notes and Excisions.

the Lord. And Joshua made a league with the Hivites, and the leaders of the congregation took an oath upon it.

Three days after they had made the league, they heard that the Hivites were their neighbors, and dwelt among them. So the children of Israel journeyed to their cities, and Joshua summoned the Gibeonites and asked, "Why have you deceived us, saying, 'We are from very far,' when you dwell among us?"

They answered, "Because your servants were told that the Lord your God had commanded his servant Moses to give you all the land, and to destroy the inhabitants. We feared for our lives, and did this thing. And now, behold, we are in your hands, to do with us as it seems good and right in your eyes."

Joshua delivered them from the hand of the children of Israel, so that they were not slain; but he made them that day hewers of wood and drawers of water for the congregation and for the altar of God.

## "You Sun, Stand Still!"

*10-19*  Now when Adonizedek, king of Jerusalem, heard how the inhabitants of Gibeon had made peace with Israel, he feared greatly, because Gibeon was a great city, like one of the royal cities, and all its men were mighty. Therefore he sent word to Hoham, king of Hebron, and to Piram, king of Jarmuth, and to Japhia, king of Lachish, and to Debir, king of Eglon, saying, "Come up, and help me, that we may smite Gibeon; for they have made peace with Joshua and with the children of Israel." The five kings of the Amorites went up, they and all their armies, and encamped before Gibeon, and made war against it.

Then the men of Gibeon sent word to Joshua at the camp of Gilgal, saying, "Come up to us quickly and save us! For all the kings of the Amorites who dwell in the mountains have gathered against us."

So Joshua ascended from Gilgal, he and all the people of war with him, all the mighty men of valor.

And the Lord said to Joshua, "Fear them not. Not a man of them shall withstand you."

Joshua came upon them suddenly, for he went up from Gilgal all through the night. And the Lord routed them before Israel, and slew them with a great slaughter at Gibeon, and chased them along the ascent to Beth-horon, and smote them to Azekah and to Makkedah. And as they fled before Israel, the Lord cast down great stones from heaven upon them, and they died; and more died from the hailstones than were slain by the sword.

Then spoke Joshua to the Lord on the day when the Lord delivered up the Amorites to the children of Israel; and he said in the sight of Israel, "O sun, stand still upon Gibeon; and you, moon, in the valley of Aijalon!" And the sun stood still, and the moon stayed, until the people had avenged themselves upon their enemies. Is not this written in the Book of Jashar: "The sun stood still in the midst of heaven, and hastened not to go down about a whole day." And there was no day like that before it or after it.

Then Joshua returned, and all Israel with him, to the camp at Gilgal. But the five kings fled, and hid themselves in a cave at Makkedah. When Joshua was told, he said, "Roll great stones against the mouth of the cave, and set men by it to guard them. But stay not yourselves. Pursue your enemies; smite their rear; let them not enter their cities."

And when Joshua and his men had made an end of slaying their fleeing enemies, and the remnant which remained had escaped into the fortified cities, all the people returned to the camp at Makkedah; and none in the land dared move his tongue against any of the children of Israel.

Then said Joshua, "Open the mouth of the cave, and bring out those five kings to me."

And they did so. Joshua said to the captains who were with him, "Come near; put your feet upon the necks of these kings." They came near, and put their feet upon the necks of the kings. And Joshua said to them, "Fear not, nor be dismayed. For thus will the Lord do to all your enemies against whom you fight."

Afterward Joshua slew them, and hanged them on five trees; and they remained hanging upon the trees until evening. At sundown Joshua commanded, and his men took them down off the trees and cast them into the cave in which they had been hidden, and laid great stones at the mouth of the cave, which remain to this very day.[3]

[3] See JOSHUA, Chapters 11-19, in Notes and Excisions.

## The Cities of Refuge

**20-22**  The Lord said to Joshua, "Say to the children of Israel, 'Set apart the cities of refuge, of which I spoke to you through Moses, that he who kills unwittingly may flee there from the avenger. And when he who flees to one of these cities shall come to the gate of the city, and declare his cause to the elders, they shall take him into the city and give him a place, that he may dwell among them. And he shall dwell there, after standing before the congregation for judgment, until the death of the high priest in those days; then the slayer may return to his home, to the city from which he fled.'"

And they set apart Kedesh in Galilee; and Shechem in the hills of Ephraim; and Kirjath-arba, which is Hebron, in the hills of Judah. And on the other side of the Jordan, eastward, they assigned Bezer in the land belonging to the tribe of Reuben; and Ramoth in Gilead, belonging to the tribe of Gad; and Golan in Bashan, belonging to the tribe of Manasseh. These were the cities set apart by Israel for themselves and for the stranger who sojourned among them, so that whoever killed a person without intent could flee there for safety, and not die at the hand of the avenger, until he stood for judgment before the congregation.[4]

## Joshua's Death

**23-24**  A long time after the Lord had given rest to Israel from their enemies round about, Joshua grew old and stricken with age. And he summoned all Israel, and their elders, and their leaders, and their judges, and their officers, and said to them, "You have seen all that the Lord your God has done to these nations for your sake; for the Lord your God, he it is who has fought for you. Behold, I have divided among you by lot the nations that remain, as an inheritance for your tribes, with all the nations that I have cut off from the Jordan, even to the Great Sea in the west. The Lord your God shall drive them out of your sight, and you shall possess their land as the Lord has promised you.

"Therefore, be very courageous to keep and to do all that is written in the book of the law of Moses, and turn not aside from it to the right hand or to the left. Take good heed to love the Lord your God. Else, if you in

[4] See JOSHUA, Chapters 21-22, in Notes and Excisions.

135

any wise follow in the ways of the nations that remain among you, and marry with them, know for a certainty that they shall become snares and traps for you, and scourges in your sides, and thorns in your eyes, until you perish in this good land which the Lord your God has given you.

"Behold, this day I am going the way of all flesh. Remember, and inscribe on your hearts and in your souls, that not one thing has failed of all the good words which the Lord your God spoke concerning you; all have come to pass, and not one has failed. But even as all the good has come upon you, so the Lord will bring upon you all the evil if you transgress the covenant of the Lord your God, and serve other gods and bow yourselves down to them. Therefore put away the strange gods among you, and incline your heart to the Lord God of Israel."

The people answered, "Far be it from us that we should forsake the Lord to serve other gods." And Joshua said to them, "You are witnesses against yourselves that you have chosen the Lord to serve him." They answered, "We are witnesses!"

So Joshua made a covenant with the people that day, and set them a statute and an ordinance at Shechem. Joshua wrote these words in the book of the law of God; and he took a great stone and set it up there under an oak which was by the sanctuary of the Lord. And he said to all the people, "Behold, this stone shall be a witness against us, for it has heard all the words that the Lord spoke to us; thus it shall be a witness against you lest you deny your God."

Then Joshua let the people depart, every man to his inheritance. After these events Joshua, the son of Nun, the servant of the Lord, died, being a hundred and ten years old. And they buried him in his inheritance at Timnath-serah, which is in Ephraim, on the north side of the hill of Gaash.

And Israel served the Lord all the days of Joshua, and all the days of the elders who outlived Joshua.

And the bones of Joseph, which the children of Israel brought up from Egypt, they buried in Shechem, in a parcel of ground which Jacob had bought from the sons of Hamor; and it became the inheritance of the descendants of Joseph.

# JUDGES
## *A Succession of Apostasies*

❲ In Judges we encounter what many scholars consider the earliest writing in the Bible. The claim has been made that Deborah's song, Jotham's fable, Samson's riddle, and some of the customs and rites described in this book antedate any part of the Five Books of Moses. The writing, too, retains evidence of the book's antiquity, in spite of the numerous rewritings it must have gone through.

This short book is obviously incomplete, and does not cover the accounts of all the judges in that period. The events in the lives of the most important of them, Eli and Samuel, are presented in the book following; and certain judges are implied, though not given by name. The period covered by the rule of the judges is difficult to estimate because of the accounts completely omitted, and because in those accounts given, the length of rule of each judge is either not stated, or given in round numbers. The authors of Judges seem to assume the existence of a more detailed chronological record of the time, well known in that day. Many chronologists estimate that the judges ruled over a period of about two hundred to two hundred and fifty years.

The essence of Judges seems to contradict much that was given in the preceding book. Instead of a glorious succession of victories in which the children of Israel, under the leadership of Joshua, uproot and destroy idolatry, and move from victory to victory, this is a record of successive apostasies, in which they constantly come under the spell of the native pagan religions. They are bitterly punished; but when the people cry out to the Lord for help, he sends them a deliverer who is prophet and judge and military leader all in one.

A number of such deliverers are mentioned in Judges: Othniel, Ehud, Shagmar, Tola, and Jair; Ibzan, Elon, and Ebdon; Deborah, Gideon,

Jephthah and Samson. Detailed accounts are given of only the last four, but these four narratives have become favorites in the literature of the world from generation to generation.

Although Judges logically ends with the death of Samson, two unrelated stories follow: one about the adventures of a thief named Micah; and the other about a civil war among the tribes, which is brought about by a dreadful act committed by some of the citizens of Gibeah. The stories were presumably included because they were about events of importance occurring in the days of the judges. ([

## The Rise of the Judges

*1-3*    After the death of Joshua, the children of Israel asked the Lord, "Who shall go up first against the Canaanites?" And the Lord said, "Judah shall go up. Behold, I have delivered the land into his hand."

Then Judah said to Simeon his brother, "Come up with me to fight against the Canaanites in the land allotted to me, and I will go up with you to fight for the land allotted to you."

So Simeon went up with him. And the Lord delivered the Canaanites and the Perizzites into their hand. They slew ten thousand of them at Bezek. And there they captured the king, Adoni-bezek. He fled, and they pursued him and caught him, and cut off his thumbs and his great toes. Adoni-bezek cried out, "Seventy kings, with their thumbs and their great toes cut off, picked crumbs under my table. As I have done, so God has requited me." And they brought him to Jerusalem, and there he died.

Afterward the children of Judah went down to fight the Canaanites who dwelt in the hills and in the valley. And Judah went up against the inhabitants of Hebron; and from there, against the inhabitants of Debir. Judah also took Gaza, with its coast, and Askelon, with its coast, and Ekron, with its coast.

The Lord was with Judah, and he drove out the inhabitants of the hills; but he could not drive out the inhabitants of the valley, because they had chariots of iron. And the children of Benjamin did not drive out the Jebusites who dwelt in Jerusalem; Manasseh did not drive out the inhabitants of Beth-shean and her towns; Ephraim did not drive out the Canaanites who dwelt in Gezer; Zebulun did not drive out the inhabitants of Kitron and Nahalol; neither did Asher drive out the inhabitants of Accho and

Zidon; nor did Naphtali drive out the inhabitants of Beth-shemesh; but they dwelt among the Canaanites, the inhabitants of the land.

The children of Israel had served the Lord during all the days of Joshua, and all the days of the elders who outlived Joshua, who had seen the great works which the Lord had wrought for Israel. But that generation had been gathered to their fathers; and there arose after them a generation which knew not the Lord. They forsook the Lord God of their fathers, who had brought them out of Egypt, and followed the gods of the people round about them. They forsook the Lord and served Baal and Ashtaroth. Then the anger of the Lord kindled against Israel, and he delivered them to their enemies, who plundered them. And wherever they went out, the hand of the Lord was against them.

Yet when the people cried out to the Lord, he raised up judges, who saved them from their plunderers. And when the Lord raised up a judge, then the Lord was with the judge, and saved them from their enemies all the days of the judge. But whenever a judge died, the people turned back to follow other gods, and served them and bowed down to them. And the children of Israel who dwelt among the Canaanites, the Hittites, the Amorites, the Perizzites, the Hivites and Jebusites took their daughters as wives, and gave their own daughters to their sons, and served their gods.

Therefore the anger of the Lord was kindled against Israel, and he gave them into the hand of the king of Mesopotamia; and the children of Israel served him eight years. But when Israel cried out again to the Lord, he raised up a deliverer for them, Othniel, the son of Kenaz, Caleb's younger brother. The spirit of the Lord came upon him, and he judged Israel; and he went out to war, and the Lord delivered the king of Mesopotamia into his hand.

Othniel judged Israel, and the land had rest for forty years. Then Othniel, the son of Kenaz, died.

## The Story of Ehud

3    The children of Israel did evil again in the sight of the Lord; and the Lord strengthened Eglon, the king of Moab, against them. Eglon gathered about him the children of Ammon and Amalek, and smote Israel, and took possession of the city of palm trees. And Israel served Eglon for eighteen years. But when the people cried out to the Lord, the

Lord raised up a deliverer for them in Ehud, the son of Gera, a Benjamite, a left-handed man.

Now Ehud carried a gift from the children of Israel to Eglon, the king of Moab. And Ehud made for himself a double-edged dagger, which he girded upon his right thigh under his garment. He brought the gift to Eglon, who was a very fat man, and after he had presented the gift to him, Ehud sent away the people who had carried it. Then he said to the king, "I have a secret message for you, O King!" And the king sent all his attendants out of his presence.

Ehud followed the king to his private summer chamber, and when they were alone, he said, "I have a message from God for you." Ehud put out his left hand and took the dagger from his right thigh, and thrust it into Eglon's belly; and the hilt went in after the blade, and the fat closed over it. Then Ehud went out, and shut the doors of the chamber, and locked them and went away.

When he had gone the servants came; and they saw that the doors of the chamber were locked; and they waited for a long time. When the king still did not open the doors of his chamber, they took a key and opened the doors; and behold, there lay their lord dead upon the floor.

While they had waited, Ehud escaped and made his way to Seirah. And as soon as he reached the hills of Ephraim, he sounded the trumpet, and the children of Israel came down to him from the hills. Ehud said to them, "Follow me, for the Lord has delivered your enemies the Moabites into your hand."

They followed him, and seized the fords of the Jordan, and did not permit a Moabite to pass over. Then they slew about ten thousand Moabites, all lusty, all men of valor; and not a man escaped.

Thus Moab was subdued that day under the hand of Israel. And the land had rest for eighty years.


## Deborah and Barak

4    When Ehud died, Israel again did that which was evil in the sight of the Lord. And the Lord gave them over to Jabin, king of Canaan, who reigned in Hazor. The commander of his army was Sisera, who dwelt in Harosheth of the Gentiles. Sisera had nine hundred chariots of iron, and for twenty years he cruelly oppressed the children of Israel.

At that time Deborah, a prophetess, the wife of Lapidoth, judged Israel.

And she sat under the palm tree of Deborah between Ramah and Bethel in the hills of Ephraim, and the people came up to her for judgment.

Deborah sent for Barak, the son of Abinoam, of the tribe of Naphtali, and said to him, "Has not the Lord God of Israel commanded, 'Go to Mount Tabor with ten thousand men from Naphtali and Zebulun; and I will draw out Sisera and his chariots and his host to the river Kishon; and I will deliver him into your hand.'?"

Barak said to her, "If you will go with me, I will go; but if you will not go with me, I will not go." And she answered, "I will surely go with you. But this journey which you take will not bring you glory, for the Lord will deliver Sisera into the hand of a woman."

Then Deborah arose, and went with Barak to Kedesh. And Barak summoned the men of Naphtali and Zebulun to Kedesh, and ten thousand men gathered round him.

When Sisera was told that Barak, the son of Abonoam, had gone up to Mount Tabor, he gathered together his nine hundred chariots of iron and all the people who were with him, from Harosheth to the river Kishon.

And Deborah said to Barak, "Up! For this is the day in which the Lord shall deliver Sisera into your hand!"

So Barak went down from Mount Tabor followed by ten thousand men. And the Lord routed Sisera and all his chariots and all his army before Barak, so that Sisera alighted from his chariot and ran away on foot. But Barak pursued the chariots and the army to Harosheth, and they all fell by the sword; and there was not a man left.

Sisera fled to the tent of Jael, the wife of Heber the Kenite, for there was peace between Jabin the king and the house of Heber. And Jael came out to meet Sisera and said to him, "Turn in, my lord, turn in to my tent, and fear not." And when he entered the tent, she covered him with a robe. He said to her, "Give me, I pray you, a little water to drink, for I am thirsty." And Jael opened a skin of milk and gave him a drink and covered him. Again he said to her, "Stand at the door of the tent, and if any man comes to inquire of you, 'Is there any man here?' you shall say, 'No.'"

But when Sisera lay weary and fast asleep, Jael went to him softly, with a tent peg and a hammer in her hand, and she drove the tent peg through his temple into the ground.

As Barak pursued Sisera, Jael came out to meet him and said to him, "Come, I will show you the man whom you seek." And when Barak entered her tent, behold, Sisera lay dead, with the tent peg in his temple.

Thus God subdued Jabin on that day. And the children of Israel prospered, and their hand prevailed against Jabin, king of Canaan.

## *Deborah's Song*

5     Then sang Deborah and Barak, the son of Abinoam, on that day:
        "Hear, O kings; give ear, O princes! I to the Lord will sing,
I will sing to the Lord, the God of Israel.

"When you came out of Seir, O Lord, when you marched from the field of Edom, the earth trembled and the heavens shook, and the mountains melted before you.

"In the days of Jael, the highways were deserted, and travelers kept to the byways. The inhabitants of the villages disappeared, they disappeared in Israel, until I Deborah, arose, arose as a mother in Israel.

"Then war entered through the gates; yet was there a shield or a spear to be seen among forty thousand in Israel?

"My heart goes out to the governors of Israel, who offered themselves willingly to defend the people.

"Awake, awake, Deborah! Awake and sing a song! Rise up, Barak, son of Abinoam, and lead away your captives.

"Out of Ephraim came those whose root is in Amalek; and then came Benjamin among your people; out of Machir came the lawgivers; and out of Zebulun the writers with the pen; and the princes of Issachar joined with Deborah as the rest of Issachar joined with Barak. The people of Zebulun risked their lives, and those of Naphtali exposed themselves to death, on the high places of the field.

"The kings of Canaan came; they fought in Taanach by the waters of Megiddo.

"From the heaven the stars fought, the stars in their courses fought against Sisera.

"The river of Kishon, that ancient river, swept them away.

" 'Curse Meroz,' said the angel of the Lord. 'Curse bitterly its inhabitants!'

"For they came not to the help of the Lord, to the help of the Lord against the mighty.

"Blessed above all women shall be Jael, the wife of Heber the Kenite, blessed shall she be above all women in the tent. He asked for water and she gave him milk; she brought him curds in a lordly bowl. She put her hand to the tent peg, and her right hand to the hammer; and with the hammer she smote Sisera; the tent peg pierced his temples. At her feet he sank, he fell; and where he fell, there he lay dead.

"The mother of Sisera looked out of the window, and she cried through the lattice, 'Why is his chariot so long in coming?' And the wisest of her ladies answered, 'They are dividing the spoil: to every warrior a maiden or two; to Sisera garments of diverse colors, dyed garments of embroidery worthy of the victor.'

"Thus may all your enemies perish, O Lord! but let those who love you be like the sun when he goes forth in his might."

And the land had rest for forty years.

## For God and for Gideon

6-8  The children of Israel did evil in the sight of the Lord, and the Lord gave them into the hand of Midian seven years.

When Israel had sown the fields, the Midianites came up, and the Amalekites, and the children of the east, and encamped against them, and destroyed the yield of the earth and left no sustenance in Israel, neither sheep, nor ox, nor ass. For they came up with their cattle and their tents, and they came like locusts in number and laid waste the land. Israel was greatly impoverished because of the Midianites; and the people made for themselves hiding places in the mountains, and in caves and in strongholds; and they cried out for help to the Lord.

Then there came an angel of the Lord and sat under an oak at Ophrah, which belonged to Joash the Abi-ezrite, as his son Gideon was threshing out wheat in the wine press to hide it from the Midianites. And the angel said to Gideon, "The Lord is with you, mighty man of valor!"

Gideon answered, "If the Lord is with us, why then has all this befallen us? And where are all his wondrous works of which our fathers told us, saying, 'Did not the Lord bring us up from Egypt?' But now the Lord has forsaken us, and delivered us into the hand of Midian."

The angel said, "You shall save Israel from the Midianites." And Gideon answered, "O my lord, how can I save Israel? Behold, my family is the poorest in Manasseh, and I the least in my father's house." The angel said, "The Lord will be with you, and you shall smite the Midianites as one man."

143

Then answered Gideon, "If now I have found favor in God's sight, depart not, I pray you, until I bring food and set it before you; then show me a sign."

Gideon went in, and made ready a kid and unleavened cakes of meal; and he brought the food out and presented it to him under the oak. The angel touched the meat and unleavened cakes with the tip of the staff in his hand, and a fire rose up out of the rock and consumed the food. Then the angel disappeared from his sight. Gideon cried out, "Alas for me, O Lord God! For I have seen an angel of the Lord face to face!" And the Lord said to him, "Fear not; you shall not die."

That same night the Lord said to Gideon, "Take your father's bullock and pull down your father's altar to Baal, and cut down the linden grove beside it. Then build an altar to the Lord upon the top of this rock, and sacrifice a bullock as a burnt offering with the wood of the grove you shall cut down."

Gideon took ten menservants, and did as the Lord had spoken to him; and because he feared his father's household, and the men of the city, he did it by night. When the men of the city rose in the morning, behold, the altar of Baal was broken, and the linden grove beside it was cut down. They said to one another, "Who has done this thing?" And they were told, "Gideon, the son of Joash, has done this."

The men of the city went to Joash and demanded, "Bring out your son, that he may die." But Joash said to all those who stood against him, "Will you contend for Baal, and do you want to save him? If he is a god, let him contend for himself, because his altar has been destroyed."

At that time the Midianites and the Amalekites and the children of the east joined forces, and encamped in the valley of Jezreel. But the spirit of the Lord came upon Gideon, and he sounded the alarm upon the trumpet, and his kinsmen gathered round him. Then he sent them as messengers throughout Manasseh and Asher and Zebulun and Naphtali, and they all came at his call. Gideon and the men with him camped beside the well of Harod, so that the army of Midianites was north of them, by the hill of Moreh, in the valley.

And the Lord said to Gideon, "The people who are with you are too many for me to give the Midianites into their hand, lest Israel boast and say, 'My own hand has saved me.' Therefore proclaim, 'Whoever is afraid, let him return home.'" And there returned twenty-two thousand of the people, and ten thousand remained. Then the Lord said, "There are still too many. Bring them down to the water's edge, and I will test them for you there. Each one who laps the water with his tongue, as a dog laps, you shall set off by himself." And the number of those who lapped, putting their hand to their mouth, was three hundred; but all the rest knelt down to drink. And the Lord said to Gideon, "By these three hundred men who lapped will I save you; and let all the others go, each man to his home."

Gideon divided the three hundred men into three companies, and he put into the hands of all of them trumpets, and empty jars with torches inside them. Then he said to them, "When we come to the outskirts of the Midianite camp, as I do, so shall you do. When I blow my trumpet, then blow your trumpets also on every side of the camp, and shout, 'For the Lord and for Gideon!' "

So Gideon, and the men who were with him, came to the outskirts of the camp at the beginning of the middle watch when the new guard had been set; and they blew their trumpets, and broke the jars, and held the torches in their left hands, and they cried out, "The sword for the Lord and for Gideon!"

Gideon and his men stood, each in his place, encircling the camp; and the enemy ran, and shouted, and fled as far as the border of Abel-meholah. And the men of Israel pursued them as they fled. The men of Naphtali and of Asher and of Manasseh joined Gideon and his three hundred men, and pursued the Midianites.

Gideon came to the Jordan and passed over, he and the three hundred men with him, pursuing Zebah and Zalmunna, the kings of Midian. And when he captured them he asked, "What manner of men were those whom you slew at Tabor?" They answered, "As you are, so were they; each one like a king." And Gideon said, "They were my brothers, the sons of my mother. As the Lord lives, if you had saved them I would not slay you." And he said to Jether, his firstborn, "Up and slay them." But the boy did not draw his sword, because he was still a youth. Then Gideon slew them, and took the crescents that were on their camels' necks.

And the men of Israel said to Gideon, "Come, rule over us, you, and your son, and your son's son also. For you have saved us from the Midianites." But Gideon answered, "I will not rule over you, neither shall my son rule over you. Only the Lord shall rule over you."

So Midian was subdued. And the land had peace for forty years in the days of Gideon.[1]

[1] See JUDGES, Chapters 6-8, in Notes and Excisions.

# The Bramble That Would Be King

8-9    Gideon had threescore and ten sons, for he had many wives. And his concubine who lived in Shechem also bore him a son, whom he named Abimelech.

And it came to pass that as soon as Gideon was dead, the children of Israel again went astray after Baalim, and made Baal-berith their god. They remembered not the Lord their God who had saved them from their enemies on every side; nor did they show kindness to the house of Gideon according to the goodness he had shown to Israel.

Now Abimelech, Gideon's son, went to Shechem to his mother's kinsmen, and said to them, "Which is better for you, that all the sons of Gideon rule over you, or that only one rule over you? Remember also that I am of your bone and your flesh." His mother's kinsmen told the men of Shechem these words, and their hearts inclined to follow Abimelech, for they said, "He is our brother." They gave him seventy pieces of silver from the temple of Baal-berith, with which Abimelech hired vain and worthless fellows to follow him. Then Abimelech went to his father's house at Ophrah and slew his brothers, and only Jotham, the youngest son of Gideon, escaped, for he hid himself. Then the men of Shechem and Beth-millo assembled and made Abimelech their king.

When this was told to Jotham, he went to the top of Mount Gerizim and cried out to the people:

"Listen to me, you men of Shechem, that God may listen to you!

"The trees once went out to anoint a king over them, and they said to the olive tree, 'Reign over us!' But the olive tree answered, 'Should I leave my oil, with which God and man are honored, to rule over the trees?' Then the trees said to the fig tree, 'Come you, and reign over us!' But the fig tree answered, 'Should I forsake my sweetness and my good fruit, to wear myself out ruling over the trees?' Then the trees said to the vine, 'Come you, and reign over us!' But the vine answered, 'Should I leave my wine, which cheers God and man, to hold sway over the trees?' Then all the trees said to the bramble, 'Come you, and rule over us.' And the bramble answered, 'If in truth you anoint me king over you, then you must come and take refuge in my shade, or else a fire will come out of the bramble and devour the cedars of Lebanon.'

"Now, therefore, if you have dealt uprightly in making Abimelech your king, and if you have dealt well with Gideon and his house, and have done to him as he deserved — for my father fought for you and saved you from Midian — then rejoice this day in Abimelech, and let him also rejoice in you! But if not, let fire come out from Abimelech and devour the men of Shechem; and let fire come out from the men of Shechem and Beth-millo and devour Abimelech!"

Then Jotham fled to Beer and hid there, for fear of Abimelech his brother.

And after Abimelech ruled over Israel three years, God sent an evil spirit between Abimelech and the men of Shechem; and the men of Shechem dealt treacherously with him.

Abimelech rose up by night, and all the men who were with him, and they lay in wait against Shechem in four companies. And Abimelech took the city and slew the people that were in it, and razed the city and sowed it with salt.

Then Abimelech encamped against Thebez and took it. But there was a strong tower within the city, and all the men and women fled to it, and shut themselves in. Abimelech came to the tower and besieged it, and drew near the door of the tower to set it on fire. Then a certain woman threw an upper millstone upon Abimelech's head, and broke his skull. He called hastily to his armor-bearer, "Draw your sword and slay me, lest men say of me, 'A woman slew him.'" And the young man thrust him through, and Abimelech died.

Thus God requited the wickedness Abimelech had committed in killing his brothers; and God also made the wickedness of the men of Shechem fall back upon their heads; and upon them came the curse of Jotham, the son of Gideon.[2]

## Jephthah's Daughter

10-12    After Abimelech there arose, to defend Israel, Tola, the son of Puah, a man from the tribe of Issachar; and he judged the people for twenty and three years. After him arose Jair the Gileadite; and he judged Israel for twenty and two years. But when Jair died, the people again served Baal and Ashtaroth, and the gods of Syria and Zidon, and Moab and Ammon, and the gods of the Philistines. Then the anger of the Lord kindled against Israel and he delivered them to the Philistines and the Ammonites.

[2] See JUDGES, Chapter 9, in Notes and Excisions.

The children of Israel were oppressed and crushed, and they cried out to the Lord, "We have sinned against you, because we have forsaken our God and have served Baalim." And the Lord said to them, "Go and cry for help to the gods whom you have chosen; let them save you in the time of your distress." But the children of Israel repented, and they put away the strange gods from among them and served the Lord. And the Lord was grieved over the misery of Israel.

Now Jephthah the Gileadite, son of a harlot, was a mighty man of valor; but his father's other sons drove him out, saying, "You shall not inherit in our father's house." And Jephthah fled to the land of Tob. When Ammon made war against Israel, the elders of Gilead went to fetch Jephthah, and they said to him, "Come and be our captain, that we may fight against Ammon." And Jephthah answered, "Did you not hate me, and drive me out of my father's house? Why now have you come to me when you are in distress?" The elders of Gilead said to him, "We turn to you now, that you may go with us and fight against Ammon, and be our head over all the inhabitants of Gilead." And Jephthah said, "If you bring me home again to fight against Ammon, and the Lord delivers them up to me, will I be your head?" And the elders answered, "The Lord be witness between us if we do not do according to your words."

Then Jephthah went with the elders of Gilead, and the people made him head and captain over them, and Jephthah vowed to the Lord in Mizpeh, "If you will indeed deliver the children of Ammon into my hands, then whatever comes out of the door of my house to meet me when I return shall belong to the Lord, and I will offer it up as a burnt offering."

So Jephthah passed over to fight against the Ammonites, and Ammon was subdued before the children of Israel.

Then Jephthah returned to Mizpeh to his home, and behold, his daughter, his only child, came out dancing to meet him.

When Jephthah saw her, he tore his garment and cried, "Alas, my daughter! You have brought me very low, for I have made a vow to the Lord and I cannot take my vow back." And she answered, "My father, if you have made a vow to the Lord, do to me according to your vow; for the Lord has avenged you upon your enemies the children of Ammon. But let this be done for me. Grant me two months, that I may go to the mountains and bewail my youth, I and my friends." And Jephthah said, "Go!" He sent her away for two months; and she departed, she and her companions.

At the end of two months she returned to her father, who did with her according to his vow. And it became a custom that the daughters of Israel went up four days each year to lament the daughter of Jephthah the Gileadite.

Jephthah judged Israel six years. Then he died and was buried in Gilead.

After Jephthah, Israel was judged by Ibzan of Bethlehem seven years, and by Elon the Zebulonite ten years. After him Abdon, the son of Hillel, judged Israel eight years.[3]

## The Birth of Samson

13      The children of Israel again did evil in the sight of the Lord, and he delivered them to the Philistines for forty years.

Now there was a certain Danite named Manoah, whose wife was barren. And an angel of the Lord appeared to the woman and said to her, "Behold, you shall conceive and bear a son. Therefore, drink no wine or strong drink, and eat no unclean thing! For lo, the child shall be a Nazarite to God from birth. No razor shall come upon his head; and he shall begin to deliver Israel from the Philistines."

The woman came to her husband and told him, "A man of God came to me, and his face was like the face of an angel of God, very awesome. I asked him not whence he came, nor did he tell me his name; but he said to me, 'You shall bear a son, and the child shall be a Nazarite from the day of his birth to the day of his death.'"

Manoah entreated the Lord and said, "O my Lord, let the man of God come again to us, and teach us how we shall rear the child that is to be born."

And the angel came again to the woman as she sat in the field, but Manoah her husband was not with her. So the woman ran in haste to her husband and said, "The man has appeared who came to me that day."

Manoah followed his wife, and went to the man and asked, "Are you the man who spoke to this woman?" He said, "I am." Manoah asked, "Now if your words come to pass, how shall we bring up the child?" And the angel answered, "Of all that I said to the woman, let her take heed." Manoah said to the angel, "I pray you, let us detain you until we have prepared food for you." But the angel answered, "Though you detain me,

[3] See JUDGES, Chapter 12, in Notes and Excisions.

I will not eat of your food; and if you wish to make an offering, you must offer it to the Lord." For Manoah did not know that he was the angel of the Lord. Then Manoah asked, "What is your name, so that when your words come to pass, we may honor you?" And the angel said, "Why do you ask for my name, seeing that it is hidden?"

So Manoah made the offering upon the rock. And when the flame rose up toward heaven from the altar, the angel ascended in the flame of the altar. Manoah and his wife looked on; then they fell on their faces to the ground. But the angel of the Lord appeared no more to them.

And Manoah said to his wife, "We shall surely die, because we have seen God." But she answered, "If the Lord wished to kill us, he would not have received our offering, nor would he have told such things as these."

The woman bore a son, and called him Samson. And the child grew, and the Lord blessed him.

## Samson's Riddle

14    Samson went down to Timnah and saw there a woman, one of the daughters of the Philistines. He returned to his father and mother and said, "I have seen in Timnah a daughter of the Philistines; get her for me as my wife." His father and mother answered, "Is there not a woman among all the daughters of our people, that you must take a wife from the uncircumcised Philistines?" But Samson said to his father, "Get her for me; she pleases me well."

His father and his mother did not know that this was brought about by the Lord; that he sought an occasion against the Philistines, who at that time had dominion over Israel.

Then Samson went down to Timnah; and when he reached the vine-yards a young lion came roaring at him. The spirit of the Lord came upon Samson, and he tore the lion asunder as he would have torn a kid. But he did not tell his father or his mother what he had done. He went down and spoke with the woman, and she pleased Samson well.

After a time, he returned to Timnah to wed the woman. And when Samson turned aside to see the carcass of the lion, behold, there was a swarm of bees and honey in it. He took some honey in his hands, and ate as he went on. When he came to his father and mother, he gave some to them and they ate. But he did not tell them he had taken the honey from the carcass of the lion.

His father went down to the woman, and Samson gave a feast there; for such was the custom of young men at that time. And when the people saw him, they brought thirty guests to be with him.

Samson said to them, "Let me give you a riddle. And if you can solve it within the seven days of the feast, I will give you thirty linen garments and thirty festal garments; but if you cannot solve it, then you shall give me thirty linen garments and thirty festal garments." They answered, "Let us hear your riddle."

Samson said to them: "Out of the eater came forth food, and out of the strong came forth sweetness."

But they could not solve the riddle. And they said to Samson's wife, "Entice your husband to tell the riddle, else we shall burn you and your father's house. Have you called us here to impoverish us?"

Samson's wife wept before him, and said, "You love me not, for you have put a riddle to my people and have not told it to me." And he answered, "I have not told it to my father or my mother. Shall I then tell it to you?" She wept before him the seven days of their feast; and on the seventh day he told her, because she urged him so hard. And she told the riddle to her people.

The men of the city said to Samson on the seventh day before the sun went down: "What is sweeter than honey? And what is stronger than a lion?"

And he said to them: "If you had not plowed with my heifer, you had not found out my riddle."

Then the spirit of the Lord came upon him, and he went down to Ashkelon and smote thirty men, and took their garments and gave them to those who had solved the riddle. And in his anger he went back to his father's house. But Samson's wife was given to his companion, who had been his friend.

## Samson's Revenge

15    After a while, at the time of the wheat harvest, Samson went to visit his wife with a gift; and he said, "I will go to my wife in her chamber."

But her father would not let him go in, and said, "I thought that you hated her. Therefore I gave her to your companion. Is not her younger sister fairer than she? Take her instead, I pray you." Samson answered, "This time I shall be blameless when I do the Philistines harm."

And he went and caught three hundred foxes, and turned them tail to tail; and he put a torch between each pair of tails. Then he set the torches on fire, and let the foxes go into the fields of the Philistines. And fire consumed the shocks, and the standing grain, and also the olive orchards.

The Philistines asked, "Who has done this?" And they were told, "Samson, the son-in-law of the Timnite, did this because his wife was given to his companion."

So the Philistines came up and destroyed her and her father with fire.

Samson said to them, "Because you have done this, I will be avenged upon you." And he smote them hip and thigh with great slaughter. Then he went down to dwell in the cleft of the rock of Etam.

The Philistines came up, and encamped in Judah, and spread themselves in Lehi. And the men of Judah asked, "Why have you come up against us?" They answered, "We have come to bind Samson, to do to him as he has done to us."

So three thousand men of Judah went to the rock of Etam, and said to Samson, "Do you not know that the Philistines rule over us? What have you done to us?" And Samson answered, "As they did to me, so have I done to them." They said to him, "We have come to bind you, so that we may hand you to the Philistines." And Samson answered, "Swear to me that you will not fall upon me yourselves." They said, "No; we will bind you and give you up to them, but we will not kill you."

They bound him with two new cords and brought him from the rock. And when he came to Lehi, the Philistines shouted as they met him. But the spirit of the Lord came mightily upon Samson, and the cords upon his arms became like flax that is burnt with fire, and his bonds dropped from off his hands. Then he saw the fresh jawbone of an ass, and took it in his hand, and with it he slew a thousand men.

And Samson judged Israel twenty years in the days of the Philistines.

## Samson and Delilah

16-18 Samson went to Gaza, and saw there a harlot and went in to her.
When the Gazites were told, "Samson has come here," they lay in wait for him all night, saying, "In the morning we shall kill him."

But Samson rose at midnight, and tore out the doors of the city gate, with the two posts, bar and all, and carried them off upon his shoulders to the top of the hill that faces Hebron.

After a time, Samson loved a woman in the valley of Sorek whose name was Delilah. And the lords of the Philistines came to her and said, "Entice him, and find out where his great strength lies and by what means we may overcome him; and we will give you, each one of us, eleven hundred pieces of silver."

Delilah said to Samson, "Tell me, I pray you, in what lies your great strength, and with what you could be bound to be subdued."

Samson answered, "If they bind me with seven fresh withes, then shall I become weak, and be like any other man."

The lords of the Philistines brought her seven fresh withes, and she bound him with them. Then she said to him, "The Philistines are upon you, Samson!" For there were men hidden in an inner chamber, who lay in wait.

And Samson broke the withes like a strand of flax when it touches fire.

Delilah said to him, "You have mocked me, and told me lies. Now tell me, I pray you, with what you might be bound."

And he said to her, "If they bind me fast with new ropes that have not been used before, I shall become weak and be like any other man." So Delilah took new ropes and bound him with them. Then she said to him, "The Philistines are upon you, Samson!" And men lay in wait in the inner chamber. But Samson snapped the ropes from off his arms like a thread.

Delilah said to him, "Up to this time you have mocked me, and told me lies. Tell me with what you might be bound."

And he said to her, "If you weave the seven locks of my head with the web of a loom, and fasten them in with the pin of the loom, then I shall become weak as any other man."

While he slept, Delilah wove his hair into the web, and fastened it with the pin, and called out, "The Philistines are upon you, Samson!"

But he awoke from his sleep, and plucked away the pin of the beam and the web.

Delilah said to him, "How can you say 'I love you,' when your heart is not with me? You have mocked me these three times, and have not told me in what your great strength lies."

She pressed him each day with her words, and urged him, until his soul was vexed to death. And he said to her, "I have been a Nazarite since the day I was born. If I were shaved, my strength would leave me."

And when Delilah saw that he had told her all that was in his heart, she sent for the lords of the Philistines, saying, "Come this once, for he has shown me all that is in his heart." Then they came up to her, and brought the money with them.

Delilah made Samson sleep upon her lap, and she sent for a man to shave off his seven locks of hair. Then she called out, "The Philistines are upon you, Samson!"

He awoke from his sleep and said, "I will go out as at the other times."

But the Philistines seized him, and put out his eyes, and brought him down to Gaza, where they bound him with fetters of brass and made him grind at the mill in the prison. However, the hair of Samson's head began to grow again after it was shaved.

The lords of the Philistines gathered to offer a great sacrifice to Dagon their god, and to rejoice; for they said, "Our god has delivered Samson our enemy into our hand."

And when their hearts were merry, the people said, "Call for Samson, that he may amuse us."

They brought Samson out of the prison, and set him between the pillars of the temple. And Samson said to the lad who held him by the hand, "Let me feel the pillars upon which the temple rests, that I may lean against them."

Now the temple was full of men and women; all the lords of the Philistines were there, and on the roof there were about three thousand men and women who watched while Samson was brought out.

Then Samson called to the Lord, "O Lord God, remember me, I pray you, and strengthen me, I pray you, only this once, O God, that I may be avenged upon the Philistines for my two eyes."

Samson took fast hold of the two middle pillars upon which the temple was supported, of the one with his right hand, and of the other with his left. And Samson said, "Let me die with the Philistines."

He pushed with all his might, and the temple fell upon the lords and upon all the people who were in it. So those whom he slew at his death were more than those he had slain in his life.

Then his kinsmen came down and took him, and buried him between Zorah and Eshtaol in the burying place of Manoah his father.[4]

[4] See JUDGES, Chapters 17-18, in Notes and Excisions.

## The Wickedness of Gibeah

*19-21*   In those days, when there was no king in Israel, a certain Levite
who dwelt on the far side of Ephraim took a concubine from
Bethlehem-Judah. And she played the harlot, and went away from him
to her father's house. After four months her husband went after her, to
speak kindly to her and to bring her back, taking with him a servant and a
couple of asses. And when the girl's father saw him, he rejoiced, and kept
him there three days.

On the fourth day, they rose early to depart; but the father said to his
son-in-law, "Comfort yourself with food, and afterward you shall go your
way." So they sat down, and ate and drank together. Then the father
said to the man, "I pray you, tarry for the night, and let your heart be
merry." Therefore he lodged there again. The man rose early on the fifth
day to depart, and the father said, "Comfort your heart, I pray you." So
they tarried until afternoon. Then the father-in-law said, "Behold, the
day draws toward evening. Stay for the night, and tomorrow go early on
your way."

But the man would stay no longer. He rose, and departed with his
concubine, his servant, and the asses. When they neared Jebus the day
was far spent, and the servant said to his master, "Come, let us turn into
this city of the Jebusites for the night." His master answered, "We will not
turn into the city of a stranger, that does not belong to the children of
Israel; we will go on to Gibeah or Ramah."

They went on their way; and the sun went down upon them when they
were near Gibeah, which belongs to Benjamin. So they turned aside to
lodge there. And he went and sat down in the broad place of the city, for
no man had taken them into his house to lodge. And behold, there came an
old man from his work in the field at evening. Now the man was from
the hills of Ephraim, and dwelt in Gibeah; but the men of the place were
Benjamites. When he saw the wayfarer the old man asked, "Whither do
you go? And from whence do you come?"

The Levite answered, "We are passing from Bethlehem in Judah to the
farther side of Ephraim, from whence I am. And no man has asked me
into his house. Yet we have fodder for the asses, and bread and wine for
ourselves, and there is no want of anything."

The old man said, "Peace be with you. Let all your needs be my care.
Only do not lodge in the street."

155

So he brought them to his home, and gave fodder to the asses; and they washed their feet, and ate and drank. As they were making their hearts merry, behold, the men of the city, certain base fellows, surrounded the house and beat upon the door, and said to the master of the house, "Bring out the man who came into your house, that we may know him."

The old man answered, "No, my brothers, I pray you, do not behave so wickedly, seeing that this man has come into my home. Do not commit this folly. Behold, here is my daughter, a maiden, and this man's concubine. I will bring them out to you, but to this man do not so vile a thing."

But the men would not listen to him. So the man took his concubine and brought her out to them, and they abused her all night; and when the day began to break, they let her go. Then the woman came at dawn, and fell down at the door of the house where her lord was, till it was light. Her lord rose in the morning and opened the door of the house, and behold, the woman lay there with her hands upon the threshold. He said to her, "Up, let us be going!" But there was no answer.

Then the man put her body upon an ass, and went to his home. And when he came into his house, he took a knife and laid hold of the body of his concubine, and divided her limb by limb into twelve pieces, which he sent to all the borders of Israel. And those who saw it said, "Such a deed has never been done from the day the children of Israel came up out of Egypt to this day. Consider it; take counsel; and speak out."

Then all the children of Israel went out, from Dan to Beersheba, and assembled as one man to the Lord at Mizpah. The heads of the tribes of Israel presented themselves in the assembly of the people of God, four hundred thousand swordsmen. And the people said, "Tell us, how did this wickedness come to pass?"

And the husband of the slain woman told them. Then the people rose as one man, saying, "None of us shall return home. We will go up by lot against Gibeah." So all the men of Israel gathered against the city, and they sent men throughout the tribe of Benjamin, saying, "What wickedness is this among you? Give up the base fellows in Gibeah, that we may put them to death, and put away such evil from Israel."

But the Benjamites would not listen. And they gathered outside of the cities to go to battle. Now the Benjamites numbered at that time, outside of the cities, twenty-six thousand swordsmen, besides the inhabitants of Gibeah, who numbered seven hundred picked men. Among all these there were seven hundred men who were left-handed, each one of them could sling stones at a hair and not miss.

The children of Israel asked counsel of God, and said, "Which of us shall go up first to battle against Benjamin?" And the Lord said, "Judah shall go up first."

So they put themselves in battle array against those at Gibeah. And the Benjamites came out of Gibeah, and struck to the ground on that day twenty-two thousand men. But the men of Israel took courage, and again put themselves in battle array in the same place. And on the second day the Benjamites struck down eighteen thousand men.

The children of Israel went up to Bethel, to the house of God, and wept before the Lord and fasted until evening. And they asked counsel of the Lord. Phineas, the grandson of Aaron, ministered before the ark in those days, and he said, "Shall we again go out to battle against Benjamin our brother, or shall we cease?" And the Lord said, "Go up, for tomorrow I will deliver them into your hand."

They went up against the Benjamites on the following day, and put themselves in battle array against Gibeah, as at the other times. When the children of Benjamin came out against the people, the children of Israel said: "Let us flee, and draw them away from the city." For they had trusted men, lying in wait, whom they had set against Gibeah. And at the appointed sign the men lying in wait would make a great beacon of smoke rise up out of the city.

Then the men of Israel retired in the battle, and the Benjamites began to smite and kill; and they said, "They are smitten before us, as at the first battle."

But when the beacon began to rise out of the city in a pillar of smoke, the Benjamites looked behind them; and behold, the whole of the city went up in smoke to heaven. Then the men of Israel turned on them, and the Benjamites were dismayed, for they saw that evil had come upon them. They turned toward the wilderness; but the battle overtook them. The men of Israel encircled the Benjamites and chased them, and when the Benjamites fled toward the rock of Rimmon, they followed hard after. So that on that day there fell of Benjamin twenty-five thousand swordsmen, all men of valor. Then the men of Israel turned back and set on fire all the cities.

Now the men of Israel had sworn at Mizpah, "None of us shall give his daughter in marriage to a Benjamite."

But the people wept in the house of God and said, "O Lord God of

Israel, why has this come to pass, that there should be today one tribe lacking in Israel?"

Then the elders of the congregation said, "We may not give them our daughters as wives, for thus we have vowed. But each year there is the feast of the Lord in Shiloh at the north side of Bethel. Therefore, let the Benjamites lie in wait in the vineyards, and when the daughters of Shiloh come out to dance, the Benjamites may catch their wives from among the daughters of Shiloh."

And the Benjamites did so. They returned to their inheritance, and rebuilt the cities, and dwelt in them. And the children of Israel departed, each man to his tribe and his family, and each man to his inheritance.

In those days there was no king in Israel; every man did that which was right in his own eyes.[5]

[5] See JUDGES, Chapters 20-21, in Notes and Excisions.

# I SAMUEL
## The Establishment of the Hebrew Kingdom

❰ When the Bible was first translated into Greek, about two centuries B.C.E., the books now known as I and II Samuel and I and II Kings appeared under the title of "The Kingdoms." But in the days before printing it was necessary, for technical reasons, to divide this large book (which runs to nearly one hundred thousand words in English) into four equal parts; and these were named: "The First Book of Kings," "The Second Book of Kings," "The Third Book of Kings," and "The Fourth Book of Kings." But since the first part contains a record of the life and acts of Samuel, the last and greatest of the judges — and a prophet held in such high esteem that his name was revered by the ancients next only to that of Moses — the first two books of "The Kingdoms" in the Hebrew Scriptures were named in Samuel's honor, even though his death is recorded seven chapters before I Samuel ends.

Among all the ancient narratives in the books of the Bible, I Samuel is one of the most effective, in spite of the variance of style, indicating different sources, and in spite of the duplications which tend to confuse the reader. (For in this book a number of events are told twice and thrice, with only minor changes and embellishments. The end of Eli's family is given twice; David is twice introduced to Saul's family; Saul is crowned three times under different circumstances; and Saul's pursuit of David in the hills of Hachilah is related in two separate chapters, then repeated as a more unified story only two chapters later.) But the essential power of the narrative becomes at once apparent when these duplications are eliminated.

This book gives the rise and fall of one of the noblest and most tragic figures in the Chronicles: Saul, a poor farmer's son, who, through no ambition of his own, becomes the first king of Israel. He proves himself spiritually, as he was physically, head and shoulders above most of his people; slow to anger, brave in adversity, passionate in devotion, humble before his God, kindly even to his enemies, and generous in judgment — tipping the scale of justice in favor of the troubled. But he learns that what might be considered a virtue in a farmer may be regarded as a fault in a king. As a result, the prophet who lifted him from obscurity to the throne turns against him; court intrigues beset him; his own son gives allegiance to his opponent; and his son-in-law seeks alliance with the enemies of Israel. And finally, Saul goes to war with the bitter foreknowledge that he and his sons will perish that day on the battlefield.

I Samuel might have been called "The Book of Saul," for it is essentially the story of the first king in Israel — from his humble beginnings, when he goes in search of his father's asses, to the day of his tragic death on the field of battle. ⟨[

## The Birth of Samuel

**1-2**    Now there was a certain man in Ramathaim-zophim, an Ephraimite named Elkanah, and he had two wives; the name of the one Hannah, and the name of the other Peninnah. Peninnah had children, but Hannah had none.

This man went up out of his city each year to Shiloh, to worship and to sacrifice to the Lord. And after Elkanah made his offering, he gave portions of the sacrificial meat to Peninnah his wife, and to all her sons and daughters; and to Hannah he gave a double portion, for he loved Hannah. But her rival would provoke her and make her fret, because the Lord had not given her a child; and so it was year by year when they went up to the house of the Lord. And once Hannah was so vexed that she wept and would not eat.

Her husband said to her, "Hannah, why do you weep? And why is your heart grieved? Am I not better to you than ten sons?"

But Hannah rose up after they had eaten in Shiloh, and went to the house of the Lord, where Eli the priest sat upon a seat beside the doorpost of the temple. She was in bitterness of soul, and prayed to the Lord and wept. And she vowed, "If you will indeed look upon the suffering of your handmaid, and grant me a son, then I will give him to the Lord for all the days of his life, and no razor shall touch his head."

As she went on praying before the Lord, Eli the priest observed her mouth. Now Hannah spoke in her heart, and her lips moved, but her voice could not be heard; therefore Eli thought she was drunk. And he said to her, "Put away your wine from you."

Hannah answered, "My lord, I am a woman in sorrow. I have drunk neither wine nor strong drink, but have poured out my soul before the Lord. Do not consider me a daughter of the wicked. Out of my grief have I spoken."

Then Eli said, "Go in peace, and the God of Israel grant your petition!"

So the woman went her way, and she ate, and her face was no longer sad. The Lord remembered Hannah; and when she bore a son she called him Samuel (The Lord Heard Me). And when she had weaned him, she took him up with her, with three bullocks, and one measure of flour, and a bottle of wine, and brought him to the house of the Lord in Shiloh. And she said to Eli the priest, "My lord, I am the woman who stood here praying. I prayed for this child, and the Lord granted my petition. Therefore, as long as he lives he shall be lent to the Lord."

Then Hannah prayed, and said:

"My heart rejoices in the Lord, my strength is exalted in him; there is none holy as the Lord, for there is none besides him; there is no rock like our God.

"Boast no more so proudly; let no arrogance come from your mouth; for the Lord is a God of knowledge, and by him our actions are weighed. Those who were sated have hired themselves out for bread, and those who were hungry now hunger no more. She who was barren has borne seven, and she who had many children has grown lonely.

"The Lord makes poor and the Lord makes rich; he raises the poor out of the dust and lifts the beggars from the dunghill, to set them among princes and to bring them into the inheritance of glory. For the pillars of the earth are the Lord's, and he has set the world upon them.

"He will guard the feet of his holy ones, and the wicked shall be put to silence in darkness; for not by might shall a man show his strength."

## Eli's Grief

2      Now the sons of Eli were base men, and they did not regard the Lord. And Eli, who was very old, heard of the evil his sons did in Israel. He said to his sons, "Why do you do such things? For I hear of your evil deeds from all the people. My sons, you make the Lord's people

transgress. If one man sins against another, the judge shall judge him; but if a man sins against the Lord, who shall plead for him?" But they would not listen to the voice of their father.

Now there came a man of God to Eli, and said to him, "Thus says the Lord: 'Why do you honor your sons above me, and fatten yourselves upon the offerings of Israel my people? Those who honor me I will honor, and those who despise me shall be lightly esteemed. Behold, the day is near when I will cut off your father's house, and there shall not be an old man left in your household. And this shall be a sign for you: your two sons, Hophni and Phinehas, shall both die on the same day. And I will raise up for myself a faithful priest, who shall do according to that which is in my heart and in my mind.' "

## Samuel's Youth

3 The child Samuel ministered before the Lord in the presence of Eli, clad in a linen garment. And each year his mother made him a little robe, and brought it to him when she came up with her husband to offer the yearly sacrifice. The child Samuel grew, and he was in favor with the Lord and with men.

And it came to pass at that time, when Eli was lying down in his place, before the lamp of God went out in the temple, and Samuel was lying down near the ark of God, that the Lord called, "Samuel!" He answered, "Here am I." And he ran to Eli and said, "Here am I, for you called me." Eli said, "I did not call; lie down again." So Samuel went and lay down.

The Lord called again, "Samuel!" And Samuel went to Eli and said, "Here am I, for you did call me." Eli answered, "I did not call, my son; lie down again."

The Lord called Samuel a third time. Samuel went to Eli and said, "Here am I, for you did call me." Then Eli perceived that the Lord was calling the child. But Samuel did not know it, for the word of the Lord had not yet been revealed to him. Therefore Eli said to Samuel, "Go, lie down; and if you are called again, you shall say, 'Speak, Lord, for your servant hears.' "

Samuel went and lay down in his place. And the Lord came and called as at the other times, "Samuel! Samuel!" Then Samuel answered, "Speak, for your servant hears."

The Lord said to Samuel, "Behold, I will do a thing in Israel at which both ears of everyone who hears it will tingle. On that day I will bring about all that I have spoken concerning Eli's house. Because his sons made themselves vile, yet he restrained them not, the iniquity of Eli's house shall not be purged by sacrifice or offering."

Samuel lay until morning, and then he opened the doors of the house of the Lord. And Samuel feared to tell Eli. But Eli called Samuel to him and said, "Samuel, my son, what was it that the Lord said to you?"

Then Samuel told him everything, and hid nothing from him.

Eli said, "It is the Lord. Let him do what seems to him good."

## The Death of Eli

4    Now Israel went out against the Philistines to battle, and en-
camped beside Ebenezer, while the Philistines encamped at Aphek. And when they joined battle, Israel was smitten, and the slain in the field numbered about four thousand men.

When the people returned to the camp, the elders of Israel said, "Why has the Lord smitten us today before the Philistines? Let us fetch the ark of the Lord here from Shiloh, that he may come among us and save us from our enemies."

So the people sent to Shiloh for the ark. And when the ark of the Lord was brought into the camp, all Israel sent up a shout so great that the earth trembled. And when the Philistines heard the shout, they asked, "What does it mean, this great shout in the camp of the Hebrews?" Then they understood that the ark of the Lord had reached the camp, and they were afraid. They said, "Woe to us! For who shall deliver us from these mighty Gods? These are the Gods who smote the Egyptians with all manner of plagues! Be strong, and acquit yourselves like men, O Philistines, that you be not slaves to the Hebrews as they have been to you; acquit yourselves like men, and fight."

The Philistines fought, and Israel was smitten; and each man fled to his tent and there was great slaughter, for there fell of Israel thirty thousand footmen. And the ark of God was taken; and the two sons of Eli, Hophni and Phinehas, were slain.

On that same day a Benjamite ran from the battle and came to Shiloh, with his clothes rent and with earth upon his head. And when he arrived, lo, Eli sat upon a seat by the wayside watching, his heart anxious for the ark of God. And when the man came into the city and told the townspeople, they all cried out. Eli heard the outcry, and he asked, "What is the meaning of this tumult?"

Now Eli was ninety and eight years old, and his eyes so dimmed that he could not see. And the man said to Eli, "I am he who fled today from the battle." Eli asked, "What has happened there, my son?" And the messenger answered, "Israel has fled before the Philistines, and there has been great slaughter among the people; and your two sons, Hophni and Phinehas, are dead; and the ark of God has been captured."

When the man mentioned the ark of God, Eli fell backward from his seat beside the gate, and his neck broke, and he died.

## The Return of the Ark

5-7    The Philistines took the ark of God, and brought it from Ebenezer to Ashdod, and into the temple of Dagon. And on the morrow, when the people of Ashdod arose, behold, Dagon had fallen upon his face to the ground in front of the ark of the Lord.

The hand of the Lord was heavy upon those of Ashdod, and he afflicted them with boils. The men of Ashdod said, "The ark of the God of Israel shall not abide with us, for his hand is heavy upon us and upon Dagon our god. Let the ark be carried to Gath." So they took the ark there.

But the Lord afflicted the men of Gath, both young and old, and boils broke out upon them. Therefore they sent the ark to Ekron.

But when the ark of God reached Ekron, the Ekronites cried out, "They have brought the ark of the God of Israel to us to slay us!" And they summoned all the lords of the Philistines and said, "Send away the ark of the God of Israel, and let it go back to its own place, so that it may not slay us!"

The Philistines sent for the priests and diviners, and asked, "What shall we do with the ark of the Lord? Tell us how we shall send it back to its place." And they answered, "If you send away the ark of the God of Israel, do not send it empty, but with a trespass offering of five golden images of the boils that plague you, and five golden images of the mice that ravage the land. And you shall give glory to the God of Israel. Then perhaps he will lighten his hand upon you, and upon your gods, and upon your land. Make a new cart and take two milch kine which have never been yoked, and yoke the kine to the cart. Then lay the ark upon the cart, and put the trespass offering of gold in a coffer beside it, and send it away. If it goes by way of its own border to Bethshemesh, know that he has done us this great evil; but if not, then we shall know it was not his hand that afflicted us."

The men did so. And the kine took the straight way to Bethshemesh, lowing as they went, and turned not aside to the right or to the left; and the lords of the Philistines followed them to the border.

The people of Bethshemesh were reaping their wheat in the valley. When they lifted up their eyes and saw the ark, they rejoiced. And they sent messengers to Kiriath-jearim, saying, "The Philistines have sent back the ark of the Lord. Come down for it."

So the men of Kiriath-jearim came, and took the ark to the house of Abinadab on the hill, and consecrated Eleazar his son to care for it.

Samuel came and spoke to all the house of Israel, saying, "If you return to the Lord with all your heart, and put away the strange gods, he will deliver you from the Philistines."

Then the people put away Baalim and Ashtaroth, and served the Lord only.

And Samuel judged the children of Israel in Mizpah.

The hand of the Lord was against the Philistines all the days of Samuel. The cities which they had taken from Israel were restored to Israel, from Ekron to Gath. And there was peace between Israel and the Amorites.[1]


# The Anointing of Saul

7-10  Samuel judged Israel all the days of his life. And he went from year to year in circuit to Bethel, and Gilgal, and Mizpah, and judged Israel in all those places. His return was to Ramah, for there was his home; and there he built an altar to the Lord.

When Samuel was old, he made his sons judges over Israel. The name of his firstborn was Joel, that of his second Abijah; and they were judges in Beersheba. But his sons did not walk in his ways, and turned aside after gain, and took bribes and perverted justice. The elders of Israel came to Samuel at Ramah and said to him, "Behold, you are old and your sons do not walk in your ways. Choose a king for us to judge us like all the nations."

[1] See I SAMUEL, Chapters 6-7, in Notes and Excisions.

This displeased Samuel. But he prayed to the Lord. And the Lord said to him, "They have not rejected you, but they have rejected me from reigning over them. Listen to their voice; however, forewarn them solemnly, and tell them the manner of king who shall reign over them."

Samuel told the words of the Lord to the people who had asked of him a king. And he said, "This will be the manner of king who will reign over you: he will take your sons and appoint them to his chariots, and to be his horsemen, and to run before his chariots. And he will appoint captains over thousands and captains over fifties; and set them to till his ground, and to reap his harvest, and to make his instruments of war. And he will take your daughters to be his confectioners and cooks and bakers. And he will take your fields and your vineyards and your olive groves, indeed the best of them, and give them to those who serve him. And he will take a tenth of your seed, and of your vineyards, to give to his officers. And he will take your menservants and maidservants, and your best young men, and your asses, to do his work. And you shall be his slaves. In that day, because of the king you shall have chosen, you will cry out; but the Lord will not hear you."

The people refused to listen to Samuel, and they answered, "Nevertheless, we will have a king over us, that we may be like all the nations, and that our king may judge us, and lead us in our battles."

When Samuel repeated the words of the people in the ears of the Lord, the Lord said to him, "Listen to their voice, and choose a king for them."

Now there was a man of Benjamin whose name was Kish, the son of Abiel, a mighty man of valor. And he had a son whose name was Saul, a young man and handsome, and among the children of Israel there was not a handsomer person than he. And from his shoulders and upward he was taller than any of the people.

The asses of Kish, Saul's father, were lost one day, and Kish said to his son, "Take one of the servants with you, and go seek the asses."

They passed through the hills of Ephraim and through the land of Shalisha, but found them not; then they passed through the land of Shaalim, and the animals were not there; and they passed through the land of the Benjamites, but found them not.

When they came to the land of Zuph, Saul said to his servant, "Come, let us return, lest my father cease being troubled about the asses and become anxious about us."

But the servant answered, "Behold, now, there is in this city a man of

God, and he is an honorable man; all that he says comes to pass. Let us go to him; perhaps he can tell us where we should go." Then said Saul, "But if we go, what shall we bring the man? For the bread is gone and there is no present to take to the man of God. What have we?" The servant answered, "I have here at hand the fourth part of a shekel of silver. You can give that to the man of God, to tell us where we should search."

So they went toward the city. And as they climbed up the hill, they met young maidens going out to draw water, and inquired of them, "Is the seer here?" For he that is now called a "prophet" was aforetime called a "seer."

They answered, "He is. But make haste now, for there is a sacrifice today upon the altar on the high place. Find him before he goes up. About this time you shall find him."

They went up to the city, and as they entered, behold, Samuel came toward them.

When Samuel saw Saul, the Lord said to him, "Behold, the man who shall reign over my people."

Saul drew near Samuel at the gate and said, "Tell me, I pray you, where is the seer's house?" Samuel answered, "I am the seer. Go up ahead of me to the altar, for you shall eat with me today; and tomorrow I will let you go, and will tell you all that is in your heart. As for the asses that were lost three days ago, set your mind at rest, for they have been found. In whom does all of Israel delight, if not in you?"

Saul answered, "Am I not a Benjamite, of the smallest of the tribes of Israel? And is not my family the least of all the families of the tribe of Benjamin? Why then do you speak thus to me?"

But Samuel took Saul and his servant, and brought them into the hall, and seated them at the head of all the guests, who were about thirty persons. And Saul ate with Samuel that day. When they came down from the height to the city, Samuel spoke with Saul on the housetop. And at the break of day Samuel called to Saul, "Up, that I may send you on your journey."

Saul rose, and they both went out, he and Samuel, into the street. As they were reaching the outskirts of the city, Samuel said to Saul, "Bid your servant pass on ahead of us, but you stand here, that I may reveal to you the word of God." And the servant passed on.

Then Samuel took a vial of oil and poured it upon Saul's head, and kissed him and said, "Has not the Lord anointed you to be prince over his inheritance? When you depart from me today, go to the plain of Tabor, and there you shall meet three men going up to God at Bethel, one carrying three kids, another carrying three loaves of bread, and another carrying a bottle of wine. They will salute you and give you two loaves of bread, which you shall receive from their hands. After that, you shall meet a group of prophets coming down from the altar on the height, with a lyre, a tambourine, a flute, and a harp; and they shall prophesy. Then the spirit of the Lord will come upon you, and you shall prophesy with them. When these signs come to pass, do as the occasion requires, for God is with you. And you shall go down to Gilgal. Seven days shall you wait, until I come to you and tell you what to do."

And it was so; and all those signs came to pass that day. When the group of prophets met Saul, the spirit of God came upon him and he prophesied. And those who knew Saul and saw him among the prophets said one to another, "What has come over the son of Kish? Is Saul also among the prophets?" Therefore it became a proverb: "Is Saul also among the prophets?"

And when Saul finished prophesying he returned home. Saul's uncle asked, "Where did you go?" Saul answered, "To seek the asses; and when we saw we could not find them, we went to Samuel." His uncle said, "Tell me, I pray you, what Samuel said to you." And Saul answered, "He told us clearly that the asses had been found." But about the matter of the kingdom, of which Samuel spoke, Saul told him nothing.

Samuel called the people together at Mizpah and said to them, "Thus says the Lord God of Israel, 'You have said, "Set a king over us!" Now therefore, present yourselves before the Lord by your tribes to draw lots.'"

When Samuel brought all the tribes of Israel near to draw lots, the tribe of Benjamin was chosen. When he brought the tribe of Benjamin near to draw lots by families, the family of the Matrites was chosen. And when he brought the family of Matrites near to draw lots, Saul, the son of Kish, was chosen.

But when they looked for Saul, he could not be found. Therefore they inquired of the Lord. And the Lord answered, "Behold, he has hidden himself among the baggage."

They ran and brought him from there. And when he stood among the people, he was taller than any of the others from his shoulders and upward.

Samuel said to the people, "See him whom the Lord has chosen! There is none like him among all the people!"

And the people shouted, "Long live the king!"

Then Samuel sent the people away, each man to his home.

And Saul also went home to Gibeah, and there went with him a band of men whose hearts God had touched.

But there were others who grumbled, "How can this man help us?" And they tried to shame him and brought him no present. But Saul held his peace.

## The Reproof of Saul

**11-15**  Now Nahash the Ammonite came up and besieged Jabesh-gilead.

And the men of Jabesh said to him, "Make a pact with us, and we will serve you." Nahash answered, "On this condition will I make a pact with you: that I may gouge out the right eye of every one of you, as a reproach against all Israel."

The elders of Jabesh said to him, "Give us seven days' respite that we may send messengers to all the borders of Israel. Then, if there are none to save us, we will come out to you."

The messengers went to Gibeah, the city of Saul, and told the tidings to the people; and all the people wept aloud. Saul came out of the field, following the oxen, and he asked, "What troubles the people that they weep?" And they told him the tidings brought by the men of Jabesh.

The spirit of God came upon Saul when he heard the tidings, and his anger kindled greatly. He took a yoke of oxen and hewed them in pieces, and sent them throughout the borders of Israel by messengers, saying, "Whoever fails to follow Saul and Samuel, so shall it be done to his oxen!"

The fear of the Lord fell upon the people, and they came out as one man. And when Saul numbered them in Bezek, the men of Israel were three hundred thousand, and the men of Judah thirty thousand. Then Saul said to the messengers, "Say to the men of Jabesh, 'Tomorrow, by the time the sun is hot, you shall have help!'"

On the morrow Saul divided the people into three companies; and they came into the midst of the enemy camp at the morning watch, and slew the Ammonites until the heat of the day; and those who remained were scattered, so that no two of them were left together.

The people said to Samuel, "Who are those that said, 'Shall Saul reign over us?' Bring them out that we may put them to death." But Saul answered, "No man shall be put to death this day, for today the Lord has wrought salvation in Israel."

Then said Samuel to the people, "Come, let us go to Gilgal and renew the kingdom there." So all the people went to Gilgal; and there they made Saul king before the Lord; and there they sacrificed peace offerings; and Saul and all the men of Israel rejoiced.

After Saul had reigned two years, the Philistines assembled to fight against Israel, thirty thousand chariots and six thousand horsemen, and men in numbers like the sand of the seashore. And they came up and camped at Michmash, east of Beth-aven. When the men of Israel saw that they were in peril, they hid themselves in caves and in thickets, and among rocky crags and in pits. And some went over the Jordan to the land of Gad and Gilead. As for Saul, he remained in Gilgal, and all the people followed him trembling.

Saul waited seven days, according to the time set by Samuel, but Samuel came not to Gilgal; and the people began to scatter. Then Saul said, "Bring a burnt offering here to me, and the peace offerings." And as he had finished making the burnt offering, behold, Samuel came; and Saul went out to meet him, that he might salute him.

Samuel asked, "What have you done?" And Saul answered, "Because I saw that the people were scattering, and that you came not within the time appointed, and that the Philistines had gathered at Michmash, I said, 'Now the Philistines will come down upon me, and I have not entreated the favor of the Lord.' I therefore forced myself, and offered a burnt offering." Samuel said to him, "You have done foolishly. You have not kept the commandment of the Lord, who might have established your kingdom over Israel forever. Now your kingdom shall not endure. For the Lord has found a man after his own heart to be captain over his people."

Then Samuel arose and departed from Gilgal.

Saul numbered the people who were still with him, about six hundred men. Then Saul, and Jonathan his son, and the people with them, abode in Gibeah, while the Philistines encamped at Michmash.

Now there was no smith to be found throughout the land of Israel, for the Philistines had said, "Lest the Hebrews make themselves swords or spears." And every one of the Israelites had to go down to the Philistines to sharpen his plowshare, and his colter, and his axe, and his mattock. So in the day of battle, there was neither sword nor spear to be found in the hand of any of the people who were with Saul and Jonathan, and only Saul and Jonathan his son had them.

Now it came to pass one day that Jonathan, the son of Saul, said to his armor-bearer, "Come, let us go secretly to the garrison of the Philistines. For there is no restraint on the Lord to save by many or by few." His armor-bearer answered, "Do what is in your heart. I am with you."

Then said Jonathan, "We will pass over to these men, and disclose ourselves to them. If they say to us, 'Stand still until we reach you!' then we will stand still in our place. But if they say, 'Come up to us!' then we will go up, for this shall be a sign to us that the Lord has delivered them into our hand."

They disclosed themselves to the garrison, and the Philistines said, "Behold, the Hebrews come out of the holes where they have hidden themselves." And they called to Jonathan and his armor-bearer, "Come up to us, and we will show you something."

Jonathan said to his armor-bearer, "Come up after me."

And Jonathan climbed up upon his hands and his feet, with his armor-bearer following him, and the Philistines fell before Jonathan, and his armor-bearer slew them after him. And in that first slaughter by Jonathan and his armor-bearer there were about twenty men left dead, within as it were half a furrow's length in an acre of land. And there was terror in the camp, in the field, and among all the people; and the earth quaked, so that it grew into a terror from God.

And Saul's watchmen in Gibeah looked, and behold, the enemy melted away. Then said Saul to the people who were with him, "Count now, and see who has gone from us." And when they had counted, Jonathan and his armor-bearer were not there.

Then Saul and all the people with him joined in the battle. And the men of Israel who had hidden in the hills of Ephraim, when they heard that the Philistines were fleeing, they also followed after them in the battle.

So the Lord saved Israel that day, and the battle passed beyond Bethaven.

And Saul adjured the people, saying, "Cursed be the man who eats any food until evening, and I am avenged upon my enemies." So none of the people tasted food. And when they came into the forest and saw honeycomb on the ground, no man put his hand to his mouth, for the people feared the oath.

But Jonathan had not heard his father charge the people with the oath; therefore he put out the staff in his hand and dipped its tip in a honeycomb, and put his hand to his mouth; and his eyes brightened. One of the people said, "Your father charged the people with an oath, saying,

'Cursed be the man who eats any food this day.'" Then said Jonathan, "See, I pray you, how refreshed I am since I tasted a little of this honey. If the people had eaten freely today of the spoil of their enemies, how much greater would have been the slaughter of the Philistines!"

They smote the Philistines that day from Michmash to Aijalon, though the people were faint. And Saul said, "Let us go down after the Philistines by night, and plunder them until the morning light, and let us not leave a man of them."

And Saul asked counsel of God, "Shall I go down after the Philistines?" But God answered him not. Saul said to the people, "Draw near, and let us see how this sin has arisen. For, as the Lord lives who saved Israel, though it be in Jonathan my son, he shall surely die."

But there was not a man among all the people who answered him. Then said he, "We shall draw lots. You take one side, and I and Jonathan my son will be on the other side." The people answered, "Do as seems good to you." And the lot fell on Saul and Jonathan.

Then Saul said, "Cast lots between me and Jonathan my son." And it fell on Jonathan. Saul said to him, "Tell me what you have done." Jonathan told him, "I did but taste a little honey on the end of my staff, and lo, I must die."

But the people said to Saul, "Shall Jonathan die, who has wrought this great salvation of Israel? God forbid! As the Lord lives, not one hair of his head shall fall to the ground!" So the people rescued Jonathan from death.

Then Saul pursued the Philistines no more, and the Philistines returned to their own place.

Thus Saul took the kingdom over Israel, and fought against enemies on every side: against Moab, and Ammon, and Edom, and the kings of Zobah, and the Philistines. And he did valiantly, and smote the Amalekites, and saved Israel from those who plundered them.

Then Samuel came to Saul and said, "Thus says the Lord of hosts, 'I remember what Amalek did to Israel, how he lay in wait for him when he came up from Egypt. Now go and smite Amalek; and spare them not, but slay both man and woman, infant and suckling, ox and sheep, camel and ass."

Saul summoned the people and numbered them in Telaim, two hundred thousand footmen and ten thousand men of Judah. And Saul came to the city of Amalek and lay in wait in the valley. He said to the Kenites,

"Go, depart, leave the Amalekites lest I destroy you with them, for you showed kindness to all the children of Israel when they came up out of Egypt." So the Kenites departed.

And Saul smote the Amalekites, and utterly destroyed them with the edge of the sword. But Saul and the people spared Agag, the king, and the best of the sheep, and the oxen, and the lambs, and all that was good.

Samuel came to Saul and said, "What is the meaning of this bleating of sheep in my ears, and the lowing of the oxen which I hear?" Saul answered, "They have brought them from the Amalekites, for the people spared the best of the sheep and of the oxen to sacrifice to the Lord. The rest we have utterly destroyed."

Then Samuel said, "When you were little in your own sight, were you not made the head of the tribes and anointed king over Israel? Now the Lord sent you on a journey and said, 'Go and utterly destroy the sinners the Amalekites!' Why then did you not obey the voice of the Lord?"

Saul answered, "Yes, I have obeyed the voice of the Lord, and have gone the way which the Lord sent me, and brought Agag, the king of Amalek, and have utterly destroyed the Amalekites. But the people took the sheep and oxen to sacrifice to the Lord in Gilgal." And Samuel said, "Has the Lord as great delight in burnt offerings and sacrifices as in obedience to his voice? Behold, to obey is better than to sacrifice. For rebellion is like the sin of witchcraft, and stubbornness like iniquity and idolatry. Because you have rejected the word of the Lord, he has also rejected you."

Saul said to Samuel, "I have sinned, for I have transgressed the commandment of the Lord. Pardon my sin and return with me, that I may worship the Lord." And as Samuel turned to go away, Saul laid hold of his robe, and it tore. Samuel said to him, "Even so has the Lord torn the kingdom of Israel from you this day, and given it to one better than you."

Then Saul said, "I have sinned; yet honor me now, I pray you, before the elders of my people and before Israel, and return with me, that I may worship the Lord." So Samuel turned back after Saul, and Saul worshiped the Lord.

Then said Samuel, "Bring before me Agag, the king of the Amalekites." And Agag came to him trembling and said, "Indeed bitter, how bitter is death!" Samuel said, "As your sword has made women childless, so shall your mother be childless among women." And Samuel hewed Agag in pieces before the Lord in Gilgal.

Then Samuel went to Ramah, and Saul went to his home in Gibeah. And Samuel came no more to see Saul to the day of his death. Nevertheless, Samuel mourned for Saul.

## The Secret Anointing

16 The Lord said to Samuel, "How long will you mourn for Saul, seeing I have rejected him? Fill your horn with oil, and go to Jesse the Bethlehemite. For I have provided a king for myself among his sons."

Samuel said, "If Saul hears of it, he will kill me."

And the Lord said, "Take a heifer with you, and say, 'I have come to sacrifice to the Lord.' And call Jesse to the sacrifice."

Samuel went to Bethlehem. And the elders of the town came to meet him trembling, and said, "Do you come peaceably?" He answered, "Peaceably; I have come to sacrifice to the Lord; purify yourselves and come with me."

Samuel sanctified Jesse and his sons, and called them to the sacrifice. And when they came, he looked at Eliab. But the Lord said to Samuel, "Look not on his face, nor at the height of his stature, because I have rejected him. For man looks at the outward appearance, but the Lord looks at the heart."

Then Jesse called Abinadab, and made him pass before Samuel. And he said, "Neither has the Lord chosen this one."

Then Jesse made Shammah pass before him, and Samuel said, "Neither has the Lord chosen this one."

Jesse made seven of his sons pass before Samuel; and Samuel said to Jesse, "The Lord has not chosen these. Are all your sons here?" Jesse answered, "There remains only the youngest, who tends the sheep." Samuel said, "Send and fetch him."

Jesse sent, and the boy was brought in. Now he was ruddy and handsome, and good to look upon. And the Lord said to Samuel, "Arise, anoint him; for this is he."

Then Samuel took the horn of oil and anointed him in the midst of his brothers, and the spirit of the Lord came upon David from that day forward.

And Samuel rose up and went to Ramah.[2]

[2] See I SAMUEL, Chapter 16, in Notes and Excisions.

## David and Goliath

17     Now the Philistines assembled their armies for battle at Socoh, which belonged to Judah. And Saul and the men of Israel encamped by the valley of Elah, in battle array against the Philistines. The Philistines were stationed on a mountain on the one side, and Israel was stationed on a mountain on the other side; and there was a valley between them.

And there went out from the camp of the Philistines a champion named Goliath, of Gath, whose height was six cubits and a span. He had a helmet of brass upon his head, and he was clad in a coat of mail that weighed five thousand shekels of brass. He had brass greaves upon his legs, and carried a brass spear between his shoulders. The staff of his spear was like a weaver's beam, and his spear's head weighed six hundred shekels of iron. And a shield-bearer went ahead of him.

Goliath stood and cried out to the armies of Israel, "Choose a man for yourselves, and let him come down to me. If he is able to kill me, then we will be your servants; but if I kill him, then shall you be our servants, and serve us. I defy the armies of Israel this day. Give me a man that we may fight together."

When Saul and all Israel heard those words, they were dismayed.

And Goliath drew near morning and evening, and presented his challenge for forty days.

Now the three eldest sons of Jesse, Eliab, Abinadab and Shammah, had followed Saul into battle. David was the youngest, and he went back and forth to feed his father's sheep at Bethlehem.

Jesse said to David his son, "Take this parched grain and these ten loaves to your brothers at the camp, and carry these ten cheeses to the captain of their thousand. And see how your brothers fare."

David rose early in the morning and left the sheep with a keeper, and went as Jesse had commanded him; and he came to the entrenchment as the army was going forth to fight and had raised the shout of battle. David left the food with the keeper of supplies, and ran into the army and greeted his brothers. And as he talked with them, behold, there came up the champion Goliath, and David heard his challenge. And the men fled from Goliath and were afraid.

David said to the men nearby him, "What shall be done for the man who kills this Philistine and takes away the reproach from Israel? For who is this uncircumcised Philistine, that he should defy the armies of the living God?" And the men answered, "The man who kills him, the king will enrich with great riches, and will give him his daughter, and make his father's house free in Israel. So shall be done to the man who kills him."

Eliab heard when David spoke to the men, and his anger blazed against him. He said, "Why came you here? And with whom have you left those few sheep in the desert? I know your pride, and the wickedness of your heart. For you came down that you might see the battle."

David answered, "What have I now done?" And he turned away from him toward another, and spoke in the same manner.

When the words which David spoke were repeated to Saul, he sent for him. And David said to Saul, "Let no man's heart fail because of Goliath. Your servant will go and fight with this Philistine." Saul said, "You are not able to go against him. For you are but a boy, and he a warrior from his youth."

David answered, "Your servant kept his father's sheep, and when there came a lion and took a lamb from the flock, I went out after him and struck him, and saved it from his mouth. And when he arose against me, I caught him by his beard, and struck him and slew him. Your servant slew the lion and also a bear, and this uncircumcised Philistine shall be like one of them, seeing he has defied the armies of the living God. The Lord who delivered me from the paw of the lion, and from the paw of the bear, will deliver me from the hand of this Philistine."

Saul said, "Go, and the Lord be with you."

Saul clad David in his armor and a coat of mail, and put a helmet of brass upon his head. And David girded on his sword over his armor, and tried to go. Then David said to Saul, "I cannot go with these." And David put them off.

He took his staff in his hand, and chose five smooth stones out of the brook, and put them in a shepherd's bag which he carried; and with his sling in his hand he drew near Goliath.

The Philistine came on and drew near David, and the man who bore his shield went ahead of him. When Goliath looked about and saw David, he scorned him, for he was only a youth, ruddy and handsome. And Goliath said to him, "Am I a dog, that you come to me with sticks? Come, and I will give your flesh to the birds of the air and to the beasts of the field."

Then said David to the Philistine, "You come to me with a sword and

with a spear and with a shield, but I come to you in the name of the
Lord, the God of the armies of Israel, whom you have defied. This day
the Lord will deliver you into my hand, and I will slay you and take
your head from you. And all this assembly shall know that the Lord saves
not with sword and spear. For the battle is the Lord's, and he will give
you into our hand."

As the Philistine drew near, David hastened, and ran toward him. He
put his hand into his bag, and took out a stone and slung it, and it struck
Goliath on the forehead, so that the stone sank into his forehead, and he
fell upon his face to the earth.

So David overpowered the Philistine with a sling and with a stone, and
slew him; but there was no sword in the hand of David. Therefore David
ran and stood over Goliath, and drew his sword out of its sheath and cut
off his head with it.

When the Philistines saw that their mighty man was dead, they fled.
And the men of Israel and of Judah arose and shouted, and pursued
them until they came to the valley and to the gates of Ekron.

As David returned after the slaughter of the Philistine, Abner, the captain of the army, took him and brought him before Saul with the head
of Goliath in his hand.

Saul took David that day, and would let him go no more to his father's
house. And Jonathan stripped off his robe and gave it to David, and his
sword, and his bow, and his girdle. Then Jonathan made a covenant with
David, because he loved him as his own soul.

## Saul's Distress

18-20  David went out wherever Saul sent him, and succeeded in all he
        undertook; and Saul set him over the men of war; and he was
favored by the people, and favored also by Saul's servants.

When they returned from a battle with the Philistines one day, the
women came out of all the cities of Israel, singing and dancing, to meet
King Saul with tambourines and instruments of music. And the women
sang to one another as they played: "Saul has slain his thousands, and
David his ten thousands."

Saul was angered, for this saying displeased him, and he said, "They
have ascribed to David ten thousands, and to me they have ascribed
thousands. What more can he have but the kingdom?" Saul eyed David

from that day forward. He removed David from his presence, and made him captain over only a thousand. But all Israel and Judah loved David.

Now Michal, Saul's younger daughter, loved David. They told Saul, and the thing pleased him. He said, "I will give her to him that she may be a snare to him, and that the hand of the Philistines may be against him." Therefore Saul ordered his servants, "Speak with David secretly, and say, 'The king delights in you, and wishes you to be his son-in-law.'"

Saul's servants spoke these words in David's ears. And he answered, "Does it seem to you a light thing to become a king's son-in-law, seeing that I am a poor man and of humble origin?"

When the servants told Saul, he said, "Thus shall you say to David, 'The king desires no dowry, except a hundred foreskins of the Philistines, so as to be avenged on the king's enemies.'" For Saul sought to make David fall by the hand of the Philistines.

It pleased David well to be the king's son-in-law. Therefore David arose and went, he and his men, and slew two hundred Philistines; and David brought their foreskins and gave them in full number to the king. And Saul gave him Michal his daughter as wife.

Saul saw and understood that the Lord was with David, and that Michal loved him. And Saul was even more afraid of David, and his enmity increased. He spoke to Jonathan his son, and to all his servants, that they should kill David. But Jonathan delighted in David, and he told him, "My father seeks to kill you. Now, I pray you, abide in a secret place and hide yourself until morning. And I will go out and stand beside my father in the field where you are; and what I learn, that I will tell you."

Jonathan spoke good of David to Saul his father, and said, "Let not the king sin against his servant David, because he has not sinned against you, and his works toward you have been good. For he put his life in his hand when he slew Goliath, and the Lord wrought a great salvation for all Israel. You saw it and rejoiced; why then will you sin against innocent blood, and slay David without cause?"

Saul listened to Jonathan, and swore, "As the Lord lives, he shall not be slain."

Jonathan called David, and told him all these things. And he brought David into Saul's presence as in times past.

Then there was war again; and David went out and fought with the Philistines, and slew them in a great slaughter; and they fled before him. And an evil spirit from the Lord came upon Saul as he sat in his house with his javelin in his hand, while David played before him on the lyre.

And Saul sought to pin David to the wall with the javelin. But as it went into the wall, David fled from Saul's presence, and he escaped that night.

Saul sent messengers to David's house to watch him, and to slay him in the morning. But Michal, David's wife, told him, "If you do not save yourself tonight, tomorrow you will be slain." So Michal let David down through a window, and he fled. Then she placed an image in his bed, and put a pillow of goat's hair at the head of it, and covered it with a cloth. And when Saul's messengers came to take David, she said, "He is sick."

Saul sent the messengers again, saying, "Bring him to me in the bed." But when the messengers came in, behold, there was an image in the bed, with a pillow of goat's hair at the head of it. Saul said to Michal, "Why have you deceived me so, and let my enemy escape?" And Michal answered, "Because he said to me, 'Let me go, or else I will kill you.'"

Now David fled to Samuel at Ramah, and told him all that Saul had done to him. And he and Samuel went up to dwell in Naioth. Saul sent messengers to take David there. But when they saw the company of prophets prophesying, and Samuel standing as head over them, the spirit of God came upon the messengers and they also prophesied.

## Jonathan's Loyalty

20     Then David fled from Naioth in Ramah, and came to Jonathan and said to him, "What is my sin, that your father seeks my life?" Jonathan answered, "You shall not die! My father does not do anything, either great or small, but that he reveals it to me. Why should my father hide this from me? It is not so."

And David swore, "Your father knows that I have found favor in your eyes and he says, 'Let not Jonathan know this, lest he be grieved!' But truly there is only a step between me and death."

Then Jonathan said, "David, whatever your soul desires, I will do for you." And David answered, "Tomorrow is the new moon, when I should not fail to sit at the meal with the king. But let me go, that I may hide in the field. If your father misses me, then say, 'David asked leave of me that he might run to Bethlehem his city, for it is the yearly sacrifice there for all his family.' And if he says, 'It is well,' then I shall have peace; but if he is very angry, then know that he is determined on evil. But who shall tell me if your father answers you roughly?"

Jonathan said to David, "When I have sounded my father, shall I not disclose it to you? Tomorrow is the new moon, and you will be missed because your seat will be empty. On the third day, hide yourself in the field where the stone rises. And I will shoot three arrows to the side of it, as though I shot at a mark. And behold, I will send a lad to find the arrows. If I say to the lad, 'The arrows are on *this* side of you,' take them and come, for there is peace for you and no hurt; but if I say to the boy, 'The arrows are *beyond* you; go your way,' then flee, for the Lord has sent you away."

So David hid himself in the field, and when the new moon had come the king sat down to his meal with Abner by his side, but David's place was empty. Nevertheless, Saul said nothing that day. For he thought, 'Something has befallen him.' On the second day David's place was still empty. And Saul asked Jonathan, "Why has not the son of Jesse come to the meal either yesterday or today?" And Jonathan answered, "David earnestly asked leave of me to go to Bethlehem."

Then Saul's anger kindled against Jonathan, and he said, "Do I not know that you have chosen the son of Jesse to your own shame? For as long as he remains alive, you shall not be established, nor your kingdom. Therefore bring him to me, for he shall surely die."

Jonathan answered, "Why should he be slain? What has he done?" But Saul threw a javelin at him, and Jonathan knew his father had determined to slay David. Jonathan rose from the table in fierce anger and ate no food that day, for he was grieved for David.

In the morning Jonathan went out into the field at the appointed time, and a little lad was with him. He said to the lad, "Run, find the arrows which I shoot." And as the lad ran, he shot an arrow beyond him, and when the lad came to the place of the arrow which Jonathan had shot, Jonathan cried out, "Is not the arrow beyond you?" And Jonathan cried out again after the lad, "Make haste, and stay not." Jonathan's lad gathered up the arrows and came to his master. Jonathan gave his weapons to the lad and said, "Go, carry them to the city." And as soon as he was gone, David came out of his hiding place, and they kissed one another, and they wept. And Jonathan said to David, "Go in peace! We have sworn in the name of the Lord, saying, 'The Lord be between us, and our descendants, forever!'"

David departed, and Jonathan returned to the city.

## David's Flight

**21-24** David went to Ahimelech the priest, in Nob. And Ahimelech came trembling to meet David, and asked, "Why are you alone?" David answered, "The king has sent me on a secret errand, and he said, 'Let no man know of the errand on which I send you.' And I have appointed my young men to meet at such and such a place. Give me five loaves of bread, or whatever you have at hand."

The priest answered, "I have no common bread at hand, but there is holy bread; if only your young men have kept themselves from women." David answered, "Of a truth, women have been kept from us these three days."

So the priest gave him holy bread.

And David said to Ahimelech, "Is there not here a spear or a sword? For I have brought neither my sword nor any weapons with me, because the king's business required haste."

And the priest said, "The sword of Goliath the Philistine, whom you slew in the valley of Elah, is here. If you wish to take that, take it, for there is no other here."

David said, "There is none like that; give it to me."

Now a certain servant of Saul was there that day, detained before the Lord. He was an Edomite named Doeg, and chief of the herdsmen that belonged to Saul; and he witnessed all this.

David fled in fear of Saul and went that day to Achish, the king of Gath. And the servants of Achish said to him, "Is not this David about whom they sang, 'Saul has slain his thousands, and David his ten thousands'?"

David considered these words in his heart, and was afraid of the king of Gath. He changed his behavior before them and feigned madness, and scrabbled on the doors of the gate, and let his spittle fall upon his beard.

Then said Achish to his servants, "You see the man is mad! Why then have you brought him to me? Have I need of madmen that you brought this fellow into my presence?"

David departed, and escaped to the cave Adullam. And when his brothers and all his father's house heard of it, they went there to him. And everyone who was in distress, and everyone who was in debt, and everyone who was discontented gathered round him, and he became captain over them. And there were with him about four hundred men.

Saul learned where David was, and of the men with him, and he said to the courtiers who stood about him, "Hear now, you Benjamites! Will the son of Jesse give every one of you fields and vineyards? Will he make you captains of thousands, and captains of hundreds, that all of you have conspired against me, and none disclosed to me that my son had made a league with the son of Jesse?"

Then answered Doeg the Edomite, who said, "I saw the son of Jesse coming to Nob, to Ahimelech, who gave him food, and the sword of Goliath the Philistine."

The king sent for Ahimelech the priest, and all the priests in Nob. And Saul said, "Why have you conspired against me, you and the son of Jesse, in that you have given him bread and a sword, so that he should lie in wait for me as at this time?"

Then Ahimelech answered the king, "Who among all your servants is so faithful as David, the king's son-in-law, who goes at your bidding and is honored in your house? Let not the king impute anything to his servant, who has known nothing of all this."

The king said, "You shall surely die, Ahimelech, you and all your father's house." And the king said to the footmen who stood about him, "Slay the priests, because they are with David, and because they knew that he fled and did not disclose it to me." But the men would not put out their hands against the priests of the Lord.

So the king said to Doeg, "You slay the priests!" And Doeg the Edomite turned upon them, and on that day slew fourscore and five persons who wore the linen garment of the priest.

One of Ahimelech's sons, named Abiathar, escaped and fled to David. And Abiathar told David how Saul had slain the Lord's priests. David said to him, "I knew that day in Nob, when Doeg the Edomite was there, that he would surely tell Saul. Thus I have occasioned the death of all the persons of your father's house. Abide with me, and fear not; for he who seeks my life seeks yours, but with me you shall be safeguarded."

Then word was brought to David, "Behold, the Philistines fight against Keilah, and are robbing the threshing floors." David's men said to him, "We are afraid here in Judah; how much more then if we go to Keilah against the armies of the Philistines?"

David inquired of the Lord. And the Lord answered him, "Arise, go down to Keilah, for I will deliver the Philistines into your hand." So David and his men went to Keilah and fought with the Philistines, and saved the inhabitants.

Saul was told that David had come to Keilah. Saul said, "God has given him into my hand, for he is shut in by entering a town that has gates and bars." And Saul summoned all the people to go down there to besiege David and his men.

But David and his men, who were about six hundred, departed from Keilah, and went wherever they could go. David dwelt in the strongholds of the wilderness, and remained in the hills of Ziph. Saul sought him every day.

Then the Ziphites came to Saul at Gibeah, saying, "Does not David hide himself in the strongholds of the wood, on the hill of Hachilah, which is south of Jeshimon? O King, come down; and our part shall be to deliver him into the king's hand."

Saul said, "Go, I pray you, and see where his haunt is and who has seen him there, for he is very cunning. Observe all his haunts where he hides himself, and return to me with the certainty. Then I will go with you. And if he is in the land, I will search him out among all the thousands of Judah."

But there came a messenger to Saul, saying, "Hasten and come, for the Philistines have invaded the land!"

So Saul gave up pursuing David, and went against the Philistines. And David left, and dwelt in the strongholds at Engedi.

When Saul returned from following the Philistines, he was told, "David is in the wilderness of Engedi."

So Saul took three thousand chosen men, and went to seek David among the rocks of the wild goats. He came to the sheepcotes along the way where there was a cave, and Saul went in to cover his feet.

Now David and his men were lodged inside the innermost parts of the cave. David rose, and noiselessly cut off the skirt of Saul's robe. But afterward David's heart smote him, and he said to his men, "The Lord forbid that I should do this to my master, to stretch out my hand against the Lord's anointed." David checked his men with these words, and would not let them rise against Saul.

When Saul left the cave, David also went out, and called after him, "My lord the king!"

Saul looked behind him, and David bowed with his face to the earth and said, "Why do you listen to men who say, 'David seeks your hurt'? See the skirt of your robe in my hand; I cut it off, yet did not kill you. I have not sinned against you, yet you hunt my soul to take it. The Lord judge between us and avenge me, but my hand shall not be upon you.

As says the proverb of the ancients, 'Wickedness proceeds from the wicked.' After whom does the king of Israel come? Whom do you pursue? After a dead dog? After a flea? The Lord judge between us."

When David finished speaking, Saul said, "Is this your voice, my son David?" And Saul lifted up his voice and wept. And he said, "You are more righteous than I, for you have rewarded me with good, whereas I have rewarded you with evil."

And Saul went home. But David and his men returned to the stronghold.

## David and Abigail

25-27    When Samuel died, and all the Israelites gathered together to mourn him, and buried him at Ramah, David rose and went down to the wilderness of Paran.

Now there was a man in Maon who had three thousand sheep and a thousand goats, and he was shearing his sheep in Carmel. The man was named Nabal, and his wife Abigail. She was a woman of good understanding, and beautiful, but the man was churlish and ill-mannered.

David heard in the wilderness that Nabal was shearing his sheep. And David sent for ten young men and said to them, "Go up to Carmel, to Nabal, and greet him in my name. And thus shall you say to him, 'Peace to you, and peace to your house, and peace to all that you have! I have heard that you have shearers. Now your shepherds who have been with us, we did them no hurt, nor did they miss anything all the while they were in Carmel. Therefore let the young men find favor in your eyes, for we come on a feast day. I pray you, give whatever comes to your hand to your servants, and to your son David.'"

But when David's young men spoke to Nabal according to these words, Nabal answered, "Who is David? And who is the son of Jesse? There are many servants nowadays who break away from their masters. Shall I then take my bread, and my water, and the meat which I have prepared for my shearers, and give it to men whom I know not?"

The young men returned, and they told David.

David said to his men, "Each man gird on his sword."

And each man girded on his sword, and David also; and there followed David about four hundred men, while two hundred remained with the baggage.

But one of the young men told of their coming to Abigail, Nabal's wife. Abigail made haste, and took two hundred loaves of bread and two skins of wine, and five dressed sheep, and five measures of parched grain, and a hundred clusters of raisins, and two hundred cakes of figs, and loaded them on asses. And she said to her servants, "Go on before me. I shall come after you." But she told not her husband Nabal.

As she rode on the ass and came down by the covert of the hill, behold, David and his men came toward her, and she met them.

Now David had said, "Surely in vain have I protected all that belongs to this fellow. He has returned me evil for good. So and more also may God do to the enemies of David if I leave to him by morning, of all that belongs to him, even as much as a stray dog."

When Abigail saw David, she hastened to alight from the ass, and bowed to the ground. She fell at his feet and said, "Upon me, my lord, upon me let this iniquity fall; but first hear the words of your handmaid. Let not my lord regard this wicked man Nabal. (For as his name is, so is he; Nabal is his name, and villain is its meaning.) But I, your handmaid, saw not the young men whom you sent. Therefore, my lord, let this gift which your handmaid has brought be given to the young men who follow you. And when the Lord shall deal well with you, remember your handmaid."

David said to Abigail, "Blessed be the Lord who sent you to meet me. And blessed your advice, which has kept me from avenging myself with my own hand."

So David accepted from her that which she had brought, and said, "Go in peace to your house. See, I have listened to you."

Abigail returned to Nabal, and, lo, he was holding a feast in his house, like the feast of a king; and Nabal's heart was merry within him, for he was very drunk. Therefore she told him nothing until the morning light. But in the morning, when the wine had gone out of Nabal, and his wife told him these things, his heart died within him and he became like a stone. About ten days later the Lord smote Nabal; and he died.

When David heard that Nabal was dead, he said, "Blessed be the Lord, who kept his servant from evil, and returned the wickedness of Nabal upon his own head."

And the servants of David came to Abigail at Carmel, and they said, "David sent us to you, to take you to him as his wife."

Abigail arose, and mounted upon an ass, with five of her maidens following her. And she went after the messengers of David, and became his wife.

David also took Ahinoam of Jezreel; and they were both of them his wives. Now when Saul heard of this he gave Michal his daughter, David's wife, to Paltiel, the son of Laish, who was of Gallim.

And David said in his heart, "I shall perish one day by the hand of Saul, unless I speedily escape into the land of the Philistines. Then Saul will despair of following me!"

David passed over with the six hundred men who were with him to Achish, king of Gath. And David dwelt with Achish at Gath, he and his men, each man with his household, and David with his two wives. And when Saul was told that David had fled to Gath, he sought him no more.

David said to Achish, "If I have found favor in your eyes, give me a place in some town in the country, that I may dwell there. For why should your servant dwell in the royal city with you?"

Then Achish gave him Ziklag. And David dwelt in the country of the Philistines a full year and four months.[3]

## The Witch of Endor

28    In those days the Philistines gathered their armies together to fight against Israel. And Achish said to David, "Know assuredly that you shall go out with me to battle, you and your men." David answered, "You will be shown what your servant can do." And Achish said to David, "Therefore I will make you the protector of my head forever."

Now Samuel was dead, and all Israel had lamented him and buried him in Ramah, his own city. And Saul had put away the wizards, and those who divined by spirits.

The Philistines encamped at Shunem; and Saul gathered his forces together at Gilboa. When Saul saw the army of the Philistines, his heart trembled. And Saul inquired of the Lord. But the Lord answered him not, neither by dreams, nor by prophets.

Then said Saul to his servants, "Seek out for me a woman who divines by a spirit, that I may go and inquire of her." And his servants said, "Behold, there is such a woman at Endor."

Saul disguised himself, and put on other garments, and went, he and two men with him, and they came to the woman at night. Saul said, "I

[3] See I SAMUEL, Chapters 26-27, in Notes and Excisions.

pray you, divine for me by a spirit, and bring up for me him whom I shall name." The woman answered, "You know what Saul has done, how he has cut off wizards and those who divine by a spirit. Why do you set a snare for my life?"

Saul vowed to her, "As the Lord lives, no punishment shall fall upon you for this!" Then said the woman, "Whom shall I bring up for you?" And he said, "Bring up Samuel."

When the woman saw Samuel, she cried out to Saul in a loud voice, "Why have you deceived me? For you are Saul." And the king answered, "Be not afraid. What do you see?" The woman said, "I see an old man coming up, and he is covered with a robe."

Saul perceived that it was Samuel, and he bowed to the ground. Samuel asked, "Why have you disturbed me?" And Saul answered, "I am in great distress, for the Philistines war against me, and God has turned away from me and answers me no more. Therefore I have called you, that you may make known to me what I should do."

Then said Samuel, "Why do you ask me, seeing that the Lord has turned away from you? The Lord has torn the kingdom from you and given it to David, because you did not obey the voice of the Lord, and did not execute his fierce wrath upon Amalek. Moreover the Lord will deliver Israel also with you into the hand of the Philistines. And tomorrow you and your sons shall be with me."

Saul fell his full length upon the earth, and was sorely afraid, because of the words of Samuel; and there was no strength in him, for he had not eaten all that day.

The woman came to Saul and saw that he was deeply troubled, and she said to him, "Behold, your handmaid has obeyed your voice and taken her life in her hand. Now, I pray you, listen to the voice of your handmaid, and let me set a morsel of bread before you; and eat, that you may have strength when you go on your way." He refused and said, "I will not eat."

But his servants, together with the woman, urged him; and he listened to them. So he rose from the ground and sat upon the bed. And the woman set food before Saul and before his servants, and they ate. Then they rose, and went away that night.

# Saul's Death

29-31  Now the Philistines assembled their armies at Aphek; and the Israelites pitched their camp by a fountain in Jezreel. The lords of the Philistines passed on by hundreds and by thousands, and David and his men passed on in the rear with Achish.

Then said the princes of the Philistines, "What do these Hebrews here?" Achish answered, "Is not this David, the servant of Saul, king of Israel, who has been with me for days and years? I have found no fault in him since he came to me."

But the Philistines were angry with him, and they said, "Make this fellow return to the place you appointed for him, and let him not go with us into battle lest in the battle he become our adversary. Is not this the David of whom they sang: 'Saul slew his thousands, and David his ten thousands'?"

Then Achish called David and said to him, "As the Lord lives, you have been upright. And I have found no fault in you since the day you came to me. Nevertheless, the lords do not favor you. Therefore return in peace, so that you do not displease the lords of the Philistines."

David asked, "But what have I done? And what fault have you found in your servant, that I may not fight against the enemies of my lord the king?"

Achish answered, "You are blameless in my sight. But the princes of the Philistines have said, 'He shall not go with us into battle.' Now rise early, and as soon as there is light, depart."

So David and his men rose early in the morning, to return to the land of the Philistines. And the Philistines went up to Jezreel.

Now the Philistines fought against Israel; and the men of Israel fled before them, and fell slain on Mount Gilboa. The Philistines followed hard upon Saul and upon his sons; and they slew Jonathan, and Abinadab, and Malchishua, the sons of Saul. The battle went against Saul, and the archers hit him, and he was sorely wounded by them.

Then said Saul to his armor-bearer, "Draw your sword and thrust me through with it, lest these uncircumcised ones come and thrust me through, and mock me."

But his armor-bearer would not, for he was afraid. Therefore Saul took his own sword and fell upon it. And when his armor-bearer saw that Saul was dead, he also fell upon his sword and died with him.

Thus died Saul and his three sons, and his armor-bearer and all his men, that same day together.

And when the men of Israel who were on the other side of the valley, and those who were on the other side of the Jordan, saw that the men of Israel had fled, and that Saul and his sons were dead, they forsook their cities. And the Philistines came and dwelt in them.

On the morrow, when the Philistines came to strip the slain, they found Saul and his three sons fallen on Mount Gilboa. They cut off Saul's head and stripped off his armor, and sent messengers into the land of the Philistines round about, to carry the tidings to the house of their idols and to the people. Then they put his armor in the house of Ashtaroth, and they fastened his body to the wall of Bethshan.

But when the inhabitants of Jabesh-gilead heard what the Philistines had done to Saul, all the valiant men rose and went through the night, and took the body of Saul and the bodies of his sons from the wall of Bethshan; and they came to Jabesh and burnt them there. And they took the bones, and buried them under a tree at Jabesh, and fasted seven days.[4]

[4] See I SAMUEL, Chapter 30, in Notes and Excisions.

# II SAMUEL
## King David's Reign

❡ The book of II Samuel covers the period of forty years during which King David reigned over Israel. To subsequent generations of Jews, David's reign seemed to belong to a golden age, and the character of King David without blemish. Yet the narrative in II Samuel devotes as much space to the portrayal of the weaknesses and faults of David as it does to his greatness and strength. He is shown as both rash and timid; cruel to enemies and ruthless to any who might endanger him; exhibiting favoritism to some of his wives, to some of his children, and to some of his kindred; and condoning the crime of rape within his own family by silence and inaction until it festers into murder and revolt. All this is given fully in the narrative. But the sins and shortcomings of King David are used as a painter might use shadows in portraying sunlight — to underscore the greatness of David, the sweet singer of Israel, and his devotion to his people and his God.

To his own people, in his own time, David was a national and military hero, under whose rule Israel and Judah were united, and the yoke of the oppressive enemies surrounding them was removed. David's rule lasted forty years, and each year was a year of war; but he rewarded his people with victory after victory over Philistia, Ammon, Moab, Edom and Syria. The people who fought under him, with him, and for him had as their battle hymn a cry against injustice and the corruption sanctioned under idolatry.

To the future generations of his people, in their darkest moments, David was an inspiration. His character and achievements inspired Ezra and Nehemiah when they returned from exile to rebuild the temple and the walls of Jerusalem five hundred years after David's death. And nearly three hundred years after Ezra and Nehemiah, the Maccabees drew strength from the memory of David, the wise ruler and great Psalmist — the man of abundant faith. ⟨[

## David, King of Judah

**1-2** Now after the death of Saul, when David had returned from battle with the Amalekites, he remained two days at Ziklag. And on the third day a young man came from Saul's camp, with his clothes torn and dust upon his head; and when he came near David, he fell to the earth and did obeisance.

David said to him, "From whence do you come?" And he answered, "I escaped out of the camp of Israel." David asked, "I pray you, tell me how went the battle?" And he answered, "The people fled, and many of them have fallen; and Saul and Jonathan his son are dead also."

David asked the young man, "How do you know that Saul and Jonathan his son are dead?" And the young man told him, "As I happened by chance upon Mount Gilboa, behold, Saul leaned upon his spear; and lo, the chariots and horsemen followed close upon him. When he looked behind him, he saw me and called, 'Who are you?' And I answered, 'I am an Amalekite.' He said to me again, 'I pray you, stand beside me and slay me, for anguish has come upon me but my life is still in me.' So I stood beside him and slew him, because I was sure that he could not live after he had fallen; and I took the crown that was upon his head, and the arm band that was on his arm, and brought them here to my lord."

David tore his garments, as did all the men who were with him; and they mourned and fasted until evening for Saul, and for Jonathan his son, and for the people of the Lord, because they had fallen by the sword.

Then David said to the man who had brought the tidings, "How were you not afraid to stretch out your hand to destroy the Lord's anointed? Your blood be upon your own head, for your mouth has testified against you, saying, 'I have slain the Lord's anointed.'" And he called out to one of the young men, "Go near and strike him." The young man struck him, and he died.

And David lamented with this lamentation over Saul and over Jonathan his son. (Behold, it is written in the Book of Jashar.)

"How are the mighty fallen! Tell it not in Gath, nor in the streets of Ashkelon; lest the daughters of the Philistines rejoice, lest the daughters of the enemy exult.

"O mountains of Gilboa, let there be no dew, let there be no rain upon you, for there the shield of the mighty was cast away — the shield of Saul, as though he had not been anointed.

"From the blood of the slain, from the fat of the mighty, the bow of Jonathan turned not back, and the sword of Saul returned not empty.

"Saul and Jonathan, beloved and loving, in their life and in their death they were not divided! They were swifter than eagles; they were stronger than lions.

"O daughters of Israel, weep for Saul, who clothed you in scarlet, who adorned your garments with gold. How are the mighty fallen in the midst of battle!

"O Jonathan, I am distressed for you, my brother Jonathan. Your love to me was more wonderful than the love of women.

"How are the mighty fallen, and the weapons of war perished!"

And it came to pass after this that David inquired of the Lord, "Shall I go into any of the cities of Judah?" And the Lord said to him, "Go."

So David went to Hebron, he and his two wives, Ahinoam and Abigail, and he took the men who were with him, each with his household. And they settled in the cities of Hebron. The men of Judah came, and there they anointed David king over the house of Judah.

But Abner, the son of Ner, captain of Saul's army, took Ish-bosheth, the son of Saul, and brought him over to Mahanaim; and made him king over Gilead, and over the Ashurites, and over Jezreel, and over Ephraim, and over Benjamin, and over all Israel. Ish-bosheth, Saul's son, was forty years old when he began to reign over Israel, and reigned two years. But the house of Judah followed David. And David was king in Hebron over the house of Judah seven years and six months.

Now Abner and the servants of Ish-bosheth went out from Mahanaim to Gibeon. And Joab, David's nephew, and the servants of David went out from Hebron; and they all met by the pool of Gibeon. They sat down, the one on the one side of the pool, and the other on the other side of the pool.

Abner said to Joab, "Let the young men now arise and perform before us." Joab answered, "Let them arise."

Then arose twelve Benjamites for Ish-bosheth, and twelve of the servants of David. Each one seized his adversary by the head, and thrust a sword into his side; so that they fell down together. And there was a fierce battle that day, in which Abner and the men of Israel were beaten by the servants of David.

The three sons of Zeruiah, David's sister, were there, Joab and Abishai and Asahel; and Asahel was as light of foot as a wild roe. Asahel pursued Abner. Abner looked behind him and said, "Turn aside from following me; why should I strike you to the ground? How then would I face Joab your brother?" But he refused to turn aside; therefore Abner struck him so that the spear came out behind him; and he fell there and died in that place. And all who came to the place where Asahel had fallen and died stood still.

The Benjamites gathered around Abner and became a single troop, and stood on the top of a hill.

Then Abner called to Joab, "Shall the sword devour forever? Know you not that it will be bitterness in the end? How long will it be, then, before you bid the people leave off pursuing their brothers?" Joab answered, "As God lives, unless you had spoken, the people would have pursued their brothers until morning."

So Joab blew the trumpet, and all the people stopped and pursued Israel no more, nor did they fight any more. And Abner and his men walked all that night through the plain, and passed over the Jordan, and went through Bithron to Mahanaim, where Ish-bosheth ruled over Israel.

## David, King of Israel

3-5 Now there was a long war between the house of Saul and the house of David, but David grew stronger and stronger, while the house of Saul grew weaker and weaker. And while there was war between Ish-bosheth and David, Abner's strength grew in the house of Saul.

But one day Ish-bosheth said to Abner, "Why have you gone in to Rizpah, my father's concubine?" Abner was angered at these words and said, "Am I a dog's head, that you accuse me concerning this woman?" And Ish-bosheth could not answer Abner a word, because he feared him.

Then Abner sent messengers to David on his behalf, saying, "Make a league with me, and my hand shall be with you to bring over all Israel to you."

David answered, "I will make a league with you. But one thing I require: you shall not see my face unless you bring my wife Michal when you come to see me."

And at the same time David sent messengers to Ish-bosheth, saying, "Send to me my wife Michal."

Ish-bosheth took Michal from her husband, Paltiel, the son of Laish, and sent her to David. And her husband went along weeping behind her as far as Bahurim. Then Abner commanded him, "Go, return!" And he returned.

Abner had communicated with the elders of Israel, saying, "In times past you sought for David to be king over you. Now then do it. For the Lord has said of David, 'By the hand of my servant David I will save my people Israel from all their enemies.'"

So Abner went to David at Hebron, and twenty men with him; and David made a feast for them. Abner said to David, "I will gather all Israel to my lord the king, that they may make a league with you, and that you may reign over all that your heart desires." Then David sent Abner away, and he went in peace.

When Joab and the army with him returned from pursuing a troop, and brought great spoil with them, they were told, "Abner, the son of Ner, came to the king, and he has sent him away in peace." Joab went to the king and said, "What have you done? Why is it that you have sent Abner away? You know that he came to deceive you, and to learn about your going out and your coming in and all that you do."

And when Joab left David, he secretly sent messengers after Abner, who overtook him at the well of Sirah and brought him back to Hebron. Joab took him aside at the gate to speak with him quietly, and struck him there so that he died.

Thus Joab slew Abner, because he had slain Asahel his brother in the battle at Gibeon.

When David heard of it, he said, "I and my kingdom are guiltless before the Lord for the blood of Abner, the son of Ner. Let it rest on the head of Joab, and all his father's house."

And to Joab, David said, "Put on sackcloth, and mourn for Abner." King David himself followed the bier. And when they buried Abner in Hebron, the king wept at his grave, and he lamented over Abner and said:

"Your hands were not bound, nor your feet put in fetters; as a man falls before the wicked, so did you fall."

And all the people wept again over him.

When Saul's son heard that Abner was dead in Hebron, his hands grew feeble, and all Israel was troubled.

Now Saul's son had two captains; the one named Baanah, and the other Rechab, sons of Rimon, a Benjamite. Baanah and Rechab entered

Ish-bosheth's house during the heat of the day, when he took his rest at noon. They came into his bedchamber where he lay on his bed, and slew him, and beheaded him, and took his head, and fled through the plain all night. They brought the head of Ish-bosheth to David at Hebron, and said to the king, "Behold the head of Ish-bosheth, the son of Saul your enemy!"

And David answered them, "When wicked men slay a righteous person in his own house, shall I not require his blood from them?"

Then David commanded his young men, and they slew Rechab and Baanah, and hanged them near the pool in Hebron. But they took the head of Ish-bosheth, and buried it at Hebron in the sepulcher of Abner.

Then all the tribes of Israel came to David at Hebron; and David made a league with them before the Lord, and they anointed David king over Israel.

David was thirty years old when he began to reign. He reigned in Hebron over Judah seven years and six months. And to David sons were born in Hebron: the firstborn was Amnon, of Ahinoam the Jezreelitess; the second was Chileab, of Abigail, the wife of Nabal the Carmelite; the third was Absalom, the son of Maacah, the daughter of the king of Geshur; the fourth was Adonijah, son of Haggith; the fifth was Shephatiah, the son of Abital; and the sixth was Ithream, born to Eglah, another of David's wives. All these were born before David was anointed king over Israel.[1]

## The Ark in Jerusalem

5-8    The Philistines heard that David was anointed king over Israel, and they went out to seek him. And they came up and spread themselves in the valley of Rephaim. David inquired of the Lord, "Shall I go up against the Philistines?" And the Lord said, "Go up." David went to Baal-perazim, and smote them there. But the Philistines came again, and spread themselves in the valley of Rephaim. And when David inquired of the Lord, he said, "You shall make a circuit behind them, and come upon them opposite the mulberry trees. And when you hear a rustling in the tops of the mulberry trees, bestir yourself, for then shall the Lord go out before you to smite the host of the Philistines."

David did so, and he smote the Philistines from Geba to Gezer.

[1] See II SAMUEL, Chapter 5, in Notes and Excisions.

Again David gathered together thirty thousand of the chosen men of Israel, and he went with them to Baal-judah to bring up from there the ark of God. They brought the ark out of the house of Abinadab in Gibeah and set it upon a new cart, and Uzzah and Ahio, the sons of Abinadab, drove the cart while David and the house of Israel played before the Lord on harps and lyres and all manner of instruments. And David danced before the Lord, clad in the linen robe of a priest.

So David and all the house of Israel brought up the ark with shouting, and with the sound of the trumpet. And as the ark of the Lord came into the city of David, Michal, Saul's daughter, looked out of a window and saw King David dancing and leaping; and she despised him in her heart.

They brought in the ark and set it in its place in the midst of the tabernacle that David had pitched for it, and David offered burnt offerings and peace offerings before the Lord. Then he blessed the people, and he distributed among the whole multitude of Israel, to each one a cake of bread, a portion of meat, and a flagon of wine.

And David returned to bless his household. Michal came out to meet him, and said, "How glorious was the king of Israel today, who displayed himself before the handmaids of his servants as the vain shamelessly display themselves!" David answered, "It was before the Lord that I danced, before the Lord, who chose me to rule over the people of Israel. As for the handmaids of whom you have spoken, by them shall I be held in honor."

Michal, the daughter of Saul, had no child to the day of her death. But David took more wives and concubines out of Jerusalem after he came from Hebron; and more sons and daughters were born to him there. These are the sons born to him in Jerusalem: Shammuah, Shobab, Nathan, Solomon, Ibhar, Elishua, Nepheg, Japhia, Elishama, Eliada, and Eliphalet.[2]

## The Last Pretender

9-10    David asked, "Is there anyone left of the house of Saul, that I may show him kindness for Jonathan's sake?"

Now there was a servant of the house of Saul whose name was Ziba. And when they summoned him to David, Ziba said to the king, "Jona-

[2] See II SAMUEL, Chapters 7-8, in Notes and Excisions.

than has a son left, who is lame." (Jonathan's son, whose name was Mephibosheth, was five years old when the tidings came of the death of Saul and Jonathan. His nurse took the child up; and as she made haste to flee, he fell, and became lame.)

The king said to Ziba, "Where is he?" And Ziba answered, "Behold, he is in the house of Machir, at Lo-debar."

King David brought him from the house of Machir. And Mephibosheth, the son of Jonathan, grandson of Saul, fell on his face before David. And he said, "Behold your servant!" David said to him, "Fear not, for I will surely show you kindness for the sake of Jonathan your father, and will restore to you all the land of Saul your grandfather, and you shall always eat at my table."

Then the king called Ziba and said to him, "I have given to your master's son all that belonged to Saul and to his house. You therefore, and your sons and your servants, shall till the land for him and bring in its fruit. But Mephibosheth, your master's son, shall always eat at my table."

Then said Ziba to the king, "As the king has commanded, so shall your servant do." [3]

## David and Bathsheba

11    It came to pass one eventide that David rose from his bed and walked upon the roof of the king's house, and from the roof he saw a woman washing herself; and the woman was very beautiful to look upon. David sent to inquire about the woman, and he was told, "Is not this Bathsheba, the daughter of Eliam, the wife of Uriah the Hittite?"

David sent messengers to bring her; and she came to him, and he lay with her. Then she returned to her house. And the woman conceived, and sent and told David, "I am with child."

David sent word to Joab, the commander of his armies, "Send me Uriah the Hittite." And when Uriah came to him, David asked of him how Joab did, and how the people fared, and how the war prospered. Then David said to Uriah, "Go down to your home, and wash your feet."

Uriah departed from the king's house, and a present from the king followed him. But Uriah slept at the door of the king's house with all the servants of his lord, and did not go to his home.

* See II SAMUEL, Chapter 10, in Notes and Excisions.

When David was told, David asked Uriah, "Have you not come from a journey? Why then did you not go down to your home?" And Uriah answered, "The ark, and Israel, and Judah abide in tents; and my lord Joab, and the servants of my lord, are encamped in the open field; shall I then go to the pleasures of my home?" David said to him, "Tarry here today, and tomorrow I will let you depart." So Uriah remained in Jerusalem that day. And on the morrow David called him to eat and drink in his presence, and Uriah was made drunk; and at even he went out to lie on his bed with the servants of his lord, but he did not go down to his home.

In the morning David wrote a letter to Joab, and sent it by the hand of Uriah. In the letter he wrote, "Set Uriah in the forefront of the hottest battle and retire from him, that he may be smitten and die."

Joab assigned Uriah to a place where he knew there were valiant men of the enemy. And the men came out and fought with Joab; and some of David's people fell, and Uriah the Hittite died also.

Then Joab sent word to David concerning the war, and charged the messenger, "When you have finished telling of all the matters of war to the king, and if the king's anger rises and he says to you, 'Why did you approach so near the city when you fought? Knew you not that they would shoot from the wall? Who killed Abimelech? Did not a woman throw a piece of millstone upon him from a wall, so that he died in Thebez? Why did you go near the wall?' Then say to him, 'Your servant Uriah the Hittite is dead also.'"

And the messenger came to David and told him all that Joab had sent him to tell. Then David said to him, "Thus shall you say to Joab, 'Let not this thing displease you, for the sword devours now one and now another; make your battle strong against the city and overthrow it.'"

When the wife of Uriah heard that her husband was dead, she mourned for him. And when the days of mourning were over, David brought her to his house, and she became his wife, and bore him a son.

But the thing that David had done displeased the Lord.


## Nathan's Parable

12    The Lord sent Nathan the prophet to David. And Nathan said to the king, "There were two men in a certain city, the one rich and the other poor. The rich man had many flocks and herds, but the

poor man had nothing save one little ewe lamb, which he had bought and nourished. It grew up with him and with his children; it ate of his own food and drank from his own cup; and it was to him like a child. And there came a guest to the rich man, but he would not take of his own flock and of his own herd to prepare food for the wayfarer who had come to him. He took the poor man's lamb, and prepared it for his guest."

David's anger kindled, and he said to Nathan, "As the Lord lives, the man who has done this shall surely die; and he shall restore the lamb fourfold, because he did this, and because he had no pity!"

Nathan answered, "You are that man! Thus says the Lord God of Israel, 'I anointed you king over Israel, and I delivered you from the hand of Saul, and I gave you your master's house, and the house of Israel and of Judah; and if that had been too little I would have given you much more. Why then have you despised the commandment of the Lord? You have killed Uriah the Hittite with the sword of the Ammonites, and you have taken his wife to be your wife. Therefore the sword shall never depart from your house. Behold, I will raise up evil against you out of your own house, and I will take your wives and give them to your neighbor, and he shall lie with them in the sight of the sun. You did it secretly; but this thing shall be done before all Israel, and in broad daylight!' "

David said to Nathan, "I have sinned against the Lord." And Nathan answered, "Because by this deed you have given great occasion to the enemies of the Lord to blaspheme, the child that is born to you shall die." Then Nathan departed.

And the Lord struck the child that Uriah's wife bore to David, and it became very sick. David besought God for the child; and he fasted, and lay all night upon the ground. The elders of his house went to him to raise him up; but he would not rise, neither would he eat with them.

On the seventh day the child died. And David's servants feared to tell him that the child was dead, for they said, "While the child was yet alive, we spoke to him and he would not listen to us. How then can we tell him that the child is dead?"

But when David saw that his servants were whispering, he asked, "Is the child dead?" And they answered, "He is dead."

David rose from the ground, and washed, and anointed himself, and changed his apparel; and went into the house of the Lord and worshiped. Then he went to his own house and asked for food, and when it was set before him, he ate.

His servants said to him, "You fasted and wept for the child while it was alive; but when the child was dead, you rose and ate bread." He answered, "While the child was still alive, I fasted and wept, for I said, 'Who can tell whether God will be gracious to me and let the child live?' But now that he is dead, why should I fast? Can I bring him back again? I shall go to him, but he shall not return to me."

And David comforted Bathsheba his wife, and went in to her and lay with her; and she bore a son, whom he named Solomon. And the Lord loved him.[4]

## The Rape of Tamar

13  Absalom, the son of David and Maacah, had a fair sister named Tamar; and Amnon, David's firstborn, loved her. Amnon so desired her that he fell ill because of his love for his half sister Tamar. For she was a virgin, and Amnon found it hard to harm her.

Now Amnon had a friend, a cousin named Jonadab, and Jonadab was a very cunning man. He said, "Why are you, a king's son, becoming leaner from day to day? Will you not tell me?" Amnon answered, "I love Tamar, my brother Absalom's sister." Jonadab said to him, "Lie down upon your bed as if you are ill; and when your father comes to see you, say to him, 'I pray you, let my sister Tamar come and give me food, that I may eat it from her hand.'"

So Amnon lay down as if he were ill, and when the king came to see him, Amnon said, "I pray you, let Tamar my sister come, that I may eat from her hand."

David sent for Tamar, and she went to her brother Amnon's house, where he was lying down. She took dough and kneaded it, and made cakes in his sight, and baked them. Then she set them before him, but he refused to eat. Amnon said, "Let everyone withdraw from me." And they all went out.

Then Amnon said to Tamar, "Bring the food into my chamber, that I may eat from your hand." Tamar took the cakes which she had made, and brought them into his chamber. But when she came near for him to eat them, he took hold of her and said, "Come lie with me, my sister." She answered, "No, my brother, do not force me. Do not commit this folly. And I, whither shall I carry my shame? And as for you, you will be one of the base men in Israel. I pray you, speak to the king, for he will

[4] See II SAMUEL, Chapter 12, in Notes and Excisions.

not withhold me from you." Amnon would not listen to her, but being stronger than she, forced her and lay with her.

Then Amnon hated her exceedingly, so that the hatred with which he hated her was greater than the love with which he had loved her. Amnon said to her, "Arise, begone!" And she said to him, "This wrong in sending me away is greater than the other which you did to me."

But he called for his servant and said, "Put this woman out, and bolt the door after her!" And his servant put her out and bolted the door after her.

Now she wore a garment of many colors, for such were the robes worn by the king's daughters, who were virgins. Tamar put ashes on her head, and rent her garment of many colors; and she laid her hand on her head, and went her way crying.

Absalom said to her, "Has Amnon your brother been with you? But now hold your peace, my sister." So Tamar remained desolate in her brother Absalom's house.

When King David heard of all these things, he was greatly angered. But Absalom spoke to his brother Amnon neither good nor bad.

After two full years had passed, Absalom had sheepshearers in Baal-hazor, which is near Ephraim; and he invited all the king's sons. He came to the king and said, "Behold now, your servant has sheepshearers; let the king, I beseech you, and his servants go to the sheepshearing feast with your servant."

The king answered, "No, my son, let us not all go, lest we be a burden to you." Then said Absalom, "If you cannot go, I pray you, let my brother Amnon go with us." The king asked, "Why should he go with you?" But Absalom pressed him, so that he let Amnon and all the king's sons go with him.

Now Absalom had commanded his servants, "Mark when Amnon's heart is merry with wine, and when I say to you, 'Strike Amnon!' then kill him!" And the servants of Absalom did to Amnon as Absalom had commanded. Then all the king's sons rose and fled.

While they were on the way, tidings came to David, "Absalom has slain all the king's sons, and there is not one of them left."

The king arose, and tore his garments, and lay upon the earth; and all his servants stood by with their garments torn. Then Amnon's cousin Jonadab said, "Let not my lord suppose that they have slain all the king's sons, for Amnon alone is dead. Absalom has been determined on this since the day Amnon forced his sister Tamar."

And the young man who kept watch lifted up his eyes and saw many young people coming by way of the hillside behind him.

Jonadab said to the king, "Behold, the king's sons come, as your servant said."

As he finished speaking, the king's sons came, and they lifted up their voice and wept; and the king also and all his servants wept bitterly.

But Absalom fled to his grandfather Talmai, king of Geshur. And David mourned for his son every day.

Absalom remained at Geshur three years.

And the soul of King David longed for Absalom; for he was comforted concerning Amnon, seeing that he was dead.

## The Woman of Tekoah

14 Now Joab, the son of David's sister, perceived that the king's heart longed for Absalom. So he brought from Tekoah a wise woman, and said to her, "I pray you, pretend to be a mourner, and put on mourning apparel, and be like a woman who has long mourned for the dead. Then go to the king and speak in this manner to him." And Joab put the words in her mouth.

When the woman of Tekoah spoke to the king, she fell on her face to the ground, and did obeisance and said, "Help, O King!" The king asked, "What troubles you?" And she answered, "I am a widow. And your handmaid had two sons, who fought together in the field with none to part them; and one struck the other and slew him. Now the whole family has risen against your handmaid, and they say, 'Deliver up him who slew his brother, that we may kill him!' Thus they would leave to my husband neither name nor remainder upon the earth."

The king said to the woman, "Go to your home. And whoever says ought to you, bring him to me, and he shall not touch you any more." Then said she, "Let your handmaid, I pray you, speak one word more to my lord the king." And he said, "Say on."

And the woman said, "Why then have you thought such a thing against the people of God, in that the king does not bring home again his banished one? For we must all die, and are as water spilt on the ground, which cannot be gathered up again; nor is God a respecter of persons. Yet the Lord devises means for his banished not to be expelled from him."

The king said to her, "Hide not from me, I pray you, the thing that I shall ask: Is not the hand of Joab in all this?" And the woman answered, "My lord is as wise as an angel of God."

Then the king said to Joab, "Bring the young man Absalom home again." Joab fell to the ground and thanked the king; and then he arose and went to Geshur, and brought Absalom to Jerusalem.

The king said, "Let him go to his own house, but let him not see my face." So Absalom returned home, but saw not the king's face.

Now in all Israel there was no man so praised for his beauty as Absalom; from the sole of his foot to the crown of his head there was no blemish in him. And at each year's end when he cut off his hair because it was so heavy on him, it weighed two hundred shekels in the king's weight.

Absalom dwelt two full years in Jerusalem, and saw not the king's face. Therefore Absalom summoned Joab to send him to the king, but Joab would not come to him. He sent a second time, and Joab would not come. So Absalom said to his servants, "See, Joab's field is near mine, and he has barley there; go, set it on fire." And Absalom's servants set the field on fire.

Then Joab went to Absalom's house and asked him, "Why have your servants set my field on fire?" Absalom answered, "I sent for you, saying, 'Come, that I may send you to the king to ask, Why have I returned from Geshur? It would have been better for me to have remained there.' Now let me see the king's face; and if there is iniquity in me, let him kill me."

Joab went to the king and told him. And when David called for Absalom, he came and bowed to the ground before him; and the king kissed Absalom.

## Absalom's Revolt

15-18   After this, Absalom arranged for chariots and horses, and fifty men to run before him. And he would rise early and stand beside the gate, and when any man had a controversy which should come to the king for judgment, Absalom called to him and said, "It is clear that your cause is right, but there is no man deputed of the king to hear you." And he would add, "O that I were judge in the land, so that any man who had a suit or cause might come to me, and I would give him justice!"

And when a man came near to do obeisance to him, he would put out his hand and embrace him. In this manner Absalom stole the hearts of the men of Israel.

After four years Absalom said to the king, "I pray you, let me go and pay my vow to the Lord in Hebron. For your servant made a vow while at Geshur."

The king answered, "Go in peace."

So Absalom arose and went to Hebron. But he sent spies throughout the tribes of Israel, saying, "As soon as you hear the sound of the trumpet, you shall say, 'Absalom reigns in Hebron!'" And Absalom took with him two hundred men from Jerusalem, who went in innocence and knew nothing.

Absalom sent for Ahithophel the Gilonite, David's counselor. And the conspiracy was strong, for the people with Absalom continually increased.

A messenger came to David, saying, "The hearts of the men of Israel turn to Absalom." And David said to all his servants who were with him in Jerusalem, "Let us flee! Else none of us shall escape from Absalom. Make speed to depart, lest he overtake us and smite the city with the sword."

The king went forth, and all his household after him. And he left behind ten concubines to care for the palace. All the people wept as they crossed over the brook Kidron, toward the way of the wilderness. And the king, and the people following him, tarried in a place far off.

Then lo, Zadok came, and the Levites with him, bearing the ark of God. The king said to Zadok, "Carry back the ark of God into the city. If I find favor in the eyes of the Lord, he will bring me back and show me both it and his habitation. But if he says: 'I have no delight in you,' behold, here I am; let him do to me as seems good to him." The king said also to Zadok the priest, "Return to the city in peace, and your two sons with you, Ahimaaz your son, and Jonathan, the son of Abiathar. See, I will tarry in the plain until word comes from you."

Therefore Zadok and Abiathar carried the ark of God back to Jerusalem, and they waited there.

David went up the Mount of Olives, and wept as he went; and he had his head covered, and walked barefoot. And all the people with him, each covered his head, and they went up weeping.

David was told, "Ahithophel is among the conspirators with Absalom."

And David said, "O Lord, I pray you, turn the counsel of Ahithophel into foolishness."

When David came to the top of the ascent, behold, Hushai the Archite came to meet him with his coat rent, and earth upon his head. David said, "If you pass on with me, you will be a burden to me. But if you return to the city and say to Absalom, 'I will be your servant, O King, as I have been your father's servant in time past,' then you may defeat the counsel of Ahithophel. Have you not there with you Zadok and Abiathar the priests? And whatever you hear in the king's house, you shall tell to Zadok and Abiathar. They have with them Ahimaaz, Zadok's son, and Jonathan, Abiathar's son; and by them you shall send me word of everything that you hear."

So Hushai, David's friend, came into the city as Absalom entered Jerusalem.

When David was a little past the top of the hill, Ziba, the servant of Mephibosheth, met him, with a couple of asses saddled, and upon them two hundred loaves of bread and a hundred clusters of raisins, and summer fruit, and a bottle of wine. And Ziba said to the king, "The asses are for the king's household to ride on; the bread and summer fruit for the young men to eat; and the wine for such as may be faint to drink."

The king asked, "Where is your master's son?" And Ziba answered, "He abides at Jerusalem, for he said, 'Today the house of Israel will restore to me the kingdom of my father.'"

When King David reached Bahurim, there came out a man of the family of the house of Saul named Shimei; and he came out cursing. He cast stones at David and at the servants of the king, and thus he cursed, "You man of blood! You man of wickedness! The Lord has returned upon you all the blood of the house of Saul, in whose stead you have reigned. And the Lord has delivered the kingdom into the hand of Absalom your son."

Then said Abishai, the son of Zeruiah, to David, "Why should this dead dog curse my lord the king? Let me go, I pray you, and take off his head." The king answered, "Let him curse. Behold, my son seeks my life; how much more now may this Benjamite do so? Let him curse, for the Lord has bidden him. It may be that the Lord will requite me good for his cursing this day."

And David and his men went on their way, while Shimei went along on the hillside opposite, and cursed as he went, and threw stones and cast dust.

Now Absalom and the men of Israel came to Jerusalem, and Ahithophel with him. When Hushai, David's friend, came to Absalom, he said, "Long live the king! Long live the king!" Absalom asked Hushai, "Is this your kindness to your friend? Why did you not go with him?" And Hushai answered, "Whom the Lord and the people choose, his will I be and with him will I abide. As I served in your father's presence, so will I in your presence."

Then said Absalom to Ahithophel, "Give your counsel as to what we shall do." Ahithophel answered, "Let me choose twelve thousand men, and I will pursue David this night. I will come upon him while he is weary and weak-handed, and make him afraid; and all the people who are with him shall flee. I will strike the king only, and I will bring all the people back to you. And all the people will be at peace." The saying pleased Absalom and the elders of Israel.

Then said Absalom, "Call Hushai the Archite also, and let us hear what he says." And Hushai said to Absalom, "The counsel Ahithophel has given at this time is not good. You know your father and his men are mighty, and are embittered, like a bear robbed of her whelps in the field; and your father is a man of war; he will not lodge among the people. He is hidden in a pit, or in some other place. And when some of the people are slain at first, whoever hears of it will say, 'There has been slaughter among those who follow Absalom.' Then even he who is valiant, whose heart is like the heart of a lion, will melt; for all Israel knows that your father is a mighty man and that those with him are valiant. Therefore I counsel that all Israel be gathered round you, from Dan to Beersheba, and that you go to battle in your own person. So shall we come upon him, and we will light upon him as the dew falls on the ground; and of him and of all the men with him there shall not be left so much as one."

Absalom and the men of Israel said, "The counsel of Hushai the Archite is better than the counsel of Ahithophel." And when Ahithophel saw that his counsel was not to be followed, he saddled his ass and went to his home, and put his household in order, and hanged himself.

Hushai sent word to the king, "Do not lodge this night in the plains, but pass over, lest the king be swallowed up and all the people who are with him."

David rose and all the people with him, and they passed over the Jordan. By the morning light there was not one of them who had not gone over. And David went on to Mahanaim.

David mustered the people with him, and set captains of thousands and captains of hundreds over them. And he sent out a third of the men under Joab, and a third under Abishai, and a third under Ittai the Gittite. Then the king said, "I will go out with you also."

But they answered, "You shall not go out, for if we flee they will not care about us; not even if half of us die will they care about us. But you are worth ten thousand of us. Therefore it is better that you help us from the city." The king said to them, "What seems best to you I will do."

And the king stood by the gate side while the people came out by hundreds and by thousands.

The king commanded Joab and Abishai and Ittai, "Deal gently for my sake with the young man, with Absalom." And all the people heard when the king charged the captains concerning Absalom.

So the men went out into the field against Israel, and the battle was in the forest of Ephraim. The men of Israel were slain by the servants of David, and there was a great slaughter that day of twenty thousand men.

Absalom chanced to meet the servants of David as he rode upon his mule, and the mule went under the thick boughs of a great oak, and Absalom's heavy hair caught in the oak, and he was left hanging between heaven and earth while the mule that was under him went away. A certain man saw this and told Joab, "Behold, I saw Absalom hanging in an oak." Joab said to the man, "Why did you not strike him there to the ground? I would have given you ten shekels of silver and a girdle."

The man answered, "Though I should receive a thousand shekels of silver, I would not put out my hand against the king's son, for in our hearing the king charged you and Abishai and Ittai, saying 'Beware that none touch the young man Absalom.'"

Then said Joab, "I cannot tarry thus with you." And he took three darts in his hand, and thrust them through the heart of Absalom while he was still alive in the oak. The ten young men who bore Joab's armor surrounded Absalom, and slew him.

Joab blew the trumpet, and the people returned from pursuing Israel. They cast Absalom into a great pit in the forest, and raised over him a great heap of stones; and all Israel fled, each one to his own home.

Then said Ahimaaz, the son of Zadok, "Let me bear the tidings to the king, how the Lord has avenged him of his enemies." Joab answered, "You shall not bear tidings this day, because the king's son is dead."

And Joab said to the Cushite, "Go, tell the king what you have seen." The Cushite bowed to Joab, and ran.

Now David was sitting between the two gates; and the watchman went up to the roof over the gate by the wall. And when he lifted up his eyes and looked, he saw a man running alone. The watchman cried out and told the king. And the king said, "If he is alone, there are tidings in his mouth." Then the watchman saw another man running and he called to the porter, "Behold, another man running alone!" And the king said, "He also brings tidings." The watchman said, "I think the running of the first man is like the running of Ahimaaz, the son of Zadok." And the king answered, "He is a good man and comes with good tidings."

Ahimaaz called to the king, "All is well!" And he bowed with his face to the earth and said, "Blessed be the Lord your God, who has delivered up the men who lifted their hand against my lord the king!" The king asked, "Is the young man Absalom safe?" And Ahimaaz answered, "When Joab sent your servant, I saw a great tumult, but I know not what it was." The king said to him, "Turn aside, and stand here." Ahimaaz turned aside and stood still.

Then the Cushite came, and he said, "Tidings, my lord the king! The Lord has avenged you this day upon all those who rose against you." And the king asked him, "Is the young man Absalom safe?" The Cushite answered, "The enemies of my lord the king, and all those who rise to harm you, be as that young man is."

The king went up to his chamber over the gate, and wept; and as he went, he said, "O my son Absalom, my son Absalom! Would I had died for you, O Absalom, my son, my son!"

## The King Returns

19-21   Joab was told, "Behold, the king weeps and mourns for Absalom."

The victory of the day was turned into mourning for all the people when they heard how the king grieved for his son. And the people entered by stealth into the city, like people who are ashamed when they flee in battle.

Joab came into the house of the king and said, "You have shamed the faces of all your servants, who on this day have saved your life, and the lives of your sons and daughters, and the lives of your wives and your concubines, in that you love your enemies and hate your friends. You have declared that you regard neither princes nor servants, for if on this day Absalom had lived and all of us had died, that would have pleased

you well. Now therefore arise, go out and speak comfortingly to your servants. I swear by the Lord that if you do not go out to them, not one will
tarry with you this night. And that will be worse for you than any of the
evils that have befallen you from your youth until now."

The king arose, and took his seat in the gate. The people were told,
"Behold, the king sits in the gate." And all the people came before him.

The men of Judah, as one man, sent word to the king, saying, "Return
to us in Judah, you and all your servants."

So the king returned, and reached the Jordan. And the people of Judah
came to Gilgal to meet him, and to conduct the king over the Jordan.[5]

## David's Song

22    On the day that the Lord delivered David from his enemies, and
from Saul, he spoke to the Lord the words of this song:

"The Lord is my rock and my fortress and my deliverer; in him will
I trust! He is my shield and the horn of my salvation, my lofty tower and
my refuge, my savior, who saves me from violence.

"When the waves of death encompassed me, and the floods of ungodly
men made me afraid; when the sorrows of hell surrounded me, and I was
bound in the snares of death; in my distress I called upon the Lord, and
cried out to my God. And he heard my voice; my plea came to his ears.

"Then the earth shook and trembled; the foundations of the heavens
moved; darkness was under his feet. He rode upon the wings of the
wind! And the channels of the sea appeared, the foundations of the world
were uncovered at the rebuke of the Lord, at the blast of his nostrils.

"He drew me out of many waters; he delivered me from my strong enemy and from those who hated me. The Lord rewarded me according to
my righteousness, according to the cleanness of my hands.

"To the merciful you show mercy, with the upright you are upright, with
the pure you show yourself pure, and to the corrupt you show your op-
position. You save the afflicted, but your eyes are upon the haughty that
you may humble them.

"You are my lamp, O Lord; and the Lord lightens my darkness. And
who is God, save the Lord? And who is a rock, save our God? God is my
strength and power, and he makes my way perfect. Your gentleness has

[5] See II SAMUEL, Chapters 19-21, in Notes and Excisions.

made me great. You have girded me with strength to battle; those who rose up against me you have subdued.

"I will give thanks to you, O Lord; I will sing praise to your name!"

## David's Last Words

**23-24** Now these are the last words of David, son of Jesse, the sweet psalmist of Israel:

"The spirit of the Lord spoke to me and his word was upon my tongue. The God of Israel said, 'He who rules over men must be just, ruling in the fear of God. And he shall be like the light of the morning when the sun rises, like a morning without a cloud, like the tender grass springing out of the earth, clear shining after rain.

"'But the sons of wickedness shall be like thorns thrust away, because they cannot be taken with the hands, but the man who touches them must be armed with iron and the staff of a spear; and they shall be burned in their place.'" [6]

* See II SAMUEL, Chapters 23-24, in Notes and Excisions.

# I KINGS, 1-11
## Solomon's Rule

❰ The first half of I Kings records the rule of King David's son Solomon, tenth in line of succession, who was proclaimed king of Israel. The kingdom David had established by the sword, his son attempted to secure and enrich through diplomacy and trade. King Solomon sought the friendship of his neighbors throughout his reign, and established pacts with many kings. Often he cemented the pact, after the custom of his times, by marrying the daughter of his new ally, and in some instances also taking the favorite maid of the princess as his concubine. So numerous were his pacts that his court of women numbered a thousand wives and concubines. Yet the offspring of King Solomon are mentioned as only one son and two daughters, borne by his favorite wife.

In addition to his policy of friendship pacts, King Solomon established a navy for trade with distant lands, and imported peacocks, monkeys, gold and ivory from, it is conjectured, South Africa or far-off India. Even his great stables of horses, which became renowned through neighboring kingdoms, were used as an important source of income from the nations who recognized the value of chariots in warfare.

During the major part of his reign, Solomon also engaged in an elaborate building program, and established the house of the Lord, the palace of the king, and the cities of the kingdom.

In the minds of his people Solomon became a synonym for splendor and wisdom. Yet the Solomon story, as given in I Kings, is startlingly brief. Nearly half of the eleven chapters on his reign dwell on David's old age, and contain lists of chiefs and princes and detailed descriptions of the temple and the royal palace, while only about a dozen pages give the chronicle of this monarch. Solomon's marital reputation is based on the brief statement that he "loved many strange women" and that he had "seven hundred wives, princesses, and three hundred concubines: and his wives turned away his heart." His reputation for wisdom (other than his choice of wisdom when God offers him a choice of gifts, and the example of his wise judgment between two mothers) rests upon the books attributed to him: The Proverbs, The Song of Songs, and, in the Apocrypha, The Wisdom of Solomon. ⟨[

# The Death of David

*1-2*    Now King David was old and stricken in years; and although they covered him with clothes, he still remained cold. Therefore his servants said to him, "Let a young maiden be sought for our lord the king, and let her wait upon him, and let her lie in his bosom, that our lord the king may be warm."

So they sought for a fair maiden throughout Israel, and found Abishag, a Shunammite, and brought her to the king. The maiden was very fair, and ministered to him; but the king knew her not.

Now Adonijah, David's fourth son, exalted himself, saying, "I will be king." And he arranged for chariots and horsemen, and fifty men to run before him. His father had not restrained him at any time, saying, "Why have you done so?" And also he was a very handsome man, and he was next in succession to Absalom.

Adonijah conferred with Joab, his cousin, and with Abiathar the priest; and they became his followers and helped him. But Zadok the priest, and Benaiah, the son of Jehoiada, and Nathan the prophet, and Shimei, and Rei, and David's mighty men were not with Adonijah.

Adonijah sacrificed sheep and oxen and fatlings by the stone of Zoheleth, which is beside En-rogel; and he invited all his brothers, the king's sons, and all the men of Judah who were the king's servants. But Nathan the prophet, and Benaiah, and the mighty men, and Solomon his brother, he did not call.

Nathan spoke to Bathsheba, the mother of Solomon, saying, "Have you not heard that Adonijah proclaims himself king, and David our lord knows it not? I pray you, let me give you counsel, that you may save your own life and the life of your son. Go to King David and say to him, 'Did you not, my lord, swear to me, "Assuredly Solomon your son shall reign after me?" Why then does Adonijah reign?' And while you still talk with the king, I will come in and confirm your words."

Bathsheba went to the king in his chamber, where Abishag ministered to the king, and bowed to him and said, "My lord, you swore by the Lord your God, saying, 'Assuredly Solomon your son shall reign after me, and he shall sit upon my throne.' And now, behold, Adonijah reigns. O King, the eyes of all Israel are upon you, to tell them who shall sit upon your throne after you!"

And while she still talked with David, Nathan the prophet came in. He bowed to the king, and said, "My lord, O King, have you said, 'Adonijah shall reign after me, and he shall sit upon my throne'? For he has gone down this day, and has slain oxen and sheep and fatlings in abundance, and has invited all the king's sons, and the captains of the army, and Abiathar the priest; and behold, they eat and drink before him and say, 'Long live King Adonijah!' But me, your servant, and Zadok the priest, and Benaiah, and your servant Solomon, he has not called."

Then King David answered, "By the Lord who has redeemed my soul, assuredly Solomon shall reign after me!"

Bathsheba did reverence to the king and said, "May my lord live forever!"

And King David said, "Call Zadok the priest, and Nathan the prophet, and Benaiah, the son of Jehoiada." And when they came before him, the king said to them, "Take with you the servants of your lord, and have Solomon my son ride upon my own mule, and bring him to Gihon; and let Zadok the priest and Nathan the prophet anoint him there king over Israel. And blow the trumpet, and say, 'Long live King Solomon!' For he shall be king in my stead, and I have appointed him ruler over Israel and Judah."

So Zadok and Nathan and Benaiah went down, and had Solomon ride upon King David's mule, and brought him to Gihon. Zadok the priest took a horn of oil out of the tabernacle and anointed Solomon. And they blew the trumpet, and all the people said, "Long live King Solomon!" And the people went up after him, playing on pipes and rejoicing.

Adonijah and all the guests who were with him heard of this as they finished feasting. And Jonathan, the son of Abiathar the priest, said to Adonijah, "Our lord King David has made Solomon king." Then all the guests were afraid, and rose up, and each man went his way.

Adonijah feared because of Solomon; and he rose, and went, and caught hold of the horns of the altar. Solomon was told, "Behold, Adonijah fears King Solomon; for lo, he has caught hold of the horns of the altar, saying, 'Let King Solomon swear to me first that he will not slay his servant with the sword.'"

Solomon said, "If he shows himself a worthy man, not a hair of his head shall fall to the earth; but if wickedness is found in him, he shall die."

So they brought Adonijah down from the altar. He came and bowed to King Solomon, and Solomon said to him, "Go to your home!"

Now the days of David drew near their end, and he charged Solomon his son, "I go the way of all flesh; be strong and show yourself a man, and walk in the way of the Lord your God. Keep his statutes, and his commandments, and his ordinances, and his testimonies, as it is written in the law of Moses, that you may prosper in all that you do. Moreover, you know also what Joab, the son of Zeruiah my sister, did to me, and to the two captains of the hosts of Israel, Abner, the son of Ner, and Amasa, the son of Jether, whom he slew, and shed the blood of war in times of peace. Therefore do not let him go down to the grave in peace. But show kindness to the sons of Barzillai the Gileadite, and let them be of those who eat at your table. For they came to me when I fled because of Absalom your brother."

Then David slept with his fathers, and was buried in the city of David. And the time that David reigned over Israel was forty years: seven years he reigned in Hebron, and thirty and three years he reigned in Jerusalem.


## The Reign of Bathsheba's Son

2-3    Solomon sat upon the throne of David his father, and his kingdom was firmly established.

Then Adonijah came to Bathsheba, the mother of Solomon, and said, "You know that the kingdom was mine, and that all Israel expected me to reign. But the kingdom has turned about and become my brother's, for it was his from the Lord. Now that I ask one favor of you, deny me not." She answered, "Say on." And Adonijah said, "I pray you speak to Solomon the king, for he will not say 'No' to you, that he give me Abishag the Shunammite as my wife." Bathsheba said, "I will speak for you to the king."

Bathsheba therefore went to Solomon. And he rose up to meet her, and bowed to her, and had a seat placed for her at his right side. Then she said, "I wish to make one small request; deny me not. Let Abishag the

Shunammite be given to Adonijah as his wife." King Solomon answered, "Why do you ask Abishag the Shunammite for Adonijah? It is as if you asked for him the kingdom also, since he is my elder brother." Then King Solomon swore by the Lord, saying, "God do so to me, and more also, if Adonijah has not spoken this word at the cost of his life. As the Lord lives who has set me on the throne of David my father, Adonijah shall be put to death this day."

And King Solomon sent Benaiah, the son of Jehoiada, who struck Adonijah so that he died.

And to Abiathar the priest, Adonijah's follower, the king said, "Go to Anathoth, to your own fields, for you deserve death. But I will not put you to death, because you bore the ark of the Lord before David my father, and because you shared in my father's afflictions."

When the tidings came to Joab — for Joab had turned to follow Adonijah, though he had not followed Absalom — he fled to the tabernacle of the Lord and caught hold of the horns of the altar.

Solomon sent Benaiah, saying, "Go, strike him down and bury him, that you may avenge me and my father for the innocent blood which Joab shed."

So Benaiah slew Joab, and he was buried in his own house in the wilderness.

The king sent for Shimei and said to him, "Build yourself a house in Jerusalem and dwell there, and do not go out from there to any other place. For on the day you go out and pass over the brook Kidron, know for a certainty that you shall die, and your blood will be upon your own head." Shimei answered, "As my lord the king has said, so will your servant do."

But at the end of three years, two of Shimei's slaves ran away to Gath. Shimei saddled his ass, and went to Gath to seek them, and brought his slaves back.

Solomon was told that Shimei had gone from Jerusalem to Gath, and had returned. And the king sent for Shimei and said to him, "Did I not make you swear by the Lord, and forewarn you that on the day you went abroad anywhere you would surely die?"

Then the king commanded Benaiah, who went out and struck Shimei so that he died. And the kingdom was established in the hand of Solomon.

Solomon became allied with Pharaoh, king of Egypt, and took Pharaoh's daughter, and brought her into the city of David until he had finished building his own house and the house of the Lord and the wall of Jerusalem round about. The people still sacrificed at the altars on the high places, because no house had been built for the Lord in those days. And Solomon loved the Lord, walking in the statutes of David his father. And the king went to Gibeon to sacrifice there, for that was the great high place; and a thousand burnt offerings did Solomon offer upon that altar.

## Solomon's Wisdom

3-4    In Gibeon the Lord appeared to Solomon in a dream and said, "Ask; what shall I give you?" Solomon answered, "O Lord my God, you have made your servant king in the place of David my father, and I am like a little child who knows not how to go out or come in. Your servant is in the midst of your people, a great people, whom you have chosen. Therefore give your servant an understanding heart to judge your people, that I may discern between good and evil."

The request pleased the Lord, and he said, "Because you have not asked for yourself a long life, or riches, or the life of your enemies, but have asked for understanding to discern justice, lo, I give you a wise and understanding heart, so that there has not been one like you before, nor shall your like arise after you. And I give you also that which you have not asked, both riches and honor, so that there shall not be any among the kings to compare with you, all your days. And if you will walk in my ways and keep my commandments, as your father David did, then I will lengthen your days."

Solomon awoke; and behold, it was a dream.

Then there came to the king two women, who stood before him. One woman said, "O my lord, I and this woman dwell in the same house; and I gave birth to a child. And on the third day after I was delivered, this woman also gave birth to a child. And we were together, and there was no one else in the house save we two. Then this woman's child died in the night, because she lay on it. And she arose at midnight, and took my son while your handmaid slept, and laid her dead child beside me. When I rose in the morning to nurse my child, behold, it was dead; but when I looked at it in the morning light, behold, it was not the son I had borne." The other woman said to the king, "No, the living child is my son and the dead one is hers." And the first woman answered, "No, the dead child is her son and the living one is mine."

The king said, "Bring me a sword." And when a sword was brought to him, he said, "Divide the living child in two, and give half to the one, and half to the other." Then spoke the woman to whom the living child belonged, because her heart yearned for her son, "O my lord, give her the living child, but do not slay it." The other said, "Let it be neither mine nor yours, but divide it." And the king answered, "Give the living child to the first woman, and do not slay it, for she is the mother."

All Israel heard of the king's judgment, and they saw that the wisdom of God was in him. So King Solomon was king over all Israel. And he reigned over all the kingdoms from the river to the land of the Philistines and to the border of Egypt; they brought gifts and served Solomon all the days of his life.

And Solomon had forty thousand stalls of horses for his chariots, and twelve thousand horsemen. And officers provided provisions for King Solomon, and for all who came to the King's table, each one in his month; they permitted nothing to be lacking.

Solomon's wisdom excelled the wisdom of all the people of the east country, and the wisdom of Egypt. And his fame was known in all nations round about. He uttered three thousand proverbs, and his songs were a thousand and five. He spoke of trees, from the cedar that grows in Lebanon to the hyssop that springs out of the wall; he spoke also of beasts and of birds, and of creeping things and of fishes. And there came men from all peoples to hear the wisdom of Solomon, and from all the kings of the earth, who had heard of his wisdom.

And Judah and Israel dwelt safely, each man under his vine and under his fig tree, from Dan to Beersheba, all the days of Solomon.[1]

## Solomon's Buildings

5-8    Now Hiram, king of Tyre, sent his servants to Solomon when he heard that they had anointed him king in the place of his father, for Hiram had always loved David. And Solomon sent word to Hiram, "You know that David my father could not build a house for the name of the Lord because of the wars about him on every side. But the Lord my God has given me peace. And I purpose to build a house for the

[1] See I KINGS, Chapter 4, in Notes and Excisions.

name of the Lord my God. Therefore command that they hew for me cedars of Lebanon; and my servants shall be with yours, for you know there are not among us any who have the skill of hewing timber like the Sidonians."

When Hiram heard the words of Solomon, he rejoiced greatly. And he sent word to him, "I will do all you desire concerning timber of cedar and timber of cypress. My servants shall bring it down from Lebanon to the sea, and I will convey it by sea in floats to the place that you will appoint."

So Hiram gave Solomon cedar and cypress. And Solomon gave Hiram twenty thousand measures of wheat for his household, and twenty measures of pure oil. Thus Solomon gave to Hiram year by year. And there was peace between Hiram and Solomon, and they made an alliance together.

King Solomon raised a levy out of Israel of thirty thousand men. And he sent them to Lebanon, ten thousand a month in relays. They would be in Lebanon one month, and two months at home. And Solomon had seventy thousand who carried burdens, and eighty thousand hewers in the mountains, besides the three thousand and three hundred chief officers who had charge of the people carrying on the work. At the king's command they brought great stones, costly stones, to lay the foundation of the house. And Solomon's builders and Hiram's builders prepared the timber, and the stonesetters prepared the stones.

In the fourth year of Solomon's reign over Israel, in the month of Ziv, which is the second month, he began to build the house of the Lord. In that year the foundation was laid; and in the eleventh year of Solomon's reign, the house of the Lord was finished throughout. Thus Solomon was seven years in building it.

And the house of the Lord was built of stone made ready at the quarry, so that there was neither hammer nor axe nor any tool of iron heard in the house while it was being built.

The walls of the house he built with boards of cedar, and he covered the floor with planks of cypress. And the cedar was carved with gourds and open flowers.

Within the house he prepared a sanctuary for the ark of the Lord which was twenty cubits in length, twenty cubits in width, and twenty cubits in height, overlaid with pure gold. And there he set an altar which was made of cedar.

And for the sanctuary Solomon made two cherubim of olivewood, each ten cubits high. The wing of each was five cubits, and from the tip of one wing to the tip of the other wing was ten cubits. And both cherubim were of the same measure and form. He set them within the sanctuary; and the wings of the cherubim were outstretched, so that the wing of one touched the one wall, and the wing of the other touched the other wall, and their wings touched one another in the center of the sanctuary. And he overlaid the cherubim with gold.

For the entrance of the sanctuary Solomon made doors of olivewood. And he built the inner court with three rows of hewn stone, and a row of cedar beams.

And he carved all the walls of the house round about with figures of cherubim and palm trees and open flowers, within and without.

Solomon also built his own house, the house of the forest of Lebanon, which was a hundred cubits in length and fifty cubits in width and thirty cubits in height. It was covered with cedar, and the chambers lay on forty-five pillars, fifteen in a row. He made a hall of pillars, which was fifty cubits in length and thirty cubits in width. And he made a hall of the throne where he might judge, and it was finished with cedar from floor to floor. His house where he might dwell, in the other court, was of like workmanship; and he made also a house for Pharaoh's daughter, whom he had taken as his wife.

The foundation was of costly stones, great stones, stones of ten cubits and stones of eight cubits. And the great court round about had three rows of hewn stone, and a row of cedar beams, like the inner court of the house of the Lord. And Solomon was in the building of his own house thirteen years.

Then King Solomon sent and fetched Hiram out of Tyre. Hiram was a widow's son of the tribe of Naphtali, and his father was a man of Tyre, a worker in brass. Hiram was filled with wisdom and understanding, and was skilled in all works in brass. He came to King Solomon, and brought all the vessels for the house of the Lord.

Then Solomon assembled the elders of Israel, and the heads of the tribes, and the princes of Israel, that they might bring up the ark of the covenant out of the city of David, which is Zion.

And the priests brought in the ark of the Lord to its place, into the sanctuary, to the most holy place, under the wings of the cherubim. For the cherubim spread their wings over the place of the ark and covered it and its staves, so that the ends of the staves were seen from within the holy place but were not seen from without.

There was nothing in the ark save the two tablets of stone which Moses put in there at Horeb, where the Lord made a covenant with the children of Israel when they came out of the land of Egypt.

And when the priests came out of the holy place, a cloud filled the house of the Lord, so that the priests could not minister because of the cloud; for the glory of the Lord had filled the house of the Lord.

Then spoke Solomon, "O Lord, I have built you a house to dwell in, a settled place for you to abide in forever!" And the king turned about, and blessed all the congregation of Israel.[2]

## Solomon's Cities and Navy

9   At the end of twenty years, when Solomon had completed the house of the Lord, and the house of the forest of Lebanon, he gave to Hiram, king of Tyre, twenty cities in the land of Galilee. For Hiram had furnished Solomon with cedar trees and cypress trees, and with gold, according to his need. Hiram came to see the cities which Solomon had given him, and they pleased him not. He said, "What cities are these which you have given me, my brother?" And he called them Cabul (Barren or Worthless), for Hiram had sent to Solomon one hundred and twenty talents of gold.

And this is the reason for the tax which King Solomon levied: for building the house of the Lord, and his own house, and Millo, and the wall of Jerusalem, and Hazor, and Meggido, and Gezer.

Pharaoh, the king of Egypt, had gone up and taken Gezer and burnt it to the ground, and slain the Canaanites who dwelt in it, and given the city as a present to his daughter, Solomon's wife. And Solomon rebuilt Gezer; and he built Lower Beth-horon, and Baalath, and Tadmor in the wilderness; and all the cities of storage, and the cities for his chariots, and the cities for his horsemen, and all that Solomon desired to build in Jerusalem, and in Lebanon, and in all the land of his dominion.

Then King Solomon made a navy of ships in Ezion-geber, which is near Eloth on the shore of the Red Sea, in the land of Edom. And Hiram sent his servants, shipmen who had knowledge of the sea, with the servants of Solomon. And they went to Ophir, and brought from there four hundred and twenty talents of gold to King Solomon.[3]

[2] See I KINGS, Chapters 6-8, in Notes and Excisions.
[3] See I KINGS, Chapter 9, in Notes and Excisions.

## The Queen of Sheba

10    When the queen of Sheba heard of Solomon's fame, she came to
      test him with hard questions. She arrived in Jerusalem with a very
great retinue, with camels that bore spices and much gold and precious
stones. And when she appeared before Solomon, she spoke with him of all
that was in her heart.

Solomon answered all her questions, and there was not anything which
he could not understand. And when the queen had tested Solomon's wisdom, and seen the house that he had built, the food served at his table,
his servants, the attendance of his ministers and their apparel, his cup-
bearers, and the offering he made in the house of the Lord, she said to the
king, "It was a true report that I heard in my own land of your acts and of
your wisdom. But I did not believe it until I came, and my eyes saw it.
Behold, your wisdom and prosperity exceed the fame of which I heard.
Happy are your servants, who stand always in your presence and hear
your wisdom! Blessed be the Lord your God, who delights in you and has
set you on the throne of Israel!"

She gave the king a hundred and twenty talents of gold, and precious
stones, and an abundance of spices. And Solomon gave to the queen whatever she desired, besides that which he gave her of his royal bounty.

Then she went to her own country, she and her servants.

## Solomon's Wealth

10    The navy of King Solomon brought gold from Ophir, and in great
      plenty, sandalwood and precious stones. The king made from the
sandalwood pillars for the house of the Lord, and for the king's house,
and also lyres and harps for the singers. No such sandalwood has ever
been seen to this day.

And the weight of gold that came to Solomon in one year was six hundred and sixty-six talents, besides that which came from the merchants
and the traders, and from the kings of the mingled peoples, and from the
governors of the country.

The king made three hundred shields of beaten gold, three pounds of
gold going to each shield, to adorn the house of the forest of Lebanon.
Moreover, the king made a great throne of ivory, and overlaid it with the

finest gold. The throne had six steps, and twelve lions stood there, one at each end of the six steps. And there was not the like of it in any kingdom.

All the king's drinking vessels were of gold, and all the vessels of the house of the forest of Lebanon. None were of silver because it was not accounted of value in the days of Solomon.

The king had a navy of ships at Tarshish with the navy of Hiram. Once every three years the fleet of ships would come bringing gold and silver, ivory, and apes and peacocks.

Thus King Solomon exceeded all the kings of the earth in riches and in wisdom. And all the rulers of the earth sought his presence to hear the wisdom which God had put in his heart. And they each brought him a present, vessels of silver and vessels of gold, and garments, and armor, and spices, and horses, and mules, year by year.

And Solomon gathered together chariots and horsemen; and he had a thousand and four hundred chariots, and twelve thousand horsemen. And the king made silver in Jerusalem as abundant as stone, and cedar as abundant as the sycamore trees of the valley.

## Solomon's End

11 Now King Solomon loved many foreign women. Besides the daughter of Pharaoh, he had women of the Moabites, Ammonites, Edomites, Sidonians, and Hittites, from the nations concerning whom the Lord had said to the children of Israel: "You shall not go among them, neither shall they come among you; for surely they will turn your heart toward their gods." But Solomon clung to these in love.

He had seven hundred wives, princesses, and three hundred concubines; and his wives turned away his heart. For when Solomon was old his wives turned his heart toward other gods. And Solomon went after Ashtoreth, the goddess of the Sidonians, and after Milcom, the god of the Ammonites. Then Solomon built an altar for Chemosh, the god of Moab, on the hill before Jerusalem, and for Molech, the god of the children of Ammon. And so did he for all his foreign wives, who sacrificed to their own gods.

The Lord was angry with Solomon and said to him, "Since you have not kept my covenant and my statutes, I will surely tear the kingdom from you. For the sake of David your father I will not do it in your day, but I will tear it out of the hand of your son. And for the sake of David my servant, and for the sake of Jerusalem, which I have chosen, I will not tear away all the kingdom, but I will give one tribe to your son."

The Lord stirred up adversaries against Solomon. And one, Jeroboam, the son of Nebat, an Ephraimite, lifted his hand against the king. And this was the reason:

The man Jeroboam was a mighty man of valor; and Solomon, seeing that the young man was industrious, put him in charge of the laborers from the house of Joseph. At that time, when Jeroboam went out of Jerusalem, the prophet Ahijah the Shilonite met him on the way. Ahijah had clad himself in a new garment, and the two were alone in a field.

Ahijah took hold of his new garment and tore it in twelve pieces. And he said to Jeroboam, "Take ten of these pieces, for thus says the Lord, the God of Israel, 'Behold, I will tear the kingdom from Solomon and will give ten tribes to you. For Solomon has not walked in my ways to do that which is right in my eyes. Yet to his son I will give one tribe, that David my servant may have a lamp always before me in Jerusalem, the city in which I have chosen to put my name.'"

Solomon sought therefore to kill Jeroboam. But Jeroboam fled to Shishak, king of Egypt, and he remained in Egypt until Solomon's death.

The rest of the acts of Solomon, and his wisdom, are they not recorded in the Book of the Acts of Solomon?

And Solomon reigned in Jerusalem over all Israel forty years. Then he slept with his fathers, and was buried in the city of David; and Rehoboam his son reigned in his stead.[4]

[4] See I KINGS, Chapter 11, in Notes and Excisions.

# I KINGS, 12-22
# II KINGS
## *A Kingdom Divided*

❲ The books I Kings and II Kings are arbitrarily divided into two sections of equal length. The first part of I Kings (Chapters 1-11) records King Solomon's rule. However, the second half of I Kings, along with the whole of II Kings, presents a continuous narrative of the divided kingdoms of Judah and Israel, and the trials of the people during two centuries under the rule of the kings of Israel and three and a half centuries under the rule of the kings of Judah. While the historical record of this period is not always sufficient or clear, the role of the prophets, in their attempts to point out the path of justice, is unmistakable. Though the rise to power of forty kings is presented, none loom so large as to compare with either Elijah or Elisha, or even some of the unnamed men of God. Throughout this recital we are told that though kings may be given the power to rule, their power is superseded by truth and justice.

The account of the two kingdoms as given in I Kings and II Kings is incomplete and sometimes confusing; and often events are presented out of their chronological order. The writers of these books assumed that their readers were acquainted with other and more complete chronicles of the same events, to which they constantly refer.

The reader may find it helpful to have before him a chronology of the rulers of the two kingdoms, and for this reason the following chart has been prepared, although the dates are still in dispute.   ❲

# THE DIVIDED KINGDOMS

## (All dates* are B.C.E.)

| ISRAEL | | JUDAH | |
|---|---|---|---|
| Jeroboam | (933-912) | Rehoboam | (933-917) |
| Nadab | (912-911) | Abijam | (917-915) |
| Baasha | (911-888) | Asa | (915-875) |
| Elah | (888-887) | | |
| Zimri | (887) | | |
| Omri | (887-876) | | |
| Ahab | (875-854) | Jehoshaphat | (875-851) |
| Ahaziah | (854-853) | | |
| Joram or Jehoram | (853-843) | Jehoram | (851-844) |
| Jehu | (843-816) | Ahaziah | (844-843) |
| Jehoahaz | (816-800) | Athaliah | (843-837) |
| Joash or Jehoash | (800-785) | Joash | (837-798) |
| Jeroboam II | (785-745) | Amaziah | (798-780) |
| Zachariah | (744) | Uzziah (also called | |
| Shallum | (744) | Azariah) | (780-740) |
| Menahem | (743-737) | Jotham | (740-735) |
| Pekahiah | (737-736) | Ahaz | (735-720) |
| Pekah | (736-734) | | |
| Hoshea | (733-722) | | |

| | | | |
|---|---|---|---|
| Shalmaneser V captures Israel in 722: end of kingdom of Israel. | | Hezekiah | (720-692) |
| | | Manasseh | (692-638) |
| | | Amon | (638) |
| | | Josiah | (638-608) |
| | | Jehoahaz | (608) |
| | | Jehoiakim | (608-597) |
| | | Jehoiakin | (597) |
| | | Zedekiah | (597-586) |

Babylonian captivity and destruction of Jerusalem in 587.

* The dates in this table are approximate, and may vary slightly from other sources whose base of calendar calculations varies.

## Israel's Secession

*12-13** Rehoboam, the son of Solomon, went to Shechem, for all Israel had come there to make him king. But when Jeroboam the Ephraimite, who was still in Egypt, heard of it, he returned. And Jeroboam and all the congregation of Israel came and spoke to Rehoboam, saying, "Your father made our yoke heavy. Now therefore lighten the yoke he put upon us, and we will serve you." Rehoboam said to them, "Depart for three days, then come to me again for an answer." So the people departed.

King Rehoboam consulted the old men who had stood before Solomon his father, and said, "What do you advise me to answer the people?" They said, "If you will be a servant to the people, and speak good words to them, then they will be your servants forever."

But Rehoboam turned away from their counsel and consulted the young men who had grown up with him. And the young men said to him, "Speak thus to the people: 'You say, "Your father made our yoke heavy, therefore lighten it for us." But you shall find my little finger thicker than my father's loins. And now, whereas my father burdened you with a heavy yoke, I will add to your yoke. My father chastised you with whips, but I will chastise you with scorpions.'"

Jeroboam and all the people returned to Rehoboam on the third day, as the king had appointed. And the king answered the people roughly, and spoke to them after the counsel of the young men. When the people of Israel saw that the king would not listen to them, they said to him, "What portion have we in David? We have no inheritance in the son of Jesse. To your tents, O Israel! Now look to your own house, David!" And the people departed.

Rehoboam reigned over those who dwelt in the cities of Judah; but when he sent Adoram, who was in charge of the tribute, the people of Israel stoned him to death. And King Rehoboam fled to Jerusalem.

So Israel rebelled against the house of David. And they summoned Jeroboam to the congregation, and made him king over Israel. And the house of David was followed by the tribe of Judah only.

But Jeroboam said in his heart, "If the people go up to offer sacrifices in the house of the Lord in Jerusalem, then will their hearts turn again to their lord, to Rehoboam, king of Judah, and they will kill me." Where-

* I KINGS.

upon the king took counsel and made two calves of gold, and he said to the people, "It is too much for you to go up to Jerusalem. Behold your gods, O Israel, who brought you up out of the land of Egypt." And he set one golden calf in Bethel, and the other he put in Dan. And he appointed priests for them.[1]

## Jeroboam's Fate

**14-15**  At that time, while Rehoboam ruled in Judah, Abijah, the son of Jeroboam, king of Israel, fell ill. Jeroboam said to his wife, "Rise, I pray you, and disguise yourself, that you may not be known as my wife, and go to Shiloh; for there is Ahijah the prophet, who told me that I would be king. Take with you ten loaves and a jar of honey, and find out from him what will become of our child."

Jeroboam's wife did so. When she came to Ahijah's house, he could not see her, for his eyes were dimmed by age. But the Lord said to Ahijah, "Behold, the wife of Jeroboam comes to ask you about her son, for he is ill. Thus and thus shall you say to her, for she shall feign to be another woman."

And when Ahijah heard the sound of her feet as she came in at the door, he said, "Come in, wife of Jeroboam. Why do you feign to be another? As for me, I have heavy tidings for you. Go, tell Jeroboam, 'Thus says the Lord God of Israel: "Forasmuch as I exalted you among the people, and made you prince over them, and tore the kingdom away from the house of David and gave it to you, yet you have done evil beyond that done by all those who went before you. You have made images, and cast me behind your back. Behold, I will bring evil upon the house of Jeroboam, and will take away the remnant of his household as a man takes away dung, until it is all gone. Anyone belonging to Jeroboam who dies in the city the dogs shall eat, and anyone who dies in the field the birds of the air shall eat!"'

"Therefore return, and when your feet enter the city, the child shall die. And all Israel shall mourn for him and bury him. For he alone of Jeroboam's house shall come to the grave, because in him there is found some good toward the Lord God of Israel.

"Moreover, the Lord will raise up a king over Israel who shall cut off the house of Jeroboam that day. And what can I tell you more? The

---

[1] See I KINGS, Chapter 13, in Notes and Excisions.

Lord will smite Israel as a reed is shaken in the water, and root up all Israel out of this good land which he gave to their fathers, and scatter them beyond the river, because they have followed other gods and provoked the Lord to anger."

Jeroboam's wife departed, and went to Tirzah. And when she came to the threshold of the door, the child died. And they buried him, and all Israel mourned for him.

The rest of the acts of Jeroboam, how he warred and how he reigned, behold, they are written in the Book of the Chronicles of the Kings of Israel.

Jeroboam reigned two and twenty years. Then Nadab his son succeeded him.[2]

## The Building of Samaria

16  Then were the people of Israel divided into two parts: half of them followed Tibni, the son of Ginath; and the other half followed Omri. But the people who followed Omri prevailed against the people who followed Tibni; so Tibni died, and Omri reigned.

King Omri bought the hill of Shemer for two talents of silver, and built on it a city; and named it Samaria, after Shemer, the owner of the hill. And Omri did evil in the eyes of the Lord; he did more evil than all those that were before him.

Then Omri slept with his fathers, and was buried in Samaria. And Ahab his son reigned after him.

Ahab took to wife Jezebel, the daughter of Ethbaal, king of the Sidonians; and he served Baal and worshiped him. And he reared up an altar to Baal in the house of Baal, which he had built in Samaria. And Ahab did more to provoke the anger of the Lord God of Israel than all the kings of Israel who were before him.

## The Miracles of Elijah the Prophet

17  Now Elijah the Tishbite, who was of Gilead, said to Ahab, the son of Omri, who reigned over Israel in Samaria, "By the Lord God of Israel, before whom I stand, there shall be neither dew nor rain — except by my word."

[2] See I KINGS, Chapters 15-16, in Notes and Excisions.

Then the word of the Lord came to Elijah, saying, "Go eastward, and hide by the brook Cherith, that is before the Jordan. You shall drink from the brook, and I have commanded the ravens to feed you there."

So Elijah went, and he dwelt by the brook Cherith. And the ravens brought him bread and meat in the morning, and bread and meat in the evening; and he drank from the brook. But after a while the brook dried up, because there had been no rain in the land.

Then the word of the Lord came to him, saying, "Arise, go to Zarephath, which belongs to Sidon, and dwell there. Behold, I have commanded a widow there to feed you."

So Elijah rose and went to Zarephath. And when he came to the gate of the city, he saw a widow gathering sticks. He called to her, "I pray you, bring me a little water, that I may drink." And as she was going to bring it, he called and said, "I pray you, bring me also a morsel of bread." She answered, "As the Lord your God lives, I have only a handful of flour in a barrel, and a little oil in a cruse; and I am gathering sticks so that I may prepare it for my son and myself, that we may eat it and not die." Elijah said to her, "Fear not. Go and do as you have said. But make a little cake of it first and bring it to me. After that make some for yourself and your son. The barrel shall not be emptied of flour, nor the cruse of oil, until the day that the Lord sends rain upon the earth."

The widow went and did as Elijah had said. And he and her household had food for many days. The flour was never spent, nor did the oil fail.

After these things happened, the son of the widow became ill, and there was no breath left in him. She said to Elijah, "Have you come to me to call my sin to remembrance, and to slay my son?"

He answered, "Give me your son." And he carried the child to the upper chamber, where he abode, and laid him upon the bed. Then he stretched himself upon the child three times, and cried out to the Lord, "O Lord, I pray you, let this child's soul come in to him again."

The Lord heard Elijah's cry, and the child revived. Elijah took him down and gave him to his mother, and said, "See, your son lives." And the woman answered, "Now I know that you are a man of God, and that the word of the Lord in your mouth is truth."

## The Prophets of Baal

*18*     After three years the word of the Lord came to Elijah, saying, "Go, show yourself to Ahab, and I will send rain upon the land." So Elijah went to Ahab, king of Israel.

Now there was a famine in Samaria; and Ahab called Obadiah, who was in charge of the household, and said, "Go through the land to all the springs of water. Perhaps we may find grass to save the horses and the mules, so that we do not lose all the animals."

They divided the land between them to pass through, Ahab going one way and Obadiah another. And as Obadiah was on his way, Elijah met him.

Obadiah fell on his face and said, "Are you my lord Elijah?" He answered, "I am. Go tell your master that I am here." Obadiah said, "What is my sin, that you would deliver me into the hands of Ahab to be slain? For there is no place where my lord has not sent to seek you. You say, 'Go tell your master that I am here.' But as soon as I am gone, the spirit of the Lord may carry you off I know not where. And when I tell Ahab, and he cannot find you, he will slay me." Elijah answered, "As the Lord lives, before whom I stand, I will show myself before Ahab today."

So Obadiah told Ahab, and the king came to meet Elijah. When Ahab saw him, he said, "Are you he who has troubled Israel?" Elijah answered, "It is not I who have troubled Israel, but you and your father's house have done so. For you have forsaken the commandments of the Lord, and worship Baalim. Therefore gather all of Israel at Mount Carmel, and also the four hundred and fifty prophets of Baal, and the four hundred prophets of the groves, who eat at Jezebel's table."

Ahab sent word to the children of Israel, and gathered the prophets together on Mount Carmel. And Elijah came before the people and said:

"How long will you waver between two opinions? If the Lord is God, follow him; and if Baal is god, then follow him."

But the people answered not a word.

Then Elijah said to them, "I alone remain as a prophet of the Lord, whereas Baal's prophets number four hundred and fifty. Let them bring two bullocks, and choose one for themselves as an offering, and place it on the wood with no fire under. Then I will prepare the other bullock, and lay it on the wood with no fire under. You shall call upon your gods, and I will call upon the Lord. And whichever God answers by fire, let him be God."

All the people answered, "It is well spoken."

The prophets of Baal took a bullock and prepared it, and called on Baal from morning until noon, "O Baal, hear us!" But there was no answer.

At noon, Elijah mocked them, "Cry louder! Either Baal is talking, or on a chase, or on a journey, or perhaps he sleeps and must be wakened."

They cried louder, and cut themselves after their custom with swords and lances until the blood gushed out upon them. When midday was past, they prayed until the time of the evening sacrifice. But still there was neither voice, nor any answer.

Elijah said to the people, "Come nearer." And all the people came near him. He repaired the altar, which had been broken down. Then Elijah took twelve stones, according to the number of the tribes of Israel, and with the stones he built an altar in the name of the Lord. He made a trench about the altar; he put the wood in order, and prepared the bullock, and laid him on the wood. Then he said, "Fill four jars with water, and pour it on the offering and the wood." When they did so, he said, "Do it a second time." And they did it a second time. Then he said, "Do it a third time." And they did it a third time. And the water ran round about the altar and filled the trench.

At the time of the evening sacrifice, Elijah came near and said, "Lord God of Abraham, Isaac, and of Israel, let it be known this day that you are God in Israel, and that I am your servant, and that I have done all these things at your command! O Lord, hear me, that the people may know you are the Lord God, and that you have turned their heart back again!"

Then the fire of the Lord came down and consumed the sacrifice, and the wood, and the stones, and the dust, and licked up the water that was in the trench. And when all the people saw this, they fell on their faces and cried out, "The Lord, he is God! The Lord, he is God!"

Elijah said to them, "Seize the prophets of Baal; do not let one of them escape." They seized the prophets of Baal, and Elijah brought them down to the brook Kishon, and slew them there.

Then Elijah said to Ahab, "Go now, and eat and drink. For there shall soon be a sound of rain."

So Ahab went up to eat and drink. And Elijah went to the top of Carmel. There he cast himself upon the ground, and put his face between his knees, and said to his servant, "Go now and look toward the sea, and tell me what you see." His servant looked and said, "I see nothing." Elijah said, "Go seven times."

At the seventh time, the servant said, "Behold, a little cloud the size of a man's hand arises out of the sea." Then Elijah said, "Go up, say to Ahab, 'Prepare your chariot and get down, lest the rain stop you.'" Ahab hastened, and went to Jezreel. And in a little while the heaven grew black with clouds and wind, and there was a great downpour. And the hand of the Lord was on Elijah; and he girded up his loins and ran before Ahab to the entrance of Jezreel.

## Elijah's Flight

19-20　When King Ahab told Jezebel his queen all that Elijah had done, and how he had slain the prophets, Jezebel sent a messenger to Elijah, saying, "So let the gods do to me, and more also, if I do not avenge my prophets by this time tomorrow."

Elijah fled to Beersheba, which belonged to Judah, and left his servant there. But he himself went the length of a day's journey into the wilderness, and came and sat down under a juniper tree, and said, "It is enough; now, O Lord, take away my life."

He fell asleep under the juniper tree, and behold an angel touched him and said, "Arise and eat."

Elijah looked, and there at his head was a cake baked on the hot stones, and a cruse of water. He ate and drank, and then lay down again. The angel of the Lord came a second time, and touched him and said, "Arise and eat, because the journey before you is long."

Elijah rose, and ate and drank. And he went on the strength of that meal forty days and forty nights to Horeb, the mountain of God. There he hid in a cave.

And the word of the Lord came to him, "What do you here, Elijah?" He answered, "The children of Israel have forsaken your covenant and thrown down your altars and slain your prophets. Only I am left, and they seek my life also." The Lord said, "Go out, and stand upon the mount."

And behold, a great and strong wind tore at the mountains and broke the rocks before the Lord, but the Lord was not in the wind; after the wind an earthquake, but the Lord was not in the earthquake; and after the earthquake a fire, but the Lord was not in the fire; and after the fire a still small voice. When Elijah heard the voice, he covered his face with his mantle and went out, and stood at the entrance of the cave. And behold, a voice said to him, "What do you here, Elijah? Go, return to the wilderness of Damascus. And anoint Hazael king over Aram; and Jehu, the son of Nimshi, king over Israel; and Elisha, the son of Shaphat, you shall anoint prophet in your place. And the one who escapes the sword of Hazael shall Jehu slay; and the one who escapes from the sword of Jehu shall Elisha slay."

So Elijah departed, and found Elisha, the son of Shaphat, as he was plowing behind twelve yoke of oxen; and Elijah cast his mantle upon him. Elisha left the oxen, and ran after Elijah and said, "Let me, I pray you, take leave of my father and mother, and then I will follow you." Elijah answered, "Go back again." Elisha returned, and took a yoke of oxen and slaughtered them, and boiled the meat and gave it to the people, and they ate. Then he followed Elijah, and ministered to him.[3]

## Naboth's Vineyard

**21-22**  Now Naboth the Jezreelite had a vineyard near King Ahab's place in Jezreel. And the king said to Naboth, "Give me your vineyard, that I may have it for an herb garden since it is near my home. And I will give you for it a better vineyard, or I will give you its value in money." Naboth answered, "The Lord forbid that I should give up the inheritance of my fathers."

Ahab returned home displeased. He lay down upon his bed, and turned away his face, and would not eat. Jezebel his wife asked, "Why is your spirit so heavy that you do not eat?" He answered, "Because I spoke to Naboth, and said to him, 'Give me your vineyard for money, or, if it pleases you, I will give you another vineyard for it.' But he answered, 'I will not give you my vineyard.'" Jezebel said to him, "Do not you govern the kingdom of Israel? Arise and eat, and let your heart be merry, for I will give you the vineyard of Naboth the Jezreelite."

She wrote letters in Ahab's name, and sealed them with his seal, and sent the letters to the elders and nobles who lived in the city where Naboth dwelt. And she wrote, "Proclaim a fast, and set two men to bear witness against Naboth, saying, 'You blasphemed God and the king.' Then stone him to death."

The elders and the nobles of the city did as Jezebel had ordered them.

---

[3] See I KINGS, Chapter 20, in Notes and Excisions.

And when Jezebel heard that Naboth was dead, she said to Ahab, "Arise, take possession of the vineyard which Naboth refused to give you, for Naboth is dead."

And Ahab went down to take possession of the vineyard. But the word of the Lord came to Elijah, saying, "Go down to meet Ahab, king of Israel. Behold, he is in Naboth's vineyard. Say to him, 'In the place where dogs licked the blood of Naboth shall dogs lick your blood.'"

Ahab said to Elijah, "Have you found me out, O my enemy?" Elijah answered, "I have found you out, because you have sold yourself to do evil. Therefore evil will come upon you, and the Lord will cut off your posterity. And of Jezebel the Lord said, 'The dogs shall eat Jezebel by the tower of Jezreel. And anyone belonging to Ahab who dies in the city the dogs shall eat, and anyone of his who dies in the field the birds of the air shall eat.'"

When Ahab heard these words, he tore his clothes, and put on sackcloth, and fasted and went about sadly. And the word of the Lord came to Elijah the Tishbite, saying, "Because Ahab has humbled himself before me, I will not bring the evil in his day. But in his son's days I will bring the evil upon his house." [4]

## Fire from Heaven

1[*]  After the death of Ahab, the seventh king of Israel, Ahaziah his son became king. And Ahaziah fell down through a lattice of his upper chamber and lay sick. The king sent messengers to inquire of Baal-zebub the god of Ekron whether he would recover.

The messengers returned and told him, "There came a man to meet us who said, 'Go, return to the king who sent you, and say to him, "Thus says the Lord: 'Is there no God in Israel that you send to inquire of Baal-zebub the god of Ekron? Therefore you shall not rise up from your bed, but shall surely die.'"'" The king asked, "What manner of man told you these words?" They answered, "He was a hairy man, with a girdle of leather about his loins." And he said, "It is Elijah the Tishbite."

Then the king sent a captain of fifty with his fifty men after Elijah. And behold, Elijah was sitting on the top of a hill. The captain said to him, "Man of God, the king sent me to bring you to him." Elijah answered, "If

[4] See I KINGS, Chapter 22, in Notes and Excisions.
[*] II KINGS.

I am a man of God, then let fire come down from heaven and consume you and your men, if you plan to take me to your king." And fire came down from heaven which consumed the captain and his fifty men.

Again the king sent a captain of fifty with his men. And fire came down which consumed them also.

The king sent a third captain and his men. And the third captain fell on his knees before Elijah and besought him, "O man of God, let my life, and the life of these fifty, your servants, be precious in your sight, and spare us!"

Then an angel said to Elijah, "Go down with him; be not afraid."

Elijah rose and went down with the captain; and Elijah said to the king, "Because you sent messengers to inquire of the god of Ekron, you shall not rise from your bed, but shall surely die."

And Ahaziah died, according to the word of the Lord spoken through Elijah.

As for the rest of the acts of Ahaziah, are they not recorded in the Book of the Chronicles of the Kings of Israel?

## Elijah's Ascent to Heaven

2      And it came to pass when the Lord was about to take up Elijah into heaven by a whirlwind, that Elijah and Elisha were on their way from Gilgal.

Elijah said to Elisha, "Wait here, I pray you, for the Lord has sent me to Bethel." Elisha answered, "As the Lord lives, I will not leave you!" So they went down together to Bethel.

The sons of the prophets who were at Bethel came out to Elisha and said to him, "Know you that the Lord will take your master away from you today?" He said, "Yes, I know it. Hold your peace."

And Elijah said to him, "Elisha, wait here, I pray you, for the Lord has sent me to Jericho. But Elisha answered, "As the Lord lives, and as my soul lives, I will not leave you!" So they went on to Jericho.

The sons of the prophets who were at Jericho came to Elisha and said, "Know you that the Lord will take your master away from you today?" He answered, "Yes, I know it. Hold your peace."

Again Elijah said to him, "Wait here, I pray you, for the Lord has sent me to the Jordan." But Elisha answered, "As the Lord lives, I will not leave you!" So the two went on.

And fifty of the sons of the prophets watched them from afar, as they both stood beside the Jordan. Elijah took off his mantle, and rolled it up, and struck the waters; and the waters parted, so that the two of them went over on dry ground.

When they had gone over, Elijah said to Elisha, "Ask what I shall do for you before I am taken away." Elisha answered, "I pray you, let your spirit be upon me twofold." Elijah said, "You have asked a hard thing. Nevertheless, if you see me when I am taken from you, it shall be as you have asked; but if not, it shall not be so."

As they still went on, and talked, behold, a chariot of fire appeared, and horses of fire, which parted them asunder; and Elijah went up by a whirlwind to heaven.

Elisha saw it and cried out, "My father, my father! The chariot of Israel and its horsemen!" Then he saw Elijah no more.

Elisha took hold of his own clothes and tore them in two pieces. And he took up Elijah's mantle, which had fallen from him, and went back and stood beside the bank of the Jordan. There he took the mantle of Elijah, and with it struck the water; and the waters parted. Then Elisha crossed over.

When the sons of the prophets at Jericho saw him, they asked, "Does the spirit of Elijah now rest on Elisha?" And they came to meet him, and bowed to the ground before him.


# The Miracles of Elisha

### The Blessing of the Waters

2      The men of a certain city said to Elisha, "Behold, the site of this city is pleasant, as my lord can see; but the water is not good, and the land is barren." He answered, "Bring me a new jar, and put salt in it." And they brought it to him.

Then Elisha went to the springs, and cast the salt in them and said, "Thus says the Lord, 'These waters are healed: no longer shall death come from them, or barren land.'" So the waters were made wholesome, in accord with Elisha's words.

## The Curse of the She-Bears

Elisha went from there to Bethel, and as he was on the way, little children came out of the city and mocked him, "Go on, you baldhead! Go on, you baldhead!"

Elisha looked at them, and cursed them in the name of the Lord. Then two she-bears came out of the wood, and tore forty-two of the children.

And Elisha went from there to Mount Carmel, and from Mount Carmel he returned to Samaria.

## The Desert Springs

3     Now Mesha, king of Moab, was a sheep-breeder, and rendered to the king of Israel a hundred thousand lambs, and a hundred thousand rams, with the wool. But when Ahab was dead, the king of Moab rebelled against Jehoram the new King of Israel.

King Jehoram, the son of Ahab, sent word to Jehoshaphat, the king of Judah, saying, "The king of Moab has rebelled against me. Will you go with me to battle against Moab?" He answered, "I will. I am as you are; my people as your people."

So the king of Israel and the king of Judah and the king of Edom went out. But after they had circled the desert of Edom for seven days, there was no water for the army, or for the cattle which followed them.

The king of Israel said, "Alas! For the Lord has called these three kings together to deliver them into the hand of Moab!" But Jehoshaphat asked, "Is there not a prophet here, that we may inquire of the Lord through him?" And one of the king of Israel's servants answered, "There is Elisha, the son of Shaphat, who poured water on the hands of Elijah."

So the king of Israel and Jehoshaphat and the king of Edom went to him. And Elisha said to the king of Israel, "As the Lord lives, were it not that I respect the presence of Jehoshaphat, king of Judah, I would not look at you. But for his sake, bring me a minstrel."

When the minstrel played, the spirit of the Lord came upon Elisha. And he said, "Thus says the Lord, 'Make this valley full of ditches. There shall be no wind, or rain; yet the valley shall be filled with water, that you may drink, both you and your beasts. And the Moabites will be delivered into your hand.'"

In the morning, at the time of the meat offering, behold, water came by way of Edom until the country was filled with it.

When the Moabites heard that the kings had come to fight against them, they gathered all those who were able to put on armor, and stood at the border. And when they rose early in the morning, and the sun shone upon the water, and the Moabites saw that the water on the other side was red as blood in the sunrise, they said, "This is blood! The kings are surely slain! They have fought one another! Now, Moab, to the spoil."

But when they came to the camp of Israel, the Israelites rose up and struck the Moabites so that they fled before them, and they pursued the Moabites even into their own country. And they beat down the cities, and on every good piece of land cast stones, and they stopped up the wells of water and felled the trees.

When the king of Moab saw that the battle went heavily against him, he took with him seven hundred swordsmen to break through to the king of Edom, but they could not. Then he took his eldest son, who was to have reigned after him, and offered him up as a burnt offering upon the wall.

And there was great indignation against Israel.


## Miracle in a Flask

4 Now a certain woman, who was the wife of one of the sons of the prophets, came to Elisha, saying, "Your servant, my husband, is dead; and you know that he feared the Lord. But a creditor has come to take my two sons as slaves for a debt."

Elisha said to her, "Tell me, what have you in the house?" She answered, "I have not anything of worth except a flask of oil." Then Elisha said, "Go, borrow empty vessels from all your neighbors, and borrow many. When you return home, shut the door upon yourself and your sons, and pour the oil into all the vessels, setting aside each which is filled."

So she went from him and shut the door upon herself and her sons, who had brought the vessels to her, and into the vessels she poured the oil from the flask. When all the vessels were full, she said to her son, "Bring me another vessel." And he answered, "There is not another." Then the oil stopped.

She came and told the man of God. And Elisha said, "Go, sell the oil and pay your debt, and you and your children live on the rest."

## The Kind Shunammite

One day Elisha went to Shunem, where there was a wealthy woman; and she invited him to eat. From then on whenever Elisha passed that way, he turned in to eat at her home. And she said to her husband, "This holy man of God often passes our way. Let us build a little chamber on the roof, and put in it for him a bed, and a table, and a stool, and a candlestick; and then when he comes to us he shall turn in there."

And one day when he came there, and turned into the chamber, Elisha said to his servant Gehazi, "Say now to her, 'Behold, you have shown us all this care; what may be done for you? Would you wish to be spoken for to the king, or to the captain of the army?' "

She answered, "I dwell among my own people."

Elisha then asked Gehazi, "What can be done for her?" Gehazi answered, "Verily, she has no child, and her husband is old." Then Elisha said, as she stood in the doorway, "About this season next year you shall embrace a son." She answered, "No, my lord, do not deceive your handmaid."

But the woman bore a son at that season, when the time came round, as Elisha had foretold.

When the child was grown, he went out one day to his father among the reapers. And he said to his father, "My head! My head!" His father said to a servant, "Carry him to his mother."

And when the child was brought to his mother, he sat upon her lap until noon; and then he died.

She went up, and laid him on the bed of the man of God, and shut the door upon him and went out.

And she went to her husband, and said, "Send me one of the servants, and one of the asses, that I may hasten to the man of God." He asked, "Why do you go to him today? It is neither the new moon nor the Sabbath." And she answered, "It is for my welfare."

Then she saddled an ass, and said to her servant, "Drive, and do not slacken unless I bid you." So she hastened to the man of God at Mount Carmel.

When Elisha saw her from afar, he said to Gehazi, "Behold, yonder is the Shunammite. Run to meet her and ask, 'Is it well with you? Is it well with your husband? Is it well with the child?' "

And she answered, "It is well."

But when she came to the man of God, she caught hold of his feet; and Gehazi came near to thrust her away. But the man of God said, "Let her alone, for her soul is bitter with sorrow, and the Lord has not revealed it to me."

Then she said, "Did I ask for a son? Did I not say, 'Do not deceive me'?"

Elisha said to Gehazi, "Take my staff in your hand, and go. If you meet anyone, do not salute him; if anyone salutes you, answer him not; but hasten and lay my staff upon the face of the child."

The mother of the child said, "As the Lord lives, and as your soul lives, I will not leave without you." So Elisha rose and followed her.

Gehazi went on ahead of them, and laid the staff upon the face of the child; and there was no response. Therefore he returned to meet Elisha, and told him, "The child has not awakened."

When Elisha came in, he saw that the child was dead. He shut the door upon the two of them, and prayed to the Lord. Then he went up and lay upon the child, and put his mouth upon the child's mouth, and his eyes upon the child's eyes, and his hands upon the child's hands, and stretched himself out upon the child. And the body of the child grew warm. Then Elisha walked to and fro in the chamber, and went up and stretched himself again upon the child. And the child sneezed seven times, and opened his eyes.

Elisha called Gehazi and said, "Call the Shunammite." And when she came in, he said, "Take up your son."

She fell at his feet, and bowed herself to the ground. Then she took up her son and went out.

## The Feeding of a Multitude

Elisha came again to Gilgal, when there was famine in the land.

And a man from Baal-shalisha brought the man of God twenty loaves of barley, and full ears of corn in the husk.

Elisha said to his servant, "Give it to the people, that they may eat." But his servant said, "What? Should I set this before a hundred men?"

Elisha said again, "Give it to the people, that they may eat. For thus says the Lord, 'They shall eat their fill, and shall leave some.'"

So he set it before the people, and they ate, and left some of it, according to the word of the Lord.

## The Curing of the Leper

5    Now Naaman, captain of the armies of the king of Syria, was a great man and honorable. He was also a mighty man of valor, but he was a leper. The Syrians had gone out in raiding bands and had brought away captive from the land of Israel a little maid, who waited on Naaman's wife. And she said to her mistress, "Would God my lord were with the prophet who is in Samaria! For he would cure him of his leprosy."

Naaman was told, "Thus and thus said the maid who is from the land of Israel."

Naaman departed, and took with him ten talents of silver, six thousand pieces of gold, and ten changes of garments. And he brought a letter from the king of Syria to the king of Israel which read, "Now when this letter comes to you, know that I have sent with it Naaman my servant, that you may cure him of his leprosy."

The king of Israel read the letter, and then he rent his clothes and said, "Am I God, to kill or to make alive, that he sends me a man to cure of his leprosy? Assuredly he seeks a quarrel with me!"

But when Elisha heard that the king of Israel had rent his clothes, he sent word to him, "Why have you rent your clothes? Let him come to me, and he shall know that there is a prophet in Israel."

So Naaman came with his horses and with his chariot, and waited at the door of Elisha's house. Elisha sent a messenger to him, saying, "Go and wash in the Jordan seven times, and your flesh shall be restored, and you shall be clean."

But Naaman was angered and said, "I thought he would surely come out to me, and stand, and call on the name of the Lord his God, and strike his hand over the place, and cure the leper. Are not Abana and Pharpar, the rivers of Damascus, better than all the waters of Israel? Could I not wash in them and be clean?" So he turned away in a rage.

His servants came near and said, "If the prophet had bid you do some great thing, would you not have done it? How much rather, then, when he says to you, 'Wash, and be clean'?"

Then Naaman went down and dipped himself seven times in the Jordan; and his flesh became like the flesh of a little child, and he was cured. He returned to Elisha, he and all his retinue, and stood before him. He said, "Now I know there is no God in all the earth other than the God of Israel. Therefore, I pray you, accept a gift from your servant."

But Elisha answered, "As the Lord lives, whom I serve, I will take nothing." Naaman urged him, but he refused.

Naaman said, "I pray you, let there be given to your servant two mule-loads of this earth, for your servant will henceforth offer neither burnt offerings nor sacrifices to any god, but to the Lord. In this thing may the Lord pardon your servant: When my master goes into the house of Rimmon to worship, leaning on my arm, and I bow in the house of Rimmon, may the Lord pardon your servant for this." Elisha said to him, "Go in peace." So Naaman departed.

But when he had gone a little way, Gehazi, Elisha's servant, said to himself, "Behold, my master has spared Naaman the Syrian in not taking from him that which he brought, but as the Lord lives, I will run after him and take something from him."

Gehazi followed Naaman; and when Naaman saw Gehazi running after him, he alighted from the chariot to meet him and said, "Is all well?" Gehazi answered, "All is well. My master has sent me, saying, 'Behold, two young men from Mount Ephraim have just now come to me. Give them, I pray you, a talent of silver and two changes of garments.'"

Naaman bound two talents of silver in two bags, with two changes of garments, and gave them to the servant.

When Gehazi returned and went in to his master, Elisha asked, "Where have you been, Gehazi?" He answered, "Your servant has not gone anywhere." And Elisha said, "Was not my spirit with you when the man turned from his chariot to meet you? Is this a time to accept money and garments, olive orchards and vineyards, sheep and oxen, menservants and maidservants? The leprosy of Naaman shall cling to you and to your descendants forever."

And Gehazi went out of Elisha's presence a leper, as white as snow.

## The Iron Axehead

6-7    The sons of the prophets said to Elisha, "The place where we dwell with you is too small for us. Let us go, we pray you, to the Jordan, and each man take a log there, and let us build a place there where we may dwell." He answered, "You may go." One said, "I pray you, come with your servants." And he answered, "I will come."

So he went with them. And when they came to the Jordan, they cut down wood. But as one was felling a log, the axehead fell into the water; and he cried out, "Alas, master! It was borrowed!" Elisha asked, "Where did it fall?" And the man showed him the place. Then Elisha cut off a stick and cast it in there, and the iron axehead floated up. Elisha said, "Take it." And the man put out his hand, and took it.

## The Blinding of the Host

The king of Syria was warring against Israel, and took counsel with his servants, saying, "In such and such a place shall be my camp."

Elisha sent word to the king of Israel, "Beware that you do not pass such a place, for there the Syrians have come." And the king avoided the place of which the man of God had warned him, and saved himself more than once or twice.

The king of Syria was troubled by this, and he called his servants and said to them, "Will you not show me who among us has warned the king of Israel?" One of his servants answered, "None, O King! But Elisha the prophet tells the king of Israel the words that you speak even in your bedchamber!"

The king said, "Find out where he is, that I may capture him." And the king was told, "Behold, he is in Dothan."

Then the king sent horses and chariots, and a great army; and they came by night and surrounded the city. When Elisha's servant rose early and went out, behold, an army surrounded the city with horses and chariots.

The servant said to Elisha, "Alas, my master! What shall we do?" And he answered, "Fear not, for those who are with us are more than those who are with them." Elisha prayed and said, "Lord, I pray you, open his eyes, that he may see." And the Lord opened the eyes of the young man, and he saw that the mountain was full of horses and chariots of fire round about Elisha.

And when the Syrians came down to him, Elisha prayed to the Lord, "Smite them, I pray you, with blindness." And God smote them with blindness in accord with Elisha's prayer.

Then Elisha said to the Syrians, "This is not the place, nor is this the city. Follow me, and I will bring you to the man whom you seek." But he led them to Samaria. And when the Lord opened their eyes, behold, they were in the midst of Samaria.

The king of Israel asked Elisha, when he saw them, "My father, shall I smite them?" Elisha answered, "You shall not smite them. Set bread and water before them, that they may eat and drink, and go to their master."

So he prepared a great feast for them. And when they had eaten and drunk, he sent them away, and they went to their master in peace.

And the raiding bands of Syria came no more into the land of Israel.[5]

## The Shield of the Shunammite

8      There was a great famine in the land. And Elisha spoke to the woman whose son he had restored to life, saying, "Arise, and go with your household to settle wherever you can. For the famine will endure seven years."

The woman departed with her household, and dwelt in the land of the Philistines for seven years. At the end of the seven years she returned, and she went to the king to petition for her house and her land.

The king was talking with Gehazi, the servant of the man of God, saying, "Tell me all the great things that Elisha has done." And as he was telling the king how Elisha had restored to life one who had been dead, behold, the woman petitioned the king for her house and her land.

Gehazi said, "O King, this is the woman, and this is her son, whom Elisha restored to life."

And when the king questioned the woman, she told him. So the king appointed an officer to her, saying, "Restore all that was hers, and all that the field has yielded since the day she left the land until now."

## The Murder of Ben-hadad

8      Elisha came to Damascus when Ben-hadad, the king of Syria, was sick. And the king was told, "The man of God has come here." The king said to Hazael, "Take a present in your hand, and go to meet the man of God, and inquire of the Lord through him, 'Shall I recover from this disease?'"

So Hazael took a present of every good thing of Damascus, forty camel-loads, and came and stood before Elisha and said, "Ben-hadad, king of Syria, has sent me to you, saying, 'Shall I recover from my disease?'" Elisha answered, "Go, say to him, 'You shall certainly recover.' But to you I will reveal that the Lord has shown me he will surely die." And the man of God wept.

[5] See II KINGS, Chapter 7, in Notes and Excisions.

Hazael asked, "Why does my lord weep?" And Elisha answered, "Because I know the evil that you will do to the children of Israel. Their strongholds you will set on fire, and their young men you will slay by the sword, and you will dash their children to pieces, and rip up their women with child."

Hazael said, "Is your servant a dog that he should do this?" Elisha answered, "The Lord has shown me that you shall be king over Syria."

So Hazael departed from Elisha and came to his master, who asked, "What said Elisha to you?" He answered, "He told me you would surely recover."

But on the morrow he took a thick cloth and dipped it in water, and spread it over the king's face, so that he died. And Hazael reigned in his stead.[6]

## Jezebel's End

8-9     In the twelfth year of Joram, king of Israel, Ahaziah, king of Judah, began his reign. Ahaziah was two and twenty years old when he began to reign; and he walked in the way of the house of Ahab, for he was the son-in-law of the house of Ahab; and he did evil in the sight of the Lord. He went with Joram, the son of Ahab, to the war against Hazael, king of Syria; and the Syrians wounded Joram.

King Joram went back to be healed of his wounds in Jezreel; and Ahaziah, king of Judah, went down to see him.

At the same time, Elisha called one of the sons of the prophets and said to him, "Take this flask of oil in your hand, and go to Ramoth-gilead. When you come there, look for Jehu, the son of Jehoshaphat, and go in, and make him rise from among his kinsmen, and lead him to an inner chamber. Take oil, and pour it on his head, and say, 'Thus says the Lord: "I have anointed you king over Israel!"' Then open the door, and flee."

So the young man, the prophet, went to Ramoth-gilead. And when he came, behold, the captains of the army were in council. And he said, "I have an errand for you, O Captain!" Jehu asked, "For which one of us?" And he answered, "For you, O Captain."

Jehu rose, and went into the house. And the young man poured the oil on his head and said, "Thus says the Lord God of Israel, 'I have anointed you king over Israel. And you shall smite the house of Ahab your

[6] See II KINGS, Chapter 8, in Notes and Excisions.

245

master, that I may avenge the blood of my servants the prophets, and the blood of all the servants of the Lord, at the hand of Jezebel. For the whole house of Ahab shall perish. And dogs shall eat Jezebel in the fields of Jezreel, and there shall be none to bury her.'" Then the young man opened the door, and fled.

Jehu returned to the servants of his lord, and one asked, "Is all well? Why did this mad fellow come to you?" Jehu answered, "You know the man and his talk." They said, "Tell us now." And Jehu answered, "He spoke to me, saying, 'Thus says the Lord, "I have anointed you king over Israel!"'"

Then they hastened, and each man took his garment, and put it under him on the stairs, and blew the trumpet, and proclaimed, "Jehu is king!"

And Jehu commanded, "Let none escape from the city to tell this in Jezreel."

Jehu rode in a chariot, and went toward Jezreel with his men; for Joram lay there, and Ahaziah had come down to see Joram. And the watchman on the tower at Jezreel spied the company of Jehu. He said to the king, "I see a company."

Joram answered, "Send a horseman to meet them, and let him ask, 'Do you come in peace?'"

So one went on horseback to meet Jehu, and said, "Thus says the king, 'Do you come in peace?'" Jehu answered, "What have you to do with peace? Turn in behind me!"

Then the watchman informed the king, "The messenger went up to them, but he does not return."

The king sent out a second man on horseback. Again the watchman reported, "He went up to them, but does not turn back. And the driving is like the driving of Jehu, the son of Nimshi; for he drives furiously."

Joram answered, "Make ready." And his chariot was made ready. Then Joram, king of Israel, and Ahaziah, king of Judah, went out, each in his chariot, and they went out against Jehu, and met him in the field of Naboth the Jezreelite.

When Joram saw Jehu, he said, "Is it peace, Jehu?" Jehu answered, "What peace is there, so long as the whoredoms and witchcrafts of your mother Jezebel are so many?"

Joram fled, and called to Ahaziah, "There is treachery, O Ahaziah!"

Jehu drew his bow with his full strength, and struck Joram between his shoulders, and the arrow went out at his heart, and he sank down in his chariot.

Then Jehu said to Bidkar his captain, "Cast him into the portion of the field belonging to Naboth the Jezreelite. For remember how the Lord pronounced this against him. Therefore, cast him there according to the word of the Lord."

When Ahaziah saw this, he fled by way of the garden house. Jehu followed him and ordered, "Strike him also." They struck him at the ascent of Gur. And he fled to Megiddo, and died there.

When Jehu came to Jezreel, Jezebel heard of it. She painted her face, and adorned her head, and looked out of the window. As Jehu entered in at the gate, he lifted up his face to the window and called, "Who is on my side? Who?" And two or three eunuchs looked out at him.

Jehu said, "Throw her down." So they threw her down; and some of her blood sprinkled the wall, and the horses; and he trod her underfoot.

When Jehu came in, he ate and drank, and said, "Go, see now to this cursed woman and bury her, for she is a king's daughter."

They went out to bury her; but they found no more of her than the skull and the feet and the palms of her hands. They returned and told Jehu. And he said, "This fulfills the word of the Lord, which he spoke by his servant Elijah the Tishbite, saying, 'In the fields of Jezreel dogs shall eat the flesh of Jezebel.'"

## The Reign of Terror

10-12 Now Ahab had seventy sons in Samaria. So Jehu wrote letters and sent them to the rulers of Jezreel, and to those who brought up Ahab's children, saying, "As soon as this letter comes to you, select the best of your master's sons and set him on his father's throne, and fight for your master's house."

But they were exceedingly afraid, and said, "Behold, two kings could not withstand him; how then shall we?" And they sent word to Jehu, "We are your servants, and will do all that you bid us. We will not make anyone king. Do that which is good in your eyes."

Then he wrote a second letter to them, saying, "If you are on my side, take the heads of your master's sons, and come to me at Jezreel by tomorrow at this time."

They slew the king's sons, seventy persons, and put their heads in baskets, and sent them to Jezreel.

When the messenger told Jehu, "They have brought the heads of the king's sons," he said, "Lay them in two heaps at the entrance of the gate until morning."

And in the morning he went out, and said to all the people, "You are guiltless! It was I who conspired against my master and slew him. But who has slain all these?"

Then Jehu slew all who remained of the house of Ahab in Jezreel, all his great men, and his kinsfolk, and his priests, until none remained.

And he departed and went to Samaria. At the shearing-house of the shepherds on the way, Jehu met the brothers of Ahaziah and said, "Who are you?" They answered, "We are the brothers of Ahaziah, and we go down to salute the children of the king and the queen."

Jehu said to his men, "Take them alive."

And at the pit of the shearing-house they slew two and forty men, and spared none of them.

Jehu assembled all the people, and said to them, "Ahab served Baal a little, but Jehu will serve him much. Therefore call together the prophets of Baal, all his servants, and all his priests, for I have a great sacrifice to make to Baal." But Jehu did this in cunning, that he might destroy the worshipers of Baal. And Jehu said, "Proclaim a solemn assembly for Baal."

Jehu sent word throughout Israel; and all the worshipers of Baal came, so that not a man was left who had not come.•And they entered the house of Baal; and the house of Baal was full from one end to another.

Jehu said to the man in charge of the vestry, "Bring out vestments for all the worshipers of Baal." And the men brought out vestments for them.

Then Jehu went into the house of Baal and said, "Search, that there may be here with you none of the servants of the Lord, but the worshipers of Baal only." And when they went in to offer sacrifices and burnt offerings, Jehu stationed fourscore men outside, and said to them, "If any of the men I have brought together escape, he who lets him go shall pay for it with his life." And as soon as he made the burnt offering, Jehu ordered the guard and the captains, "Go in and slay them!"

They slew them with the sword; and then they went into the inner chamber of the house of Baal, and brought out the images and burned them. And they tore down the image of Baal, and tore down the house of Baal, and made it a privy, which it is to this day.

Thus Jehu rooted out Baal from Israel.

And the Lord said to Jehu: "Because you have done to the house of Ahab according to all that was in my heart, your children to the fourth generation shall sit on the throne of Israel."

Now the rest of the acts of Jehu, and all that he did, are they not written in the Book of the Chronicles of the Kings of Israel?

And Jehu slept with his fathers, and he was buried in Samaria. Jehoahaz his son reigned in his stead; and Jehu reigned over Israel, in Samaria, twenty-eight years.[7]

## Elisha's Last Miracle

13    In the twenty-third year of Joash, son of Ahaziah, king of Judah, Jehoahaz, son of Jehu, began to reign over Israel in Samaria. And he did that which was evil in the sight of the Lord. The anger of the Lord kindled against Israel, and he delivered them into the hand of Hazael, king of Syria, and into the hand of Ben-hadad, the son of Hazael.

Now Elisha had fallen ill of the sickness of which he was to die. And Joash, king of Israel, came to him and wept, "O my father! My father! The chariot of Israel and its horsemen!"

But Elisha said to him, "Take a bow and arrows." And he took a bow and arrows. Then Elisha said, "Put your hand upon the bow." The king put his hand upon it, and Elisha laid his hands upon the king's hands. He said, "Open the window eastward." The king opened it. Then Elisha said, "Shoot!" And he shot.

Elisha said to him, "You have shot the arrow of the Lord's deliverance, and the arrow of deliverance from Syria! For you shall strike the Syrians in Aphek, until you have consumed them." Then Elisha said, "Take the arrows!" The king took them. And Elisha said to the king of Israel, "Strike upon the ground." The king struck thrice, and stopped.

The man of God was angered, and said, "You should have struck five or six times; then you would have struck Syria until you had consumed it, whereas now you shall strike Syria but thrice."

So Elisha died, and they buried him.

At that time bands of Moabites invaded the land at the coming in of the year. And as they were burying a man, behold, they spied a band of raiders. So they cast the man into the sepulcher of Elisha; and when the man touched the bones of Elisha, he revived and stood up on his feet.

[7] See II KINGS, Chapters 11-12, in Notes and Excisions.

## The Thistle and the Cedar

*14-16*   In the second year of Joash, the twelfth king of Israel, Amaziah became king of Judah. He was twenty-five years old when he began to reign, and he ruled twenty-nine years in Jerusalem. As soon as the kingdom was firmly in his hands, he slew the servants who had slain the king his father. But the children of the murderers he did not slay, according to that which is written in the book of the law of Moses: "The fathers shall not be put to death for the children, and the children shall not be put to death for the fathers; but every man shall die for his own sin."

Then Amaziah sent messengers to the king of Israel, saying, "Come, let us look one another in the face." And the king of Israel sent word back to the king of Judah, "The thistle of Lebanon sent word to the cedar in Lebanon, saying, 'Give your daughter to my son as his wife.' And there passed a wild beast of Lebanon and trod down the thistle. Now you have indeed smitten Edom, and your heart has grown proud. Glory in this and stay at home; why should you meddle to your hurt, so that you fall and Judah with you?"

But Amaziah would not take his counsel.

Therefore Jehoash went up, and he met Amaziah, the king of Judah, at Bethshemesh. And Judah fled before Israel. The king of Israel captured Amaziah at Bethshemesh, and came to Jerusalem, and broke down the wall of the city from the gate of Ephraim to the corner gate; and he took all the gold and silver and all the vessels in the house of the Lord and in the king's treasury, also hostages, and returned to Samaria.

Now the rest of the acts of Jehoash and his might, and how he fought with Amaziah, are they not written in the Book of the Chronicles of the Kings of Israel?

Jehoash slept with his fathers, and was buried in Samaria with the kings of Israel; and Jeroboam his son reigned after him.[8]

[8] See II KINGS, Chapters 14-16, in Notes and Excisions.

## The Fall of the Kingdom of Israel

17     In the twelfth year of Ahaz, king of Judah, Hoshea, the son of Elah, began his reign over Israel in Samaria. Against him came up Shalmaneser the Fifth, king of Assyria; and Hoshea became his vassal and paid him tribute.

But when Shalmaneser found out that Hoshea had sent emissaries to So, the king of Egypt, and brought no tribute to Assyria as he had done year by year, the king of Assyria came to the kingdom of Israel and besieged it for three years.

In the ninth year of Hoshea, the king of Assyria took Samaria and carried Israel away into captivity, and settled them in the cities of the Medes. And there was left the tribe of Judah only.

For the children of Israel had sinned against the Lord their God. They had built altars on the high places in all their cities, from the watchtower to the fortified city. And they had set up images on every high hill and under every green tree. They worshiped all the host of heaven, and served Baal as did the heathen. And they caused their sons and daughters to pass through the fire.

They rejected the Lord their God, and the covenant he had made with their fathers, and followed vanity, and became vain; therefore the Lord removed them from his sight.

And the king of Assyria brought people from Babylon and from Cuthah and from Avah and from Hamath and from Sepharvaim, and settled them in the cities of the children of Israel; and they took possession of Samaria and inhabited its cities.[9]

## Sennacherib's Invasion of Judah

18-19    Now in the third year of Hoshea, king of Israel, Hezekiah, the son of Ahaz, king of Judah, began to reign. He was twenty-five years old when he became king, and he reigned twenty-nine years in Jerusalem.

He did that which was right in the sight of the Lord, according to all that David had done. He removed the altars on the high places, and broke the images, and cut down the sacrificial groves, and broke in pieces

[9] See II KINGS, Chapter 17, in Notes and Excisions.

251

the brazen serpent that Moses had made. For in those days the children of Israel burned incense to it, and called it Nehushtan. He trusted only in the Lord, and departed not from the commandments which the Lord had given through Moses.

And the Lord was with him, and he prospered. He rebelled against the king of Assyria, and served him not. He smote the Philistines as far as Gaza and its borders, from the tower of the watchman to the fortified city.

In the fourteenth year of the reign of King Hezekiah, Sennacherib, the new king of Assyria, came up against all the fortified cities of Judah, and took them.

The king of Judah sent word to the king of Assyria at Lachish, saying, "I have offended you; withdraw from me, and whatever you put on me as penalty I will bear."

The king of Assyria demanded from Hezekiah three hundred talents of silver and thirty talents of gold. And at that time Hezekiah removed the gold from the doors of the temple, and from the pillars, and gave the gold to the king of Assyria. Hezekiah also gave him all the silver that was found in the house of the Lord, and in the treasures of the king's house.

Nevertheless, the king of Assyria sent Tartan and Rabsaris and Rab-shakeh from Lachish with a great army against Jerusalem. And they came and stood by the conduit of the upper pool, which is on the highway of the laundryman's field. When they called out for the king, there came out to them Eliakim, the son of Hilkiah, who was overseer of the palace, and Shebna the scribe, and Joah, the son of Asaph the recorder.

Rab-shakeh said to them, "Tell your King Hezekiah, 'Thus says Sennacherib, the great king of Assyria, "In whom do you trust, that you rebel against me? Behold, you trust in the staff of this broken reed Egypt, on which if a man lean, it will go into his hand and pierce it. So is Pharaoh, king of Egypt, to all who trust in him."' Now, I pray you, give pledges to my lord the king of Assyria, and I will deliver to you two thousand horses if you are able on your part to set riders upon them. How then will you turn away the face of one captain of the least of my master's servants, and put your trust in Egypt for chariots and horsemen?"

Eliakim and Shebna and Joah said to Rab-shakeh, "Speak, we pray you, in the Syrian language, for we understand it; and do not talk with us in Judean within hearing of the people on the wall."

But Rab-shakeh said to them, "Has my master sent me to your master, and to you, to speak these words? Has he not sent me also to the men who sit on the wall?" Then Rab-shakeh stood up and cried out with a loud voice in Judean, "Hear the word of the great king, the king of Assyria! Thus says the king, 'Let not Hezekiah deceive you, for he shall not be able to deliver you out of my hand; nor let Hezekiah make you trust in the Lord, saying, "The Lord will surely deliver us." ' Do not heed Hezekiah; for thus says the king of Assyria, 'Make an agreement with me by a payment of tribute, and come out to me; and then each man among you may eat of his own vine and of his own fig tree, and drink the waters of his own cistern, until I come and take you away to a land like your own land, a land of grain and wine, a land of bread and vineyards, a land of olive and of honey, that you may live, and not die. But do not heed Hezekiah when he tries to persuade you, saying, "The Lord will deliver us." Has any of the gods of the nations delivered his land out of the hand of the king of Assyria? Where are the gods of Hamath, and of Arpad? Where are the gods of Sepharvaim, Hena, and Ivah? Have they delivered Samaria out of my hand? Who among all the gods of the countries have delivered their country out of my hand, that the Lord should deliver Jerusalem out of my hand?' "

But the people held their peace and answered not a word.

Then Eliakim and Shebna and Joah went to Hezekiah with their garments rent, and told him the words of Rab-shakeh. King Hezekiah covered himself with sackcloth, and went into the house of the Lord. And he sent Eliakim and Shebna and the elders of the priests, covered with sackcloth, to Isaiah the prophet.

They said to Isaiah, "Thus says Hezekiah, 'This day is a day of trouble, and a rebuke, and disgrace, for the children have reached the hour of birth, and there is no strength to bring them forth. It may be that the Lord our God will hear the words of Rab-shakeh, whom the king of Assyria has sent to reproach the living God, and reprove those words. Therefore pray for the remnant that is left.' "

Isaiah answered, "You shall say to your master, 'Thus says the Lord: "Be not afraid of the words you have heard, with which the servants of the king of Assyria have blasphemed me. Behold, he shall return, and I will cause him to fall by the sword in his own land!" '

"And this is the word that the Lord has spoken concerning Sennacherib: 'Whom have you reproached and blasphemed? Against whom have you raised your voice and lifted up your eyes? Against the Holy One of Israel! By your messengers you have reproached the Lord, and said, "With the multitude of my chariots I have come up to the heights of the mountains, to the sides of Lebanon, and will cut down the tall cedar and the choice cypress; and I will enter into the forest of Carmel." Because your rage against me and your tumult have come up to my ears, I will put my ring in your nose, and my bridle between your lips, and I will turn you back on the way by which you came.'

"And this also is the word of the Lord concerning the king of Assyria, 'He shall not come into this city, nor shoot an arrow there, nor come before it with a shield, nor cast up mounds against it. By the way that he came, by that same way shall he return, and shall not come into this city! For I will defend this city and save it, for my own sake and for the sake of my servant David.'"

That night the angel of the Lord smote in the camp of the Assyrians a hundred and eighty-five thousand. And when Sennacherib rose early in the morning, behold, all the men in his army were dead.

So Sennacherib, king of Assyria, departed, and went back, and dwelt at Nineveh. And as he was worshiping in the house of Nisroch his god, Adrammelech and Sharezer, his sons, slew him with the sword, and escaped into the land of Ararat. And his son Esarhaddon reigned in his stead.

## Isaiah's Forecast

20    In those days Hezekiah was ill to the point of death. And the prophet Isaiah came to him and said, "Thus says the Lord, 'Set your house in order, for you shall die.'"

Hezekiah turned his face to the wall and prayed, "I beseech you, O Lord, remember now how I walked before you in truth, and have done that which is good in your sight!" And he wept bitterly.

As Isaiah left the king, and before he had gone as far as the middle courtyard, the word of the Lord came to him, saying, "Return, and tell Hezekiah, the captain of my people, 'Thus says the Lord: "I have heard your prayer; I have seen your tears. Behold, I will heal you. On the third day you shall go up into the house of the Lord. And I will add to your life fifteen years; and I will deliver you and this city from the king of Assyria, for my own sake and for the sake of my servant David."'"

When Isaiah told the king, he asked, "What shall be the sign that the Lord will heal me?" Isaiah answered, "This sign you shall have: Shall the shadow on your sundial go forward ten steps, or go back ten steps?" Hezekiah answered, "Rather let the shadow turn back ten steps."

Isaiah the prophet cried out to the Lord; and he brought the shadow back ten steps, from which it had gone down on the step-sundial of Ahaz.

At that time Berodach-baladan, son of Baladan, king of Babylon, sent messengers with a present to Hezekiah, for he had heard that Hezekiah had been sick. Hezekiah listened to them, and showed them all his precious things, the silver and the gold, and the spices and the precious ointments, and all his armor, and all his treasures. There was nothing in his house or in his dominion that Hezekiah did not show them.

Isaiah came to King Hezekiah and asked, "What said these men? From whence did they come to you?" Hezekiah answered, "They came from a far country, from Babylon." And Isaiah asked, "What did they see in your house?" Hezekiah answered, "There is nothing among my treasures that I have not shown them."

Then Isaiah said to the king, "Hear the word of the Lord: 'Behold, the days are at hand when all that is in your house, and that which your fathers stored up to this day, shall be carried into Babylon: nothing shall be left. And the sons which you shall have, they shall be taken away; and they will be eunuchs in the palace of the king of Babylon.'"

The rest of the acts of Hezekiah, and all his might, and how he made a pool and a conduit and brought water into the city, are they not written in the Book of the Chronicles of the Kings of Judah?

And Hezekiah slept with his fathers; and Manasseh his son succeeded him.

## The Reforms of Josiah

21-23    Manasseh was twelve years old when he began to reign, and he
         reigned thirty-one years in Jerusalem. He reared up altars to Baal; and worshiped all the hosts of heaven, and served them.

And the Lord spoke through his servants the prophets, saying, "Because Manasseh has made Judah sin with his idols, behold, I will stretch over Jerusalem the line of Samaria, and the plummet of the house of Ahab; and I will wipe Jerusalem as a man wipes a dish, wiping it and turning it upside down. And I will forsake the remnant of my inheritance, and deliver them to their enemies."

Moreover, Manasseh shed much innocent blood, besides the sin which he made Judah sin. And then Manasseh slept with his fathers, and was buried in the garden of his own house; and Amon his son succeeded him.

Amon also did evil in the sight of the Lord, as his father Manasseh had done. His servants conspired against him, and slew the king in his own house. But the people of the land slew those who had conspired against the king, and made Josiah his son king in his place.

Josiah was eight years old when he began to reign, and he reigned thirty-one years in Jerusalem. And he walked in the way of David his forefather, and turned not aside to the right hand or to the left.

In the eighteenth year of his rule, King Josiah sent Shaphan the scribe to the house of the Lord, saying, "Go to Hilkiah the high priest, that he may take the silver which the keepers of the door have gathered from the people; and let them deliver it to those who have charge of the work of the house of the Lord, to give to the carpenters and builders and masons, and to buy timber and hewn stone to repair the house."

And Hilkiah the high priest said to Shaphan the scribe, "I have found the book of the law in the house of the Lord." Hilkiah gave the book to Shaphan, and he read it.

Then Shaphan went to the king and said, "Your servants have gathered the money that was in the temple, and have given it to the workmen in charge of the work in the house of the Lord. Hilkiah the priest also gave me this book." And Shaphan read from the book of the law to the king.

When the king heard the words of the book, he rent his clothes. And the king communed with Hilkiah the priest, and Ahikam, son of Shaphan, and Achbor, and Shaphan the scribe, and Asahiah, a servant of the king's, saying, "Go, inquire of the Lord for me, and for the people and for all Judah, concerning the words of this book; for great must be the wrath of the Lord against us, because our fathers have not done according to all that is written in it concerning us."

So they went to Huldah the prophetess, who dwelt in another part of Jerusalem. And she told them, "Thus says the Lord God of Israel, 'Tell the man who sent you to me, behold, I will bring evil upon this place and upon its inhabitants, according to the words of the book which the king of Judah has read, because the people have forsaken me. But to the king of Judah who sent you, thus shall you say, "Because you humbled yourself before the Lord when you heard what I spoke against this place, I also have heard you. Behold, I will gather you to your fathers in peace, and your eyes shall not see the evil which I will bring upon this place." ' "

And they brought to the king the words of Huldah.

The king sent for the elders of Judah and of Jerusalem. And he went up into the house of the Lord, and with him all the people, both small and great; and he read to them from the book of the covenant which had been found in the house of the Lord.

The king made a covenant before the Lord to keep his commandments and his testimonies and his statutes. And all the people confirmed the covenant.

Then the king commanded Hilkiah the high priest, and the priests of the second order, and the keepers of the door, to bring out of the temple all the vessels made for Baal and for all the host of heaven; and he burned them outside of Jerusalem in the fields of Kidron, and carried the ashes to Bethel.

And he removed the idolatrous priests whom the kings of Judah had ordained to burn incense to Baal, to the sun, and to the moon, and to the planets, and to all the host of heaven.

And he demolished Tophet, which is in the valley of the children of Hinnom, that no man might make his son or daughter pass through the fire to Molech.

And he took away the horses that the kings of Judah had given to the sun, at the entrance to the house of the Lord, and burned the chariots of the sun with fire.

And the altars on the roof of the upper chamber of Ahaz, which the kings of Judah had made, and the altars which Manasseh had made in the two courts of the house of the Lord, the king demolished and broke down, and cast their dust into the brook Kidron. Then he broke the images and cut down the groves.

Moreover, Josiah put away the wizards and the idols and all the abominations that were in Judah and in Jerusalem, that he might follow the law written in the book which Hilkiah the priest found in the house of the Lord.

Before him there was no king like Josiah who turned to the Lord with all his heart and with all his soul and with all his might; nor after him arose any like him.

Now the rest of the acts of Josiah, and all that he did, are they not written in the Book of the Chronicles of the Kings of Judah?

In his days Pharaoh Nechoh, king of Egypt, went up against the king of Assyria to the river Euphrates; and King Josiah went against him, and was slain at Megiddo. His servants carried him in a chariot, dead, from Megiddo to Jerusalem, and buried him in his own sepulcher.

And the people of the land took Jehoahaz, the son of Josiah, and anointed him king in his father's stead.

## The Fall of Judah

23-25   Jehoahaz was twenty-three years old when he began to reign; and he reigned three months in Jerusalem. Then Pharaoh Nechoh put him in bonds at Riblah, and made Eliakim, brother of Jehoahaz, king in his place. And Pharaoh changed the king's name to Jehoiakim, and took Jehoahaz to Egypt; and he died there.

Jehoiakim was twenty-five years old when he began to reign, and in his days Nebuchadnezzar, king of Babylon, came up, and Jehoiakim became his vassal for three years. Then Jehoiakim turned and rebelled against the king of Babylon.

Jehoiakim ruled eleven years in Jerusalem; and when he died, his son Jehoiakin became king.

Jehoiakin was eighteen years old, and he reigned in Jerusalem three months. At that time the servants of Nebuchadnezzar, king of Babylon, came up against Jerusalem, and the city was besieged. Jehoiakin, the king of Judah, surrendered to the king of Babylon, he, and his mother, and his servants, and his princes, and his officers. And the king of Babylon took them captive.

Nebuchadnezzar carried off all the treasures of the house of the Lord and the treasures of the king's house, and broke up all the vessels of gold which Solomon had made for the temple of the Lord. And he carried away all the mighty men of valor, and all the craftsmen, and the smiths; none remained save the poorest of the land. Thus he carried away to Babylon Jehoiakin the king, and the king's mother, and the king's wives, and his officers, and the mighty of the land; all of them he carried into captivity from Jerusalem to Babylon.

Then the king of Babylon made Mattaniah, Jehoiakin's uncle, king in his stead, and changed his name to Zedekiah. And Zedekiah reigned eleven years in Jerusalem.

And it came to pass that Zedekiah rebelled against the king of Babylon. In the ninth year of his reign, Nebuchadnezzar came against Jerusalem, and built siege walls round about. And the city was besieged until the eleventh year of King Zedekiah's reign. On the ninth day of the fourth month of that year famine prevailed in the city, and there was no food for the people.

Then the city was breached, and all the men of war fled at night by way of the gate between the two walls, which was by the king's garden, while the Chaldeans were surrounding the city; and the king went toward the plain. But the army of the Chaldeans pursued the king, and overtook him in the plains of Jericho; and all his army had scattered from him.

So they took Zedekiah and brought him to the king of Babylon at Riblah. And they slew his sons before his eyes; then put out his eyes and bound him with fetters of brass, and carried him away to Babylon.

In the fifth month, on the seventh day of the month, Nebuzar-adan, captain of the guard of the king of Babylon, came to Jerusalem. He burnt the house of the Lord, and the king's house, and all the houses of Jerusalem, and every great man's house. And the army of the Chaldeans, who were with the captain of the guard, broke down the walls of Jerusalem round about. Now the rest of the people who had been left in the city, and the fugitives who had fallen away to the king of Babylon, with the remnant of the multitude, Nebuzar-adan carried away as captives. But the captain left some of the poorest of the land as vine-dressers and husbandmen.

So Judah was carried away from their land into captivity to Babylon.

# I and II CHRONICLES
## A Late Version of I and II Kings

❰ In length, I and II Chronicles approximate I and II Kings, and in content they cover the period of "The Kingdoms," but from a markedly different approach: whereas the books of Samuel and Kings stress the historical and prophetic developments in Israel, I and II Chronicles are more concerned with the ecclesiastical development and the growth of the priestly tradition. Though the events are much the same, the underscoring differs.

In the Greek, the Chronicles are called Paralipomenon, which means "Things Left Out," for apparently this material was intended to supplement I and II Samuel, I and II Kings, and other books of history which have since been lost.

I Chronicles begins with a nine-chapter genealogy, from Adam to the days of King Saul and his children to the ninth generation. The tenth chapter recounts King Saul's defeat in battle, his death, and the passing of the kingdom to David, son of Jesse. The rest of the book (Chapters 11-29) retells the story of King David's life and reign; his devotion in gathering materials for the temple and establishing the Levites in their many duties; and his instructions to Solomon on the building of the temple and its administration. The book ends with David's death, "Full of years, riches, and honor"; and we are reminded that all the acts of King David are to be found in the Book of Samuel the Prophet, the Book of Nathan the Prophet, and the Book of Gad the Seer.

II Chronicles recounts the deeds of King Solomon in the first nine chapters, but adds nothing basically new to the story as given in I Kings. Great stress is laid on Solomon's dedication to the building of the temple, and on his development of the institution of sacrifices. Here, as in I Kings, mention is made of the lavish palace Solomon built for Pharaoh's daughter, his wife, and the reason for building it is given: "For he said, 'My wife shall not dwell in the house of David, king of Israel, because the house was holy into which the ark of the Lord had come.'"

The remainder of II Chronicles (Chapters 10-36) presents a terse history of the southern kingdom of Judah, from the death of Solomon to the Babylonian captivity. This is easier to follow than the same account in II Kings, since it is not constantly interrupted and confused with events occurring in the northern kingdom of Israel during the same period; but it is also less colorful than the earlier account. Large sections of the Chronicles are presented in synopsis form, often lacking verbs and connectives.

There are several striking features in Chronicles. Although the two books, like those of Samuel and Kings, cite facts and figures about battles, armies, tribute exacted or paid, temple vessels, and so on, all too frequently the same facts bear different figures in the two accounts. Sometimes the discrepancies are slight, and often the divergence is quite great. Varying reasons for these discrepancies have been given by different scholars. But their existence still remains puzzling.

The first mention of Satan in the Hebrew Scriptures is made in Chronicles. This would indicate that the books of I and II Chronicles were compiled rather late, since the concept of Satan does not appear in the early period of Israel.

Perhaps the most striking feature of the two books of Chronicles is the importance they attribute to King David as founder of the tradition of the temple.

II Chronicles ends where the book of Ezra begins — with the proclamation by King Cyrus of Persia, permitting Jewish captives in Babylonia to return to Palestine to help in the rebuilding of the temple at Jerusalem. ❪

# DANIEL
## A Chronicle of Miracles and Prophecies

❴ This concise work of twelve short chapters, written partly in Hebrew and partly in Aramaic in the original, is the only purely apocalyptic work in the Hebrew Scriptures. Like all apocalyptic literature, it is written almost entirely in symbolic language and contains references to the future, and even to the end of time. To interpret the symbols in this slender book, numberless works have been written in the past twenty centuries; and the end is not yet in sight.

Not only is practically every word in this book subject to diverse interpretations, but even the place of the book in the Bible has produced stormy differences. In the Hebrew Scriptures, Daniel comes before Ezra, because the events it records took place in the days of the Babylonian captivity just preceding the events recorded in the book of Ezra. Many scholars maintain that the language and historical allusions of Daniel indicate it could not have been written before the days of the Maccabees (some four centuries after the Babylonian captivity); others cite Daniel's wisdom as having become so proverbial during his own lifetime that the prophet Ezekiel (who lived early in the Babylonian captivity) could exclaim ironically to the king of Tyre: "You are wiser than Daniel!" (Ezekiel, 28:3). But whatever the period in which the work was completed, the events in the book of Daniel place it, chronologically, before Ezra, even though there is dispute among scholars as to its historical value.

In the Greek translation of the Bible (and in subsequent versions based on the Greek, including the King James Authorized Version and all versions based on the King James Bible) Daniel is placed fourth among the major prophets, because of the interpretation given to his visions and forecasts of the future.

The Greek version differs in another important respect from the Hebrew book from which it is taken: In the third chapter of the book, the Greek version contains a long section not found in the Hebrew, known as the Song of the Three Holy Children; and in the end two additional chapters appear, known as Susanna and the Elders, and Bel and the Dragon. These are now included in Roman and Greek Catholic Bibles; in Protestant Bibles they appear among the Apocrypha when the Apocrypha are given.

The Book of Daniel, apart from its theological and eschatological implications, includes stories which are universal in their appeal. ⟨[

## *Daniel Before the King*

1    In the third year of the reign of Jehoiakin, king of Judah, came Nebuchadnezzar, king of Babylon, to Jerusalem, and besieged it. And the Lord gave the king of Judah into his hand, with part of the vessels of the house of God, which he carried off to Shinar; and he brought the vessels into the treasure house of his god.

Then the king told Ashpenax, the chief of his eunuchs, to bring certain of the children of Israel, of the king's descendants and of the princes — children in whom there was no blemish, and who were skillful and wise, and such as had ability to serve in the king's palace — to whom they might teach the learning and language of the Chaldeans.

Now among these were Daniel, Hananiah, Mishael, and Azariah, whom the chief eunuch renamed Belteshazzar, Shadrach, Meshach, and Abednego. And to these four God gave knowledge and vision, and skill and learning; and Daniel had understanding in all visions and dreams.

At the end of the time that the king had appointed, they were brought in before Nebuchadnezzar, and the king spoke with them. But among them all was found none like Daniel, Hananiah, Mishael, and Azariah; therefore they stood before the king. And in all matters of wisdom and understanding that the king inquired of them, he found them ten times wiser than all the magicians and astrologers in his realm. And Daniel continued until the first year of King Cyrus.

# The Feet of Clay

2      In the second year of his reign Nebuchadnezzar dreamed a
dream which troubled his spirit. The king commanded the magi-
• cians, the astrologers, the sorcerers, and the Chaldeans, to be summoned.
So they came and stood before him. And the king said to them, "I
have dreamed a dream, and my spirit is troubled." Then said the Chaldeans to the king in Syriac, "O King, live forever! Tell your servants the
dream, and we will show you its interpretation."

The king answered, "The dream has gone from me. If you will not
make known to me the dream and its interpretation, you shall be cut in
pieces, and your houses made a dunghill. But if you declare the dream
and the interpretation of it, you will receive from me gifts and great
honor." The Chaldeans answered, "There is not a man upon the earth
who can do so! No ruler has asked such a thing of any magician or
astrologer or Chaldean. It is a difficult thing that the king asks, and none
can reveal it except the gods."

At this the king became very angry, and decreed that all the wise men
in Babylon should be slain. And they sought Daniel and his companions,
to slay them also.

Daniel asked Arioch, the captain of the king's guard, who had gone out
to slay the wise men of Babylon, "Why is the king's decree so hasty and
so harsh?" And Arioch made the matter known to him.

Daniel went in and petitioned the king to grant him time, and he
would declare to the king the dream and its interpretation. Then Daniel
went to his house and told Hananiah, Mishael, and Azariah, that they
might pray with him to God concerning this secret, so that Daniel and his
companions would not perish with the rest of the wise men of Babylon.
And the secret was revealed to Daniel in a vision of the night.

Daniel said, "Blessed be the name of God, for wisdom and might are
his! He changes the times and the seasons. He removes kings, and sets
them up. He gives wisdom to the wise, and knowledge to those who understand. He reveals the deep and secret things. He knows what is in the
darkness, and the light dwells with him. I thank you and praise you, O
God of my fathers, who has revealed to us the king's concern."

Therefore Daniel went in to Arioch and said to him, "Destroy not the
wise men of Babylon. Bring me in before the king, and I will tell him
the interpretation."

Arioch brought Daniel before the king in haste, and said, "I have found a man among the captives of Judah who will make known to the king the interpretation of his dream." The king said to Daniel, "Are you able to make known to me both the dream I dreamed and its interpretation?"

Daniel answered, "The secret which the king has demanded, the wise men, the astrologers, the magicians, the soothsayers cannot reveal to the king. But there is a God in heaven who reveals secrets and makes known what shall be in the days to come. Your dream and the visions of your head are these:

"You, O King, dreamed of a great image of surpassing brightness; and its form was terrible. The head was of fine gold, the breast and arms of silver, the belly and thighs of brass, the legs of iron, the feet part of iron and part of clay. Then you saw a stone which struck the image upon the feet that were of iron and clay, and broke them into pieces. Then the iron, the clay, the brass, the silver, and the gold, were broken into pieces together, and became like the chaff of summer threshing floors; and the wind carried them away until no trace was left of them. And the stone which smote the image became a great mountain, and filled the whole earth.

"That was your dream. And this is its interpretation:

"You, O King, are a king of kings; for the God of heaven has given you power and strength and glory. And wherever the children of man dwell, the beasts of the field and the birds of heaven, he has given into your hand and made you ruler over them all. You are this head of gold.

"And after you shall arise another kingdom inferior to you, and a third kingdom of brass, which shall rule over all the earth. And the fourth kingdom shall be strong as iron; for, as iron breaks into pieces and crushes all things, so shall it break and crush. And as you saw the feet and toes, part of potters' clay and part of iron, so shall the kingdom be a divided kingdom. And as the toes of the feet were part of iron and part of clay, so the kingdom shall be in part strong and in part brittle.

"And in the days of those kings the God of heaven will set up a kingdom which shall never be destroyed; and the kingdom shall not be left to other people, but it shall break in pieces and consume all these kingdoms, just as you saw the stone break into pieces the iron, the brass, the clay, the silver, and the gold. The great God has made known to the king what shall come to pass. The dream is certain and the interpretation of it certain."

The king answered, "Truly, your god is the God of gods, and the Lord of kings, and a Revealer of secrets, seeing you could reveal this secret."

Then the king gave Daniel many great gifts, and appointed him ruler over the whole province of Babylon, and chief of the governors over all the wise men in his realm. And Daniel requested of the king, and he appointed Shadrach, Meshach, and Abed-nego over the affairs of the province of Babylon. But Daniel remained at the court of the king.

## The Trial by Fire

3    Nebuchadnezzar the king had made an image of gold, whose height was sixty cubits and its breadth six cubits, which he set up in the plain of Dura, in the province of Babylon. Then the king sent for the princes, the governors, the captains, the judges, the treasurers, the counselors, the magistrates, and all the rulers of the provinces, to come to the dedication of the image which he had set up. When they gathered together and stood before the image, a herald cried out, "To you it is commanded, O people, nations of all languages, that when you hear the sound of the horn, pipe, harp, sackbut, dulcimer, and every kind of music, you must fall down and worship the golden image that Nebuchadnezzar the king has set up. And whoever does not obey, in the same hour shall be cast into the midst of a burning fiery furnace."

After that time certain Chaldeans came to the king and said, "O King, live forever! You, O King, have made a decree that all shall fall down and worship the golden image. Yet there are certain Jews whom you have set over the affairs of the province of Babylon, Shadrach, Meshach, and Abed-nego; and these men, O King, have no regard for you. They serve not your gods, nor worship the golden image which you have set up."

Then Nebuchadnezzar in his rage and fury sent for Shadrach, Meshach, and Abed-nego. And when they were brought before him, the king asked, "Is it true that you do not serve my gods, or worship the golden image which I have set up? Now if you are ready at the sound of the music to fall down and worship the image which I have made, it is well; but if you worship not, you shall be cast into a burning fiery furnace; and who is that God that will deliver you out of my hands?"

And they answered, "O King, be it known to you that we will not serve your gods, nor worship the golden image which you have set up. Our God, whom we serve, is able to deliver us from the burning fiery furnace, and he will deliver us from your hand, O King."

Then was Nebuchadnezzar full of fury. He commanded that the furnace should be heated seven times more than it was wont to be heated. And he commanded the most mighty men in his army to bind Shadrach, Meshach, and Abed-nego, and to cast them into the fiery furnace.

These men were bound in their cloaks, their tunics, and their hats, and were cast into the furnace. And because the king's order was urgent, and the fire exceedingly hot, the flame of the fire slew the men who took up Shadrach, Meshach, and Abed-nego. And the three men fell down bound into the midst of the furnace, unharmed.

Then Nebuchadnezzar the king was alarmed, and rose in haste and said to his counselors, "Did we not cast three bound men into the fire?" They answered, "True, O King." And he said, "Lo, I see four men walking in the midst of the fire, and they are not harmed; and the form of the fourth is like that of an angel."

Nebuchadnezzar came near the mouth of the fiery furnace and called, "Shadrach, Meshach, and Abed-nego, you servants of the most high God, come out!"

Then Shadrach, Meshach, and Abed-nego came out from the midst of the fire. And the princes, the governors, the captains, and the king's counselors saw these men, upon whose bodies the fire had no power, and not a hair of their heads was singed, neither were their cloaks changed, nor the smell of fire passed on to them.

Nebuchadnezzar said, "Blessed be the God of Shadrach, Meshach, and Abed-nego, who has sent his angel and delivered his servants, who trusted in him, and have changed the king's word, and yielded their bodies, that they might not serve nor worship any god except their own God. Therefore I make a decree that any who speak anything amiss against the God of Shadrach, Meshach, and Abed-nego shall be cut in pieces, and their houses shall be made a dunghill, because there is no other God who can rescue in this manner."

Then the king promoted Shadrach, Meshach, and Abed-nego in the province of Babylon.[1]

[1] See DANIEL, Chapter 3, in Notes and Exclsions.

## Nebuchadnezzar's Madness

**4**   Nebuchadnezzar the king, to all people, nations of all languages on the earth:

Peace be with you!

I, Nebuchadnezzar, was at rest in my house, and flourishing in my palace, when I had a dream which made me afraid, and the visions in my head troubled me. Therefore I made a decree for all the wise men of Babylon to come before me, that they might make known to me the interpretation of my dream. Then came the magicians, the astrologers, the Chaldeans, and the soothsayers; but they could not give me the interpretation of it. But at the last Daniel came in before me, and I told him the dream, saying, "O Daniel, because I know that the spirit of the holy God is in you, and no secret is difficult for you, tell me the meaning of my dream: I saw a tree in the center of the earth, and the height of it was great. The tree grew and was strong, and reached to heaven, and it could be seen to the ends of the earth. The leaves of it were fair, and its fruit abundant, and it had food for all. The beasts had shade under it, and the birds dwelt in its boughs, and all flesh was fed from it. Then I saw in my vision a watcher, a holy one, come down from heaven. And he cried aloud, 'Hew down the tree and cut off its branches; shake off its leaves and scatter its fruit. Let the beasts get away from under it, and the birds from its branches. But leave the stump of its root in the earth, bound with a band of iron and brass, in the tender grass of the field; and let it be wet with the dew of heaven. And let his portion be with the beasts in the grass of the earth. Let his heart be changed from man's, and let a beast's heart be given to him; and let seven years pass over him.'

"This dream I, King Nebuchadnezzar, have dreamed. Now you, Daniel, declare its meaning, as all the wise men of my kingdom are not able to make it known to me."

Daniel was dismayed for a time, and his thoughts troubled him. Then Daniel answered, "My lord, would that your dream were for those who hate you, and the interpretation of it for your enemies! You have grown and become strong until your greatness reaches to heaven and your dominion to the ends of the earth. And this, O King, is the decree of the Most High: you shall be driven from men, and shall dwell with beasts of the field; and you shall eat grass like an ox. And seven years shall pass

over you, until you know that the Most High rules in the kingdom of men
and gives it to whomsoever he will."

All this was fulfilled.

And at the end of seven years I, Nebuchadnezzar, lifted my eyes to
heaven, and my understanding returned to me; and I blessed the Most
High, and I praised and honored him, who lives forever, and whose dominion is everlasting, and whose kingdom endures from generation to
generation.

## The Writing on the Wall

5     Belshazzar the king, son of Nebuchadnezzar, gave a great feast
to a thousand of his lords. And they brought gold and silver vessels which his father Nebuchadnezzar had taken out of the temple in
Jerusalem, that the king, his princes, his wives, and his concubines, might
drink out of them. They drank wine, and praised the gods of gold and
of silver, of brass, of iron, of wood, and of stone.

In that same hour there appeared the fingers of a man's hand, and
wrote upon the plaster of the wall of the king's palace; and the king saw
the hand that wrote. Then the king's face paled, and his thoughts troubled him so that his joints were loosed, and his knees struck one against
another.

The king cried out for the astrologers, the Chaldeans, and the soothsayers. And the king said to the wise men of Babylon, "Whoever reads
this writing, and tells me what it means, shall be clothed in scarlet and
have a chain of gold about his neck, and shall be third to the ruler of
the kingdom." But none could read the writing or make known to the
king what it meant. Then was King Belshazzar greatly troubled, and his
lords were dismayed.

Now the queen, when she heard of the words of the king and his lords,
came into the banquet hall, and said, "O King, live forever! Let not your
thoughts trouble you. For there is a man in your kingdom, named Daniel, in whom there is wisdom like that of the gods. The king Nebuchadnezzar, your father, made him master of the magicians, astrologers, Chaldeans, and soothsayers. Forasmuch as an excellent spirit and knowledge
were found in this Daniel, now let him be called, and he will show the
interpretation."

Then Daniel was brought in before the king. And the king said to him, "Are you that Daniel whom the king my father brought from Judah with the captives? I have heard of you, that the spirit of the gods is in you, and that light and understanding and wisdom are found in you. Now if you can read the writing on the wall, and make known to me the interpretation of it, you shall be clothed in scarlet and have a chain of gold about your neck, and shall be the third ruler in the kingdom."

Daniel answered, "Give your rewards to another; but I will read the writing to the king, and make known to him the interpretation.

"O King, the most high God gave Nebuchadnezzar your father a kingdom and honor and glory. And because of his greatness nations of all languages trembled and feared him. But when his heart and mind hardened in pride, he was deposed from his kingly throne, and his glory taken from him; and he dwelt with the wild asses and ate grass, and his body was wet with the dew of heaven, until he knew that the most high God rules the kingdom of men.

"And you his son, O Belshazzar, have not humbled your heart, though you knew all this, but have lifted yourself up against the Lord of heaven. The vessels of his temple have been brought before you, and you and your lords, your wives and your concubines have drunk wine from them; And you have praised the gods of silver and gold, of brass, of iron, of wood, and of stone — which see not, nor hear, nor know. Yet the God in whose hand is your breath you have not glorified.

"Then was the hand sent to write upon your wall, and this is what was written:

*MENE, MENE, TEKEL, UPHARSIN.*

"This is the interpretation:

"MENE: God has numbered the days of your kingdom.

"TEKEL: You have been weighed in the balance, and found wanting.

"PERES: Your kingdom shall be divided and given to the Medes and Persians."

Then Belshazzar commanded, and they clothed Daniel in scarlet, and put a chain of gold about his neck, and proclaimed him the third ruler in the kingdom.

In that night Belshazzar, the king of the Chaldeans, was slain. And Darius the Mede took the kingdom.

## Daniel in the Lions' Den

**6**     It pleased Darius to set over the kingdom a hundred and twenty
governors. And over them he set three presidents, of whom
Daniel was first, to whom the governors might give accounts, so that the
king should suffer no loss. And Daniel distinguished himself above the
others because of the excellent spirit in him; and the king thought to set
him over the whole realm.

Then the presidents and princes sought to find occasion against Daniel;
but they could find none, for he was faithful, nor was any error or fault
found in him. Then said these men, "We shall not find any occasion
against this Daniel unless we find it concerning the law of his God."

And they assembled before the king and said, "King Darius, live forever! All the presidents of the kingdom, the governors, and the princes,
the counselors and the captains have met and agreed on a royal decree:
that whoever shall ask a petition of any god or man for thirty days, save
of you, O King, shall be cast into the den of lions. Now, O King, establish
the decree and sign the writing, that it may not be changed, according to
the law of the Medes and Persians, which does not alter."

Wherefore King Darius signed the decree.

Now when Daniel knew that the decree had been signed, he went into
his house, and knelt and prayed as he always did. Then these men assembled, and found Daniel praying and making supplication before his
God.

They spoke in the king's presence concerning the king's decree, and
asked, "Have you not signed a decree that every man who asks a petition
of any god or man within thirty days save of you, O King, shall be cast
into the den of lions?" The king answered, "This is true, according to the
law of the Medes and the Persians, which does not alter." They said, "That
Daniel, who is of the captives from Judah, has no regard for you, O
King, or the decree that you have signed, for he petitions his God three
times each day."

When the King heard these words he grieved, and set his heart on saving Daniel. And he labored until sundown to deliver him. But these
men said, "Know, O King, that it is a law of the Medes and the Persians
that no decree or statute which the king establishes may be changed."

Then the king commanded, and they brought Daniel and cast him into
the den of lions. And a stone was brought and laid upon the mouth of

the den; and the king sealed it with his own signet, and with the signet of his lords. Then the king went to his palace and passed the night fasting; no music was played before him, and sleep left him.

The king rose very early, and went in haste to the den of lions. And he cried in a lamenting voice, "O Daniel, servant of the living God, has your God, whom you serve continually, been able to deliver you from the lions?" Daniel answered, "O King, live forever! My God has sent his angel, and has shut the lions' mouths so that they have not harmed me. For I have been found innocent before him. And also to you, O King, have I done no harm."

Then was the king exceedingly glad, and commanded that they should take Daniel up out of the den. So Daniel was taken up out of the den, and no manner of hurt was found upon him, because he believed in his God.

And the king commanded, and they brought those men who had accused Daniel, and cast them into the den of lions, them and their children and their wives; and the lions attacked them and broke all their bones.

Then King Darius wrote to all the people who dwell on the earth:

"Peace be with you! I make a decree that in all my dominion men tremble before the God of Daniel; for he is the living God, and steadfast forever, and his kingdom shall not be destroyed, and his dominion shall endure to the end. He delivers and rescues, he works miracles and wonders in heaven and earth; he who has delivered Daniel from the power of the lions."

So Daniel prospered in the reign of Darius, and also in the reign of Cyrus the Persian.[2]

## The Vision of the Four Beasts

7-8    In the first year of Belshazzar, king of Babylon, Daniel had a dream, and he wrote down the dream and told the sum of the matter:

"I saw in my vision by night the four winds of heaven strive upon the great sea. And four great beasts came up from the sea, different one from the other.

"The first was like a lion, and had eagle's wings. I watched it until the

[2] See DANIEL, Chapter 6, in Notes and Excisions.

wings of it were plucked off, and it was lifted up from the earth and made to stand like a man, and a man's heart was given to it.

"And behold, there was another beast, like a bear, which raised itself up on one side, and it had three ribs between its teeth. And it was told, 'Arise, devour much flesh.'

"After this I beheld another, like a leopard, which had upon its back four wings of a bird. The beast had also four heads; and dominion was given to it.

"After this I saw in the night visions, and behold, a fourth beast, dreadful and terrible, and exceedingly strong; and it had great iron teeth. It devoured and broke in pieces, and stamped the residue with its feet. And it was different from all the other beasts, and it had ten horns. I considered the horns, and behold, there came up among them another little horn, before whom three of the first horns were plucked up by the roots; and behold, in this horn were eyes like the eyes of man, and a mouth speaking great things.

"I watched till the thrones were cast down, and the Ancient One, whose garment was white as snow, and the hair of his head like pure wool, sat down. His throne was fiery flame, and his heels burning fire. A fiery stream flowed before him; and a thousand thousands ministered to him, and ten thousand times ten thousand stood before him. The judgment was set, and the books were opened.

"I beheld the great beast slain, and his body destroyed and given to the burning flame. As for the rest of the beasts, they had their dominion taken away, but their lives were prolonged for a season and a time.

"I saw a vision in the night, and behold, with a cloud of heaven there came the Ancient One, like a son of man. And there was given him dominion, and glory, and a kingdom, that all peoples, nations of all languages, should serve him. His dominion was to be an everlasting dominion, and his kingdom one which shall not be destroyed.

"I, Daniel, was grieved in my spirit, and the visions troubled me. I came near to one of those who stood by, and asked him for the meaning concerning all this. So he made known to me the interpretation: 'The great beasts, which are four, are four kings who shall arise on the earth. But the saints of the Most High shall receive the kingdom, and possess it forever.'

"Then I desired to know the truth about the fourth beast, which was different from all the others, whose teeth were of iron and his nails of brass, and among the ten horns in his head a horn that had eyes, and a mouth that spoke very great things. And he said, 'The fourth beast shall be the fourth kingdom upon earth, which shall be different from all kingdoms, and shall devour the whole earth. And the ten horns are ten kings that shall arise; and another shall rise after them; and he shall be different from the first, and he shall subdue the three kings. He shall speak great words against the Most High, and shall wear out the saints of the Most High, and he shall think to change the seasons and the law. This shall be granted to him for a time, and times and half a time.

" 'But the judgment shall sit, and they shall take away his dominion to consume and destroy it to the end. And the kingdom and dominion, and the greatness of the kingdom under the whole heaven, shall be given to the people of the saints of the most High, whose kingdom is everlasting.'

"This was the end of my vision. As for me, Daniel, my thoughts troubled me; but I kept the matter in my heart." [3]

## Daniel's Prayer

9      In the first year of Darius, who was made king over the realm of the Chaldeans, I, Daniel, meditated in the books concerning the desolation of Jerusalem, whereof the word of the Lord came to Jeremiah the prophet.

And I prayed to the Lord my God, and made confession, "O Lord, who keeps covenant with those who love you and keep your commandments, we have sinned and have rebelled, and have turned aside from your commandments; and we have not listened to your servants the prophets, who spoke in your name to our kings and to all the people of the land. O Lord, righteousness belongs to you, but to us confusion of face. Yes, all Israel has transgressed your law; and so there has been poured upon us the curse and the oath which are written in the law of Moses, the servant of God.

"O Lord, I pray you, let your anger be turned away from your city Jerusalem, your holy mountain. Hear the prayer of your servant, O our God, and cause your face to shine upon your sanctuary, which is desolate."

And while I was speaking in prayer, the man Gabriel whom I had seen in the vision at the beginning approached close to me, flying swiftly, about the time of the evening offering. And he said to me, "At the begin-

[3] See DANIEL, Chapters 7-8, in Notes and Excisions.

ning of your supplications a word went forth, and I have come to declare it, for you are greatly beloved; therefore consider the word and understand the vision.

"Seventy weeks are decreed upon your people and your holy city, to finish the transgression, and to make an end of sin, and to forgive iniquity, and to bring in everlasting righteousness, and to seal vision and prophet, and to anoint the most holy place.

"Know therefore and understand that from the going forth of the word to restore and to build Jerusalem to one anointed, a prince, shall be seven weeks; and for threescore and two weeks it shall be built again, but in troubled times.

"And after the threescore and two weeks shall an anointed one be cut off and be no more; and the city and the sanctuary be destroyed by the people of a prince who shall come, but his end shall be with a flood; and to the end there shall be war and desolation."

## The Great Wars

**10-12** In the third year of Cyrus, king of Persia, word was revealed to Daniel concerning a great war; and he gave heed to the word, and had understanding of the vision.

In those days I, Daniel, was mourning for three weeks. And as I stood beside the great river, the Tigris, I beheld a man clothed in linen, whose loins were girded with fine gold. His body was like beryl, his face had the appearance of lightning, his eyes were like flaming torches, his arms and legs in color like burnished brass, and his voice was like the voice of a multitude.

When I heard the voice I fell into a deep sleep, with my face toward the ground. And behold, a hand touched me, which set me tottering upon my hands and knees. And he said to me: "O Daniel, man greatly beloved, give heed to the words that I speak, and stand upright; for now have I been sent to you."

And when he had spoken, I stood up trembling. Then said he, "Fear not, Daniel, for from the first day that you set your heart to understand, and to humble yourself before your God, your words have been heard; and I have come because of your words.

"Behold, there shall arise three kings in Persia; and a fourth shall be far richer than them all; and when he has grown strong through his riches, he shall stir up all against the realm of Greece. Then a mighty king shall arise, who shall rule with great dominion and do according to his will. But his kingdom shall be broken, and divided toward the four winds of heaven.

"The king of the south shall come out and fight with him, with the king of the north. And in those times there shall be many who stand up against the king of the south; also the children of the violent among your people shall lift themselves up to establish the vision, but they shall fail. Then the king of the north shall come, and cast up siegeworks, and take a well-fortified city. And the arms of the south shall not withstand him.

"At the time of the end the king of the south shall push against him; but the king of the north shall come upon him like a whirlwind, with chariots and with horsemen and with many ships; and he shall enter into the countries, and shall overflow, as he passes through. He shall enter also into the glorious land, and many countries shall be overthrown. He shall stretch out his hand upon the countries, and the land of Egypt shall not escape. And he shall have power over the treasures of gold and of silver, and over all the precious things of Egypt.

"But tidings out of the east and out of the north shall trouble him, and he shall go forth with great fury to destroy. And he shall plant the tents of his palace between the seas and the holy mountain; yet he shall come to his end, and none shall help him.

"At that time shall arise the great prince Michael, who will stand for the children of your people; and there shall be a time of trouble such as has never been since there was a nation. But at that time your people shall be delivered, everyone whose name shall be found written in the book. And many of those who sleep in the dust of the earth shall awake, some to everlasting life, and some to shame and everlasting dishonor. And those who are wise shall shine like the brightness of the firmament; and those who turn many to righteousness like the stars forever and ever.

"But you, O Daniel, shut up the words and seal the book, even to the time of the end."

Then I, Daniel, looked, and behold, there stood two others, one on this side of the bank of the river, and the other on that side of the bank of the river. And I said to the man clothed in linen, "How long shall it be to the end of these wonders?"

The man lifted his right hand and his left hand toward heaven; and I heard him swear by him who lives forever that it shall be for a time, times, and half a time; and when they have made an end of shattering the power of the holy people, all these things shall be finished.

I heard, but I understood not, and I said, "O, my lord, what shall be the latter end of these things?" And he answered, "Go your way, Daniel, for the words are shut up and sealed till the time of the end."

# EZRA and NEHEMIAH
## Men with a Mission

⟨ During the Babylonian captivity, which lasted about half a century (587-538 B.C.E.), the exiled people experienced a great sense of remorse and a spiritual revival. In exile they fortified their religious life with unprecedented zeal. The prophets Zachariah and Haggai were leaders in stirring the people to rebuild the temple. Later Nehemiah, the Babylonian courtier, succeeded in rebuilding the temple and the walls of Jerusalem, and with Ezra, the priest and scribe, re-established the holy law — in spite of almost insurmountable difficulties.

Ezra is generally credited with zealously rededicating the people to the law; and Nehemiah, the more polished writer and more urbane character, with enabling Ezra to inaugurate a solemn return of the people to the letter of the law, and to observance of the ritual.

Ezra and Nehemiah are inseparable from Chronicles; and their names appear in apocryphal and pseudepigraphic works — I, II, III and IV Esdras (or Ezdras). The first two books in the Apocrypha are given as I and II Esdras; and in the Pseudepigrapha, III and IV Ezdras appear after the Book of Enoch. Parts of the excluded Esdras are duplications of the Ezra accepted by the canon, and parts are apocalyptic, filled with visions and revelations, after the manner of the Book of Daniel.

The Book of Ezra and the Book of Nehemiah show how loyalty and devotion to a cause may overcome grave difficulties, as well as how such zeal may at times engender hardships and dangers — hardships and dangers which are so clearly protested in the Book of Ruth and in the Book of Jonah. ⟨

## The Return from Captivity

**1-2*** Now in the first year of Cyrus, king of Persia, the Lord stirred up the spirit of the king, and he made a proclamation throughout his kingdom, and put it also in writing, saying:

"Thus says Cyrus, king of the Persians: 'The Lord God of heaven, who has made me king of the whole world, has charged me to build him a house in Jerusalem, which is in Judah. Therefore, whoever among his people so desires, let him go up to Jerusalem and rebuild the house of the Lord God of Israel. And whoever remains where he now sojourns, let him help with silver, and with gold, and with goods, and with beasts, besides the freewill offerings for the house of God in Jerusalem.'"

Then rose up the heads of the families of Judah and of Benjamin, and the priests and the Levites, with all those whose spirit God had aroused to rebuild the house of the Lord in Jerusalem. And those who remained behind strengthened their hands with vessels of silver, with gold, with goods, with cattle, and with other precious things.

Cyrus the king also brought out the holy vessels which Nebuchadnezzar had taken from Jerusalem, and gave them to be delivered to the governor of Judea.

Now the children of Israel who had been carried away by Nebuchadnezzar and returned again to Judah were forty-two thousand and three hundred and sixty, besides their servants and their maids, of whom there were seven thousand three hundred and thirty-seven: and among them were two hundred singing men and women. And they came again to Jerusalem, each one to his city.[1]

## The Rebuilding of the Temple

**3** In the second year of their return to Jerusalem, in the second month, Zerubbabel, the son of Shealtiel, and Jeshua, the son of Jozadak, and their brothers the priests and all those who had come out of captivity, appointed the Levites — from twenty years old and upward — to set forward the work of the house of the Lord. And when the builders laid the foundation of the temple, the priests in their vestments came

---

* The Book of Ezra.
[1] See EZRA, Chapter 2, in Notes and Excisions.

forward with trumpets, and the Levites with cymbals, to praise the Lord. They sang together, "For the Lord is good, his mercy endures forever."

And the people shouted with great joy. But many of the priests and Levites, old men who had seen the first house, when the foundation of this house was laid before their eyes, wept with a loud voice; so that the people could not distinguish the noise of the shout of joy from the noise of the weeping of the people.[2]

## Epistle to Artaxerxes

4-5   Now when the adversaries of Judah and Benjamin heard that the children of the captivity were building the temple, they came to Zerubbabel, and to the heads of the fathers of Israel, and said, "Let us build with you, for we seek your God as you do; and we have sacrificed to him since the days of Esar-haddon, king of Assur, who brought us here." But Zerubbabel and the fathers of Israel answered, "We alone will build to the Lord God of Israel, as King Cyrus has commanded us."

Then the people of the land harried them in the rebuilding, and hired counselors to frustrate their purpose, all the days of Cyrus, king of Persia.

And when Artaxerxes became king of Persia, Rehum the chancellor and Shimshai the scribe wrote a letter against those who dwelt in Judea and in Jerusalem. This is the letter written in the Syrian tongue which they sent:

"To Artaxerxes the king, from your servants in Samaria:

"Be it known to the king that the Jews who returned from you to us in Jerusalem are rebuilding that rebellious and wicked city, and have repaired the walls, and are now laying the foundation of the temple.

"Be it known to the king that when this city and its walls are set up again, they will not only refuse to pay tribute and toll, but also rebel against kings. Now because we have maintenance from the king's palace, and it is not fitting for us to see the king's dishonor, we have sent and informed the king."

Then the king sent an answer in this manner: "Peace! And now the letter which you sent to us has been plainly read before me. Then I decreed, and diligent search has been made, and it has been found that this city has from of old time made insurrection against kings, and that

[2] See EZRA, Chapter 3, in Notes and Excisions.

rebellion and sedition have been made in it. There have been mighty kings also over Jerusalem, who ruled over all countries beyond the river; and toll, tribute, and custom were paid to them. Now, therefore, make a decree to cause these men to cease, and that this city be not rebuilt until a decree shall be made by me. And take heed that no more be done in it, and that they proceed no further to the annoyance of kings."

When the copy of King Artaxerxes' letter was read before Rehum, and Shimshai the scribe, and their companions, they went up in haste to Jerusalem and made the workers cease by force and power. So ceased the work on the house of God which is in Jerusalem.[3]

## The Completion of the Temple

6    Then Darius became king of Persia, and he decreed that a search be made in the house of the archives, where the treasures were stored in Babylon. And there was found a scroll, and on it a record thus written:

"In the first year of Cyrus the king he made a decree concerning the house of God in Jerusalem, saying, 'Let the house be built, the place where they offer sacrifices, and let its foundations be strongly laid.

'Now therefore Tattenai, governor beyond the river, and Sheltar-bozenai, and your companions, let the work of this house of God alone, that the governor of the Jews and the elders of the Jews may rebuild the house of God in its place. Also, I have made a decree that whoever shall alter this word, let timber be pulled down from his house, and let him be hanged thereon; and let his house be made a dunghill. And may the God who has caused his name to dwell there destroy all kings and peoples who shall put their hand to alter or to destroy this house of God in Jerusalem. I, Darius, have made a decree; let it be done with speed.' "

And the elders of the Jews built and finished the house of the Lord according to the commandment of the God of Israel, and according to the decree of Cyrus and Darius, kings of Persia. And this house was finished on the third day of the month of Adar, which was in the sixth year of the reign of Darius.

Then the children of Israel, the priests and the Levites, and the rest of the returned captives dedicated the house of God with joy.

[3] See EZRA, Chapter 5, in Notes and Excisions.

# Ezra Returns to Jerusalem

7     Now after these things, in the reign of Artaxerxes, king of Persia, Ezra, son of Seraiah, went up from Babylon; and he was a ready scribe in the law of Moses, which the Lord God of Israel had given; and the king granted him all his requests according to the hand of the Lord his God upon him. And there went up with him to Jerusalem in the seventh year of Artaxerxes the king some of the children of Israel, and some of the priests, and the Levites, and the singers, and the porters. And he came to Jerusalem in the fifth month of that year.

Now this is a copy of the letter which the king gave to Ezra the priest:

"Artaxerxes, king of kings, to Ezra the priest, the scribe of the law of the God of heaven: Perfect peace!

"And now I make a decree that all those of the people of Israel, and their priests and Levites in my realm, who are minded of their own free will to go up to Jerusalem may go with you. For you are sent by the king and by his seven counselors to inquire concerning Judah and Jerusalem, according to the law of your God.

"And I, Artaxerxes the king, make a decree to all the treasurers who are beyond the river. Whatever Ezra the priest shall require of you, let it be done speedily. Whatever is commanded by the God of heaven, let it be diligently done for the house of the God of heaven, lest there be wrath against the realm of the king and his sons.

"And you, Ezra, after the wisdom of your God, appoint magistrates and judges who may judge all the people beyond the river, all such as know the laws of your God; and teach those who know them not. And whoever will not do the law of your God and the law of the king, let judgment be executed speedily upon him, whether it be to death, or to confiscation of goods, or to imprisonment."

Ezra thanked the Lord and said, "Blessed be the Lord God of our fathers, who has put such a thing as this in the king's heart, to beautify the house of the Lord in Jerusalem; and has extended mercy to me before the king and his counselors and before all the king's mighty princes." [4]

[4] See EZRA, Chapter 8, in Notes and Excisions.

# Ezra's Sorrow

8-10 "And I, Ezra, was strengthened, and the hand of the Lord my
God was upon me, and I gathered together the chief men of
Israel to go up with me. We departed from the river Ahava on the
twelfth day of the first month, to go to Jerusalem; and the hand of God
was upon us, and he delivered us from such as lay in ambush along the
way.

"Then the princes came to me and said, 'The people of Israel, and the
priests, and the Levites, have not separated themselves from the peoples
of the land, or their abominations; and they have taken their daughters
in marriage for themselves and for their sons, so that the holy seed has
mixed with that of the peoples of the land.'

"When I heard this, I rent my mantle and sat down appalled. There
were assembled about me everyone who trembled at the words of the
God of Israel, because of the transgression of those who had been captives. And at the evening sacrifice I fell upon my knees and prayed, 'O
my God, I am ashamed and blush to lift up my face to you, my God; for
our iniquities rise over our heads, and our trespass reaches to the heavens. From the days of our fathers we have trespassed against you, and
for our iniquities we, our kings and our priests, have been delivered to the
sword, to captivity, and to shame, as at this day. Now for a little space
grace has been shown by the Lord our God, to leave us a remnant, and
to give us a foothold in his holy place.

"'Our God has not forsaken us in our bondage, but has extended mercy
to us in the sight of the kings of Persia, to set up the house of our God,
to repair its ruins, and to give us protection in Judah and Jerusalem.
And now, O our God, what shall we say after this? For we have forsaken
your commandment. O Lord God of Israel, you are righteous, for a
remnant have escaped, as at this day. Behold, we are before you in our
sins.'"

Now while Ezra prayed and made confession, weeping and casting
himself down before the house of God, there assembled about him a great
congregation of men and women and children; and the people wept bitterly. Shechaniah, the son of Jehiel, said to Ezra, "We have trespassed
against our God, and have taken wives from the peoples of the land; yet
there is hope in Israel concerning this matter. Let us make a covenant
with our God to put away all the wives, and such as are born of them, ac-

cording to the counsel of my lord and of those who tremble at the commandment of our God; and let it be done according to the law."

Then Ezra rose and went into the chamber of Johanan, the son of Eliashib, and he fasted; for he mourned because of the transgression of the returned captives. And a proclamation was made throughout Judah and Jerusalem to all those returned from captivity that they should gather together in Jerusalem.

The men of Judah and Benjamin assembled in Jerusalem within three days. And all the people sat in the broad place before the house of God, trembling because of this matter, and because of the great rain. Ezra the priest stood up, and said to them, "You have transgressed, and have taken foreign wives, and so increased the sins of Israel. Now therefore make confession to the Lord God of your fathers and do his pleasure, and separate yourselves from the peoples of the land and from the foreign wives."

The congregation answered in a loud voice, "As you have said, so we must do. But the people are many, and it is the time of much rain, and we are not able to stand in the open; nor is this a work for one day or two, for there are many who have transgressed in this matter. Let those in our cities who have taken foreign wives come at appointed times, and with them the elders and judges of every city, until the fierce wrath of our God over this is turned away."

And they did so. They sat down in the first day of the tenth month to examine the matter. And they finished with all the men who had taken strange wives by the first day of the first month.[5]


*The chronicle of Nehemiah, the son of Hachaliah.*


# The Rebuilding of the Walls

*1-3* [*]   In the month of Chislev, in the twentieth year, as I was in Shushan the palace, Hanani, one of my brothers, and certain men of Judah came, and I asked them concerning the Jews who had escaped captivity, and concerning Jerusalem. And they said to me, "The remnant in the province are in great misery and reproach; the wall of Jerusalem is broken down, and its gates have been burned."

[5] See EZRA, Chapter 10, in Notes and Excisions.
[*] The Book of Nehemiah.

When I heard these words I wept and fasted, and prayed before the God of heaven, "I beseech you, O Lord, God of heaven, the great and terrible God, who keeps the covenant and shows mercy to those who love him and observe his commandments, let your ear be attentive and your eyes open, that you may hear the prayer of your servant, which I pray before you day and night for the children of Israel your servants, confessing the sins which we have sinned against you. Both I and my father's house have sinned. O Lord, I beseech you, let your ear be attentive to the prayer of your servant, and of those who fear your name; and prosper your servant this day, I pray you, and grant him mercy in the sight of this man." For I was the king's cupbearer.

And it came to pass in the month of Nisen, in the twentieth year of Artaxerxes the king, when wine was served him, I took up the wine and gave it to the king. Now I had not been sad before in his presence. Therefore the king asked, "Why is your face sad, seeing you are not sick? This is nothing else but sorrow of heart." Then I was frightened and said, "May the king live forever! Why should not my face be sad, when the city, the place of my fathers' sepulchers, lies waste, and its gates have been destroyed by fire?"

Then the king asked, "For what do you make request?" So I prayed to the God of heaven. And I said, "If it please the king, and if your servant has found favor in your sight, send me to Judah, to the city of my fathers' sepulchers, that I may rebuild it." And the king said to me, the queen sitting beside him, "How long will your journey be? And when will you return?" So I set him a time; and it pleased the king to send me. Moreover, I said to the king, "If it please the king, let letters be given me to the governors beyond the river, that they may let me pass till I come into Judah; and a letter also to Asaph, the keeper of the king's forest, that they may give me timber to make beams for the gates, and for the wall of the city, and for the house that I shall dwell in."

And the king granted my request, according to the good hand of my God upon me.

Then I came to the governors beyond the river, and gave them the king's letters. Now the king had sent with me captains of the army and horsemen. And when Sanballat the Horonite and Tobiah the Ammonite heard of this, it grieved them exceedingly that a man had come to seek the welfare of the children of Israel.

So I came to Jerusalem, and was there three days. And I arose in the night, I and a few men with me, and told no man what God had put in my heart to do in Jerusalem. And there was no beast with me save the beast that I rode upon. I went out by the gate of the valley, before the dung port, and viewed the walls of Jerusalem, which were broken, and its gates, which had been destroyed by fire. Then I went on to the gate of the fountain, and to the king's pool. But there was no place for the beast that was under me to pass. And I went up in the night by the brook and viewed the wall; and turned back, and entered through the gate of the valley, and so returned. The rulers knew not where I went nor what I did; neither had I as yet told the Jews, nor the priests, nor the nobles, nor the rest who did the work.

Later I said to them, "You see the distress we are in, how Jerusalem lies waste and its gates burned. Come, let us rebuild the wall of Jerusalem, that it may no longer be a reproach to us." Then I told them of the hand of my God which was good upon me; and also the words the king had spoken to me. And they said, "Let us rise up and build."

So they strengthened their hands for the good work.[6]


## Sanballat's Reproach

4-5    When Sanballat heard that we were rebuilding the wall, he was
       angered and indignant. And he said to the people of Samaria, "What are these feeble Jews doing? Will they revive the stones out of the heaps of rubbish?" Tobiah the Ammonite was by him and said, "If a fox goes up on it, he will break down their stone wall."

But we built the wall until all of it was joined together. For the people had a mind to work. And when Sanballat and his men heard that the walls of Jerusalem were joined, and that the breaches had begun to be stopped up, they were very angry, and conspired to fight against Jerusalem and to hinder the work.

We made our prayer to God, and set a guard on watch against them day and night. And I said to the nobles and to the rest of the people, "Be not afraid of them. Remember the Lord, great and terrible, and fight for your brothers, your sons and your daughters, your wives and your homes."

And from that time on, half of my servants worked while the other half held the spears, the shields and the bows. Those who built the wall and those who carried burdens, each one worked with one hand and

* See NEHEMIAH, Chapter 3, in Notes and Excisions.

with the other held his weapon. For the builders, each one had his sword girded at his side while he built.

And I said to the nobles and the rulers and the rest of the people, "The task is great, and we are separated on the wall, far from one another. Therefore in the place where you hear the sound of the trumpet, come to us; our God will fight for us." So we labored, half of us holding spears from the break of day until the stars appeared. At the same time said I to the people, "Let everyone with his servant lodge within Jerusalem, that they may be a guard for us at night, and labor during the day."

So neither I, nor my brothers, nor my servants, nor the men of the guard who followed me, none of us took off our clothes; and each one that went to the water had his weapon.

Then there arose a great outcry from the people and their wives. Some said, "We, our sons and our daughters are many; therefore we must have grain, that we may live." Some said, "We have mortgaged our lands, vineyards and houses, that we might buy grain because of the famine." And there were some also who said, "We have borrowed money for the king's tribute upon our lands and vineyards. Our flesh is like the flesh of our brothers, our children like their children; and yet we bring our sons and daughters to slavery for debt, and some of our daughters are slaves already; nor is it in our power to redeem them, for others have our lands and our vineyards."

Then I rebuked the nobles and the rulers, and I summoned a great assembly against them. And I said to them, "It is not good what you do. Ought you not to walk in the fear of our God because of the reproach of the heathen our enemies? I pray you, let us leave off this usury. Restore to them this very day their lands, their vineyards, their olive orchards, and their houses."

Then said they, "We will restore these to them and require nothing from them; we will do as you say." And I took an oath from them that they would do according to their promise. Also I said, "May God shake out from his house, and from his labor, every man who does not fulfill this promise."

And the congregation said "Amen!" and praised the Lord.

And the people did according to this promise.[7]

[7] See NEHEMIAH, Chapter 5, in Notes and Excisions.

## Sanballat's Deception

6-7    Now when Sanballat and Tobiah and Geshem the Arabian, and the rest of our enemies heard that there was no breach left in the wall of Jerusalem, though at that time I had not set up the doors in the gates, they sent word to me, saying, "Come, let us meet in one of the villages in the plain of Ono." But they thought to do me harm. And I sent messengers to them, saying, "I am doing a great work; how can I let the work cease while I come down to you?" Yet they sent word to me four times in this manner, and I answered them in the same way.

Then Sanballat sent his servant to me in like manner a fifth time, with an open letter in his hand, in which was written, "It is reported among the nations that you and the Jews plan to rebel: For this purpose you build the wall, and that you may become their king. Now it will be reported to the king of Persia. Come therefore, and let us take counsel together." Then I sent word to him, saying, "No such things have been done as you say. You imagine them in your heart."

Afterward I went to the house of Shemaiath, the son of Delaiah, and he said, "Let us meet in the house of God, within the temple, and let us shut the doors! For they will come to slay you; yes, in the night they will come to slay you." And I answered, "Should such a man as I flee? What man like myself would go into the temple to save his life? I will not go in." And I perceived that God had not sent him, but that Tobiah and Sanballat had hired him.

So the wall was finished in fifty-two days. And when our enemies heard of it, they were downcast; for they perceived that this work was wrought by our God.

And when the wall was built, and I had set up the doors, and the gatekeepers, the singers, and the Levites had been appointed, I gave my brother Hanani and Hananiah, the ruler of the palace, charge over Jerusalem. And I said to them, "Let not the gates of Jerusalem be opened until the sun is hot; and while they still stand on guard, let the doors be shut and barred. And from the inhabitants of Jerusalem appoint guards to stand watch, each one opposite his home." Now the city was wide and large, but the people in it were few, for houses had not yet been built.

And my God put it into my heart to gather together the nobles, the rulers, and the people, that they might be reckoned by genealogy. And I found a register of the genealogy of those who had come up at the first, and found recorded in it those whom Nebuchadnezzar had carried away, and who had returned to Jerusalem and Judah, each to his own city.

The whole congregation together was forty-two thousand three hundred and threescore, besides their servants, of whom there were seven thousand three hundred and thirty-seven; and they had two hundred and forty-five singing men and singing women.

So the priests, and the Levites, and the gatekeepers, and the singers, and all Israel, dwelt in their cities.[8]

## The Reading of the Law

8-12     And when the seventh month had come, and the children of Israel were in their cities, all the people assembled as one man in the broad place before the water gate; and they asked Ezra the scribe to bring the book of the law of Moses, which the Lord had given to Israel.

And Ezra the priest brought the law before the congregation, both men and women, and all who could hear with understanding, and he read from it in the broad place before the water gate from early morning until midday, and the people were attentive. Ezra the scribe stood on a pulpit of wood which they had made for the purpose. And he opened the book in the sight of all the people, for he stood higher than they; and when he opened it, the people rose up. Ezra blessed the Lord, the great God. And the people answered, "Amen! Amen!" And they bowed their heads, and worshiped the Lord with their faces to the ground.

Nehemiah, who was the governor, and Ezra the priest, and the Levites who taught the people, said to them, "This day is holy to the Lord your God; mourn not, nor weep." For all the people wept when they heard the words of the law. They said, "Go your way, eat and drink, and send portions to those who have nothing prepared for them; for this day is holy. And grieve not, for the joy of the Lord is your strength."

So the people went their way to eat and to drink, and to send portions, and to rejoice, because they had understood the words that were declared to them. They went to the hills to bring olive branches and branches of pine and myrtle and palm, to make booths, as it is written. And they made themselves booths, each one on the roof of his house, and

[8] See NEHEMIAH, Chapter 7, in Notes and Excisions.

in their courts, and in the courts of the temple, and in the broad place at the water gate, and at the gate of Ephraim.[9]

# The Reforms by Nehemiah

13    They read from the book of Moses in the hearing of the people, and in it was found that the Ammonite and Moabite should not come into the congregation of God, because they did not meet the children of Israel with bread and water, but hired Balaam to curse them; although our God turned the curse into a blessing. When the congregation heard the law, they separated from Israel all the mixed peoples.

Now before this, Eliashib the priest, overseer of the chambers of the house of our God, was allied to Tobiah; and he prepared for Tobiah a great chamber where before they had put the offerings, the frankincense, the vessels and the tithes of grain, the new wine and the oil, which were given by commandment to the Levites, the singers, and the gatekeepers; and the offerings for the priests.

But in all this time I was not in Jerusalem, for in the thirty-second year of Artaxerxes I went to the king. And after a certain time I obtained leave of the king and came to Jerusalem. Then I discovered the evil that Eliashib had done in preparing for Tobiah a chamber in the courts of the house of God. It grieved me bitterly, and I cast out from the chamber all that belonged to Tobiah. Then I commanded, and they cleansed the chambers, and brought back into them the vessels of the house of God, with the offerings and the frankincense.

And I perceived that the portions of the Levites had not been given them; so that the Levites and the singers, who did the work, had fled each one to his field. So I gathered them together and brought them to their place. Then all Judah brought the tithe of the grain and the new wine and the oil into the storehouses.

In those days I saw in Judah some treading wine presses on the Sabbath, and bringing in sheaves, and loading asses; as also wine, grapes, figs, and all manner of burdens, which they brought into Jerusalem on the Sabbath day. And I testified against them on the day on which they sold the food. In the city dwelt men of Tyre, who also brought fish and all manner of wares and sold them on the Sabbath to the children of Judah, and in Jerusalem. Then I contended with the nobles of Judah, and said

[9] See NEHEMIAH, Chapters 8-12, in Notes and Excisions.

to them, "What evil thing is this, that you profane the Sabbath day?"

And when it began to be dark, at the gates of Jerusalem before the Sabbath, I commanded that the gates should be shut, and ordered that they should not be opened until after the Sabbath. And I set at the gates some of my servants to guard that no burden might be brought in on the Sabbath day. So the merchants of all kinds of wares lodged outside Jerusalem once or twice. Then I said to them, "Why do you lodge near the wall?" From that time forth they came no more on the Sabbath. And I commanded the Levites to purify themselves, and that they should come and guard the gates, to sanctify the Sabbath day.

In those days also I saw Jews who had taken wives of Ashdod, of Ammon, and of Moab; and their children spoke in the speech of Ashdod, and could not speak in the language of Judah. I contended with them and cursed them, and struck certain of them, saying, "You shall not give your daughters to their sons, nor take their daughters for your sons or for yourselves. Did not Solomon, king of Israel, sin in this way? Yet among the nations there was no king like him, beloved of his God, and God made him king over all Israel; nevertheless foreign women caused even him to sin. Shall we then let you do this great evil?"

Thus I cleansed them, and assigned the duties of the priests and the Levites, and provided for the wood offering at the times appointed, and for the first fruits.

Remember me, O my God, for good.

## PART THREE
# The Books of the Prophets
# נְבִיאִים

*An Anthology of Four Centuries of Hebrew Prophecy*

⟨[ Every sacred literature has its prophets; but in none does the prophet assume so lofty a place of honor, and of power, as recorded in our Bible. Other ancient nations have extolled their ruling princes, or revered their philosopher-orators, or clothed in majesty their military heroes. The ancient Hebrews reserved the highest place of dignity for their soul-searching poet-prophets.

These outspoken seers may have appeared as gadflies to the priests, and as annoyances to the princes; the Jezebels may have repeatedly tried to kill them and to wipe out all remembrance of them; but the people loved them. These lonely seekers after God's justice would come out of their solitary contemplation and appear, like apparitions, in the most crowded places, denouncing corruption, their voices like the call of trumpets. And while the kings might continue to envy Assyrian and Babylonian power, and the priests to be swayed by the rituals of Baal and Molech, the poor and the oppressed of the land listened to their prophets, and were comforted.

The prophets in Israel and Judah were many; and there is a clear distinction between the earlier prophets of Israel and those of the Books of the Prophets.

The "seer" and the "prophet" are mentioned quite early in the Bible. According to an ancient tradition, all men to whom the Lord had "spoken" were accounted prophets. By this definition, Adam was the first of the prophets; and Abraham, Isaac and Jacob were counted among them. And there were many others. In the Hebrew Scriptures, Moses appears as the Prophet of Prophets; and the Five Books of Moses are assumed to be the work of his hand. These books are followed in the Bible by what is called in the Hebrew Scriptures the Books of the Former Prophets: Joshua, Judges, I and II Samuel, I and II Kings. In these works appear Joshua and all the judges, Samuel, Nathan and Gad, Elijah, Elisha and Abijah — all prophets by definition, since the Lord had "spoken" to all of them.

As the Bible narration progresses through the Books of the Former

Prophets, a gradual transformation takes place in the "seer" and the "prophet," who turns from the man who had spoken *with* God to the man who spoke *for* God — the man inspired by God, who appears in the market place, or in the temple, or even in the house of the king, to denounce evildoing and to proclaim that "obedience to God is nobler than sacrifice."

But it is not until we reach what is called in the Hebrew Scriptures the Books of the Latter Prophets that we are introduced to a small group of poet-prophets who were preoccupied with the troubled events of their own times, yet who dealt with human aspirations and frustrations so probingly that their words have retained their luster and relevance to this day.

When we refer to the prophets of the Bible, we usually refer to the men of the Books of the Prophets, who foretold what would happen to him who lived by folly, and to the nation that persisted in vain ambitions; and they prophesied, not mystically or by clairvoyance, but in the clearness of their vision and the wisdom of their hearts. Their place in the history of literature as poet-prophets is immutable not only because of their poetic power, but as much because they were steeped in the vision of a world worthy of humanity, and that would seem good in the eyes of the Lord.

Each, each in his own way, told of his abhorrence of social iniquity, of reckless luxury and pride, of cruelty and corruption in high places; and each enunciated the meaning of the acceptance of a Divine Discipline — the love of peace, the cleansing of the heart of falsehood, the rejection of lust and wickedness, the love of one's neighbor, and above all, the duty of each man to refuse to follow the multitude to do evil.

The essence of their utterances is presented for the most part in poetry that has made the Books of the Latter Prophets the crown and glory of the Bible.

The "literary" prophets are traditionally divided into the major prophets and the minor prophets — the terms "major" and "minor" neither a measure of them as poets or prophets, nor an index of the order of their appearance, but referring merely to the volume of their work included in the Scriptures. Though the order of the major prophets (Isaiah, Jeremiah and Ezekiel) has remained fixed in all versions, the order of the minor prophets varies in different versions, and is presented in some according to their length — the longest coming first and the shortest last. In other standard versions Malachi appears last, although other prophets lived after his time. In this version the Books of the minor prophets are arranged chronologically to accord with the time in which, according to most scholars, they were written.

The Books of the Prophets cannot be read like the earlier parts of the Bible, which present, mainly, a sequence of allegorical or historical narratives beginning with Creation and ending with the story of Nehemiah, who rebuilt the walls of Jerusalem in the days of the prophets Malachi and Obadiah. The Books of the Prophets should be read as an anthology of Hebrew poetry covering about four centuries. And we should realize that the poetry includes not only a number of different poets, who wrote from first to last four hundred years apart, but also that the work of each poet-prophet incorporates a group of different poems on differing themes.

The Books of the Prophets in the standard versions usually appear without breaks or signposts, excepting for chapterizations, which do not always indicate a change in theme, and the reader has no way of knowing where one poem ends and where another poem begins. (A parallel would be the attempt to read *Leaves of Grass* by Walt Whitman in an edition where his four hundred poems are presented without separate titles or headings, and in an unbroken torrent of lines.) For this reason the poems, or poetic sections, are given titles in this version, although these obviously are intended only as signposts to the themes treated in each section or poem.

Though the Books of the Prophets are almost entirely a collection of the poetry of a group of poet-prophets, no attempt has been made here to present their work in verse form. For added to the general difficulties of translating Hebrew into English, there is the specific difficulty that Hebrew poetry does not depend on rhyme, and its meter is of less importance than the sharpness, the sonority, or the plaintive sound of the syllables conveying the thought; and intensity of emotion is very often attained by imagery, by repetition, or by the choice of words which fall upon the ear harshly or softly, sweetly or stridently. To marshal the translated words into lines of a fixed meter often widens the gap between the English and the original, because of these subtle untranslatable differences. In the Books of the Prophets, as in the subsequent Books which are basically poetic works, the attempt is made here to retain the lyrical, lamenting, or ecstatic quality of the original, as well as the dramatic, often blatant imagery, although conveyed through the humbler medium of prose.

The importance of the "literary" prophets to us is as much in what they had to say to their generation that is still valid for us today as in the medium they employed. In a way, they were like men who can see, among blind men in distress. They take the blind by the hand and lead them to safety, and along the way they describe vividly what they see around them. And for a moment we, the blind, perceive, however dimly, the glory that was in their sight.

The Books of the Prophets begin with Isaiah the First, who lived in the days of the Assyrian King Shalmaneser, some seven and a half centuries before the Christian Era; and ends with Jonah, whose career in the days of King Jeroboam II (eighth century B.C.E.) was, according to modern scholars, not recorded until the days of Alexander the Great about four centuries later. Even had they all lived in the same century, their differences as poets would distinguish them one from another, as would the circumstances of their personal lives. Isaiah was an aristocrat, Amos a herdsman, Ezekiel a priest and visionary, Hosea a courtier, and so on. The differences in their lives are reflected in their work. Isaiah, the man of royal descent, attempts to quiet the tempests in his heart with reasoned thought; Ezekiel, the priest in exile, is harsh in statement, and uses words that are turbulent, fearless and disturbing; Amos, the lonely herdsman, is often violent in expression; Jonah has a gentle touch of humor in his work.

Separately, the poet-prophets in this anthology differ from each other as much as would any other group of poets who lived in a period covering four centuries — just as the works of the great poets of England from Marlowe and Shakespeare to Masefield and Eliot differ. Their subject matter, their imagery, their approach, have little in common. We who read the prophets in English (more exactly, in the English of the specific period when the translation was made) cannot appreciate the great diversity in their work. In Hebrew the basic outlines of their differences can still be distinguished; though even in Hebrew the differences have been sanded down by successive scribal editing.

Collectively, the poet-prophets of this anthology seem to have a singleness of purpose which overrides their separate differences. In times of trouble they proclaim that man's fate lies in his own hands if he will but submit to the Divine Discipline, which requires of him, not offerings and sacrifices alone, but also a contrite heart. **([**

# ISAIAH (I)
## *The Eloquent*

❡ Probably the best known of the Hebrew prophets is Isaiah. What is not so well known is that there are three or more poet-prophets discernible in the Book of Isaiah, unequal in the volume of their contributions, or as poets, and belonging to quite different periods.

According to one theory, this came about when the books of the Bible were assembled and the scrolls had definite limits as to maximum and minimum length. When documents to be inscribed were too long, they were divided into two or more scrolls; when they were too short, two or more documents were combined on one scroll and, in the instance of this book, under a single heading.

The Books of the Prophets were not included in the Bible until about the second century before the Christian Era, and the original Book of Isaiah (Chapters 1-39) must have been found too short for an independent scroll, and was therefore combined with the work of at least two other poet-prophets of a later date, whose separate names were not recorded.

About the first Isaiah we know a great deal. According to rabbinic tradition, he was born around 742 B.C.E. into the royal family of Judah, and was on intimate terms with the king all his life. He married when young, and had two sons, to whom he gave symbolic names after the custom of his times. His discourses were political in nature; and he urged King Hezekiah to ally himself with Assyria, but to keep free of alliances with Egypt.

Isaiah (I) clearly begins with Chapter 6, in which the poet-prophet introduces himself in the traditional manner of his day. Chapters 1-35 of this book are a collection of only remotely related poems, with a few repetitions in theme but none in treatment. His denunciation of luxury and corruption is invariably gentle, reasoned, muted, and eloquent. The

299

remainder of the book, Chapters 36-39, records in prose two events: Sennacherib's unsuccessful siege of Jerusalem; and King Hezekiah's recovery from a severe illness — events already recorded in almost identical words in II Kings and II Chronicles. ⟪

## Isaiah's Call

6 *   In the year that King Uzziah died, I saw the Lord upon a throne, high and lifted up, and his train filled the temple. About the throne stood the six-winged angels, and they chanted to one another:

"Holy, holy, holy is the Lord of hosts: the whole earth is full of his glory!"

And I said, "Woe to me, I am undone! I am a man with unclean lips, and my eyes have seen the King, the Lord of hosts!"

Then flew one of the angels to me with a glowing coal in his hand, which he had taken with tongs from off the altar; and he touched my mouth with it and said, "Lo, this has purged your sin."

And I heard the voice of the Lord saying, "Whom shall I send and who will go for us?"

Then said I, "Here am I; send me!"

And the Lord said, "Go, tell this people, 'You will surely hear, but you will not understand; you will surely see, but you will not perceive!' Make the heart of this people fat, make their ears heavy, and shut their eyes; lest, seeing with their eyes and hearing with their ears and understanding with their heart, they return and be healed."

Then said I, "O Lord, for how long?"

And he answered, "Until their cities are laid waste, and their houses are without dwellers, and their fields are desolate, and the forsaken places in the land are many. Yet a remnant will return, and will be like the oak whose substance is in them when they have cast their leaves. So the holy seed will be preserved."

* The call of the prophet (Chapter 6) has been transposed to the beginning of this book. Chapter 1 follows.

## *Though Your Sins Be as Scarlet*

1    Hear, O heavens, and give ear, O earth, for the Lord has spoken:
"Children have I nourished and brought up, and they have rebelled against me. The ox knows its owner, and the ass its master's crib;
but Israel does not understand or consider me."

O sinful nation, laden with iniquity, offspring of evildoers, children who
deal corruptly! They have forsaken the Lord; they have provoked the
Holy One of Israel to anger.

Now your country lies desolate; your cities are burned with fire; strangers devour your land in your very presence.

And the Daughter of Zion is deserted, like a booth in a vineyard, like
a city besieged.

If the Lord of hosts had not left us a few survivors, we would have been
as Sodom and Gomorrah.

Hear the word of the Lord, you rulers of Sodom, give ear to the law of
our God, you people of Gomorrah! "To what purpose is the multitude
of your sacrifices?" says the Lord. "I am sated with the burnt offerings of
rams, with the fat of well-fed beasts; nor do I delight in the blood of bullocks or of lambs or of he-goats. Who has required this when you come
before me?

"Bring me no more vain oblations; your incense is abhorrent to me.
Your celebration of the new moons and your appointed feasts my soul
hates; they are a burden I weary of bearing. And when you spread out
your hands, I will hide my eyes; when you make many prayers, I will not
listen. For your hands are full of blood.

"Go, wash yourselves clean! Put away your evil! Learn to do good; seek
justice; relieve the oppressed; defend the fatherless, and plead for the
widow. Come now and do these things; and though your sins be as scarlet, they shall become white as the snow; though they be crimson-red,
they shall become like wool.

"If you are willing and obedient, you will eat from the fruit of the land;
but if you refuse and rebel, the sword shall devour you," says the Lord.

The rebels and sinners shall be destroyed together; those who forsake
the Lord shall be consumed. They shall be like an oak whose leaves have
withered, like a garden that has no water. Their mighty men shall become as hemp, and their work as a spark; and they shall both burn together with none to quench them.

## Swords into Plowshares

2    It shall come to pass, in the latter days, that the house of the Lord shall be established at the top of the mountains; and all nations shall flow to it; and many peoples shall come and say:

"Let us go up to the mountain of the Lord, to the house of the God of Jacob! And he will teach us his ways, that we may walk in his paths. For out of Zion shall go forth the law, and the word of the Lord from Jerusalem."

Then shall he judge the nations and rebuke many peoples; and they shall beat their swords into plowshares, and their spears into pruning hooks; nation shall not lift up sword against nation; neither shall they learn war any more.

## O House of Jacob!

2    O house of Jacob, come, let us walk in the light of the Lord!

For you have forsaken your people, the house of Jacob, because they are soothsayers like the Philistines and rejoice in the children of strangers. Their land is filled with silver and gold, and there is no end to their treasures; their land is filled with horses, and there is no end to their chariots; and their land is filled with idols!

They worship the work of their own hands, they worship that which their fingers have fashioned; and men bow down to them; the lowly and the great alike humble themselves before them.

O Lord, forgive them not!

## The Lord Alone Shall Be Exalted

2    Enter into the rock, and hide yourself in the dust, for fear of the Lord and for the glory of his majesty. For the day of the Lord of hosts shall come upon the proud and the lofty as well as on those who have been brought low; upon all the cedars of Lebanon, so high, and upon the oaks of Bashan; upon the high mountains and every high tower; upon every fortified wall, and all the ships of Tarshish.

The proud shall be bowed down and the haughty made low, and the Lord alone shall be exalted in that day.

In that day a man shall take his idols of silver and his idols of gold, which he made for himself to worship, and cast them to the moles and the bats, and hide them in the clefts of the rocks, for fear of the Lord and for the glory of his majesty, when he arises to shake the earth terribly.

## Because the Daughters of Zion Are Haughty

3-4    The Lord said, because the daughters of Zion are haughty, and walk with outstretched necks and wanton eyes, walking mincingly as they go, and making a tinkling with their feet, the Lord will smite with a scab the heads of the daughters of Zion and lay bare their secret parts.

On that day the Lord will take away the bravery of their tinkling ornaments, and their cauls, and their head-tires, round like the moon; their chains and bracelets; their mufflers and bonnets; the ornaments of their legs; and the headbands, the earrings and rings and nose jewels; the changeable suits of apparel and the mantles; the wimples, the crisping pins, the glasses; and the fine linen, and the hoods and the veils.

Instead of perfume there will be rottenness; and instead of a girdle, rags; and instead of well-set hair, baldness; and instead of a stately robe, a girding of sackcloth; and burning shame instead of beauty.

Their lovers shall fall by the sword, their mighty men in battle. And they shall sit upon the ground, desolate, and mourn.

On that day seven women shall take hold of one man and plead, "We will eat our own bread, and wear our own apparel, only let us be called by your name, to take away our reproach!"

But when the Lord shall have washed away the filth of the daughters of Zion, and shall have purged the blood of Jerusalem by the spirit of justice, in that day shall the branch of the Lord be beautiful and glorious, and the fruit of the earth shall be great for the survivors in Israel.

And the glory of the Lord will be a canopy for shade from the heat of the day, and a shelter for refuge from rain and storm.

## My Beloved Had a Vineyard

5    My beloved, my well-beloved, had a vineyard on a very fertile hill. He fenced it in; he cleared away the stones; he planted it with choice vines. He built a tower in the midst of it, and in the tower he

made a wine press; and he waited for his vineyard to yield choice grapes. But it brought forth wild grapes.

O men of Judah, inhabitants of Jerusalem, judge, I pray you, between me and my vineyard! What more could I have done for my vineyard that I have not done? When I looked for it to yield good grapes, why did it bring forth wild grapes?

Now come, let me tell you what I will do to my vineyard. I will take away its hedge, and it shall be devoured; I will tear down its wall, and it shall be trampled; and I will lay it waste. It shall not be pruned or hoed, but briers and thorns shall cover it. And I will command the clouds to rain no rain upon it.

For this vineyard of the Lord of hosts is the house of Israel; the men of Judah are his pleasant vines. And where the Lord looked for justice, he saw oppression; where he looked for righteousness, he heard a cry.

## Those Who Call Evil Good

5-8   Woe to those who call evil good, and good evil; who change darkness into light, and light into darkness; who make the bitter sweet, and the sweet bitter!

Woe to those who are wise in their own eyes and prudent in their own sight!

Woe to those who are mighty to drink wine, and men of strength to mix strong drink; who justify the wicked for reward and take away the righteousness of the righteous!

As the tongue of fire devours the stubble, as the flame consumes the chaff, so shall their root be turned to rottenness and their blossom go up like dust. For they have rejected the law of the Lord, and scorned the word of the Holy One of Israel! [1]

## The People Who Walked in Darkness

9   The people who walked in darkness have seen a great light; they who dwelt in the land of the shadow of death, upon them the light shone. You have multiplied the nation and increased their joy, which is as the joy of the harvest and the rejoicing of men who divide the spoil.

[1] See ISAIAH, Chapters 6-8, in Notes and Excisions.

For you have broken the yoke of his burden, you have broken the rod of his oppressor as in the day of Midian. For every boot stamped with fierceness and every garment rolled in blood; but this shall be for fuel of the fire.

For a child is born to you, to you a son is given, and the government shall be upon his shoulder. And his name will be "Wonderful Counselor," "The Mighty God," "The Everlasting Father," and "The Prince of Peace." That his government shall be increased, there shall be no end of peace upon the throne of David, and upon his kingdom, to order it and to establish it with justice through righteousness from now and forever.

## The Proud and Arrogant

9-10    All the people of Israel who say in their pride and arrogance of heart, "The bricks have fallen, but we will build with hewn stones; the sycamores are cut down, but we will replace them with cedars," all these shall know that the Lord will raise up their adversaries against them, and join their enemies together — the Syrians in front and the Philistines behind — to devour Israel with open mouth.

For all this his anger is not turned away; his hand is stretched out still.

The people seek not the Lord of hosts; therefore the Lord will cut off from Israel head and tail, palm branch and reed, in one day. The elder and honorable man, he is the head; the prophet who teaches lies, he is the tail. For those who lead this people cause them to err; and those led by them are destroyed.

The Lord will have no joy in their young men, nor mercy on their fatherless and widows. For every one of them is an evildoer, and every mouth speaks folly.

For all this his anger is not turned away; his hand is stretched out still.

Woe to you who decree iniquitous decrees; who falsify in writing to take away their right from the poor, that widows may be your prey, that you may rob the fatherless! What will you do on the day of visitation, in the desolation which will come from afar? To whom will you turn for help? Where will you leave your glory? Without me you shall crouch under the captives or fall under the slain.

For all this God's anger is not turned away; his hand is stretched out still.

He will raise a signal for a nation afar off; and lo, swiftly and speedily shall it come. None amongst them shall be weary or stumble; none shall sleep or slumber; the girdles of their loins shall not be loosed, nor a latchet of their shoes be broken. They shall come with arrows sharp, and bows bent, their horses' hoofs like flint, their wheels like the whirlwind. Their roaring shall be like a lion; like young lions they shall roar and seize their prey and carry it off — and there shall be none to stop them.[2]

## A Little Child Shall Lead Them

**11-12**  There shall come forth a shoot out of the stem of Jesse, and a branch shall grow out of his roots; and the spirit of the Lord shall rest upon him — the spirit of wisdom and understanding, the spirit of counsel and might, the spirit of knowledge and of the fear of the Lord. And he shall not judge by what his eyes see, or reprove by what his ears hear; but with justice shall he judge the poor, and decide with equity for the meek of the earth. With the rod of his mouth, with the breath of his lips, shall he slay the wicked. Righteousness shall be the girdle of his loins, and faithfulness the girdle of his waist.

In that day the wolf shall dwell with the lamb, and the leopard shall lie down with the kid; and the calf and the young lion and the fatling together; and a little child shall lead them all. The cow and the bear shall feed as their young ones lie down together; the lion shall eat straw like the ox. And the sucking child shall play at the hole of the asp, and the weaned child shall put his hand on the adder's den. They shall not hurt or destroy one another in all my holy mountain.

For the earth shall be full of the knowledge of the Lord, as the waters cover the sea.

In that day the root of Jesse shall stand as a signal to the peoples, and him shall the nations seek; and his dwelling shall be glorious. In that day the Lord will set his hand a second time to recover the remnant of his people, and will gather the dispersed of Israel, and the scattered of Judah, from the four corners of the earth.

And the Lord will utterly destroy the tongue of the Egyptian sea. And there shall be a highway for the remnant of his people to cross over dryshod, as there was for Israel when he came up from the land of Egypt.[3]

---

[2] See ISAIAH, Chapter 10, in Notes and Excisions.
[3] See ISAIAH, Chapter 12, in Notes and Excisions.

## Warning to Babylon

13    Lament, O Babylon, for the day of the Lord is at hand! As destruction from the Almighty will it come! Pangs and throes will seize you; you will be like a woman in labor. Behold, the day of the Lord is coming, cruel with wrath and fierce anger!

The stars in heaven and the constellations will not shine that day; the sun will be darkened at his rising, and the moon will withhold her light through the night.

The Lord will punish the wicked for their iniquity, and end the arrogance of the proud, and lay low the haughtiness of the tyrant. On that day in Babylon a man will be rarer than gold, more rare than the pure gold of Ophir. The heavens will tremble, and the earth will move out of its orbit, at the wrath of the Lord of hosts in the day of his fierce anger.

"Behold," says the Lord, "I will stir up the Medes against you, who shall have no regard for silver, and no delight in gold. And their bows will shatter your young men; they will have no pity on the fruit of the womb; their eye will not spare the children."

And Babylon, the glory of the kingdoms, the beauty of the Chaldeans, will be like Sodom and Gomorrah when God overthrew them. Never again will it be inhabited, or dwelt in from generation to generation. No Arab will pitch his tent there, nor shepherds make their fold there. But wild beasts of the desert will hide there, and owls will fill the houses; there the young owls will dwell and the he-goats will dance. The wild beasts will howl in the desolate houses, in the pleasant palaces.

The day is near, the day of the Lord is at hand!


## The Lord Will Have Compassion

14    The Lord will have pity on Jacob and compassion on Israel, and he will return them to their own land. And the stranger will join them, and cling to the house of Jacob. On that day the Lord will give Israel rest from sorrow, and from fear, and from hard bondage; and on that day you will take up this parable against the king of Babylon:

How the oppressor has ceased!

The Lord has broken the staff of the wicked, the scepter of rulers who smote the people in wrath, who ruled the nations in anger.

Now the whole earth is at rest and the people break into singing. Even the fir trees rejoice, and the cedars of Lebanon call out: "Since you are laid low, O Babylon, none come to fell us!"

Sheol beneath is preparing to receive you; the dead stir up for you the chiefs of the earth, all the kings of the nations, who speak out and say to you: "Are you also become weak as we?" Your pomp and the sound of your music is brought down to the grave; the maggots are your bed, the worms your coverlet.

How you have fallen, O bright and morning star! How you are cut down to the ground, you who weakened the nations! You said in your heart, "I will ascend into heaven; I will set my throne above the stars of God; I will rise over the heights of the clouds; I will be like the Most High!"

Yet you shall be brought down to Sheol, to the utmost depths of the pit, and those who gaze at you will say: "Is this the king of Babylon, who made the earth tremble and kingdoms shake, who made the world a desert and destroyed its cities, who never opened the doors to let his prisoners go?"

## Rejoice Not, Philistia!

14-23    Rejoice not, Philistia, because the rod which smote you is broken.
For out of the serpent's root will come a basilisk, and its fruit will be a flying serpent. The firstborn of the poor will feed, and the needy lie down in safety; but I will kill your root with famine, and the remnant I shall slay.

Howl, O gate! Cry, O city! Dissolve in fear, O Philistia! For smoke comes out of the north, and in his ranks there is no straggler! [4]

## The Prophecy of Desolation

24    Behold, the Lord will make the earth empty and desolate, and turn it upside down, and scatter its inhabitants. And it shall be, as with the people, so with the priest; as with the servant, so with his master; as with the maid, so with her mistress; as with the buyer, so with the seller; as with the lender, so with the borrower; as with the creditor, so

[4] See ISAIAH, Chapters 15-23, in Notes and Excisions.

with the debtor — the land shall be emptied and despoiled; for the Lord has spoken this word.

The earth mourns; the world withers; and the haughty people languish. The earth is defiled by its inhabitants because they have transgressed the laws, changed the ordinance, broken the everlasting covenant. Therefore a curse devours the earth, and those who dwell in it are desolate.

The new wine fails; the vine withers; all the merry-hearted sigh. The mirth of timbrels ceases; the sound of rejoicing ends; the joy of the harp is stilled. No more do they drink wine with a song, and the strong drink is bitter to those who drink it. Broken down is the city of confusion; every house is shut, that none may enter. All joy is darkened; the mirth of the land is gone. Only desolation is left in the city; in the gate, only ruin.

Fear, and the pit, and the snare are upon you, O inhabitant of the earth! He who flees in fear shall fall into the pit, and he who climbs out of the pit shall be caught in the snare; for the windows of heaven are opened, the foundations of the earth tremble. The earth is rent asunder, shakes violently, reels like a drunkard, and it shall fall and not rise again.

On that day the Lord will punish the high who are on high, and the kings of the earth. And they will be gathered together as prisoners are gathered in a dungeon, and after many days they will be punished.

On that day the moon will be confounded, and the sun ashamed.

## Lo, This Is Our God!

25-27 Lo, this is our God! We have waited for him, and he will save us; we have waited for him and rejoice in his salvation! On this mountain the Lord of hosts will make a feast for the peoples of the earth, a feast of wine on the lees, of fat things full of marrow, of wine well refined. And on this mountain he will destroy the covering and the mask that covers all people and masks all nations. He will wipe away the tears from all faces; the fear of death he will swallow up forever. And the reproach of his people he will take away from off the earth; for the Lord has spoken.

On that day we shall sing this song in the land of Judah:

"We have a strong city; God will appoint salvation as the walls and as the bulwarks. Open the gates, that the righteous nation which keeps the truth may enter. Trust in the Lord forever; for in the Lord God is everlasting strength.

"The Lord brings down those who dwell on high; the lofty city he lays low and brings down to the dust, that the foot may trample it, even the foot of the poor and the steps of the needy."

The path of the just is straight, in the way of your judgments, O Lord! We have waited for you; your name is the desire of our souls. Our soul has yearned for you in the night, our spirit in the morning. For when your judgments are upon the earth, O Lord, the peoples of the world will learn justice.[5]

## Woe to the Drunkards!

28      Woe to the crown of pride, the drunkards of Ephraim, whose beauty is a fading flower! Behold, the Lord has one mighty and strong, one like a storm of hail and a destroying tempest, like a flood of mighty waters overflowing, one who shall cast to earth the pride of the drunkards of Ephraim and trample it under foot.

On that day the Lord of hosts shall be a crown of glory, a diadem of beauty to the remnant of his people; a spirit of justice to him who sits in judgment, and of courage to those who turn back the tide of battle at the gate.

But these also have erred through wine: the priest and the prophet reel through strong drink, they falter in vision, they stumble in judgment.

Whom shall one teach knowledge, and to whom make clear the tradition? To those who are just weaned and drawn from the breast. For it must be taught precept upon precept, line upon line; here a little, there a little. With stammering lips and in a strange tongue it shall be spoken to this people, to whom it was said, "This is the rest wherewith you may give rest to the weary." But they would not listen.

Hear the word of the Lord, you scoffers who rule the people of Jerusalem! Because you have said, "We have made a covenant with death, and with Sheol an agreement, that when the scourge passes through it shall not come near us; for we have made lies our refuge, and falsehood our hiding place," thus says the Lord: "Behold I am laying in Zion a foundation stone, a precious cornerstone, a sure foundation; he who believes shall not be in haste. Justice shall be the line, and righteousness the plummet. Hail shall sweep away the refuge of lies, and the waters shall overflow your hiding place. Your covenant with death shall be annulled,

[5] See ISAIAH, Chapters 26-27, in Notes and Excisions.

your agreement with Sheol broken. The overwhelming scourge shall pass through and tread you down. Each time it passes it shall smite you; and it shall pass through by day and by night, and strike terror in your hearts when you understand the message. The bed will be too short to stretch out upon; and the coverlet too narrow for a man to wrap himself in it."

## The Parable of the Plowman

28 Give ear, attend, listen to my speech: Does the plowman, intent on sowing, plow unceasingly? Does he open and break the clods with the harrow unendingly? When the ground is plowed and harrowed, does he not spread the black cumin and scatter it, and seed the wheat and barley and rye in their appointed places? For his God instructs him and teaches him aright.

The black cumin is not threshed with a threshing instrument, nor is a cartwheel rolled over it, but the cumin must be beaten with a staff and with a rod. Is the seeding wheat to be crushed? No, it is not to be threshed forever, or broken by the wheel of the cart, or crumbled by the hoofs of the horses.

This also comes from the Lord of hosts, wonderful in counsel, great in wisdom.

## Sennacherib's Invasion

29 Jerusalem, O Jerusalem! Woe to you, city where David encamped!

Go on with your cycle of feasts, year following year; but I will distress you and there shall be mourning in Jerusalem. I will lay siege to you, and raise up forts to hem you in. Then your voice, like the voice of a ghost, shall come from the ground, shall come low out of the dust. But your foes shall be as numerous as particles of fine dust, as chaff carried by the wind.

Suddenly, in an instant, the Lord of hosts shall visit your enemies with thunder and earthquake, with whirlwind and tempest and devouring flame. And all the nations who war against Jerusalem and distress her shall vanish like a nightmare. As a hungry man dreams that he is eating, but awakes, and his hunger is still there; as a thirsty man dreams that he is drinking, but awakes, and his thirst is still with him; so shall it be with the nations who war against you, O Jerusalem, O Mount Zion!

## *You Who Reel*

29      You who are drunk, but not with wine, who reel, but not with
        strong drink — stupefy yourselves and remain in a stupor; blind
yourselves and be blind! For the Lord has poured over you a deep sleep
and has closed your eyes; he has covered the heads of your prophets.

And the vision of all this has become to you like the writing in a book
that is sealed. Men take it to the learned and say, "Read this, we pray
you!" and he replies, "I cannot, for the book is sealed." Then they take it
to him who is not learned and say, "Read this, we pray you!" and he replies, "I cannot, for I am not learned."

And the Lord says: "Because these people draw near, and honor me
with their lips, but their hearts are far from me, and their fear of me is a
commandment learned by rote, behold, the wisdom of their wise men
shall depart from them; the prudence of their prudent men shall be hidden."

And you who plot your plots deep and hide them from the Lord, and in
the darkness where you work, you say, "Who sees us? And who knows
us?" How perverse you are! Shall the potter be regarded like the clay,
that the thing made should say of him who made it, "He made me not,"
or the thing formed say of him who formed it, "He lacks understanding"?

## *The Rebellious Children*

30-31   "Woe to the rebellious children," says the Lord, "who seek coun-
        sel, but not of me, that they may add sin to sin. They set out to
go down to Egypt (and have not sought my counsel), to take refuge in
the stronghold of Pharaoh, and shelter in the shadow of Egypt! Therefore
the strength of Pharaoh shall turn to your shame, and your trust in Egypt
to your confusion. They shall be ashamed of a people who cannot profit
them, who can bring them but shame and disgrace.

"Go now, and write it for them upon a tablet, and inscribe it upon a
scroll, that it may be a witness against them forever. For they are a rebellious people who say to their seers, 'You must not see!' and say to their
prophets, 'You must not prophesy the truth! Speak softly to us, and prophesy illusions; turn aside out of the path, and let us hear no more of the
Holy One of Israel!'

"Because you despised the prophet's word, and trusted in cunning and oppression, the guilt shall be for you like a breach in a high wall ready to fall, that breaks in an instant, that crashes like a potter's vessel, so shattered that there cannot be found of it a fragment to take fire from the hearth, or water from the cistern."

For thus says the Holy One of Israel, "In repentance and joy can you be saved; in quietness and trust shall be your strength!" But you said, "No, we will flee upon horses and ride upon swift steeds!" Therefore shall those who pursue you be swift. A thousand shall flee at the rebuke of one; and at the rebuke of five shall you flee until you are left like a flagstaff upon a mountain, like a signal upon a hill.

Woe to those who go down to Egypt for help, and rely on horses and trust in chariots because they are many, and in horsemen because they are strong, but look not to the Holy One of Israel, nor seek the Lord! Now the Egyptians are men, and not God; and their horses flesh, and not spirit. When the Lord stretches out his hand, both the helper and the helped shall fall down; they shall all perish together.

## You Women at Ease

32     Rise up, you women who are at ease, complacent daughters of Jerusalem! Listen to my voice! Many days and many years shall you be troubled, you complacent ones, and tremble, you confident ones. Strip, make yourselves bare, gird yourselves with sackcloth!

Beat your breasts for the pleasant fields and fruitful vines, for the soil of your people covered with thorns and briers, for all the joyous houses in the joyful city. Because the palace shall be forsaken, and the teeming city shall be deserted. The ramparts and the watchtowers shall become dens to delight the wild asses, and the pasture of flocks.

Until the spirit is poured upon us from on high, and the wilderness shall again become a fruitful field, and the fruitful field become vast as a forest.

Then justice shall rule the wilderness, and righteousness the fruitful field. And the effect of righteousness will be peace, and quietness forever. And my people shall dwell peacefully in their habitations, secure in their dwellings, and in quiet resting places.

## Woe to the Plunderer

**33-34** Woe to you, plunderer, who yourself have not been plundered;
and to you who deal falsely, though none dealt falsely with you!

Behold, the valiant men cry without, and the ambassadors of peace
weep bitterly. The highways lie waste; the wayfarers have ceased; the
land mourns and languishes; Lebanon withers in shame, and Sharon is
like a wilderness; both Bashan and Carmel are leafless. For the covenant
has been broken; its witnesses have been mocked at.

"Hear, you who are far off," says the Lord, "and you who are near,
acknowledge my might!"

The sinners in Zion are filled with fear; trembling has seized the ungodly, and they ask, "Who among us can dwell with a devouring fire?
Who among us can dwell with eternal flames?" He who walks uprightly
and speaks the truth; he who despises gain won by oppression, and
keeps his hand free from the touch of a bribe; he who will not hear of
bloodshed, or look upon evil. He will dwell on the heights, secure on the
rocks; his bread shall be given him; his water will be sure.

Your eyes shall then see Jerusalem as a quiet habitation, a tabernacle
that shall not be taken down; whose stakes shall never be removed, nor
any of its cords be broken.

There the glorious Lord will be for us a place of broad rivers, where no
galley shall pass. For the Lord is our judge, the Lord is our lawgiver, the
Lord is our king; he will save us.[6]

## The Eyes of the Blind

**35-39** Say to those fearful of heart, "Be strong, fear not! Behold, your
God will come and save you!"

Then the eyes of the blind shall be opened, and the ears of the deaf un-
stopped. The lame man shall leap like a hart, and the tongue of the
dumb sing out. The waters shall break out in the wilderness, and streams
in the desert; the parched ground shall become like a pool, and the
thirsty land like springs of water. In the haunt of jackals, herds shall
gather; there the grass and reeds and rushes shall grow.

And a highway shall be there, and it shall be called the holy way. The

* See ISAIAH, Chapter 34, in Notes and Excisions.

unclean shall not pass over it; but it shall be for God's wayfarers. And even fools shall not err upon it. No lion shall be found there, nor any ravenous beast; but the redeemed shall walk there, the ransomed of the Lord shall return by it. And they shall come to Zion with songs upon their lips, and everlasting joy upon their heads. They shall find joy and gladness, and sorrow and sighing shall flee away.[7]

[7] See ISAIAH, Chapters 36-39, in Notes and Excisions.

# ISAIAH (II)
## The Comforter

❲ About the person of Isaiah (II), author of Chapters 40-55 in the Book of Isaiah, we know practically nothing. We surmise from his work that he lived fully two centuries after Isaiah (I), and that he lived in exile in Babylon. From the ebullience of his work — the variety of sounds he describes, the bright colors and pageantry of his metaphors, and the tumultuous atmosphere he constantly creates — it is assumed he was quite young at the time the poems were written. But that is about all we can guess at. He has become known as the "Unknown Author" — and the "unknown author" has become universally loved, although he left only a slender collection of disconnected poems, which occupy no more than a dozen pages in the Bible.

Beyond his greatness as a poet (whose imagery in translation is inevitably dimmed), Isaiah (II) is among the first of the prophets of Israel to create an entirely new concept of the Creator. The Lord is not a God of vengeance, but a comforting God, a forgiving God, a Rock of refuge, in whom every breaking heart can find comfort.

A vast literature has arisen about Isaiah the "Unknown" (often called the Second Isaiah, or, more commonly, Deutero-Isaiah), much of it devoted to his prophecies concerning life after the Day of Judgment — his "eschatological prophecies." This speculation is based principally on the four poems (which some scholars believe may have been interpolated) known as "The Songs of the Servant."

Through the centuries the songs by Isaiah (II) have given comfort and joy. The first utterance from this prophet is: "Be comforted, be comforted, my people, says the Lord"; and his last utterance begins with the reassuring: "You shall go out in joy and be led forth in peace." ❲

## Be Comforted, My People

*40*     "Be comforted, be comforted, my people," says the Lord. "Speak
to the heart of Jerusalem, and tell her that her time of servitude
is ended, that her punishment is over, that she has received from
the Lord's hand double for all her sins."

A voice cries out in the wilderness: "Prepare a way for the Lord; make
straight through the desert a highway for our God! Every valley shall be
raised, and every mountain shall be lowered; the crooked shall be made
straight, and the rough ground leveled. And the glory of the Lord shall be
revealed; all flesh shall see it together. For the mouth of the Lord has
spoken it."

The voice said: "Proclaim!" And I, the prophet, asked, "What shall I
proclaim?" And the voice said: "Proclaim that all flesh is as grass, and all
its beauty as the flower of the field. The grass dries up, the flower withers;
only the word of the Lord endures forever."

O you who bring glad tidings to Zion and good tidings to Jerusalem,
climb to the top of a high mountain! Lift up your voice fearlessly, and say
to the cities of Judah:

"Behold your God! Behold, the Lord your God is coming in his might,
and his arm will rule! And like a shepherd who feeds his flock, he will
gather the lambs in his arms and carry them in his bosom, and gently
lead all that are with young."

## Who Has Measured the Waters?

*40*     Who has measured the waters in the hollow of his hand, and
computed the heavens with a span, and meted out the dust of
the earth in a measure, and weighed the mountains in scales, and the
hills in a balance?

Who has probed the spirit of the Lord, or, as his counselor, has taught
him? Whose counsel has he sought; and who instructed him in judgment,
and taught him in knowledge, and pointed out the way of understanding?

Lo, to him all the nations are as a drop from a bucket, or accounted as
fine dust on a scale; the weight of the islands are a mote to him, and the
whole of Lebanon not enough for fuel, nor its beasts for a burnt offer-

ing. All the nations are as nothing before him; as less than nothing are they accounted.

To whom, then, will you liken God? The idol cast by the smelter, and overlaid with gold by the goldsmith? Do you not know, or have you not heard, and were you not told from the beginning — since the foundation of the earth was established — that it is the Lord who sits above the circle of the earth, and all its inhabitants are as grasshoppers? It is he who stretched out the heavens like a curtain, and spread them like a tent to dwell in; it is he who brings princes to nothing, and turns to naught judges of the earth. Scarcely are they planted, scarcely are they sown, and scarcely has their stock taken root in the earth, when he blows upon them and they wither, and the whirlwind carries them away like straw.

Why do you say, O Jacob, and you, O Israel, "My way is hidden from the Lord; justice is passed over by my God"? Do you not know, and have you not heard, that the everlasting God, the Creator of the earth, neither weakens nor wearies, that his understanding is beyond probing? It is he who gives strength to the weak; and to the weary, power. Even youths grow faint and weary, and young men fall; but those who wait upon the Lord renew their strength, they mount up as on the wings of eagles; and those who trust in the Lord shall run and not tire, they shall go on and not grow faint.

## Fear Not, For I Am with You

41    "And you, Israel my servant, Jacob my chosen, seed of Abraham whom I befriended — you whom I gathered from the remote parts of the earth, and said to you: 'I have chosen you as my servant, and have not spurned you' — fear not, for I am with you; be not dismayed. I will give you strength; I will uphold you with my victorious arm!

"Behold, all those incensed against you shall be shamed and confounded; those who strive against you shall perish and come to nought. You shall seek them, but you shall not find them; those who war against you shall be as nothing, as a thing without substance.

"Fear not, for I, the Lord your God, hold your right hand and say to you: 'Fear not, for I am with you!' "

## *When the Poor and Needy Seek Water*

*41*    "When the poor and needy seek water, and their tongues are parched with thirst, I the Lord will answer them, I the God of Israel will not forsake them.

"I will open rivers on the heights and fountains in the valleys; I will make the desert a pool of water, and the dry land, springs of water. In the wilderness I will plant the cedar, the acacia, the myrtle and the olive; in the desert the cypress, the larch and the pine will thrive together. So men may see, and know, and consider, and understand, that the hand of the Lord has done this, that the Holy One of Israel has created it."

## *The First Song of the Servant*

*42*    Behold my servant, whom I uphold; my chosen, in whom I delight! I have put my spirit upon him, and he will go forth to bring justice to the nations. He will not shout or raise his voice, or make himself heard in the street; he will not break a bending reed or quench a flickering wick; but he will raise justice to truth. He will not fail or be discouraged until he has established justice upon the earth. And the islands shall wait for his teachings.

## *Sing to the Lord a New Song*

*42-43*    Sing to the Lord a new song! Let his praise be heard from the ends of the earth! Let the sea roar, and the islands with all their inhabitants! Let the desert and its cities raise their voice, and the villages of Kedar be heard! Let the inhabitants of Sela sing joyfully, let them shout from the top of the mountains: "Glory to the Lord!"

The Lord will go forth like a mighty warrior; he will stir up his rage like a man of war; he will cry out against his enemies: "For long, for too long have I held my peace, and kept still, and restrained myself! Now will I cry out like a woman in labor, gasping and panting at once. I will lay waste mountains and hills and dry up their herbs; I will make the rivers into islands and dry up the pools. And I will guide the blind in paths they have never known, and make the darkness light before them, and make

the crooked roads straight. All these things will I do and not leave undone. But those who trust in graven images, those who say to molten
idols, 'You are our gods' — they shall be turned back in shame."[8]

## The Man Who Feeds on Ashes

*44*     A man hews down a cedar, or an oak or a cypress, which the
Lord planted and the rain nourished; and he takes part of the
tree for fuel, and kindles a fire and bakes bread; and of the rest he carves
an idol, and bows down before it and worships it, and prays to it, saying,
"Deliver me, for you are my god!"

But he does not consider in his heart to say, "Is there knowledge or
understanding in him who says, 'Half of the tree I burned in the fire, and
on its embers I baked bread and roasted meat; and the rest I shall make
into an idol and bow down before the block of wood'!"

That man feeds on ashes, and has been misled, so that he can no longer
save himself and say, "Is there not a lie in my right hand?"

## Not for Price or Reward

*44-46*     "Remember these things, O Jacob and Israel: I have blotted out
your sins and erased your transgressions; I have redeemed you!"

Sing, O heavens, for the Lord has done it; break into song, O mountains, O forest, and every tree in it! For the Lord has redeemed Jacob,
and glorifies himself in Israel.

Thus says the Lord your Redeemer: "I am the Lord, Creator of all
things, who stretched out the heavens above and spread out the earth
below; who frustrates the omens of impostors and makes of diviners fools;
who turns wise men backward and makes their knowledge foolish; who
said to Jerusalem, 'You shall be inhabited again,' and to the cities of Judah, 'You shall be rebuilt upon the waste places'; who said to the deep,
'Be dry! For I will dry up your rivers'; and who said to Cyrus, 'I will un-
gird the loins of kings, to open their doors before you; I will give you
treasures hidden in darkness, and the riches of secret places, that you
may know it is I the Lord who call you by your name, for the sake of
Jacob my servant, and Israel my chosen. I am the Lord, and there is no
other besides me, there is no other God.'

[*] See ISAIAH, Chapters 42-44, in Notes and Excisions.

"Woe to him who strives with his Maker, as a potsherd with the potters of the earth! Does the clay say to him who fashions it, 'What are you making?' "

Thus says the Lord, the Holy One of Israel, "Ask me of the things that are to come, concerning my sons and concerning the work of my hands. I have raised Cyrus in victory, and I will make level all his ways. For he shall rebuild my city, and he shall set my exiles free, not for price or for reward." [9]

## The Downfall of Babylon

47    "Come down, come down and sit in the dust, O virgin daughter of Babylon; sit on the ground without a throne, O daughter of the Chaldeans! No longer shall you be called tender and delicate! Take the millstones and grind the grain; remove your veil, make bare the leg, uncover the thigh, pass through the rivers. For I will take vengeance, and no man shall intercede.

"Go into the darkness and sit in silence, O daughter of the Chaldeans! No longer shall you be called the mistress of kingdoms! O complacent one, given to pleasures, you who say to yourself, 'I am, and there is no one besides me!' Your wisdom and your knowledge have led you astray. Disaster shall come upon you, and you shall not be able to charm it away. Sudden destruction shall fall upon you, and you shall not know how to avert it.

"I was angry with my people, and I placed them in your hand. But you showed them no pity; upon the aged you laid your yoke heavily; and you said in your heart, 'I shall be their mistress forever.' Secure in your wickedness, you said, 'No one sees me.' Therefore will I take vengeance, inexorable vengeance," says the Redeemer, the Lord of hosts, the Holy One of Israel.

## No Peace for the Wicked

48    The Lord your Redeemer, the Holy One of Israel, says, 'I the Lord am your God, who teaches you for your own profit, who leads you in the way you should go. O that you would hearken to my

[9] See ISAIAH, Chapters 45-46, in Notes and Excisions.

commandments! Then your peace would be as a river, your prosperity constant as the waves of the sea, your offspring as many as the sands, your descendants as the dust of the earth; and your name would never be cut off from before me."

Go out from Babylon, flee from the Chaldeans, and with a joyful voice declare to the ends of the earth: "The Lord has redeemed his servant Jacob! When he led them through the desert they knew no thirst; he made the waters flow for them out of a rock; he cleft the rock and the waters gushed out."

"But there is no peace for the wicked," says the Lord.

## The Second Song of the Servant

49    Listen, O isles! And you people afar, hearken to me! The Lord has called me from the womb, and given me my name. He has made my mouth like a sharp sword, and he has hidden me in the shadow of his hand. He has fashioned me like a polished arrow and concealed me in his quiver; and he said to me: "You are my servant Israel, in whom I will be glorified."

But I said, "In vain have I labored; my strength I have spent for nought. Yet surely my right is with the Lord, and my reward with my God."

And now says the Lord, who called me from the womb to be his servant, to bring Jacob back to him, and that Israel be gathered to him, "It is too light a thing that you should be my servant to bring back the tribes of Jacob and to restore the offspring of Israel; I will also give you as a light to the nations, that my salvation may reach to the ends of the earth."

## Sing, O Heavens

49    Sing, O heavens; be joyful, O earth! Break into song, O mountains! For the Lord has comforted his people, and has pity upon the afflicted.

Zion had said, "The Lord has forsaken me; the Lord has forgotten me!"

Can a woman forget her nursing child, that she should have no compassion upon her son? "Though these may forget," says the Lord, "I will not forget you. Behold, I have engraved you upon the palms of my hands;

your walls are always before my eyes. Hasten, hasten your children, while yet your destroyers and those who laid you waste are leaving. Lift up your eyes and behold how they gather themselves together and come to you. You shall put them on as an ornament, and gird yourself with them like a bride. For your wasted and desolate places shall be restored, and the land shall be filled with inhabitants.

"Behold, I will lift up my hand to the nations, and they shall bring back your sons to your bosom, and carry home your daughters on their shoulders. Kings shall be your foster fathers, and queens your nursing mothers. They shall bow down with their faces to the earth and lick the dust of your feet. And you shall know that I am the Lord, and none who trust in me shall be put to shame."

## The Third Song of the Servant

50    The Lord God has given me the tongue of the disciple, that I may know how to sustain with words him who is weary. Each morning, each morning he wakens my ear to hear as disciples hear; and I have not been rebellious or turned away. I gave my back to the smiters, and my cheek to those who plucked off my hair; nor did I hide my face from the shame of being spat upon.

The Lord God will help me, therefore I am not confounded, therefore have I set my face like flint. My vindicator is near; who will contend with me? Who is he who will condemn me?

Whoever among you fears the Lord and obeys the voice of his servant, though he walk in darkness without a gleam of light, let him trust in the name of the Lord and rely upon his God! [10]

## Awake! Awake!

51-52    Awake! Awake! Put on strength, O arm of the Lord! Awake as in the days of old, in the generations of ancient times. The redeemed of the Lord shall return and come with singing to Zion; and everlasting joy shall be upon their heads. They shall know gladness and joy; and sorrow and sighing shall flee away.

Awake! Awake! rise up, O Jerusalem, you who have drunk at the hand

[10] See ISAIAH, Chapter 51, in Notes and Excisions.

of the Lord the cup of his fury, you who have drained the beaker to the dregs! Hear this, you who are afflicted, who are drunk, but not with wine: Thus says the Lord, the Lord your God who pleads the cause of his people:

"Behold, I have taken from your hand the cup of my fury; you shall not drink from it again. And I will put it into the hand of your tormentors, who said to you, 'Bow down, that we may go over you!' who made your back a street for them to walk over."

Awake! Awake! Put on your strength, O Zion! Put on your beautiful garments, O Jerusalem, the holy city! Shake yourself from the dust; loose yourself from the bonds upon your neck, O captive daughter of Zion!

How beautiful upon the mountains are the feet of the heralds who bring good tidings, who announce good tidings of peace and of salvation, who say to Zion: "Your God reigns!"

Break into joyful song all together; sing together, you waste places of Jerusalem; for the Lord has comforted his people, he has redeemed Jerusalem. The Lord has bared his holy arm in the eyes of all the nations; and to the ends of the earth they shall witness the salvation of our God!

Depart, depart, touch no unclean thing; purify yourselves, you who bear the vessels of the Lord. And you shall not go out in haste, neither shall you depart in flight; for before you and behind you shall go the Lord God of Israel.

## The Fourth Song of the Servant

52-53    Behold, my servant shall prosper! He shall be exalted and extolled very high! As he amazed many (for his visage was so marred and his form unlike that of other men), so shall he startle many nations. Kings shall shut their mouths because of him; for that which had not been told them they shall see, and that which they had not heard they shall perceive.

Who would have believed our report? And to whom has the arm of the Lord been revealed? For he grew up like a sapling, like a root out of the ground. He had no comeliness that we should look upon him, or beauty that we should delight in him. He was despised and forsaken by men.

Yet it was our grief and our sorrow that he carried, while we accounted him stricken and afflicted by God. He was wounded because of our transgressions, and bruised for our iniquities. The chastisement of our welfare was upon him, and with his stripes we were healed. We, like sheep, went astray; we turned each one his own way; and the Lord laid upon him the iniquity of us all.

When he was oppressed, he humbled himself; he did not open his mouth. As a lamb led to the slaughter, as a sheep before the shearers, he opened not his mouth. He was cut off from the land of the living, and for our transgressions he was stricken to death. They made his grave with the wicked and his tomb with the evil-rich, although he had done no violence, nor was there any deceit in his mouth.

Yet it pleased the Lord to crush him with grief. No, through the suffering of his soul and through his affliction, shall my righteous servant make many righteous, and their sins he shall bear. Therefore will the Lord give him a portion among the great, and he shall divide the spoil with the mighty, because he bared his soul to death and was numbered with the transgressors, yet bore the sins of many, and for transgressors interceded.

## O Barren One

54 "Sing, O barren one, who did not bear! Break into song, you who have not known the pain of labor! For more are the children of the desolate one than the children of her who is married," says the Lord. "Enlarge your tent, stretch out the curtains of your habitations, lengthen the cords and strengthen the stakes. For your children shall possess the inheritance of the nations, and fill with inhabitants the desolate cities."

You shall forget the shame of your youth, and remember no more the reproach of your widowhood. For your Maker is your husband, the Holy One of Israel is your Redeemer. The Lord regarded you like a wife forsaken and grieved in spirit, the Lord regarded you, O Jerusalem, like the wife of one's youth, when she is cast off.

"For a brief moment have I forsaken you," says your God, "but with great compassion will I bring you back to me. In my anger I hid my face from you for a moment, but now I will have compassion on you with everlasting kindness. For this day is to me like the days of Noah: as I swore then that the floods should never again cover the earth, so have I sworn now never again to be angry with you or rebuke you. Though the mountains may depart and the hills be removed, my kindness shall not depart from you, nor shall my covenant of peace be removed.

"O afflicted one, tossed by the tempest and without comfort! Behold, I will set your stones in bright colors, and lay your foundations with sapphires, and make your windows of agate, and your gates of carbuncles, and your borders of precious stones. All your sons shall be taught by the Lord; great shall be the peace of your children; for in righteousness shall you be established. You shall be far from oppression, for you shall have nothing to fear; and you shall be far from destruction, for I shall not let it come near you," says the Lord.

## As the Rain Comes Down

55     "Ho, everyone who thirsts, come to the waters; and he who has no money, come, buy and eat! Come, buy wine and milk without money and without price. Why do you spend money for that which is not bread, and the earnings from your labor for that which does not satisfy? Listen to me, and you shall eat what is good and delight your soul with it.

"Listen to me, and your soul shall live; I will make an everlasting covenant with you as I did with David. Seek the Lord while he may be found, call upon him while he is near. Let the wicked forsake his ways, and the unrighteous man his thoughts. Let them return to the Lord and he will have pity on them, and to our God, for he will abundantly pardon them.

"For my thoughts are not like your thoughts, neither are your ways like my ways," says the Lord. "As the heavens are higher than the earth, so are my ways higher than your ways, and my thoughts than your thoughts. But as the rain and snow come down from heaven, and do not return there but water the earth and make it give seed to the sower and bread to the eater, so shall be the word that goes forth from my mouth; it shall not return to me except it accomplish the purpose for which it was uttered.

"You shall go out in joy and be led forth in peace; the hills and mountains shall break into song before you; the trees in the field shall clap their hands. Instead of the thorn shall come up the fir tree; in place of the brier shall come up the myrtle. And they shall be to the Lord a memorial, an everlasting sign that shall not be cut off."

# ISAIAH (III)
## *Poet of Great Faith*

❨ The writer of the last part of the Book of Isaiah, chapters 56-66, is commonly known as Trito-Isaiah, or the Third Isaiah. Here we are in the presence of a quite different poet; and some scholars maintain that in these few chapters several poets are represented. The poet attempts to emulate the Second Isaiah, but nowhere reaches his poetic heights. Even more pronounced than the difference in style is the difference in theme. This poet is preoccupied with matters of ritual. He dwells on the proper way to keep the Sabbath, and on the blessings of those who keep it as prescribed; and he assumes stature principally in his great faith in God and loyalty to his people. ❨

## *Aliens Who Join the Lord*

56    Let not the alien who has joined himself to the Lord say, "Surely
      the Lord will make a distinction between me and his people"; nor
let the eunuch say, "In the eyes of the Lord, I am a dry tree."
    For thus says the Lord, "The eunuch who keeps my Sabbaths, and holds fast to my covenant, even him will I bring into my house and within my walls, and I will give him a name better than 'son' or 'daughter,' an everlasting name which shall not be cut off.
    "And the alien who joins himself to the Lord, to serve him and to love the name of the Lord, who keeps the Sabbath and profanes it not, and holds fast to my covenant, even him will I bring to my holy mountain and to my house of prayer; his burnt offering and his sacrifices shall be accepted upon my altar. For my house shall be called a house of prayer for all peoples.

"Thus," says the Lord God, who gathers the dispersed of Israel, "will I gather others to them, besides those who are already gathered."

## O Sons of Sorcerers

57     Draw near, you sons of sorcerers, offspring of adulterer and harlot! Against whom do you make sport? Against whom do you open wide your mouth and put out your tongue? Are you not the children of sin, the seed of falsehood? Are you not those who inflame themselves under every leafy tree? With the smooth stones of the lake your lot is cast!

Upon a high and lofty mountain have you made your bed; and there you went to offer sacrifice. Behind the door and doorpost you set up the symbol of your idols. You have made a pact with them, with those you love, and appeared before the king with oil and offerings of perfumes.

Whom did you so fear and dread that you denied me, that you did not remember me? Because I held my peace so long, you feared me not. I shall proclaim your deeds, I shall expose your ways; and they shall not profit you; let your idols deliver you when you cry out. The wind shall scatter them, and the breezes bear them off. But those who take refuge in me shall possess the land and inherit my holy mountain.

## Cry Aloud!

58-59     Cry aloud, cry aloud! Lift your voice like a trumpet! Declare to my people, declare to the house of Jacob their transgressions!

Each day they seek me, they delight in drawing near; like a people who have not forsaken the ordinance of their God, they ask, "Why have we fasted and you see us not? Why do we humble ourselves and you heed us not?"

Behold, on the day of your fast you pursue your affairs; you perform all your labor; you multiply strife and contention, to smite with the fist of wickedness. Is such the fast that I have chosen, a day for a man to bow down his head like a bulrush? Will you call this a fast to the Lord?

Is not this the fast that I have chosen? A day to loose the fetters of wickedness, to undo the bands of the yoke, to let the oppressed go free; a day to give your bread to the hungry, and to bring the homeless into your home; a day when you cover the naked, and do not hide from your own flesh and blood. Then, when you call, the Lord will answer; when you cry out, he will say, "Here I am!"

When your soul goes out to the hungry and you serve the afflicted, your light shall rise in the darkness, your gloom shall turn into noonday. And the Lord will guide you always, he will satisfy your thirsting soul; you will be like a garden that has been watered, like a spring whose waters never fail. Your descendants shall rebuild the ancient ruins; you shall raise up the foundations of many generations. And you shall be called "repairer of the breach," "restorer of the paths." [11]

## Arise! Shine!

60    Arise! Shine! For the glory of the Lord is upon you! Behold, darkness shall cover the earth, and thick darkness the peoples, but upon you the glory of the Lord shall be seen. The nations shall come to your light, and kings to the brightness of your rising.

Lift your eyes and see! They all gather together, they come to you! Your sons shall come from afar, and your daughters shall be carried at the side. Then you shall see and be radiant, and your heart shall swell; for the riches of the sea shall flow toward you, the wealth of the nations shall come your way. Caravans of camels shall cover your land, the dromedaries of Midian and Ephah, bringing gold and frankincense.

The sons of strangers shall rebuild your walls, and their kings shall minister to you. Though in my great anger I smote you, in my great mercy I shall have compassion on you. Your gates shall always be open; by day and by night they shall not be closed, that men may bring their wealth to you, their kings leading them. For the nation and the kingdom that will not serve you shall perish; those nations shall be laid waste.

The glory of Lebanon shall come to you; the fir, the pine and the larch shall adorn my sanctuary. And the sons of those who oppressed you shall come bending their knees; those who despised you shall bow down at your feet; they shall call you "the city of the Lord," "the Zion of the Holy One of Israel."

Whereas you have been forsaken and hated so long, I will make you a joy from generation to generation. And you shall know that I am your Savior, and I, the Mighty One of Jacob, your Redeemer. Instead of brass I will bring you gold; instead of iron, silver; instead of wood, brass; in-

[11] See ISAIAH, Chapters 58-59, in Notes and Excisions.

stead of stones, iron. I will make peace your officers, and righteousness your taskmasters. Violence shall no more be known in your land, nor waste or destruction within your borders. You shall call your walls Salvation, and your gates Praise.

Your sun shall go down no more, nor your moon wane; for the Lord will be your everlasting light. Your days of mourning shall be ended. All your people shall be righteous; they shall inherit the land forever, as the branch of my planting, as the work of my hands, in which I may be glorified. The least shall become great, and the smallest grow into a mighty nation.

I the Lord will hasten the day in its time.

## The Call of the Prophet

61     The spirit of the Lord God is upon me, because the Lord has anointed me to bring good tidings to the humble. He has sent me to bind up the brokenhearted, to proclaim liberty to the captives, to open the gates for those who are imprisoned, to comfort all who mourn, and to give to the mourners in Zion beauty instead of ashes, the oil of joy instead of sorrow, the mantle of praise in place of the garment of dejection; that they may be called "the trees of righteousness," "the planting of the Lord," in which he may be glorified.

As a bridegroom puts on his diadem, and a bride adorns herself with her jewels, as the earth in spring brings forth her shoots, so the Lord God will cause justice and praise to spring forth among the nations.

## For Zion's Sake

62     For Zion's sake I will not hold my peace, and for Jerusalem's sake I will not rest, until her vindication shines forth and her salvation is bright as a flame. The nations shall see your righteousness, and all the kings your glory. You shall be called by a new name, which the mouth of the Lord shall determine. You shall be like a crown in the hand of the Lord, like a royal diadem in the hand of your God.

None shall again call you "Forsaken," or your land, "Desolate." You shall be called "My Delight," and your land "The Wedded"; for as a young man weds a virgin, so shall your sons wed you; and as the bridegroom rejoices in his bride, so shall your God delight in you.

The Lord has sworn by his right hand, and by the arm of his strength, "I will no more give your grain as food to your enemies; and the sons of strangers shall not drink the wine for which you have labored!"

Pass through, pass through the gates! Prepare the way for the people! Build up, build up the highway, clear away the stones, raise a banner for the people! Behold, the Lord has proclaimed to the ends of the earth: "Say to the daughters of Zion, 'Your salvation is at hand!' And to the people say, 'Your name shall be "The Redeemed of the Lord!"' And to the city of Jerusalem say, 'You shall be called "The Sought After," "The Unforsaken!"'"

## A Day of Vengeance

63      Who is this that comes from Edom, clothed in crimson, marching in the greatness of his strength?

"It is I, who have promised justice, who am mighty in redemption."

Why is your apparel red, and your garments like those of one who treads the wine press?

"I have trodden the wine press, and with none to help me. I trod the nations in my anger, I trampled them in my fury; and their blood has stained my garments. For in my heart it was a day of vengeance, my year of redemption. I looked about me, but there was none to help; I looked in astonishment, but there was none to uphold. So my own arm helped me, and my fury upheld me. I trod down the people in my anger; in my fury I shattered them and brought them to the dust."

## Look Down from Heaven

63-64    Look down from Heaven, and behold from your habitation in holiness and glory; where is your zeal and your might, and your yearning pity toward me? Are they restrained from me? For you are our Father, although Abraham knows us not, and Israel does not acknowledge us. You, O Lord, are our Father, and your name everlastingly "Our Redeemer."

O Lord, why have you made us err, and wander from your ways? Why do you harden our hearts from fearing you? Turn, turn your face again to your servants, the tribes of your heritage!

We are yours! Would that the heavens were rent and you would appear; that the mountains might quake and the nations tremble at your presence; that we might see the fearful things unheard of since the beginning of time.

We have become like a garment defiled, like a wilting leaf; our guilt bears us away like the wind. There is no one to call upon your name, for you have hidden your face from us, and we are delivered up to our sins.

O Lord, you are our Father! We are the clay and you our potter; we are all the work of your hand. Be not angry with us, O Lord, nor remember our guilt forever! Behold, your holy cities are a wasteland, Zion a wilderness, Jerusalem a desolation. Our holy and beautiful house, where our fathers praised you, has been burned, and all the cherished things in it laid waste.

Will you restrain yourself over these things, O Lord?

Will you remain silent, O Lord, and afflict us beyond measure?

## Behold, My Servants Shall Eat

65    "Behold, my servants shall eat, but you shall go hungry; behold, my servants shall drink, but you shall thirst; behold, my servants shall rejoice, but you shall be put to shame; behold, my servants shall sing with gladness, but you shall weep with sorrow of heart and wail with vexation of spirit," says the Lord God.

The Lord shall slay you, and to God's elect your name shall remain as a curse; but he shall call his servants by another name. And he who prays for a blessing shall bless himself by the God of truth; he who takes an oath shall swear by the God of truth.

"Behold," says the Lord, "I am creating a new heaven and a new earth; and former things shall be forgotten, nor come to mind. You shall be glad and rejoice in that which I create. For I shall create Jerusalem as an exultation, and my people as a joy; and I will rejoice in Jerusalem and exult in my people. And the voice of weeping in her midst shall be heard no more.

"Before they call I will answer; while yet they speak I will hear them. The wolf and the lamb shall feed together; the lion shall eat straw like the ox; and dust shall be the food of the serpent. They shall do no harm in all my holy mountain."

## The Heaven Is My Throne

66   "The heaven is my throne and the earth is my footstool," says the
Lord. "Where is the house that you would build for me? Where
is the place that would be my resting place? For all these things my
hand has made, and thus they came to be.

"Yet I will have regard for him who is humble and of a contrite spirit,
and trembles at my word; on this man will I look. But he who slaughters
an ox as if he slew a man, and sacrifices a lamb as if he cut off a dog's
head, and makes a meal offering as if it were swine's blood, and prepares
the memorial offering of frankincense as if he blessed an idol — according to the path he has chosen will I choose the outrages against him, and
the fears that I will bring upon him."

Hear the word of the Lord, you who tremble at his word: "Your brothers who hate you, who cast you out and mock, 'Let the Lord show his
glory, that we may gaze upon your joy!' — they shall be put to shame."

Behold, the Lord will come in fire; his chariots shall be like the whirlwind, and his rebuke like flames.

"I shall come," says the Lord, "to gather all the nations; and they shall
see my glory. And from new moon to new moon, from sabbath to sabbath, all flesh shall worship before me," says the Lord.

# JEREMIAH
## *The Sorrowful*

◖ About the personal life of Isaiah the Comforter we know practically nothing; about the personal life of Jeremiah we know a great deal. One stands in deep shadow; the other in broad daylight.

Jeremiah, the son of a wealthy priestly family, was born in or about 645 B.C.E. in the Benjamite village of Anathoth, not far from Jerusalem. His early youth, it is surmised, was a happy one; for though he spent most of his mature life in metropolitan Jerusalem, the imagery of his poetry is steeped in pleasurable impressions of rural Anathoth and its environs.

At the age of nineteen, in 626 B.C.E., Jeremiah entered the temple ministry and moved to Jerusalem, where he remained for over forty turbulent years. His life spanned the vigorous struggle of the good King Josiah to purify religion; Josiah's tragic death in battle against Pharaoh Nechoh of Egypt; the brief rule of confusion by Josiah's son Jehoahaz (who was carried off to Egypt and his throne given to his brother Jehoiakim); and Jehoiakim's rule, evil and foolish in Jeremiah's eyes. The king had the prophet arrested, thrown into a pit and put into stocks, and ordered his recorded prophecies burned. Then came the first Babylonian invasion of 597 B.C.E., when Jehoiakim's son Jehoiakin, king of Judah, was taken into captivity along with many leaders of the nation, including the prophet Ezekiel. Jeremiah remained in Jerusalem, and saw Zedekiah, placed upon the throne by the Babylonian king, revolt against his Babylonian master, counter to Jeremiah's constant warnings; and finally he saw Jerusalem besieged a second time, and the Jewish state completely destroyed. Jeremiah was not carried off in the second Babylonian captivity, but was permitted to remain with the remnant of the poor under the governorship of the good Gedaliah.

Jeremiah's earliest prophecies show the conviction that to see what was wrong in the affairs of his people and not to speak out against them was evil; and in the blackest hour of his nation's loss he continued to voice his belief that their greatest calamity was not attack and conquest from without, but moral corrosion from within. The people responded to his prophecies with hatred. And there is some obscurity about Jeremiah's end. According to one tradition, at the time Governor Gedaliah was murdered (described in Chapters 40-41) Jeremiah was taken to Egypt by his detractors; and when he persisted in castigating them in his sermons, they stoned him to death. Jeremiah was then sixty or sixty-one years old.

One reason we know so much about the events in Jeremiah's life is because he had a devoted disciple, Prince Baruch, who acted as scribe to the prophet. Baruch lacked the gift of poetry, but he faithfully recorded all that befell the prophet. We know of Baruch's activities on the prophet's behalf from the Book of Jeremiah, as well as from the record in a separate book, bearing Baruch's name, among the books of the Apocrypha.

Jeremiah was the most prolific of the literary prophets. The Book of Jeremiah is the longest among the Books of the Prophets; and the second longest in the entire Bible; to Jeremiah also is attributed the authorship of Lamentations; and the historian Josephus, in his *Antiquities of the Jews,* mentions another work of Jeremiah's, an Elegy for King Josiah, which presumably still existed in his times.

The Book of Jeremiah falls into three parts: laments and exhortations on moral reform (Chapters 1-24); the experiences of the prophet recorded in prose by Baruch (Chapters 26-45); and prophecies against foreign nations (Chapters 25 and 46-51). The last chapter (52) repeats what has already been recorded in II Kings (24:18; 25:1-27).

This division is only a generalization, however, for the various sections in the entire book, particularly the poetry sections, do not appear in consecutive order. The lack of proper sequence in some of the material has been pointed up by the knowledge that Jeremiah prophesied under five different kings, as well as after the final destruction of Jerusalem, and it is obvious that his utterances under Josiah could not have been made after the murder of Governor Gedaliah, as some of them appear in the work. Scholars interested in the historical aspects of the Book of Jeremiah have rearranged the contents and made new tables of continuity. But if the book is read as a collection of poetry, it is not necessary to disturb or change the order as it appears in the Bible.

Jeremiah's poetry reflects his life of bitterness and anguish, and his world of famine, pestilence, and war. His lamentations have given us the word "jeremiad"; and his sorrow of more than twenty-five centuries ago can still touch us to the quick. ❬[

*The word of the Lord that came to Jeremiah, son of Hilkiah, of the priests of Anathoth in the land of Benjamin, in the days of Josiah, king of Judah. It came also in the days of King Jehoiakim, the son of Josiah, and until the end of the eleventh year of King Zedekiah, in the fifth month of the captivity of Jerusalem.*

# The Call of the Prophet

1 The word of the Lord came to me, saying, "Before I formed you in the womb, I knew you, and before you were born I sanctified you; and I ordained you a prophet to the nations."

Then said I, "Ah, Lord God! Behold, I cannot speak, for I am a mere youth."

But the Lord said, "Say not, 'I am a mere youth'; for you shall go to whomever I send you, and whatever I command you to say you shall speak. Be not afraid, for I am with you. Behold, I put my words in your mouth; I set you this day over nations and over kingdoms, to root out and to pull down and to destroy evil, and to build and to plant in my name."

Then came the word of the Lord, saying, "Jeremiah, what do you see?"

And I said, "I see an almond branch that hastens to bloom."

Then said the Lord, "You have seen well, for I will hasten my word to perform it."

And the word of the Lord came to me a second time, saying, "Jeremiah, what do you see?"

And I said, "I see a seething pot which faces from the north."

Then the Lord said to me, "Out of the north evil shall break upon all the inhabitants of the land. For lo, I will call all the families of the kingdoms of the north, and they shall come to the gates of Jerusalem, and against its walls round about, and against all the cities of Judah. And I will utter my judgments against those who have forsaken me, and have burned incense to other gods, and worshiped the works of their own hands. Gird up your loins; arise and speak to them all that I command you; be not dismayed. For I have made you this day a fortified city and an iron pillar against the kings of Judah, and its princes, and its priests, and against the people of the land. They shall fight against you, but in vain; for I am with you."

## I Remember the Affection of Your Youth

'2    The word of the Lord came to me, saying, "Go, cry out in the hearing of Jerusalem, 'Thus says the Lord: "I remember the affection of your youth, and your love as a bride; how you followed me in the wilderness, in a land that was not sown." '

"Israel is the Lord's hallowed portion, his first fruits of the harvest; all that devour him shall be held guilty; evil shall come upon them," says the Lord.

## The Broken Cisterns

2    Hear the voice of the Lord, O house of Jacob, and all the families of the house of Israel: "What wrong have your fathers found in me, that they went far from me and walked after things of nought, and are become nought?

"They did not say, 'Where is the Lord who brought us up out of Egypt, who led us through the wilderness, through a land of drought and the shadow of death, a land where no man dwelt?' Yet I brought them through it into a plentiful country, to eat its fruit and to enjoy its goodness.

"But when they entered they defiled my land, and made my heritage an abomination. The priests did not ask, 'Where is the Lord?' Those who handle the law knew me not; the rulers transgressed against me; the prophets prophesied to Baal, and walked after things that do not profit.

"Be astonished, O you heavens," says the Lord, "for my people have committed two evils: they have forsaken me, their fountain of living waters, and have hewed out for themselves cisterns, broken cisterns, that can hold no water."

## The Noble Vine

2      "I had planted you as a noble vine, a wholly good seed," says the
Lord. "How then have you turned into the degenerate plant of
a strange vine to me? For though you wash yourself with lye and scrub
yourself with soap, still the markings of your guilt stand out before me.

"How can you say, 'I am not defiled. I have not gone after the idols'?
See your way in the valley, know what you have done. You are a swift
young camel traversing her ways; a wild ass used to the wilderness, sniff-
ing the wind in her desire; who can hinder her in her lust?

"As the thief is ashamed when he is discovered, so is the house of Israel
ashamed — they, and their kings, and their priests, and their prophets,
who said to a clump of wood: 'You are my father!' and to a stone: 'You
gave me birth!' But in the time of their trouble they called to me, 'Arise
and save us!'

"Where are the gods that you have made? Let them arise and save you
in the time of your trouble, if they can. For as many as the number of
your cities are your gods, O Judah!

"In vain have I smitten your children; they received no correction. Your
own sword has devoured your prophets, like a destroying lion.

"Why say my people, 'We will come no more to you'? Can a maiden forget her ornaments, or a bride her attire? Yet my people have forgotten me
days without number.

"If a man puts away his wife, and she goes from him and becomes another's, shall he return to her again?

"You have played the harlot with many lovers; and would you yet return to me?" says the Lord. "Lift up your eyes to the high hills and tell
me, where have you not been lain with? Yet you had a harlot's brazen-
ness, and refused to be ashamed.

"Did you not just now cry out to me, 'My father, you are the friend
of my youth. Will he bear grudge forever?'

"Behold, you have spoken, but you have done evil things, and have had
your way."

## *Return, O Israel!*

3-4    "Return, O faithless Israel!" says the Lord. "I will not frown upon
you, for I am merciful. I will not bear a grudge forever. Only acknowledge your iniquity, your transgressions against the Lord your God.

"Return, O faithless children! And I will take you, one from a city and
two from a family, and bring you to Zion. And I will give you shepherds
according to my heart, who will feed you on knowledge and on understanding. In those days the house of Judah shall walk with the house of
Israel; they shall come together out of the north to the land I have
given as an inheritance to your fathers.

"Return, O faithless children; I will heal your faithlessness."

Here we are, we have come to you; for you are the Lord our God.
Truly vain have proved the hills, the uproar on the mountains; truly in the
Lord our God is the salvation of Israel.

Let us lie down in our shame, let our confusion cover us; for we have
sinned against the Lord, we and our fathers; we have not listened to the
voice of the Lord our God.[1]

## *Hear This, O Foolish People*

5    Proclaim this in the house of Jacob, and announce it in Judah:
"Hear this, O foolish people; you who have eyes and see not, who
have ears and hear not! Do you not fear me? Do you not tremble at my
presence? It is I who placed the sand as a boundary for the sea, an everlasting barrier that it cannot pass. Though the waves toss, they cannot
prevail; though they roar, they cannot pass over it. But this people with
the rebellious heart has revolted; they have turned aside and gone off.
For among my people are wicked men who lie in wait like fowlers: they
set a trap to catch men. As a cage full of birds, so are their houses full
of deceit. They have become great and rich; they have grown fat and
sleek. They surpass in deeds of wickedness, but never uphold the cause
of the fatherless or the rights of the needy. Shall I not punish them for
these things?" says the Lord. "Shall I not be avenged on a nation such as
this?"

An appalling and horrible thing has come to pass in the land: the

[1] See JEREMIAH, Chapter 4, in Notes and Excisions.

prophets prophesy in the service of falsehood; the priests gain power through their means; and my people love to have it so. But what will you do when the end comes?

## O You Children of Benjamin

6-7     O you children of Benjamin, flee from Jerusalem! Blow the trumpet in Tekoa, and raise a signal in Beth-hacherem! Evil and destruction loom out of the north!

For thus says the Lord of hosts: "Hew down her trees, set up a siege against Jerusalem. This is a city to be punished. As a cistern wells up with its waters, so does Jerusalem well up with her wickedness. Sounds of violence and robbery are heard in her midst; the sight of grief and wounds are always before me. Be warned, O Jerusalem, lest my soul be estranged from you; lest I make you desolate, a land uninhabited."

Thus says the Lord, "Stand on the roads and look, and ask for the old paths, for the good way, and walk in it, that you may find rest for your souls. But they said, 'We will not walk in it.' So I set my watchmen over you, saying, 'Listen for the sound of the trumpet!' But they said, 'We will not listen.' Therefore hear, you nations, and know, O congregation, what shall befall them. Hear, O earth; behold, I will bring evil upon this people, the fruit of their thoughts, because they would not listen to my words, and rejected my law. I will lay stumbling blocks before this people, and the fathers and sons shall stumble against them; the neighbor and his friend shall perish together.

"Behold," says the Lord, "a people comes from the north, cruel and without mercy. Their voice is like the roar of the sea; they ride upon horses, set in array as men of war against you, O daughter of Zion!" Go not forth into the field, nor walk on the way; for the sword of the enemy and terror are all around you. O daughter of my people, gird on sack-cloth, cover yourself with ashes; mourn as for an only son, with bitter lamentation; for the plunderer shall suddenly come upon you! [2]

² See JEREMIAH, Chapter 7, in Notes and Excisions.

## *If a Man Fall*

7-8    "I will put an end, in the cities of Judah and the streets of Jerusalem, to the voice of mirth and the voice of gladness, the voice
of the bridegroom and the voice of the bride; for the land shall be desolate," says the Lord.

"At that time, they shall bring out of their tombs the bones of the kings
of Judah and the bones of the princes and the priests, the bones of the
prophets and the bones of the inhabitants of Jerusalem; and they shall
spread them before the sun, and the moon, and all the host of heaven
which they have loved and served and worshiped. They shall not again
be gathered nor buried; they shall be left as dung upon the earth. And on
that day death shall be chosen rather than life by all of this evil family
who remain in the places to which I have driven them.

"And you shall say to them, 'Thus says the Lord: "If a man falls, does
he not attempt to rise again? Why then do the people of Jerusalem per-
petually slide back? They cling to deceit, they refuse to repent. None
speak the truth, and no one repents his wickedness. Everyone turns away
in his own course, like a horse that rushes headlong into battle. The
stork in the heavens knows her appointed time; the swallow and the
crane observe the time of their coming; but my people know not the
ordinance of the Lord. The wise men are ashamed, they are dismayed;
for lo, they have rejected the word of the Lord, and what wisdom is in
them?"'

"From the least of them to the greatest, each one is greedy for gain;
from prophet to priest, each one deals falsely. They have healed the hurt
of my people lightly, saying, 'Peace, peace,' when there is no peace. They
have committed abominations, yet know no shame. Therefore they shall
be among those who fall, and in the hour of their punishment, they shall
stumble."

## *The Prophet's Grief*

8-9    Though I try to take comfort against sorrow, my heart is full of
pain within me. For I hear the cry of my people far and wide
through the land: "Is not the Lord in Zion? Is not her King with her?"
For the wound of my people am I wounded and seized with anguish;

341

I mourn, and terror has grasped me. Is there no balm in Gilead? Is there no physician there? Why then do not my people recover?

Oh that my head were waters, and my eyes a fountain of tears, that I might weep day and night for the slain of my people!

## Call the Mourning Women

9 Consider, and send out a call for the mourning women! Let them make haste and come, and take up their wailing for us, until our eyes run down with tears, and our eyelids gush with waters. For a voice of wailing is heard out of Zion, "How we are ruined! We are greatly confounded, because we have forsaken our land and given up our dwellings!" Hear the word of the Lord, O you women, and teach wailing to your daughters and lamentation to your neighbors. For death peers into our windows and has entered our palaces, cutting down the children in the street, the young men on the highway.

Thus says the Lord, "Let not the wise man glory in his wisdom; neither let the strong man glory in his strength; and let not the rich man glory in his riches. But let him who glories glory only in this: that he understands, and knows me, that I am the Lord who exercises mercy, and justice, and righteousness upon the earth. For in these things I delight," says the Lord.[3]

## The Approach of Doom

10 Gather up your wares from the ground, O you who live under the siege! For thus says the Lord: "Behold, this time I will sling out the inhabitants of the land!"

Woe is me for my hurt! Though I said to myself, "This is a sickness I can bear," my wound is heavy. My tent is plundered, all my cords are broken; my children have gone from me, and are no more. There is no one to spread out my tent, to set up my curtains.

For the shepherds have become brutish and do not inquire of the Lord; therefore they have not prospered, and all their flock is scattered.

Hark! A great commotion comes out of the north country, the noise of the brute who comes to make the cities of Judah a dwelling place of jackals.

[3] See JEREMIAH, Chapter 10, in Notes and Excisions.

O Lord, I know that the way of man is not of his own choosing; it is not in man to direct his steps as he walks. Correct me, O Lord, but not in your anger, lest you bring me to nothing.

Pour out your wrath upon the nations who know you not, upon the families who do not call on your name; for they have devoured Jacob and consumed him, and made desolate his habitation.

## What Does My Beloved Want?

11    What does my beloved want in my house? Is it to fulfill her many evil desires? For it is only when she does evil that she rejoices.

The Lord has made you like a leafy olive tree, fair and with goodly fruit. But the Lord, who planted you, has pronounced evil against you, because of the evil in Israel and in the house of Judah; with a great roar he has kindled a fire upon the tree, and the branches are consumed.

## Plot Against the Prophet

11    The Lord gave me knowledge, and I knew; he showed me what they were plotting. I was like a docile lamb led to the slaughter; I knew not their devices against me, saying, "Let us destroy the tree with its fruit, let us cut him off from the living, that his name may be remembered no more."

O Lord of hosts, who judges righteously the thoughts in men's hearts, let me see your vengeance upon them, for to you have I confided my cause.

Concerning the men of Anathoth who seek my life, and who say, "If you are not to die by our hand, you must not prophesy in the name of the Lord!" thus says the Lord of hosts, "Behold, I will punish them; the young men shall die by the sword; their sons and their daughters shall die by famine; no remnant shall be left. For I will bring evil upon the men of Anathoth in their year of reckoning."

# Why Do the Wicked Prosper?

12 You are righteous, O Lord, yet let me plead before you:
Why do the wicked prosper? Why are the treacherous secure? You have planted them and they have taken root; they grow and bring forth fruit. You are near in their mouth, but far from their heart.

Yet you know me, O Lord; you see me and try my heart toward you. Then hear me: pull them out like sheep for the day of slaughter! How long shall the land mourn, and the herbs of the field wither, for the wickedness of those who dwell there and say, "God will not see our end!"

# I Have Forsaken My House

12 "I have forsaken my house, I have abandoned my heritage, I have given the dearly beloved of my soul into the hands of her enemies. My heritage has become to me like a lion in the forest and cried out against me; my heritage has become to me like a bird of prey, with the vultures round about her.

"Many shepherds have destroyed my vineyard, they have trodden my portion under foot, they have made my pleasant portion a wasteland. Upon all the high hills plunderers have come, for the sword of the Lord shall devour from one end of the land to the other, and no living thing shall have peace. They have sown wheat and reaped thorns; they have worn themselves out without profit. They shall be shamed of their harvest, because of the fierce anger of the Lord." [4]

# Lament for the King

13 Say to the king and to the princes, "Humble yourselves! For the crown of your glory shall come down, your beautiful crown."
The cities of the south shall be closed up, with none to open them; Judah shall be carried away captive!

Lift up your eyes and behold those who come from the north. Where is the flock, the beautiful flock, that was given you? What will you say on the day when they punish you, when they set over you those whom

[4] See JEREMIAH, Chapter 13, in Notes and Excisions.

you yourself have trained? Shall not your pangs be those of a woman in labor?

And if you say in your heart, "Why have these things befallen me?" — for the greatness of your iniquity they have befallen you. Can the Ethiopian change his skin, or the leopard his spots? So also you cannot do good who are accustomed to do evil. Therefore I will scatter you like stubble in the wind of the wilderness.

"This is your lot, the portion measured out to you," says the Lord, "because you have forgotten me and trusted in falsehood. I have seen your abominations on the hills in the fields. Woe to you, O Jerusalem! You will not soon be made clean."

## Judah Mourns

14    Judah mourns and her gates languish; they bow down in black to the ground, and the cry of Jerusalem rises. The nobles send their lads for water; they come to the cisterns and find none; they return with their vessels empty; they are ashamed and confounded, and cover their heads. For the ground is cracked from lack of rain upon the earth.

The plowmen are ashamed, they cover their heads. The hind in the field forsakes her young because there is no grass. The wild asses stand upon the heights, they gasp for air like jackals; their eyes fail because there is no herbage.

Though our sins bear witness against us, O Lord, protect us for your name's sake. O hope of Israel, its savior in time of trouble, why should you be like a stranger, like a wayfarer who tarries for a night? Why should you be like a man overcome, like a mighty man who cannot help? Yet you, O Lord, are in our midst, and we call upon your name; desert us not!

## The Prophet's Despair

15    Woe to me, my mother, that you gave birth to a man of strife, a man of contention to the whole land! I have not lent or borrowed, yet all men curse me.

The Lord said, "I will cause your enemies to entreat you in the time of their affliction. Yet I will make you pass with your enemies into a strange land which you know not."

O Lord, remember me, and avenge me upon my persecutors! Know that for your sake I have suffered taunts. When I found your words, I ate them, and they were the joy of my heart. I sat not in the assembly of the merrymakers, nor rejoiced; I sat alone because of your hand upon me, for you have filled me with indignation.

Why is my pain unending, and why does my wound refuse to be healed? Will you be to me like a deceitful stream, like waters that fail?

The Lord says, "If you bring forth the precious out of the vile, you shall be as my mouth. And I will make you to this people like a fortified wall; they may fight against you, but they will not prevail. For I am with you, and I will save you from the hand of the wicked and redeem you from the hand of the terrible."

## You Shall Take No Wife

16    The word of the Lord came to me, saying: "You shall take no wife, nor have sons or daughters in this place. For the sons and daughters, and their mothers and their fathers, in this land shall die grievous deaths. They shall not be buried or lamented; they shall lie like dung upon the ground. They shall perish by the sword and by famine, and be food for the scavengers of heaven and of earth.

"Enter not into the house of mourning; neither go there to lament nor to bemoan. For I have taken away my peace from this people, and my compassion. Great and small alike shall die in this land; they shall have no burial; none shall lament them or break bread in mourning to comfort the living for the dead.

"Before your eyes, and in your days, I will put an end in this land to the sound of mirth and the voice of gladness, to the voice of the bridegroom and the voice of the bride.

"I will send for many fishers to fish for them; and afterwards I will send for many hunters, and they shall hunt them from every mountain and every hill, and from out of the clefts of the rocks. For my eyes are upon all their ways; they are not hidden from me; and I will repay their sin doubly.

"Yet behold, the day will come," says the Lord, "when it shall no more be said, 'As the Lord lives, who brought the children of Israel out of the

PARABLE OF THE POTTER

land of Egypt'; and instead it shall be said, 'As the Lord lives, who brought the children of Israel from the lands of the north, and from all the lands to which he had driven them, to restore them again to the land of their fathers.'"

## The Sin of Judah

17    The sin of Judah is written with a pen of iron, diamond-pointed; it is engraved upon the tablet of their heart, and upon the horns of their altar. O you who sit upon the mountain in the field, I will give your substance and all your treasure for booty. You shall lose the heritage I gave you, and I will cause you to serve your enemies in a strange land, for you have kindled a fire in my nostrils which shall burn forever.

## Blessed Is the Man

17    Cursed is the man who trusts in man, who makes flesh his strength and whose heart turns away from the Lord. He shall be like a tree in the desert, in the parched places of the wilderness, in a salt land, uninhabited.

Blessed is the man who trusts in the Lord and whose hope is the Lord. He shall be like a tree planted by the river, which spreads its roots in the waters and fears not when heat comes, but whose leaves are ever green; not anxious in the year of drought, and never ceasing to yield fruit.[5]

## Parable of the Potter

18    The word came to Jeremiah from the Lord, saying, "Arise and go down to the potter's house, and there you will hear my words." Then I went down to the potter's house, and beheld him working at his wheel. And when the vessel which he made of the clay became marred in the hand of the potter, he remade it into another vessel, as it seemed good to the potter to make it.

Then the word of the Lord came to me, saying, "O house of Israel, like clay in the potter's hand, so are you in mine. If at any time I speak

[5] See JEREMIAH, Chapter 17, in Notes and Excisions.

concerning a nation or a kingdom, to pluck up and to pull down and to destroy it, and if that nation or that kingdom turns away from the evil which caused me to speak against it, I repent of the evil that I thought to inflict upon them. And if at any time I speak concerning a nation or a kingdom, to build it up and to plant it, and if that nation or that kingdom does evil in my sight and does not obey my voice, then I repent of the good that I planned to bestow upon them. Therefore, speak to the men of Judah and to the inhabitants of Jerusalem and say, 'Return now every man from his evil ways!' And if they refuse, and follow their own devices, and act each according to the promptings of his evil mind, then you shall say to them, Thus says the Lord:

" 'The virgin of Israel has done a deadful thing. My people have forgotten me; they have stumbled off the ancient paths, to make their land an astonishment, a perpetual horror. Therefore I will scatter them as with an east wind; I will look upon their back and not their face in the day of their calamity.' " [6]

## Parable of the Broken Flask

**19**    Thus said the Lord, "Go and get a potter's earthen flask, and take with you elders of the people and priests, and go down to the valley of Ben-Hinnom, at the entry of the east gate, and there proclaim:

" 'Hear the word of the Lord, O kings of Judah and inhabitants of Jerusalem! "Behold, I will bring such evil upon this place that whoever hears of it, his ears shall tingle. Because the people have forsaken me, and have filled this place with the blood of innocents, and burned their sons as offerings to Baal, therefore the day comes when this place shall no longer be called Tophet, or the Valley of Ben-Hinnom, but the Valley of Slaughter. The men of Judah and Jerusalem will fall by the sword before their enemies; and their bodies I will give as food to the birds of the heaven, and to the beasts of the earth. Everyone who passes shall hiss because of all the plagues in it." '

"Then shall you break the flask in the sight of the men with you and say, 'As one breaks an earthen vessel, which cannot be made whole again, even so will the Lord break this people and this city.' " [7]

---

[6] See JEREMIAH, Chapter 18, in Notes and Excisions.
[7] See JEREMIAH, Chapters 19-20, in Notes and Excisions.

WOE TO THE SHEPHERDS

## Cursed Be the Day

20 Cursed be the day on which I was born! Let not the day on which
my mother bore me be blessed. Cursed be the man who brought
the tidings to my father: "A son is born to you!" making him very glad.
Let that man be like the cities which the Lord destroyed without
mercy; let him hear a cry in the morning, and an alarm at noon, because
he did not let me die at birth, that my mother might have been my
grave.

Why was I born to see toil and sorrow, and my days consumed in
shame? [8]

## Two Ways Before You

21-22 Thus says the Lord, "Behold, I set before you the way of life and
the way of death. He who abides in this city shall die by the
sword, and by famine, and by pestilence; but he who leaves, and surren-
ders to the Chaldeans who besiege it, shall live. For I have set my face
against this city for evil and not for good. It shall be given into the hand
of the king of Babylon, and he shall burn it with fire.

"Behold, I am against you, O dweller of the valley and rock of the
plain!" says the Lord. "You who say, 'Who will come down against us?
Who will enter our habitations?' I will punish you according to the fruit
of your deeds; I will kindle a fire in your forests that shall devour all that
is round about," says the Lord. [9]

## Woe to the Shepherds

23 "Woe to the shepherds who destroy and scatter my flock," says
the Lord to the shepherds of his people. "You have driven them
away and have not cared for them. Behold, I will visit upon you the
evil of your doings. Then will I gather the remnant of my flock out of
all the countries to which I have driven them, and I will bring them
back to their fold; and they shall be fruitful and multiply. And I will set

[8] See JEREMIAH, Chapter 21, in Notes and Excisions.
[9] See JEREMIAH, Chapter 22, in Notes and Excisions.

over them shepherds who will feed them and care for them; and they shall fear no more, nor be dismayed; neither shall they lack in anything.

"Behold, the day is coming when I will raise to David a righteous shoot, and he shall reign as king and prosper; he shall execute justice and righteousness in the land. In his days Judah shall be saved, and Israel again dwell in safety. And he shall be called: The Lord of Our Righteousness."

## Concerning the Prophets

23 My heart within me is broken, all my bones ache; I am like a drunken man, like a man whom wine has overcome, because of the Lord, because of his holy words. For the land is full of adulterers; and because of them the land mourns, the pleasant places are dried up. Their course is evil and their power is not right. Both the prophet and the priest are ungodly.

"Therefore," says the Lord, "their way shall be like slippery places in the dark, along which they shall be thrust and fall; for I will bring evil upon them in the year of reckoning."

I have seen the folly in the prophets of Samaria: they prophesied to Baal and made my people err. I have seen the prophets of Jerusalem: they committed adultery and walked in lies; they strengthened the hands of evildoers so that none would turn away from their wickedness. They have all become like the inhabitants of Sodom and Gomorrah.

"Behold," says the Lord, "I will feed them with wormwood and make them drink the water of gall. They speak out of a vision in their own heart, and not out of the mouth of the Lord.

"They say to those who despise me, 'You shall have peace!' And they say to everyone who walks in the stubbornness of his own heart, 'No harm shall befall you!' "

"I have not sent these prophets, yet they ran; I have not spoken to them, yet they prophesied. I have heard these prophets who prophesy lies in my name say: 'I have dreamed, I have dreamed!' The prophet who has a dream, let him tell his dream; and he who has my word, let him tell my word faithfully. What has the chaff to do with the wheat? Is not my word like a fire, or like a hammer that shatters the rock?

"Behold, I am against these prophets who use their tongues and speak in my name. I am against those who prophesy false dreams, and make my people err by their lies. I will bring everlasting reproach upon them, and perpetual shame which shall not be forgotten."

## The Parable of the Figs

24-28    After Nebuchadnezzar, king of Babylon, had carried away captive the king and princes of Judah, and their smiths, to Babylon, the Lord showed me two baskets of figs placed before the temple. One basket had very good and ripe figs, and the other had figs so bad that they could not be eaten.

Then the Lord said, "Jeremiah, what do you see?"

And I answered, "I see figs; the good ones are very good, and the bad ones so bad they cannot be eaten."

And the Lord said, "Like these good figs, so will I regard the captives of Judah. I will guard them for good, and bring them back from the land of the Chaldeans to this land; and I will build them and not tear them down; I will plant them and not pluck them up. I will give them the heart to know me, that I am the Lord; and they shall be my people, and I will be their God. As for the bad figs, which cannot be eaten, as I will destroy them so will I destroy Zedekiah, king of Judah, and his princes, and the remnant of the people in Jerusalem, and those who dwell in Egypt. I will deliver them to become a reproach and a taunt in all the kingdoms of the earth, a proverb and a curse in all places to which I shall drive them. And I will send the sword, famine, and pestilence among them, until they are wiped off from the land that I gave to them and their fathers." [10]

## A Letter to the Exiles

29    Now these are the words of the letter from Jeremiah the prophet in Jerusalem to the elders and priests and prophets taken captive to Babylon; and it was sent by the hand of Elasah, son of Shaphan:

"Thus says the Lord of hosts, the God of Israel, to all who were carried away captive from Jerusalem to Babylon:

" 'Build houses and live in them; plant gardens and eat their fruit. Take wives and have sons and daughters; multiply and do not be dimin-

[10] See JEREMIAH, Chapters 25-28, in Notes and Excisions.

ished. Seek the welfare of the city to which you have been taken and pray for it, for in its peace shall you find peace. Let not the prophets and diviners in your midst delude you; neither listen to their dreams. They prophesy falsely; I have not sent them.

"'And after seventy years have passed in captivity, I will visit you and fulfill my promise to restore you to this place. Then when you call upon me and pray to me, I will hear you; when you seek me, you shall find me. I will gather you from all the nations, from all the places to which I have driven you; and I will bring you again to the place from which I have sent you into exile.'" [11]

## Be Not Dismayed

30    "Fear not, O my servant Jacob," says the Lord; "be not dismayed, O Israel. Lo, I will save you from afar, and your offspring from the land of their captivity. Your affliction is incurable, and your wound grievous. There is no one to bind your wound; you have no medicine to heal you. All your lovers have forgotten you; they do not seek you, for I have wounded you with the wound of an enemy, with the chastisement of a cruel one, because your guilt is great and your sins are many. But all those who devour you shall be devoured; all your adversaries, every one of them, shall go into captivity; those who plunder you shall be plundered; and all those who prey upon you shall become prey. For I will restore your health to you, and I will heal your wounds.

"Behold, I will free from captivity the tents of Jacob and have mercy upon his dwelling places. The city shall be rebuilt upon its mound, and the palace shall appear upon its wonted place. And out of them shall come songs of thanksgiving, and the voices of those who make merry. I will multiply them, and they shall not be diminished; I will glorify them, and they shall not be small. Their children shall be as in days of old; their congregation shall be established before me; and I will punish all who oppress them. Their prince shall be one of themselves; their ruler shall proceed from their midst. I will cause them to draw near, to approach me. And they shall be my people, and I will be their God."

[11] See JEREMIAH, Chapter 29, in Notes and Excisions.

## *The People Who Were Left*

31  Thus says the Lord: "The people who escaped the sword will find
grace in the wilderness. Again will I build you, and you shall be
built, O virgin of Israel! Again shall you be adorned with timbrels, and
go forth in the dances of those who make merry. Again shall you plant
vineyards upon the mountains of Samaria; the planters shall plant, and
shall enjoy the fruit. For there shall be a day when the watchmen will
call upon Mount Ephraim: 'Arise, and let us go up to Zion, to the Lord
our God.'

"Sing with gladness for Jacob! Announce, praise, and say: 'O Lord,
save your people, the remnant of Israel.'

"Behold, I will bring them from the north, and gather them from the
uttermost parts of the earth, and with them the blind and the lame, the
woman with child, and she who is in labor, together; a great company
shall they return here.

"With weeping shall they come, with supplications will I lead them. I
will lead them by the waters of streams, in a straight path on which they
shall not stumble; for I am a father to Israel, and Ephraim is my firstborn.

"Hear the word of the Lord, O you nations! Declare it in isles afar off!
'He who scattered Israel will gather him and keep him, as a shepherd
keeps his flock. For the Lord has ransomed Jacob, and redeemed him
from the hand of one stronger than he. And they shall come and sing upon
the heights of Zion, and flow together to the goodness of the Lord, to the
grain, and to the wine, and to the oil; to the young of the flock and
of the herd; their soul shall be like a watered garden; they shall not pine
any more.'

"Then shall the virgin rejoice in the dance, and the young men and
the old together. For I will turn their mourning into joy, and will comfort
them," says the Lord.

## *Refrain from Weeping*

31-33  Thus says the Lord: "A voice is heard in Ramah, lamentation and
bitter weeping; Rachel weeping for her children refuses to be
comforted for her children, because they are not.

"Refrain your voice from weeping, and your eyes from tears. For your work shall be rewarded," says the Lord, "and your children shall return to their own border.

"I have heard Ephraim bemoaning himself, 'You have chastised me, and I was chastised, as a bullock unaccustomed to the yoke. Turn me and I shall be turned, for you are the Lord my God.'

"Is Ephraim my dear son? Is he my beloved child? Though I spoke against him, I earnestly remember him still; my heart yearns for him, I will surely have compassion upon him," says the Lord.

"Behold, the day is coming when I will sow the house of Israel and of Judah with the seed of man and the seed of cattle. And as I have watched over them in the past to pluck up and to break down, to overthrow and to destroy and to afflict, so will I watch over them to build and to plant.

"In those days they shall say no more, 'The fathers have eaten sour grapes, and the children's teeth are set on edge!' But every man who eats sour grapes, his teeth shall be set on edge; every man shall die for his own iniquity.

"Behold, in days to come I will make a new covenant with the house of Israel and the house of Judah. And in their heart will I write it. And I will be their God, and they shall be my people. They shall not need to teach each man his neighbor, and each man his brother, saying, 'Know the Lord!' For they shall all know me, from the least of them to the greatest; and I will remember their sin no more." [12]

# The Broken Pledge

34-35    The king Zedekiah made a covenant with all the people in Jerusalem, to proclaim liberty to them; that every man should let his Hebrew slaves go free, and none should make a bondsman of his brother. And they obeyed; but afterwards the princes and the people brought back into bondage the slaves they had set free.

Then the word of the Lord came to Jeremiah, saying, "I made a covenant with your fathers on the day that I brought them out of Egypt, out of the house of bondage, saying: 'At the end of seven years you shall let go every man his brother who has been sold to you.'

"Now you had done right in my sight in proclaiming liberty, every man to his bondsman; but you turned and profaned my name when you brought them back into bondage. Behold, I will proclaim liberty to the

[12] See JEREMIAH, Chapters 32-34, in Notes and Excisions.

sword, to pestilence, and to famine, and I will cause you to be removed to all the kingdoms of the earth. The men who broke this covenant I will give into the hand of their enemies; their dead bodies shall be food for birds of prey and beasts of the field. And Zedekiah and his princes will I give into the hand of the king of Babylon's army, which has gone away from you. Behold, I will command, and cause them to return to this city; and they will fight against it, and take it, and turn it; and I will make the cities of Judah a desolation, without an inhabitant." [13]

## The Recording of the Prophecies

36      This word came to Jeremiah from the Lord: "Take a scroll and write upon it all that I have spoken to you against Israel and Judah, from the first day that I spoke to you to this day. It may be that when Judah hears of the evil which I purpose to do to them, they may turn back each man from his evil way, that I may forgive their iniquity and their sin."

Then Jeremiah called Baruch, the son of Neriah; and Baruch wrote down upon a scroll all the words of the Lord which he had spoken to Jeremiah. And Jeremiah commanded Baruch, saying, "Since I am not allowed to go into the house of the Lord, go you upon a fast day, and read within the hearing of the people the words that you have written down; and also read them to all of Judah who come here from their different cities."

Baruch read from the scroll in the house of the Lord. And when Michaiah, son of Gemariah, heard the words of the Lord from the scroll, he went to the king's house, to the scribe's chamber; and all the princes sat there. Michaiah told them what Baruch had read in the hearing of the people. And the princes sent Jehudi, son of Nethaniah, to summon Baruch. So Baruch took the scroll in his hand and came to them. They said to him, "Sit down now, and read it to us." And Baruch read it to them.

When they had heard all the words, the princes turned in fear to one another, and they said to Baruch, "We will surely tell the king all these words. Go, hide yourself, you and Jeremiah, and let no man know where you are."

They went into the court to the king and told him all they had heard, but they left the scroll in the chamber of the scribe. So the king sent

[13] See JEREMIAH, Chapter 35, in Notes and Excisions.

Jehudi to fetch the scroll; and Jehudi read from it to the king, in the hearing of all the princes who stood about the king.

Now the king was in the winter house, and there was a fire burning in the brazier before him. As Jehudi read three or four columns, the king cut them off with a knife and cast them into the fire in the brazier, until all the scroll was consumed.

Then the word of the Lord came to Jeremiah, saying, "Take another scroll, and write upon it all the words that were on the first one which the king of Judah has burned."

Jeremiah took another scroll, and gave it to Baruch the scribe, who wrote down from the mouth of Jeremiah the words of the scroll which the king of Judah had burned; and there were added to them besides many like words.

## Jeremiah Imprisoned

37 Now when the Chaldeans raised their siege of Jerusalem, in fear of Pharaoh's army, Jeremiah left Jerusalem to go to the land of Benjamin. And at the gate of Benjamin, a sentry, whose name was Irijah, seized the prophet, saying, "You are deserting to the Chaldeans." Jeremiah answered, "It is false." But Irijah would not listen to him, and brought him to the princes. The princes were angry with Jeremiah, and struck him, and put him into the dungeon in the house of Jonathan the scribe, for it had been made a prison.

When Jeremiah had remained there many days, Zedekiah the king sent for Jeremiah, and asked him secretly in his house, "Is there any word from the Lord?" Jeremiah answered, "There is. You shall be delivered into the hand of the king of Babylon." And Jeremiah said to the king, "How have I sinned against you or the people, that you have put me in prison? Where now are your prophets who prophesied, 'The king of Babylon will not fight against you'? I pray you, O my lord the king, let me not be returned to the prison, lest I die there."

Then Zedekiah commanded that they commit Jeremiah to the prison of the court; and they gave him daily a loaf of bread from the bakers' street, until all the bread in the city was spent.

So Jeremiah remained in the prison of the court.

## Jeremiah Rescued

38    The princes heard that Jeremiah had said to the people, "Thus
      says the Lord, 'He who remains in this city shall die by the sword,
by famine, and by pestilence; but he who goes over to the Chaldeans
shall live. For this city will surely be given into the hand of the army of
the king of Babylon.'" And the princes said to the king, "We beseech
you, let this man be put to death! For his words weaken the hands of our
men of war, and of all the people. This man seeks not the welfare of our
people, but its ruin."

Zedekiah answered, "Behold, he is in your hands, for the king can do
nothing against you."

Then the princes took Jeremiah and let him down into a pit in the
court prison. There was no water in the pit, but mire; and into the mire
sank the prophet.

Now when Ebedmelech the Ethiopian, an officer in the king's house,
heard that they had put Jeremiah into the pit, he went to the king and
said, "My lord the king, these men have dealt wickedly with the prophet
Jeremiah, whom they have cast into the pit, for he will surely die there."

The king ordered Ebedmelech, "Take thirty men with you, and draw
Jeremiah out of the pit before he dies."

So Ebedmelech took the men with him and went to the king's house
under the treasury, and gathered cast-off clothes and old rags, and lowered them into the pit by cords to Jeremiah. And he said, "Put the rags
and clothes between your armpits and the cords." And Jeremiah did so;
then they drew him up out of the pit.

And Jeremiah remained hidden in the prison of the court.

## The Secret Meeting

38    Zedekiah the king sent secretly for Jeremiah and said to him, "I
      will ask you a question; conceal nothing from me." And Jeremiah
answered, "If I declare it to you, will you not put me to death? And if
I give you counsel, will you heed me?"

Zedekiah swore secretly, "As the Lord lives, who made my soul, I will
not put you to death, nor give you into the hands of the men who seek
your life."

Then said Jeremiah, "Thus says the Lord, the God of Israel: 'If you will surrender to the king of Babylon's princes, this city shall not be burned, and you and your house shall live; but if you will not surrender, this city shall be given into the hand of the Chaldeans, and they shall burn it, and you shall not escape them.'"

Zedekiah said to Jeremiah, "Let no man know of these words, and you shall not die. But if the princes hear that I have talked with you, and they demand of you, 'Tell us what you have said to the king and what the king said to you,' say to them, 'I presented my petition to the king that he would not return me to the pit to die there.'"

Then all the princes came to Jeremiah and asked him; and he told them the words that the king had commanded. So they left him in peace, for the conversation had not been overheard.

And Jeremiah remained in the prison of the court until the day that Jerusalem was taken.

## The Fall of Jerusalem

39-40   In the ninth year of Zedekiah, king of Judah, in the tenth month, came Nebuchadnezzar, king of Babylon, and all his army against Jerusalem, and besieged it. And in the eleventh year of Zedekiah, in the fourth month, on the ninth day of the month, the city was breached.

All the princes of the king of Babylon came in and sat in the middle gate, and when Zedekiah and his men of war saw them, they fled, and went out of the city at night by way of the king's garden, and escaped to the plain. But the Chaldeans pursued them, and overtook them in the plains of Jericho. And when they had captured the king, they brought him to Nebuchadnezzar at Riblah in the land of Hamath, where he passed judgment upon him. The king of Babylon slew the sons of Zedekiah before his eyes, and he slew all the nobles of Judah. Then he put out Zedekiah's eyes, and bound him in fetters to take him to Babylon.

The Chaldeans burned the king's house and the houses of the people, and broke down the walls of Jerusalem. And Nebuzaradan, the captain of the guard, carried off to Babylon the survivors of the people who remained in the city. But he left some of the poor of the people, who had nothing in the land of Judah, and gave them vineyards and fields in that day.

Now Nebuchadnezzar charged the captain of the guard concerning

Jeremiah, saying, "Take him and look after him well; and do him no harm, but do to him even as he shall say to you."

So Nebuzaradan sent for Jeremiah, and took him out of the court prison and said to him, "The Lord your God has pronounced this evil upon this place. And now, behold, I free you from the chains upon your hands. If it seems good to you to come with me to Babylon, come, and I will look after you well; but if not, behold, all the land is before you, to go wherever it seems good and right to you to go. You may go to Gedaliah, the son of Ahikam, whom the king of Babylon has made governor over the cities of Judah, and dwell with him among your people."

Then went Jeremiah to Gedaliah in Mizpah to dwell among the people left in the land.[14]

## The Murder of Gedaliah

*41*    Now it came to pass in the seventh month that Ishmael, of the seed royal, and ten men with him, came to Gedaliah in Mizpah, and there they broke bread together. And as they ate, Ishmael arose, and the ten men who were with him, and they slew Gedaliah, and all the Jews who were with the governor of the land, and the Chaldeans who were there, and the men of war.

Then Ishmael carried away captive all the rest of the people in Mizpah, and the king's daughters whom Nebuzaradan had committed to Gedaliah; and he departed to go over to the Ammonites. But Johanan, the son of Kareah, and the captains of the forces who were with him, heard of the evil Ishmael had done, and they set out to fight him, and overtook him at the great waters of Gibeon. When the people with Ishmael saw Johanan and his men, they were glad, and Ishmael's captives went over to Johanan. But Ishmael escaped with eight of his men, and they made their way to the Ammonites.

Then Johanan took the people whom Ishmael had brought out of Mizpah to the habitation of Chimham, which is near Bethlehem; for they feared the Chaldeans because Ishmael had slain Gedaliah, whom the king of Babylon had made governor over the land.

[14] See JEREMIAH, Chapter 40, in Notes and Excisions.

## Jeremiah in Egypt

**42-43** All the people, from the least to the greatest, came to Jeremiah the prophet and said to him, "We beseech you, pray for us to the Lord your God, for we are left but a few of many, as your eyes can see — and guide us in the way we should go and the thing we should do."

Jeremiah said to them, "I will pray to the Lord; and whatever the Lord shall answer you, that I will declare to you. I will withhold nothing from you."

And they said to Jeremiah, "The Lord be witness between us that we will do all things that the Lord shall command us to do; whether they are pleasant or painful, we will obey the voice of the Lord our God."

After ten days the word of the Lord came to Jeremiah. And he called Johanan and his captains, and all the people, and said to them, "Thus says the Lord God of Israel, to whom you sent me with your supplications: 'If you will remain in this land, I will build you up and not pull you down. Fear not the king of Babylon, for I am with you. I will show my mercies to you, that he may have mercy upon you and let you remain in your own land. But if you say, "We will go to Egypt, and dwell there where we shall see no more war, nor hear the trumpet, nor hunger for bread," then it shall come to pass that the sword which you fear shall overtake you in the land of Egypt; and there the famine which you dread shall follow close behind you; and there you shall die. As my anger has been poured out upon the inhabitants of Jerusalem, so shall it be poured out upon you if you enter Egypt.'"

When Jeremiah had made an end of speaking, Johanan and all the proud men said to him, "You speak falsely! The Lord our God has not sent you to say this, but Baruch, the son of Neriah, has set you against us, to give us into the hand of the Chaldeans, that they may put us to death or take us as captives to Babylon!"

Then Johanan and his captains took the remnant of Judah, along with Jeremiah the prophet and Baruch his scribe, and they went to the land of Egypt, and settled in Tahpanhes.

## *You Have Seen All the Trouble*

*44-50*   The word that came to Jeremiah concerning the Jews who dwelt
in the land of Egypt: "Thus says the Lord, the God of Israel: 'You
have seen all the trouble I have brought down upon Jerusalem and upon
the cities of Judah. Behold, this day they are a desolation and no man
dwells in them, because of the wickedness which they committed, in
that they went to offer incense and to serve other gods. Therefore my fury
was poured forth, and was kindled in the cities of Judah and the streets
of Jerusalem.' "

And now, thus says the Lord, "Why do you commit this great evil
against your own souls with the works of your hands, burning incense
to other gods in the land of Egypt, where you have gone to dwell? Have
you forgotten the wicked deeds of your fathers, and the wicked deeds
of the kings of Judah, and your own wicked deeds in the land of Judah?
For I will punish those who dwell in Egypt as I have punished Jerusalem."

Hear the word of the Lord, all you of Judah who are in the land of
Egypt: "Behold, I have sworn that my name shall no more be named in
the mouth of any man of Judah in all the land of Egypt, saying, 'As the
Lord God lives!' And this shall be as a sign to you that I will punish you
in this place. Behold, I will give Pharaoh Hophra, king of Egypt, into the
hand of his enemies as I gave Zedekiah, king of Judah, into the hand of
Nebuchadnezzar, king of Babylon, his enemy who sought his life." [15]

## *Jeremiah to Seraiah*

*51-52*   The word of Jeremiah the prophet to Seraiah, son of Neriah, when
he went with Zedekiah, king of Judah, to Babylon in the fourth
year of his reign. Jeremiah recorded in a book all that would befall Babylon. And he said to Seraiah:

"When you come to Babylon, see that you read all that I have written,
and say, 'O Lord, you have spoken concerning this place, to cut it off, so
that none shall remain in it, man or beast, but that it shall be desolate
forever.' And when you have finished reading, take a stone and tie it to

[15] See JEREMIAH, Chapters 45-51, in Notes and Excisions.

this scroll, and throw it into the midst of the Euphrates, and say, 'Thus shall all Babylon sink, and shall not rise again, because of the evil that I will bring upon her.'"

And here end the words of Jeremiah.[16]

[16] See JEREMIAH, Chapter 52, in Notes and Excisions.

# EZEKIEL
## *Prophet of the Exile*

❲ The entire Book of Ezekiel is written in the prose-poetry of the mystic, full of symbolical allusions which are not easily subjected to analysis. Yet these visions clearly imply the harsh realities which a people in great adversity must face. The book divides itself into three parts: the prophecy of the doom of his people for their sins as a nation (Chapters 1-32); the hope of each person to gain redemption through repentance (Chapters 33-40); and the vision of the restoration of Zion, with the people ruled over and protected by God (Chapters 41-48).

Ezekiel presumably recorded this book himself, and he did not incline toward filling it with personal data. We know only that he was born toward the end of the sixth century in the kingdom of Judah and, like Jeremiah, was a descendant of a distinguished priestly family. But while Jeremiah was left in Jerusalem during the first Babylonian captivity of 597 B.C.E., Ezekiel was taken along with the king and his nobles and many of the community leaders. And he settled in the Babylonian village of Tel Abib, where he remained for the rest of his life.

Ezekiel has been called "the Fearless" because, although he employed visions in which to convey his castigation of the people for their sins, his tirades against idolatry and social injustice were always clear and painfully unsparing. Nevertheless, the people in exile turned to him in their darkest hour. For he taught the concept of personal responsibility for guilt — that "only the soul that sins shall die" — and in his new concept of personal redemption through repentance, the sorrowful exiles found consolation. ❳

*The word of the Lord which came to Ezekiel the priest, in the land of the Chaldeans, in the fifth year of King Jehoiakin's captivity.*

# The Vision of the Glory

*1-3*      I looked, and behold, a whirlwind came out of the north driving a great cloud, with fire in its midst the color of amber, so that a brightness was round about it. And in the midst of the fire was the likeness of four living creatures. And this was their appearance: each had the form of a man; each had four faces; and each had four wings. Their legs were straight, and instead of feet they had hoofs like those of a calf, and they sparkled like burnished brass. Under their wings they had the hands of a man. And their wings were joined one to another so that they turned not when they went, but went together straight forward. Their faces were one of a man and one of a lion, on the right side; and one of an ox and one of an eagle, on the left side. As for their wings, two were joined one to another, and two covered their bodies. The fire was bright, and the living creatures ran to and fro in its midst like flaming torches with the speed of lightning.

As I observed the living creatures with the four faces, behold, a wheel appeared beside each; and the wheels were the color of beryl. The four wheels looked the same; each appeared as a wheel within a wheel, high and dreadful; and their rims were full of eyes all around. And when the living creatures moved, the wheels moved beside them; and when the living creatures stood still, the wheels stood still beside them.

The firmament above the heads of the living creatures was the color of crystal. And above the firmament over their heads appeared the semblance of a throne made of sapphire; and upon the semblance of the throne appeared the likeness of a man. And from his loins upward and from his loins downward I saw as it were the appearance of fire, with the brightness of the rainbow in the cloud. Such was the appearance of the likeness of the glory of the Lord.

And when I saw it, I fell upon my face, and I heard a voice that said: "Mortal man, rise upon your feet, and I will speak with you!" And the spirit entered into me and set me upon my feet. And he said to me, "I send you to the children of Israel, a rebellious nation. They and their fathers have transgressed against me, for they are hard-faced and hard-hearted children. You shall say to them, 'Thus says the Lord God!' And whether they listen to you or not, yet shall they know that there is a prophet among them.

"And you, mortal man, fear them not. Though you dwell among scorpions, be not afraid or dismayed, and speak my words to them. Be not you rebellious like that rebellious house; open your mouth and eat what I give you!"

And behold, a hand was stretched out to me, and lo, a scroll was in it. The scroll was spread before me, and there was writing on both sides, words of lamentation and mourning and woe. And the voice said to me, "Mortal man, eat this scroll; then go and speak to the house of Israel." And I ate it; and it was in my mouth as the sweetness of honey. And the voice said, "Go to the house of Israel and speak to them. You are not sent to a strange people of a strange speech and a slow tongue, whose words you cannot understand. Surely, if I sent you to them, they would listen. But the house of Israel will not listen to you because they are impudent and hard-hearted. Behold, I have made your face strong against their faces; like adamant harder than flint have I made your forehead. All the words that I shall speak to you, hear them with your ears and receive them in your heart; then go to those in captivity, to the children of your people, and tell them: 'Thus says the Lord God!'"

Then the spirit took me up, and I heard behind me the sound of the wings of the living creatures as they touched one another, and the sound of the wheels beside them — like the sound of rushing waters. Though the hand of the Lord was strong upon me, I went in bitterness until I came to those in captivity who dwelt by the river Chebar, at the Hill of Grief. And I sat down where they sat, and remained there silent and astonished among them seven days.[1]

## Forecast of the Siege

4-6    At the end of seven days the word of the Lord came to me, saying, "Mortal man, take a brick and lay it before you, and portray upon it the city of Jerusalem and build a fort against it; and cast up a mound against it; set the camp also against it, and battering rams round about. Moreover, take an iron plate and place it as a wall of iron between you

[1] See EZEKIEL, Chapter 3, in Notes and Excisions.

and the city; then set your face toward it. This shall be a sign to the house of Israel.

"Then lie down upon your left side; and lie there according to the number of days that you shall bear their iniquity. But first take wheat, and barley, and beans, and lentils, and millet, and make yourself bread of them, according to the number of days that you shall lie upon your side — three hundred and ninety days shall you eat of it. And the food you eat shall be by weight, and the water you drink shall be by measure, for thus will Jerusalem besieged eat bread by weight, with fearfulness, and drink water by measure, in dismay.

"For I have set Jerusalem in the midst of many nations; and she has rebelled against my ordinances in doing wickedness more than any of the nations round about her. Therefore, thus says the Lord God: 'Behold, I am against you! I will do to you that which I have never done and never will do again. The fathers shall eat their sons, and the sons shall eat their fathers, and all those who remain I will scatter to the winds. A third part shall die of pestilence and famine, a third part shall fall by the sword, and a third part I will scatter to the winds. Thus shall my anger be accomplished, and they shall know that I, the Lord, have spoken in my zeal.' " [2]

## The Day of Doom

7-11     The word of the Lord came to me, saying, "An end, an end shall come upon the four corners of the land of Israel! Now the end is upon you, and I will judge you according to your deeds and punish you for all your abominations! The day of trouble is near. My eyes will not spare you, nor will I have pity. He who is in the field shall die by the sword; and he who is in the city, famine and pestilence shall devour.

"Those who escape shall escape to the mountains, like doves of the valleys, all of them mourning, each one for his iniquity. All hands shall be feeble, and all knees weak as water. They shall gird themselves in sackcloth, and horror shall cover them. Shame shall be upon their faces, and baldness upon all heads.

"They shall fling their silver into the streets, and their gold shall be an unclean thing; their silver and their gold shall fail them in the day of the wrath of the Lord; it shall not satisfy their souls or fill their stomachs, for it has been the stumbling block of their iniquity. Their beautiful orna-

[2] See EZEKIEL, Chapter 6, in Notes and Excisions.

ments which they made into images I will give to strangers as prey, and to the wicked of the earth as plunder.

"When panic comes, they will seek peace, and there shall be no peace. Calamity will fall upon calamity, and rumor follow rumor; and they shall seek a vision from the prophet, but in vain. Instruction shall perish from the priest, and counsel from the elders. The king shall mourn, the prince shall be clothed in desolation, and the people of the land shall be enfeebled. According to their deeds will I judge them, and they shall know that I am the Lord!" [3]

## Forecast of the Exile

*12-14* The word of the Lord came to me again, saying, "O mortal man, you dwell in a rebellious household, for though they have eyes they see not, and though they have ears they hear not. Therefore remove all you possess in broad daylight and within their sight, as for exile; carry out your possessions on your shoulders in the twilight. And when the rebellious household asks you, 'What are you doing?' say to them: 'Thus says the Lord: "This burden concerns the prince in Jerusalem as much as all the house of Israel. Thus shall they all go into captivity. The prince shall bear his burden in the twilight, and cover his face so that he sees not the ground. My net will I spread upon him, and he shall be taken in my snare. I will bring him to Babylon, to the land of the Chaldeans; yet he shall not see it, for he shall die there. And I will scatter all his troops and draw my sword after them; I will scatter them among the nations and disperse them in many lands."'

"There is a proverb in Israel: 'The days go by and every vision is forgotten.' Tell the people they shall no more use this as a proverb; and say to them, 'The days are at hand for every vision to be fulfilled.' There shall be no more vain visions and flattering divination within the house of Israel; and the word which I speak shall be fulfilled." [4]

[3] See EZEKIEL, Chapters 8-11, in Notes and Excisions.
[4] See EZEKIEL, Chapters 12-14, in Notes and Excisions.

## The Worthless Vine

15 The word of the Lord came to me, saying, "How is the wood of the vine better than any other wood? In what way is it better than the branches of the trees of the forest? Can wood be taken from it to make any useful thing? Can even a peg be made of it to hang a vessel on it? Behold, it is thrown into the fire as fuel; the flames devour both ends of it and the middle is singed. Is it good for anything? When it was whole, it was used for nothing; how much less can it be useful for anything when the fire has consumed it, and it is singed!"

Therefore, thus says the Lord, "As the wood of the vine among the trees of the forest, which I have given to the fire for fuel, so will I give the inhabitants of Jerusalem. I will set my face against them. Though they come out from one fire, another shall devour them. And I will make the land desolate, for they have acted faithlessly," says the Lord.

## Allegory of the Faithless Wife

16 Again the word of the Lord came to me, saying, "Mortal man, make known to Jerusalem her abominations, and say to her, 'Your birthplace was the land of Canaan; your father was an Amorite, your mother a Hittite. And on the day you were born, your navel cord was not cut, nor were you washed in water to cleanse you; you were not rubbed with salt, nor were you swaddled. No eye pitied you, to do any of these for you, but you were cast out in the open field with loathing on the day that you were born.

"'And when I passed by and saw you, I said to you: "Live!" And I caused you to grow like a plant in the field. And you grew up, and you came to full beauty; and behold, the time for love was upon you. But you were still naked and bare. Then I spread my skirt over you and covered your nakedness; I swore that you would be mine and entered into a covenant with you. Then I washed you and anointed you with oil; and I clothed you in an embroidered cloak, and shod you with sealskin, and covered you with silk. And I put a bracelet upon your hand and a chain around your neck, a ring upon your nose and earrings in your ears. And I placed a beautiful crown upon your head. You were decked with gold and silver, your raiment was of fine linen and silk and embroidered work.

You ate fine flour, and honey and oil, and you grew exceedingly beautiful. And the fame of your beauty went out among the nations.

" 'But you trusted in your own beauty and played the harlot because of your fame. You took the jewels and the gold and the silver which I had given you and made yourself images, and you set my oil and my incense before them. Moreover, you took the sons and daughters whom you had borne to me and sacrificed them to be devoured by fire. And in all your abominations you did not remember the days of your youth, when you were naked and bare, and wallowing in your blood.

" 'You were like a wife who commits adultery, who takes strangers instead of her husband. You gave gifts to your lovers and bribed them to come to you.

" 'Therefore have I stretched out my hand and diminished your food, and delivered you to the will of those who hate you, the daughters of Philistia, who are ashamed of your lewdness. Behold, I will gather all your lovers and expose you to them. And I will judge you as the adulteress and the murderer are judged. I will turn you over into their hands, and they shall strip you of your jewels and your clothes, and leave you naked and bare. Then they will stone you with stones and pierce you with swords.

" 'So will my jealousy depart from me, and I will be calm and be angry no more.' "

## As Is the Mother

16-17 "Everyone who uses proverbs shall use this proverb about you, saying, 'As is the mother, so is the daughter.' For you are the daughter of the mother who loathed her husband and her children. And you are the sister of the sisters who loathed their husbands and their children. Your mother was a Hittite; your elder sister is Samaria and your younger sister is Sodom. Yet you were corrupted more than they in all your ways. Sodom your sister has not done, she and her daughters have not done what you and your daughters have done; nor has your sister Samaria committed half the abominations you have committed.

"Therefore," says the Lord God, "I will deal with you as you have done, you who have despised the oath and have broken the covenant." [5]

[5] See EZEKIEL, Chapter 17, in Notes and Excisions.

# The Fathers Who Ate Sour Grapes

18    The word of the Lord came to me again, saying: "What does this
      proverb concerning Israel mean, 'The fathers ate sour grapes, and
the children's teeth are set on edge'?

"As I live," says the Lord, "you shall have no occasion to use this proverb in Israel any more. Behold, all souls are mine; as the soul of the
father, so also the soul of the son is mine; only the soul that sins shall die.

"But if a man is just, and does that which is right, and has not lifted
up his eyes to idols; if he has not oppressed any, or harmed any by
violence; if he has not lent for usury, and has given of his bread to the
hungry, and covered the naked with a garment; if he has executed true
justice between man and man, and dealt truly, he shall surely live.

"The soul that sins shall die. The son shall not bear the iniquity of the
father, nor shall the father bear the iniquity of his son. The righteousness
of the righteous shall be upon him, and the wickedness of the wicked
shall be upon him. But if the wicked will turn from all the sins he has
committed, and does that which is lawful and right, he shall surely live;
he shall not die. All his transgressions shall not be mentioned to him; in
the righteousness which he has done he shall live.

"Have I any pleasure at all that the wicked should die," says the Lord,
"and not rather that he should repent his ways and live?"

# Lament for the Princes

19    "Take up a lament for the princes of Israel, and say, 'Your mother
      was a lioness; among lions she couched, and nourished her whelps
among young lions. She brought up one of her whelps, and it became a
young lion; it learned to catch prey. Then the people heard that he
devoured men, and they assembled against him, and caught him in their
pit, and brought him in chains to the land of Egypt, that he should prey
on men no more.

"'Now the mother waited long for his return; and when her hope
was gone, she took another of her whelps and reared him as a young lion.
And he went up and down among the lions and learned to catch prey.
And he too devoured men. He made their palaces desolate and laid waste
their cities, and the land was full of the noise of his roaring.

" 'Then the people set against him on every side, and they spread nets for him, and he was taken in their pit. And they put him in a cage in chains, and brought him to the king of Babylon. There they placed him in a den, that his roaring should no more be heard upon the mountains of Israel.' " [6]

## The Fire and the Sword

**20-22**  The word of the Lord came to me, saying: "O mortal man, set your face toward the south and prophesy against the forest of the south, and say: 'Thus says the Lord, "Behold, I will kindle a fire in you which shall devour every green tree and every dry tree; and the flame shall not be quenched until every face, from north to south, shall be scorched by it." '

"Set your face toward Jerusalem, and prophesy against the land of Israel, and say, 'Thus says the Lord, "Behold, I am against you! I will draw my sword from its sheath and it will cut off from you the righteous with the wicked." ' Sigh, therefore, O mortal man! Sigh before them with heartbreaking and bitter sighs. And when they ask you, 'Why do you sigh?' you shall answer, 'Because of the tidings which I bring you, at which every heart must melt, and all hands grow feeble, and every spirit faint! A sword, a sword is furbished to flash like lightning, and sharpened for slaughter. It is given to the slayer, and it shall fall upon my people and upon the princes of Israel! Therefore I sigh.'

"Prophesy, O mortal man! Wring your hands! For the sword shall fall a second time, and come down still a third time and bring terror upon them, until their hearts melt and their ruins are many: the work of the sword which flashes like lightning and is sharpened for slaughter!" [7]

## Allegory of the Two Sisters

**23-26**  The word of the Lord came again to me, saying, "O mortal man, there were two women, the daughters of one mother, and their names were Aholah and Aholibah. Samaria is Aholah, and Jerusalem is Aholibah.

[6] See EZEKIEL, Chapters 19-20, in Notes and Excisions.
[7] See EZEKIEL, Chapter 22, in Notes and Excisions.

"And Aholah played the harlot when she was mine; and she doted on her lovers, on the Assyrians her neighbors, who were clothed in blue, captains and rulers all of them, lusty young men, riding upon horses. Therefore I have given her into the hand of her lovers, into the hand of the Assyrians upon whom she doted.

"Aholibah was even more corrupt in her inordinate passion than her sister. She doted upon the Assyrians her neighbors, captains and rulers clothed in full armor, horsemen riding upon horses, all of them lusty young men. She saw the images of the Chaldeans portrayed in vermilion, with girdles on their loins and turbans on their heads, all of them princes in appearance; and she sent messengers to them in Chaldea. And the Babylonians came to her bed of love with their lust.

"O Aholibah, thus says the Lord: 'Behold, I will rouse up your lovers against you and bring them from every side, the Babylonians and all the Chaldeans, and Pekod and Shoa and Koa, and all the Assyrians with them, all of them lusty young men, captains and rulers, all of them riding upon horses. They shall come against you with chariots and with an assembly of armed men, and shall surround you with buckler and shield and helmet.

" 'You sent for them from afar, and they came. For them you anointed yourself and painted your eyes and decked yourself with ornaments; you reclined upon your stately couch, and set your table before it. And they went in to you as to a harlot.

" 'In your sister's footsteps have you walked; therefore will I give her cup into your hand. You shall drink deep of it and be filled with drunkenness and sorrow, with astonishment and desolation; you shall be scorned and derided, for your sister's cup is full to brim, and you shall drink it and drain it.' " [8]


## *Lament for Tyre*

27-33   The word of the Lord came to me, saying: "Now, mortal man, make a lament for Tyre, and say to her who dwells at the entry of the sea, and is a merchant to the people of many isles:

" 'O Tyre! You have said, "I am of perfect beauty!" Your shores are in the heart of the seas; your builders have perfected your beauty. They have fashioned your ships from the fir trees of Senir, and for masts they

[8] See EZEKIEL, Chapters 24-26, in Notes and Excisions.

have taken cedars from Lebanon. Of the oaks of Bashan have they made your oars; the Ashurites have made your benches of ivory brought from the isles of Chittim. For your sails you spread out fine linen from Egypt; blue and purple from the isles of Elisha are your awnings.

"'The inhabitants of Sidon and Arvad were your rowers; your wise men, O Tyre, were your pilots. The elders of Gebal and its wise men were your calkers. All the ships of the sea with their mariners came to trade for your wares. Men of Persia and of Lud and of Phut were in your army, your men of war; the men of Arvad with your army were upon your walls round about; the Gammadims were the watchmen in your towers; they hung their shields upon your walls, they made your beauty perfect.

"'Tarshish traded with you; with silver, iron, tin and lead they traded in your fairs.

"'Javan, Tubal and Meshech traded slaves and vessels of brass in your market. Those of the house of Togarmah traded horses and horsemen and mules for your wares.

"'The men of Dedan were your merchants; they brought you horns of ivory and ebony. Syria traded with you, and filled your fairs with emeralds, purple, and embroidered work, fine linen, and coral and agate.

"'Judah and the land of Israel traded in your market with wheat and honey, and oil and balm. Damascus traded with the wine of Helbon, and white wool.

"'Vedan and Javan paid for your goods with iron, cassia and calamus. Dedan traded precious cloth for chariots.

"'Arabia and all the princes of Kedar were your merchants in lambs and rams and goats. The merchants of Sheba and Raamah filled your fairs with spices and precious stones and gold.

"'Heran and Canneh and Eden, the merchants of Sheba, Asshur and Chilmad, were your merchants. These were your merchants in wrappings of blue and embroidered work.

"'The ships of Tarshish sang your praise in your markets. You were replenished and made glorious in the midst of the sea.

"'But your rowers shall bring you into deep waters on the day of your ruin; the east wind shall shatter you in the heart of the sea.

"'Your riches and your fairs, your mariners and your pilots, your calkers and the traders of your wares, all your men of war and all your company on that day shall sink into the sea.

"'At the cry of your pilots the uplands shall quake. All who handle the oar, all the pilots of the sea shall come down from their ships; they shall stand on the shore and cry out bitterly. They shall cast dust upon their heads; they shall shave their heads and gird themselves with sackcloth, and they shall weep for you in bitterness of heart.

"'And they shall take up a lament for you, saying, "What city was there like Tyre! When your wares went out on the seas you satisfied many peoples; you enriched the kings of the earth with the abundance of your wealth! Now that you are shattered by the sea, in the depths of the waters, and your wares and all your company have fallen with you, the inhabitants of the isles are appalled at you and their kings are afraid; their faces are troubled. The merchants among the peoples hiss at you; you have come to a terrible end, and shall never be any more."'" [9]

## The Leaders of Israel

34-36  And the word of the Lord came to me, saying, "O mortal man, prophesy against the shepherds of Israel, prophesy and say to them, 'Thus says the Lord God:

"'"Woe to the shepherds of Israel who have fed themselves! Should not the shepherds feed the sheep? You eat the fat, you clothe yourselves with the wool and slaughter the fatlings, but you feed not the flock. The weak you have not strengthened, the sick you have not healed; neither have you bound up the wounded, nor brought back those which have strayed, nor sought those that were lost. But with force and cruelty have you ruled over them."'

"And my flock was scattered because there was no shepherd; they became food for the beasts of the field. My sheep wandered over all the mountains and upon every high hill; yes, my flock was scattered over the face of the whole earth, and none did search or seek for them."

"Therefore, you shepherds, hear the word of the Lord: 'Because my flock became prey to every beast of the field, because my shepherds cared not for my flock, but cared for themselves, therefore, O shepherds, I will require my flock at your hand, nor shall the shepherds feed themselves any more.'

"Behold, I will search for my sheep and seek them out. I will deliver them out of all the places where they have been scattered in the day of clouds and darkness. I will gather them from the countries and bring

[9] See EZEKIEL, Chapters 28-33, in Notes and Excisions.

them to their own land, and feed them upon the mountains of Israel by the rivers and in all the habitable places of the country. I will feed them in a good pasture, and upon the high mountains of Israel shall be their fold.

"I will feed my flock, and I will cause them to lie down," says the Lord God. "I will seek' those who were lost, and bring back those who were driven away, and bind up the broken, and strengthen the sick.

"And I will set up one shepherd over them, and he shall be their shepherd. And I, the Lord, will be their God, and my servant David prince among them. And I will make with them a covenant of peace, and will cause the evil beasts to cease out of the land; and they shall dwell safely in the wilderness, and sleep in the woods.

"I will make them and the places round about my hill a blessing; and I will cause the shower to come down in its season; and the tree of the field shall yield her fruit, and the earth shall yield her increase; and they shall be safe in their land.

"They shall no more be prey to the nations; neither shall the beast of the land devour them; but they shall dwell safely, with none to make them afraid. Thus shall they know that I, the Lord their God, am with them, and that they, the house of Israel, are my people." [10]

## The Valley of Dry Bones

37-39 The hand of the Lord was upon me, and carried me out in the spirit, and set me down in the midst of a valley which was full of bones. And behold, there were very many bones in the open valley; and lo, they were very dry.

And God said to me, "Prophesy over these bones, and say to them: 'O you dry bones, hear the word of the Lord! Thus says the Lord God: Behold, you shall live! I will lay sinews upon you, and bring flesh upon you, and cover you with skin, and put breath in you, and you shall live.' "

So I prophesied as I was commanded; and as I prophesied, there arose a noise as the bones came together, bone to its bone. And I beheld, and lo, there were sinews upon them, and the flesh came upon them and the skin covered them, but there was no breath in them.

Then said God to me, "Prophesy to the wind and say, Thus says the

[10] See EZEKIEL, Chapters 35-36, in Notes and Excisions.

Lord God: 'Come from the four corners and breathe upon these slain, that they may live.' "

So I prophesied as he commanded me, and the breath came into them, and they lived, and stood up upon their feet, an exceedingly great army.

Then God said to me, "These bones are the whole house of Israel! Behold, they say, 'Our bones are dry, and our hope is lost.' Prophesy and say to them, Thus says the Lord: 'O my people, I will open your graves and cause you to come up out of them, and bring you back into the land of Israel. And I will put my spirit in you, and you shall live. And you shall know that I, the Lord, have spoken, and performed it.' " [11]

## The Vision of the New Temple

*40-48*  In the twenty-fifth year of our captivity, in the fourteenth year after Jerusalem had been smitten, the hand of the Lord was upon me and brought me in a vision to the land of Israel, and set me down upon a very high mountain, where, to the south, there appeared a city being built.

And there, standing at the gate, was a man holding a line of flax in one hand and a measuring reed in the other.

The man said to me, "Look with your eyes, and hear with your ears, and set down in your heart all that I shall show you; then declare all that you have seen to the house of Israel."

He measured the breadth of the entry of the gate, and the length of the gate. Then he brought me into the outer court, and lo, there were chambers, and a pavement made for the court round about, and thirty chambers were upon the pavement.

After that he brought me toward the south, and behold, a gate toward the south, and he measured its posts and its arches.

He brought me to the inner court by the south gate. And outside the inner gate were the chambers of the singers of the inner court. And he said to me, "This chamber toward the south is for the priests, the keepers of the house; and the chamber toward the north is for the priests, the keepers of the altar."

Then he measured the court, a hundred cubits foursquare, and the altar that was before the house.

Afterward he brought me to the temple. I saw also the height of the

[11] See EZEKIEL, Chapters 37-39, in Notes and Excisions.

house round about; the foundations of the side chambers were a full reed of six great cubits. The posts of the temple were squared. And the temple and the sanctuary had two doors. And there were carved on the doors of the temple cherubim and palm trees.

Then the man said to me, "The north chambers and the south chambers are holy chambers, where the priests shall lay the most holy things."

Afterward he brought me to the gate facing east. And behold, the glory of the God of Israel came from the east, and his voice was like the sound of many waters, and the earth shone with his glory. And I heard the Lord speaking to me out of the house, saying, "This is the place of my throne, and the place for the soles of my feet, where I will dwell in the midst of the children of Israel forever. My holy name shall the house of Israel no more defile, neither they nor their kings. O mortal man, show this house to Israel, that they may be ashamed of their iniquities."

Then the man brought me to the door of the house, and behold, waters issued from under the threshold, eastward. He led me to the outer gate, and when the man had measured a thousand cubits, the waters had reached to my ankles. Again he measured a thousand cubits, and the waters reached to my knees; again he measured a thousand cubits, and now the waters reached my loins; and when he measured another thousand cubits, it had become a river that I could not pass over. So the man brought me back to the bank of the river. And when I returned, behold, there were many trees on both sides.

And he said to me, "These waters issue toward the east country, and go down into the desert and go to the sea. Wherever the river will come, there everything will live. And there will be a great multitude of fish in the waters, and fishermen shall spread forth their nets from Engedi as far as Eneglaim; and the fish will be like the fish of the great sea. And upon the banks of the river will grow trees whose leaves will never wither, nor their fruit ever fail. The fruit shall be good for food, and the leaves for healing. And the name of this city shall be: 'The Lord Is There.' " [12]

[12] See EZEKIEL, Chapters 40-48, in Notes and Excisions.

# THE TWELVE MINOR
# PROPHETS

❮ These twelve poet-prophets are grouped together although they did not live in the same century, their calls to phophesy were aroused by different circumstances, and their prophetic insight into similar events varied greatly. The poetry which has been preserved for us ranges in volume from twenty-one brief verses by Obadiah to two hundred and eleven verses by Zechariah; and their disparity as poets is as great. In the Septuagint they are arranged in order of length, the longest coming first and the shortest last. In this book they appear in their chronological order:

AMOS, a herdsman of Tekoa, prophesied in the days of Jeroboam II, king of Israel, sometime between 765 and 750 B.C.E.

HOSEA, the son of Beeri, preached or prophesied in the kingdom of Israel about the same time that Amos stirred up the people against the king with his utterances, for Hosea also prophesied in the days of Jeroboam II.

MICAH, a younger contemporary of Isaiah (about 730 B.C.E.), was born in the village of Moresheth-Gath near the Egyptian border, and his work has some affinity with the poetry of Amos and Hosea, and shows their influence.

ZEPHANIAH, who lived about the same time as Micah, was apparently the son of a noble family.

NAHUM the Elkonite (about 610 B.C.E.) poured out his wrath against the Assyrians in prophecies on the fate of Nineveh and its idols.

HABAKKUK, it is surmised, lived in the days of, or soon after, Nahum, but we know neither his family origins nor his birthplace; and it has been suggested that he used an Assyrian pseudonym to hide his identity because he prophesied the ultimate destruction of the powerful and dreaded Chaldeans.

HAGGAI (about 520 B.C.E.) is mentioned by both Ezra and Nehemiah as one of the prophets who inspired the people in the rebuilding of the Temple of Jerusalem.

ZECHARIAH, son of Berechiah, the grandson of Iddo, lived in the days of Haggai and was associated with him, and he too spurred the people to rebuild the Temple and the city of Jerusalem.

MALACHI (about 450 B.C.E.) is apparently not the name of the prophet, but a pseudonym meaning "My Messenger." His distinctive style is emphasized by the asking and the answering of a question in a stylized manner.

OBADIAH (about 425 B.C.E.) has the distinction of having the shortest book in the Hebrew Scriptures.

JOEL, the son of Pethoel (about 400 B.C.E.) left a remarkable sheaf of poems on minor themes; and some scholars are of the opinion that several poets are represented in this slender collection.

JONAH, the son of Amittai, is included among the prophets because the story of his experience at sea includes his prayer of repentance in traditional prophetic form, and because he so strongly exemplifies the prophetic idea that God is concerned with Nineveh as much as with Jerusalem, and considers "Egypt, my people, and Assyria, the work of my hands," as much as "Israel, my inheritance." Although Jonah's period is specifically given as in the days of Jeroboam II (II Kings, 14:25), which would make him a contemporary of Amos, many scholars believe that the Book of Jonah was not written until about 350 B.C.E. ❨[

# AMOS
## The Herdsman of Tekoa

*The words of Amos, who was among the herdsmen of Tekoa, concerning Israel in the days of Uzziah, king of Judah, and of Jeroboam, king of Israel.*

## For Three Transgressions

**1-2**    The Lord roars from Zion, and utters his voice from Jerusalem; and the habitations of the shepherds mourn, the top of Carmel withers.

Thus says the Lord: "For three transgressions of Damascus, and for four, I will not reverse the punishment; because they have threshed Gilead with sledges of iron. I will send a fire into the house of Hazael and it shall devour the palaces of Ben-hadad; and I will break the bar of Damascus, and cut off the inhabitants from the plain of Aven, and him that holds the scepter from Beth-Eden; and the people of Aram shall go into captivity to Kir."

Thus says the Lord: "For three transgressions of Moab, and for four, I will not reverse the punishment; because he burned the bones of the king of Edom into lime. I will send a fire upon Moab, and it shall devour the palaces of Kerioth; and Moab shall die with tumult, with shouting, and with the sound of the trumpet. And I will cut off the judge and slay all the princes with him."

Thus says the Lord: "For three transgressions of Judah, and for four, I will not reverse the punishment; because they have despised the law of the Lord and have not kept his commandments, and their lies have caused them to stray from the paths their fathers walked. I will send a fire upon Judah, and it shall devour the palaces of Jerusalem."

Thus says the Lord: "For three transgressions of Israel, and for four, I will not reverse the punishment; because they sell the righteous for silver and the needy for a pair of shoes. They pour dust upon the head of the poor and frustrate the way of the humble.

"Yet it was I who destroyed the Amorite before them, whose height was like the cedar and who was strong as the oak; I destroyed his fruit from above and his roots from below.

"And it was I who brought you up out of the land of Egypt, and led you forty years through the wilderness, to possess the land of the Amorite.

"And I raised up some of your sons as prophets, and some of your young men as Nazarites. Is it not thus, O you children of Israel? But you gave the Nazarites wine to drink, and commanded the prophets, 'Prophesy not!'

"Behold, I shall make you pressed, as a cart full of sheaves is pressed. Flight shall fail the swift, and strength shall leave the strong; neither shall the mighty save himself, and he who handles the bow shall not stand firm. He who rides a horse shall not escape; and the most courageous among the mighty shall flee away naked in that day." [1]

## You Only Have I Known

3      "O Israel, you only have I known of all the families of the earth," says the Lord. "Therefore I will punish you for your iniquities."

Will two walk together except they are agreed? Will a lion roar in the forest unless he has prey? Will a young lion cry out of his den if he has taken nothing?

Will a bird fall in a snare upon the earth where there is no lure for it? Will the trap spring up from the ground and have caught nothing at all?

Shall a trumpet be blown in the city, and the people not tremble? Shall evil befall a city, and the Lord has not done it?

Surely the Lord God will do nothing without revealing his secret to his prophets.

When the lion has roared, who does not fear? When the Lord God has spoken, who will not prophesy?

Proclaim it in the palaces at Ashdod, and in the palaces of Egypt, and say: "Assemble upon the mountains of Samaria, and behold the confusion

[1] See AMOS, Chapters 1-2, in Notes and Excisions.

and oppression in her midst. For those who store up violence and robbery in their palaces, know not how to do right."

Therefore thus says the Lord God: "An adversary shall surround your land; he shall take away your strength, your palaces shall be plundered.

"As the shepherd rescues out of the mouth of the lion two legs, or a piece of an ear, so shall the children of Israel who dwell in Samaria be rescued."

# O Kine of Bashan

4 O you kine of Bashan, who are in the mountain of Samaria, you who oppress the poor and crush the needy, and who say to their masters, "Bring, that we may feast!" The Lord God has sworn by his holiness that the days shall come when he will take you away with hooks, and your posterity with fishhooks.

"Come to Bethel and transgress; at Gilgal multiply transgression; bring your sacrifices every morning, your tithes after three days, and offer a sacrifice of thanksgiving with leaven, and proclaim the freewill offerings. For this you love to do, O children of Israel," says the Lord.

"I have withheld the rain from you when there were yet three months to the harvest. And I sent rain upon one city and no rain upon another. One field was rained upon, and the field on which the rain fell did not wither. So two or three cities wandered to drink water in one city, and were not satisfied; yet have you not returned to me," says the Lord.

"I have smitten you with blasting and mildew; when your gardens and your vineyards and your fig trees and your olive trees flourished, the palmerworm devoured them; yet have you not returned to me," says the Lord.

"I have sent among you a pestilence after the manner of Egypt. Your young men have I slain with the sword, and have taken away your horses; and I have made the stench of your camps come up into your nostrils; yet have you not returned to me," says the Lord.

"I have overthrown some of you, as Sodom and Gomorrah were overthrown, and you were like a firebrand plucked out of the burning; yet have you not returned to me," says the Lord.

"Therefore prepare to meet your God, O Israel!"

## Hear This Dirge

5   Hear this dirge which I take up, O house of Israel! "The virgin
of Israel has fallen; she shall not rise again. She is forsaken upon
her land; there is none to raise her up."

For thus says the Lord God: "To the city from which a thousand went
forth, a hundred shall return; and to those from which a hundred went
forth, ten shall return to the house of Israel."

Seek the Lord and you shall live, lest he break out like a fire in the
house of Joseph, and devour it, and there be none to quench it in Bethel.

O you who turn justice to wormwood and cast righteousness to the
ground, seek him who made the stars, who turns the morning light into
the shadow of death, who darkens the day into night, who calls for the
waters of the sea and pours them out upon the face of the earth — the
Lord God of hosts is his name!

For I know your manifold transgressions, your mighty sins, you who
afflict the just, and take a bribe, and turn aside the poor.

Therefore thus says the Lord, the God of hosts: "There shall be wailing
in the broad places, and in all the streets they shall say, 'Alas, alas!' They
shall call the husbandman to mourn, and in all the vineyards there shall
be lamentation. For I will pass through your midst.

"I hate, I despise your feast days, and I take no delight in your solemn
assemblies. Though you offer me burnt offerings and meal offerings, I
will not accept them. Take away from me the noise of your songs; I will
not listen to the melody of your viols. But let justice flow like the waters,
and righteousness like a mighty stream."

## Those at Ease in Zion

6   "Woe to those who are at ease in Zion, and trust in the mountain
of Samaria, who are named chief of the nations, to whom the
house of Israel come! Go down to Gath of the Philistines; are they any
better than these kingdoms? Or is their border greater than your border?

"Those who lie upon beds of ivory and stretch themselves upon their
couches, and eat the lambs out of the flock and the calves out of the
midst of the stall; who chant to the sound of the viol and invent instruments of music, like David; who drink wine in bowls and anoint them-

selves with choice ointments, but are not grieved for the affliction of Joseph; it is they who shall go captive with the first of those who go captive, and their revelry shall come to an end," says the Lord.

"Do horses race upon the rock? Or does one plow there with oxen? You have turned justice into gall, and the fruit of righteousness into hemlock. Behold, I will raise up against you a nation, O house of Israel," says the Lord, the God of hosts, "and they shall afflict you from the entrance of Hamath to the brook of the wilderness!" [2]

## Amos at Bethel

7      Amaziah the priest of Bethel sent to Jeroboam, king of Israel, saying, "Amos has conspired against you in the midst of the house of Israel; the land is not able to bear all his words. For thus Amos says, 'Jeroboam shall die by the sword, and Israel shall surely be led away captive out of their own land.'"

And Amaziah said to Amos, "O seer, flee to the land of Judah, and there eat bread, and prophesy there. But prophesy not again at Bethel. For it is the king's sanctuary and the king's court."

Then answered Amos to Amaziah, "I was no prophet, neither was I a prophet's son; but I was a herdsman. And the Lord took me as I followed the flock, and said to me, 'Go, prophesy to my people Israel.' Now therefore hear the word of the Lord.

"You say, 'Prophesy not against Israel, and preach not against the house of Isaac.' Therefore thus says the Lord, 'Your wife shall be a harlot in the city; your sons and your daughters shall fall by the sword; your land shall be divided by line; and you shall die in an unclean land. And Israel shall surely be led away captive!'"

## The Basket of Summer Fruit

8      The Lord God showed me a basket of summer fruit, and he said, "Amos, what do you see?" And I answered, "A basket of the-end-of-the-summer fruit."

Then said the Lord, "The end has come upon my people Israel; I will not again pardon them any more. The songs of the temples shall be

[2] See AMOS, Chapter 7, in Notes and Excisions.

dirges on that day; the dead bodies shall be many in every place; they shall be cast out in silence."

Hear this, O you who swallow up the needy and destroy the poor of the land, saying, "When will the new moon be gone, that we may sell grain; and the Sabbath, that we may set out wheat?" Making the measure small and the price great, falsifying the balances, so that you may buy the poor for silver and the needy for a pair of shoes, and sell the refuse of the wheat.

The Lord has sworn by the excellency of Jacob, "Surely I will never forget any of your evil deeds. I will make the sun go down at noon, and darken the earth in the clear day. I will turn your feasts into mourning, and all your songs into lamentation. I will put sackcloth upon all loins, and baldness on every head. And I will make it like the mourning for an only son, and like the end of a bitter day.

"Behold, the days come," says the Lord God, "when I will send a famine on the land. Not a famine of bread or a thirst for water, but a famine and a thirst for hearing the words of the Lord. They shall wander from sea to sea, and from the north to the east; they shall run to and fro to seek the word of the Lord, but shall not find it."

## I Saw the Lord

9    I saw the Lord standing beside the altar, and he said: "Smite the lintel of the door until the posts shake. Cut off the chiefs, and I will slay the rest of them with the sword.

"He who flees shall not flee far, and he who escapes shall not be rescued. Though they dig down to Sheol, thence shall my hand take them; though they climb up to heaven, I will bring them down. And though they hide at the top of Carmel, or flee from my sight to the bottom of the sea, I shall search and find them. Though they go into captivity before their enemies, there will I command the sword, and it shall slay them.

"Lo, I will command," says the Lord, "and I will sift the house of Israel among all nations as grain is sifted in a sieve. Yet shall not the least grain fall upon the earth. All the sinners of my people who say, 'The evil shall not overtake us or confront us,' shall die by the sword.

"In that day I will raise up the house of David that is fallen, and close up the breaches, and rebuild it as it was in days of old.

"Behold, the days come when the plowman shall overtake the reaper, and the treader of grapes him who sows the seed.

"I will bring back my people to Israel from captivity; and they shall rebuild the ruined cities and inhabit them; they shall plant vineyards and drink the wine; they shall plant gardens and eat the fruit.

"And I will plant them upon their land, and they shall no more be pulled up out of the land which I have given them," says the Lord your God.

# HOSEA
## The Compassionate

*The word of the Lord that came to Hosea in the days of Jero-*
*boam, king of Israel.*

## Allegory of a Marriage

1-3    And the Lord said to Hosea, "Go, take a harlot as your wife; for
the land has committed harlotry in departing from the Lord."
So Hosea took Gomer, the daughter of Diblaim; and she bore him a
son. And the Lord said to Hosea, "Call him Jezreel, for yet a little
while and I will avenge the blood of Jezreel upon the house of Jehu,
and bring to an end the kingdom of Israel. On that day I will break the
bow of Israel in the valley of Jezreel."

Then Gomer bore a daughter. And God said to Hosea, "Call her Lo-
ruhamah (The Unpitied), for I will no longer have pity on the house of
Israel."

Gomer gave birth to another son, and God said to Hosea, "Call him Lo-
ammi (Not My People), for you are not my people, and I will not be
your God."

(Yet the number of the children of Israel shall again be as the sands
of the sea, which cannot be measured or numbered. And it shall come
to pass that where it is written, "You are not my people," it shall be said
to them, "You are the children of the living God." Then shall Judah and
Israel be gathered together, and appoint for themselves one head, and
shall go up out of the land; for great shall be the day of Jezreel. And you
shall say to your brothers, Ammi (My People), and to your sisters, Ruhamah (She Has Obtained Pity).

Say to your children, "Plead with your mother, plead! Let her put away her adulteries, lest I strip her naked as on the day she was born, and put her out. And I will not have mercy upon you, her children; for you are the children of harlotry.

"Your mother said, 'I will follow my lovers who give me my bread and water, my wool and my flax, my oil, and my wine to drink!' Behold, I will hedge her way with thorns, and raise a wall against her so that she shall not find her paths. She shall run after her lovers, but she shall not overtake them; she shall seek them, but shall not find them.

"Then shall she say, 'I will return to my husband, for then was it better with me than now.' But I will withhold the grain and wine from her, and withdraw my wool and flax, given to cover her nakedness. I will end all her mirth; all her feast days, her new moons and her Sabbaths, and her solemn feasts. I will destroy her vines and her fig trees, of which she said, 'These my lovers gave me.' And I will punish her for the days on which she offered incense to strange gods, and decked herself with jewels, and followed her lovers, and forgot me," says the Lord.

"Behold, I will allure her, and bring her into the wilderness, and speak tenderly to her. And I will return to her her vineyards, and give her the valley of Achor as a door of hope. She shall respond there as in the days of her youth, as on the day she came up out of Egypt. And she shall call me Ishi (My Husband) and not again call me Baali (My Master). For I will take away from her mouth the names of the strange gods, and they shall no more be remembered.

"On that day will I make a covenant for them with the beasts of the field, and the birds of heaven, and the creeping things of the ground; and I will break the bow and banish forever the sword, and will make them lie down in safety.

"And I will betroth her to me forever in righteousness and in justice, in lovingkindness and in compassion; I will betroth her to me in faithfulness." [1]

## Because There Is No Truth

4   Hear the word of the Lord, O Israel! The Lord has a controversy with the inhabitants of the land, for there is no truth, or mercy, or knowledge of God in it.

[1] See HOSEA, Chapter 3, in Notes and Excisions.

By swearing, by lying, by killing, by stealing, and by adultery they go on, and add bloodshed to bloodshed. The land mourns, and those who dwell in it languish.

Therefore shall you stumble in the day, and the prophet shall stumble with you in the night. My people are destroyed for lack of knowledge. They ask counsel at their stock, and their staff declares it to them. They sacrifice upon the tops of the mountains, and offer upon the hills, under oaks and poplars and elms, because their shade is good.

Because you have rejected knowledge, I will reject you; seeing you have forgotten the law of your God, I will forget your children.

## Hear This, O Priests!

5-6     "Hear this, O priests! Listen, O house of Israel! You have been a snare at Mizpah, and a net spread out upon Tabor.

"Though I rebuked them, the revolters came out for slaughter; Ephraim went knowingly against my commandments.

"Therefore Israel and Ephraim shall fall in their iniquity. Ephraim shall be desolate in the day of rebuke. I will go out against him like a lion, and like a young lion I will tear and go away. I will take away, and there shall be none to rescue.

"O Ephraim, what shall I do with you? For your goodness is like the morning cloud and early dew that vanish when the sun rises.

"Therefore I have hewn them by the prophets; I have slain them by the words of my mouth. For I desire abiding faith, not sacrifice; the knowledge of God rather than burnt offerings."

## Come, Let Us Return

6     Come, let us return to the Lord; for he has torn, and he will heal us; he has smitten, and he will bind us up.

After two days will he revive us; on the third day he will raise us up, and we shall live in his presence.

His going forth is sure as the morning; and he shall come to us as the rain, as the latter rain that waters the earth.

## Ephraim

7      Ephraim has mingled with the peoples; strangers have devoured his strength, and he knows it not. Yes, gray hairs are here and there upon him, yet he knows it not.

Ephraim has become like a silly dove, without understanding; they call to Egypt, they go to Assyria.

Even as they go, I will spread my net upon them; I will bring them down like birds from the heaven.[2]

## They Have Sown the Wind

8-10    Set the trumpet to your lips! For they have transgressed my covenant and trespassed against my law. They have set up kings, but not of my choice; they have anointed princes, but without my knowledge; out of their silver and gold they have fashioned idols.

They have sown the wind, and they shall reap the whirlwind. The bud shall yield no meal; and if it yield, strangers shall swallow it up.

Ephraim has made many altars, but all of them altars of sin. Israel has forgotten his maker, and built palaces. Judah has multiplied fortified cities. But I will send a fire upon the cities, and it shall devour the palaces within.

The days of recompense have come! Israel shall know it. Ephraim is stricken, their root is dried up, they shall bear no fruit. The high places of Aven, the sin of Israel, shall be destroyed. Thorn and thistle shall come up on their altars. They shall say to the mountains, "Cover us," and to the hills, "Fall on us."

You have plowed wickedness, and you have reaped iniquity; you have eaten the fruit of lies. For you trusted in your ways, in the strength of your mighty men.

A tumult shall arise among your people, and all your fortresses shall be razed. Thus it shall be done to you because of your great wickedness: in a morning the king of Israel shall be utterly cut off.

[2] See HOSEA, Chapter 7, in Notes and Excisions.

## When Israel Was a Child

11    "When Israel was a child, then I loved him, and I freed him from
      Egypt. I taught Ephraim to walk, and led him by the hand. But
he knew not that I healed him, that I drew him with bands of love, that
I fed him gently.

"How shall I give you up, Ephraim? How shall I surrender you, Israel?
My heart is turned within me; my compassion is kindled. I will not execute the fierceness of my anger; I will not return to destroy Ephraim,
for I am God and not man, the Holy One in your midst, and I will not
come in fury.

"They shall walk after the Lord; he shall roar like a lion; and when
he roars, the children shall come trembling from the west. They shall
come trembling like a bird out of Egypt, like a dove out of the land
of Assyria. They shall come home again," says the Lord.

## Ephraim Feeds on Wind

12-13    "Ephraim feeds on wind and follows after the east wind," says
         the Lord. "All the day he multiplies lies and desolation. He is a
merchant who balances deceit in his scales; he is fond of oppression. He
says in his heart, 'I have become rich, and my wealth is my power.'

"When Ephraim spoke, the people were in awe; he exalted himself
in Israel; but when he became guilty through Baal, he died. And now
they sin more and more; and out of their silver they make idols and
images, according to their understanding, and all the work of their own
craftsmen. Therefore shall they be like the morning cloud, and like
the dew that early passes away, like the chaff driven from the threshing
floor by the storm, like the smoke that goes up out of the chimney."

## The Iniquity of Ephraim

13    The iniquity of Ephraim is bound up; his sin is laid up in store;
      he is an unwise son.

Shall I ransom them from Sheol? Shall I redeem them from death? Ho,
your plagues, O death! Ho, your destruction, O Sheol! Compassion shall
be hidden from my eyes!

Though he be fruitful among the reed plants, an east wind shall come; the wind of the Lord shall come up from the wilderness. And his spring shall become dry, his fountain shall dry up; all that is precious in his treasure shall be plundered.

## As the Fragrance of Lebanon

14    Return, O Israel, return to the Lord your God and say to him, "Take away our iniquity and receive us graciously. For in you the fatherless find mercy!"

"I will heal their faithlessness," says the Lord; "I will love them freely. I will be as the dew of the skies to Israel. He shall grow like the lily in the field; his roots shall go deep, his branches spread wide; and his beauty shall be like the olive tree, and his fragrance as the fragrance of Lebanon.

"Those who dwell in my shadow shall flourish; they shall revive and blossom like the vine, and their fragrance shall be like the wine of Lebanon.

"O Ephraim, I am like a leafy cypress tree; your fruit comes from me.

"Whoever is wise, let him understand these things. Whoever is prudent, let him discern them. For the ways of the Lord are right, and the just walk in them."

# MICAH
## Prophet of the Poor

*The word of the Lord that came to Micah concerning Samaria
and Jerusalem.*

## As Wax Before the Fire

**1**    Hear, all you people; listen, O earth and all that is in it! Let the
Lord God be witness against you, the Lord from his holy temple!
Behold, the Lord will come forth out of his place, and come down
and tread upon the high places of the earth. And the mountains shall
melt under him; the valleys shall be cleft asunder as wax before the fire,
as waters that pour down a steep place.

For the transgressions of Jacob will all this come to pass, for the sins of
the house of Israel.

What is the transgression of Jacob? Is it not Samaria? And what is the
sin of Judah? Is it not Jerusalem?

"Therefore," says the Lord, "I will make Samaria a heap of ruins; I will
pour down her stones into the valley, and uncover her foundations. All
her carved images shall be shattered, and burned with fire, and all her
idols will I lay waste. For they were bought with the hire of a harlot,
and to the hire of a harlot shall they return."

For this will I lament, and go stripped and naked; I will wail like the
jackal, and mourn as do the owls. For her wound is incurable: it has come
to Judah, it has come to the gate of my people, even to Jerusalem.[1]

[1] See MICAH, Chapter 1, in Notes and Excisions.

## *Those Who Oppress*

2  Woe to those who plan iniquity, and devise evil upon their beds! In the morning light they practice it, because it lies in the power of their hand. They covet fields and take them by violence; they covet houses and seize them. So they oppress a man and his household, a man and his inheritance.

Therefore thus says the Lord, "Behold, against them do I plan a disaster from which they shall not remove their neck; neither shall they walk haughtily again, for this shall be an evil time.

"For you rise up as the enemy of my people; you pull off the robe from those who pass by in trust and they become like men returning from war. The women of my people you have cast out from their pleasant houses; from their children you have taken away my glory forever."

Arise and depart! For this is not your resting place.

## *Hear, O Princes*

3  Hear, O heads of Jacob, and you princes of the house of Israel! Thus says the Lord concerning the prophets who make my people err, who cry "Peace! Peace!" when their mouths are full, but when nothing is given them, declare war.

It shall be night for you, without vision, and darkness for you, without divination. The sun shall go down upon these prophets, and the day shall become black as the night over them. The seer shall be put to shame, the diviners confounded. They shall all cover their lips, for they shall have no answer from God!

Hear this, heads of the house of Jacob and princes of the house of Israel, you who abhor justice and pervert all equity! Your heads judge for reward; your priests teach for hire; your prophets prophesy for money. Yet they lean upon the Lord and say, "Is not the Lord in our midst? No misfortune can befall us!" Because of you, Zion shall be plowed like a field, Jerusalem shall become a heap of ruins, and the mountain of the house of the Lord like a high place in the forest.

## *In the Latter Days*

**4**    In the latter days it shall come to pass that the mountain of the house of the Lord shall be established, and exalted above the hills; and the peoples shall flow to it. And many nations shall come and say, "Let us go up to the mountain of the Lord, into the house of the God of Jacob; and he will teach us of his ways, and we will walk in his paths." For the law shall go forth from Zion, and the word of the Lord from Jerusalem.

Then shall he judge between many peoples, and rebuke strong nations. And they shall beat their swords into plowshares, and their spears into pruning hooks; nation shall not lift up sword against nation; neither shall they learn war any more. But they shall sit each man under his vine and under his fig tree, and none shall make them afraid.

"In that day," says the Lord, "I will assemble her lame, and gather her outcasts and her afflicted, and I will make them into a strong nation! And the Lord shall reign over them in Mount Zion from thenceforth, forever-more."

## *Hill of Zion*

**4**    And you, O tower of the flock, hill of the daughter of Zion, to you shall it come; yes, the former dominion shall come, the kingdom of the daughter of Jerusalem.

Why do you cry out? Have you no king? Has your counselor perished? Pangs have seized you like a woman in labor.

Labor to bring forth, O daughter of Zion, like a woman in travail; for now shall you go forth out of the city, and you shall dwell in the field, and you shall go to Babylon. There shall you be rescued; there shall the Lord redeem you from the hand of your enemies.

## *Many Nations Assemble*

**4**    Many nations assemble against you, who say, "Let her be defiled, let our eye gaze upon Zion."

But they know not the thoughts of the Lord, neither understand they his counsel, for he has gathered them like sheaves to the threshing floor.

Arise, O daughter of Zion! For I will make your horn iron and your hoofs brass; and you shall shatter many peoples; and you shall devote their gain to the Lord, their substance to the Lord of the whole earth.

## Though You Be Little

5     And you, Bethlehem Ephrathah, though you be little among the thousands of Judah, yet out of you shall come forth one who is to be ruler in Israel, whose beginnings are from the beginning.

And he shall stand and feed his flock in the strength of the Lord, in the majesty of the name of the Lord his God; and they shall endure; for then shall he be great to the ends of the earth.

And the remnant of Jacob shall be in the midst of many peoples, as the dew from heaven, as the showers upon the grass, that tarry not for men, nor wait for the sons of men.

## O My People!

6     "Hear, you mountains, the Lord's controversy, and you, enduring rocks, the foundation of the earth! For the Lord has a controversy with his people, and he will plead with Israel!

"O my people, what have I done to you? How have I wearied you? Testify against me!

"For I brought you up out of Egypt and redeemed you from the house of bondage, and I sent before you Moses, Aaron and Miriam.

"O my people, remember now what Balak, king of Moab, devised, and the answer of Balaam, son of Beor, that you may know the righteousness of the Lord.

"You ask, 'Wherewith shall I come before the Lord, and bow myself before God on high? Shall I come before him with burnt offerings, with yearling calves? Will the Lord be pleased with thousands of rams, with ten thousands of rivers of oil? Shall I give my firstborn for my transgression, the fruit of my body for the sin of my soul?'

"It has been told you, O man, what is good, and what the Lord does require of you: only to do justly, to love mercy, and to walk humbly with your God."

## *Hark, the Voice of the Lord!*

6      Hark! The voice of the Lord cries to the city: "Are there yet
       treasures of wickedness in the house of the wicked, and the scant
measure that is abominable?

"Shall I account those pure who have the wicked balances and the bag
of deceitful weights?

"Your rich men are full of violence; your inhabitants have spoken lies,
and the tongue in their mouth is deceitful.

"I will make you desolate because of your sins.

"You shall eat, but not be satisfied. You shall sow, but shall not reap;
you shall tread the olives, but not anoint yourself with oil, and the vintage, but shall not drink the wine!"

## *The Gleanings of the Vintage*

7      Woe to me! For I am like the last of the summer fruit, like the
       grape gleanings of the vintage when there is no cluster to eat. The
good man has perished from the earth, and the upright among men is no
more. They all lie in wait for blood; they hunt their brother with a net.
The best of them is like a brier; the most upright, sharper than a thorn
hedge.

They do evil diligently; the prince asks, and the judge is ready for a
bribe; and the great man utters only the wicked desire in his heart. And
so they pervert justice among them.

The day of your watchmen and of your visitation has come! Now shall
come their perplexity!

Put no confidence in a friend, nor trust in your confidante; guard the
doors of your mouth against her who lies in your bosom.

For the son does not honor the father; the daughter rises against her
mother, the daughter-in-law against her mother-in-law; and a man's
enemies are in his own house.

Therefore I will look to the Lord; I will wait for the God of my
salvation; my God will hear me.

## *Rejoice Not, My Enemy!*

7      Rejoice not, O my enemy! When I fall, I shall rise; when I sit in darkness, the Lord shall be a light to me. I will bear the indignation of the Lord because I have sinned against him, until he plead my cause and execute judgment for me. He will bring me forth to the light, and I shall behold his righteousness.

Then my enemy shall see it, and shame shall cover her who taunted me, "Where is the Lord your God?"

For who is a God like my God, who pardons the iniquity and passes over the transgressions of the remnant of his heritage? He retains not his anger forever, because he delights in mercy.

He will turn again, he will have compassion upon us; he will subdue our iniquities and cast all our sins into the depths of the sea.

O Lord, you will show the truth as promised to Jacob, and mercy to Abraham, as you have sworn to our fathers from the days of old!

# ZEPHANIAH
## *The Stern*

*The word of the Lord which came to Zephaniah, the son of Cushi, in the days of Josiah, king of Judah.*

## *The Day of God's Wrath*

1   "I will utterly consume all things from off the face of the earth," says the Lord. "I will consume man and beast; I will consume the birds of the heaven and the fish of the sea, and the stumbling blocks together with the wicked; and I will cut off man from the face of the earth.

"I will stretch out my hand against Judah, and against all the inhabitants of Jerusalem; and I will cut off the remnant of Baal from this place, and those who worship the host of heaven from the housetops; and those who worship, who swear by the Lord and swear by Malcam; those also who have turned away from the Lord and those who have not sought him."

Hold your peace, for the day of the Lord is at hand! The Lord has prepared a sacrifice, he has consecrated his guests.

"On that day," says the Lord, "there shall come a cry from the Fish Gate, and a great crashing from the hills. Wail, you inhabitants of Maktesh, for all the merchants shall be cut down, all those laden with silver cut off.

"At that time I will search Jerusalem with lamps, and I will punish the men settled upon their lees, who say in their heart, 'The Lord will do neither good nor evil!' Their wealth shall become booty, their houses a desolation; yes, they shall build houses, but shall not inhabit them, and plant vineyards, but shall not drink the wine."

399

The great day of the Lord is near; it approaches swiftly, the day on which the mighty man shall cry bitterly.

That day shall be a day of wrath, a day of trouble and distress, a day of ruin and desolation, a day of darkness and gloom, a day of the trumpets' alarm and battle cry against the fortified cities, against the high towers.

Men shall walk like blind men in distress, because they have sinned against the Lord; their blood shall be poured out like dust. Neither their silver nor their gold shall be able to save them on the day of the Lord's wrath, but the whole earth shall be devoured by the fire of his jealousy; for he will make an end, yes, a terrible and speedy end, of all those who dwell on the earth.

## The Doom of the Philistines

2      Gather yourselves together, O shameless nation; yes, gather together before the day when you pass like chaff before the fierce anger of the Lord!

Seek the Lord, all you humble of the earth, who have followed his laws; seek righteousness, that you may find refuge on the day of the Lord's anger.

Gaza shall be forsaken, Ashkelon a desolation; the people of Ashdod shall be driven out, and the people of Ekron shall be uprooted.

Woe to the inhabitants of the seacoast, the nation of the Cherethites!

The word of the Lord is against you, O land of the Philistines! The seacoast shall become the dwelling place of shepherds, and pasture for their flocks.

## The Doom of Moab

2      "I have heard the taunts of Moab, the revilings of Ammon, with which they have vaunted themselves against my people," says the Lord of hosts, the God of Israel.

"Therefore Moab shall become like Sodom, and the children of Ammon like Gomorrah: a land of nettles and of salt pits, and a wasteland forever! This shall they have for their pride, because they taunted and spoke boastfully against the people of the Lord of hosts."

## *The Doom of Assyria*

2      The Lord will stretch out his hand against the north and destroy
       Assyria. He will make Nineveh a desolation and dry as a desert.
And herds of every beast in the field shall lie down in her midst. The
cormorant and the hooting owl shall lodge upon the roofs, and porcu-
pines in all the lofts; their voices shall be heard at the windows. Desolation shall sprawl on every threshold.

The joyous city that dwelt without care, that said in her heart: "I am,
and there is none besides me!" — she shall become a lair for beasts to lie
down in! Everyone who passes by her shall hiss and shake his fist!

## *The Oppressing City*

3      Woe to the oppressing city!
       She would listen to no voice and accept no correction; she
trusted not in the Lord; she drew not near to her God.

Her princes are roaring lions, and her judges are wolves of the night,
who leave no bone for the morrow. Her prophets are wanton and treacherous persons; her priests profane that which is holy and do violence to
the law.

"Wait for the day when I arise as a witness against you," says the
Lord. "For my decision is to gather the nations, that I may assemble the
kingdoms, to pour upon them my indignation and all my fierce anger."

## *Sing, O Daughter of Zion*

3      Sing, O daughter of Zion; shout, O Israel! Be glad and rejoice
       with all your heart, O daughter of Jerusalem! The Lord has cast
out your enemy; the Lord, King of Israel, is in your midst; you shall not
see evil any more.

The Lord your God is mighty; he will save; he will rejoice over you.

"Behold," says the Lord, "I will gather all your oppressed, all who are
sorrowful for the solemn assembly, all those who have borne the burden
of reproach. I will save the lame, and gather those who were driven

away; and I shall make them praised and famed in every land where they have been put to shame.

"At that time will I bring you back again, and gather you; I will make your name a name of praise among all people of the earth when I turn back your captivity before your eyes," says the Lord.

# NAHUM
## Prophet of Doom

*The vision of Nahum concerning the downfall of Nineveh.*

## The Lord Is Slow to Anger

1    The Lord is jealous and an avenging God, and he reserves his
full wrath for his adversaries.

The Lord is slow to anger and great in power, but he will not acquit
the wicked.

The Lord has his way in the whirlwind and the storm, and the clouds
are the dust of his feet. He rebukes the sea and makes it dry; he dries
up all the rivers; Bashan and Carmel languish, the flower of Lebanon
fades. The hills tremble, the mountains melt away, the earth quakes in
the presence of the Lord — yes, the world and all who dwell in it.

Who can stand before his indignation? Who can endure the fierceness of his anger? His fury pours out like fire, and the rocks crumble before him.

The Lord is good, a stronghold in the day of trouble and a refuge for
those who trust in him.

But with an overflowing flood will he make a full end of his adversaries.

## Behold upon the Mountain

1    Behold upon the mountain the feet of the herald who brings good
tidings, who announces peace! O Judah, keep your solemn feasts,
fulfill your vows! And the wicked shall never again pass through your
borders; they shall be utterly cut off!

403

# The Destruction of the City

2-3     Keep the rampart! Set watch upon the road! Gird your loins! Fortify yourself mightily! For the shatterer has besieged you!

The shield of his warriors will be red, and his valiant men clothed in scarlet. His chariots will be like flaming torches in the day of preparation, and make the fir trees quiver. His chariots will rage through the streets, and jostle one against another in the broad places; they will appear like torches and race by like lightning.

He shall summon the nobles; and they will come stumbling, and hasten to the walls to set up the defenses.

The gates of the river shall be opened, and the palace dissolved. The queen shall be led away captive, and her maidens shall mourn her, moaning with the sound of doves, beating upon their breasts.

Nineveh shall be like a pool from which the waters flee away. "Stay! Stay!" they shall cry; but none shall pay heed.

She is empty, she is desolate and waste; and the heart melts, the knees tremble, there is much pain in every loin, and upon all the faces darkness gathers.

Where is the dwelling of the lions, and the feeding place of the young lions, where the old lion walked, where he brought his prey to the lioness, and enough for his whelps, and none made them afraid?

Woe to the bloody city, full of lies and plunder; full of the crack of the whip, the rattle of wheels, the prancing of horses, the rushing of chariots, and horsemen charging with bright sword and glittering spear — where the host of the slain lie in heaps, and there is no end to the corpses!

All who look upon you shall flee from you, crying, "Nineveh is laid waste! Who will mourn her, and where shall her comforters come from?"

Are you, Nineveh, better than the populous No-Amon on the Nile that was surrounded by waters, whose rampart was the sea, and the sea her wall? Yet she was carried away, she went into captivity; they cast lots for her honored men, and her great men were bound in chains.

You also shall be drunken and reel; you also shall seek refuge from the enemy. But your strongholds shall be like fig trees with ripe fruit: when they are shaken, the fruit falls into the mouth of the eater. Your people will be like women, and your gates set wide open to your foes, for fire shall have devoured your bars.

Draw water for the siege, fortify your strongholds; go into the clay and tread the mortar; make strong the brick kiln. There shall the fire devour you, the sword cut you off.

You have multiplied your merchants above the stars of heaven, your princes like the locusts, and your captains like the great grasshoppers which camp on the hedges in the cool of the day, but when the sun rises they flee away, and no one knows where they are.

Your shepherds slumber, O King of Assyria; your nobles sleep; your people are scattered upon the mountains.

There is no healing of your hurt, your wound is beyond curing. All who hear of your disaster shall clap their hands over you. For upon whom has not your wickedness fallen?

# HABAKKUK
## *"The Little Book of Job"*

*The burden which Habakkuk the prophet did see.*

## How Long, O Lord

**1-3**  How long, O Lord, shall I cry, and you will not hear? How long
will you show me iniquity? Plunder and violence are everywhere
before me; the law is neglected; justice never goes forth. For the wicked
beset the righteous, and justice is perverted.

Look you among the nations, and see, and be astonished! Behold, a
deed shall be wrought in your days which you would not believe though
it be told you. Lo, I raise up the Chaldeans, that bitter and hasty nation,
who shall march through the breadth of the land to seize dwelling places
that are not theirs.

They are terrible and dreadful! Their horses are swifter than leopards,
more fierce than the wolves of the desert; their horsemen come from afar,
they fly like vultures that hasten to devour. They come for violence, their
faces are set as the east wind; and they shall gather captives as one
gathers sand.

Are you not from everlasting, O Lord my God, my Holy One? We
shall not die. O Lord, you have ordained them for judgment; O Rock,
you have established them for correction. Why do you look upon those
who deal treacherously, and hold your peace when the wicked swallows
up the man more righteous than he; and make men like the fish of the sea,
like the creeping things that have no ruler over them? They take all of
them up with the angle, they catch them in their net and gather them in
their drag.

I will stand my watch, and station myself upon the tower, and wait until I hear what God will answer me.

And the Lord answered me and said, "Write the vision, and make it plain upon the tablets, that he who runs may read it as he runs:

"Behold, the wicked soul is puffed up, it is not upright in him; but the just shall live by his faith. The haughty man enlarges his desire, he cannot be satisfied; he is like death that gathers in all nations and assembles all peoples. Shall not these take up a taunting parable against him and say, 'Woe to him who increases that which is not his! Woe to him who gathers unjust gains, to set his nest so high that he may be saved from the power of disaster! For the stone shall cry out of the wall, and the beam out of the timber shall answer it! Woe to him who builds a town on bloodshed, and establishes a city by iniquity! Woe to him who says to the wood, "Awake" and to the dumb stone, "Arise!" Lo, they are overlaid with gold and silver, yet can these teach?'

"But the Lord is in his holy temple; let all the earth keep silence before him!" [1]

[1] See HABAKKUK, Chapter 3, in Notes and Excisions.

# HAGGAI
## *A Sermon*

*The words of Haggai the prophet, in the days of Darius the king, which he spoke to Zerubbabel, governor of Judah, and to Joshua the high priest.*

## Rebuilding the Temple

**1-2**  Thus speaks the Lord of hosts: "This people say, 'The time has not yet come, the time to rebuild the house of the Lord!' Is it time for them to dwell in their houses with shaded balconies while the holy temple lies in ruins?

"Consider your ways," says the Lord. "You have sown much, yet have reaped little; you eat, but you are not filled; you drink, but you still thirst; you put on garments, yet none among you is warm; and he who earns wages puts it as if into a bag with holes.

"You looked for much, and lo, it came to little; and when you brought that little home, I blew it away. Why?" says the Lord of hosts. "Because of my house that lies in ruins while you run each man to his own house. Therefore the heavens above you withhold their dew, and the earth withholds its fruit. I called for a drought upon the land, and upon all that the ground brings forth; upon men and upon cattle, and upon all the labor of men's hands.

"Speak now to Zerubbabel, and to Joshua the high priest, and to the remnant of the people, and say, 'Who among you saw the house of the Lord in its former glory? And how do you see it now? Go up to the mountain and bring down wood, and rebuild my house; and I will take pleasure in it!'

"Be strong, O Zerubbabel, and be strong, O Joshua, and be strong, all you people of the land," says the Lord. "Work, for I am with you. My spirit abides among you; fear not. A little while, and I will shake the heavens and the earth and the sea and the dry land; and I will rouse the nations, and I will fill this house with splendor. The silver is mine and the gold is mine. And the glory of this new house shall be greater than the former. And in this place will I give you peace."

# ZECHARIAH
## *"The Little Book of Ezekiel"*

*In the second year of Darius the king, this vision of the Lord came to Zechariah the prophet.*

## Man on a Red Horse

**1**     I looked in the night, and behold, a man riding upon a horse among the myrtle trees in the hollow; and behind him were others on red and speckled and white horses.

Then I asked, "O my lord, what are these?" And the man who stood among the myrtle trees answered, "These are they whom the Lord has sent to walk to and fro over the earth; and they walked to and fro over the earth, and behold, the earth is still, and at peace."

Then the angel of the Lord who spoke with me said, "O Lord of hosts, how long will you have no mercy on Jerusalem and on the cities of Judah, against whom you have been angered these threescore and ten years?" And the Lord answered the angel with good and comforting words.

And the angel who spoke with me said, "Proclaim, 'Thus says the Lord: "I am jealous for Jerusalem and for Zion with a great jealousy. Therefore will I return to Jerusalem in mercy; my house shall be rebuilt in it; and I, the Lord, shall comfort Zion, and shall yet choose Jerusalem!"'"

## The Vision of Four Horns

1    I lifted my eyes and beheld four horns. And I said to the angel who spoke with me, "What are these?" And he answered me, "These are the horns which have scattered Judah, Israel, and Jerusalem."

And the Lord showed me four craftsmen. Then said I, "What have these come to do?" And he spoke, saying, "These have come to frighten them, to cast down those who lifted up their horn against the land of Judah to scatter it."

## The Vision of the Measuring Line

2-3    I lifted my eyes again, and beheld a man with a measuring line in his hand. And I asked, "Where are you going?" And he said to me, "To measure Jerusalem, and to learn the length and breadth of it."

And behold, the angel who spoke with me went forth, and another angel went to meet him, and said to him, "Speak to this young man and tell him that Jerusalem shall be inhabited like towns without walls, because of the multitude of men and cattle within it."

"For," says the Lord, "I will be to her a wall of fire round about, and I will be the glory in her midst.

"Sing and rejoice, O daughter of Zion! Lo, I come, and I will dwell in your midst," says the Lord.

"And many nations shall be joined to the Lord on that day, and shall be his people. And the Lord shall inherit Judah as his portion in the holy land, and shall again choose Jerusalem." [1]

## The Vision of the Candelabra

4    The angel who spoke with me came again, and waked me, as a man is wakened out of his sleep. And he said to me, "Look, what do you see?" I looked and beheld a golden candelabra, with a bowl on the top of it, and seven lamps thereon, and two olive trees, one at each side of the bowl.

And I asked the angel, "What are these, my lord?" The angel said,

[1] See ZECHARIAH, Chapter 3, in Notes and Excisions.

"Know you not what these are?" And I said, "No, my lord!" Then he answered, "The seven lamps are the seven eyes of the Lord that range over the whole earth."

Then I asked, "What are these two olive trees upon the right side and upon the left side of the candelabra?" And the angel said, "These are the two anointed ones who stand beside the Lord of all the earth."

## The Vision of the Flying Scroll

5-6   I turned, and lifted my eyes, and saw a flying scroll. And the angel beside me asked, "What do you see?" And I answered, "I see a flying scroll, the length of it twenty cubits and the width of it ten cubits."

Then said he to me, "This is the record of the curse that goes out over the face of the whole earth. For everyone who steals and everyone who swears falsely shall be swept away like it. It shall enter the house of the thief, and into the house of him who swears falsely by my Name, and it shall abide in the house and consume them, with their timber and their stones." [2]

## When You Fasted

7-14   In the fourth year of King Darius, the word of the Lord came to Zechariah, saying, "Speak to all the people of the land, and to the priests, and say to them:

" 'When you fasted and mourned these seventy years, did you fast for me? And when you ate, and when you drank, did you not eat and drink for yourselves?

" 'Are not these the words proclaimed by the former prophets when Jerusalem was inhabited and prosperous, when men dwelt in the cities round about her? "Be just; show mercy and compassion every man to his brother; oppress not the widow or the fatherless, the stranger or the poor; and let none of you devise evil in his heart against his brother." '

"But they refused to listen, and turned a stubborn shoulder, and stopped up their ears, and made their hearts like adamant stone against

[2] See ZECHARIAH, Chapters 5-6, in Notes and Excisions.

the words of the Lord. Therefore, as the prophet called and they would not hear him, so they called and I would not hear them," says the Lord. "I scattered them with a whirlwind; and after them no man passed through the land or returned, for they laid the pleasant land desolate." [3]

[3] See ZECHARIAH, Chapters 9-14, in Notes and Excisions.

# MALACHI
## *The Messenger*

*The word of the Lord to Israel through Malachi, his messenger.*

## God's Love for Israel

**1** "I have loved you," says the Lord to Israel. "But you say: 'How have you loved us?' Was not Esau Jacob's brother? Yet I loved Jacob, but Esau I hated, and leveled his mountains, and laid waste his heritage and gave it to the jackals of the desert," says the Lord.

## A Son Honors His Father

**1-2** "A son honors his father, and a servant his master. If then I am your Father, where is my honor? And if I am your Master, where is my respect, O priests who despise my name?" says the Lord.

"But you say, 'How have we despised your name?' You offered polluted food upon my altar," says the Lord of hosts. "I have no pleasure in you, neither will I accept an offering at your hand.

"From the rising of the sun to its setting, my name is great among the nations. But you have profaned it. And now, O priests, this commandment is for you: If you will not listen, and if you will not lay it to your heart, to give honor to my name, then I will send a curse upon you, and I will curse your blessings. Yes, I will indeed curse them, because you do not lay it to your heart."

414

## Have We Not All One Father?

2     "Have we not all one Father? Has not one God created us all?
      Why then do we deal treacherously, every man against his
brother, and profane the covenant of our fathers?

"You have wearied the Lord with your words. Yet you say, 'How have
we wearied him?' When you say, 'Everyone who does evil is good in the
sight of the Lord, and he delights in them'; or when you ask, 'Where is
the God of justice?'"

## The Day of Judgment

3     "Behold, I will send my messenger, and he shall prepare the way
      before me! And the Lord, whom you seek, shall suddenly appear
in his temple; and the messenger of the covenant whom you delight in,
behold, he shall come," says the Lord of hosts.

"But who may abide on the day of his coming? Who shall stand when
he appears? For he shall be like a refiner's fire, and like a fuller's soap!
And as a refiner of silver he shall purify the sons of Levi, and purge
them as gold and silver. Then shall the offering of Judah and Jerusalem
be pleasant to the Lord, as in the days of old, and as in former years.

"I will draw near to you in judgment," says the Lord, "and I will be a
swift witness against the sorcerer, the adulterer, the false witness, and
against those who oppress the hireling in his wages, the widow and the
fatherless, and who defraud the stranger of his right, and fear not me,"
says the Lord.

## A Book of Remembrance

3-4     "Your words have been strong against me," says the Lord. "Yet
        you say, 'How have we spoken against you?' When you said, 'It
is vain to serve God, for what profit is it that we have kept his ordinance?
Now we deem the proud happy, and the doers of wickedness are built
up; and those who try the Lord are delivered!'

"Then those who feared the Lord spoke with one another, and the
Lord heard, and a book of remembrance was written before him of those
who feared the Lord.

"They shall be mine," says the Lord of hosts. "On the day when I make up my treasure I will spare them, as a man spares his own son who serves him.

"For behold, the day will come when all the proud, and all who do wickedly, shall be as stubble, and the day that comes shall set them ablaze and it shall leave them neither root nor branch.

"But for you who fear my name shall the sun of righteousness arise with healing in its wings," says the Lord. "Behold, I will send you Elijah the prophet before the coming of the great and dreadful day; and he shall turn the heart of the fathers to their children, and the heart of the children to their fathers, lest I come and smite the earth with destruction."

# OBADIAH
## The Plaintive

*The vision of Obadiah concerning Edom.*

## The Doom of Edom

"Behold, I shall make you small among the nations," says the Lord. "Behold, you are to be greatly despised.

"The pride of your heart has deceived you, you who dwell in the clefts of the rock, whose habitation is high. You have said in your heart, 'Who can bring me down from my heights?' Though you build your nest as high as the eagle's, and though you set it among the stars, I will bring you down from there.

"On that day I will destroy the wise men of Edom, and banish understanding from the Mount of Esau. And your mighty men, O Teman, shall be dismayed, so that every warrior shall be cut off in the slaughter.

"For the violence done to your brother Jacob, shame shall cover you, and you shall be cut off forever. On the day that you stood aloof while strangers entered Jacob's gates, and carried off his treasures and cast lots for Jerusalem, you too were as one of them.

"You should not have gazed upon your brother's disaster, or rejoiced over the children of Judah in the day of their destruction, or spoken proudly on the day of their distress. You should not have entered the gate of my people on the day of their calamity, or stood in their way to cut off those who escaped, or delivered up those who survived on that day of sorrow.

"As you have done, it shall be done to you: your dealing shall return upon your own head.

"But those who escaped shall come again to Mount Zion, and it shall be holy, and the house of Jacob shall possess their own possessions. The house of Jacob shall be a fire and the house of Joseph a flame, and the house of Esau shall be like stubble. And the fire shall devour the stubble, and none shall remain of the house of Esau."

For the Lord has spoken.

# JOEL
## *Recorder of Disaster*

*The word of the Lord that came to Joel, the son of Pethuel.*

## *The Plague of the Locust*

**1**    Hear this, old men, and give ear, you inhabitants of the land! Has this ever happened in your days, or even in the days of your fathers? Tell it to your children, and let your children tell it to theirs, and their children to another generation.

That which the palmerworm left, the locust has eaten; and what the locust left, the cankerworm has eaten; and what the cankerworm left, the caterpillar has eaten.

Awake, you drunkards, and weep! Lament like a virgin girded with sackcloth for the husband of her youth. The food offering and the drink offering is cut off from the house of the Lord, and the priests are in mourning. The field is devasted and the land mourns; for the grain is laid waste, the new wine is dried up, and the oil fails.

The husbandmen lament because the harvest in the field has perished. The vine has dried, the tree languishes; the pomegranate, the palm tree also, the apple tree, and all the trees of the orchard are withered.

Gather the elders and all the inhabitants of the land to the house of the Lord, and cry out: "Alas for the day! For the day of the Lord is at hand, and as destruction from the Almighty does it come!"

The seed is rotted under the clods; the storehouses are desolate, the bars are broken down, for the grain is withered. How the herds groan! They wander about perplexed because they have no pasture, and the flocks of sheep are desolate.

## Blow the Trumpet in Zion

**2**     Blow the trumpet in Zion, sound the alarm in my holy mountain!
Let all the inhabitants of the land tremble! The day of the Lord
comes, it is nigh; a day of darkness and of gloom, a day of clouds; when
like clouds gathering upon the mountains a great and strong people shall
appear, a devouring fire before them, behind them a burning flame. The
land that lies like the garden of Eden before them shall become a desolate wilderness when they have passed, and nothing shall escape them.

They shall appear like war horses, with a noise like chariots upon the
tops of mountains, like the crackle of flame devouring the stubble of the
field. At the sight of them the people shall be in anguish; all faces shall
darken with pain.

They shall leap upon the city; they shall run upon the wall; they
shall climb up on the houses; they shall enter in at the windows like a
thief.

The earth shall quake before them; the sun and the moon shall grow
dark, and the stars shall cease to shine.

## Proclaim Among the Nations

**3**     Proclaim this among the nations! Prepare for war! Rouse the
mighty men! Let all the men of war draw near, let them come up.
Beat your plowshares into swords, and your pruning hooks into spears;
let the weak say: "I am strong." Hasten, you nations round about; gather
together. Put in the sickle, for the harvest is ripe. Come, step down and
tread, for the wine press is full, the vats overflow. For their wickedness
is great, and the day of the Lord is near in the valley of decision!

On that day the mountains shall drip with new wine, and the hills flow
with milk, and all the brooks of Judah flow with water; and a fountain
shall spring forth from the house of the Lord that shall water the valley
of Shittim.

Egypt shall become a desolation and Edom a desert, for their violence
against Judah, for the innocent blood they have shed.

But Judah shall abide forever, and Jerusalem from generation to generation. For the Lord dwells in Zion!

And the voice of the Lord shall be heard before his army, "Rend your hearts and not your garments; turn to the Lord your God! For he is merciful, slow to anger, and abundant in kindness."

Blow the trumpet in Zion, sanctify a fast, call a solemn assembly. Summon the people, assemble the elders, gather the children, even those that suck at the breast. Let the bridegroom come out of his chamber, and from her bridal chamber the bride. Let the priests, the ministers of the Lord, weep between the porch and the altar; let them say, "Spare your people, O Lord, and make not your heritage a reproach. Why should the nations mock them and say, 'Where is their God?'"

Then will the Lord pity his people; yes, the Lord will answer them.

Fear not, O land! Be glad and rejoice, for the Lord will do great things. Be glad, you children of Zion, and rejoice in the Lord your God. For he shall give you the former rains in full measure, and they shall come down in their season. Then the threshing floors shall be full of wheat, and the vats overflow with wine and oil. And he will restore to you the loss of the years of the locust, and the cankerworm, and the caterpillar, and the palmerworm. And you shall have plenty, and be satisfied.

And the Lord will pour out his spirit upon all flesh; and your sons and daughters shall prophesy, your old men shall dream dreams, your young men shall see visions.

# JONAH
## *The Prophet Who Fled*

### *The Great Storm*

1     Now the word of the Lord came to Jonah, son of Amittai, saying, "Arise, go to Nineveh, that great city, and preach against it, for their wickedness has come up before me."

But Jonah fled from the presence of the Lord, and went down to Joppa, where he found a ship going to Tarshish. So he paid the fare and went aboard. But the Lord sent a great wind and a mighty tempest upon the sea, in which the ship was like to be shattered. Then the mariners were afraid, and each man cried out for mercy to his god; and they cast the cargo into the sea to lighten the ship.

But Jonah had gone down into the hold, and he lay there fast asleep.

The shipmaster came to him and asked, "Why do you sleep at a time like this? Arise, call upon your God! Perhaps your God will remember us and we will not perish."

And the passengers said one to the other, "Come, let us cast lots, that we may know on whose account this evil has befallen us."

So they cast lots, and the lot fell upon Jonah.

They said to him, "Tell us, we pray you, why has this disaster befallen us? What is your occupation? Whence come you? What is your country? And of what people are you?"

And Jonah answered, "I am a Hebrew; and I fear the Lord, the God of heaven, who has made the sea and the dry land."

When he told them why he had fled from the presence of the Lord, the men were terrified and asked, "What shall we do to you, that the sea may be calmed for us?"

And Jonah said, "Cast me into the sea, so that the sea shall be calmed

422

for you, for I know it is because of me that this great storm has come upon you."

Nevertheless, the men rowed hard to bring the ship to shore; but they could not. Then they cried out, "We beseech you, O Lord, let us not perish for this man's life, and lay not upon us innocent blood!"

They took Jonah and cast him into the sea, and the sea ceased from raging.

## Jonah's Prayer

1-2   Now the Lord had sent a great fish to swallow up Jonah. And he remained in the belly of the fish three days and three nights.

Then Jonah prayed to the Lord his God from the belly of the fish: "In my affliction I cried out to the Lord, and he heard me; out of the belly of Sheol cried I, and he heard my voice. The billows and the waves passed over me, and I said, 'I am cast out of your sight; how shall I ever again look upon your holy temple?' The waters surrounded me, the depths closed over me, the weeds were wrapped about my head. I went down to the foundations of the mountains, and the bars of the earth closed upon me forever. Yet you spared my life, O Lord my God! Those who trust in lying vanities forsake their own mercy. But with the voice of thanksgiving will I sacrifice to you; that which I have vowed will I pay; for salvation is of the Lord."

The Lord spoke to the fish, and it vomited out Jonah upon the dry land.

## Jonah in Nineveh

3   The word of the Lord came to Jonah a second time, saying, "Go to Nineveh and preach that which I bid you." So Jonah arose and went to Nineveh.

Now Nineveh was an exceedingly large city, three days' journey from end to end. Jonah entered the city and traveled a day's journey. And he cried out, "Within forty days Nineveh shall be overthrown!"

The tidings reached the king of Nineveh, and he rose from his throne, and took off his robe, and covered himself with sackcloth, and sat down in ashes. And he sent a proclamation throughout the city, saying, "Let neither man nor beast taste anything; let them not feed or drink water; but let them cry mightily to God! Let everyone turn from evil, and from the violence that is in their hands! Who knows but God might yet turn from his fierce anger, so that we do not perish."

## The Rebuke of Jonah

**3-4**  When God saw how the people of Nineveh turned away from evil, he relented and spared the city. But this displeased Jonah exceedingly. And he prayed, "O Lord, is not this why I fled before to Tarshish? For I knew that you are a gracious God, and compassionate, slow to anger and abundant in mercy. Therefore now, O Lord, take my life from me, for it is better for me to die than to live!"

And the Lord said, "Do you do well to be angry?"

So Jonah went out of the city and made a booth for himself, and sat in its shade to see what would happen to Nineveh.

And the Lord God made a gourd grow up over Jonah that it might be a shade over his head, to save him from discomfort. And Jonah was exceedingly glad because of the gourd. But when dawn came the next day, God prepared a worm to smite the plant, so that it withered. And when the run rose high, God prepared a fearful east wind; and the sun beat down upon the head of Jonah. And he grew faint and wished he were dead.

God said to Jonah, "Are you greatly angry because of the gourd?"

Jonah answered, "I am angry enough to wish I were dead."

Then said the Lord, "You have pity on the gourd, for which you have not labored, nor did you make it grow. It came up in a night, and in a night it perished. And should not I pity Nineveh, that great city in which there are more than six score thousand infants who cannot tell their right hand from their left?"

*PART FOUR*

# The Writings
# כתובים

*Called Hagiographa in the Septuagint*

# THE BOOKS OF THE
# HOLY DAYS

❰ There are five sections in the Bible which are known in the Hebrew Scriptures as the Five Scrolls, and each of these has become associated with a fast or a feast. The Five Scrolls are: The Song of Songs, The Book of Ruth, Lamentations, Ecclesiastes, and The Book of Esther. In this version, part of I Maccabees has been added.

The Song of Songs is a series, or a collection, of love songs, or wedding songs, which some scholars have associated with early semireligious ceremonial dances or wedding rituals. Attempts have been made by scholars to arrange the poetry in the form of a dramatic idyl, but the material is too fragmentary to submit to a rigid literary unity. Like the classic love songs of all ages, the songs in this collection are unfailing in their appeal from generation to generation. Love and marriage have always been associated with the season of spring, and The Song of Songs (also known as The Song of Solomon) has become associated with the Biblical holiday of the Passover, which usually occurs in April.

The Book of Ruth is an idyl, almost modern in form, set in the days of the judges. The claim has been often made that this story was written, centuries later, as a protest against the harsh policies on intermarriage issued by Ezra and Nehemiah, and was intended to prove that King David, so revered by his people, was a grandson of Ruth the Moabite. To succeeding generations, however, it has been a touching story of loyalty. Since the story of Ruth unfolds at the time of the grain harvest in Canaan, the Book of Ruth has become associated with the Biblical holiday of Pentecost or the Feast of Weeks, also known as the Grain Harvest Festival.

Lamentations is attributed to the prophet Jeremiah, and is a dirge, or a series of laments, on the fall of Jerusalem and the destruction of the Temple in 586 B.C.E. The final destruction of the city and the Temple took

427

place on the ninth day of the Hebrew month of Ab in that year, and according to the Bible that date late in the summer was commemorated as a fast by the people taken to Babylon. It is called Tishah B'Av. After their return from captivity, and ever since, the fast was retained by the Jews. The reading of Lamentations is part of the commemoration of the fast.

Ecclesiastes is attributed, by implication, to King Solomon. Because of íts profound despair, and many contradictions, it was among the last of the books to be accepted into the Bible. But since it was considered part of the wisdom of Solomon, which came from the Lord, it was finally admitted. Some modern scholars believe that the contradictions in this work are interpolations, intended as answers to the original pessimism expressed, and that it was only after these acceptable answers to the Preacher's despair were inserted that the work was accepted among the books of the Bible. This scroll is associated with the autumn of the year, and read during the Biblical Festival of the Booths, which marks the end of summer.

The Book of Esther is a record of grave persecution threatening the Jews of Persia, and how they were saved. The date of the happy ending of the story is recorded as the fifteenth day of the Hebrew month of Adar, and was set aside as a day of "feasting and gladness," and a day for exchanging gifts. The book gives the name of the holiday, Purim, and the reason for the name is given. Because of its more secular nature, Esther was among the last of the books accorded a place in the Bible. The story of Esther is amplified in the apocryphal work called "The Rest of the Chapters of the Book of Esther," but it does not carry the story any further. ⟪

# THE SONG OF SONGS
## A Collection of Love Songs

**1**     The song of Songs, which is Solomon's.

Kiss me with the kisses of your mouth, for your love is better than wine. Your ointments and your name have a sweet fragrance; therefore do the maidens love you.

Draw me; let us hasten; bring me, O King, into your chamber, that we may be glad and rejoice in your love better than wine!

I am black as the tents of Kedar, as the curtain of Solomon, O daughters of Jerusalem! Disdain me not because I am swarthy, because the sun has scorched me. For my mother's sons were incensed against me and made me the keeper of the vineyards, but my own vineyard have I not kept.

Tell me, O you whom my soul desires, where you feed your flock, where you make them rest at noon. Why should I be as one who is veiled beside the flocks of your companions?

I have compared you, O my love, to a steed in Pharaoh's chariot. Your cheeks and your neck are comely, with pearls and with chains of gold. We will make for your hair bangles of gold with studs of silver.


As long as the king sits at his table, my spikenard sends forth its fragrance. A bundle of myrrh is my beloved to me; he shall spend the night between my breasts. My beloved is to me as a cluster of camphire from the vineyards of Engedi.


Behold, you are fair, my beloved, you are fair; your eyes are as doves. Behold, you are fair, my beloved, and pleasant. Our couch is green; the beams of our house are of cedar, and our rafters of cypress.

2  I am a rose of Sharon, a lily of the valleys.

   As a lily among thorns, so is my love among the daughters.

As the apple tree among the trees of the wood, so is my beloved among the sons. I sat under his shadow with delight, and his fruit was sweet to my palate.

He brought me to the banqueting table, and his banner over me was love. Stay me with raisins, refresh me with apples, for I am sick with love. His left hand is under my head, and his right hand embraces me.

I charge you, O daughters of Jerusalem, by the rose and by the hinds of the field, that you stir not up nor awaken love until it please.

Behold, my beloved comes leaping upon the mountains, skipping upon the hills. My beloved is like a roe or a young hart; he stands behind our wall, he looks in at the windows, showing himself through the lattice. My beloved spoke, and said to me, "Rise up, my love, my fair one, and come away! For lo, the winter is past, the rain is over and gone; the flowers appear on the earth; the time of the singing of birds is come, and the voice of the turtle is heard in our land. The fig tree puts forth her green figs, and the vines with tender grapes give forth their fragrance. Arise, my love, my fair one, and come away!

"O my dove, who is in the clefts of the rock, in the recesses of steep places, let me see your face, let me hear your voice; for sweet is your voice, and your face is comely. Let us catch the foxes, the little foxes that spoil the vines, our vines with tender grapes."

My beloved is mine and I am his; he feeds his flock among the lilies. Until day breaks, and the shadows are gone, turn, my beloved, turn and be like a roe or a young hart upon the mountains of Bether.

3  Every night on my bed I sought him whom my soul loves; I sought him, but I found him not. I said, "I will rise now, and go about the city; in the streets and in the broad ways I will seek him whom my soul loves." I sought him, but I found him not. The watchmen who go about the city found me, and I asked them, "Saw you my beloved?" I had just left them when I found him whom my soul loves. I held him and would not let him go until I had brought him into my mother's house, into the chamber of her who conceived me.

What is this that comes up out of the wilderness like pillars of smoke, perfumed with myrrh and frankincense, with all powders of the merchant?

Behold, it is the litter of Solomon; threescore mighty men are about it, of the valiant of Israel. They all have swords and are expert in war; every man has his sword upon his thigh, because of fear in the night.

King Solomon made for himself a palanquin of the wood of Lebanon. He made its pillars of silver, the bottom of it of gold, the covering of purple, and the interior paved with the love of the daughters of Jerusalem.

Go forth, O daughters of Zion, and behold King Solomon, wearing the crown with which his mother crowned him on his wedding day, on the day of the gladness of his heart.

4    Behold, you are fair, my love; behold, you are fair! Your eyes are as doves behind your veils; your hair as a flock of goats that lie along the side of Mount Gilead. Your teeth are like a flock of ewes newly shorn which come up from the washing, all of which bear twins, and none among them is barren. Your lips are a thread of scarlet, and your mouth is comely; your temples are like a piece of pomegranate behind your locks. Your neck is like the tower of David built for an armory, whereon there hang a thousand bucklers, all shields of mighty men. Your two breasts are like twin fawns which feed among the lilies.

Until the day breaks and the shadows flee, I will get me to the mountain of myrrh, and to the hill of frankincense.

Come with me from Lebanon, my bride, look down from the top of Amana, from the top of Shenir and Hermon, from the lions' dens, from the mountains of the leopards.

You have ravished my heart, my bride, you have ravished my heart with one glance of your eyes, with one turn of your neck. How much better is your love than wine, and the fragrance of your ointments than all spices! Your lips, my bride, are like the honeycomb; honey and milk are under your tongue, and the scent of your garments is like the fragrance of Lebanon.

A garden enclosed is my bride, a spring shut up, a fountain sealed. Your plants are an orchard of pomegranates, with precious fruits, with trees of myrrh and aloes, with all the chief spices. You are a garden fountain, a well of living waters, flowing from the stream of Lebanon.

Awake, O north wind; and come, you south wind! Blow upon my garden, that its spices may let my beloved come into his garden and eat his precious fruits.

5      I have come into my garden, my bride; I have gathered myrrh and spice; I have eaten honeycomb with my honey; I have drunk wine with my milk. "Eat, O friends; drink abundantly, and be drunk with your lovers!"

I was asleep, but my heart wakened. It is my beloved who knocks, saying, "Open, my love, my dove, my undefiled. For my head is filled with dew and my locks with the drops of the night."

I have taken off my garments; shall I put them on again? I have washed my feet; shall I defile them? My beloved put in his hand by the hole of the door, and my heart yearned for him. I rose to open the door to my beloved, and my hands dripped sweet-smelling myrrh upon the handles of the bolt.

I opened to my beloved — but my beloved was gone. I sought him, but I could not find him. I called him, but he gave me no answer. The watchmen who go about the city found me, they struck me, they wounded me; the keepers of the walls took away my mantle from me.

I charge you, O daughters of Jerusalem, if you find my beloved, tell him that I am sick with love!

What is your beloved more than another, O you fairest among women? What is your beloved more than another, that you charge us so?

My beloved is white and ruddy, chief among ten thousand. His head is as fine gold, his locks are bushy, and black as a raven. His eyes are like doves beside the brook, washed with milk, and fitly set. His cheeks are as a bed of spices, as banks of sweet herbs; his lips are as lilies. His hands are as rings of gold set with beryl; his body is an ivory column inlaid with sapphires. His legs are as pillars of marble set into sockets of gold; his face is like Lebanon, excellent as the cedars. His mouth is sweet; he is altogether lovely. This is my beloved, my lover, O daughters of Jerusalem!

6      Where has your beloved gone, fairest among women? Where has your beloved turned aside, that we may seek him with you?

My beloved has gone down to his garden, to the beds of spices, to feed in the garden and to gather lilies. I am my beloved's, and my beloved is mine, who feeds his flock among the lilies.

You are beautiful, O my love, as Tirzah, comely as Jerusalem, terrible as an army with banners. Turn away your eyes from me, for they overcome me!

There are threescore queens and fourscore concubines, and maidens without number, and my dove, my undefiled, is only one; she is the only one of her mother; she is the choice one of her who bore her. The daughters saw her and called her blessed, and the queens and concubines praised her.

I went down to the garden of nuts, to see the green plants of the valley, to see whether the vine budded and the pomegranates were in flower. Before I was aware, my soul was in the chariot of my princely lover.

7    How beautiful are your feet in sandals, O prince's daughter! The joints of your thighs are like jewels, the work of a cunning workman. Your navel is like a goblet, in which wine is not lacking; your belly is like a sheaf of wheat set about with lilies. Your two breasts are like two fawns that are twins of a roe. Your neck is like a tower of ivory; your eyes as the pools in Heshbon; your nose like the tower of Lebanon looking toward Damascus.

How fair and how pleasant are you, O love, for delights!

I said, "I will climb up into the palm tree, I will take hold of its branches." Let your breasts be as clusters of grapes, and the scent of your breath like apples, and your mouth for your beloved like the best wine that goes down smoothly, causing the lips of even those who are asleep to speak.

I am my beloved's, and his desire is toward me. Come, my beloved, let us go into the field, let us lodge in the villages. Let us get up early to the vineyards; let us see whether the vine has budded, and its blossom opened, and the pomegranates be in flower; there will I give you my love!

8    O that you were as my brother, who sucked my mother's breast! Then when I found you and kissed you, none would despise me. I would lead you and bring you into my mother's house; I would give you

433

a drink of spiced wine, and the juice of the pomegranate. Your left hand would be under my head, and your right hand would embrace me.

Set me as a seal upon your heart, as a seal upon your arm; for love is strong as death; jealousy is cruel as the grave — its coals are as coals of fire. Many waters cannot quench love, neither can the floods drown it.

We have a little sister, and she has no breasts; what shall we do for our sister in the day when she shall be spoken for? If she were a wall, we would build upon her a turret of silver; and if she were a door, we would enclose her with boards of cedar.

I am a wall, and my breasts are like its towers; and in his eyes I am as one who has found peace.

Make haste, my beloved, make haste, and be as a roe or a young hart upon the mountains of spices!

# THE BOOK OF RUTH
## *An Idyl*

1    In the days when the judges ruled there was a famine in the land.

And a certain man of Bethlehem in Judah went to Moab, he and his wife Naomi, and their two sons Mahlon and Chilion; and they remained there.

Then Elimelech died, and Naomi was left with her two sons. Her sons took wives from the women of Moab; the name of the one was Orphah, and the name of the other Ruth; and the family dwelt there about ten years.

Then both Mahlon and Chilion died, so that Naomi was bereft of her sons and her husband. And she started out to return from Moab to the land of Judah, and her two daughters-in-law went along with her on the way.

Naomi said to them, "Go, return each of you to her mother's house; and may the Lord deal kindly with you, as you have dealt with the dead and with me." Then she kissed them. But they wept, and said to her, "We will return with you to your people."

Naomi answered, "My daughters, why should you go with me? Have I any more sons to be your husbands? Turn back and go your way. It grieves me much that the hand of the Lord has gone against me."

They wept again, and then Orphah kissed her mother-in-law and departed. But Ruth clung to her and said, "Entreat me not to leave you, or to refrain from following you. For wherever you go, I will go; and where you lodge, there I will lodge. Your people shall be my people, and your God my God. Where you die I will die, and there will I be buried. The Lord do so to me, and more also, if ought but death part you and me."

When Naomi saw that Ruth was steadfast, she said no more; and the

435

two went on until they came to Bethlehem. So Naomi returned from the land of Moab, and Ruth her daughter-in-law with her; and they came to Bethlehem at the beginning of the barley harvest.

2      And Ruth said to Naomi, "Let me go to the field and glean with the gleaners of the harvest." And Naomi answered, "Go, my daughter."

Now Naomi had a kinsman, a man of wealth, of the family of Elimelech; and his name was Boaz.

And when Ruth went and gleaned in the field after the reapers, she happened on a part of the field which belonged to Boaz. And behold, Boaz came from Bethlehem and said to the reapers, "The Lord be with you!" They answered him, "The Lord bless you!"

Boaz asked his servant who was in charge of the reapers, "Whose maiden is this?" And the servant answered, "It is the maiden who returned with Naomi from the country of Moab. She said, 'Pray let me glean after the reapers among the sheaves.' So she came, and has worked from morning until now."

Boaz said to Ruth, "My daughter, go not to glean in another field, but abide here with my maidens. Watch the field they reap, and follow the reapers. For I have charged the young men not to touch you. When you are thirsty, go to the vessels and drink of the water my servants have drawn."

Ruth bowed to the ground, and said to him, "Why have I found favor in your eyes, that you should take notice of me, seeing I am a stranger?"

And Boaz answered, "I have been fully told of all you have done for your mother-in-law since the death of your husband, and how you left your father and your mother, and the land of your nativity, and came to a people you did not know before. May the Lord God of Israel, under whose wings you have taken refuge, give you a full reward."

Then Ruth said, "You have comforted me, for you have spoken kindly to your handmaid, though I am not like one of your handmaids." And Boaz said to her, "At mealtime, come here and eat of the bread, and dip your morsel in the vinegar."

So Ruth sat beside the reapers; and he reached to her parched grain, and she ate, and was satisfied, and left. And when she had risen up to glean, Boaz commanded his young men, "Let her glean among the sheaves, and reproach her not. And let fall some handfuls on purpose for her, and leave them that she may glean them, and rebuke her not."

Ruth gleaned in the field until evening. Then she beat out all that she had gleaned, and it was about an ephah of barley. She took it up, and went into the city, and showed it to her mother-in-law.

Naomi said to her, "Where have you gleaned today? Blessed be he who took notice of you."

And Ruth said, "The man's name, in whose field I worked today, is Boaz." And Naomi answered, "Blessed be the Lord! For the man is near of kin to us. It is good, my daughter, that you glean with his maidens until they have finished all the harvesting."

So Ruth kept close to the maidens in the fields of Boaz and gleaned until the end of the barley harvest and of the wheat harvest; and she dwelt with her mother-in-law.

3-4     Then Naomi said to Ruth, "My daughter, shall I not seek a home for you, that it may be well with you? And is not Boaz of our kindred? Behold, he winnows barley tonight at the threshing floor. Wash and anoint yourself, and put on your fine raiment, and go down there. But do not make yourself known until Boaz has finished eating and drinking."

Ruth went to the threshing floor. And when Boaz had finished eating and drinking, and his heart was merry, he went to lie down at the end of a heap of grain. Then Ruth came softly and lay down beside him. At midnight Boaz turned, and behold, a woman lay at his feet.

He said, "Who are you?" And she answered, "I am Ruth, your handmaid." Boaz said, "May the Lord bless you, my daughter! For you have shown kindness, inasmuch as you followed not young men, whether poor or rich. All the people of my city know that you are a virtuous woman. Now it is true that I am your kinsman, but there is a kinsman who is nearer than I. Remain until morning. And if he will perform the duty of a kinsman, let him do so. But if he will not, then I will do the part of a kinsman to you, as the Lord lives."

Ruth lay at his feet until morning. Then she arose before dawn. And Boaz said to her, "Do not let it be known that a woman came to the threshing floor." Also he said, "Hold out your veil." And when Ruth held out her veil, he poured into it six measures of barley, and slung it upon her shoulder. And she returned to the city.

Then Boaz went to the gate of the city and sat down there; and behold, the kinsman of whom he had spoken came by. Boaz said to him, "Turn aside and sit down." And the man turned aside and sat down.

Then Boaz called ten elders of the city, and said to his kinsman before them, "Naomi, who has returned from Moab, is selling the parcel of land which belonged to our brother Elimelech. I disclose this to you before the elders of our people, so that if you wish to redeem it, you may do so." The man said, "I will redeem it." Then said Boaz, "On the day you buy the field from Naomi, you must also buy it from Ruth the Moabite, to raise up the name of the dead upon his inheritance."

And the man answered, "I cannot redeem it for myself, lest I mar my own inheritance. Therefore you may take the right to redeem it for yourself, for you are next of kin."

(Now in former times in Israel, to confirm all things concerning redeeming and exchanging, a man drew off his sandal and gave it to his neighbor as testimony.)

So the man said to Boaz, "Buy it for yourself." And he drew off his sandal.

Then Boaz said to the elders, and to all the people, "You are witness this day that I have bought from Naomi all that belonged to Elimelech and their sons. Moreover, I have acquired Ruth, the wife of Mahlon, to be my wife, so that the name of the dead shall not be cut off from his brothers."

And all those at the gate said, "We are witnesses. May the Lord make this woman who comes into your house like Rachel and Leah, who built up the house of Israel."

So Boaz took Ruth as his wife. And the Lord gave her a son. Then the women said to Naomi, "Blessed be the Lord, who has not left you without a kinsman; and may his name be renowned in Israel. He shall be the restorer of your life and a nourisher of your old age; for your daughter-in-law, who loves you and is better to you than seven sons, has borne him."

Naomi took the child and held him in her arms, and became his nurse. And the women who were her neighbors said, "A son has been born to Naomi." They called him Obed. Obed was the father of Jesse. And Jesse was the father of David.

# LAMENTATIONS
## *A Dirge*

1     How lonely sits the city, once so full of people! She has become
      like a widow! She who was great among the nations, she who
was a princess among the provinces, has become a bondswoman!

She weeps through the night, and the tears flow down her cheeks.
Among all her lovers she has none to comfort her; all her friends have
betrayed her, they have become her enemies.

Judah has gone into captivity to endure affliction, to dwell among the
heathen and find no rest. All her persecutors have overtaken her in her
distress.

Even the roads of Zion mourn, because none come to the solemn feasts.
All her gates are desolate, her priests sigh, and she herself is in bitterness.

Her adversaries have come to power, her enemies prosper, and her
children have gone away into captivity before the foe.

Beauty has departed from the daughter of Zion. Her princes have become like stags that find no pasture, that flee before the hunter.

In the hour of her affliction, Jerusalem recalls all the pleasant things
she had in the days of old — now that her people have fallen to the enemy and none come to her aid, now that her oppressors gaze upon her
and mock her. She sighs, she turns away, she has none to console her.

"O Lord, see and consider how despised I have become! You who
pass by, behold, and see if there is any sorrow like my sorrow, with
which the Lord has overwhelmed me in his fierce anger. From above he
has sent down fire into my bones; below he has spread a net for my feet;
he has made me desolate and faint all the day. He has crushed my mighty
men, and trodden as in a wine press the daughters of Judah.

"For these things I weep; my eyes run down with tears. The comforter
who should console me is far from me, he who should refresh my soul.

My children are distraught, for the enemy has prevailed. Zion reaches out her hands, but there are none to touch them.

"Hear, I pray you, all people, and look upon my sorrow. My maidens and young men have been taken as captives. My priests and elders have perished in the city while they sought food to still their hunger. Behold, O Lord, my distress!

"My enemies have heard of my trouble; they rejoice in what you have done. O hasten the day when they shall be as I am! Let their wickedness come before you as mine has; do to them as you have done to me for all my transgressions. For my sighs are many, and my heart is breaking."

2        How the Lord has covered the daughter of Zion with the cloud of his anger! He has hurled to the ground the glory of Israel. He has allowed the habitations of Jacob to be consumed without mercy; in his wrath he has thrown down the strongholds of the daughter of Judah; in his fierce anger he has cut off the horn of Israel; his fury has burned like a fire that devoured Jacob.

He has bent his bow like an enemy, standing with his right hand like an adversary, and has slain all that was pleasant in Zion. With violence he has stripped his tabernacle; he has spurned his altar and his sanctuary; he has destroyed the places of assembly; he has caused the solemn fasts and Sabbaths to be forgotten in Zion.

Now the gates of Zion have sunk into the ground; her bars are broken. Her kings and princes are among the Gentiles, and the Lord appears no more in visions to her prophets.

The elders of Zion sit upon the ground in silence. They have cast dust upon their heads, and girded themselves in sackcloth. The maidens of Jerusalem hang their heads. And the life of the infant ebbs away in the arms of its mother.

To what shall I liken you, that I may comfort you, O daughter of Jerusalem? Your breach is as great as the sea; who can heal you?

All who pass by clap their hands; they hiss and wag their heads and say, "Is this the city men called the perfection of beauty, the joy of the earth?" All your enemies have opened their mouths against you and say, "This is the day we have looked for! We have swallowed her up!"

The Lord has fulfilled his word: he has thrown down without mercy; he has made the enemy rejoice over you; he has exalted the strength of your foes.

Arise, cry out in the night at the beginning of the watches! Pour out your heart like water; lift up your hands to the Lord for the life of your children who faint from hunger.

See, O Lord, and consider to whom you have done this! The young and the old lie on the ground in the streets. The maidens and young men have fallen by the sword. You have slain them in your anger, O Lord; you have killed unsparingly. In the day of the Lord's anger, none escaped and none survived.

3       I am the man who has seen affliction by the rod of his wrath. He has led me into darkness, not into light. He has turned his hand against me. He has set me in dark places, like those long dead. He has hedged me about so that I cannot get out; he has made my chain heavy. And when I cry for help, he shuts out my prayer. He has turned against me like a bear lying in wait, like a lion in a secret place. He has bent his bow and made me the target of his arrow. He has filled me with bitterness and sated me with wormwood. And I cry out, "My strength and my hope, they have perished!"

Remembering my misery, the wormwood and the gall, my soul is humbled within me. "The Lord is my heritage," says my soul, "therefore will I hope!"

The Lord is good to those who wait for him, to the soul that seeks him. It is good that a man should hope and quietly wait for the salvation of the Lord. It is good for a man to bear the yoke of his youth. For the Lord will not cast off forever. Though he cause grief, yet will he have compassion in the multitude of his mercies. For he does not afflict willingly, nor grieve the children of men.

Let us search our ways, and turn again to the Lord. Let us lift up our hearts to God in the heavens, and confess that we have transgressed and rebelled. Therefore has he not forgiven us.

My enemies have hunted me like a bird, without cause. They have thrown me into a dungeon and cast stones upon me. And out of the low dungeon I called upon the Lord. You drew near in the day that I called upon you; you said: "Fear not."

O Lord, you have redeemed my life. O Lord, you have seen my wrong; be the judge of my cause. You have seen their vengeance against me, and all their devices. You have heard their taunt, O Lord. At their sitting down or standing up, I am their song.

Reward them, O Lord, according to the work of their hands. Give them sorrow of heart, and your curse. Pursue them and destroy them in anger from under the heavens of the Lord.

*4*     How the gold has dimmed! The holy stones of the sanctuary lie
        scattered in every street. The precious sons of Zion, comparable to fine gold, are esteemed like earthen pitchers, the work of the hands of the potter!

Even the jackals bare their breast to suckle their young; but the daughters of my people have become cruel, like the ostriches of the desert. The tongue of the nursing infant clings to the roof of his mouth; the young children beg for food, and none gives it to them. For the punishment of the daughter of my people is greater than the punishment of Sodom, which was overthrown in a moment. Her princes were purer than snow, their bodies more ruddy than rubies. Now their faces are blacker than soot; the skin has shriveled upon their bones; none recognize them. And those slain by the sword are better off than those who die of hunger.

The Lord has accomplished his fury; he has kindled a fire in Zion that has devoured it to its foundation. No king on earth believed, nor any of the inhabitants of the world, that the enemy would enter the gates of Jerusalem.

*5*     Remember, O Lord, what has befallen us! Consider, and behold
        our disgrace! Our inheritance has been turned over to strangers, our houses to aliens. We are orphans and fatherless; our mothers are like widows.

We must pay for the water we drink; our own wood is sold to us. Our necks are in the yoke, and our labor unceasing. We have stretched out our hand to the Egyptians and to the Assyrians to get enough bread. Our fathers have sinned, and we are punished for their iniquities. Slaves rule over us, and there are none to save us from them. We get our bread at the peril of our lives. Our skin is black from the terrible famine.

The women of Zion are ravished, and the maidens of the cities of Judah. Princes are hung up by their hands; the faces of the elders are not honored. The young men are taken to grind at the mills, and the children fall under their loads of wood. The judges have ceased giving judgment, and the musicians have ceased from their music.

The joy of the heart is gone, and the dance has turned into mourning. The crown has fallen from our head. Woe to us, that we have sinned!

For this our heart is faint; for these things our eyes are dim: the Mountain of Zion is desolate; the foxes walk upon it.

You, O Lord, are enthroned forever. Why have you forsaken us so long? Turn us toward you, O Lord, and we shall be turned; renew our days as of old. Surely you have not utterly rejected us, though your anger against us is great!

# ECCLESIASTES
## The Wisdom of the Preacher

**1**      The words of the Preacher, the son of David, king in Jerusalem:
"Vanity of vanities," said the Preacher, "vanity of vanities, all is vanity.

"What profit has a man of all his labor under the sun? One generation passes away, and another generation comes, but the earth abides forever. The sun also rises, and the sun goes down and hastens to the place where it arose. The wind goes toward the south and turns about to the north; it whirls about continually and returns again according to its circuits.

"All the rivers flow into the sea, yet the sea is not full; to the place from whence the rivers come, thither they return again. All things weary us. The mouth does not tire of speaking; the eye is not satisfied with seeing, nor the ear filled with hearing.

"That which has been is that which shall be, and that which has been done is that which shall be done, and there is no new thing under the sun."

"I, the preacher, was king over Israel in Jerusalem. And I applied my heart to seek out wisdom concerning all that occurs under heaven, and behold, all is vanity and vexation of spirit.

"That which is crooked cannot be made straight, and that which is lacking cannot be numbered. I communed with my heart, saying, 'Lo, I have wisdom above all those who were before me in Jerusalem.' And I perceived that this also is vexation of spirit. For in much wisdom is much grief, and he who increases knowledge increases sorrow."

**2**     "I said in my heart, 'Go now, I will test you with mirth; therefore enjoy pleasure.' And behold, this also is vanity.

"I sought to give myself to wine, yet guiding myself with wisdom; and how to lay hold on folly, until I could see what was good for the sons of men, which they should do under the heavens all the days of their life. I made great works; I built for myself houses; I planted vineyards; I set out gardens and orchards, and I planted trees in them of all kinds of fruits. I made pools of water to bring forth trees. I gathered also silver and gold, and the peculiar treasure of kings. I gathered together men singers and women singers, and all the delights of the songs of men. And whatever my eyes desired I kept not from them; I withheld not my heart from any joy. Then I looked on all the works that my hands had wrought. And behold, all was vanity and vexation of spirit, and there was no profit under the sun.

"I turned then to consider wisdom, and madness, and folly. Then I saw that wisdom excels folly as light excels darkness. The wise man's eyes are in his head, but the fool walks in darkness. And yet I perceived also that one event happens to them all.

"Then said I in my heart, 'As it happens to the fool, so it happens even to me; how then was I more wise?' Then I said in my heart, 'This also is vanity.' For the wise man, like the fool, in the days to come shall be forgotten.

"So I hated life, because all labor under the sun comes to nothing; for all is vanity and vexation of spirit.

"There is nothing better for a man than that he should eat and drink, and make his soul enjoy good in his labor. For to the man who pleases him, God gives wisdom and knowledge and joy; but to the sinner he gives travail, to gather and to heap up, that his portion may be given to him who pleases God. This also is vanity and vexation of spirit."

**3**     "There is a season for everything, and a time for every purpose under the heaven: a time to be born, and a time to die; a time to plant, and a time to reap; a time to kill, and a time to heal; a time to break down, and a time to build up; a time to weep, and a time to laugh; a time to mourn, and a time to dance; a time to embrace, and a time to refrain from embracing; a time to get, and a time to lose; a time to keep, and a time to cast away; a time to rend, and a time to sew; a time to keep silence, and a time to speak; a time to love, and a time to hate; a time for war, and a time for peace.

"What profit has he who works in that wherein he labors? I know that there is nothing better for men than to rejoice, and to do good as long as they live. And also that every man should eat and drink, and enjoy the good in his labor, for that is the gift of God.

"I know that whatever God does, it shall be forever. Nothing can be added to it, nor anything taken from it; and God has done it, that men should fear him.

"Moreover, I saw in the place of judgment that wickedness was there, and in the place of righteousness that iniquity was there. I said in my heart, 'God shall judge the righteous and the wicked, for there is a time for every purpose and for every work.'

"I said in my heart, 'The sons of men are but as beasts; one fate befalls them. For that which befalls the sons of men befalls beasts; as the one dies, so dies the other; yes, they have all one breath, so that a man has no pre-eminence over a beast; for all is vanity. All go to one place; all are of the dust, and all turn to dust again.'

"Wherefore I saw that there is nothing better than that a man should rejoice in his own works, for that is his portion; for who shall bring him back to see what shall be after him?"

4        "I returned and considered all the oppressions that are practiced under the sun. And I beheld the tears of the oppressed, and they had no comforter; and their oppressors were great with power, but they also had no comforter. Therefore I envied the dead more than the living; and more than either did I regard him who has not been, who has not seen the evil that is done under the sun.

"Then I returned and considered: two are better than one, because they have a good reward for their labor. And if they fall, one will lift up his fellow; but woe to him who is alone when he falls, for he has no one to help him up. Again, if two lie together, then they keep warm; but how can one be warm alone? And if a man prevail against him who is alone, two shall withstand him; and a threefold cord is not quickly broken. And better is a poor and wise youth than an old and foolish king, who will no more be admonished."

5        "Be not rash with your words, and let not your heart be hasty to utter anything before God; for God is in heaven, and you upon earth; therefore let your words be few.

"Suffer not your mouth to cause your flesh to sin; neither say before the angel, 'It was an error.' Why should you anger God with your voice, and destroy the work of your hands? For in the multitude of dreams and words there are many vanities.

"If you see oppression of the poor and violence take the place of judgment and justice, marvel not at the matter; for One higher than the highest observes them. Moreover, the profit of the earth is for all; the king himself is served by the field.

"He who loves silver shall not be satisfied with silver, nor he who loves abundance with increase: this is also vanity. When goods increase, those who eat them are increased; and what advantage is there to the owner except in looking at them with his eyes? The sleep of a laboring man is sweet, whether he eat little or much; but the glut of the rich will not let him sleep. There is a sore evil which I have seen under the sun, namely, riches kept by its owner to his own hurt. Such riches perish by evil adventures; and if he begets a son, there is nothing for him."

6      "There is another evil which I have seen under the sun, and it is common among men: a man to whom God gives wealth and honor, and he lacks nothing of all his soul desires, yet God gives him not the power to eat it, and a stranger eats it. This is vanity, and evil as a disease. If a man begets a hundred children, and lives many years, but his soul is not filled with his bounty, I say that an untimely birth is better than he. For he comes in with vanity, and departs in darkness.

"All the labor of man is for his mouth, and yet the appetite is not filled. What advantage has the wise over the fool? Or what has the poor man, who knows how to walk before the living? For who knows what is good for man in his life, all the days of his vain life which he spends as a shadow?"

7-8    "A good name is better than precious ointment, and the day of death than the day of one's birth.

"It is better to visit the house of mourning than the house of feasting, for that is the end of all men, and the living will consider it in his heart. Sorrow is better than laughter, for by the sadness of the face the heart is made wiser. The heart of the wise is in the house of mourning, but the heart of the fool is in the house of mirth. It is better to hear the rebuke of the wise than the song of fools. For as the crackling of thorns under a pot, so is the laughter of the fool.

"Surely oppression makes a wise man mad, and a bribe destroys his understanding.

"Better is the end of a thing than its beginning, and the patient spirit is better than the proud in spirit.

"Be not hasty in your anger, for anger rests in the bosom of fools.

"Wisdom is as good as an inheritance, for wisdom is a defense even as money is a defense, but the excellency of wisdom is that it preserves the life of those who have it.

"Consider the work of God, for who can make straight that which he has made crooked? In the day of prosperity be joyful, and in the day of adversity consider: God has made the one with the other, to the end that man should not find out anything that shall be after him.

"I applied my heart to know, and to search, and to seek out wisdom and the reason of things, and to know that wickedness is folly and that foolishness is madness.

"Lo, this too have I found, that God made men upright, but they have sought out many inventions." [1]

9    "For all this I considered in my heart: that the righteous and the wise, and their works, are in the hand of God. All things come alike to all: there is one event to the righteous and to the wicked, to the clean and to the unclean; as is the good, so is the sinner, and he who swears as he who fears an oath.

"This is an evil among all that is done under the sun, that there is one event to all. The hearts of the sons of men are full of evil while they live, and after that they go to the dead.

"For to him who is joined to all the living there is hope, for a living dog is better than a dead lion. The living know that they shall die; but the dead know not anything, neither have they any reward, for they are forgotten. Also their love, and their hatred, and their envy is now perished; neither have they any portion forever in anything that is done under the sun.

"Go your way, eat your bread with joy and drink your wine with a merry heart, for God has accepted your works. Live joyfully with the wife whom you love all the days of your life, for that is your portion, and your labor which you take under the sun.

"Whatever your hand finds to do, do it well; for there is no work, nor device, nor knowledge, nor wisdom in the grave, whither you go.

[1] See ECCLESIASTES, Chapter 8, in Notes and Excisions.

"I also saw that the race is not to the swift, nor the battle to the strong, neither yet bread to the wise, nor yet riches to men of understanding, nor yet favor to men of skill; but time and chance happen to them all.

"For man also knows not his time. As the fishes that are taken in an evil net, and as the birds that are caught in the snare, so are men snared in an evil time when it falls suddenly upon them.

"I have also gained wisdom in this wise: There was a little city, and few men within it; and there came a great king and besieged it, and built great bulwarks against it. Now there was found in that city a poor but wise man, and he by his wisdom saved the city; yet no man remembered that same poor man. Then said I, 'Wisdom is better than strength; nevertheless, the poor man's wisdom is despised and his words are not heard.'"

10    "The words of wise men spoken in quiet are heard more than the cry of him who rules among fools. Wisdom is better than weapons of war, but one sinner destroys much good.

"Dead flies cause the ointment of the apothecary to send out a stink; so does a little folly outweigh a reputation for wisdom and honor.

"If the spirit of the ruler rise up against you, leave not your place; for yielding allays great offenses.

"I have seen servants upon horses, and princes walking as servants upon the earth.

"He who digs a pit shall fall into it; and he who breaks through a fence, a serpent shall bite him.

"Surely the serpent will bite without enchantment; and a babbler is no better.

"Woe to you, O land whose king is a child, and whose princes feast in the morning! Happy the land whose king is the son of nobles, and whose princes feast in due season, for strength and not for drunkenness!

"By slothfulness the roof caves in, and through idleness of the hands the house leaks.

"Curse not the king even in your thought, and curse not the rich in your bedchamber. For a bird of the air shall carry your voice, and that which has wings shall tell the matter."

11    "Cast your bread upon the waters, and you shall find it after many days.

"If the clouds be full of rain, they empty themselves upon the earth;

and if the tree falls toward the south or toward the north, in the place where the tree falls, there shall it be.

"He who observes the wind shall not sow, and he who regards the clouds shall not reap.

"In the morning sow your seed, and do not rest until evening; for you know not which shall prosper, whether this or that, or whether both shall be alike good.

"Truly the light is sweet, and a pleasant thing it is for the eyes to behold the sun. If a man lives many years, let him rejoice in them all; yet let him remember the days of darkness, for they shall be many.

"Rejoice, O young man, in your youth, and let your heart cheer you in the days of your youth; but know that for all these things God will bring you to judgment.

"Therefore remove sorrow from your heart, and put away evil from your flesh; for childhood and youth are also vanity."

12    "Remember your Creator in the days of your youth, before the evil days come and the years draw nigh when you will say, 'I have no pleasure in them'; before the sun, or the light, or the moon, or the stars are darkened, or the clouds return after the rain; in the day when the keepers of the house shall tremble, and the strong men shall bow themselves, and the grinders cease because they are few, and those who look out of the windows are darkened, and the doors shall be shut in the streets; when the sound of the grinding is low, and one shall rise up at the voice of a bird, and all the daughters of music shall be brought low; when they shall be afraid of that which is high, and fears shall be in the way, and the grasshopper shall be a burden, and desire shall fail, because man goes to his long home, and the mourners go about the streets; before the silver cord be loosed, or the golden bowl be broken, or the pitcher be broken at the fountain, or the wheel broken at the cistern; and the dust return to the earth as it was; and the spirit return to God who gave it.

"Vanity of vanities," said the Preacher, "all is vanity."

Moreover, because the Preacher was wise, he still taught the people knowledge. He sought to find out acceptable words; and that which was written was upright, and the words of truth.

The words of the wise are like goads, and like nails fastened by the masters of assemblies, which are given from one shepherd.

Let us hear the conclusion of the wise Preacher: "Fear God and keep his commandments, for this is the whole duty of man. For God shall bring every work into judgment, with every secret thing, whether it be good, or whether it be evil."

# THE BOOK OF ESTHER
## *Fast into Feast*

**1**     Now in the days of Ahasuerus — this is the Ahasuerus who
reigned from India to Ethiopia, over a hundred and twenty-seven
provinces — the king, in the third year of his reign, gave a feast for all
the princes and nobles of his provinces, and showed them the riches of
his glorious kingdom for a hundred and fourscore days.

When these days had passed, the king gave for all the people who
were present in Shushan a seven-day feast in the court of the garden of
the king's palace. There were hangings of white cotton and blue, fastened with cords of fine linen and purple upon silver rings and pillars
of marble; and the couches were of gold and silver, upon a pavement of
green and white and shell and onyx. The drinks were served in vessels
of gold, each vessel different one from another, and royal wine in abundance.

Vashti the queen also gave a feast for the women in the royal house
which belonged to King Ahasuerus.

On the seventh day, when the heart of the king was merry with wine,
he ordered his seven chamberlains to bring Vashti the queen before the
king wearing the crown royal, to show the people and the princes her
beauty, for she was fair to look upon. But the queen Vashti refused to
come at the king's command by his chamberlains. Therefore the king became enraged, and his anger burned within him.

The king asked the wise men, who knew the times, "What shall we do
to the queen Vashti, according to law, because she has not obeyed the
command of the king?"

And one answered, "Vashti the queen has done wrong not only to the
king, but also to all the princes and people in the provinces of the king
Ahasuerus. For when this deed of the queen becomes known to all

women, it will cause them to disobey their husbands. If it please the king, let a royal decree be sent out, and written among the laws of the Persians and the Medes, so that it may not be altered, that Vashti come no more before King Ahasuerus, and that the king give her royal estate to another better than she. Thus when the king's decree is proclaimed throughout his empire, all wives will give honor to their husbands, both to high and low."

This saying pleased the king and the princes. And the king sent letters to every province, to every people in their own language, so that every man should rule in his own house.

2      After these things, when the wrath of King Ahasuerus subsided, he remembered Vashti and what she had done, and what was decreed against her.

Then said the king's servants who ministered to him, "Let fair young maidens be sought for the king. And let the king appoint officers in all the provinces of his kingdom to gather together all the fair young maidens at the palace, in the custody of Hegai, the king's chamberlain, keeper of the women. And let the maiden who pleases the king best be queen instead of Vashti."

Now in Shushan there was a certain Jew named Mordecai, a Benjamite who had been carried away from Jerusalem with the captives taken by Nebuchadnezzar. And Mordecai brought up Hadassah, called Esther, his uncle's daughter, for she had neither father nor mother. And the maiden was fair to look upon.

So it came to pass, when the king's decree was proclaimed, and when many maidens assembled in Shushan, that Esther also was brought to the king's house, to the custody of Hegai.

The maiden pleased Hegai, and she obtained kindness from him; and he speedily gave her seven maidens from the king's house to serve her; and he assigned her and her maidens to the best place in the house of women.

Now when each maiden's turn came to go to the king Ahasuerus, whatever she desired was given her when she left the house of the women. In the evening she went; and on the morrow she returned to the second house of the women, where dwelt the concubines. She came no more to the king, unless the king delighted in her and she was called by name.

When the turn came for Esther to go to the king, she asked for nothing but what Hegai appointed. And Esther obtained favor in the sight of all those who looked upon her. So Esther went to King Ahasuerus in his house royal, in the seventh year of his reign. And the king loved Esther above all the women, and she obtained grace and favor in his sight more than all the others, so that he set the royal crown upon her head and made her queen instead of Vashti.

Then the king gave a great feast for all his princes and servants, a feast for Esther; and he proclaimed a holiday and distributed gifts.

And when the maidens were gathered together the second time, then Mordecai sat at the king's gate. Esther had not yet made known to the king her kindred or her people, as Mordecai had charged her; for Esther did the bidding of Mordecai just as when she was brought up by him.

In those days, while Mordecai sat at the king's gate, two of the king's chamberlains, Bigthan and Teresh, who guarded the door, sought to lay hands on the king. The matter became known to Mordecai, who told it to Esther the queen; and Esther informed the king in Mordecai's name. And when the matter was examined it was found to be so. Therefore Bigthan and Teresh were both hanged on a tree; and it was recorded in the Book of the Chronicles in the presence of the king.

3 After these events King Ahasuerus promoted Haman, the son of Hammedatha the Agagite, and set him above all the princes. And the king's servants who were at the king's gate bowed down before Haman, for the king had so commanded concerning him. But Mordecai bowed not, nor did him honor.

Then the king's servants asked Mordecai, "Why do you ignore the king's command?" They spoke daily to him, and when he paid no heed to them, they told Haman. When Haman saw that Mordecai bowed not, he was full of wrath. But he scorned the thought of laying hands on Mordecai alone, for they had told him of Mordecai's people. Wherefore Haman sought to destroy all the Jews, the people of Mordecai, throughout the kingdom of Ahasuerus.

Then Haman said to the king, "There is a certain people scattered abroad and dispersed in all the provinces of your kingdom; and their laws are different from other peoples; neither do they keep the king's laws. Therefore it is not to the king's profit to suffer them to live. If it please the king, let it be decreed that they may be destroyed; and I will pay ten thousand talents of silver to those in charge of this matter, to bring into the king's treasury."

The king took his ring from his hand, and gave it to Haman, the enemy of the Jews, and said, "The silver is yours, and the people also, to do with them as seems good to you."

Then the king's scribes were called, and a decree was issued according to that which Haman had ordered; and it was sent to the governor in each province, according to the writing and language of the people. And it was written in the name of the king, and sealed with the king's ring.

And the letters were sent by posts into all the king's provinces, to destroy, to kill, and to cause to perish all Jews, both young and old, little children and women, in one day, upon the thirteenth day of the twelfth month, which is the month of Adar, the day set by the *pur*, which is the lot cast. The posts went out, being hastened by the king's command, and the decree was given in Shushan the palace.

And the king and Haman sat down to drink; but the city Shushan was perplexed.

4      When Mordecai learned of all that was done, he rent his clothes and put on sackcloth and ashes. He went into the midst of the city and cried out loud and bitterly; and came even before the king's gate, though none might enter the king's gate when clothed in sackcloth. And in every province, wherever the king's decree came, there was great mourning among the Jews, and fasting and weeping and wailing, and many lay in sackcloth and ashes.

When Esther's maids came and told her, the queen was grieved. She sent garments to clothe Mordecai, and to take away his sackcloth; but he accepted them not. Then Esther summoned Hatach, one of the king's chamberlains, whom he had appointed to attend her, and sent him secretly to Mordecai to find out why he was in mourning. Hatach went to Mordecai before the king's gate; and Mordecai told him of all that had happened, and of the sum of money that Haman had promised to pay to the king's treasury for the destruction of the Jews. Also he gave him the copy of the decree that was issued from Shushan to show to Esther, and to charge her to go to the king and plead for her people.

Hatach returned and told Esther the words of Mordecai. Again Esther sent word with Hatach to Mordecai: "All the king's people know the law that whoever, whether man or woman, comes to the king into the inner court without being summoned, he is put to death, except those to whom the king holds out the golden scepter, that he may live. But I have not been called to the king these thirty days."

Then Mordecai sent this answer to Esther: "Think not that you shall escape in the king's house, any more than all the Jews. For if you hold your peace at this time, then deliverance shall arise to the Jews from another source, but you and your father's house shall be destroyed. For who knows whether you have not come to the kingdom for just such a time as this?"

Esther bade them return to Mordecai this reply: "Go, gather together all the Jews who are in Shushan, and fast for me three days, and I and my maidens will fast also. Then will I go to the king unbidden. And if I perish, I perish."

So Mordecai went his way, and did all that Esther had commanded him.

5      On the third day Esther put on her royal apparel, and stood in the inner court of the king's house. And when the king, who sat upon his royal throne, saw Esther the queen standing in the court, she obtained favor in his sight, and the king held out to Esther the golden scepter in his hand.

Then the king asked, "What is your request, Queen Esther? It shall be given you, even to the half of my kingdom." And Esther answered, "If it seem good to the king, let the king and Haman come tomorrow to the banquet that I have prepared for them."

Then Haman went out that day joyful and with a glad heart. But when he saw Mordecai at the king's gate, and that he neither stood up nor moved for him, he was full of indignation. Nevertheless, Haman restrained himself. And when he came home, he sent for his friends, and Zeresh his wife. And Haman told them of the glory of his riches, and all the things in which the king had advanced him above the other princes.

Moreover, Haman said, "Esther the queen lets no man come with the king to the banquets she prepares, but tomorrow I am invited also with the king. Yet all this avails me nothing, so long as I see Mordecai the Jew sitting at the king's gate."

Then said Zeresh his wife and all his friends, "Let a gallows be made fifty cubits high, and tomorrow speak to the king that Mordecai may be hanged on it. Then go in merrily with the king to the banquet."

The counsel pleased Haman, and he caused the gallows to be made.

6      On the night before the banquet the king could not sleep. And he asked for the Book of the Chronicles, and they read it to him. And in it was found written that Mordecai had told of Bigthan and

Teresh, the king's chamberlains who had sought to lay hands on the king Ahasuerus.

The king asked, "What honor has been done to Mordecai for this?" Then answered the king's servants, "Nothing has been done for him." And the king asked, "Who is in the court?" Now Haman had come into the outer court of the king's house, to speak to the king to hang Mordecai on the gallows which had been prepared. And the king's servants answered, "Behold, Haman stands in the court." The king said, "Let him come in." So Haman came in.

And the king said to Haman, "What shall be done for the man whom the king wishes to honor?" Now Haman thought to himself, "Whom would the king wish to honor other than myself?" And Haman answered the king, "For the man whom the king wishes to honor, let the royal apparel be brought which the king wears, and the horse which the king rides upon, and the crown royal which is set upon his head; and let the horse and apparel be delivered to the hand of one of the king's most noble princes, that he may array the man whom the king wishes to honor, and bring him on horseback through the streets of the city and proclaim before him: 'Thus is it done to the man whom the king wishes to honor.'"

Then the king answered, "Make haste, and take the apparel and the horse, as you have said, and do so to Mordecai the Jew, who sits at the king's gate. Let nothing fail of all that you have spoken!"

Haman took the apparel and the horse, and arrayed Mordecai, and brought him on horseback through the streets of the city, and proclaimed before him, "Thus is it done to the man whom the king wishes to honor!"

Then Mordecai returned to the king's gate. But Haman hastened to his home like one in mourning, with his head covered; and he told Zeresh his wife and his friends everything that had befallen him. And while they were still talking with him, the king's chamberlains came to bring Haman to the banquet which Esther had prepared.

7    So the king and Haman came to banquet with Esther the queen. And the king said again to Esther at the banquet of wine, "What is your request, Queen Esther? It shall be granted to you, even to the half of my kingdom."

Then Esther the queen answered, "If I have found favor in your eyes, O King, let my life be spared me at my petition, and that of my people at my request; for we have been sold, I and my people, to be destroyed, to be slain, and to perish. If we had been sold as bondsmen and bonds-women, I had held my tongue, although our enemy would never repair the king's loss."

The king asked, "Where is he who dares presume in his heart to do so?" And Esther said, "The adversary and enemy is this wicked Haman."

Then Haman was afraid. And when the king rose in his wrath and went into the palace garden, Haman knelt down to beg for his life of Esther the queen; for he saw that there was evil determined against him by the king.

When the king returned from the palace garden, and found Haman fallen upon the couch on which Esther sat, he said, "Will he also force the queen before me in the house?" As the words left the king's mouth, Haman's face darkened. And Harbonah, one of the chamberlains, said to the king, "A gallows fifty cubits high, which Haman has made for Mordecai, stands at the house of Haman." Then the king said, "Hang him upon it!"

So they hanged Haman on the gallows which he had prepared for Mordecai.

8      The king Ahasuerus gave the house of Haman to Esther the queen. And Mordecai came before the king, for Esther revealed what he was to her. The king took off his ring, which he had taken from Haman, and gave it to Mordecai. And Esther set Mordecai over the house of Haman.

Esther spoke again to the king, and fell down at his feet, and besought him with tears to put away the evil decree of Haman the Agagite against the Jews.

Then the king Ahasuerus said to Esther the queen and to Mordecai the Jew, "Behold, I have given Esther the house of Haman, and him they have hanged upon the gallows because he laid his hand upon the Jews. Write now, in the king's name, for the Jews as it pleases you, and seal it with the king's ring; for that which is written in the king's name, and sealed with the king's ring, may no man reverse."

Then were the king's scribes summoned; and it was written according to all that Mordecai commanded, to the lieutenants and the deputies and rulers of the provinces, to each people in their language. And he wrote in the name of King Ahasuerus, and sealed it with the king's ring, and sent letters by posts on horseback, and riders on mules, camels, and young dromedaries, annulling Haman's decree. So the posts hastened and pressed on by the king's command.

Mordecai went out from the presence of the king in royal apparel of blue and white, and with a great crown of gold, and with a garment of fine linen and purple. And the city of Shushan rejoiced and was glad.

The Jews had light, and gladness, and joy, and honor. And in every province, wherever the king's decree came, the Jews celebrated a feast and a good day.

9-10      Now on the twelfth month, that is, the month of Adar, on the thirteenth day, the day when the enemies of the Jews hoped to have power over them (though it was turned to the contrary), the Jews assembled together throughout the provinces of King Ahasuerus to lay hands on such as sought to harm them. And the rulers and officers of the king helped the Jews, because the fear of Mordecai had fallen upon them.

On the fourteenth day they rested, and made it a day of feasting and gladness and of sending gifts to one another.

Mordecai wrote all these things down, and sent letters to all the Jews who were in all the provinces of King Ahasuerus, both near and far, that they should keep the fourteenth day of the month Adar, and the fifteenth day of the same, each year as the days which were turned for them from sorrow to joy, and from mourning to a good day; and that they should make them days of feasting and joy, and of sending gifts to one another and gifts to the poor.

And the Jews undertook to do as Mordecai had written to them.

They called these days Purim, for Haman, the enemy of the Jews, had cast the *pur*, that is, the lot, to consume and destroy them, and his wickedness had returned upon his own head. And the Jews ordained, and took it upon themselves and upon their descendants, to keep these two days each year throughout every generation.

And the decree of Esther confirmed these matters of Purim, and it was recorded in the book.[1]

[1] See ESTHER, Chapter 10, in Notes and Excisions.

*I Maccabees is a historical narrative of considerable length that covers a period of more than thirty years—beginning with the revolt instituted by Mattathias of Modin against Antiochus IV, and ending with an account of the relationship of his children to republican Rome. The first four chapters, which are included in this version, give the upsurge of the revolt under the Maccabees, their victories under Judas, son of Mattathias, in 165 B.C.E., and the cleansing of the Temple in Jerusalem—which gave rise to the Holiday of Lights, called Hanukkah. I Maccabees is not included in the traditional Hebrew Scriptures; it is now found among the Apocrypha.*

# I MACCABEES
## Rededication of the Temple

**1**     And it happened that after Alexander, son of Philip the Macedonian, had conquered Darius, king of the Persians and Medes, that he reigned in his stead, the first over Greece. Then he waged many wars, and won many strongholds, and took spoils of many nations, until the earth was subdued before him. Whereupon he was exalted, and his heart lifted up.

He gathered a mighty army, and ruled over countries and nations and kings who became tributary to him. And after these things he fell sick, and perceived he would die.

He called his loyal servants, such as were honorable and had been brought up with him from his youth, and divided his kingdom among them while he was yet alive.

So Alexander reigned twelve years, and then died. And his servants ruled, each one in his place. After his death, they all put a crown upon themselves, as did their sons after them for many years; and evils were multiplied upon the earth.

And there came out of them a wicked root, Antiochus surnamed Epiphanes, son of Antiochus the king, who had been a hostage at Rome, and he reigned in the hundred and thirty-seventh year of the kingdom of the Greeks.

In those days there went out of Israel wicked men who persuaded many, saying, "Let us make a covenant with the heathen round about us, for since we departed from them we have had much sorrow." Then certain of these people went to the king, who gave them permission to follow the ordinances of the heathen. Whereupon they built a gymnasium in Jerusalem according to the custom of the heathen, and forsook the holy covenant, and were dedicated to do mischief.

Now when Antiochus established his kingdom, he sought to reign over Egypt, that he might have the dominion over two realms. Therefore he went to Egypt with a great multitude — with chariots, and elephants, and horsemen, and a great navy — and he made war against Ptolemy, king of Egypt. Ptolemy was afraid of him, and fled; and many were wounded to death.

After Antiochus had smitten Egypt, he went up against Israel and Jerusalem with a great multitude, and entered proudly into the sanctuary, and took away the golden altar, and the candlestick of light, and all its vessels. And he took the table of the shewbread, and the pouring vessels, and the vials, and the censers of gold, and the veil, and the crowns, and the golden ornaments that were before the temple. He took also the silver and gold and precious vessels which he found in the hidden treasury. And when he had taken all away, he made a great massacre.

There was great mourning in Israel, in every place where they went. The princes and elders mourned; every bridegroom took up a lament; and the bride in her bridal chamber sorrowed.

After two years had expired Antiochus sent his collector of tribute to the cities of Judah; and he came to Jerusalem with a great multitude, and spoke words of peace to them in deceit; for when they believed him, he suddenly fell upon the city and killed many people. And after he had plundered the city, he set it on fire, and pulled down its houses and walls on every side. But the women and the children they took captive, and they took possession of the cattle.

Then they rebuilt the city of David with a great and strong wall, and with mighty towers, and made it a stronghold for themselves. They brought into it wicked men, and fortified themselves in it. They stored it also with armor and food, and hoarded there all the spoils of Judah. Thus Jerusalem became an evil adversary to Israel. They shed innocent blood on every side of the sanctuary, and defiled it. The people of Jerusalem had fled because of them, and the city became the habitation of strangers, and strange to those who had been born in it. Her sanctuary was laid waste, her feasts were turned into mourning, her Sabbaths into reproach, her honor into contempt.

Moreover King Antiochus sent a decree throughout his whole kingdom that all under his rule must become one people, and each one abandon his own laws. The heathen agreed to obey the decree of the king; and also many of the Israelites consented to accept the king's religion, and sacrificed to idols, and made their souls abominable with all manner of profanation. And whoever would not obey the decree of the king, the king ordered that he should die.

Now in the one hundred and forty-fifth year of the Greek rule, on the fifteenth day of the month of Kislau, the Greeks built idol-altars throughout the cities of Judah. And wherever a man was found with any book of the covenant, the decree of the king was that he should be put to death. And thus did they every month by this authority, and killed as many as were found.

On the twenty-fifth day of each month they sacrificed upon the idol-altar. And on that day they put to death certain women who had caused their children to be circumcised, and slew the infants and those who had circumcised them.

Yet many in Israel were fully resolved to die rather than to profane the holy covenant; and so they died.

And there was great wrath upon Israel.

2     In those days arose Mattathias, the son of John, son of Simeon, a priest of the sons of Joarib, who dwelt in Modin. And he had five sons: Joannan (called Caddis); Simon (called Thassi); Judas (called Maccabeus); Eleazer (called Avaran); and Jonathan (called Apphus).

When Mattathias saw the blasphemies committed in Judah and Jerusalem, he said, "Woe that I was born to see this misery of my people and the holy city! Her temple has become like a man without glory. Her vessels are carried away into captivity, her infants are slain in the streets, her young men with the sword of the enemy! Behold, our sanctuary, our beauty and our glory, is laid waste and profaned by the stranger. To what end shall we live any longer?" Then Mattathias and his sons rent their clothes, and put on sackcloth, and mourned.

In the meanwhile the king's officers, such as compelled the people to revolt, came into Modin, and summoned Mattathias and his sons, and many of Israel, to make them sacrifice. Then the king's officers said to Mattathias, "You are a leader and a great man in this city, strengthened with sons and brothers. Therefore you come first to fulfill the king's command, so that you and your house shall be numbered among the king's friends, and you and your children honored with silver and gold and many rewards."

Mattathias answered in a loud voice, "Though all the nations under the king's dominion obey him and give consent to his commands, yet will I and my sons and my brothers walk in the covenant of our fathers. We will not heed the king's words to depart from our religion, either to the right hand or to the left."

Now when he had finished speaking these words, there came forward one of the Jews in the sight of all to sacrifice on the altar according to the king's command. And when Mattathias saw this thing, he was inflamed with zeal; neither could he forbear to show his anger. Wherefore he ran and slew the man upon the altar. He also killed the king's commissioner who compelled men to sacrifice to idols, and pulled down the altar. Thus dealt Mattathias zealously for the law of God.

And Mattathias called out through the city in a loud voice, "Whoever is zealous of the law and maintains the covenant, let him follow me!"

So he and his sons fled to the mountains, and left all they possessed in the city. And many who sought justice went down into the wilderness to dwell there — they, and their children, and their wives, and their cattle.

When the king's officers at Jerusalem were told that certain men who had broken the king's commandment had gone down into the secret places of the wilderness, they pursued them with a great army; and having overtaken them, fought against them on the Sabbath day. But first the officers said to them, "Let that which you have done so far suffice. Come out and obey the command of the king, and you shall live."

They answered, "We will not come out, nor will we obey the king's command to profane the Sabbath day. Let us die in our innocence; heaven and earth shall testify for us that you put us to death wrongfully."

So the king's men went against them in battle on the Sabbath, and slew them with their wives and children, to the number of a thousand people.

When Mattathias and his friends learned of this, they mourned, and they said to one another, "If we all do as our brothers have done, and do not fight for our lives and laws against the heathen, they will quickly root us out of the earth." And at that time they agreed, saying, "Whoever comes to make battle with us on the Sabbath day, we will fight against him. We will not die like our brothers, who were murdered in their places of refuge."

Then came to Mattathias a company of Assideans, who were mighty men in Israel, devoted to the law, and who had fled from persecution. So they joined their forces, and struck sinful men in their anger and wicked men in their wrath. Mattathias and his friends pulled down the idol-altars; and any uncircumcised children they found within the borders of Israel, they circumcised. So they recovered the law out of the hand of the heathen and out of the hand of the king; nor did they permit the sinner to triumph.

When the time drew near for Mattathias to die, he said to his sons, "Be zealous for the law, and give your lives for the covenant of your fathers. Remember the valiant acts of our forefathers in their time; so shall you also receive honor. Fear not the words of the sinful man. Today he shall be lifted up; and tomorrow he shall have returned to the dust, and his thought come to nothing. Therefore, my sons, be valiant. Show yourselves in behalf of the law, for by it shall you obtain glory.

"Behold, I know that your brother Simon is a man of good judgment; listen to him always; he shall be as a father to you. As for Judas Maccabeus, he has been mighty and strong from his youth. Let him be your captain and fight the battle of the people. Gather about you all those who observe the law and avenge the wrong of your people."

So he blessed them; and he died; and his sons buried him in the sepulcher of his fathers at Modin; and all Israel lamented for him.

3    Then his son Judas Maccabeus rose up in his stead. And all his brothers helped him, and so did all those who had held with his father. And they fought with cheerfulness the battle of Israel. Judas put on a breastplate, and girt himself in warlike harness, and he went into battle, protecting the host with his sword. In his acts he was like a lion, and like a lion's whelp roaring for his prey. For he pursued the wicked, and sought them out, and destroyed those who vexed his people. The wicked shrank in fear of him, and the workers of iniquity were troubled, because salvation prospered in his hand. He also grieved many kings, and made Jacob glad with his acts. He went through the cities of Judah, destroying the ungodly and turning wrath away from Israel; so that he was renowned to the utmost part of the earth, and he gathered around him such as were ready to die.

Now when Seron, a prince of the army of Syria, heard that Judas had gathered about him a company of the faithful to go out with him to war, he said to himself, "I will gain honor in the kingdom if I fight Judas and his men, who despise the king's command." So he went up, with a mighty host to help him, to be avenged upon the children of Israel.

And when he came near the ascent of Bethhoron, Judas went out to meet him with a small company. And the men, when they saw the army coming to meet them, said to Judas, "Being so few, how shall we be able to fight against so great and so strong a multitude, seeing that we are ready to faint from fasting all the day?"

And Judas answered, "With God in heaven it is all one to save with a great multitude or a small company. For the victory of battle depends not on the numbers of the army, since strength comes from heaven. They come against us in great pride and wickedness to destroy us and our wives and our children. But we fight for our lives and our laws. Therefore the Lord himself will overthrow them before us. And as for you, be not afraid of them!"

As he left off speaking, he leaped suddenly upon the enemy, and Seron and his army were overthrown before him. Judas and his men pursued them along the descent of Bethhoron to the plain, where were slain about eight hundred of the foe, and the remainder fled into the land of the Philistines.

Then the dread of Judas and his brothers began to fall upon the nations round about them; for his fame reached the king, and all the nations talked of the battles of Judas.

When Antiochus heard these things, he was full of indignation, and he gathered together all the forces of his realm. He opened his treasury and paid his soldiers for a year, commanding them to be ready whenever he should need them. And he appointed Lysias, a nobleman, as overseer of the affairs of the king from the river Euphrates to the borders of Egypt. Moreover, he delivered to him half of the forces, and elephants, and charged him to send an army to destroy and root out the strength of Israel; and to put strangers in all their quarters, and divide the land by lot.

Then Lysias chose Ptolemy and Nicanor and Gorgias, three mighty men of the king's friends, and with them he sent forty thousand footmen, and seven thousand horsemen, to go to the land of Judah to destroy it, as the king had commanded.

So they went forth with all their power, and pitched their camp near Emmaus in the country of the plain. The merchants of the country heard of their coming, and they went to the camp with much silver and gold to buy as slaves the children of Israel, who were about to be conquered.

When Judas and his brothers saw the forces encamped upon their borders, they said one to another, "Let us restore the decayed estate of our people, and let us fight for our people and the sanctuary."

Then the congregation gathered, that they might be ready for battle, and that they might pray and ask mercy and compassion. They assembled at Maspha, which was the place where they had prayed in times of old in Israel; and the congregation fasted and put on sackcloth. Then they cried out toward heaven, "Your sanctuary is trodden down and profaned, and your priests are brought low. Behold, the heathen have assembled to destroy us. How shall we be able to stand up against them, except you, O God, be our help?"

Then they sounded the trumpets. And after this Judas appointed captains over his forces. But as for those who were building houses, or had just married, or were planting vineyards, or were afraid, those he commanded to return to their home, according to the law. The camp removed, and pitched on the south side of Emmaus. And Judas said to his men, "Arm yourselves, and be in readiness against the morning, that you may fight these nations who have assembled to destroy us. For it is better for us to die in battle than to see the calamities of our people and our sanctuary. As is the will of God in heaven, so let it be!"

*4-16*    Then Gorgias took five thousand footmen and a thousand of the best horsemen, and went out of the camp at night, that he might rush in upon the camp of the Jews and strike them suddenly. And the men from the fortress were his guides. When Judas learned of it, he himself left the camp and the valiant men with him, that he might strike the king's army, which was at Emmaus, while yet their forces were dispersed.

Gorgias came at night into the camp of Judas, and when he found no man there, he said, "These fellows flee from us"; and he sought them in the mountains.

But as soon as it was day, Judas showed himself in the plain with three thousand men, who nevertheless had neither armor nor swords. And they saw the camp of the heathen, strong and well harnessed, and surrounded by horsemen expert in war.

Judas said to his men, "Fear not their numbers; neither be afraid of their attack. Remember how our fathers were saved when Pharaoh pursued them. Perhaps the Lord will have mercy upon us and destroy this enemy before us this day, that the heathen may know there is one who delivers and saves Israel."

So they joined in battle, and the enemy fled into the plain.

Then Judas said to his people, "Be not greedy for the spoils, inasmuch as there is a battle before us, and Gorgias and his host are nearby in the mountain. Stand now against our enemies and overcome them, and after that you may boldly take the spoils."

As Judas was still speaking, there appeared part of the enemy from the mountain. And when they perceived that the Jews had put their host to flight, and were burning the tents, they were afraid. And seeing the host of Judas in the plain ready to fight, they fled into the land of strangers. Then Judas returned to the tents, where they found much gold, and silver, and blue silk, and purple of the sea, and great riches.

After this they went home, and sang a song of thanksgiving, and praised the Lord in heaven because his mercy endures forever.

Thus Israel had a great deliverance that day.

Now those of Gorgias' men who had escaped went to Lysias and told him what had happened. And when he heard of it he was confounded and discouraged that such things as the king had commanded him had not come to pass. In the year following, Lysias gathered together sixty thousand choice footmen, and five thousand horsemen, and marched to subdue Judas and his men. He came to Idumea, and pitched his camp at Bethsura, where Judas met him with ten thousand men.

And when Judas saw the mighty army, he prayed, "Blessed are you, O Savior of Israel! Let this army be confounded in their power and their horsemen, and shut them up in the hand of your people Israel. Cast them down with the sword of those who love you, and let all those who know your name praise you with thanksgiving."

So they joined battle, and there were slain of the host of Lysias about five thousand men.

When Lysias saw his army put to flight, and how Judas' men were ready either to live or to die valiantly, he returned to Antiochia.

And Judas said to his brothers, "Behold, our enemies are discomfited. Let us go up to cleanse and dedicate the sanctuary."

Upon this all his host went up to Mount Zion. But when they saw the sanctuary desolate, and the altar profaned, and the gates burned, and shrubs growing in the courts as if in a forest, they fell upon the ground in a lament.

Then Judas appointed certain men to fight against those who were in the fortress, until he had cleansed the sanctuary. And he chose priests to cleanse it, and to carry out the defiled stones. They pulled down the altar which was profaned, and built a new altar of whole stones, according to the law. They made up the sanctuary, and the things that were within the temple, and hallowed the courts. They made also new holy vessels, and into the temple they brought the candlestick, and the altar, and the table. And upon the altar they burned incense; and they lighted the lamps that they might give light in the temple; and they set the loaves of holy bread upon the table, and spread out the veils, and finished all the work which they had undertaken.

Now on the twenty-fifth day of the ninth month, which is called the month of Kislau — in the one hundred and forty-eighth year — they rose early and offered a sacrifice according to the law upon the new altar which they had built. And it was dedicated with singing, and citherns, and harps, and cymbals. Then the people worshiped, and praised God in heaven. And they kept the dedication of the altar eight days, and offered the burnt offering with gladness, and sacrificed the sacrifice of deliverance with praise. They decked the front of the temple with crowns of gold and with shields, and the gates and the chambers they rebuilt, and hung new doors upon them. Thus was there great gladness among the people.

Moreover Judas and his brothers, with the whole congregation, ordained that the days of the dedication of the altar should be kept in their season from year to year for the space of eight days with mirth and with gladness.[1]

[1] See I MACCABEES, Chapters 5-16, in Notes and Excisions.

# THE BOOK OF JOB
## *The Great Debate*

❡ The prophecies of the prophets and their poetry dwell on the theme of the justice of the Lord, and the punishment of those who depart from the covenant to do evil. From the prophet Jeremiah we hear the sudden faint plaint that he was afflicted, though he had done no harm. And this theme, that suffering is not always punishment for sin, and that those who do evil often prosper, is developed in full symphonic length in the great epic The Book of Job.

The book begins and ends with a prose folktale, told in stark and simple language. The body of the book, presented in unequaled poetry, falls into four parts. First comes Job's lament, stating the case of his fate and calling God to trial. Then follows a debate between Job and the three friends who have come to console him in his hour of trouble. His friends insist that he must have sinned or he would not suffer, and Job vehemently denies the charge. Then Job soliloquizes on the futility of the debate. And finally God's overwhelming reply surges out of the whirl-wind, humbling Job and silencing his plaint, but vindicating him of his friends' charge. The epic ends as it began, simply and calmly, in the al-most traditional folktale manner.

Between the central debate and Job's soliloquy appear four speeches by a young man named Elihu (which most scholars agree must be an in-terpolation, and which do not rise to the heights of the rest of the poetry of the epic); and these speeches are preceded by another interpolation (Chapter 28), a magnificent poem on man's search for wisdom, which, however, has no relation to the rest of the Book of Job.

So highly was the Book of Job regarded by the ancients that its author-ship was ascribed to Moses.

The lofty imagery in this book, and the scope of its theme, have caused many scholars and literary critics to call it the Matterhorn and the Everest of prophetic poetry. ⟨[

## Job's Misfortunes

**1-2**    There was a man in the land of Uz whose name was Job; and he was just and upright, one who feared God and shunned evil. There were born to him seven sons and three daughters, and he owned seven thousand sheep, three thousand camels, five hundred yoke of oxen, five hundred she-asses, and a very great household; so that this man was the greatest of all the men in the east.

His sons held a feast in their houses, each one upon his day, and invited their three sisters to eat and to drink with them. And when the days of their feasting had gone the round, Job would rise early in the morning and offer sacrifices according to their number, for Job said in his heart, "It may be that my sons have sinned, and renounced God in their hearts." Thus did Job continually.

Now there came a day when the sons of God presented themselves before the Lord, and Satan came also among them. And the Lord said to Satan, "Whence come you?" Then Satan answered the Lord, "From roaming to and fro over the earth." And the Lord said, "Have you observed my servant Job? For there is none like him, so perfect and upright a man, who fears God and shuns evil." Then Satan answered the Lord, "Does Job fear God for nought? Have you not made a hedge about him, and about his house, and about all that he has on every side? You have blessed the work of his hands, and his substance has increased in the land. But put out your hand now and touch all that he has, and he will renounce you to your face." And the Lord said to Satan, "Behold, all that he has is in your power. Only upon his person you may not lay your hand."

So Satan left the presence of the Lord.

And it fell upon a day, when Job's sons and daughters were eating and drinking wine at their eldest brother's house, that a messenger came to Job and said, "The oxen were plowing, and the asses feeding beside them, when the Sabeans fell upon them and took them away and slew the servants, and I alone have escaped to tell you."

While he was speaking, there came another messenger and said, "God's fire has fallen from heaven and consumed the sheep and the servants, and I alone have escaped to tell you." He was still speaking when there arrived another messenger and said, "The Chaldeans came in three bands, and fell upon the camels and seized them, and slew the servants with a sword, and I alone have escaped to tell you."

While he was still speaking, there came also another messenger and said, "Your sons and your daughters were eating and drinking wine at the home of their eldest brother; and behold, there came a great wind from the wilderness that struck the four corners of the house, and it fell upon the young people, and they are all dead; and I alone have escaped to tell you."

Then Job arose, and rent his mantle, and shaved his head, and he fell upon the ground and said:

"Naked did I come out of my mother's womb, and naked shall I return; the Lord gave and the Lord has taken away; blessed be the name of the Lord."

In all this Job did not sin, or charge God with injustice.

There was another day when the sons of God presented themselves before the Lord, and Satan came also among them. The Lord said to Satan, "Whence did you come?" And Satan answered, "From roaming to and fro over the earth." The Lord said to Satan, "Have you observed my servant Job? There is none like him, so perfect and upright a man, who fears God and shuns evil. And still he holds fast his integrity, although you moved me against him to destroy him without cause." Satan answered, "All that a man has will he give for his life. Put out your hand now, and touch his bone and his flesh, and he will renounce you to your face." The Lord said to Satan, "Behold, he is in your hand; only spare his life."

So Satan left the presence of the Lord, and afflicted Job with boils from the sole of his foot to the crown of his head.

Job sat down among the ashes and scraped himself with a potsherd; and his wife said to him, "Do you still hold fast to your faith? Curse God, and die." But he answered, "You speak as one of the foolish women would speak. Shall we receive good at the hand of God, and shall we not receive evil?"

And in all this Job did not sin with his lips.

Now when Job's three friends heard of the evil that had befallen him, they came each from his own place: Eliphaz the Temanite, and Bildad the Shuhite, and Zophar the Naamathite; and they arranged to meet and come together to comfort him. When they lifted their eyes and saw him from afar, they did not recognize him. They wept aloud and rent each one his mantle, and sprinkled dust upon their heads. Then they sat down with him upon the ground for seven days and seven nights, and none spoke a word, for they saw that his grief was very great.

## Job's Lament

3  Then Job opened his mouth and spoke: "Perish the day on which I was born, and the night on which it was said, 'There is a man-child conceived!' May that day be darkness; let not God regard it from above, neither let the sun shine upon it. May darkness and the shadow of death claim it for their own; may a cloud dwell upon it; may all that makes the day black terrify it. Let it not be joined to the days of the year, or be counted in the number of the months.

"Lo, let that night be desolate; may no joyful voice be heard in it. May the stars of its twilight be dark; let it wait for light, but may none come; let it never behold the dawn, because it did not shut up the doors of my mother's womb, and hid not sorrow from my eyes.

"Why did I not die at birth? For now I would have lain still and been quiet; I should have slept, and had been at rest. Or as an untimely birth I had not been; as infants who never saw light. There the wicked cease from troubling, and there the weary are at rest. There the prisoners are at ease together; they hear not the voice of the oppressor. The small and great are there alike, and the servant is free from his master.

"Why is light given to him who is in misery, and life to the bitter in soul, who longs for death and seeks it more than hidden treasure? Why is light given to a man whom God has hedged in? For my sighs come with my food, and my groans with the water that I drink. For the thing which I feared has come upon me; that of which I was afraid has overtaken me. I am not at ease, neither have I rest, nor am I quiet; yet trouble continues to come."

## The Speech of Eliphaz

4-5    Then Eliphaz the Temanite spoke and said, "If we try to reason with you, will you be grieved? Behold, you have instructed many, and strengthened weak hands. Your words have upheld him who was falling, and gave firmness to feeble knees. But now when it has come upon you, you grow faint; it touches you, and you are troubled. Is this your confidence, your hope, your fear of God? Have the innocent ever perished? Or have the righteous ever been cut off? As I have seen it, they who plow guilt and sow trouble reap sorrow. By the wrath of God they perish, and by the breath of his anger they are consumed. The teeth of the young lions are broken, and the old lion perishes for lack of prey.

"Now a thing was secretly brought to me, and my ear received a whisper of it. In thoughts from the visions of the night, when deep sleep falls on men, fear came upon me, and trembling which made all my bones shake. Then a spirit passed before my face, and I heard a voice saying, 'Shall mortal man be more just than God? Shall a man be purer than his Maker? Behold, he puts no trust even in his servants, and he charges his angels with error. How much less trust has he in those who dwell in houses of clay, whose foundation is dust, who are crushed as the moth? Between morning and evening they are destroyed; they perish forever without any noticing it. They die, but without wisdom.'

"Call now if there are any who will answer you. To which of the holy ones will you turn? As the foolish man is killed by anger, so does jealousy slay the dolt. Affliction does not arise from the dust, neither does trouble spring out of the ground; but man is born to trouble, even as the sparks fly upward. As for me, I would seek God, and to God would I commit my cause. For he does great things and unsearchable, marvelous things without number. He gives rain to the earth and sends water upon the fields. He sets up on high those who are low; those who mourn he lifts up with his help. He frustrates the crafty, so that their hands cannot accomplish their devices. He catches the cunning in their own wiles, and the counsel of the schemers is brought to a sudden end, they grope at noonday as in the night; but he saves the poor from the hand of the mighty.

"Happy is the man whom God corrects; therefore despise not the chastening of the Almighty. For he makes sore, and he binds up; he wounds, and his hands make whole. He will deliver you from six troubles, and in seven no evil shall touch you. In famine he will redeem you from death,

473

and in war from the power of the sword. And you shall come to your grave at a full age, as a shock of grain comes in its season."

## *Job's Reply*

6-7    Job answered and said, "Oh that my grief were weighed, and my calamity laid in the balances! For now it would be heavier than the sands of the sea. The arrows of the Almighty are within me, and my spirit drinks their poison; the terrors of God are arrayed against me. Does the wild ass bray when he has grass? Or does the ox low over his fodder? Can the tasteless be eaten without salt? Or is there any taste in the white of an egg? What my soul refuses to touch, that has become my loathsome food. Oh that I might have my request, and that God would grant me the thing that I long for! Even that it would please God to crush me; that he would loose his hand and cut me off! What is my strength, that I should hope? And what is my end, that I should be patient?

"To him who is afflicted his friends should show kindness, even if he forsakes the fear of the Almighty. But my brothers are treacherous as a torrent. You see my misfortune and are afraid. Did I say, 'Give me of your substance'? Or, 'Deliver me from the enemy's hand'? Or, 'Redeem me from the hand of oppressors'? Teach me, and I will hold my tongue; and cause me to understand in what I have erred. How forcible are upright words! But what does your arguing prove? You would cast lots over the fatherless, and dig a pit for your friend. Look upon me! Surely it is evident to you that I do not lie. Return, I pray you, let there be no injustice! Return, for my cause is righteous. Is there injustice on my tongue? And cannot my palate discern perversity?

"Is there not an appointed time to man upon earth? Are not his days like the days of a hireling? As a servant who longs for the evening, and as a hireling who looks for his wages, so am I given months of emptiness, and wearisome nights are apportioned to me. When I lie down, I say, 'When shall I arise, and the night be gone?' I am full of tossings to the dawning of the day. My flesh is clothed with worms and clods of dust; my skin is broken and loathsome; my days are swifter than a weaver's shuttle, and are spent without hope.

"Oh, remember that my life is as the wind; my eyes shall no more see good. As the cloud is consumed and vanishes, so is he who goes down to the grave. Therefore I will not restrain my mouth; I will speak in the anguish of my spirit; I will complain in the bitterness of my soul. When I think, 'My bed shall comfort me, my couch shall ease my complaint,' then you frighten me with dreams and terrify me with visions, so that my soul chooses death rather than these my bones. I loathe my life; I would not live forever. Let me alone, for my days are vanity.

"What is man, that you should magnify him; that you should set your heart upon him; that you should visit him every morning and try him every moment? If I have sinned, what shall I do, O Watcher of men? Why have you set me as your target, so that I am a burden to myself? Why do you not pardon my transgression and take away my iniquity? For now I shall lie down in the dust; and you will seek me, but I will not be there."

## Bildad's Speech

8 Then answered Bildad the Shuhite and said, "How long will you speak such things, and the words of your mouth be like a strong wind? Does God pervert justice? If your children have sinned against him, he has cast them away for their transgressions. If you would seek God betimes and make your supplication to the Almighty, if you were pure and upright, surely now he would make the habitation of your righteousness prosperous. Can the rush grow without water? While it is yet green, and not cut down, it withers before any other plant. So are the paths of all who forget God; he shall lean upon his house, but it shall not stand; he shall hold it fast, but it shall not endure.

"But God will not cast away a perfect man; neither will he help the evildoers. He will yet fill your mouth with laughter, and your lips with rejoicing. They who hate you will be clothed in shame; and the dwelling place of the wicked shall come to nought."

## Job's Reply

9-10 Then answered Job, "But how should man debate with God? If he contend with him, he cannot answer God one of a thousand. For God is wise in heart and mighty in strength. Who can harden himself against him and prosper? He who removes the mountains and overturns them in his anger, he who can shake the earth out of its place and make its pillars tremble, who commands the sun and it rises not, and seals up the stars — lo, he goes by me and I see him not. He passes, but I perceive him not. Behold, he takes away; who can hinder him? Who will say to him, 'What is this you do?' How shall I answer him, or choose my words to reason with him? Though I were innocent, yet would I not know how to plead, for I would be making supplication to my judge. If I had called and he had answered me, yet would I not believe that he listened to my voice. For he can break me with a tempest, and multiply my wounds without cause. He will not suffer me to take my breath, but fills me with bitterness. If I speak of strength, lo, he is strong; and if of judgment, who shall appoint me a time to plead? If I justify myself, my own mouth shall condemn me. Though I were perfect, my own words would prove me perverse. Therefore I say, 'It is all one; he destroys the perfect and the wicked.'

"The earth is given into the hand of the wicked. He covers the faces of the judges; if it is not he, who then is it? For he is not a man, as I am, that I should answer him, that we should come together in judgment. Neither is there any arbiter between us, who might lay his hand upon us both. Let him take his rod away from me, and let not his terror make me afraid; then would I speak and not fear. For my soul is weary.

"I will speak in the bitterness of my soul. I will say to God, 'Show me why you contend with me. Does it seem good to you that you should oppress me, that you should despise the work of your hands and shine upon the counsel of the wicked? Have you eyes of flesh, and see as man sees? Are your days numbered as the days of man, or your years as man's years, that you search out my sin, although you know that I am not wicked? Your hands have fashioned me, yet you seek to destroy me. You have clothed me with skin and flesh, and knit me together with bones and sinews. You have granted me life and preserved my spirit. Yet these things you hide in your heart. If I sin you watch me, but will not acquit me of my iniquity. If I am wicked, woe to me! And if I am innocent, yet I cannot lift up my head, being filled with shame, seeing my affliction.

" 'I am full of confusion! You hunt me like a fierce lion. You renew your witnesses against me and increase your indignation. Why have you brought me forth out of the womb? It were better if no eye had seen me, if I were carried from the womb to the grave. Are not my days few? Cease, then, and let me alone, that I may take comfort a little before I go whence I shall not return, to the land of darkness and the shadow of death!' "

476

## Zophar's Speech

**11**      Then Zophar the Naamathite spoke and said, "Oh that God would
speak, and open his lips against you, that he might show you the
hidden wisdom! But you should know that God exacts of you less than
your iniquity deserves. Can you by searching find out God, and reach to
the limits of the Almighty? If he calls for judgment, who can hinder him?
For he knows vain men, and when he sees wickedness, shall he not consider it? If you stretch out your hands toward him, and let not injustice
dwell in your tents, surely then you will be steadfast and shall not fear.
You will forget your misery, and remember it only as waters that pass
away. You will shine, and be as the morning. You will be secure in your
hope, and rest in safety. When you lie down, none shall make you
afraid; yes, many will respect you. But the eyes of the wicked will fail
them; they will find no refuge, and their only hope will be to die."

## Job's Reply

**12-14**      And Job answered, "No doubt but you are the people, and wisdom shall die with you! But I have understanding as well as you.
I have become as one mocked by his neighbor, the just man laughed to
scorn. In the thought of him who is at ease there is contempt for the un-
fortunate whose foot slips. The tents of robbers prosper, and they who
provoke God are secure. Ask the beasts and they shall teach you, and the
birds of the air and they shall tell you. Or speak to the earth and it shall
teach you, and the fishes of the sea shall declare to you, that the hand of
the Lord has wrought all this — that in his hand is the soul of every living
thing, and the breath of all mankind. With him is wisdom and might; he
has counsel and understanding. Behold, he breaks down, and it cannot be
built again. He withholds the waters, and they dry up. Again he sends
them out, and they flood the earth. The deceived and the deceiver are
his. He leads counselors astray and makes fools of judges. He loosens the
bonds of kings and binds their loins with the waist-cloth. He removes the
speech of the self-confident and takes away the understanding of the
elders. He pours contempt upon princes and shames the strong with
weakness. He increases the nations, then destroys them. He takes away
the heart of the chiefs of the people of the earth, and makes them wander

aimlessly. They grope in the dark without light, and he makes them stagger like drunken men.

"Lo, my eye has seen all this, my ear has understood it. What you know, I know also. Surely I would speak to the Almighty, and I desire to reason with God. But you are forgers of lies, you are all physicians of no value. Oh that you would hold your peace, and your silence were your wisdom! Hear now my reasoning, and listen to the pleadings of my lips. Will you speak wickedly for God? And talk deceitfully for him? Will you contend for God? Hold your peace. Let me speak, and let come on me what may:

"Though he slay me, yet will I trust in him; but I will maintain my ways before him. This will be my salvation, for a faithless man shall not come before him. Listen diligently to my words, and let my declaration be in your ears. Behold now, who is he who will contend with me? For if I hold my tongue, I shall die. Only do not two things to me; then will I not hide myself from your face. Withdraw your hand from me, and let not your terror make me afraid. Then call, and I will answer; or let me speak, and answer me. Make known to me my transgressions and my sin. Wherefore do you hide your face and treat me as your enemy? Will you pursue a fallen leaf or dry stubble?

"Man, born of woman, is of few days and full of trouble. He comes forth like a flower and is cut down. He flees as a shadow that cannot endure. Upon such a one do you open your eyes to bring him into judgment with yourself? His days are determined. You have appointed his bounds which he may not pass. There is hope for a tree, if it be cut down, that it will sprout again, and through the scent of water it will bud and put forth new boughs. But when a man dies and wastes away, where is he? Till the heavens be no more, he will not awake or be roused out of his sleep. Oh that you would hide me in my grave until your wrath is past!"

## Eliphaz Speaks a Second Time

15    Then answered Eliphaz, "Your mouth utters your guilt, for you choose the tongue of the crafty. Your own words condemn you, and not I; your own lips testify against you. Are you the first man who was born? Were you created before the hills? Have you heard God's secret? What know you that we know not? What do you understand which is not known to us? Are the consolations of God small in your eyes? Why does

your heart carry you away, that you turn against God and let such words leave your mouth? What is man that he should be innocent, and he who is born of woman that he should be righteous? Behold, he puts no trust even in his holy ones; even the heavens are not clean in his sight. How much more abominable is man, who drinks iniquity like water? Let him not trust in vanity, deceiving himself; for vanity shall be his recompense. It shall be accomplished before his time, and his branch shall not be green. He will shed his unripe grapes as the vine, and cast off his flower as the olive. For the congregation of the profane shall be barren, and fire shall consume the tents of the bribers.

"They conceive mischief, they incubate deceit, and they give birth to wickedness."

## Job Answers Eliphaz

16-17    Then Job answered, "If your soul were in my soul's stead, I could heap up words against you and shake my head at you. But I would strengthen you with my words, and the solace of my lips should lessen your grief. Though I speak, my grief is not allayed; and though I forbear, am I eased? How weary I am now! God has torn me in his wrath and persecuted me. He hast cast me into the hands of the wicked. I was at ease, but he has broken me asunder; he has taken me by my neck and dashed me to pieces, and set me up as his target. His archers surround me. On my eyelids is the shadow of death, although there is no violence in my hands, and my prayer is pure. Even now, behold, my witness is in heaven, and he who vouches for me is on high. My friends scorn me. But my eyes pour out tears to God. Would that one could plead for a man with God, as one pleads for his neighbor!

"My spirit is broken, my days are extinct, the grave is ready for me. My eyes are dim with sorrow, and all my members as a shadow. Upright men shall be astonished at this, and the innocent shall stir up against the hypocrite. But you, all of you, return; for I cannot find one wise man among you. My days are past, my purposes are broken, even as the thoughts of my heart. I have said to corruption, 'You are my father,' and to the worm, 'You are my mother and my sister.' Where then is my hope? Will it go down with me to the grave?"

## Bildad Speaks a Second Time

18     Then answered Bildad, "How long will you make snares of words? Consider, and then we will speak. Why are we accounted as beasts, and become unclean in your sight? Shall the earth be forsaken for your sake? And the rock removed out of its place? Surely the light shall be darkened in the tent of the wicked, and his lamp be put out. Terrors shall make him afraid on every side. Calamity shall be ready when he halts. His roots will dry up underneath him; and above, his branch will be cut off. His name and remembrance will perish from the earth. He will be driven from light into darkness, and out of the world they shall chase him. He shall have neither son nor grandson among his people, nor any remaining wherever he lives. Surely such is the fate of the wicked, and the destiny of those who know not God."

## Job Answers Bildad

19     Job answered and said, "How long will you vex my soul and crush me with words? Ten times have you reproached me, yet are not ashamed to return to deal harshly with me. If, indeed, I have erred, does not my error remain with myself? If indeed you must magnify yourselves and reproach me, remember it was God who caused my downfall, and enclosed me in his net. Behold, I cry out, 'Violence!' But no one answers. I cry for help, but there is no judgment! He has fenced me in so that I cannot pass. He has stripped me of my glory and taken the crown from my head. My hope he has plucked up like a tree. Those who once dwelt in my house regard me as a stranger; I am an alien in their sight. My spirit is strange even to my wife. Street urchins despise me. My close friends abhor me, and those whom I loved have turned against me.

"Have pity upon me, O my friends, for the hand of God has touched me! Oh that my words were written down, that they were inscribed in a book, that with an iron pen and lead they were engraved in the rock forever! For I know that my redeemer lives, and that he shall stand up upon the earth; and I shall see God."

## Zophar Speaks a Second Time

20    Then answered Zophar, "Know you not this of old, that since
        ever man was placed upon the earth, the triumph of the wicked
is short-lived, and the joy of the godless but for a moment? Though his
ambition mount to the heavens, and his head reach the clouds, yet shall
he perish like his own dung. Those who have seen him shall say, 'Where
is he?' He shall fly away as a dream, and none shall find him. Though
wickedness be sweet in his mouth, though he hide it under his tongue,
yet his bowels shall turn it into the gall of asps within him. That which
he labored for shall he restore; according to the substance he has gotten
shall he make restitution. Because he has oppressed the poor, and violently taken away the house which he did not build, his prosperity shall
not endure. In the fullness of his abundance he shall be in straits; and
the hand of everyone in misery shall be lifted against him. God will cast
the fury of his wrath upon him, and rain it upon him while he is eating. He
shall flee from the iron weapon, and the brass bow shall strike him down.
The increase of his house shall depart; his goods shall flow away in the
day of wrath. For such is the portion of the wicked man from God, and
the heritage appointed to him."

## Job Answers Zophar

21    Job answered and said, "Suffer me to speak; and after I have
        spoken, you may mock me. Hear me, and be astonished. For even
when I think of it I am terrified, and horror takes hold of my flesh. Why do
the wicked live, grow old, and mighty in power? Their children are established in their sight, and their offspring before their eyes. Their houses
are safe from fear, and the rod of God is not upon them. Their bull gen-
ders and fails not; their cow calves and does not cast her calf. They send
out their little ones like a flock, and their children dance to the timbrel
and the harp, and rejoice in the sound of the pipe. They spend their days
in prosperity. That is why they say to God, 'Depart from us! For we desire not the knowledge of your ways. What is the Almighty that
we should serve him? And what would it profit us if we were to pray to
him?'

"How often is the lamp of the wicked put out? And how often does calamity befall them? God, who distributes sorrow in his anger, so that men are as stubble before the wind and as chaff the storm carries away, does he store up the punishment of the wicked for his children? Let him punish the wicked himself, that they may know their guilt. Let their own eyes see their destruction, and drink the wrath of the Almighty. For what regard has the wicked about his house after him, when the number of his months is suddenly cut off? One dies in his full strength, being wholly at ease and content. And another dies in bitterness of soul, never having tasted of good. Yet they shall lie down in the dust, and the worms shall devour them both. Behold, I know your thoughts. For you say, 'Where is the house in which the wicked dwelt?' Ask those who go by the way. Have they not told you that the wicked man is spared disaster? Who shall rebuke him for what he has done? He is carried to the grave, and a watch is kept over his tomb. Even the clods of the valley are sweet to him, and many men are drawn to honor his memory."

## Eliphaz Speaks a Third Time

22    Then Eliphaz answered Job and said, "Is it any pleasure to the Almighty that you are righteous? Or is it gain to him that you make your ways perfect? Is it for your fear of him that he reproves you? Is it not that your wickedness is great, and your iniquities without number? For you must have taken a pledge from your brother for nought, and stripped the naked of their clothing. You must have withheld water from the thirsty and bread from the hungry. You must have sent the widows away empty, and broken the arms of the fatherless. That is why snares are round about you, and sudden fear besets you in darkness, so that you cannot see, as one covered by a flood. Behold the stars, how high they are! Is not God in the height of heaven above them? Receive, I pray you, the law from his mouth, and cherish his words in your heart! If you return to the Almighty, and put iniquity far from your tents, then the Almighty shall be your treasure. For then shall you delight in the Almighty, and lift up your face to God. You shall pray to him and he shall hear you; and light shall shine upon your ways."

## *Job Answers*

**23-28**    Then Job answered, "Oh that I knew where I might find him!
I would place my cause before him and fill my mouth with arguments. I would know the words which he would answer me, and understand what he would say to me.

"Will he plead against me with his great power? No. He would heed me. But lo, I go forward and he is not there, I go backward and I cannot find him. He knows well that my foot has held fast to his steps, that his way have I kept and not turned aside. I have not gone back from the commandment of his lips, and I have treasured the words of his mouth more than food. But when he decides none can turn him! Whatever pleases him, that he does. Therefore am I in terror before him, and my spirit is crushed.

"Behold, as wild asses in the desert, the poor of the earth go forth to their work. They reap their grain in the field, and they glean the vintage of the wicked. They lie all night without clothing, and have no covering against the cold. They go naked and hungry; they tread the wine presses of the wicked, yet suffer from thirst. Men groan from out of the city, and the wounded cry out; yet God pays no heed to their plight. The murderer rises with the light to kill the poor and needy, and in the night he is as a thief. The eye of the adulterer waits for the twilight, saying, 'No eye shall see me,' and disguises his face. In the dark they break into houses which they marked for themselves in the daytime. They dislike the light, for the morning is to them as the shadow of death. They prey on the woman who can have no child, and give no aid to the widow. Wherever they rise, no man is sure of life. Yet God gives them safety, and they rest in it, though his eyes are upon their ways. If it is not so, let my words be proven false." [1]

## *Job's Soliloquies*

**29-37**    "Oh that I were as in months past, as in the days when God's
lamp shone upon my head, and by his light I walked through darkness! When the Almighty was with me, when I went forth to the gate of the city and prepared my seat in the street, the young men withdrew,

[1] See JOB, Chapters 25-28, in Notes and Excisions.

and the aged stood up, and the voice of the nobles was hushed. Then the ear that heard me blessed me; then the eye that saw me testified for me, that I delivered the poor and the fatherless, and he who had none to help him; that I made the widow's heart sing for joy! I was eyes to the blind and feet to the lame and father to the needy. My root spread out to the waters, and the dew lay all night upon my branch. Men gave ear to me, and kept silence for my counsel; and they waited for my words as one waits for the rain. I chose out their way, and sat as their chief, and dwelt as a king in the army, as one who comforts the mourners.

"But now they who are younger than I, and whose fathers I disdained to set with the dogs of my flock, now hold me in derision. I have become their taunt, and as a byword am I to them. They abhor me, and spare not to spit in my face. Because God has loosed my cord, and afflicted me, they also have let loose the bridle before me. He has cast me into the mire, and I am become like dust and ashes.

"I cry to you, and you do not answer! I stand up, and you do not look at me! You have become cruel to me; with the might of your hand you persecute me. You lift me up to the wind; you make me ride upon it, and dissolve my substance in the storm. Why? Did I not weep for him who was in trouble? Was not my soul grieved for the poor? Yet when I looked for good, evil came to me; and when I waited for light there came darkness. My harp has turned to mourning, my lute to the voice of those who weep.

"If I have walked with vanity, of if my foot has hastened to deceit; if my step has turned out of the way, and my heart has followed my eyes; if my heart has been enticed by a woman, or I have lain in wait at my neighbor's door; if I despised the cause of my manservant or my maidservant when they contended with me — (Did not he who made me in the womb make him also?); if I have withheld the poor from their desire, or caused the eyes of the widow to fail; or have eaten my morsel myself alone, while the fatherless went hungry; if I have seen any perish for want of clothing, or the needy without covering; if I have lifted up my hand against the fatherless; if I have made gold my hope, or fine gold my confidence; if I rejoiced in the disaster of him who hated me, or lifted myself up when evil found him; if, like Adam, I covered my transgressions by hiding my iniquity in my bosom; if I feared the multitude, or the contempt of the mighty terrified me so that I kept silence and went not out of the door — then let me be weighed in a just scale; for my God knows my integrity!

"Oh that I had one who would hear me! Oh that the Almighty would answer me!" [2]

## God's Words to Job

**38-41**  Then the Lord answered Job out of the whirlwind: "Who is this that darkens counsel by words without knowledge? Gird up your loins like a man; for I will ask of you, and you shall answer me:

"Where were you when I laid the foundation of the earth? Declare, if you have the understanding. Who determined its measures, if you know? Upon what were the foundations fastened, and who laid its cornerstone, when the morning stars sang together, and all the sons of God shouted for joy? Who restricted the sea with boundaries when it broke forth as if it had issued from the womb, when I made the cloud its garment, and a swaddling band for it of thick darkness, and prescribed for it my decree, and set bars and doors, and said, 'This far shall you come, but no further, and here shall your proud waves be stayed'?

"Have you ever commanded the morning, and caused the daybreak to know its place, that it might take hold of the ends of the earth and shake the wicked out of it? Have you entered into the springs of the sea? Or searched the recesses of the deep? Have the gates of death been revealed to you, or the doors of the shadow of death? Can you show me the way to the dwelling of light, and to the house of darkness, that you may follow it to its boundaries? Have you entered the treasuries of the snow, or seen the storehouse of the hail which I have reserved against time of trouble, against the day of battle?

"Show me the place where the light parts, or the east wind scatters upon the earth. Who has divided the torrents, and made a way for the lightning of the thunder, to cause it to rain upon the earth, and satisfy the waste and desolate ground, and make the tender grass to grow? Who has begotten drops of dew, or drops of rain? Out of whose womb came the ice? Who has gendered the hoary frost of heaven, and covered the waters as with stone, and caused the face of the deep to be frozen?

"Can you bind the cluster of the Pleiades, or loose the bands of Orion? Know you the laws of the heavens? Can you lift up your voice to the clouds and command them, that abundance of waters may cover you? Who has put wisdom in the mind, or understanding in the heart? Will you

---

[2] See JOB, Chapters 32-37, in Notes and Excisions.

hunt the prey for the lioness, or satisfy the appetite of the young lions when they crouch in their dens? Who provides food for the raven when his young ones cry to God and wander for lack of food?

"Know you the time when the wild goats of the rock bring forth? Or when the hinds calve? Who has set the wild ass free, and made the wilderness his home, and the salt land his dwelling place, and the mountains his pasture? Will the unicorn be content to serve you, and abide by your crib? Can you bind him with his band in the furrow, and will he harrow the valleys for you? Will you trust him, because his strength is great, to bring home your seed, and gather the grain of the threshing floor? Gave you wings to the peacock, or feathers to the ostrich?

"Have you given the horse his height? Have you clothed his neck with quivering power? Can you make him leap as a young grasshopper? The glory of his snorting is terrible. He paws in the valley and rejoices in his strength; he goes out to meet the armed men. He mocks at fear and turns not back from the sword. The quiver rattles against him, the glittering shield and the spear; yet he swallows the ground with fierceness and rage at the sound of the trumpet and the smell of battle.

"Does the hawk soar by your wisdom, and stretch her wings toward the south? Does the eagle mount at your command, and make her nest high upon the crag of the rock? From there she spies her prey, and where the slain are, there is she.

"Behold now the behemoth, which I made with man! He eats grass like an ox; but observe the strength in his loins, and the force in the muscles of his belly. His tail is like a cedar, and the sinews of his thighs are closely knit together. His bones are like rods of brass or bars of iron. Only he who made him can make the sword to approach him. Surely the mountains bring forth food for him, where all the beasts of the field do play. He lies down in the shadow among the reeds and tall grass; the willows of the brook surround him. He drains a lake to slake his thirst; he hastens not; he is confident he can drink the Jordan dry. Can you take him by his eyes, or pierce his nose with a nose-ring?

"Can you draw out the leviathan with a fishhook? Shall your friends make a banquet of him, or divide him among the merchants? Can you fill his skin with barbed irons or his head with fish spears? If you try to lay your hand upon him, and remember the battle, you will not try it again! Shall not one be cast down even at the sight of him?

"None is so fierce who dares stir him up; who then is able to stand before me? Whatsoever is under the whole heaven is mine!"

486

## Job's Retraction

42  Then Job answered the Lord and said, "I know that you can do all things, and that no thought can be hidden from you. I have uttered that which I understood not, things too wonderful for me, which I knew not. Hear, I beseech you, and I will speak. I have heard of you by the hearing of the ear, but now my eye sees you. Therefore I abhor myself, and repent in dust and ashes!"

## Job Is Comforted

42  Then the Lord said to Eliphaz the Temanite, "My wrath is kindled against you and against your two friends. For you have not spoken of me what is true, as has my servant Job. Now, therefore, take seven bullocks and seven rams, and go to my servant Job, and make a burnt offering; and my servant Job shall pray for you. For his sake I will not deal harshly with you according to your folly."

So Eliphaz and Bildad and Zophar did as the Lord commanded them; and the Lord accepted Job's prayer for his friends.

And the Lord turned Job's fortune, and gave Job twice as much as he had before. Then came to Job all his brothers and sisters, and all those who had known him before, and ate with him in his house, and comforted him over all the evil that the Lord had brought upon him. And each man gave him a piece of gold, or a ring of gold.

So the Lord blessed the end of Job's life more than the beginning; for he now had fourteen thousand sheep, and six thousand cattle, and a thousand yoke of oxen, and a thousand she-asses.

He had also seven sons and three daughters. And he named the first daughter Jemimah, and the second Keziah, and the third Keren-happuch. And in all the land there were no women so fair as the daughters of Job. And their father gave them inheritance among their brothers.

After this Job lived a hundred and forty years, and saw his sons and his sons' sons to the fourth generation. Then Job died, being old and full of days.

# THE BOOK OF PROVERBS
## A Collection of Sayings and Gnomic Poetry

❡ Every ancient literature has its collection of proverbs. Often the proverb is an object lesson, summing up a conclusion on a universal experience, which finds its parallels in places thousands of miles, and many centuries, apart. More often the proverbs themselves have traveled and survived those centuries. Frequently great collections of proverbs have been attributed to a favorite king or religious leader. There are collections of sayings attributed to the Buddha, Lao-Tze, Confucius and Zoroaster; the Shinto sayings, Kami-no-michi; and the still earlier collection of Egyptian sayings, The Wisdom of Amen-em-ope, which were read four or five centuries before David, and are quoted in Proverbs (22:17-23:14).

The Book of Proverbs is a collection of sayings and observations attributed in the Bible to King Solomon. "Solomon's wisdom," the Bible tells us, "excelled the wisdom of all the people of the east . . . He uttered three thousand proverbs; and his songs were a thousand and five." (I Kings, 4:30-32). The Book of Proverbs is therefore also known as The Proverbs of Solomon, although many scholars believe that this collection was assembled seven or eight centuries after King Solomon's time.

Proverbs covers a multitude of subjects, from conceit and deceit, wealth and poverty, indolence and diligence, friendship and enmity, to adultery and the appreciation of a good wife. As in most large collections of proverbs, some cancel each other out, for the sayings accumulated over a long period, during which there existed differences of opinion, and differences in conclusions.

Late editors of The Proverbs of Solomon added a lengthy preamble on wisdom and folly. And they included several short poems at the beginning of the book, and appended two oracles by Agur and Lemuel, ending with the famous acrostic mistranslated as "a virtuous woman."

In this version all the proverbs are included, excepting duplications; material which is merely a variant of a preceding observation (as, for example, 6:6-11 and 24:30-34) and so similar as to be another version of the same expression; and text in which an idea already expressed is given in different forms successively. ⟨[

## *Happy the Man Who Finds Wisdom*

*1-4*    Happy is the man who finds wisdom, and the man who obtains understanding. For wisdom is better than silver and fine gold, more precious than rubies; and all the things you can desire are not to be compared with her. Long life is in her right hand; in her left hand are riches and honor. Her ways are ways of pleasantness, and all her paths are peace. She is a tree of life to those who lay hold of her; and happy are those who hold her fast.

The Lord by wisdom founded the earth; by understanding he established the heavens; by his knowledge the depths were broken up, and the skies drop down the dew.

My son, keep sound wisdom and discretion; let them not depart from your eyes. Then will you walk on your way securely, and your foot will not stumble. When you lie down, you shall not fear; you shall lie down and your sleep shall be sweet.

Withhold not good from those to whom it is due when it is in the power of your hand to do it. Say not to your neighbor: "Go, and come again, and tomorrow I will give," when you have it with you.

Devise not evil against your neighbor, seeing he dwells trustingly beside you. Strive not with a man without cause, when he has done you no harm.

The curse of the Lord is on the house of the wicked, but the habitation of the just he blesses. The wise shall inherit honor, but the fools carry away disgrace.[1]

[1] See PROVERBS, Chapters 1, 3 and 4, in Notes and Excisions.

## The Lips of a Strange Woman

5 The lips of a strange woman drop honey, and her mouth is smoother than oil; but in the end she is bitter as wormwood, sharp as a two-edged sword. Her feet lead down to death; her steps lead down to hell. She finds not the level path of life; her ways are unstable and she knows it not.

Now therefore, my son, listen to me, and depart not from the words of my mouth. Remove your way far from her, and come not nigh the door of her house, lest you give your honor to others and your years to the cruel; lest strangers be filled with your substance and your labors be in the house of an alien; and in the end, when your flesh and your body are wasted, you will say, "How I have hated instruction, and my heart despised reproof! I obeyed not the voice of my teachers, nor inclined my ear to those who taught me! I well nigh came to an evil end in the midst of the congregation."

Drink waters out of your own cistern, and running waters out of your own well. Why should your springs be dispersed abroad, your streams of water in the streets? Let them be for yourself alone, and not for strangers. Let your fountain be blessed; and rejoice in the wife of your youth. As a loving hind and a pleasant doe, let her breasts satisfy you at all times; be always ravished with her love. Why should you, my son, be ravished with the wife of another?

For the ways of man are before the eyes of the Lord, and he ponders all his goings. The wicked shall be ensnared by his own iniquities, and held by the cords of his sins. He shall die for lack of instruction; in his great folly he shall go astray.

## If You Are Snared

6 My son, if you become surety for your neighbor, if you have given your pledge for a stranger, if you are snared by the words of your mouth and caught by the words of your lips — do this now, my son, and save yourself, seeing that you have come into the power of your neighbor.

Give no sleep to your eyes, or slumber to your eyelids. Save yourself, as a gazelle from the hand of the hunter, as a bird from the hand of the fowler.

## Go to the Ant, You Sluggard

6    Go to the ant, you sluggard; consider her ways and be wise. For though she has no chief or overseer or ruler, yet she provides her food in the summertime, and gathers her provisions at the harvest.
How long will you sleep, O sluggard?
When will you arise from your sleep?

## The Fate of the Schemer

6    A base person, a wicked man, is he who walks about with crooked speech, who winks his eyes, who scrapes his feet, who points with his finger.
Perverseness is in his heart; he sows discord. Therefore calamity shall suddenly come upon him, and suddenly will he be broken and beyond healing.

## Six Things the Lord Hates

6    There are six things which the Lord hates, yes, seven which are an abomination to him: haughty eyes, a lying tongue, and hands that shed innocent blood, a heart that devises wicked imaginations, feet swift in running to evil, a false witness who utters lies, and he who sows discord among brothers.

## Beware the Adulteress

6    My son, keep the commandment of your father, and forsake not the teaching of your mother. Bind them always upon your heart; tie them about your neck.
When you go out it shall lead you, when you sleep it shall watch over you, and when you awake it shall talk with you.

THE BOOK OF PROVERBS

For the commandment is a lamp, and the law is a light, and reproofs of instruction are the way of life; to guard you from the evil woman, from the flattering tongue of the adulteress. Lust not after her beauty in your heart; neither let her snare you with her eyelids. For on account of an adulteress a man may be brought down to a crust of bread; and the adulteress hunts for the precious life.

Can a man take fire into his bosom and his clothes not be burned? Or can one walk upon hot coals and his feet not be scorched? So he who goes in to his neighbor's wife; whoever touches her shall not go unpunished.

Men do not despise a thief if he steals to satisfy his hunger. But if he is found, he shall restore sevenfold, he shall give all the substance of his house.

He who commits adultery with a woman is devoid of understanding; only he does it who would destroy his own soul. Wounds and dishonor shall he get, and his reproach shall not be wiped away; for jealousy is the rage of a man, and he will not spare in the day of vengeance. He will not regard any ransom; neither will he rest content though you give him many gifts.

## At the Window of My House

7-8    At the window of my house I looked out through my lattice; and I beheld among the thoughtless ones, I discerned among the youths, a young man void of understanding, passing through the street near her corner, and he went the way to her house; in the twilight, in the evening of the day, in the blackness of night and the darkness.

And behold, there met him a woman with the attire of a harlot, and wily of heart. She is clamorous and willful, her feet abide not in her house; now she is in the streets, now in the broad places, and lies in wait at every corner. So she caught him, and kissed him, and with an impudent face she said to him:

"Sacrifices of peace offerings were due from me and today have I paid my vows. Therefore I came out to meet you, diligently to seek your face, and I have found you. I have spread my couch with coverlets, with striped cloths of the yarn of Egypt. I have perfumed my bed with myrrh, aloes, and cinnamon. Come, let us take our fill of love until the morning; let us solace ourselves with loves. For my husband is not at home, he is gone on a long journey; he has taken a bag of money with him; he will not come home until the full moon."

With her fair speech she causes him to yield, with the flattering of her lips she carries him away. He goes after her as an ox goes to the slaughter, as a bird hastens to the snare, and knows not that it is at the cost of his life.

Listen to me now, my sons, and attend to the words of my mouth. Let not your hearts incline to her ways, go not astray in her paths. For she has cast down many wounded, and her slain are a mighty host. Her house is the way to Sheol, going down to the chambers of death.[2]

## The House Wisdom Built

9    Wisdom has built her house; she has hewn out her seven pillars. She has prepared her meat, she has mingled her wine; she has also set her table. She has sent forth her maidens; she cries out upon the highest places of the city, "Whoever is thoughtless, let him turn in here." To him who is void of understanding she says, "Come, eat of my bread and drink of the wine which I have mingled. Leave off your thoughtlessness, and live; walk in the way of understanding."

## Reproof of the Scoffer

9    He who corrects a scoffer earns for himself shame, and he who reproves a wicked man gets himself reviled. Reprove not a scoffer, lest he hate you; reprove a wise man, and he will love you. Give instruction to a wise man and he will be still wiser; teach a righteous man and he will increase in learning.

The fear of the Lord is the beginning of wisdom, and the knowledge of the Holy One is understanding. For by me your days shall be multiplied, and the years of your life increased. If you are wise, you are wise for yourself; and if you scorn, you alone shall bear it.

[2] See PROVERBS, Chapter 8, in Notes and Excisions.

## The Woman Folly

9 The woman Folly is clamorous; she is thoughtless and knows nothing. She sits at the door of her house, on a seat in the high places of the city, to call to those who pass by, "He who is thoughtless, let him turn in here."

And to him who lacks understanding she says, "Stolen waters are sweet, and bread eaten in secret is pleasant." But he knows not that the dead are there, that her guests are in the depths of hell.

## The Proverbs of Solomon

10-22 A wise son makes a glad father, but a foolish son is the grief of his mother.

Treasures of wickedness profit no one, but righteousness delivers from death.

He becomes poor who deals with an idle hand, but the hand of the diligent makes rich.

He who gathers in summer is a wise son, but he who sleeps at harvest is a shameful one.

He who walks uprightly walks securely, but he who perverts his ways shall come to grief.

Hatred stirs up strife, but love covers all transgressions.

The rich man's wealth is his strong city; the destruction of the poor is their poverty.

He who hides hatred has lying lips, and he who utters slander is a fool.

In a multitude of words there is room for transgressions, but he who controls his lips acts wisely.

The lips of the righteous feed many, but the foolish die for lack of understanding.

It is like sport to the fool to do wrong, as is wisdom to a man of understanding.

As vinegar is to the teeth, and smoke to the eyes, is the sluggard to those who send him.

A false scale is an abomination to the Lord, but a just weight is his delight.

When pride comes, then comes shame; but with the lowly is wisdom.

Riches are of no avail in the day of wrath, but righteousness saves from death.

When a wicked man dies, his hope perishes; and the expectation of his children perishes with him.

A talebearer reveals secrets, but the faithful conceal the matter.

For want of guidance a people will fall, but in many counselors there is safety.

A gracious woman obtains honor, and a strong man obtains riches.

Like an ornament of gold in a swine's snout, so is beauty in a woman without taste.

The generous soul shall be enriched, and he who satisfies shall himself be satisfied.

He who withholds grain, the people shall curse; but blessings shall fall upon the head of him who sells it.

He who trusts in his riches will fall, but the righteous will flourish like a green leaf.

He who troubles his own house shall inherit the wind, and the foolish shall be servant to the wise of heart.

He who loves knowledge loves correction, but he who hates reproof is brutish.

A good woman is a crown to her husband; she who brings him shame is like rot in his bones.

A righteous man has regard for the life of his beast, but even the tender mercies of the wicked are cruel.

The way of a fool seems right in his own eyes; he who is wise listens to counsel.

A fool's vexation is soon known, but a prudent man conceals shame.

Deceit is in the heart of those who devise evil, but the conselors of peace have joy.

Lying lips are an abomination to the Lord; those who deal truthfully are his delight.

A prudent man conceals his knowledge, but the fool proclaims his foolishness.

Care in the heart of a man bows him down, but a good word makes him glad.

From the fruit of his mouth the good man eats good, and the faithless, violence.

The sluggard desires, and gains nothing, while the diligent is amply rewarded.

Wealth gained by vanity shall be diminished, but he who gathers by labor shall increase.

Hope deferred makes the heart sick, but desire fulfilled is a tree of life.

The teaching of the wise is a fountain of life, that one may avoid the snares of death.

A wicked messenger falls into evil, but a faithful messenger brings healing.

Poverty and shame come to him who refuses correction, but he who accepts reproof shall be honored.

He who walks with wise men shall be wise, but the companion of fools shall suffer harm.

A good man leaves an inheritance to his children's children, but the wealth of the sinner is laid up for the righteous.

Much food is in the tillage of the poor, but much is swept away by injustice.

He who spares the rod hates his son; he who loves his son chastens him betimes.

The wise woman builds her house, but the foolish one tears it down with her own hands.

When there are no oxen, the crib is empty; but by the strength of the ox comes abundance.

A scoffer seeks wisdom and finds it not, but knowledge is easy for him who has discernment.

The heart knows its own bitterness, and a stranger cannot share in its joy.

There is a way which seems right to a man, but in the end it leads to death.

The thoughtless believe every word, but the prudent man watches his every step.

He who is soon angry deals foolishly, and a man of wicked devices is hated.

The poor is hated even by his neighbor, but the rich have many friends.

He who despises his neighbor sins, but happy is he who is gracious to the humble.

In all labor there is profit, but mere talk tends only to penury.

He who is slow to anger has great understanding, but he who becomes easily angered exalts folly.

A tranquil heart prolongs life, but envy is a rot in the bones.

He who oppresses the poor blasphemes his Maker, but he who has mercy on the needy honors him.

A soft answer turns away wrath, but harsh words stir up anger.

A soothing tongue is a tree of life, but perverseness in it wounds the spirit.

In the house of the righteous there is much treasure, but in the revenues of the wicked, only trouble.

A merry heart makes a cheerful countenance, but by sorrow of heart the spirit is broken.

All the days of the poor are sorrowful, but he of a merry heart has a continual feast.

Better is little, with the fear of the Lord, than great treasure, and with it trouble.

Better a dinner of herbs where love is than a roasted ox with hatred.

A wise son makes a glad father, but a foolish one despises his mother.

To the wise the path of life goes upward, away from Sheol below.

The Lord is far from the wicked, but he is near to the righteous.

The wrath of a king is like a messenger of death, and a wise man will pacify it.

How much better it is to get wisdom than gold, to get understanding rather than silver.

Pride goes before destruction, and a haughty spirit before a fall.

A wellspring of life it is to teach the wise, but to teach the fool is folly.

Pleasant words are like honey, sweet to the soul and health to the body.

A perverse man sows strife, and a whisperer separates friends.

He who is slow to anger is better than the mighty, and he who rules his temper than he who conquers a city.

The lot is cast, but disposing of it is from the Lord.

Better a dry morsel in peace than a house full of feasting with strife.

The refining pot is for silver and the furnace for gold, but the Lord tries the heart.

An evildoer heeds wicked lips, and a liar heeds the mischievous tongue.

He who mocks the poor blasphemes his Maker, and he who is gladdened by calamity will not go unpunished.

A rebuke cuts deeper into one who has understanding than a hundred stripes into a fool.

Let a man meet a bear robbed of her whelps rather than a fool bent on his folly.

He who rewards evil for good, evil shall not depart from his house.

He who justifies the wicked, and he who condemns the righteous, both are an abomination to the Lord.

Why is there a price in the hand of a fool to buy wisdom, seeing that he has no understanding?

He who begets a fool does it to his sorrow, and the father of a fool has no joy.

A merry heart is good medicine, but a broken spirit dries up the bones.

Even a fool, when he holds his peace, is accounted wise; when he shuts his lips, he is esteemed as prudent.

With wickedness comes contempt, and with dishonor comes disgrace.

The words of a man's mouth are as deep waters; the wellspring of wisdom is as a flowing brook.

A fool's mouth is his ruin, and his lips are the snare of his soul.

The words of a gossip are wounds that go down into the innermost parts of the belly.

The lazy is brother to the wastrel.

The rich man's wealth is his strong city, and like a high wall in his own conceit.

Before destruction the heart of man is haughty, but humility goes before honor.

The spirit of a man will endure illness; but a broken spirit who can bear?

A man's gift makes room for him, and brings him before great men.

Death and life are in the power of the tongue, and those who indulge it shall eat its fruit.

He who finds a good wife finds a great good, and obtains favor of the Lord.

The poor entreat, but the rich answer insolently.

There are friends that one has to his own hurt, but there is a friend who sticks closer than a brother.

Better are the poor who walk with integrity than the rich with lying lips.

Wealth gains many friends; poverty separates them.

Many will entreat the favor of the noble, and everyone is a friend to him who gives gifts.

Even the brothers of the poor hate him; how much more do his friends go far from him!

Luxury is not fitting for a fool; much less for a servant to rule over princes.

House and riches are an inheritance from fathers; a prudent wife is from the Lord.

There are many devices in a man's heart, but it is the purpose of the Lord that shall be established.

Wine is a mocker, strong drink is riotous; and whoever is deceived by it is not wise.

The sluggard will not plow when it is cold; therefore he shall beg at the harvest, and have nothing.

Who can say, "I have made my heart clean, I am pure from my sin"?

The hearing ear and the seeing eye, the Lord has made them both.

Love not sleep, lest you come to poverty; open your eyes, and you shall have plenty of bread.

There is gold and there are rubies, but the lips of knowledge are more precious than either.

Bread of deceit is sweet to a man, but afterwards his mouth shall be filled with gravel.

The glory of young men is their strength, and the beauty of old men their hoary head.

He who closes his ear to the cry of the poor, he shall cry out himself, and not be heard.

He who loves pleasure will be a poor man; he who loves wine and oil will not be rich.

It is better to dwell in a desert than with a contentious and fretful woman.

The horse is prepared for the battle, but victory is of the Lord.

A good name is more desirable than great riches, and a good reputation than silver and gold.

Train a child in the way he should go, and even when he is old he will not depart from it.

The lazy man says, "There's a lion in the streets; I will be killed if I go out."

The mouth of a strange woman is a deep pit; he whom the Lord abhors shall fall into it.

## *Words of the Wise*

**22-24** Incline your ear, and listen to the words of the wise, and apply your heart to acquire them. For it is a pleasant thing if you keep them within you.

Rob not the poor, because he is poor, nor oppress the afflicted; for the Lord will plead their cause and despoil the life of those who despoil them.

Make no friendship with a man given to anger, and stay away from a man of wrath, lest you learn his ways and ensnare your soul.

Remove not the ancient landmark which your fathers have set.

Toil not to become rich, for riches can certainly make themselves wings and fly away like an eagle toward heaven.

Eat not the bread of the miserly, nor desire his dainties. For as he thinks in his heart, so is he! "Eat and drink!" he will say to you, but his heart is not in his words.

Speak not in the ears of a fool, for he will despise the wisdom of your words.

Through wisdom a house is built, and by understanding it is established, and by knowledge the chambers are filled with all precious and pleasant riches.

A wise man is strong; a man of knowledge increases strength.

If you faint in the day of adversity, your strength is small indeed.

Fret not because of evil men, nor be envious of the wicked, for there is no future for the evil man, and the candle of the wicked shall be put out.

Prepare your work outside, make everything ready for yourself in the field; and afterwards build your house.

Be not a witness against your neighbor without cause, and deceive not with your lips. Say not, "I will do to him as he has done to me; I will render to the man according to his work."

## *Who Has Woe?*

**23** Who has woe? Who has sorrow? Who has strife? Who has wounds without cause? Who has redness of eyes? Those who tarry long over wine, those who seek mixed wines.

Look not upon the wine when it is red, when it gives its color to the cup. It may slide down smoothly, but in the end it bites like a serpent and stings like an adder.

Your eyes will behold strange things, and your heart utter confused things. You will be like one who lies down in the midst of the sea, or like one who lies upon the top of a mast; and you will say, "They have stricken me, and I felt it not. They have beaten me, and I knew it not. When shall I awake? I will seek it yet again."

## A Little Sleep

24     I went by the field of the slothful, and by the vineyard of the man void of understanding. And lo, it was overgrown with thistles and covered with nettles, and the stone wall was broken down.

Then I beheld, and considered well; I saw, and received instruction. "Yet a little sleep, a little slumber, a little folding of the hands to sleep" — so shall poverty come upon you like a runner, and want like an armed man.

## Further Proverbs of Solomon

*These also are proverbs of Solomon, which the men of Heze-kiah, king of Judah, copied out.*

25-29    The heaven for height, and the earth for depth, and the heart of kings, is unsearchable.

Be not hasty to strive, lest you know not what to do in the end, and your neighbor put you to shame.

A word fitly spoken is like apples of gold in baskets of silver.

As clouds and wind without rain, so is he who boasts of a gift not yet given.

Have you found honey? If you eat too much of it, you will become ill.

Let your foot be seldom in your neighbor's house, lest he weary of you.

Confidence in an unfaithful man in time of trouble is like a broken tooth, and a foot out of joint.

As vinegar upon a wound, so is he who sings songs to a sorrowing heart.

If your enemy is hungry, give him bread to eat, and if he is thirsty, give him water to drink; for you will heap coals of fire upon his head, and the Lord will reward you.

The north wind brings rain, and a backbiting tongue an angry face.

As cold waters to the thirsty, so is good news from a far country.

He who cannot control his temper is like a city without defenses.

As snow in summer and rain in harvest, so honor is not fitting for a fool.

Answer not a fool according to his folly, lest you also be like him.

Answer a fool according to his folly, lest he be wise in his own eyes.

As a thorn that goes up in the hand of a drunkard, so is a parable in the mouth of a fool.

As the door turns upon its hinges, so does the sluggard upon his bed.

He who meddles in strife not concerning him is like one who catches a dog by the ears.

For lack of wood the fire goes out; and where there is no gossip, contention ceases.

Flattering lips and a wicked heart are like an earthen vessel overlaid with silver dross.

He who digs a pit shall fall into it, and he who rolls a stone shall have it come back upon him.

A lying tongue hates those whom it has wounded, and a flattering mouth works ruin.

Boast not of tomorrow, for you know not what the day may bring.

Let another man praise you, and not your own mouth; a stranger, and not your own lips.

Wrath is cruel and anger is overwhelming, but who can stand before jealousy?

Open rebuke is better than love that is hidden.

The sated loathe even honey, but to the hungry every bitter thing is sweet.

Your own friend, and your father's friend, forsake not; and go not to your brother's house in the day of your calamity: better a neighbor who is near than a brother far off.

As iron sharpens iron, so a man sharpens the face of his friend.

Hell and death are never satisfied; so too the eyes of man are never satisfied.

The wicked flee when no man pursues, but the righteous are as bold as a lion.

A poor man who oppresses the poor is like a sweeping rain which leaves no food.

Those who forsake the law praise the wicked, but those who keep the law contend with them.

He who augments his substance by usury and unjust gain shall gather it for him who has pity on the poor.

As a roaring lion and a ranging bear, so is a wicked ruler over a poor people.

He who tills his land shall have plenty of bread, and he who follows after worthless persons shall have plenty of poverty.

He who rebukes a man shall afterward find more favor than he who flatters with the tongue.

When the wicked rise, men hide themselves; but when the wicked perish, the righteous increase.

When the righteous are in authority, the people rejoice; but when the wicked rule, the people mourn.

A man who flatters his neighbor spreads a net for his feet.

When a ruler listens to falsehood, all his servants become wicked.

Correct your son and he will give you rest, he will give delight to your soul.

Where there is no vision, the people perish.

See you a man who is hasty in his words? There is more hope for a fool than for him.

An angry man stirs up strife, and a wrathful man abounds in transgression.

A man's pride shall bring him low, but the humble in spirit shall obtain honor.

An unjust man is abhorred by the just; and he who is upright is abhorred by the wicked.

# The Oracle of Agur

*The words of Agur, the son of Jakeh: the oracle.*

30     Two things have I asked of you; deny them not to me before I die. Remove far from me vanity and lies, give me neither poverty nor riches; feed me with my allotted bread, lest I be full, and deny you

and say, "Who is the Lord?" Or lest I be poor, and steal, and use profanely the name of my God.

There are three things that are never satisfied, yes, four that say not, "Enough": the grave; and the barren womb; the earth, never satisfied with water; and the fire that never says, "Enough."

There are three things which are too wonderful for me, yes, four which I cannot understand: the way of an eagle in the air; the way of a serpent upon a rock; the way of a ship in the midst of the sea; and the way of a man with a maiden.

There are three things which make the earth tremble, and four which it cannot endure: a servant when he reigns; and a churl when he is filled with food; an odious woman when she is married; and a handmaid who is heir to her mistress.

There are four things upon the earth which are little, but they are exceedingly wise: the ants, who are not strong, yet provide their food in the summer; the conies, who are feeble, yet make their homes in the crags; the locusts, who have no king, yet all march out in ranks; the spider, which you can take in your hands, yet it is in the palaces of kings.

There are three things which are stately in their march, yes, four which are stately in their gait: the lion, which is mightiest among beasts and turns not away before any; the greyhound; the he-goat also; and the king, against whom there is no rising up.

If you have done foolishly in exalting yourself, or if you have thought evil, lay your hand upon your mouth: for as the churning of milk brings forth curd, and the wringing of the nose brings forth blood, so the forcing of wrath brings forth strife.

## The Oracle of Lemuel

*The words of King Lemuel: the oracle which his mother taught him.*

31    O my son, give not your strength to women, nor your ways to
       that which destroys kings. It is not for kings, O Lemuel, it is not
for kings to drink wine, nor for princes to say, "Where is strong drink?"
Lest they drink and forget the law, and pervert the justice due to any
who are afflicted.

Give strong drink to him who is ready to perish, and wine to the bitter in soul; let him drink and forget his poverty, and remember his misery no more.

Open your mouth for the dumb, in the cause of all such as are left desolate. Open your mouth, judge righteously, and plead the cause of the poor and needy.

# A Woman of Valor

31 A woman of valor who can find? She is more precious than rubies. The heart of her husband safely trusts in her; she does him good all the days of her life.

She seeks wool and flax, and works willingly with her hands. She is like the merchant-ships which bring their wares from afar. She rises while it is yet night, and gives food to her household, and their tasks to her maidens. She considers a field, and buys it; with the fruit of her hands she plants a vineyard. She girds her loins with strength, and makes strong her arms. She perceives that her merchandise is good.

Her lamp does not go out at night. She puts her hand to the distaff and her hands hold the spindle. She stretches out her hand to the poor and reaches out her hand to the needy. She is not afraid of the snow for her household, for all her household are clothed in scarlet. She makes for herself coverlets; her clothing is fine linen and purple. Her husband is known in the gates, when he sits among the elders of the land. She makes linen garments and sells them, and delivers girdles to the merchants.

Strength and dignity are her clothing, and she fears not the future. She opens her mouth with wisdom, and the law of kindness is on her tongue. She looks well to the ways of her household, and eats not the bread of idleness.

Her children rise up and call her blessed; her husband also, and he praises her, saying, "Many daughters have done valorously, but you excel them all."

Grace is deceitful, and beauty is vain; but a woman who fears the Lord, she shall be praised. Give her of the fruit of her hands, and let her works praise her in the gates.

# THE BOOK OF PSALMS
## A Collection of Hymns, Chants and Prayers

❦ Every sacred literature has its collection of prayers, hymns and lit-
anies, and some contain over a thousand songs — like the Hindu hymns of
the Rig-Veda — while others are slender collections of personal supplications.

The Book of Psalms in the Bible is a collection of one hundred and fifty
religious songs, many of them intended for recitation or choral singing to
the accompaniment of instrumental music; and they accumulated over a
period of about seven centuries. These religious poems are perhaps the
best known of all the books in the Bible. They are used by the faithful on
waking to a new day and at the day's end; they are recited on every
gay or solemn occasion; and there are secular groups whose members
read a psalm each day for pleasure and comfort.

Scholars find the Psalms difficult to classify since they vary so much
in length, in form, and in content. Some of the psalms are very short —
Psalm 117 contains only fifteen words in the original Hebrew; others are
very long — Psalm 119 has a hundred and seventy-six couplets. In form
they include dramatic lyrics, personal supplications, monologues, national
prayers, hymns with and without refrains, choral lyrics, and unison chants.
And there are nine psalms composed in extremely involved acrostics, following the Hebrew alphabet. These are of interest primarily to scholars
of acrostic literature.

While the Song of Songs, Proverbs and Ecclesiastes are attributed to
King Solomon, the Book of Psalms is attributed to King David. In the collection itself, however, the Seventy-second Psalm ends with the notation:
"The prayers of David the son of Jesse are ended." Songs in all parts of
the collection are attributed to Moses, to Solomon, and to Levites of the
families of Asaf and of Korah; and many are considered to be anonymous.

Many psalms are personal prayers in time of sorrow or need. Some are personal songs of gratitude. A large number are exultant lyrics on the majesty and the glory and the goodness of the everlasting God; and these are known as the *Hallel* or Hallelujah psalms. There are the psalms in praise of wisdom, psalms which commemorate historical events, psalms to the glory of nature, psalms which express unshaken faith in justice and truth, psalms of thanksgiving for national victory; and there are psalms which have been called "vindictive" or "imprecatory," which call down the wrath of the Lord upon enemies and the wicked.

Some psalms appear twice in identical wording (such as Psalm 14, which is repeated in Psalm 53; and Psalm 40: 13-17, which is repeated in Psalm 70); many others are found in quite similar versions, particularly the exhortations in praise of God. Several psalms contain two or more unrelated songs, without any signposts, combining a plea for help in trouble with a prayer for vengeance. A number of psalms are beautiful when sung, and with the proper *responsa*, although their special quality is not as evident when they are silently read. Many of the psalms, particularly those we can identify as belonging to a very early period, employ imagery and concepts completely obscure to us in our times, and the Hebrew in which they were composed can be only dimly approximated in contemporary English.

Yet despite the diversity of the psalms, and the poetic images of a pre-scientific age, they encompass in brief all the faith in the glory of life and its Creator which is expressed variously throughout the books of the Bible; and the Book of Psalms has been justly called "a Bible in miniature."

The psalms given in this version might be grouped into personal supplications, expressions of personal faith, psalms of gratitude, hymns, Hallel psalms, national psalms, and some pleas for vengeance. They are not placed in this order, but follow the numerical sequence in which they appear in the Book of Psalms. All psalms omitted are variants of those included. ❨

## Like a Tree Beside a River *

**1**     Happy is the man who has not walked in the counsel of the
wicked, nor stood in the way of sinners, nor sat in the seat of the
scornful. He shall be like a tree planted beside a river, that brings forth
its fruit in season, whose leaf does not wither; and all that he does shall
prosper.

Not so the wicked, but they are like the chaff which the wind blows
away. The wicked shall not rise in judgment, nor sinners in the congregation of the righteous. For the Lord regards the way of the righteous, but
the way of the wicked shall perish.

## My Shield and My Glory

**3**     O Lord, how my enemies have multiplied! How many have risen
against me, saying, "There is no help for him in God!" But you,
O Lord, are my shield and my glory; you lift up my head. I cry out to
you, and you answer me from your holy mountain. I lay me down and
sleep; I wake again, for the Lord sustains me. I have no fear though ten
thousand foes surround me.

Arise, O Lord! Save me, O my God! Alway you have smitten my
enemies upon the cheek, you have broken the teeth of the wicked. Salvation belongs to the Lord; your blessing be upon your people.

## Hear Me When I Call

**4**     Hear me when I call, O God, you who have freed me when I was
in distress! Have mercy upon me and hear my prayer!

O sons of men, how long will you turn my glory into shame? How long
will you love vanity and seek after falsehood? Know that the Lord has set
apart the godly as his own. Tremble, and sin no more. Commune with
your heart and be still. Offer the sacrifices of righteousness, and put your
trust in the Lord.

O Lord, lift up the light of your countenance upon us. You have put

---

* There are no summations of omitted psalms in the Notes and Excisions, since
they are all variants of psalms included.

gladness in my heart; in peace will I lay me down and sleep; for you, O Lord, make me dwell in safety.

## Rebuke Me Not

6      O Lord, rebuke me not in your anger, nor chasten me in your wrath! Have mercy upon me, O Lord, for I am weak. Heal me, for my bones are shaken and my soul is grieved.

Return, O Lord, and deliver my soul. Save me for your mercy's sake. For in death there is no remembrance of you; in the grave who will praise you? I am weary with my moaning; all the night I flood my bed with my tears; my eye is dim from grief because of my enemies.

Depart from me, evildoers, for the Lord has heard my supplication; he has accepted my prayer. Now all my foes shall be shamed and terrified; they shall turn back, and be suddenly ashamed.

## When I Consider Your Heavens

8      O Lord, our Lord, how great is your name in all the earth, as is your glory in the heavens! Out of the mouth of babes and nurslings have you ordained strength to still the enemy and the avenger.

When I consider your heavens, the work of your fingers, the moon and the stars, which you have established, what is man that you are mindful of him? And the son of man that you should think of him? Yet you have made him but a little lower than the angels, and crowned him with glory and honor. You have given him dominion over the works of your hands; you have put all things under his feet: all sheep and oxen, all the beasts of the field and the birds of the air, the fish of the sea, and whatever passes through its paths.

O Lord, how glorious is your name in all the earth!

## I Trust in Your Mercy

13      How long, O Lord, will you forget me? How long will you hide your face from me? How long shall I take counsel in my soul, having sorrow in my heart all day? How long shall my enemy be ex-

alted over me? Consider and hear me, O Lord my God! Bring light to my eyes, lest I sleep the sleep of death; lest my enemies say they have prevailed against me; lest those who trouble me rejoice when I fall.

But I trust in your mercy; my heart shall rejoice in your salvation. I will sing to the Lord, because he has dealt bountifully with me.

## God Is with the Righteous

14    The fool has said in his heart, "There is no God!" They are corrupt; they have done abominable things. There is none that does good. The Lord looked down from heaven upon the children of men to see if there were any who were wise and sought God. But they have all gone astray, they have all become impure; there is none that does good, no, not one. Do not all the workers of evil know it, who devour my people as they would eat bread, and call not upon the Lord?

Then were they in great fear: for God is with the generation of the righteous. You would put to shame the counsel of the poor, but the Lord is his refuge.

## Who Shall Enter Your Tabernacle?

15    Lord, who shall enter your tabernacle? Who shall dwell upon your holy mountain? "He who walks uprightly, and acts justly, and speaks the truth in his heart; he who does not slander with his tongue, nor does evil to his neighbor, nor takes up a reproach against his friend; he in whose eyes a vile person is despised, but who honors those who fear the Lord; he who swears to his own hurt, and changes not; he who does not put out his money to usury, nor take a bribe against the innocent; he who does these things shall never be moved."

## Preserve Me, O God

16    Preserve me, O God, for in you do I put my trust! O my soul, you have said to the Lord, "I have no good but in you!" As for the saints on earth, they are the excellent ones in whom is my delight.

Let sorrows be multiplied for those who hasten after another God. Their drink offerings of blood I will not offer, nor take their names upon my lips. O Lord, you are the portion of my inheritance.

My lines have fallen in pleasant places; yes, I have a goodly heritage. I will bless the Lord, who has given me counsel. I have set the Lord before me always; he is at my right hand, I shall not stumble.

My heart is glad and rejoices, for you will not abandon me in Sheol; neither will you suffer the good to see corruption. You will show me the path of life; in your presence is fullness of joy, in your right hand bliss for evermore.

## The Heavens Declare the Glory of the Lord

19    The heavens declare the glory of God, and the firmament reveals his handiwork. Day speaks to day, and night speaks to night; and there is no speech nor language where their voice is not heard. Their words have gone out to the end of the world. In them has he set a tabernacle for the sun, which comes out like a bridegroom coming from his chamber, like a strong man rejoicing to run a race. It rises at one end of heaven and its circuit is to the other end; and nothing is hidden from its heat.

The law of the Lord is perfect, and restores the soul; the testimony of the Lord is certain, making the simple wise. The precepts of the Lord are right, rejoicing the heart; the commandment of the Lord is pure, enlightening the eyes; the fear of the Lord is clean, enduring forever; the judgment of the Lord is true and righteous altogether. More to be desired are they than fine gold; sweeter are they than honey. By them am I, your servant, warned; in keeping them is my reward.

Cleanse me, O Lord, from hidden faults. Keep me from presumptuous sins, that they may not have dominion over me. Then shall I be innocent of great transgression. Let the words of my mouth and the meditation of my heart be acceptable to you, O Lord, my Rock, and my Redeemer!

## Why Have You Forsaken Me?

22    My God, my God, why have you forsaken me? Why are you so far from me, from the words of my outcry? O my God, I call by day and you hear me not, and in the night, but you are silent. Yet you

are holy, you who are enthroned upon the praises of Israel. In you did our fathers trust; they trusted and you saved them. They cried out to you and were delivered; they trusted in you and were not put to shame.

But I am as a worm, scorned by men and despised by the people. Those who see me laugh me to scorn; they shake their heads saying, "He trusted in the Lord to save him. Let the Lord deliver him!"

Yet you are he who took me from the womb; you made me secure upon my mother's breast. Upon you have I been cast from my birth; you are my God since I was born. Be not far from me, for trouble is near, and there is none to help. Many surround me, strong bulls of Bashan beset me; they gape at me with mouths open wide. My heart has become like wax and melts; my tongue clings to my palate. For you have brought me into the dust of death. The wicked encircle me; like a lion they are at my hands and my feet; they look, and gloat over me; they divide my garments among them, and cast lots for my raiment. O my Lord, be not far from me! Hasten to help me! Deliver my soul from the sword; save me from the mouth of the lion!

I will declare your name to my brothers; I will praise you in the midst of the congregation. For the Lord does not despise or abhor the afflicted; neither does he hide his face from them, but hears when they cry out. Let the humble eat and be satisfied; let them seek the Lord and praise him. All the earth shall remember the Lord and turn to him; and all the kindreds of the nations shall worship before him. For the kingdom is the Lord's, and he is the ruler over all the nations.

## The Lord Is My Shepherd

23      The Lord is my shepherd; I shall not want. He makes me to lie down in green pastures; he leads me beside the still waters; he restores my soul. He leads me in the paths of righteousness for his name's sake. Even though I walk through the valley of the shadow of death, I will fear no evil, for you are with me; your rod and your staff, they comfort me. You prepare a table before me in the presence of my enemies; you anoint my head with oil; and my cup runs over. Surely goodness and mercy shall follow me all the days of my life, and I will dwell in the house of the Lord forever.

## The Earth Is the Lord's

24    The earth is the Lord's, and the fullness thereof; the world, and those who dwell in it. For he has founded it upon the seas and established it upon the floods. Who shall ascend the mountain of the Lord, and who shall stand in his holy place?

He who has clean hands and a pure heart, he who has not lifted up his soul to vanity, nor taken the name of God in vain, he shall receive a blessing from the Lord, and righteousness from the God of his salvation.

Lift up your heads, O gates, and open your doors, that the King of glory may come in! Who is the King of glory? The Lord, strong and mighty, the Lord, mighty in battle, the Lord of hosts, he is the King of glory!

## The Lord Is My Light

27    The Lord is my light and my salvation; whom shall I fear? The Lord is my strength; of whom shall I be afraid? When the wicked, my enemies and my foes, came to destroy me, they stumbled and fell. Though a host should encamp against me, my heart shall not fear; though war rise against me, yet will I be confident.

One thing have I asked of the Lord, that will I seek after: that I may dwell in the house of the Lord all the days of my life. For in time of trouble he will hide me in his pavilion; in the shelter of his tabernacle he shall conceal me. He shall set me high upon a rock.

Teach me your way, O Lord, and lead me along an even path. Deliver me not to the will of my enemies. False witnesses have risen against me, and such as breathe violence. I would have been overcome, had I not believed in the goodness of the Lord in the land of the living!

Place your hope in the Lord; be of good courage, and he will strengthen your heart. Yes, wait for the Lord.

## Joy Comes in the Morning

30    I will extol you, O Lord, for you have lifted me up and have not
      let my foes rejoice over me. O Lord my God, you have healed me;
you have restored my soul; you have kept me alive, that I should not go
down to the grave.

Sing praise to the Lord, and give thanks to his holy name. His anger
endures but a moment; his favor endures for a lifetime. Weeping may
lodge with us for a night, but joy comes in the morning.

In my prosperity I said, "I shall never be moved. O Lord, by your favor
you have made me strong as a mountain." But when you hid your face,
I was troubled. I cried to you, "O Lord, what profit is there in my blood
when I go down to the grave? Shall the dust praise you? Shall it declare
your truth? Hear, O Lord, and have mercy upon me!"

Then you turned my mourning into dancing; you took off my sackcloth
and girded me with gladness. To the end of my days, O Lord my God, I
will praise you; I will give thanks to you forever.

## Trust in the Lord

37    Fret not because of evildoers; neither be envious of wrongdoers.
      For they shall soon be cut down like grass, and wither like the
green herb.

Trust in the Lord, and do good; so shall you dwell in the land and be
fed. Delight in the Lord, and he shall give you the desires of your heart.
Rest in the Lord, and wait patiently for him.

Fret not because of the man who brings wicked devices to pass. Cease
from anger and forsake wrath. For evildoers shall be cut off, but those
who wait for the Lord, they shall inherit the earth. Yet a little while, and
the wicked shall be no more. But the humble shall inherit the earth, and
delight in the abundance of peace. The wicked have drawn out the
sword and have bent their bow, to cast down the poor and needy and
to slay the upright. But their sword shall enter into their own heart, and
their bows shall be broken. The little that a righteous man has is better
than the riches of the wicked. For the arms of the wicked shall be
broken, but the Lord upholds the righteous.

The wicked borrows and does not repay, but the righteous is generous and gives freely. Those who bless the Lord shall inherit the earth, and those who curse him shall be cut off. The steps of a good man delight the Lord; and though he may fall, he shall not be utterly cast down, for the Lord upholds him.

I have been young, and I have grown old, yet have I not seen the righteous forsaken, nor his children begging bread. For the Lord loves the just and forsakes not his saints. The mouth of a righteous man utters wisdom, and his tongue speaks of justice. The law of his God is in his heart; his steps do not falter.

I have seen the wicked in great power, and spreading himself like a green bay tree. Yet he passed away and was no more; though I sought him, he could not be found.

But salvation of the righteous is from the Lord; he is their strength in time of trouble. And the Lord helps them, and saves them from the wicked, because they trust in him.

## *Hear My Prayer*

39    I said, "I will take heed to my ways, that I sin not with my tongue; I will keep a curb upon my mouth while the wicked are before me."

I was dumb with silence, I held my peace; my pain was held in check. My heart grew hot within me; while I was musing, the fire kindled. Then I spoke out:

"Lord, let me know the measure of my days, let me know how short-lived I am. Behold, you have made my days as a handsbreadth, and my life is as nothing before you. Surely every man walks in shadow, and only vanity is his concern; he gathers, but knows not who will use it.

"And now, Lord, for what do I wait? My hope, it is in you. Deliver me from all my transgressions; make me not the scorn of the base. Remove your stroke from me, for I am overcome by the blow of your hand.

"Hear my prayer, O Lord, and give ear to my cry; hold not your peace at my tears! For I am a sojourner with you, as were my fathers. O spare me, that I may take comfort, before I depart and am no more."

## As the Deer Pants for Water

42    As the deer pants for the waters of the brook, so my soul pants
for you, O God. My soul thirsts for God, for the living God.
When shall I come and appear before him? My tears have been my food
through the day and night, while they say to me always, "Where is your
God?"

Why are you cast down, O my soul? Why are you disquieted within
me? Hope in God, for I shall again praise him.

In the day his loving-kindness will command me, and in the night his
song shall be with me.

## Why Do I Mourn?

43    Judge me, O God, and plead my cause against an ungodly nation; deliver me from the deceitful and unjust. For you are the
God of my strength. Why do you cast me off? Why do I go mourning under the oppression of the enemy?

O send out your light and your truth, and let them lead me. Let them
bring me to your holy mountain and to your dwelling place. Then will I
go to the altar of God, to God, my exceeding joy; and I will praise you
upon my harp, O God my God.

Why are you cast down, O my soul? Why are you disquieted within
me? Hope in God, for I shall again praise him, my salvation and my
God!

## God Is Our Refuge

46    God is our refuge and our strength, a very present help in trouble.
Therefore we will not fear. Though the earth tremble and the
mountains sink in the heart of the seas, though its waters roar and
rage and the mountains totter at its swelling, yet we will not fear.

There is a river whose streams make glad the city of God, the holy
dwelling place of the Most High. God is in her midst; God shall help
her. The Lord of hosts is with us; the God of Jacob is our refuge.

## Great Is the Lord

48    Great is the Lord, and greatly to be praised in the city of our God, in the mountain of his holiness! The city of the great King is fair and the joy of the earth; God, in her palaces, has made himself known as a refuge. For lo, the kings were assembled and conspired together. But when they saw it, they were troubled and hastened away; fear took hold upon them. You broke the ships of Tarshish with an east wind. As we have heard, so have we seen in the city of the Lord of hosts; God will establish it forever.

We thought of your loving-kindness, O God, in the midst of your temple. Let Mount Zion rejoice. Let the daughters of Judah be glad, because of your judgments. Walk about Zion and go round about her; observe her towers and mark well her bulwarks and traverse her palaces, that you may tell it to the generation following. Such is God our God, forever and ever; he will guide us eternally.

## Cast Me Not Out

51    Have mercy upon me, O God! In your abundant mercy blot out my transgressions; wash me thoroughly from my iniquity; cleanse me from my sin! For I acknowledge my transgressions, and my sin is ever before me.

Behold, you desire truth in the inward soul, therefore make me know wisdom in my inmost heart. Purge me with hyssop and I shall be clean; wash me and I shall be whiter than snow. Make me hear joy and gladness, that the bones you have crushed may rejoice. Create in me a clean heart, O God, and renew the spirit within me. Cast me not out of your presence; take not your holy spirit from me.

Restore to me the joy of your salvation, and uphold me with your spirit. Then will I teach transgressors your way, and sinners shall return to you.

For you delight not in sacrifice, else would I give it. The sacrifices of God are a broken spirit; a broken and a contrite heart, O God, you will not despise.

## My Soul Waits for God

62     My soul waits for God; from him comes my salvation. He only is my rock and my defense. Trust in him at all times, O people; pour out your heart before him; God is our refuge.

Trust not in oppression, and put not vain hope in robbery; if riches increase, set not your heart upon it. God has spoken once; twice have I heard this: that power belongs to God. Also to you, Lord, O Lord, belongs mercy, for you render to every man according to his work.

## Let the Nations Be Glad

67     God be merciful to us, and bless us, and cause his face to shine upon us; that your way may be known upon earth, your saving health among all nations!

Let the peoples praise you, O God; let all the peoples praise you. O let the nations be glad and sing for joy, for you shall judge the people justly and govern the nations upon earth.

Let the peoples praise you, O God; let all the peoples praise you. The earth has yielded her increase; may God, our God, bless us!

## Let Your Compassion Revive Us

79     O God, the nations have come into your inheritance; they have defiled your holy temple; they have laid Jerusalem in ruins. The bodies of your servants they have given as food to the birds of the heaven, and the flesh of your saints to the beasts of the field. Their blood has been poured out like water. We have become a taunt to our neighbors, scorned and derided by those round about us.

How long, O Lord, will you be angry? Will your jealousy burn like fire forever? Pour out your wrath upon the nations who know you not, and upon the peoples who call not upon your name. Remember not against us our former iniquities. Let your compassion speedily revive us, for we are brought very low. Help us, O God of our salvation, for the glory of your name.

Let the sighing of the prisoner come before you; and according to the greatness of your power, preserve those appointed to death. So that we, who are your people and the flock of your pasture, will give you thanks forever, and recount your praise to all generations.

## How Lovely Are Your Tabernacles

84    How lovely are your tabernacles, O Lord of hosts! My soul longs and pines for the courts of the Lord. The sparrow has found a house, and the swallow a nest for herself where she may have her young; even so my heart longs for the courts of the Lord.

Blessed are those who dwell in your house; they will find peace praising you. Blessed is the man whose strength is in you; he shall go from strength to strength. For a day in your courts is better than a thousand elsewhere. I had rather stand at the threshold of the house of my God than dwell in the tents of wickedness. For the Lord God is a sun and a shield; the Lord bestows grace and glory. No good thing will he withhold from those who walk uprightly. Blessed is the man who trusts in you, O Lord of hosts!

## You Have Been Our Dwelling Place

90    Lord, you have been our dwelling place in all generations, before the mountains were brought forth, or ever you formed the earth and the world; even from everlasting to everlasting, you are God.

You turn man back to dust and say, "Return, O children of men." For a thousand years in your sight are but as yesterday when it is past, as a watch in the night. You sweep them away as with a flood; they are as a dream. In the morning they are like grass which springs up: in the morning it flourishes; in the evening it is cut down and withers.

For we are destroyed by your anger and troubled by your wrath. You have set our iniquities before you, our secret sins in the light of your countenance. All our days are passed away in your wrath; we spend our years like a tale that is told. The days of our years are threescore and ten; and if by reason of strength they are fourscore, yet are they filled with toil and sorrow; for they are speedily gone and we fly away. Who knows the power of your anger and your wrath? Teach us to number our days, that we may apply our hearts to wisdom. Return, O Lord, and relent concerning your servants.

O satisfy us with your mercy, that we may rejoice and be glad all our days. Make us glad according to the days in which you have afflicted us, and the years in which we have seen evil. Let your work appear to your servants, and your glory to their children. Let the graciousness of the Lord our God be upon us, and establish the work of our hands; yes, the work of our hands, establish it.

## His Truth Is Your Shield

91    He who dwells in the shelter of the Most High, and abides in the shadow of the Almighty, will say of the Lord, "He is my refuge and my fortress; my God, in him will I trust."

Surely he will deliver you from the snare of the fowler and from the noisome pestilence. He will cover you with his pinions, and under his wings will you take refuge; his truth is your shield and buckler. You will not fear the terror of the night, nor the arrow that flies by day, nor the pestilence that walks in darkness, nor the destruction that wastes at noonday. A thousand may fall at your side, and ten thousand at your right hand, but it will not come nigh you. With your eyes you will see the punishment of the wicked.

Because you have made the Lord your refuge, and the Most High your habitation, no evil shall befall you, no plague come nigh your dwelling. For he will give his angels charge over you, to guard you in all your ways. They shall bear you up in their hands, lest you dash your foot against a stone. You shall tread upon the lion and the adder; the young lion and the serpent shall you trample underfoot.

Because he has set his love upon me, I will save him. I will set him on high, because he has known my name. When he shall call upon me, I will answer him; I will be with him in trouble; I will deliver him and honor him. With long life will I satisfy him, and show him my salvation.

## O Come, Let Us Worship

95    O come, let us sing to the Lord; let us shout for joy to the Rock of our salvation! Let us come before his presence with thanksgiving, and shout joyfully to him with psalms.

For the Lord is a great God. In his hand are the depths of the earth;

the heights of the hills are his also. The sea is his and he made it, and his hands formed the dry land.

O come, let us worship and bow down; let us kneel before the Lord our Maker! For he is our God, and we are the people of his pasture and the sheep of his hand.

## O Sing to the Lord

98     O sing to the Lord a new song, for he has done marvelous things! His right hand and his holy arm have brought him the victory. The Lord has made known his salvation; his righteousness has he revealed in the sight of the nations. He has remembered his mercy and his faithfulness toward the house of Israel; all the earth has seen the salvation of our God.

Shout joyfully to the Lord; rejoice and sing praise! Sing to the Lord with the harp, with the harp and the voice of a psalm; with trumpets and the sound of cornets make a joyful noise before the Lord!

Let the sea roar, and the fullness thereof; the world, and those who dwell in it. Let the floods clap their hands; let the hills be joyful together before the Lord. For he comes to judge the earth; with righteousness he will judge the world, and the peoples with equity.

## Enter into His Gates

100     Make a joyful noise to the Lord, all the earth! Serve the Lord with gladness; come before his presence with singing.

Know that the Lord he is God; it is he who has made us and we are his; we are his people and the sheep of his pasture. Enter into his gates with thanksgiving, and into his courts with praise; give thanks and bless his name. For the Lord is good; his mercy is everlasting; and his truth endures to all generations.

## Hide Not Your Face

102     Hear my prayer, O Lord, and let my cry come to you! Hide not your face from me in my day of distress. Incline your ear to me; in the day when I call answer me speedily. For my days pass like smoke.

My heart is stricken, and withered like grass; I forget to eat my food; my bones cling to my skin.

I am like a pelican of the wilderness, like an owl of the desert, like a bird alone upon the housetop. My enemies taunt me all the day, and they curse me. I have eaten ashes like bread, and mingled my drink with tears, because of your indignation and your wrath. For you have lifted me up, and then cast me down. My days are like a lengthening shadow, and I am withered like grass.

But you, O Lord, shall endure forever, and shall be remembered from generation to generation. Arise and have mercy upon Zion! The time to be gracious to her has come. For your servants take pleasure in her stones, and love even her dust.

This shall be recorded for the generation to come; and a people who shall be created will praise the Lord. For he has looked down from the height of his sanctuary to hear the groaning of the prisoner, and to loose those appointed to death.

I say, "O my God, take me not away in the midst of my days, you whose years endure through all generations. Of old have you laid the foundation of the earth, and the heavens are the work of your hands. They may perish, but you will endure; all of them may grow old like a garment; like a vesture you may change them, and they will be changed. But you are the same always, and your years have no end."

## The Lord Is Merciful

103    Bless the Lord, O my soul, bless his holy name. Bless the Lord, O my soul, and forget not all his benefits who forgives your iniquities, who heals your diseases, who redeems your life from destruction, who crowns you with loving-kindness and tender mercies, who satisfies your old age with good things so that your youth is renewed like the eagle.

The Lord executes righteousness for all who are oppressed. The Lord is merciful and gracious, slow to anger and plenteous in mercy. He has not dealt with us according to our sins, nor rewarded us according to our iniquities. For high as the heaven above the earth, so great is his mercy toward those who fear him. Far as the east is from the west, so far has he removed our transgressions from us.

Like a father who pities his children, so the Lord pities those who fear him. For he knows our frame; he remembers that we are dust. As for man, his days are like grass; like a flower of the field, so he flourishes. For the wind passes over it, and it is gone; and that place shall know it no more. But the mercy of the Lord is everlasting upon those who fear him, upon those who remember his commandments to do them. Bless the Lord, all his works, in all the places of his dominion; bless the Lord, O my soul.

## How Manifold Are Your Works

104  Bless the Lord, O my soul! O Lord my God, you are very great! You who are clothed with honor and majesty, who covers himself with light as with a garment, who stretches out the heavens like a curtain, who lays the beams of his upper chambers in the waters, who makes the clouds his chariot, who walks upon the wings of the wind.

You laid the foundation of the earth, so that it might never be moved; you covered it with the deep as with a garment. The waters stood above the mountains; at your rebuke they fled, at the voice of your thunder they hastened away — the mountains rose, the valleys sank down to the place you founded for them — you set a boundary which they may not pass over, that they might not again cover the earth.

You send the springs to flow in the valleys; they run between the hills. They give drink to every beast of the field; wild asses quench their thirst. Beside them the birds of the heavens dwell, and sing among the branches. You water the mountains from your upper chambers; the earth is full of the fruit of your work. You cause the grass to grow for the cattle; and bring food out of the earth, and wine that gladdens the heart of man, and bread which strengthens man's heart. The trees of the Lord are full of sap, the cedars of Lebanon which he has planted, in which the birds make their nests. As for the stork, the fir trees are her home. The high hills are a refuge for the wild goats, and the rocks for the conies.

You appointed the moon for seasons; the sun knows his going down. You make the darkness, and it is night, when all the beasts of the forest creep forth and the young lions roar after their prey. The sun rises, and they go off together and lie down in their dens. Man goes forth to his work and to his labor until the evening.

O Lord, how manifold are your works! In wisdom have you made them all; the earth is full of your riches. So is that great and wide sea in which live things innumerable, both small and great. There go the ships; there too is the leviathan, which you made to play there. All these wait upon you, that you may give them their food in due season. That which you give them they gather; you open your hand, they are filled. You hide your face, and they are troubled. You take away their breath, they perish and return to their dust.

The glory of the Lord shall endure forever; the Lord shall rejoice in his work. He looks on the earth and it trembles; he touches the hills and they smoke. I will sing to the Lord as long as I live; I will sing praise to my God while I have my being. My meditation of him shall be sweet; I will rejoice in the Lord. Bless the Lord, O my soul! Hallelujah!

## He Who Fears the Lord

112    Blessed is the man who fears the Lord, who delights greatly in his commandments. His children will be mighty upon earth; the generation of the upright shall be blessed. Wealth and riches shall be in his house, and his righteousness will endure forever. To the upright he shines like a light in the darkness; he is gracious and full of compassion. A good man deals graciously and lends; he guides his affairs with discretion. He will not be afraid of evil tidings; his heart is steadfast trusting in the Lord. His heart is steady; he shall not fear. He has given to the needy; he shall be exalted forever.

## Praise the Name of the Lord

113    Praise, O servants of the Lord, praise the name of the Lord! Blessed be the name of the Lord from this time forth and forevermore. From the rising of the sun to its going down, the Lord's name is to be praised.

The Lord is high above all nations, and his glory above the heavens. Who is like the Lord our God, who dwells on high and looks down upon the earth? He lifts the poor out of the dust, and the needy out of the dunghill, that he may set them with princes, with the princes of his people. He makes the barren woman dwell in her house as a joyful mother of children. Praise the Lord!

## When Israel Went Out of Egypt

114    When Israel went out of Egypt, the house of Jacob from a people of strange language, Judah became his sanctuary and Israel his domain.

The sea saw it and fled; Jordan was driven back. The mountains skipped like rams, and the little hills like lambs.

What ailed you, O sea, that you fled? And you Jordan, that you were driven back? And you mountains, that you skipped like rams, and you little hills, like lambs?

Tremble, O earth, at the presence of the Lord, at the presence of the God of Jacob, who turned the rock into a pool of water, the flint into a fountain of waters.

## His Mercy Is Great

117    Praise the Lord, all nations! Praise him, all peoples! For his mercy is great toward us, and the truth of the Lord endures forever. Hallelujah!

## I Lift My Eyes to the Hills

121    I lift up my eyes to the hills, whence comes my help. My help comes from the Lord, who made heaven and earth!

He will not suffer my foot to slip; he who guards me will not slumber. Behold, the guardian of Israel will neither slumber nor sleep. The Lord is my guardian; the Lord is the shade upon my right hand. The sun will not smite me by day, nor the moon by night. The Lord will preserve me from all evil. He will preserve my soul. He will guard my going out and my coming in from this time forth, and forevermore.

## Our Eyes Look to the Lord

123    I lift up my eyes to you, O you who dwell in the heavens. Behold, as the eyes of servants look to the hands of their masters, and as the eyes of a maiden to the hand of her mistress, so our eyes look to the Lord our God until he has mercy upon us.

Have mercy upon us, O Lord, have mercy upon us. For our soul is filled with the scorn of those who are at ease, and with the contempt of the insolent.

## Our Soul Escaped

124    Let Israel say, "If it had not been the Lord who was on our side when men rose up against us, then had they swallowed us up alive; then the waters would have overwhelmed us, the torrent would have gone over us.

"Blessed be the Lord, who has not given us a prey to their teeth. Our soul escaped like a bird from the snare of the fowlers; the snare is broken and we have escaped. Our help is in the name of the Lord, who made heaven and earth."

## Those Who Trust in the Lord

125    Those who trust in the Lord are like Mount Zion, which cannot be moved, but abides forever. As the mountains are round about Jerusalem, so the Lord is round about his people, from this time forth and forever.

For the rod of the wicked shall not rest upon the lot of the righteous, lest the righteous put forth their hand to do wrong. Do good, O Lord, to those who are good, to those who are upright in their heart. As for those who turn aside to crooked ways, let the Lord lead them away with the wrongdoers. Peace be upon Israel!

## When the Lord Brought Back the Captives

126    When the Lord brought back the captives to Zion, we were like those who dream. Then was our mouth filled with laughter, and our tongue with singing. Then said they among the nations, "The Lord has done great things for them!"

The Lord has done great things for us, and we are glad.

Turn again our captivity, O Lord, as the streams in the dry land.

Those who sow in tears shall reap in joy; and he who goes forth and weeps, bearing precious seed, shall return with rejoicing, bearing his sheaves with him.

## Except the Lord Build the House

127    Except the Lord build the house, they labor in vain who build it. Except the Lord guard the city, the watchman is wakeful in vain. It is vain for you to rise up early, to sit up late, to eat the bread of sorrow; so he gives to his beloved sleep.

Lo, children are a heritage from the Lord, and the fruit of the womb is a reward. As arrows in the hand of a mighty man, so are the children of one's youth. Happy is the man who has his quiver full of them! They will not be put to shame when they speak with their enemies in the gate.

## He Has Cut the Cords of the Wicked

129    Israel may now say: "Many a time have they afflicted me from my youth, yet they have not prevailed against me. The plowers plowed upon my back; they made their furrows long." But the Lord is righteous; he has cut asunder the cords of the wicked.

Let them be put to shame and turned back, all those who hate Zion. Let them be like the grass upon the housetops, which withers before it springs up; with which the reaper fills not his hand, nor the binder of sheaves his arms. Those who pass by will not say to him, "The blessing of the Lord be upon you; we bless you in the name of the Lord."

## Out of the Depths I Cried Out

130    Out of the depths have I cried out to you, O Lord! Hear my voice; let your ears be attentive to my supplications! If you, O Lord, should mark iniquities, who could stand? But with you there is forgiveness, that you may be revered.

I wait for the Lord; my soul does wait, and in his word do I place my hope. My soul waits for the Lord more than the watchmen who wait for the morning, yes, more than watchmen who wait for the morning. Let

Israel hope in the Lord. For with the Lord there is mercy; with him there is plenteous redemption. And he will redeem Israel from all his iniquities.

## My Heart Is Not Haughty

131    My heart is not haughty, nor my eyes proud, O Lord! Neither
       do I exercise myself in matters too great or too high for me.
Surely, I have stilled and quieted myself, like a child whose mother has weaned him; like a weaned child is my soul.
    Let Israel hope in the Lord, from this time forth and forever.

## Like the Dew of Hermon

133    Behold, how good and how pleasant it is for brothers to dwell
       together in unity!
It is like precious ointment; it is like the dew of Hermon that descends upon the mountains of Zion. For there the Lord commanded the blessing: life forevermore.

## By the Rivers of Babylon

137    By the rivers of Babylon, there we sat down, yes, we wept when
       we remembered Zion. Upon the willows we hung up our harps.
For there, those who led us away captive required of us a song, and our tormentors required of us mirth, saying, "Sing us one of the songs of Zion."
    How could we sing the songs of the Lord in a strange land? If I forget you, O Jerusalem, let my right hand forget her cunning. If I do not remember you, let my tongue cling to the roof of my mouth; if I prefer not Jerusalem above my chief joy.

## If I Take Wing with the Morning Star

139    O Lord, you have searched me and known me. You know when
       I sit down and when I rise up; you understand my thoughts from
afar. There is not a word in my tongue, but lo, O Lord, you know it.

Such knowledge is too wonderful for me; it is too high, I cannot attain to it.

Where shall I go, and whither shall I flee from your presence? If I ascend into heaven you are there, and if I make my bed in Sheol, behold, you are there. If I take wing with the morning star, and dwell in the uttermost parts of the sea, even there would your hand lead me, and your right hand would hold me. If I say, "Surely the darkness will cover me," even night becomes light about me; yes, the darkness hides nothing from you. The darkness and the light are both alike to you.

Marvelous are your works; and that my soul knows well. And in your book all the days of my life are recorded. How precious are your thoughts to me, O God! How great is the sum of them! Were I to count them, they would outnumber the sands.

Search me, O God, and know my heart! Try me, and know my thoughts! See if there is any wicked way in me, and lead me in your way everlasting.

## *Praise the Lord*

150    Praise the Lord.
      Praise God in his sanctuary!
Praise him in the firmament of his power.
Praise him for his mighty acts.
Praise him according to his greatness.
Praise him with the sound of the trumpet.
Praise him with psaltery and harp.
Praise him with the timbrel and dance.
Praise him with stringed instruments and pipes.
Praise him upon the crashing cymbals.
Let everything that has breath praise the Lord. Hallelujah.

# Appendixes

# THE EXCLUDED BOOKS
## A Digest of the Apocrypha

There are a number of documents which were originally included in the Bible (and are still included in the Greek Orthodox and Roman Catholic Bible) but were later excluded, first by the Jews and then by the Protestants. These are the fourteen books of the Apocrypha: sometimes called deuterocanonical (or secondary to the canonical) books.

In addition to these, there existed at one time a vast number of works, most of them apocalypses, which were excluded from every canon because their authorship and dates were in doubt. The "doubtful" works are known as Pseudepigrapha. Many of the pseudepigraphic works have since disappeared; and of those that remain, many are preserved in fragmentary form. Some of them belong with the Old Testament and are Hebraic in origin, and some belong with the New Testament and are Christian in origin. Though all these works are Biblical in character, and some compare favorably in style and in their lofty teachings with many of the books included in the canon, they have always remained outside the boundary of the "inspired" books.

The Apocrypha, included as part of the Greek and Roman Catholic Bibles, and sometimes included, but only as an appendix, in the Old Testament of the Protestant Bible, should be known at least in scope and content to all Bible readers. The following digest may serve as a general introduction to these works; and they are presented in the order in which they appear in the appendix to the Authorized Version.

## I Esdras

This work in nine chapters is noted for its folktale about Zerubbabel, in the court of King Darius, who gained distinction for wisdom when he chose truth as the greatest power in the world, after others before him had argued in favor of the power of wine, of women, and of the king. The rest of the book repeats, and adds little to, the canonized books of Ezra and Nehemiah.

## II Esdras

This apocalyptic version of Ezra, in sixteen chapters, is filled with visions and mystic dreams, the prophetic parts reminiscent of the minor prophets, and the style resembling the Book of Revelation in the New Testament.

## Tobit

This symbolical legend in fourteen chapters tells about the devout Tobit, who sends his son Tobias on a business mission to a distant city. Tobias and his dog, guided by the angel Raphael disguised as a young man, come to the house of Raguel, whose young daughter Sara has been married seven times. They learn that each time, on her wedding night, Sara's husband has been killed by a demon. Tobias marries the girl and, with the aid of the angel Raphael, exorcises the demon. The story extols chastity, benevolence and prayer.

## Judith

This long short-story, in sixteen chapters, based on historical events, tells how the Jewish city of Bethulia was besieged by General Holofernes and his army and reduced to the point of surrender, when Judith, a widow of great beauty and devotion to her people, devises a plan to enter the enemy camp. When she succeeds in this, and is left alone with Holofernes, she kills him, and flees to Bethulia. At the death of the general, his army is thrown into confusion and the city is saved.

## Esther

The canonical Esther ends rather abruptly with the third verse of the tenth chapter. The apocryphal Esther picks up the story here and adds ten verses to this chapter, followed by six more chapters, which complete the story.

## The Wisdom of Solomon

This is a supreme example of Hebrew "wisdom literature" and compares favorably with Proverbs and Ecclesiastes. The first six chapters deal primarily with the immortality of the just and the punishment of the wicked; the next two chapters are devoted to the praise of wisdom; and the remaining nine chapters, written in an entirely different style from the preceding material, summarize the history of God's people from Creation, and attempt to explain the origin of idolatry. The Pauline letters frequently quote the first nine chapters of this book.

## Ecclesiasticus

This work, also known as The Wisdom of Jesus ben Sirach, contains some of the most brilliant passages to be found in the entire body of Hebrew "wisdom literature." It is the longest work in the Apocrypha, consisting of fifty-one chapters, and ending with a psalm. The book was originally written in Hebrew and translated into Greek. Today no complete Hebrew version exists, and there is great variation in the text of the different versions.

## Baruch

This, presumably, is the book of the same Prince Baruch who was the scribe and friend of the prophet Jeremiah. The apocryphal work bearing his name is obviously incomplete and disjointed. The six chapters give a message from the Jews in exile to the Jews in Jerusalem, an exhortation to wisdom, a lament, a warning against idolatry, and touch upon many other topics. The work seems to have been longer originally, for parts of it are found among other excluded books of the Bible, such as the Apocalypse of Baruch in the Pseudepigrapha.

## Song of the Three Holy Children

This prayer in sixty-eight verses, which presumably belongs in Daniel after 3:23, is by Azariah, one of the three men thrown into the fiery furnace.

## Susanna

This short short-story presumably also belongs in Daniel, though excluded from the Hebrew canon and placed among the Apocrypha in the Authorized Version. It tells of the attempted seduction of the beautiful and virtuous Susanna, the false accusation against her and her vindication by young Daniel; and it is written with a crispness of style that makes the story startlingly contemporary.

## Bel and the Dragon

This fragment also is part of the Daniel story, and tells how Daniel exposes false priests. (See DANIEL in Notes and Excisions.)

## Prayer of Manasses

This is a prayer in one long verse (alluded to in II Chronicles 33:13), presumably by Manasses, king of Judah, when he was taken captive to Babylonia. In historical chronology this would belong somewhere in II Kings, 23.

535

## I Maccabees

An authentic historical record, in sixteen chapters, covering a period of thirty-two years, beginning with the uprising of Mattathias against the oppression of Antiochus IV and ending with the murder of Simon, the son of Mattathias (135 B.C.E.).

## II Maccabees

This is a brilliant literary work purporting to be a condensation into fifteen chapters of the record given by Jason of Cyrene in five volumes; and assurance is given the reader that the author took great care to prepare his material so "that they who read might have delight, and that they who are desirous to commit to memory might have ease, and that all into whose hands it comes might have profit." Apparently there were many other works on the Maccabees. In addition to I and II Maccabees in the Apocrypha, there are also III, IV and V Maccabees in the Pseudepigrapha.

# SUMMARY OF
# PRINCIPAL LAWS IN THE
# FIVE BOOKS OF MOSES

The Five Books of Moses contain a great diversity of laws, many of which are by now of only historical interest, but many others are, in modified form, the basis of our Western law. A summary of the most important of these laws is given below, arranged alphabetically; and the source in the Authorized Version is given parenthetically, so that the reader who wishes to do so may look up the original text. Some laws are repeated, with variations, in two or more of the Five Books; in such cases the references given are arranged chronologically as they appear in the Bible.

*Adultery* is prohibited in the Ten Commandments, and repeatedly described as an offense punishable by death. (Exod. 20:14; Lev. 18:20; 20:10; Num. 5:12-31; Deut. 5:18; 22:22-24.)

*Aliens* must be treated with fairness, and the same laws apply to them as to the native, though a distinction is made in the prohibition against usury, which is lifted in the case of the stranger. (Exod. 12:49; 22:21; 23:9; Lev. 19:34; 24:22; Num. 9:14; 15:14-16; 35:15; Deut. 1:16; 23:20; 24:14-18; 27:19.)

*Animals* must be treated with kindness and compassion. And the day of rest, prescribed for all who labor, applies to the beast of burden. The ass that falls under his burden must be helped, even if the animal belongs to an enemy. (Exod. 23:4-5, 11-12; 34:26; Lev. 22:28; 25:5-7; Deut. 22:6-7; 25:4.) Vicious animals are to be killed, and the owners of vicious animals are held responsible for them. (Exod. 21:29, 35-36.)

*Apostasy* is prohibited in the severest terms. The prohibition appears in the Ten Commandments, and is repeated many times. (Exod. 20:2-5; 22-26; 22:20; 23:24; 34:12-14, 17; Lev. 18:3; 19:27-28; 20:23; Deut. 4:15-19; 5:7-10; 6:14-15; 7:5, 25; 11:16-17, 26-28; 13:1-16; 14:1-2; 16:21-22; 17:2-7; 18:9-12; 27:15; 30:17-18.)

*Arson* is to be punished, and the damage caused by the fire paid by the arsonist. (Exod. 22:6.)

*Assault* causing disability is to be fined according to the loss of time involved;

537

assault causing injury to a slave gives him the right to his freedom. (Exod. 21:18-27; Lev. 24:19; Deut. 27:24.)

*Avenger of Murder.* See *Murder*

*Beating,* as court punishment, was permitted, but limited to a maximum of "forty stripes." (Deut. 25:2-3.)

*Blasphemy* is prohibited in the Ten Commandments and repeatedly warned against; and the punishment for the offender is death by stoning. (Exod. 20:7; 22:28; Lev. 18:21; 19:12; 24:10-16, 23; Deut. 5:11.)

*Blood,* in any form, must not be eaten. (Lev. 19:26; Deut. 12:23; 15:23.)

*Breach of trust* is defined, and the penalties prescribed. (Exod. 22:7-13; Lev. 6:1-5.)

*Bribery* of judges is condemned. (Exod. 23:8; Deut. 16:19; 27:25.)

*Burglary.* See *Theft*

*Capital punishment* is to be meted out for those found guilty of a diversity of crimes. (Exod. 21:15-18; 22:18-19; Lev. 20:2, 9; Deut. 17:2-7; 21:18-21.)

*Cheating,* and all forms of "dealing falsely," is forbidden. (Lev. 19:11.)

*Circumcision* is required as part of the covenant with Abraham; and it is required of the stranger who wishes to keep the Passover. (Gen. 17:9-14; 21:4; Exod. 12:44, 48; Lev. 12:3.)

*Cities of refuge* are to be established as sanctuary for those who commit manslaughter, but whose intent to kill has not been established. (Exod. 21:13-14; Num. 35:6-32; Deut. 19:1-13.)

*Citizenship* qualifications for belonging to the congregation of the Lord. (Deut. 23:1-8.)

*Compensation for damages.* See *Restitution*

*Contempt of court* is an offense punishable by death. (Deut. 17:11-13.)

*Crossbreeding* of animals or plants is prohibited. (Lev. 19:19; Deut. 22:9-11.)

*Cursing of parents.* See *Parents*

*Damages.* See *Restitution*

*Daughters as inheritors.* See *Inheritance*

*Death* caused by an animal. See *Goring*

*Death sentence.* See *Capital punishment*

*Deuterogamic code* defines the impartiality that must be observed toward children of two wives. (Deut. 21:15-17.)

*Divorce and remarriage.* Though divorce is permitted, remarriage to a former spouse is prohibited. (Deut. 24:1-4.)

*Enslavement* for theft is to be the punishment of the thief who is unable to make restitution. (Exod. 22:3.)

*Excommunication* is prescribed for perpetrators of specific offenses. (Lev. 18:1-29; 20:3-18; Num. 9:13; 15:30; 19:20.)

*Eye-for-eye and tooth-for-tooth* law of justice defined. (Exod. 21:24-25; Lev. 24:19-22; Deut. 19:21.)

*False prophets.* See *Prophets*
*False witness.* See *Witness*
*Falsification of weights and measures.* See *Weights and measures*
*Family allotment of land.* See *Inheritance laws*
*Favoritism* in judgment is forbidden. (Exod. 23:2-3, 6; Lev. 19:15, 35.)
*Firstborn,* rights of. See *Deuterogamic code*
*Foods* not to be eaten by members of the congregation of the Lord. (Exod. 22:31; Lev. 7:24; 11:1-47; 17:15; 22:8.)
*Forbidden marriages.* See *Marriages*
*Foreigners.* See *Aliens*
*Fugitives,* protection of. (Deut. 23:15-16.)

*Goring* by an ox which had previously killed a man or another animal is held to be the responsibility of the owner, and the animal is to be stoned. (Exod. 21:28-32.)

*Hanging,* as punishment. (Deut. 21:22-23.)
*Heirs.* See *Inheritance laws*
*Honor due to parents.* See *Parents*

*Idolatry.* See *Apostasy*
*Impartiality of judges.* See *Favoritism*
*Impersonation* of a woman by a man, or by a woman as a man, is forbidden. (Deut. 22:5.)
*Imprisonment,* until guilt can be determined. (Lev. 24:12; Num. 15:34.)
*Incendiaries.* See *Arson*
*Incest* is meticulously defined; and the penalty for incest is death. (Lev. 18:6-21; Deut. 22:30; 27:22-23.)
*Inheritance laws* of each tribe, family inheritance, inheritance of daughters, and inheritance of slaves, are separately defined. (Num. 27:5-11; 33:54; 36:1-12; Deut. 21:15-17.)
*Injuries* resulting in disability or death. The punishment of the person responsible for the injury varies according to whether the injured individual is a freeman or a slave. (Exod. 21:18-23.)
*Interest.* See *Usury*

*Jealousy,* the trial procedure for wives accused by jealous husbands. (Num. 5:11-31.)
*Jubilee year* is prescribed, in which slaves are to be freed, and the land is to remain fallow at the end of seven-times-seven years. (Lev. 25:3-54; Deut. 15:1-3, 12-18.)
*Judges,* how they are to be appointed, their authority, and the importance

of their absolute impartiality is given. (Exod. 18:13-26; 23:6-8; Lev. 19:15; 24:22; Num. 11:16; Deut. 16:18; 25:1.)

*Justice*, to be strictly observed; obstruction or perversion of justice to be severely punished. (Exod. 23:1-7; Lev. 19:15, 35-36; Deut. 16:19.)

*Kidnaping* of individuals to be sold as slaves punishable by death. (Exod. 21:16.)

*Landmarks* must not be removed. (Deut. 19:14; 27:17.)

*Law*, instruction in and obedience to the law; the penalty for defiance of the law. (Lev. 18:4-5, 26; 19:19; 20:8, 22; Num. 15:30-31; Deut. 5:31-33; 6:1-3, 6-7, 17; 7:11; 8:1, 6, 11; 10:12-13; 11:18-19; 17:12-13; 26:16-17; 27:1-8; 30:15-16.)

*Laws of primogeniture.* See *Primogeniture*

*Lying* is tersely forbidden, along with theft. (Lev. 19:11.)

*Marriages* that are permitted, and marriages that are forbidden, and the special laws governing the marriages of priests. (Exod. 22:16-17; 34:12-16; Lev. 18:6-18; 20:11-21; 21:7, 13-15; Num. 25:6-8; 36:6; Deut. 7:1-7; 22:30.)

*Measures.* See *Weights and measures*

*Military laws* governing the service of all men twenty to fifty, and defining the exceptions as newlyweds and those building a house or planting a vineyard. (Num. 1:2-3; Deut. 20:5-8.)

*Miscarriage* caused by a chance hurt; the guilty party to be punished as determined by the judge. (Exod. 21:22-25.)

*Mob rule* is condemned. (Exod. 23:2.)

*Murder* is condemned in the Ten Commandments. The law is elaborated upon later by distinguishing between premeditated and accidental killing, and giving the punishment for each in the case of a freeman or a slave. (Exod. 20:13; 21:12-14, 20-23; Lev. 24:17; Num. 35:11-34; Deut. 5:17; 19:11-13; 21:1-9.)

*Mutilation,* as punishment for indecency. (Deut. 25:11-12.)

*Naturalization laws.* (Deut. 23:3, 7-8.)

*Needy people,* and the disabled and the poor, to be treated with special consideration. (Lev. 19:14; Deut. 24:14; 27:18.)

*Neighbors* are to be loved, even if they are aliens in the land. (Lev. 19:18; Deut. 10:19; 22:4.)

*Oath* of a witness is binding, and the breaking of an oath is to be punished. (Exod. 22:10-11; Lev. 6:1-7.)

*Orphans and widows* are to be treated with special consideration. (Exod. 22:22-24; Deut. 24:17; 27:19.)

*Parents* are to be honored and obeyed; the limitations on parental authority are given. (Exod. 20:12; 21:7-11, 17; Lev. 19:3; 20:9; Deut. 5:16; 21:18-21.)

*Patricide* is punishable with death. (Exod. 21:15.)

*Perjury* is forbidden in the Ten Commandments. The law is elaborated upon in other parts of the Bible. (Exod. 20:16; 23:1; Lev. 19:12; Deut. 5:20; 19:16-20.)

*Philanthropy*, particularly to the poor and the alien, is stressed. (Exod. 23:10-11; Lev. 19:9-10; 23:22; Deut. 24:19-21.)

*Pledges* may not be taken of tools needed to earn a livelihood, nor of clothing needed for warmth. (Exod. 22:26-27; Deut. 24:6, 10-13.)

*Poor.* See *Needy*

*Primogeniture*, or the rights of the firstborn son, established. (Deut. 21:15-17.)

*Property*, personal. Neither the buyer nor the seller should take advantage of each other when such property is sold. (Lev. 25:14.)

*Prophets*, false, are warned against; and the offenders are to be put to death. (Deut. 13:1-5; 18:20-22.)

*Prostitution* is forbidden; and the penalty for the daughter of a priest who becomes a prostitute is death by burning. (Lev. 19:29; 21:9.)

*Punishment* is intended for the guilty person, and no man is to be punished for the guilt of another, whether son or father. (Deut. 24:16.)

*Ransom*, when allowed and when not allowed. (Exod. 21:30; Num. 35:31.)

*Rape*, and the punishment for rape. (Deut. 22:25-26.)

*Redemption* of land. (Lev. 25:23-24.) Redemption of slaves. (Lev. 25:45-47; Deut. 15:12-18; 21:10-14.)

*Restitution*, for damages or stolen property of diverse kinds. (Exod. 21:19, 32, 35-36; 22:12, 14-15; Lev. 5:16; 6:1-7; 24:18, 21; Num. 5:7.)

*Sabbath* to be observed as a day of rest is in the Ten Commandments; the urgency to observe it is repeated many times; the penalty for desecration of the Sabbath is death by stoning. (Exod. 20:8-11; 23:12; 31:14, 17; 34:21; 35:2-3; Lev. 19:3, 30; 26:2; Num. 15:32-36.)

*Sabbatical year*, in which children of Israel must refrain from tillage — every seventh year. (Lev. 25:3-7.)

*Sacrifice* of children forbidden upon penalty of death. (Lev. 18:21; 20:2-5; Deut. 12:29-31.)

*Scourging.* See *Beating*

*Seduction* and its punishment. (Lev. 19:20-22; Deut. 22:28-29.)

*Self-defense*, resulting in death, not to be punished. (Exod. 22:2.)

*Servants.* See *Slaves*

*Slander* is forbidden. (Exod. 23:1; Lev. 19:16; Deut. 22:13-21.)

*Slaves*, as property, and who could be bought and sold. Slavery was permitted, but many laws regulated when and how the slaves could gain their freedom. (Exod. 21:2-11; Lev. 19:20; 25:39-55; Deut. 15:12; 16:10-11; 20:14; 23:15-16.)

*Sodomy* is forbidden upon the penalty of death. (Exod. 22:19; Lev. 18:22; 20:13; Deut. 23:17.)

*Sorcery* is forbidden. (Exod. 22:18; Lev. 20:27.)

*Stoning,* as punishment. (Lev. 20:2, 27; 24:16; Num. 15:32-36; Deut. 13:10; 17:5-7; 21:19-21; 22:21.)

*Strangers.* See *Aliens*

*Theft* is prohibited in the Ten Commandments; and if the thief is caught he must make restitution or be sold into slavery. (Exod. 20:15; 22:1-5; Lev. 6:2-7; 19:11; Deut. 5:19; 23:24-25.)

*Usury* is strictly prohibited, though permitted to strangers. (Exod. 22:25; Lev. 25:36-37; Deut. 23:19-20.)

*Wages* of servants are to be paid promptly. (Lev. 19:13; Deut. 24:14-15.)

*Weights and measures* must be accurate. (Lev. 19:35-37; Deut. 25:13-16.)

*Widows* are to be treated with kindness and special consideration. (Exod. 22:22-24; Deut. 24:17; 27:19.)

*Witchcraft.* See *Sorcery*

*Witness* must be truthful; false witnesses should be punished; no man should be condemned on the evidence of only one witness. (Exod. 22:10-11; 23:1; Lev. 19:12; Deut. 5:20; 17:7; 19:15-20.)

*Wizards.* See *Sorcery*

# NOTES AND EXCISIONS

All notes on the text of the Bible, and all parts omitted in the continuity but summarized here, follow the order of the books of the Bible as they appear in this volume. The chapter numbers in parentheses refer to the chapter numbers in the Authorized Version of the Bible. Redundancies within the text and lengthy identifications of people and places have been sharply edited; and the repetition of speeches or ritual instructions which are first given to one person and then repeated almost verbatim to another or others were also omitted; but these are not indicated in the Notes.

## Genesis

(Ch. 1-2) Here we seem to have two accounts of the creation of man; but they are interpreted as one account, given briefly in the first chapter and elaborated upon in the second. The First Man story is found in other sacred books: to the Chinese he is known as P'an Ku; in the Hindu scriptures he appears as Man-u; and in the Babylonian account he is known as Adami. The names of the four rivers flowing from the garden of Eden, omitted in this version, it is assumed represent the seats of all early civilizations.

(Ch. 4) An account follows here of Cain's grandchildren, and how they domesticated cattle, invented the harp and the organ, and discovered the use of brass and iron.

(Ch. 5) A genealogy is presented from Adam to Noah, son of Methuselah, showing how long-lived the people were in those early days, with Methuselah — oldest man of a long-lived race — reaching the age of nine hundred and sixty-nine years.

(Ch. 9:18-27) A brief record is given here of how Ham, Noah's youngest son and called the father of Canaan, mocks his father when he finds him drunken in his tent; and how Noah, when he becomes sober and hears of Ham's behavior, curses him with the curse that his offspring shall be servants to the offspring of his brothers Shem and Japheth.

(Ch. 10) Another genealogy follows, giving the multiplication of the nations descended from the sons of Noah, who dispersed to many parts of the earth.

(Ch. 11) The genealogy of Noah's son Shem is followed for nine generations

543

to Terah, father of Abraham, who dwelt in Ur of the Chaldees (Babylonia).

(Ch. 14) The record is given of a war between four kings, led by the king of Elam (probably Persia), against five Canaanite kings, including the king of Sodom, in the course of which Lot and his household were taken captive and their possessions confiscated. When Abraham heard of this, he joined forces with the Canaanites and battled successfully to free Lot and his household, and to have Lot's possessions returned to him. The grateful king of Sodom offered Abraham compensation from the booty, but Abraham refused to accept as much as a "thread or a shoelatchet" save only what his warriors had eaten, and the portion due to the men who had joined him against Elam. This chapter is regarded as an interpolation from another ancient but non-Israelitish source, labeled "Arabian" or "Edomite," which was at one time acceptable to Jewish tradition.

(Ch. 15) God promises Abraham that his offspring shall be as numerous as the stars of the sky, and that Canaan will be their inheritance.

(Ch. 17) Circumcision in itself was well known in Abraham's day and widely practiced among Egyptians, Moabites, Edomites, and other nations.

(Ch. 20) This chapter repeats the story told earlier (Gen. 12:11-20) in which Abraham claims that his wife is his sister; but here Egypt is replaced by Gerar, and Pharaoh by King Abimelech.

(Ch. 21:22-34) Here we have a record of a primitive pact concerning water rights between Abraham and Abimelech at Bath-Sheba.

(Ch. 25:1-18) After Sarah's death, Abraham marries a woman named Keturah. (In Biblical folklore it is assumed that the woman was Hagar, who, though separated from Abraham for all those years, had waited for him.) The record gives the children born to Abraham and Keturah. Then Abraham died, at the age of one hundred and seventy-five years, and was buried in the Cave of Machpelah. A brief genealogy follows of Ishmael's offspring.

(Ch. 26) The twice-told story (Gen. 12:11-20 and Gen. 20) appears again; but this time Isaac and Rebekah replace Abraham and Sarah in Abimelech's court.

(Ch. 36) The entire chapter is devoted to a genealogy of Esau's descendants, known as Edomites.

(Ch. 38) The Joseph story is interrupted here by the story of Tamar, a bereaved daughter-in-law of Judah, who forces him to confess his transgression against her.

(Ch. 46) A genealogy is given of the children and grandchildren who came with Jacob from Canaan to Goshen in Egypt.

(Ch. 48) Joseph and his two sons Manasseh and Ephraim visit Jacob, and he blesses them before he dies.

## Exodus

(Ch. 6) A genealogy is given, parenthetically, which indicates that Aaron and Moses were direct descendants of Abraham.

(Ch. 21-23) The miscellany of laws in these chapters cover: the manumission of slaves; the treatment of women sold in slavery; manslaughter; the penalties for striking or cursing a parent; the theft of men to be sold as slaves; bodily injury caused willfully or inadvertently; punishment for theft, arson, or trespass; seduction, perversion, and idolatry; the treatment of witches, slanderers, and falsifiers; how to treat the widow, the orphan, and the stranger; the observance of the Sabbath, the feasts, and the Jubilee; the sacrifices to be made to the Lord, and the offerings of the firstborn and first fruits. The most important of these are given in the text of this book, and all the others are included in the Summary of Principal Laws in the Pentateuch (page 537).

(Ch. 25-31) These chapters give a detailed description of: the ark and its dimensions; the mercy seat and the table for the shewbread; the six-branched candelabra made of pure gold; the ten curtains of the tabernacle and the hangings at the door; the altar and its furnishings; the oil to be used for the eternal light; the consecration of Aaron and his sons; the robes which the priests were to wear when performing their duties: the ephod, the breastplate, the embroidered coat, the miter, and the girdle; and the manner in which the priests should be consecrated.

(Ch. 35-40) These chapters give in detail the fulfillment of the Lord's command concerning the tabernacle and the ark; and repeat how the people gathered all the materials for the house of God and for the garments of the priests; and how Aaron and his sons were ordained.

## Leviticus

(Ch. 1-7) Detailed instructions are given here for the diverse sacrifices and offerings, whether of cattle or fowl or the first fruits; and the differences are indicated in the ritual between sin offerings, peace offerings and trespass offerings.

(Ch. 8-9) These chapters record the ceremony with which Aaron and his sons are consecrated as priests, and give the strange and elaborate ritual in which, after Aaron and his sons lay their hands upon the sacrificial ram and slay it, Moses takes its blood and puts some of it "upon the tip of Aaron's right ear, and upon the thumb of his right hand, and upon the great toe of his right foot"; and he does the same to Aaron's sons before he sprinkles the blood upon the altar. And when it is over, a holy fire comes down and consumes the burnt offering on the altar; and the people who witness it shout and fall upon their faces.

(Ch. 10) An incident is recorded of Nadab and Abihu, Aaron's sons, placing fire and incense in their censers in a manner offensive to the Lord, and for this offense they are consumed by a fire from heaven. But Moses commands Aaron and his remaining sons not to mourn their loss, because they are people anointed with the oil of the Lord and must show no personal grief.

(Ch. 12) The laws are given relating to the purification of women after childbirth.

(Ch. 13-17) The laws are established concerning leprosy: how to recognize it; how to cleanse the leper; and how to cleanse the house in which leprosy occurs.

(Ch. 15) Various types of uncleanliness are described, and the laws are given regulating how men and women are to achieve cleansing.

(Ch. 16) A description is given of the manner in which the high priest is to enter the holy place to perform the sin offering for himself and for the people; the use of the scapegoat in this ceremony; and the injunction to observe the Day of Atonement on the tenth day of the seventh month.

(Ch. 21-22) Additional laws for the priests are given which establish when a priest may or may not mourn the dead, and whom he may and whom he may not marry. ("He shall take a wife in her virginity. A widow, or a divorced woman, or a profane woman, or a harlot, these shall he not take.") It also prohibits any priest with a physical defect from making offerings before the altar, although he is permitted to eat of the bread of God.

(Ch. 24) After receiving instructions from the Lord concerning the oil for the eternal light and the baking of the memorial bread, Moses is told again to inform his people of the punishment for blasphemy, murder, and property damage. And we have a repetition of "Breach for breach, eye for eye, tooth for tooth: as he has caused a blemish in a man, so shall it be done to him. And he that kills a beast shall restore it; and he that kills a man, he shall be killed."

(Ch. 26-27) These two chapters contain a repetition of the prohibitions against idolatry; the reverence to be shown the Sabbath; laws on the making of vows and concerning tithes; the blessings on those who keep God's commandments and the punishment of those who walk contrary to them.

## Numbers

(Ch. 1-2) The names are listed by their tribes of all those who assisted with the census; and in full detail the numbers of each tribe, and the captains of each tribe as grouped in the armies.

(Ch. 3-4) A detailed count is recorded of the tribe of Levi, who ministered in the tabernacle and were not subject to military service.

(Ch. 5) This chapter gives a detailed description of an ancient rite in the trial of jealousy. If a man suspects his wife of infidelity, but has no proof of it, he may bring her to the tabernacle, where the priest will pronounce a curse and cause her to drink the bitter water; if she is guilty she will swell up, but if she is innocent she will show no ill effects from either the drink or the curse.

(Ch. 6) Laws are established concerning the vow of the Nazarite, who, during all the days of his separation, must not touch any wine or strong drink, or cut his hair, or come near the dead; and when the days of his separation are over, he must make the proper sacrifices.

(Ch. 7) An inventory is given of the gifts brought to the tabernacle by the princes of the tribes of Israel: wagons, oxen, golden spoons, silver chargers, silver bowls, bullocks, rams and lambs, flour mixed with oil, and frankincense — and their number and value is recorded.

(Ch. 8) The ritual for the tabernacle service is established, and the age when the Levites are permitted to perform these services is limited to between twenty-five and fifty years.

(Ch. 9) An amendment is made to the laws governing the observance of the Passover which permits those on a journey during the first day of the festival, or who cannot celebrate it for some other reason, to celebrate it the following day.

(Ch. 10) The order of the tribal armies and their leaders is given as they start the journey from Sinai to Paran.

(Ch. 15) Various offerings are described; the punishment for one who breaks the Sabbath; and the requirement that the children of Israel wear a garment with four fringes on the borders as a constant reminder of God's commandments.

(Ch. 17) Upon disaffection among the leaders of the tribes and grumbling against the authority of Aaron and the Levites, Moses orders the elders of the twelve tribes to bring a rod into the tabernacle, one rod for each tribe; and Aaron's rod is presented to represent the tribe of Levi. The next morning, when the rods are brought out again, Aaron's rod has blossomed overnight and brought forth almonds, proving that Aaron and the Levites are God's choice for the priesthood.

(Ch. 18) The priests and the Levites are given responsibility for the tabernacle and its services; their rights in the portions brought as offerings and tithes are described.

(Ch. 19) The preparation of water to be used in purification of sin ("the water of separation") is given, and how it is to be used ritually.

(Ch. 20:2-11) This records a repetition of the miracle given in Exodus 17:1-7.

(Ch. 21:10-20) The record continues with additional journeying in the desert, and wars with unfriendly natives. Here, for the first time, we find a reference to a lost book, called The Book of the Wars of the Lord.

(Ch. 25) At Shittim in Moab the children of Israel began to "commit whoredom with the daughters of Moab," and in consequence were punished with a plague which killed twenty-four thousand people before it was stayed. The story implies that the Moabites sent down their women to seduce the Israelites and weaken them; and that the leaders understood this threat and warned their men against the Moabite women, but were not heeded. Then Zimri, of the tribe of Simeon, brought Cozbi, the daughter of a Midianite chieftain, openly into camp; and Phinehas, Aaron's grandson, followed them into their tent and thrust his javelin through both the man and the woman.

(Ch. 26) In the plains of Moab, near Jericho, another census is taken of those capable of going to war; by this time only Caleb and Joshua are left in this category from all those numbered at Sinai.

(Ch. 27:1-11) The five daughters of Zelophehad, descendants of Manasseh, son of Joseph, petition for an inheritance after their father's death; and Moses establishes the precedent that daughters may inherit their father's possessions if he leaves no sons behind him, provided the daughters marry men of their own tribe.

(Ch. 28-29) A recapitulation is made of the offerings for the Sabbath, the beginning of the month, the Day of Atonement, and the holidays, as well as the daily offerings.

(Ch. 30) This chapter gives the commandments concerning vows, and particularly vows made by women; when they are binding and when they are not binding.

(Ch. 31) Here we have the record of Israel's cruel war against Midian, in which all the enemy males are slain and the women and children taken captive; after the battle Moses orders all male children and married women slain, after which there is a division of the spoils.

(Ch. 33-35) These chapters record the great victory in the war against Midian and the division of the spoils. After the recital of all the journeys of the children of Israel from the day they left Egypt until they reached the borders of Canaan, the border limits of the country to be conquered are defined; the names of the men who are to take charge of the division of the land among the tribes are enumerated; and forty-eight cities are set aside as an inheritance of the Levites — and of these cities six are to be cities of refuge, to which any man-slayer may escape until he has appeared before judges.

(Ch. 36) The law is established that daughters who inherit land or property must marry within the tribe so that inheritance is not transferred from one tribe to another.

## Deuteronomy

(Ch. 1-4) As given in this book, the first four chapters were sharply edited, as shown below, and verses 16-17 in Chapter 1 were transposed and placed at the end of the first discourse by Moses, for reasons of emphasis.

(Ch. 1:41-46) Repeats the punishment for disobedience, as given in Numbers 14:40-45.

(Ch. 2:2-37) Gives a detailed account of the command from the Lord not to fight against the Moabites or the Ammonites; and of the victory over King Sihon.

(Ch. 3:12-20) Tells how the land won from Og, king of Bashan, and the land won earlier from Sihon, king of the Amorites, was divided between the tribes of Reuben and Gad and half of the tribe of Manasseh.

(Ch. 5) The first three sentences in this chapter have been transposed to the end of the second discourse by Moses. The Ten Commandments, with minor changes, are repeated here, and the circumstances in which they were received at Sinai are recalled.

(Ch. 6-9) Moses underscores the purpose of God's law, and exhorts the Israelites to preserve their national purity; and he repeats that it is because of God's goodness that they are about to enter Canaan to possess it.

(Ch. 10-11) The many mercies of the Lord are recalled: in restoring the tablets of stone bearing the Ten Commandments upon them, which Moses broke the first time he came down from Mount Sinai; in guarding the people on their journeys; and in God's miracles and acts while they were still in Egypt and after that time.

(Ch. 12) Nearly the whole of this lengthy chapter is devoted to a repetition of the command, given so often, to destroy idolatry; and a warning against the snares of idolatry after they come into the Promised Land.

(Ch. 14) The laws are given again as to what may and what may not be eaten, as recorded in Leviticus; then follows an enumeration of the tithes for the Lord, and the tithes for the widow, the orphan and the stranger.

(Ch. 15:12-23) This deals with the manumission of Hebrew slaves; and the consecration to the Lord of the firstborn males of flocks and of herds.

(Ch. 16-24) Excepting for the passages used in the text, these chapters reiterate laws and regulations concerning the holidays, the institution of judges, how the priests and judges are to determine difficult cases, the election of a king, the rights and privileges of the priests and the Levites, cities of refuge, the punishment of false witnesses, the captive that is taken as a wife, those who may and those who may not enter into the congregation of the Lord, divorce and remarriage, and many sundry personal ordinances.

(Ch. 25) Limitations are placed on punishment by whipping; and the duty is given for a man to marry his brother's wife if the brother dies childless; and the requirement that the firstborn of such a marriage should bear the dead brother's name, so that "his name shall not be erased in Israel."

(Ch. 27) The Levites pronounce curses for idolatry, perversion, incest, murder, and disobedience to the Lord's commandments.

## Joshua

(Ch. 1:12-17) Joshua reminds the Reubenites, the Gadites and half the tribe of Manasseh (who had settled east of the Jordan), of their promise to Moses that they would help the remainder of the tribes in the conquest of Canaan.

(Ch. 7-8) Because of the theft of some of the spoils of Jericho (which had been dedicated to the house of the Lord), Joshua suffers defeat at the city of Ai. The thief is discovered, and is stoned for his crime. Then Joshua captures the city by a ruse, and reduces it to a heap of ashes.

(Ch. 11-12) These chapters record many victories, and give a list of the thirty-one kings whom Joshua conquered "in the mountains, and in the valleys, and in the plains, and in the springs, and in the wilderness."

(Ch. 13-19) After the conquest of the kings and kingdoms, the boundaries of the land (as divided among the tribes) are determined in detail; a list is given of the cities belonging to the tribe of Judah; and the narrative records the fact that the Jebusites, who inhabited Jerusalem, were not driven out by Judah; nor were the Canaanites completely routed by Ephraim.

(Ch. 21) The forty-eight cities and surrounding land given to the Levites are listed, and their location indicated.

(Ch. 22) After the wars Joshua blesses Reuben, Gad, and the one half of the tribe of Manasseh whose lands are across the Jordan. Then they return home. They set up an altar at the Jordan, which angers the rest of Israel, but they explain their act to the satisfaction of the others, and name the altar Ed (The Witness), for it was intended as a witness between them and the Lord.

## Judges

(Ch. 6-8) In this narrative there is confusion between the angel of the Lord speaking to Gideon, and Gideon being addressed by the Lord. In the version given in this text, only the angel is presented as speaking to Gideon. Omitted from the story is Gideon's quarrel with the men of Succoth and Penuel for their refusal to give provisions for his warriors during their pursuit of the Amalekites, and Gideon's vengeance after his victorious return.

(Ch. 9:24-55) The conspiracy against Abimelech by Gaal and his followers is detailed here.

(Ch. 12) Here we have a reminder of the times when human sacrifices were sometimes made in fulfillment of vows to God.

(Ch. 17-18) The account is given here of a man named Micah who steals money from his mother, then restores it; and the curious consequences which follow when she spends it on images.

(Ch. 20-21) In the war between the tribe of Benjamin and the rest of the children of Israel, the Israelites vow never to permit their daughters to marry Benjamites. This seems to be a faint and confused record of the custom of exogamous marriage, when the males of one tribe would steal their wives on certain festivals from among the daughters of another tribe.

## I Samuel

(Ch. 6:14-20) The Levites of Bethshemesh take the ark from the cart and offer sacrifices to the Lord; but because they have touched the ark and looked into it, they are stricken by the Lord.

(Ch. 7:5-14) While Samuel has gathered the people in Mizpah to judge them, the Philistines launch an attack upon them. Samuel prays for the people, and the Lord sends great thunder and helps Israel subdue the enemy.

(Ch. 16:14-23) Here we find an interpolation (from some other source) of an event which took place later in the chronology of time: we are told of an evil spirit descending on King Saul; the king sends for David to soothe him by playing on his harp, and when David plays, the evil spirit departs from Saul.

(Ch. 26) This chapter is another version of what was given earlier in 23:19-26 and 24:1-22.

(Ch. 27:8-12) While David is in Ziklag, a city in Gath, he invades the neighboring countries of the Gesurites, Gezrites and Amalekites; and he brings the booty of sheep, oxen, camels and apparel to Achish, to convince that king that the people of Israel abhor David.

(Ch. 30) While David and his men try to join the lords of the Philistines in their battle against Israel, the Amalekites attack Ziklag, burn it to the ground, and take all the women and children captive. David and his men pursue and attack the Amalekites while they are still celebrating their victory over Ziklag, and rescue the women and children. Then David takes, as spoil, all the flocks and herds, and distributes them generously.

## II Samuel

(Ch. 5:6-12) David conceives the idea of capturing the city of Jerusalem, which is in the hands of the Jebusites, and making it the seat of his kingdom. He succeeds in his undertaking; and King Hiram of Tyre makes a pact of friendship with him. And David now perceives that the Lord has established him king over Israel.

(Ch. 7-8) These two chapters deal with David's desire to build a temple in Jerusalem; but the prophet Nathan brings the word of the Lord prohibiting it. David offers a prayer. After this David fights against the Philistines, the Moabites and the Syrians. He wins great victories, and dedicates the spoils of war to the Lord.

(Ch. 10) This is the record of another war and its cause: when King Nahash the Ammonite dies, David sends men to comfort his son Hanun, but David's messengers are suspected of being spies and are dishonored. Then David sends his nephew Joab to fight the Ammonites and their allies.

(Ch. 12:26-31) The intermittent war with the Ammonites is resumed, and another victorious chapter recorded.

(Ch. 19:16-43) Upon his return, King David settles accounts with those who defected during the revolt of Absalom; those who remained loyal are reinstated in David's favor. Saul's son reveals how falsely his servant has dealt with him, and is pardoned by David. Others are banished.

(Ch. 20) A Benjamite named Sheba gathers a force and rebels against David. The king sends a force under Amasa to subdue Sheba, but Joab resents Amasa's assignment. He treacherously murders Amasa, then pursues Sheba. The credit of killing Sheba, who led the revolt, is given to a woman of the besieged city of Abel; but Joab is rewarded upon his return to Jerusalem when the king makes him head of the armies of Israel.

(Ch. 21) Here we have the record of a three-year famine, which comes as a punishment for Saul's behavior toward the Gibeonites; and of King David's bringing about the death of seven of Saul's sons. This is followed by an account of another victorious war against the Philistines.

(Ch. 23:8-39) A list is given here of all the names of "the mighty men whom David had."

(Ch. 24) David orders Joab to take a census; and through the prophet Gad, David is informed that he will be punished for the sin of numbering the people, and he is given a choice of three punishments. David chooses pestilence, and in it die seventy thousand people. The king builds an altar and prays, and the plague is ended.

## I Kings

(Ch. 4:2-19) King Solomon's scribes, recorders, priests and principal officers are given by name, and the regions of their responsibilities are enumerated. This record includes his two sons-in-law: Abinadab, who married Solomon's daughter Taphath, and Ahimaz, who married Solomon's second daughter Basmath.

(Ch. 6) This chapter gives detailed dimensions and descriptions of the temple and its adornments.

(Ch. 7) Descriptions are given of Solomon's palace and the palace he built for Pharaoh's daughter, the numerous vessels made by Hiram the craftsman, and their designs and dimensions.

(Ch. 8:15-66) A long prayer by King Solomon is given here, followed by a lavish peace offering of twenty-two thousand oxen and a hundred and twenty thousand sheep.

(Ch. 9:1-14) This part presents a vision in which the Lord promises to establish Solomon's kingdom over Israel forever if the king follows in his father's footsteps; but if he does not, he and his people will be cast out of the sight of the Lord.

(Ch. 11:14-25) A record is given of two adversaries of Solomon's, Hadad the Edomite, and Rezon, the son of Eliadah, before the uprising of Jeroboam.

(Ch. 13) At an altar in Bethel, King Jeroboam's hand withers when he tries to lay hands upon a man of God who prophesies against him; and his hand is restored to health by the prayer of the same prophet. The man of God refuses to go to the king's house; but he goes to eat in the house of another prophet, though the Lord commanded him not to do so; and for this sin he is later killed by a lion. And Jeroboam returns to his evil ways.

(Ch. 15-16) These two chapters give a digest of the reign of a number of kings of Israel and Judah. They cover the days of Abijam, Asa and Jehoshaphat, kings of Judah, and Nadab, Baasha, Elah, Zimri, Omri and Ahab, kings of Israel.

(Ch. 20) With the guidance of a prophet, King Ahab of Israel defeats the mighty Syrian King Ben-hadab; but counter to the prophet's command to utterly destroy the enemy, Ahab makes a friendly pact with Ben-hadab; and Ahab is told that he and his people will be severely punished by the Lord.

(Ch. 22) The record of how Ahab, the king of Israel, is killed and his blood licked up by the dogs as had been prophesied; the short rule by his son Ahaziah; and a brief record of the good rule of Jehoshaphat, king of Judah, and of his merchant marine which traded with Ophir (India).

## II Kings

(Ch. 7) The great famine story continues, with Elisha prophesying incredible abundance. The king's treasurer, who doubts the prophet, is trodden to death when the prophesy is fulfilled.

(Ch. 8:16-24) Thirty-two-year-old Jehoram (or Joram), married to the daughter of King Ahab of Israel, becomes king of Judah and follows in the footsteps of his evil father-in-law. The Lord, for David's sake, grants him victory over the Edomites.

(Ch. 11-12) When Ahaziah, king of Judah, dies, his mother Athalia murders all the royal descendants and proclaims herself queen. But Joash (or Jehoash), the infant son of Ahaziah, is rescued from the king's house and hidden. When the child is seven years old, he is brought out of hiding and, with the aid of Jehoiada, a friendly priest, he is anointed king; and Queen Athalia is killed. Under Jehoiada's guidance, the young king rules justly and well for thirty-nine years; then he is murdered by his servants and succeeded by his son Amaziah.

(Ch. 14:17-29) King Amaziah of Judah is slain, and his son Azariah is proclaimed king. And in the fifteenth year of Azariah's reign in Judah, Jeroboam II is made king over Israel. Jeroboam was an evil king, who ruled for forty years; and he was succeeded by his son Zachariah.

(Ch. 15) While Azariah rules well and peacefully in Judah for forty years, there is great distress in Israel. Zachariah, in the first year of his rule, is slain by Shallum, who takes over the throne; but within a month Shallum in turn is killed, and succeeded by Menahem, the son of Gadi. After six troublesome years, Menahem is succeeded by his son Pekahiah, who is no better than his predecessors, and he is killed after two years of rule by one of his military men, Pekah, who becomes the ruler of Israel.

(Ch. 16) At the time of Pekahiah and Pekah in Israel, twenty-year-old Ahaz became king of Judah, and "he did not that which was right in the sight of the Lord his God." He ruled for sixteen years, and was succeeded by his son Hezekiah.

(Ch. 17:24-41) Here we have a rather confusing record of what happened to the alien nations who were brought in to inhabit Samaria, and who continued to worship the gods and images of their forefathers.

## Daniel

(Ch. 3:23) The prayer of Hananiah, Mishael and Azariah in the fiery furnace is given in the Apocrypha under the name of The Song of the Three Holy Children.

(Ch. 6) Another version of Daniel in the lion's den is given in the Apocryphal work The History of the Destruction of Bel and the Dragon. This brief history tells how Daniel exposed idolatrous priests who worshiped an idol called Bel, and a dragon. The Babylonians, in their anger against Daniel for the anguish he caused their priests, throw Daniel into a den of seven lions. God protects Daniel from the lions, and the prophet Habakkuk is sent to feed him. On the seventh day, when King Cyrus comes to mourn Daniel's fate, he looks down into the pit and beholds Daniel unhurt. The king has Daniel drawn out; and his detractors are thrown into the den.

(Ch. 7) Though the entire Book of Daniel is apocalyptic, Chapter 7 reveals this in its purest form. Each image and act in the vision is symbolical, so that many mystic interpretations might be given to it; as, indeed, various mystic interpretations have been given to it.

(Ch. 8) This chapter presents another vision, in which Daniel sees a mighty goat (with one horn between its eyes) destroy a mighty ram having two great but unequal horns. The angel Gabriel explains to Daniel that the goat in the vision refers to Greece, and the ram with the two unequal horns to the kingdoms of Media and Persia, and that in the end Greece too shall be shattered, though not by human hands.

## Ezra

(Ch. 2) This chapter enumerates by families the people who returned from the Babylonian captivity under the leadership of Zerubbabel; their possessions; and their gifts.

(Ch. 3:1-7) A description is given here of the altar in Jerusalem for the daily offerings.

(Ch. 5) Here we have a record of how the prophets Haggai and Zechariah inspired Zerubbabel to rebuild the temple; and how their task was hindered by the governors of neighboring states.

(Ch. 8:1-30) After a list by name of all the men who accompanied Ezra from Babylon to Jerusalem, a fast is recorded; and an account of how Ezra committed into the hands of the priests the offerings he had gathered for the house of God.

(Ch. 10:18-44) This section lists the sons of the priests who had foreign wives.

## Nehemiah

(Ch. 3) A list is given of those who aided in the rebuilding instituted by Nehemiah, detailing what each group or clan accomplished.

(Ch. 5:14-19) Nehemiah tells of his generosity as governor, to set an example for the rest of the people in their rebuilding the temple and the city of Jerusalem.

(Ch. 7:5-73) A genealogy is given of those who returned from Babylon; an enumeration of their possessions; and the gifts of silver and gold to the treasury for the building program.

(Ch. 8:13-18) Ezra and the Levites reinstitute the observance of the Feast of the Tabernacles.

(Ch. 9) This chapter gives in detail the establishment of a day of solemn fast and confession of sins; and a prayer by the Levites which is a historical summation in brief from Creation to their own day.

(Ch. 10-11) The new covenant between the people and God is summarized in these two chapters, and they list those who accept the covenant (presented in reverse order); then the names are given of the people chosen by lot to dwell in Jerusalem, the remainder to dwell in other cities of Judah as enumerated.

(Ch. 12) This chapter gives a list of the priests who returned from Babylon with Zerubbabel, and the succession of high priests; and it describes the dedication of the completed walls of Jerusalem, naming those who were in charge of the celebration.

## Isaiah

(Ch. 6) The call of the prophet has been transposed to the beginning of this book.

(Ch. 7) This chapter gives a somewhat confusing narrative concerning a war waged against Jerusalem by the king of Syria allied with the king of Israel; and Isaiah's assurances to the king of Judah that they will not succeed.

(Ch. 8) The prophet proclaims again that men who fear the Lord their God need not fear their enemies.

(Ch. 10:5-34) This prophecy against Assyria is filled with local historical references.

(Ch. 12) This chapter gives Israel's song of thanksgiving for the millennium which is to come.

(Ch. 15-23) Many scholars believe that these chapters are interpolations, taken from a book of oracles. Apparently later editors were concerned that the book was too brief to fill a conventional scroll, and at this point, basing themselves on the oracular expressions of Isaiah (I) against Babylon and Philistia in the preceding chapters, added a number of oracles against Moab, Damascus, Ethiopia, Egypt and Tyre — in the manner of, but not quite in the lofty style of, the two preceding chapters.

(Ch. 26:11-13; 27) The prophecy in the two chapters preceding is amplified here, and the apocalyptic style is even more pronounced. There are references to the resurrection of the dead and to a life hereafter — concepts unknown among the Jews in the days of Isaiah (I). Scholars believe that it is quite likely that also Chapters 24-27 were interpolated some three hundred years after the time of Isaiah (I).

(Ch. 34) With slight variations, this chapter gives another expression of God's indignation against the nations.

(Ch. 36-39) These prose chapters repeat the record already given in II Kings of Sennacherib's unsuccessful siege of Jerusalem, and King Hezekiah's recovery from a grave illness.

(Ch. 42:18-25; 43; 44:1-13) The rebuke to the idolatrous, Babylon's doom, and the folly of idol-worshipers are underscored once again.

(Ch. 45:14-24; 46) These describe Israel's eventual triumph and God's omnipotence.

(Ch. 51) A promise is made that God, who had comforted Israel in the past, will redeem Zion and remove the affliction of Jerusalem in the future.

(Ch. 58:13-14; 59) These chapters repeat the admonitions to keep the Sabbath, and give a description of the sins of Israel.

## Jeremiah

(Ch. 4) The proclamation in this chapter is developed, in essence, more sharply in the next chapter.

(Ch. 7:1-33) This is a long prose declamation on the sins of the people, and a call for repentance.

(Ch. 10:1-16) A comparison is made between the heathen idols and the Lord; and the folly of idolatry is shown and condemned.

(Ch. 13:1-17) Two parables, of the linen girdle and bottles filled with wine, are presented to symbolize the faithlessness of Judah.

(Ch. 17:9-27) After a sequence of gnomic words of wisdom, the sanctity of the Sabbath is extolled.

(Ch. 18:18-23) A plot against Jeremiah is related, followed by his prayer for the punishment of his enemies.

(Ch. 19:14-15; 20:1-13) Jeremiah's persecution by Pashur (who puts the prophet in stocks), is lamented by Jeremiah, but his faith remains unshaken.

(Ch. 21:1-7) Jeremiah warns King Zedekiah not to go to war against Babylonia.

(Ch. 22) This chapter gives another series of prophecies against Judah.

(Ch. 25-28) The prophet foretells the Babylonian captivity, and the punishment which will fall upon Babylon in the end. For his bold utterance against Judah, the prophet is arrested; then he is freed. He returns to urge the king to yield to Nebuchadnezzar, king of Babylon.

(Ch. 29:15-32) The letter continues, describing the unhappy condition of those who remained behind and were not taken into exile.

(Ch. 32-34) A record is preserved here of Jeremiah's purchase of a family inheritance; his imprisonment, and his visions in prison; and his prophecy that King Zedekiah would be taken captive.

(Ch. 35) The prophet declares God's blessing on the Rechabites because they have set an example of obedience.

(Ch. 40:7-16) A warning is given Gedaliah of the conspiracy against him.

(Ch. 45-51:1-58) In these chapters appear a long series of prophecies against Egypt, the Philistines, Moab, the Ammonites, Edom, Damascus, Kedar and the kingdom of Hazor; and a bitter denunciation of Babylon.

(Ch. 52) This chapter repeats what had been already recorded in II Kings 24:18; 25:1-27.

## Ezekiel

(Ch. 3:16-27) Ezekiel is appointed watchman over the house of Israel, and then silenced until such time as he is commanded to speak again.

(Ch. 6) Another prophecy is given against Israel because of their idolatry; and Ezekiel bewails his country and his people.

(Ch. 8-11) The prophet describes his visions of idolatry in Jerusalem (and the punishment of those guilty of it) in symbolic and apocalyptic language.

(Ch. 12:21-28) A warning is issued against false prophets; and a promise of the speedy fulfillment of prophecies.

(Ch. 13-14) These chapters contain further prophecies against false prophets, and a denunciation of idolaters.

(Ch. 17) A parable about two eagles is given in this chapter, proving allegorically that the king of Babylon will take Judah into captivity.

(Ch. 19:10-14; 20:1-44) Jerusalem is likened to a vine plucked up in fury; and the prophet recalls all the mercies of the Lord to Israel, and their rebelliousness.

(Ch. 22) This is a sermon on Jerusalem's sins and inevitable punishment.

(Ch. 24) This chapter gives: a parable about a rusty pot, which symbolizes Jerusalem grown filthy; the command to the prophet not to mourn the death of his wife; and the prophet's explanation of what these things mean.

(Ch. 25-26) A series of prophecies are proclaimed against the Ammonites, Moabites, Edomites, Philistines, and Tyre.

(Ch. 28-32) These chapters contain more prophecies, in the same vein, against Tyre, Zidon, Egypt, and Nebuchadnezzar of Babylon.

(Ch. 33) The prophet is compared to a watchman for Israel, and he is informed why Jerusalem will be destroyed, and that he will be mocked for his warnings.

(Ch. 35-36) A bitter prophecy is made against Mount Seir (Edom); and a promise of the restoration and regeneration of Israel.

(Ch. 37:15-28) An allegory is given of two sticks, symbolizing the unification of Judah and Israel upon their return from captivity.

(Ch. 38-39) A prophecy against the land of Magog, interpreted by some as a prophecy against Persia.

(Ch. 40-48) The last nine chapters of Ezekiel are devoted to an extremely detailed description of the future temple of Jerusalem.

## Amos

(Ch. 1-2) The warning to Damascus, Moab, Judah and Israel is also given in prophecies against Syria, Philistia, Tyre, Edom and Ammon.

(Ch. 7:1-9) Three brief visions of destruction are symbolized here by the grasshoppers, fire, and the plumb line.

## Hosea

(Ch. 3) A second symbolical marriage is given on the part of the prophet and an adulteress.

(Ch. 7:1-7) Israel's internal corruption is described here, ending with a comparison of Ephraim to "a cake not turned."

## Micah

(Ch. 1:10-15) This gives a dirge for Israel that begins with "Tell it not in Gath!" and makes numerous references to local cities. Other parts of Micah are variations of the same theme.

## Habakkuk

(Ch. 3) This chapter presents a long prayer in the form of a psalm.

## Zechariah

(Ch. 3) A vision of the high priest Joshua accused by Satan, and Joshua's vindication by the Lord.

(Ch. 5:5-11; 6) Two more visions are given: one about a woman with a measure, symbolizing wickedness; and another about chariots drawn by horses of different colors, each going to different parts of the earth.

(Ch. 9-14) These five chapters, assumed by many scholars to be later interpolations, present mystical promises of the restoration of Jerusalem, and the doom of the faithless.

## Ecclesiastes

(Ch. 8) Advice is given to keep the king's commandments; and it is emphasized that adversity with the godly is better than prosperity with the wicked.

## Esther

(Ch. 10) This chapter, which begins here with the greatness of Ahasuerus and Mordecai's advancements, is continued in the Apocryphal Book of Esther.

## I Maccabees

(Ch. 5-16) The remainder of this book gives the further wars of Judas Maccabeus against the Greeks and other nations, and his pact with the Romans; how Judas falls in battle and is succeeded by his brother Jonathan; the slaying of Jonathan through trickery; the succession of his brother Simon; and finally, how the leadership passes from the aged Simon to his two sons Judas and John. The book of I Maccabees is regarded as a reliable historical source for the period it covers — 167-137 B.C.E.

## Job

(Ch. 25-28) Bildad repeats his earlier arguments, and Job replies to him. Chapters 26-31 are given as Job's reply to Bildad, although from their content it is clear that Chapters 27:7-23 to the end of Chapter 28 give an argument which is opposed to all that Job had previously stated, and repeats Zophar's earlier argument.

(Ch. 32-37) This entire section, in which the young man Elihu is introduced to reprove Job, is considered by many scholars to be a late interpolation.

## Proverbs

(Ch. 1-2, 3:1-12) This is a rather lengthy preamble to the greatness and rewards of wisdom, with an exhortation to obedience to the law.

(Ch. 4) Here Solomon recites what he had learned from his father and his mother in the study of wisdom and how to shun the ways of the wicked.

(Ch. 8) This chapter, like the first three chapters, is devoted to the praise of the excellency and power of wisdom.

## About the Editor

Joseph Gaer (1897–1969) was born in Yedinitz, Russia, and came to America in 1917. He was a prolific writer and editor, specializing in literature and religion. Gaer's first book, *The Magic Flight*, was a highly regarded collection of Jewish folktales. It was followed by *The Burning Bush*, a study of biblical folklore. Best known for his popular work *How the Great Religions Began*, Gaer was also a frequent consultant on many of the films with biblical themes produced in Hollywood. He served as Executive Director of The Jewish Heritage Foundation and was a member of the American Jewish Congress Commission on Jewish Affairs and the National Jewish Music Council.